101 Projects for Your **Porsche Boxster**

By Wayne R. Dempsey

Quarto.com

First published in 2010 by Motorbooks, an imprint of The Quarto Group, 100 Cummings Center, Suite 265-D, Beverly, MA 01915, USA. T (978) 282-9590 F (978) 283-2742

Motorbooks titles are also available at discount for retail, wholesale, promotional, and bulk purchase. For details, contact the Special Sales Manager by email at specialsales@quarto.com or by mail at The Quarto Group, Attn: Special Sales Manager, 100 Cummings Center, Suite 265-D, Beverly, MA 01915, USA.

ISBN-13: 978-0-7603-3554-3

Library of Congress Cataloging-in-Publication Data

Dempsey, Wayne R., 1972-
101 projects for your Porsche Boxster / Wayne R. Dempsey.
p. cm.
Includes index.
ISBN 978-0-7603-3554-3 (pbk. : alk. paper)
1. Boxster automobile--Maintenance and repair--Amateurs' manuals. I. Title. II. Title: One hundred one projects for your Porsche Boxster.
TL215.B586D46 2011
629.28'722--dc22

2010027836

Editors: Peter Schletty and Jeffrey Zuehlke

Design Manager: Jon Simpson
Designed by: Danielle Smith

Printed in China

101 Projects Website

Please visit the official website for this book: www.101Projects.com. This website contains book updates, exclusive photos not published in the book, a Porsche Boxster forum and BBS, links to sites for more information, and locations where you can purchase the parts and tools mentioned in this book.

About the Author

Wayne R. Dempsey is the author of several highly successful books, including *101 Projects for Your Porsche 911* and *How to Rebuild and Modify Porsche 911 Engines*. He has been working and playing with mechanical machines all his life. In college, Wayne earned both a BS and an MS degree in Mechanical Engineering from the Massachusetts Institute of Technology, specializing in flexible manufacturing technology. His introduction to automobiles began when he raced with the MIT Solar Electric Vehicle Racing Team. After a few years building communications satellites for Hughes Space and Communications, Wayne left to pursue an entrepreneurial calling. Literally starting in his garage, Wayne co-founded Pelican Parts, an Internet-based European automotive parts company. Today, Pelican Parts is thriving with the growth in Internet technology. Wayne currently maintains the site and has written most of the technical articles that are featured on the Pelican Parts website, www.PelicanParts.com. Wayne currently owns the 2000 3.4 Boxster conversion profiled in this book, a 2001 Aerokit 996 Carrera, a 1999 Boxster Tip, a 1999 996 Carrera convertible, a 1974 914-6 conversion, a 1972 RS clone, a 1973 RSR clone, a 1987 Porsche 959, and a 1987 Kremer Racing Porsche 962C.

Contents

SECTION 5: TRANSMISSION

SECTION 6: EXHAUST

SECTION 7: BRAKES

SECTION 8: SUSPENSION

SECTION 9: BODY

SECTION 10: ELECTRIC

SECTION 11: MISCELLANEOUS

Acknowledgments

It's obvious that a book of this magnitude does not simply write itself, but needs a cooperative effort from many people in all walks of life. A lot of people have helped me with this book over the past three years and have joined in my enthusiastic vision of what I wanted it to be. First on the list is Jared Fenton, who assisted me greatly with both the projects and photos for this book. I would like to thank my very patient wife, Nori, without whose unending support and patience this project would never have gotten finished. Also thanks to my three young children, Sean, Holly, and Patrick, to whom this book is dedicated. Special thanks and consideration are due to Tony Callas and Tom Prine of Callas Rennsport in Torrance, California, who have volunteered their time and resources on countless occasions in order to make this book great. Boxster guru Todd Holyoak deserves a notable shout-out for assisting with the 3.4 conversion project and for helping edit and review the entire book. Scott Slauson of Softronic was very helpful with reprogramming the DME and also in giving hints and tips about the cars that weren't common knowledge. Special thanks to Charles Navarro of LN Engineering for all of his help with the engine projects. Special thanks to Peter Schletty, Jeff Zuehlke, Jim Michels, Becky Pagel, the rest of the MBI staff for packaging my wordy content into a concise and useable format. Special thanks to Zack Miller for giving me more space to add more content and for putting up with my occasional irascible temper. Of course, no good Acknowledgments section would be complete without a note of thanks to my parents, Meg and Ed Dempsey. In the beginning, I'm certain they thought I was headed for trouble, but somehow they managed to turn the tide, and this book is one of many accomplishments that they have been proud of over the years. Also very helpful were Ken Fund, Tim Suddard, Jim Schrager, Joe Fabiani, Art Chavez, Lennie Yee, Paul Guard, Bruce Anderson, Gary Hand, Peter Bodensteiner, Pedro Bonilla, Jake Raby, Ray Crawford, Owen Stutton, Michael C. Harley, Stefan Wilhelmy, Joel Reiser, Scott Shores, Loren Cook, Stephen Kaspar, Hans Kopecky, Fletcher Benton, Richard Grauman, Jay Horak, Randy Leffingwell, Mike Focke, Trinidad Winters, the folks at LA Porsche Dismantlers, and a whole host of others who have given me help and encouragement with this great book.

Introduction

Since its introduction in 1997, the Porsche Boxster has earned itself a reputation as one of the world's best sports cars. Building upon Porsche's nearly 40 years of experience creating production and race cars, the Boxster has been designed and improved over the years to a state of near perfection. It has also garnered a huge, loyal following of people who love to drive it. Boxster owners tend to adore their cars and also enjoy restoring, modifying, and maintaining them to perfection. If you're one of these people, this book was written especially for you.

Information is the key to success in any project or endeavor. Without the proper knowledge, you can make costly mistakes and waste your time as you trudge through the learning process. The projects in this book aim to eliminate any guesswork that you may have while working on your Boxster. My slogan has always been, "Let me make the mistakes and warn you about them, so you won't do the same." Believe me, I've made many mistakes and learned the hard way the best and worst ways to repair, restore, and modify these cars. My lessons, as well as the lessons learned by the expert mechanics I've consulted with, are compiled here for you.

Who am I? I am the owner of one of the largest European online parts retailers, PelicanParts.com. I designed and built Pelican Parts especially for the do-it-yourself (DIY) mechanics who love to work on their own cars—people just like me. Our website has hundreds of Porsche technical articles that are the foundation for most of the projects in this book. If you like what you see in this book, then you will definitely enjoy more of the same at our website, www.PelicanParts.com.

The projects in this book are written in a format and style that should empower anyone to work on his or her car. One of the principal drawbacks to owning a Porsche is the high cost of maintaining it. You can literally save thousands of dollars in mechanic's costs simply by performing the work yourself. It is the goal of this book to get more people out working on their Boxsters—it's too much fun not to! Plus, when you personally complete a job on your Boxster, you get the added satisfaction of having done it yourself. Working on your own car can give you that emotional attachment to your Boxster that is common with Porsche owners.

This book is divided into 11 sections, each focusing on a particular system of the Porsche Boxster. The "backyard" mechanic can perform almost all of the projects contained within these pages over a weekend or two. In an attempt to appeal to everyone, some of the projects are basic and some are more advanced. Some of the projects are simply overviews of systems found on the Boxster. For example, Project 18, which covers superchargers and turbochargers, is simply meant to give you an inside look into what happens when you take your engine's performance to the next level.

Most projects follow a distinct how-to format. Step-by-step instructions tell you how to perform the job, what tools to use, and what costly mistakes to avoid. The photos that accompany the projects tell a story of their own. I've spread hints and tips throughout each project, so make sure that you read all the text and captions before you start.

In addition to this book, I've also created a bonus website that contains additional information and photos that I didn't have room to publish here in print. This bonus content is available for free at the main website for this book, www.101Projects.com. In addition, I've set up the site with a discussion forum so that you can ask questions and get feedback regarding any of the projects in the book. You can often find me and many other Boxster experts there, ready to share knowledge and exchange ideas.

Please don't be afraid to get this book dirty—take it with you underneath the car. Get it greasy. Compare the pictures in the book to your own car. Follow along step by step as you tear into each project. If this book gets dirty, then I will sleep well at night knowing that it's being put to good use.

While this book is a great guide for determining what upgrades and maintenance you need to perform on your Boxster, it's not meant to be the only book for your car. Limited by a fixed page count, I can't provide the detailed diagrams, torque settings, and factory procedures that are documented in the original factory workshop manuals. If you are planning to work on your own car, I recommend that you invest as much as you can in books and information that will help you along the way. Make sure that you review the Information Resources section in the next section of this book for my recommendations of the best places to find additional technical information for the Boxster.

This book is not meant to be read from cover to cover, but is designed to be flipped through so that you can get an idea of what projects interest you for your Boxster. I've structured the projects so that you can simply open up the book and start working on your car. I do recommend, however, that you read the "Tools of the Trade" section in the first part of the book, and also Project 1, "Jacking Up Your Car," before you start working on any of the projects.

In a detailed how-to book like this one, it's important to distinguish literally which way is up. The Boxster engine can be confusing because it's located in the middle of the car. When I refer to the front of the engine, I will be talking about the area toward the front of the car, where the belts and pulleys are located. Conversely, the back of the engine refers to where the flywheel is mounted. When referencing left or right, I'm assuming that you're sitting in the driver's seat. If I reference the passenger or driver's side, I'm assuming a left-hand drive car, as we have here in the United States. I also refer to locations on the engine by cylinder bank numbers. Cylinder numbers 1 through 3 are located on the right side of the car; cylinder numbers 4 through 6 are located on the left.

One of the features in this book that I have taken special care with is the index. I find it especially frustrating when a good book has a lousy index, where you can't find anything useful. For that reason, I've personally indexed the book according to unique words found within each project and also listed each index item under multiple names. This way, if there are different names for a part or procedure, it will still be easy to locate it within the body of the text. For example brake discs are listed as both brake discs and brake rotors, as they are sometimes called. Please feel free to use the index as one of the primary guides to the book.

Finally, remember that safety should be your number-one concern. It's very easy to get so intimately involved with working on your Boxster that you forget how fragile and vulnerable the human body can be. Have patience and think about every action you make. Think ahead as to what might happen if you slip or if something breaks. Using your head a little will go a long way toward protecting yourself.

I hope you enjoy the book, as I have spent a long time compiling this information and filtering it so that it's easy to understand and follow. If you have any feedback or questions for me, you can contact me at this book's dedicated website, www.101Projects.com. Enjoy!

Boxster Information Resources

I've always said that you can never have too much information. This is definitely true when working on an automobile. For the Porsche Boxster, there are a few really great technical resources that I refer to regularly when working on my own personal cars.

PelicanParts.com: This website has a treasure-trove of technical articles, diagrams, hints, and a neat forum/BBS tied into this book. In addition, Pelican Parts has the Internet's largest parts catalog, complete with just about everything you could want or need for your Boxster. You can even order "dealer-only" parts directly on the site, simply by typing the part number into the Pelican Parts search engine.

Bentley Manuals: I wrote this 101 Projects book specifically to complement and to be used in conjunction with the Bentley workshop manual. This manual is a reference bible for working on the Boxster, and I do not recommend that you pick up your wrench until you have one of these in hand. It contains all of the torque specs, parts information, electrical diagrams, and repair procedures that you would

find in a typical factory workshop manual. I have purposely tried not to duplicate information that is already published in the Bentley manual, instead saving room for material that is not specifically covered within it.

Porsche Owner's Maintenance Manual for Boxster: Written in a style that is very similar to the Bentley manual, this book covers material ranging from an expanded owner's guide to basic maintenance tasks. Included is a buyer's guide and overview of the various systems on the car. Also covered are some basic repair procedures and a large section of technical information compiled in a very concise format.

Porsche Service Information Manuals: These are one of the best-kept secrets in the Porsche world. Each time Porsche releases a new model of car, they create a high-quality book for their dealers explaining how the car differs from the previous model year. The book is designed to be read by the service shop mechanics, and it reviews each system on the car, documenting any new features or updates that may have been introduced with the new model. These are a bit difficult to find at times, but you can sometimes find them on eBay or automotive literature sites, or you can order them from Porsche if they have stock on hand.

Porsche Factory Workshop Manuals: Nothing beats having the same information that the techs at the dealership have, and the factory manuals offer the final word on what you need to know. The electrical diagrams, factory procedures, torque values, and detailed information overview really make the set indispensible for hardcore do-it-yourselfers.

Boxster General Maintenance & ODB II Diagnostic Guide: This 230-page book has a small front section dedicated to basic maintenance, but the real content of the book is dedicated to diagnosing problems with the engine management system. The book contains a comprehensive list of all of the trouble codes, what they mean, and what you can do to try to solve the problem.

Tools of the Trade

We've all heard the clichés about having the right tool for the job. Most of us have heard stories about a botched repair or wasted hours because somebody attempted to save a few dollars by putting off buying the right tool. Here's the nuts and bolts of it: even though all good mechanics will admit that there is no substitute for the correct tool, they will also admit that no matter how many tools you have, you will never have every tool you need. I've learned that having just the right tool for the job can turn a five-hour problem into a five-minute fix. The more you work on your car, and the more you look at tool catalogs (like the one at PelicanParts.com), you'll find that you'll cherish the art of buying and acquiring tools. But you need a good place to start. Here are some of my suggestions to get you started on your way.

THE BASIC TOOL SET

There are literally tens of thousands of tools available to perform an equal number of tasks. Fortunately, it's not likely you'll need all of them.

Your tool set should consist of some basic items:

Screwdrivers: You should have at least three flat-tip (3/32, 3/16, and 5/16), and two Phillips tip (Number 1 and Number 2) screwdrivers. Inspect the tips of your screwdrivers to be sure that they are not bent, broken, or otherwise worn. A damaged screwdriver is a quick way to strip the head of a fastener, causing an otherwise simple repair to turn into a nightmare. A ratcheting screwdriver is a useful tool as well.

Adjustable Wrench: Quality is of the utmost importance when choosing an adjustable wrench. Less expensive wrenches have jaws that will stretch, mar, and otherwise fall apart when used; this is another very good way to damage a fastener and ruin your day. A good adjustable plumber's wrench can also come in handy when you need to remove large stubborn nuts.

Pliers: No tool set would be complete without a few sets of pliers. The three basic pliers are slip-joint, adjustable (sometimes called channel-lock), and needle-nose. The important consideration when choosing most pliers is the teeth. The teeth should be sharp, and they should stay sharp, as pliers are generally used under less than ideal circumstances. Again, don't cheap-out on the pliers. The Vise-Grip brand is very good, and a set of multiple sizes will service you well over many years.

Sockets and Drivers: Aside from a variety of sizes, sockets come in either 12-point or 6-point, regular and deep versions. Twelve-point versions are more versatile, but 6-point sockets are stronger and do less damage to fasteners. Socket drives normally come in 1/4-, 3/8-, 1/2-, 3/4-, and 1-inch sizes. Your socket set should also include a good ratchet (money well spent), a 2-inch extension, a 6-inch extension, and a universal joint.

A full, complete metric set is a great starting point and will likely be the cornerstone of your collection. A good set will contain three socket ratchet drivers in three different sizes and the associated short and deep sockets. Also useful is a set of universal or swivel joints that allow you to reach difficult nuts. Start with the basic universal joint set, and then buy a swivel with built-in sockets when you need them. A deep-socket metric set is useful as well.

A really neat tool that I recently discovered is the Stanley 3/8-inch Drive Rotator Ratchet (Part Number: 89-962). This ratchet driver allows you to rotate the handle to turn the socket. But unlike other ratchet drivers, you can turn the handle clockwise and counterclockwise in a quick repeatable manner, and it will only turn the socket in one rotational direction. It's very cool, and I recommend it.

Wrenches: The combination wrench is the backbone of any good automotive tool set. There are also other varieties available, such as the double-open, double-boxed, deep-offset, and socket wrench. Ideally you'll need a range of 7- to 19-millimeter for starters (and a spare 10- and 13-millimeter will always come in handy). Recently, there have been a number of innovations in wrench technology. My favorite of these new tools are the

GearWrenches. These are combination wrenches with very fine, reversible ratchets built in. They are very useful in all circumstances, and I use the GearWrenches almost exclusively these days. I recommend the 12-piece all-metric set with the mini reversible switch (see photo, page 10). This set retails for about $125 from the tool catalog of PelicanParts.com.

Hammers: There are hundreds of different types of hammers, each in a variety of different sizes. There are ball-peen hammers, claw hammers, soft blow hammers, nonmarring, welding hammers, and picks, just to name a few. The hammer you need to be concerned with is the 16-ounce ball-peen. This is a great all-purpose hammer, but you may desire a 32-ounce if you really need to hit something hard. Buying a hammer shouldn't be rocket science, but there are some precautions. Aside from the weight and the quality of the head, the handle is an important consideration. There are now a variety of different handles: wood, fiberglass, steel, and reinforced plastic. I prefer a hardwood, like oak, for ball-peen hammers, but all my hammers have different handles, based on how I want the blow to strike certain objects. Also useful is a rubber mallet for removing parts without inflicting damage.

Allen/Hex Wrenches: There are many variations of this tool: socket drive, T-handle, and multifunction. If you're only going to have one set, a basic right-angle hex key set will give you the most versatility and serve you best. I recommend having a spare 5- and 6-millimeter, as they do wear out at the least opportune times. The next step up is the socket set that fits on the end of a ratchet driver. These are very useful for applying more torque when you need it.

Torx Sockets/Drivers: Modern Porsches contain a tremendous number of Torx fasteners. You will need a set of Torx sockets, a set of Torx screwdrivers, and a set of female Torx sockets to remove bolts like those found on the seat rails.

Torque Wrenches: No good mechanic or weekend warrior is complete without a torque wrench. The ultimate tool for assembly, the torque wrench is used to measure and restrict the amount of torque that is applied to a fastener. This is of the utmost importance, since too little torque can result in a nut falling off, or too much torque can damage a valuable part. Make sure that you get a torque wrench with both English and metric measurements labeled on it. I recommend purchasing two wrenches, one for small increments (0–25 ft-lb) and one for larger tasks (above 25 ft-lb).

Electrical Repair: You don't need a degree in physics to perform basic electrical repairs on cars, but you do need the right tools. At a minimum you'll need a test light, wire crimping pliers, wire strippers, an assortment of solderless terminals, and a good multitester. Most parts stores carry inexpensive kits that are suitable for most jobs. The automotive electronics company SUN manufactures a great hand-held voltmeter, ammeter, tachometer, and dwell meter unit, and it is available at most local auto parts stores. Wiring diagrams for your year car are also extremely valuable for the process of troubleshooting electrical problems.

Hydraulic Jack: Arguably the most important tool in your collection, it's wise not to cheap-out on this one. Although good-quality jacks are often expensive, they are definitely worth it, and they will last a long, long time. Purchase a large jack with a very large lifting throw. Weight capacity is not as important as how high you can lift with the jack. Purchase a 3- to 5-ton jack with the highest lift that you can find. Typical costs for these are in the $150–$400 range, but they are well worth it. The world's greatest floor jack is the DK13HLQ from AC Hydraulics—I discuss how fantastic this jack is in Photo 5 of Project 1. Also necessary are jack stands. I like to have two different sizes around so that I can adjust the car to different heights. See Project 1 for more details.

Shop Lamp: Another extremely useful tool is the shop lamp. My favorite type of shop lamp is the 3-foot-long fluorescent hand-held unit on a retractable cord. These allow the spring-loaded cord to be wound back into the main housing. Stay away from the shop lamps that use a standard 60-watt incandescent light bulb. These get hot and can burn you under the car or even start fires if oil or gasoline accidentally drips on them. Stick with the fluorescent lamps.

Another good lamp is the shop halogen lamp. These are extremely high-powered lamps that come with adjustable stands and metal grille covers. Although these lamps get very hot, they give out a lot of light and are especially useful for lighting up engine compartments and the underside of the car when you're working in that area.

Safety Glasses: Anyone who has worked on cars for any length of time or has worked in a machine shop knows the importance of wearing safety glasses. Never get underneath the car without them. Always make sure that you have three or four pairs around. You will undoubtedly misplace them, and you want to make sure that you have plenty of spares so that you don't avoid using them because you can't find them.

Miscellaneous: There are plenty of tools that fit into this category. Here are some that you should not be without: X-acto or craft knife, small pick, tape measure, scissors, a set of good feeler gauges, a hack saw, a set of files, and an inspection mirror. Throughout this book, I recommend specific tools that are useful or required to perform a specific task. Examples include the Motive Products brake bleeder, the Durametric code reader tool, and many others. In most cases, you will need to purchase these tools (or similar ones) in order to complete the task.

THE ADVANCED COLLECTION

The upgraded tool set is simply an extension of a basic set. As you perform more tasks, greater range of sockets, wrenches, screwdrivers, and pliers will become increasingly helpful. You should also begin purchasing diagnostic tools.

Some popular tools you might be quick to add are snap ring pliers, a socket drive Allen and Torx set, stubby wrenches, and swivel sockets.

The Dremel tool and angle grinder are two of the most destructive, yet useful, tools for working on older cars. When bolts are rusted solid and there really isn't any alternative, the grinding tools play an important role. No one should be without a Dremel tool, as it is most useful for cutting off small bolts and other pieces of metal that are difficult to reach. The Dremel tool with a flexible extension is particularly useful for reaching into tight places. Be sure to use the fiberglass reinforced cutting wheels for maximum cutting power.

Everyone who works around the house probably has a good variable-speed electric hand drill. However, what are really important are the drill bits. Bargain-basement drill bits are fine for drilling through wood, but when it comes to metal, you need the best quality you can get. Make sure that you get a good-quality set; otherwise you may end up hurting yourself or your car.

One tool that is not commonly used but can save you many hours is the electric impact wrench. This tool is similar to the air compressor impact wrenches that are used in automotive shops everywhere, except that it runs on ordinary 120-volt current. The impact wrench is especially useful for removing nuts that can't be well secured and tend to rotate when you are trying to remove them (like the shock tower nut in Project 63).

When serious engine problems are suspected, the tool most people turn to first is the "compression tester." It will provide clues to such problems as bad rings, leaking valves, or even a hole in one of the pistons. Also useful is a "leakdown tester," which works by pressurizing the cylinder and measuring how much pressure the cylinder loses over time. It should be used in conjunction with the compression tester to gain a more complete diagnosis of your engine (see Project 7).

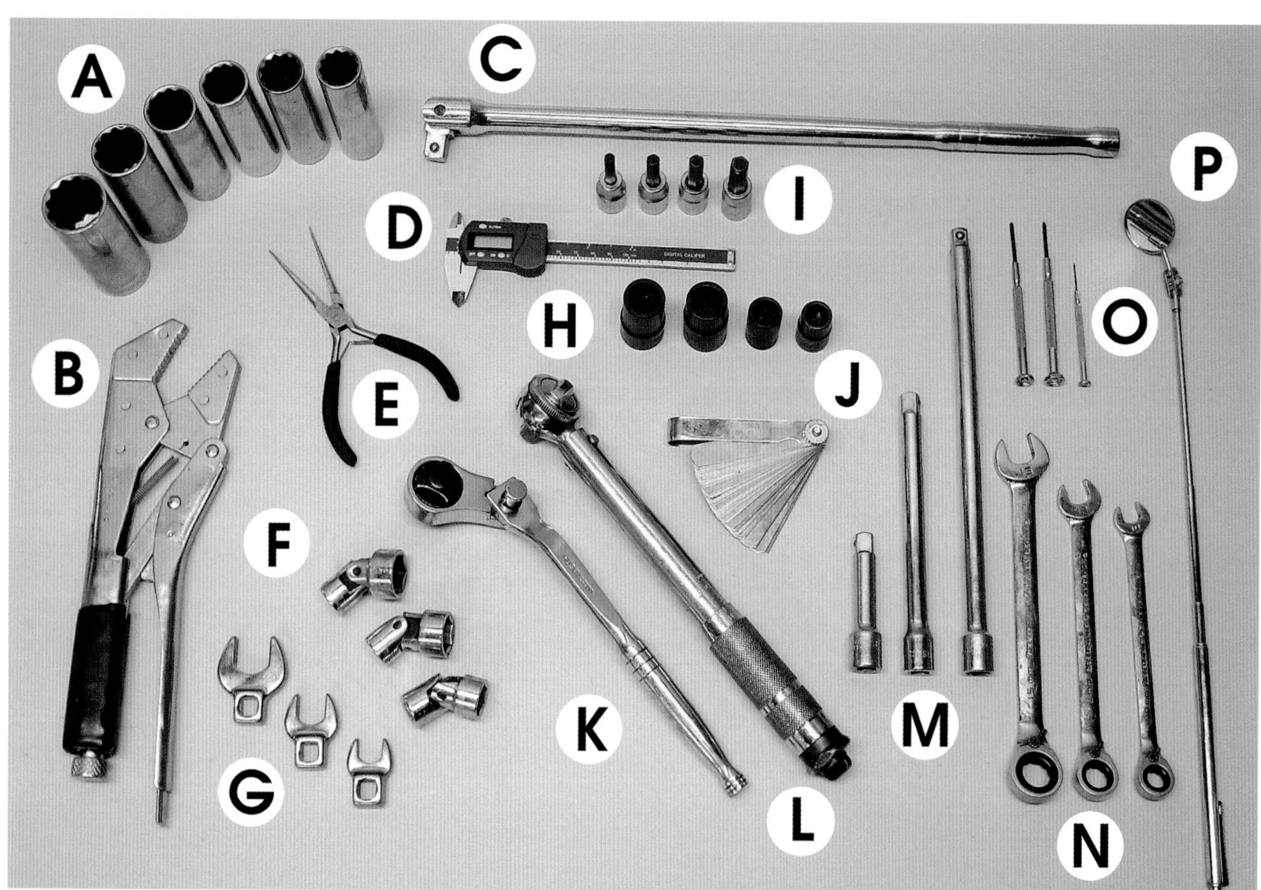

Tools: I've picked out some of the less commonplace tools for this photo. This is a collection of tools that you might not normally think to purchase, but ones that I would consider vital and use on a daily basis: **A: Deep socket metric set.** This is most useful for those large fasteners that you really need a socket for. Eventually, you will need one of the sockets in this set—might as well spring for the set all at once. **B: Locking pliers.** These are sometimes called vise grips and are very good multipurpose tools as long as they are not abused. Don't get lazy and use them instead of the proper tool for the job. **C: Breaker bar.** In conjunction with the deep socket set, you will need a tool that will give you the amount of torque that you need to remove those troublesome fasteners. **D: Digital caliper.** This is an excellent tool for making measurements of just about anything. The price on these has dropped in the past few years, so you can pick up a decent-quality unit for not too much money. **E: Needle-nose pliers.** Very handy for grabbing lost screws or nuts, or for simply installing small snap rings. Get a good-quality pair that won't bend or break on you. **F: Swivel-foot sockets.** These are great for using your sockets in hard-to-reach places, like the nut on the air conditioning compressor (see Photo 52 of Project 11). You can sometimes get away with a standard universal joint adapter for your socket driver as well. **G: Crowfoot wrenches.** These are perfect for that one nut that you just can't get to. They are particularly good for removing those hard-to-reach nuts in the engine compartment (see Photo 48 of Project 11). **H: Female Torx Sockets.** These are required for working on any modern Porsche. The really strong nuts (like the ones that hold on the seat rails) are typically of this variety and require these sockets for removal. **I: Hex wrench socket set.** Most of us have the standard set of right-angle hex wrenches; however, using a socket driver increases your ability to get into tight places and apply greater torque. **J: Feeler gauges.** You really can't get away without a set of these. They are useful for a variety of measurements in tight places. **K: Flexible ratchet.** I purchased this tool because it looked real cool—not because I could think of a unique purpose for it. However, it has become one of the most valuable tools in my collection. You don't realize the limitations of a standard ratchet until you've tried one of these. I also have an equally useful one that bends forward as well. **L: Torque wrench.** This tool is a must-have in everyone's collection. Purchase a good-quality one, and make sure that its range covers the tasks that you need to accomplish. **M: Extension set.** Extensions for your ⅜-inch drive are most useful, but other sizes can also come in handy. Some nuts are just impossible to reach with a standard-length socket and ratchet. **N: GearWrenches.** These ratcheting wrenches are some of my favorite tools. Make sure that you get the metric set with the tiny reversible lever on the end (shown in the photo). **O: Mini screwdrivers.** You don't know when you will need one, but when you do they're tremendously useful. **P: Inspection mirror.** Very useful when you just can't see into the rear of your engine compartment or around blind corners.

How to Use This Book

Time: This guide will orient you to the actual time the project takes to complete, including setup, installation, and cleanup. As everyone knows, sometimes the part that the manufacturer claimed could be installed in one hour actually takes three or four. So consider these times a ballpark average.

Tab: Another factor in deciding whether to embark on the project is cost, typically referring to the overall cost of the parts.

Talent: This estimates the mechanical knowledge and skills the project requires. They are numbered as follows:

1 = Beginner; little or no experience
2 = Beginner/Intermediate; some experience, but not a lot
3 = Intermediate; a fair amount of experience and confidence
4 = Advanced; a lot of experience and confidence
5 = Expert; you've seen and done it all

Tools: This component will identify what tools are required. Depending upon your inventory of tools, this may be a deciding factor between performing the job yourself or having your local shop take care of it.

Applicable Years: In some instances, the project may only be applicable to specific Boxster models, configurations, and model years.

More Info: Visit the link to find out more about this project.

Tip: Bits of information to help you with a quicker or better installation.

Performance Gain: Essentially, this will tell you the benefits you should see—in performance, fuel economy, or aesthetics. This measurement touches on your reason for performing the project in the first place.

Comp Modification: Points to other projects that could help you get even more out of the current project.

SECTION 1
BASICS

This section is a good place to start. If you've just purchased your Boxster and it is lacking an owner's manual, the Basics section covers what you need to know. No special tools are required, and the projects will give you a good idea of the format and tone of the rest of the book. If you've never worked on your Porsche before—don't worry. These first few projects are very simple, and are a good introduction to your car.

PROJECT 1

Jacking Up Your Car

Time / Tab / Talent: 20 minutes / $0 /

Tools: 2-ton jack, jack stands, jack pad tool

Applicable Years: All

Parts: None

More Info: www.101projects.com/Boxster/1.htm

Tip: Stack the wheels under the car as an added safety measure

Performance Gain: Starting point for all work underneath the car

Comp Modification: Check front and rear suspension bushings

About one-third of all tasks that you need to perform on your Boxster require it to be raised off of the ground. Simple enough for the experienced mechanic, the procedure of lifting a 3,000-pound car can be a bit unnerving for the amateur. In this project, I'll start out by showing you the best places to jack your car up and how to support it while you're working on it.

First, let's talk a bit about safety. Haphazard use of a floor jack can result in some pretty significant and expensive damage to you or your car. Before you begin raising the car, make sure that you have the wheels of the car blocked so that it can't roll. It's also wise to have your parking brake on as well and the car placed in first gear. You should always use jack stands in pairs to support the car—not simply the floor jack. Even if you are only lifting the car up for a few minutes, make sure that you place an emergency jack stand loosely underneath the transmission, motor, or rear differential just in case the floor jack fails.

Before you attempt to begin jacking up the car, make sure that all four wheels are carefully chocked and that the car is on a level surface. Keep in mind that if you raise up the rear of the car, the emergency brake no longer works (it works only on the two rearmost wheels of the car). If you place the car in park (automatic transmissions), it will only lock the rear wheels. Place a few 2×4 pieces of wood in front of each of the wheels to make sure that the car will not roll anywhere when you lift it up off of the ground.

The ideal places for jack stand supports are right underneath the four standard factory jack supports. Except for the emergency back-up jack stand mentioned previously, I don't recommend that you place the jack stands underneath the engine or transmission, as this can lead to instability.

I typically like to jack up the front of the car first. Use the reinforced area of the chassis shown in Photo 1. If you don't have a soft rubber pad or spare hockey puck for your jack, then fit a rolled up newspaper in between the jack and the car to avoid damage to the undercarriage of your car. Lift up the car slowly. It's perfectly okay if the car tilts while the wheels on the opposite side are still on the ground. Depending upon where you placed your jack, both front wheels may come off the ground or both wheels on one side of the car may come off the ground. Lift the car up only enough to get the jack stand underneath while it's set at its minimum height. Place the jack stand securely under the factory jack support area and slowly lower the car. If your car is spotless, I recommend placing a little bit of newspaper between the jack stand and the car to avoid scratching or scraping the underside of the chassis.

If you are lifting the front of the car, then place a jack stand under the front reinforced plate, lower the car onto the jack stand, and then repeat for the opposite side of the car. Then jack up the rear of the car in a similar fashion using the jack point shown in Photo 2. Jacking the car up from this point will typically raise the entire rear of the car, allowing you to set both rear jack stands in place at the same time. Set the height on the jack stands to be the same as the ones for the front. With the car supported on all four jack stands, you can carefully repeat the whole process to raise the car higher if needed.

Safety is of paramount importance here. Never work under the car with it suspended simply by the jack—always use jack stands. Always use a backup jack stand wherever you place your primary jack stands. One tiny flaw located in the casting process can lead to a jack stand breaking and having the car fall on top of you. If you are going to remove the wheels from the car, be sure that you loosen the lug nuts before you lift the car off the ground, otherwise the wheels will spin and you will have a difficult time getting the lug nuts off. Take the wheels and stack them in pairs underneath the car—this is an added measure of safety in case something fails.

Once you have the car up in the air and supported on the jack stands, position the jack under the engine without lifting it, and push on the car and see if it is unstable on the jack stands. If the car moves at all, you do not have it properly supported. It is far better for the car to fall off the jack stands while you are pushing on it than when you are underneath it. Really try to knock it off the jack stands—you want to make sure that it's perfectly stable. Set the floor jack underneath the engine or transmission while you're working as yet another backup support. Again, it's a wise idea to set up a spare jack stand or two as a precautionary measure against one of them failing.

When you are ready to lower the car, be aware of where you are placing your floor jack. Sometimes you will not be able to easily remove the jack when the car is lowered, or the jack handle may crush or damage part of the chassis or something else on the way down. Proceed very slowly and also be aware that some floor jacks release very quickly. Also be careful to place the car in gear, or to engage the parking brake before you lower it. The car may have a tendency to roll away right after it's put back on the ground.

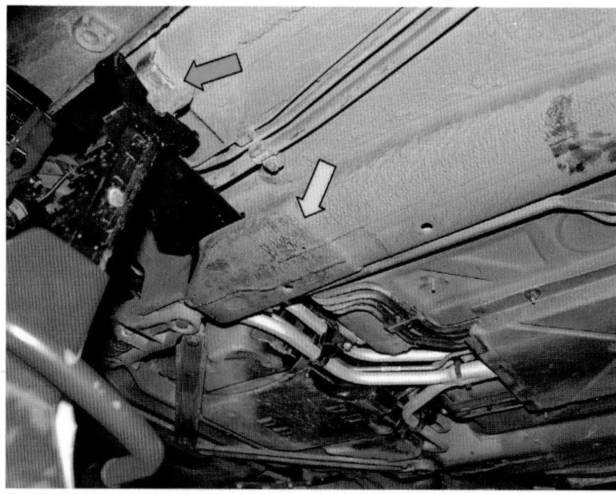

1 There is a reinforced area of the front chassis that makes for an excellent point to jack the car up with (yellow arrow). If you place your floor jack under this section, then you will be able to fit your jack stands in the standard factory jack support areas (green arrow). In this photo, the front of the car is on the left.

2 Jacking up the rear of the car can be easy—if you have a long-reach jack. My preferred spot is the rear suspension mounting point—it attaches the suspension to the chassis and is very strong. Avoid lifting the car using any part of the engine. Place your jack stands under the standard factory lift points (shown in Photo 3).

3 The best place to support the Boxster with jack stands is under the factory jack support areas. These four spots on either side of the car have metal cup pieces that act as locators for professional-style hydraulic lifts used at repair shops. Placing four jack stands at equal height on either side of the car like this creates a very stable platform for the car.

4 For better stability and ease of jacking up, you can use a jack plate tool. This tool attaches to the points under the car and gives you a nice, wide circular surface to use with your floor jack.

5 Based upon my extensive search for the perfect jack, I must recommend the DK13HLQ from AC Hydraulics. This jack is the best that I have ever seen and is exclusively available at PelicanParts.com. Manufactured with the highest quality in Denmark, this floor jack satisfies all of my requirements and has more than earned its place in my garage. With a minimum height of only 80mm (3.1 inches), the jack will easily fit under any of my lowered Porsches. On the other end, the jack has an unusually high lift of 735mm (29 inches) that enables you to raise your car up onto floor jacks in one swift motion. Combine that with the easy-to-use lift foot pedal, and you have a superior jack that's perfect for any car enthusiast, regardless of which car they happen to own.

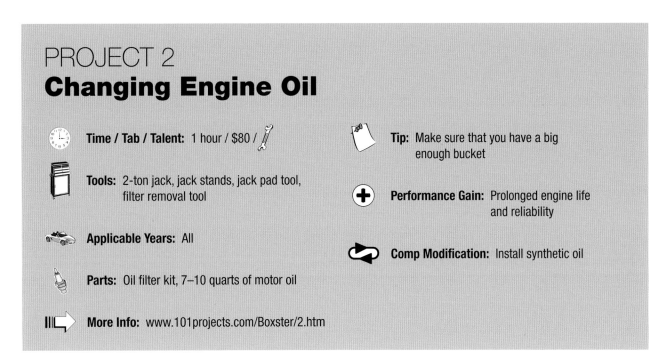

PROJECT 2
Changing Engine Oil

Time / Tab / Talent: 1 hour / $80 /

Tools: 2-ton jack, jack stands, jack pad tool, filter removal tool

Applicable Years: All

Parts: Oil filter kit, 7–10 quarts of motor oil

More Info: www.101projects.com/Boxster/2.htm

Tip: Make sure that you have a big enough bucket

Performance Gain: Prolonged engine life and reliability

Comp Modification: Install synthetic oil

One of the most common tasks to perform is replacing your engine oil. Frequent oil changes are perhaps the most important procedure you can do to maintain and prolong the life of your engine. However, with the better oils that are available today, the requirement for frequent changes is diminishing. Even though Porsche now recommends oil change intervals that are much farther apart than in the past, I usually recommend that you keep the changes under the 5,000-mile limit. If you don't drive your car too often, you should change the oil at least once a year to keep things fresh.

The first thing you need to do is to make sure that you have everything required for the job. Nothing is more frustrating than emptying your oil, only to find out that you don't have a replacement filter or enough oil. You will need an oil filter, a new drain plug sealing ring, the special Porsche oil filter removal tool, a roll of paper towels, a very large oil pan or bucket, and approximately 7–10 quarts of oil. You'll also need an 8mm hex socket tool to remove the drain plug from the bottom of the engine sump. Start by driving the car around, and let it heat up to operating temperature. You'll want to empty your oil when it's hot, because the heat makes the oil flow a lot easier, and more particles of metal and dirt will come out when the oil is emptied.

Once you get the car parked, place the oil pan bucket underneath the oil sump of the car. If your Boxster is too low to the ground to fit your oil change pan bucket underneath, then you will have to raise the car off of the ground (see Project 1). At the bottom of the engine sump there is a plug that is used for draining oil. Remove this plug carefully, and make sure you have a very large oil pan—at least a 10-quart capacity—under it, with a drip pan under the pan in case you underestimate. The oil will be very hot and will empty out extremely quickly, so be careful not to burn yourself (wear rubber gloves). There will be no time to grab any more buckets or oil pans if you underestimate, so make sure that the one you choose is big enough.

While the oil is draining, it is a good time to remove the oil filter. You want to make sure that you remove the filter with the oil pan still under the car because the oil filter is full of oil, and this oil will have a tendency to drip down out of the filter into the engine and out the drain hole. The Boxster filter is a cartridge-type filter, which is contained within a plastic oil filter housing next to the bottom sump underneath the car. You will typically need the factory oil filter housing removal tool, or a comparable one, in order to remove the housing. Remove the plastic housing, and underneath you will see the cartridge filter. Simply pull on it to remove it from the engine—it will be stuck on a pipe pointing down out of the engine. Have plenty of paper towels on hand, as oil will spill from the filter if you're not careful.

While all of your oil is draining, take the drain plug from the engine, and carefully clean it with a paper towel. When the plug is clean, replace it in the car with a new metal gasket. Torque the plug to 50 Nm (37 ft-lb).

Now install the new oil filter. Simply take the filter cartridge and place it on the oil pipe exiting the bottom of the engine. One side of the filter should be slightly beveled to enable you to easily slip the filter onto the pipe. Clean out the inside of the oil filter housing and replace the O-ring with a new one before installing the new oil filter cartridge. Slightly lubricate the O-ring with some fresh motor oil prior to installing it. Now, screw on the filter housing and make it snug tight. Torque it to 25 Nm (19 ft-lb).

Now it's time to fill up your Porsche with motor oil. A lot of people aren't really sure what motor oil to use in their car. Traditionally, the characteristics of motor oil were linked closely to its weight. Heavier-weight oils protect well against heat; lighter-weight oils flow better in cold. In general, if you live in a cold climate, you should use a 10W-40 or similar oil. This oil is a 10-weight oil that behaves and protects against heat like a 40-weight oil. In warmer climates, you should use a 20W-50 oil. This oil doesn't flow as well at the colder climates, but gives an extra "edge" on the hotter end. I have put a lot more info on motor oils on the 101Projects.com site—check there for more recommendations.

The question of whether to use synthetic or traditional "dinosaur" oil often comes up among car buffs. *Consumer Reports* (July 1996) ran an extensive test on the two types of oil, altering amongst many different brands. The testers installed freshly rebuilt engines in 75 taxicabs and then ran them through the harshest conditions on the streets of New York City. Placing different brands, weights, and formulations in the cars, they racked up 60,000 miles on the engines, tore them down, measured, and inspected the engine components for wear. The oil was changed at 3,000 miles in half of them, and the rest were changed at 6,000 miles. The results: regardless of brand, synthetic or traditional non-synthetic, weight, and oil change interval, there were no discernable differences in engine component wear in any of the engines. Their conclusion? Motor oils and the additives blended into them have improved so much over the years that frequent oil changes and expensive synthetics are no longer necessary.

Still, some people swear by synthetic oil. In practice, I don't recommend using synthetic oil if you have an older car with old seals in the engine. There have been many documented cases in which the addition of synthetic oil has caused an otherwise dry car to start leaking. If you own an older Boxster that doesn't have fresh seals in the engine, I would stick to the non-synthetics. However, if synthetic oil was the only type of oil that your engine has seen, I usually recommend sticking with it.

Fill your oil tank from the oil filler hole located in the rear trunk. Add about 5 quarts to the engine, and check the dipstick (1997–2004) or the oil level gauge (2005 and later). Continue to add about a half a quart at a time and keep checking the level. Fill it up until it reaches the top mark of the dipstick or gauge—when you start the engine, the engine oil level will automatically lower when the oil filter fills up with oil. Make sure that you put the oil filler cap back on the top of the filler hole, otherwise, you will end up with a messy trunk compartment when you drive away. While you're at it, also check the seal in the oil filler cap. A vacuum leak in this cap will cause rough running when you go to start the engine.

If you had the car up on jack stands, lower it down to the ground. Now, start up the engine. The oil pressure light should stay on for about a second or two and then go out. Hop out of the car and look at the engine underneath, then take a quick look underneath the car. Verify that there's no volume of oil seeping out of the engine. Take the car out for a drive and bring it up to operating temperature. Shut the car off and then recheck the oil level (careful, the car will be hot). At this point, I like to top the oil off at the top point on the dipstick. Make sure that you dispose of your old oil at a respectable recycling station.

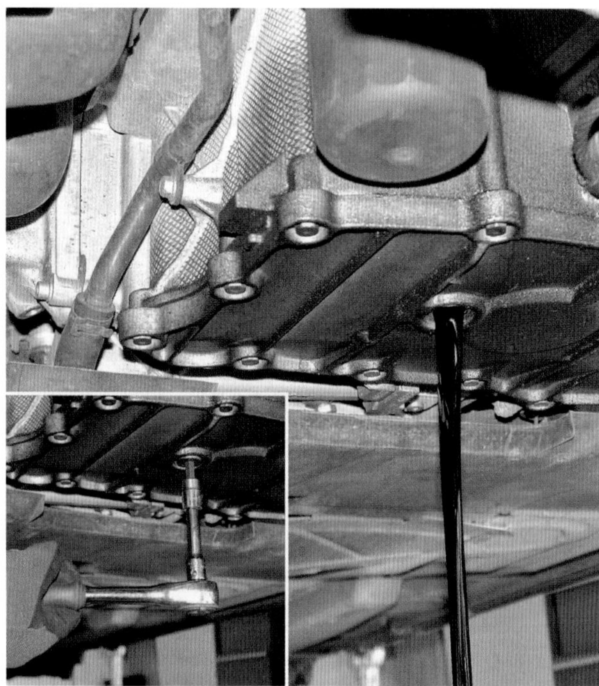

1 Begin the oil change process by removing the drain plug underneath the car. The plug should accept an 8mm hex socket tool (inset). I recommend that you replace the small metal gasket underneath the plug each time, as it helps guard against oil leaks.

2 The filter housing will probably be stuck and difficult to remove from the engine. The best way to get it off is with the Porsche oil filter housing removal tool. Simply slide the tool on and remove the housing from the engine.

3 Be sure to remember to replace the large O-ring that seals the oil filter housing to the engine. This O-ring should be included in your complete oil filter kit (inset photo).

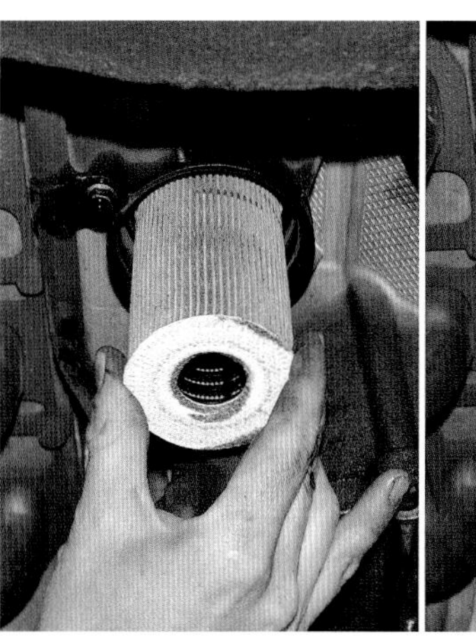

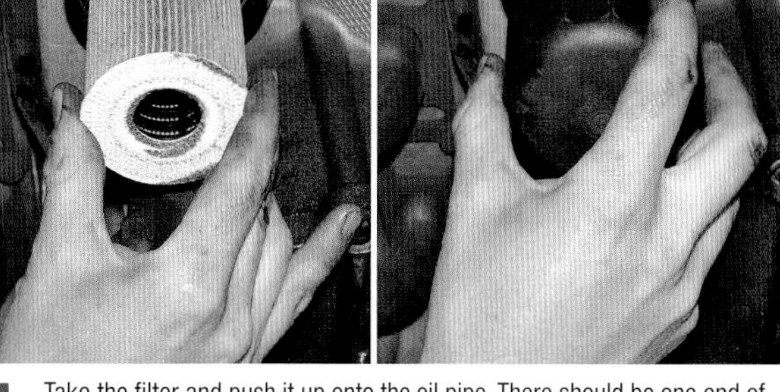

4 Take the filter and push it up onto the oil pipe. There should be one end of the filter that's slightly beveled to ease the installation process. With the filter in place, install the oil filter housing back onto the engine.

5 Fill your car with oil from the inlet in the front of the rear trunk. The oil filler hole is on the left side, and the oil cap is a light tan in color. If you're quick and skilled with the bottle, you can pour without spilling. However, most people use a funnel to help prevent a mess.

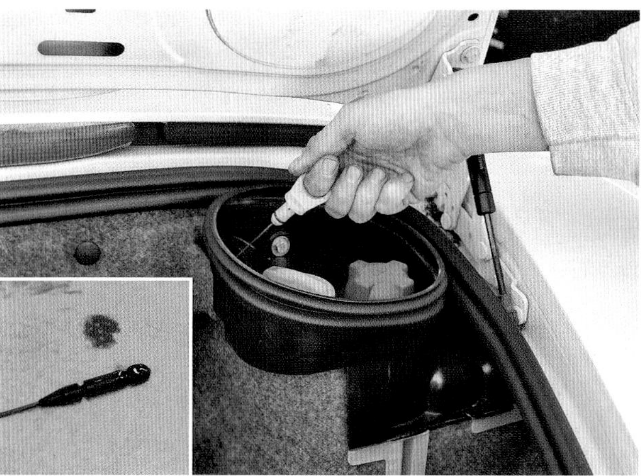

6 Pull your dipstick and check to make sure you have ample oil in your engine sump (1997–2004 only). Wipe down the end of the dipstick prior to inserting it into the engine—this will help you achieve an accurate reading.

7 Shown here is a full-flow spin-on oil filter adapter, allowing for use of a conventional spin-on oil filter, rather than requiring the use of expensive and inferior replacement cartridge-style filters. Manufactured by LN Engineering, this design makes changing your oil a somewhat simpler task. With the adapter, you no longer have to handle the filter cartridge, worry about contamination of the oil filter housing, or worry about cross-threading the cheap plastic filter housing. The spin-on oil filter adapter also helps improve the longevity of your engine by providing full flow filtration, which means 100 percent of the oil gets filtered without having oil bypass the filter (an improvement over the factory design).

PROJECT 3

Replacing Air Filters

Time / Tab / Talent: 30 minutes / $40 /

Tools: None

Applicable Years: All

Parts: Air filter, cabin pollen filter

More Info: www.101projects.com/Boxster/3.htm

Tip: Replace both air filter and pollen filter together

Performance Gain: Better airflow into your fuel injection system

Comp Modification: Install cone filter or cold air intake

You should change the air filter in your Boxster every 10,000 miles or so. The air filter protects the fuel injection system and the air intake system from dust and debris that can be sucked in under normal operation.

On the Boxster, the filter is located on the upper left side of the engine compartment. In order to reach the top of the engine compartment, you need to slightly lower the roof and raise up the rear convertible top cover (see Photo 1).

To access the filter, simply release the spring clips and pull up on the top cover—the filter should come right out of its housing. Take a look inside the filter housing—there are usually some leaves or dirt that found their way in there. Clean the housing out before installing the new filter.

For the Boxster there are basically two different types of air filters—the stock paper or cloth air filters and aftermarket units. These aftermarket units utilize an oil-soaked fabric to achieve freer airflow. The bottleneck for airflow in the Boxster engine is not necessarily the air filter. The primary advantage of the aftermarket units is that you usually only have to purchase one, and it will last the life of your car.

No matter what your friends tell you, these aftermarket filters will not add any significant horsepower to your engine. Many tests on a dynamometer have revealed that the freer-flow air filters do not suddenly "create" horsepower out of thin air. If you install one of these filters into your car and "swear" there's more horsepower, then have a friend do a blind test for you. Have him switch the filters in and out at random and see if you can tell the difference. This is what is commonly called the placebo effect—perceiving significant gains in performance just because you added a "performance part."

The downside to using these aftermarket filters is that they often do not filter as well as the factory units. In addition, the use of aftermarket filters may cause excess dirt to accumulate in the mass airflow sensor and lead to its premature failure. The bottom line is that you need to carefully research any aftermarket filter before you install it into your car and carefully clean and maintain it thereafter. I personally prefer to use the stock OEM cloth/paper filters to ensure maximum filtering and protection. Whichever one you choose, make sure that it filters as well as or better than the original Porsche specifications.

1 In order to gain access to the engine compartment on the Boxster, you need to place the convertible top into the "service position." Raise the top so that the front edge is about 10 inches above the front windshield. The rear cover or tonneau cover should be up about as far as it can go during the process of opening the roof.

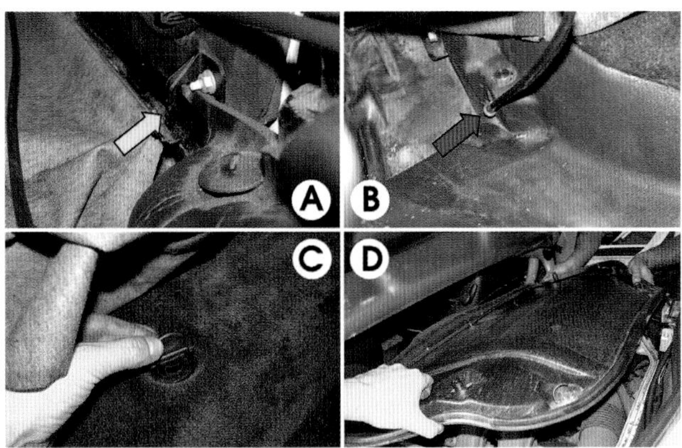

2 Once the roof is in the service position, there are a few steps that you need to take in order access the top of the engine. **A:** Disconnect the convertible top plastic fabric rod from the two connectors at the rear bulkhead (yellow arrow). **B:** Find and pull off the lower ball head of the convertible top tension cables on each side (red arrow). Push the bottom of the folding top toward the front of the car. **C:** Rotate snaps and remove rear shelf compartment from underneath the convertible top. **D:** Rotate the clips on the engine compartment cover and lift off.

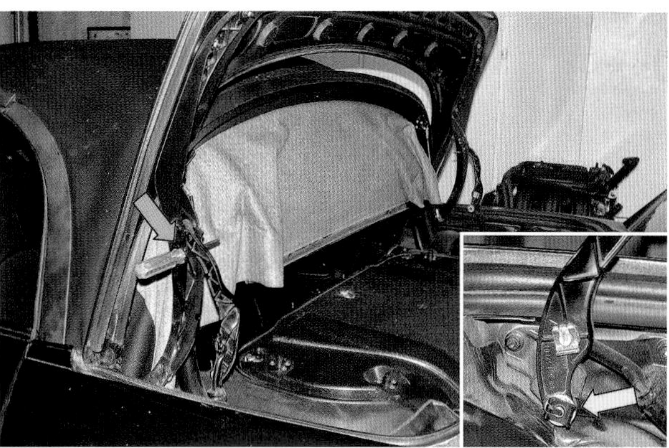

3 If you wish to have greater access to the engine compartment, you can disconnect the linkage for the rear cover and slide it up into a position closer to the front of the car. Simply disconnect the small lower circlip from each side (yellow arrow) and push the roof forward. Then hold it in place with spare screwdrivers inserted into the locking holes to keep it secure (blue arrow). Be sure to secure the rear cover (sometimes called a clamshell cover) carefully—if it falls, the two nipples on the underside may dent the rear trunk lid.

BASICS

4 The air filter is located on the left side of the engine compartment. Snap out the spring clips and pull up on the black plastic housing (green arrow), and you should be able to reach in and pull the filter out.

5 Pull up on the air filter cartridge and remove it from the car. You should then be able to easily remove the air filter and replace it with a new one (early style shown in inset photo).

6 While you're replacing the engine air filter, I recommend that you also swap out the cabin air filter as well. Sometimes known as a "pollen filter," the cabin filter is located in the front trunk on the right side of the car. Remove the plastic panel just in front of windshield on the right side (upper left) with a T-25 Torx driver. Then reach in and pull out the filter. Install the new filter in place (upper right) and replace the plastic panel.

7 Later cars have a different-style air cleaner and filter—begin by removing the two screws on the front cover (yellow arrows). Then remove the single screw that attaches the filter to the box (green arrow), and then wiggle the filter insert out. Transfer the mounting plate to the new filter and reinstall.

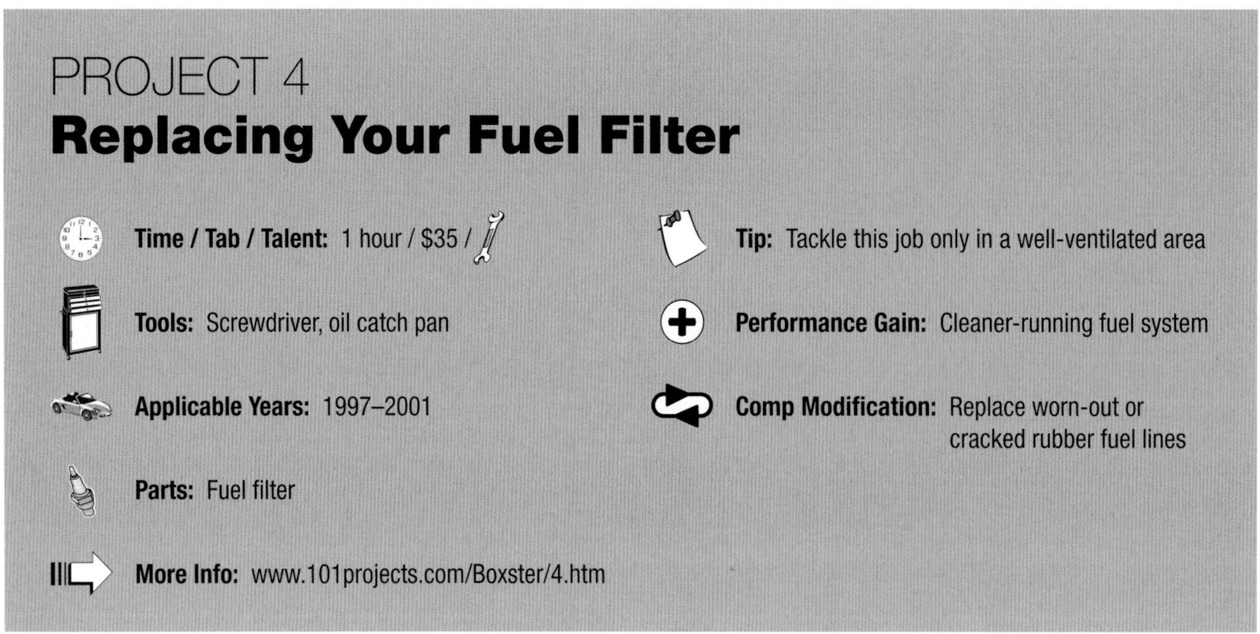

PROJECT 4
Replacing Your Fuel Filter

Time / Tab / Talent: 1 hour / $35 /

Tools: Screwdriver, oil catch pan

Applicable Years: 1997–2001

Parts: Fuel filter

More Info: www.101projects.com/Boxster/4.htm

Tip: Tackle this job only in a well-ventilated area

Performance Gain: Cleaner-running fuel system

Comp Modification: Replace worn-out or cracked rubber fuel lines

One of the basic maintenance projects that you should perform on your Porsche is the replacement of the fuel filter. Starting in 2002, Porsche moved the filter to inside the gas tank and called it a "lifetime" filter that never needs to be changed. For cars with a replaceable filter, I recommend that you replace your fuel filter about once a year or every 10,000 miles. It seems that with today's odd blended fuels, there always seems to be some gas station that has problems with dirt or grime in the gasoline that can clog your tank. I don't think quality control with gasoline stations is really what it used to be. Needless to say, I try to replace the fuel filter at least once a year.

Changing the fuel filter is not a job that I relish. It is almost guaranteed that you will spill at least some fuel on the ground and yourself as you swap out the fuel filter. Be sure to perform the replacement in a well-ventilated area. That means outdoors or in your garage with a few large fans blowing air both in and out. Have a fire extinguisher handy, wear rubber gloves, eye protection, and have a few rolls of paper towels handy—you will need them.

The fuel tank should be as low as possible—drive around until the gas tank is almost empty. This will minimize problems if something should happen to go wrong.

The first step is to jack the car up (Project 1). The Boxsters have an intelligent design when it comes to fuel flow. The fuel pump is located in the bottom of the tank and pumps fuel out of the top fuel tank cover. Why is this good? Well, when you go to change the fuel filter, you can pull out the fuel pump relay, crank the car a few times, and be assured that fuel isn't going to flow everywhere if you make a mistake. Some older cars have a gravity-fed system that takes fuel out of the bottom of the tank. With these systems, you have to disconnect the line and clamp it very quickly—otherwise, the entire tank of gas will empty out! Unfortunately, with the Boxster system, you can't get 100 percent of the fuel out, and some will spill when you disconnect the fuel filter. In addition, the filter itself will mostly be full of fuel too.

With the car up off the ground, crawl underneath the car. The filter is located behind the large plastic panel located in the very center of the car. This panel is held on with some plastic nuts (10mm head)—remove them and the panel should easily drop down. Next, remove the foam fixture piece that wraps around all of the lines in the center tunnel, and remove the two bolts that hold the plastic coolant line bracket (see Photo 1). Disconnect the fuel filter ground strap, and loosen up the clamp that holds the filter. Now you want to disconnect the lines to the filter. The Boxster filter has connections that are very easy to attach and remove. Simply push gently on the gray tabs on opposite sides of the plastic connector, and the connection should easily slide off. Take a close look at your new filter for guidance on how this quick-connect connector works. Have a small pail or bucket handy to catch the excess fuel when you release the connection.

When the connections have been released, expect quite a few ounces of gasoline to be coming your way. Be prepared (gloves, eye protection, paper towels, bucket, and a well-ventilated area). Take the filter out by pulling it toward the rear of the car, put it in your bucket, and take it and any left over or spilled gasoline outside of your garage immediately. Let the garage sit empty for about 15–20 minutes before you re-enter—it will take about that long for the fumes to clear. Then, simply reattach the new filter in place of the old one, observing the direction of the arrows located on the filter—they point in the direction of fuel flow, which is from the gas tank (front) to the engine (rear). Check that the snap-fit connections are properly seated by gently tugging on them. Reattach the ground wire (important!). Tighten the clamp that holds the filter tight. Then reinstall the foam piece and the large center panel.

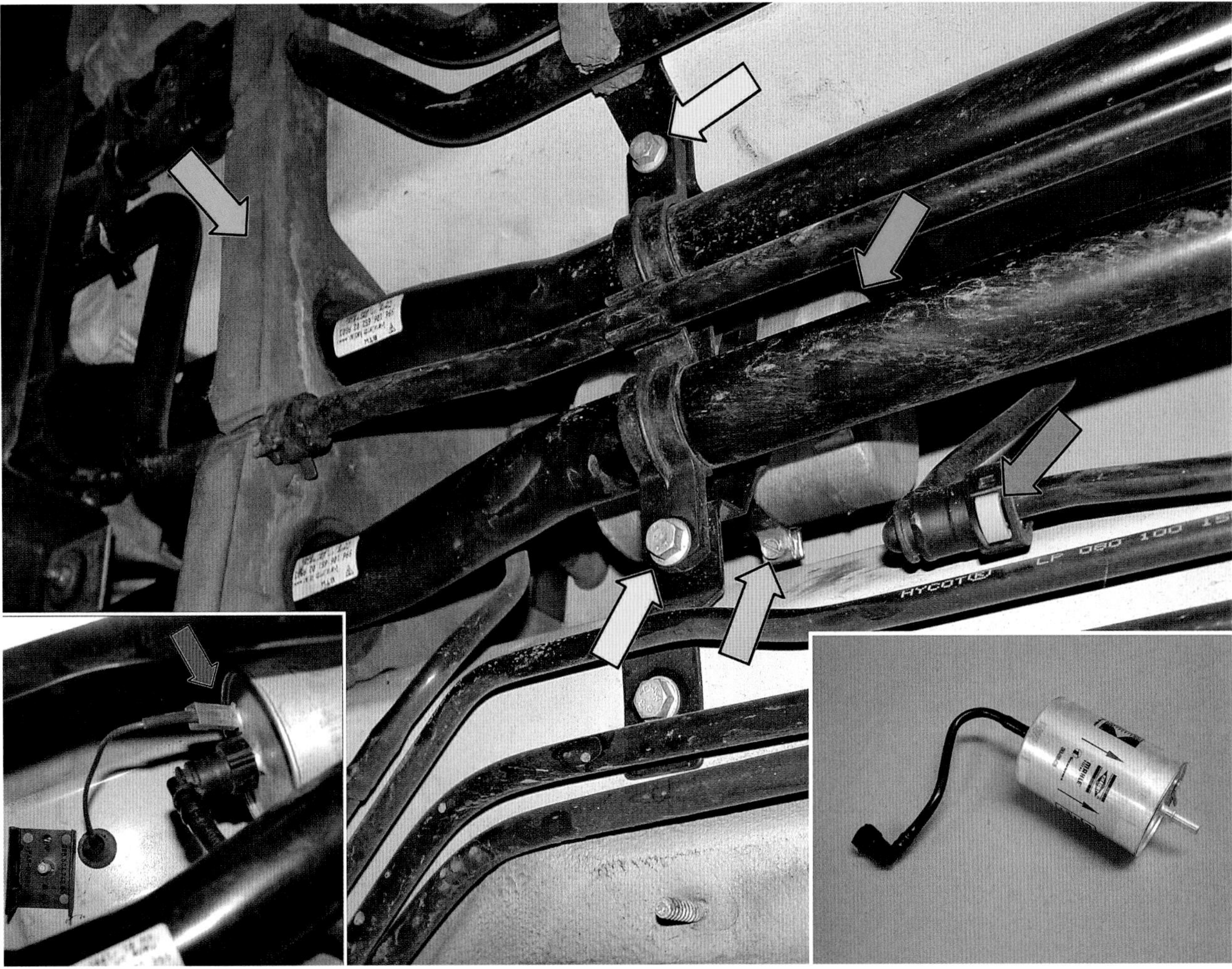

1 The filter (green arrow) is located almost dead center in the middle of the car, hidden somewhat behind the coolant pipes. The blue arrow points to the foam piece that needs to be removed so that you can pull the filter out toward the rear of the car. Removal of the filter is made easier if you remove the two screws that hold on the plastic coolant line bracket (yellow arrows). The orange arrow shows the screw that needs to be loosened in order to release the fuel filter from the clamp. The purple arrow points to one of the two tabs that must be depressed on the quick-disconnect connector. In the lower right, a brand-new fuel filter is shown. Note the arrows that indicate fuel flow direction are printed on the side of the filter. The lower left inset photo shows the small ground strap that needs to be removed from the old filter and reattached to the new one (red arrow).

PROJECT 5
Replacing Belts

Time / Tab / Talent: 1 hour / $30 /

Tools: Socket set, 24mm wrench for idler pulley

Applicable Years: All

Parts: Drive belt

More Info: www.101projects.com/Boxster/5.htm

Tip: Carry a spare main drive belt with you in case of failure

Performance Gain: No squeaky engine or water pump failure

Comp Modification: Replace water pump and/ or alternator

One of the routine maintenance items that you should perform on your Boxster is the checking and replacement of your accessory drive belt. The belts are driven off of the crankshaft and power accessories such as the water pump, power steering pump, alternator, and air conditioning compressor. There is only one belt on the car that powers it all. It should be checked periodically (every 5,000 miles, or when you change your oil).

The Boxster uses what is known as a poly-ribbed belt (having many channels or ribs on the underside of the belt). The poly-ribbed belt setup utilizes a spring-loaded belt tensioner pulley that provides the proper tension for the belt at all times, making adjustment unnecessary.

When inspecting your belts, the one thing that you want to look for is cracks (see red arrow in Photo 1). If you see any cracks at all, you should replace your belts immediately. The cracks will usually occur on the inside of the belt (the surface that typically rides on the surface of the pulley). With the poly-ribbed belts, this is the grooved surface.

With the poly-ribbed belt, replacement is a snap. Begin by gaining access to the front of the engine. Follow the instructions in Photo 1 to remove the carpet and front engine cover from the rear of the passenger compartment.

The tensioners that hold the belt tight can be easily released using a 24mm wrench. Rotate the tensioner clockwise to release the tension. Simply release the tension on the belt from the tensioner, and then the belt should simply slide off. Release the tension, and then you should be able to unwind the belt from the engine. Tip: If the belt is worn, simply release the tension on it, and snip it with some large tin cutters to pull it out of the car.

Installation of the new belt is easy. Simply slide on most of the new belt onto the pulleys, release the tension on the tensioner, and slide the belt onto the tensioner. Check to make sure that the belt is securely seated in all of the pulleys. Verify that the ribbed portion of the belt is set against the crankshaft pulley. Install the belt in the following order: **1:** Water pump, **2:** Alternator, **3:** Upper idler pulley, **4:** Power steering pump, **5:** Air conditioning compressor, **6:** Crankshaft, **7:** Flexible idler pulley, **8:** Lower idler pulley.

1 The drive belt on the Boxster is accessible through a trapdoor compartment cover that's located behind the seats. Move the seats all the way forward, and remove the rear carpet panel by releasing the small snaps that hold it in place (inset photo, upper right). The clips are screwed onto metal studs. They can be removed using a forked tool available at some shops, or simply slip your finger underneath to provide some upward pressure and pull off. Underneath the carpet, you will see the front engine cover—remove the seven bolts and two nuts (all 10mm head) that hold on the cover, and it should easily come off. The lower left inset photo shows a belt that is getting very old and showing numerous cracks in the ribbed surface.

2 With the front engine cover removed, you can see all of the various components that are driven by the main belt. On the right are the air conditioning compressor (yellow arrow) and the power steering pump (green arrow). On the left is the alternator (blue arrow). Out of view on the bottom is the water pump. The crankshaft is in the center, shown by the orange arrow. To release tension on the belt, simply place a 24mm socket attached to a breaker bar on the idler (red arrow) and turn it clockwise (lower left).

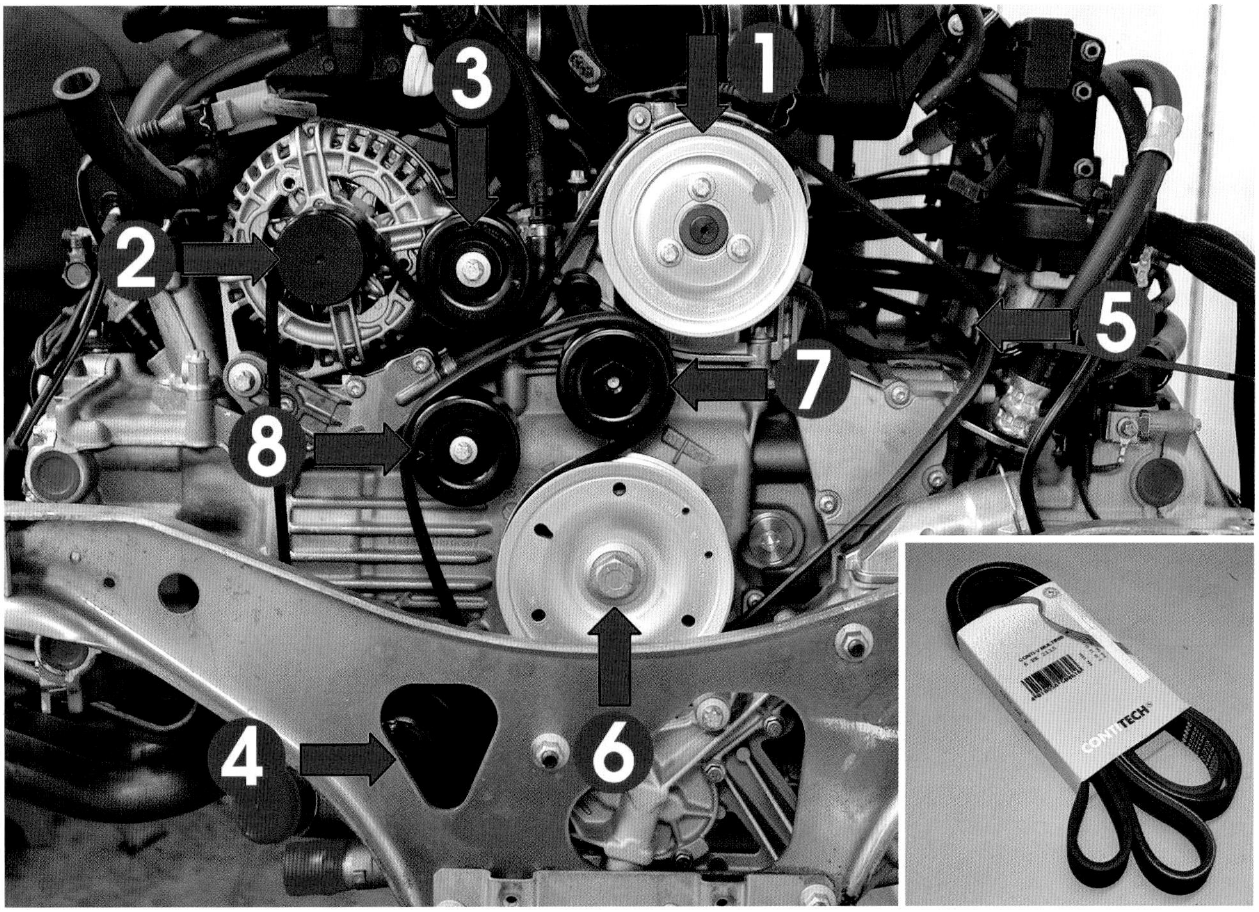

3 Here is a brand new crate 3.4-liter 996 motor direct from Porsche. The various components are **1:** Power steering pump, **2:** Alternator, **3:** Upper idler pulley, **4:** Water pump, **5:** Air conditioning compressor (not installed), **6:** Crankshaft, **7:** Tensioner pulley, **8:** Lower idler pulley. On the lower right is a photo of what a brand new belt looks like.

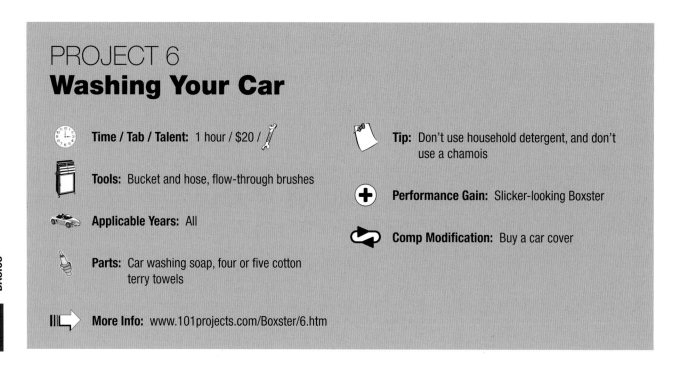

PROJECT 6
Washing Your Car

Time / Tab / Talent: 1 hour / $20 /

Tools: Bucket and hose, flow-through brushes

Applicable Years: All

Parts: Car washing soap, four or five cotton terry towels

More Info: www.101projects.com/Boxster/6.htm

Tip: Don't use household detergent, and don't use a chamois

Performance Gain: Slicker-looking Boxster

Comp Modification: Buy a car cover

One of the most basic maintenance tasks for your car is cleaning it. While this includes the art of washing your Porsche, it also includes the reconditioning and protection of both the exterior paint and the interior.

The first step in washing your car is to determine exactly what it needs. If the car is simply dusty and has been sitting in the garage, then you probably only need to wash it with plain water (no soap). Wet the car down and use a wash mitt to remove any dust that might have settled on the car inside the garage. When washing the car, remember to get the valance panels and the lower rockers. As these panels are closest to the ground, they have a tendency to get the dirtiest.

I don't recommended using a chamois to dry your car. The chamois can trap small particles of dirt in its porous material and can actually cause scratches in the surface of the paint when it's used to dry off the car. A really good alternative is 100 percent cotton terry towels. Make sure the towels have been washed at least once, and don't use a rinse or softener. The softener is an additive that can cause streaks, and it inhibits the towel's absorbency.

If your car suffers from more than simple dust accumulation, then you will need to use a bit of car wash soap. Make sure that you don't use normal household soap or detergent, as this will remove the wax from the surface of the paint. As the wax is oil-based, normal detergents will attack and remove it. The car wash soaps are very mild and shouldn't remove the layer of wax that you have on your car.

Rinse the car completely with water from a hose, taking care not to spray the water in any areas where your seals may be cracking. If your Boxster is a few years old, the overall watertight seal of the interior may not be as solid as desired. If your car does leak water, then toss some towels inside the car near the windows or under the roof to make sure that you catch any water before it reaches the carpet and seats. Also be aware not to get any water into the side snorkel area—water can collect there and then be sucked up into the engine.

After the car is completely rinsed, start drying it immediately. It's best to dry the car off out of the reach of sunlight. Pull the car into the garage and dry it off in there. Removing the car from the sun helps keep those ugly water spots from appearing.

The key to keeping the paint free of scratches is to make sure that the towels are clean and free of any debris. Handle the towels as if they were going to be used for surgery. Don't leave them outside, or if you drop them on the ground, don't use them again until they have been washed. Small particles of dirt trapped within the towels can cause nasty scratches in the paint. If you happen to encounter a water spot, use a section of a damp, clean terrycloth towel to gently rub it out.

When you are finished cleaning, it's time to tuck the car away. I recommend that you use a good-quality soft car cover if your car is spending most of its life in the garage. The cover will protect it from dust accumulation and also might help protect against items falling on the car or cats jumping on it. For cars stored outdoors, covers usually are not a great idea. They have a tendency to trap water, and the wind can make the cloth cover wear against the paint. If your car is not perfectly clean, then dirt particles trapped between the car and the cover will have a tendency to scratch the paint.

One of the most interesting new products to hit the marketplace in recent years are deionized water washing systems. I have used these on several of my cars, and I've been very pleased with the results. Available in small hand-held units, or semi-permanent installed setups, the systems filter regular tap water through a deionizing filter and provide a quick and easy way to wash your car without having to dry it—the deionized water doesn't leave any ugly water spots. These systems work pretty well, although in practice I was not able to eliminate all of the water spots from the car, so I recommend using them with a set of traditional towels as well to help dry the car.

1 One of the most innovative and time-saving products I've seen in recent years are flow-through brushes from Carrand. These are the perfect car-washing tool for busy people on the go. Simply hook up the brushes to your hose, and water flows through the brush as you're cleaning. Add an automatic soap dispenser, and you can clean an absolutely filthy car in about 10 minutes. My personal favorite is the flow-through wheel cleaning brush. It removes wheel dust and grime within about a minute of use. Used weekly, it's a great way to keep hard-to-remove grit and grime from building up on your wheels.

SECTION 2
ENGINE

The modern Porsche engines are built upon years of experience with the air-cooled 911. Porsche has taken a good, reliable design and continually modified and improved it—making the boxer six-cylinder into a reliable, water-cooled power plant. Still, there are components that wear out and need attention. This section will guide you through engine maintenance tasks and also help you to evaluate what happens when you encounter the rare engine problem.

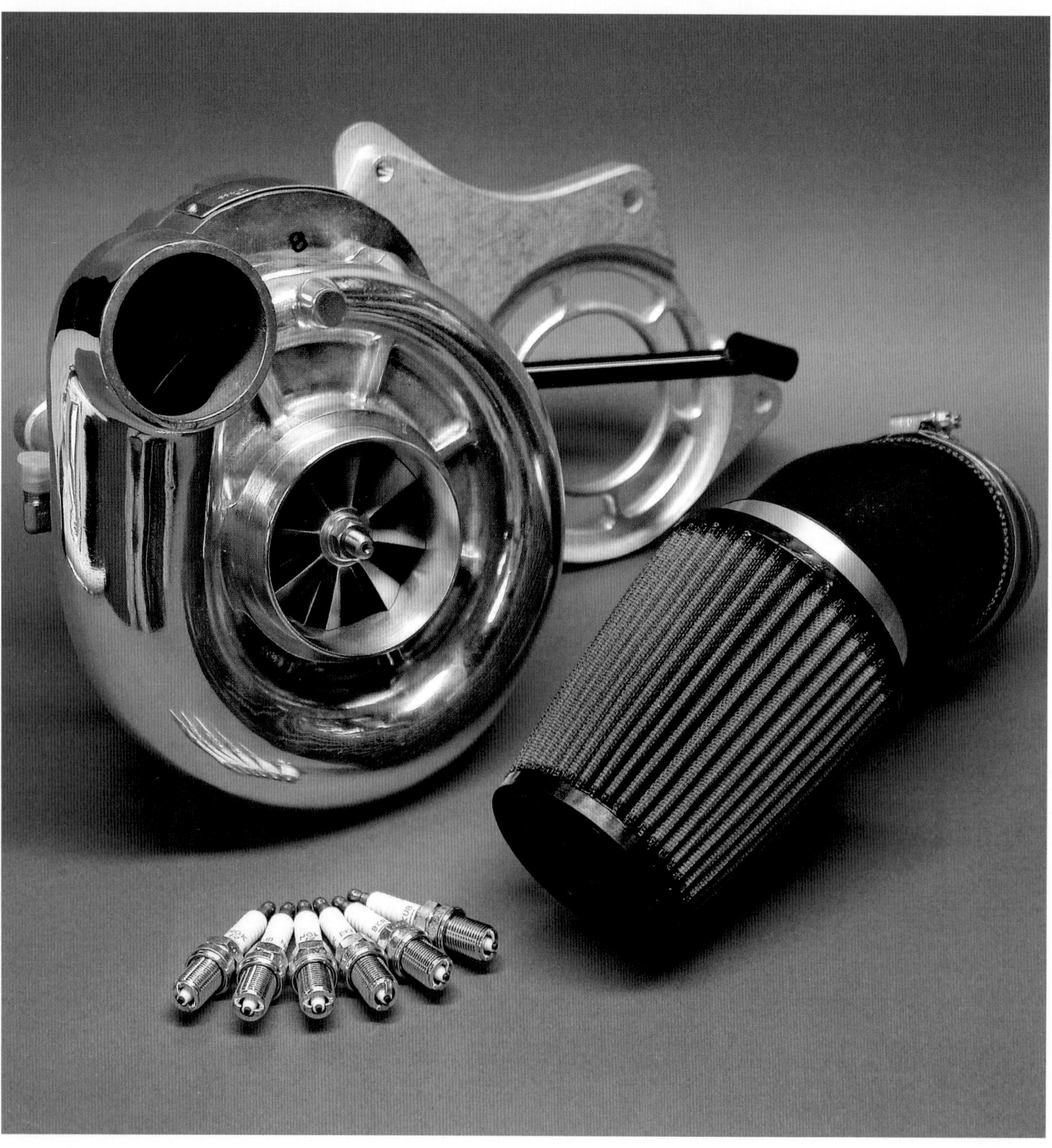

PROJECT 7
Replacing Spark Plugs/Coils

Time / Tab / Talent: 2 hours / $20 /

Tools: Spark plug wrench

Applicable Years: All

Parts: Spark plugs, spark plug tubes

More Info: www.101projects.com/Boxster/7.htm

Tip: Don't use anti-seize on the plugs when installing

Performance Gain: Cleaner, better running engine

Comp Modification: Replace spark plug tubes and/or O-rings

The replacement of your spark plugs and spark plug wires (where applicable) is a basic tune-up procedure for just about any car on the road. I recommend replacing your spark plugs every 10,000 miles, or about once a year. In reality, you can probably go longer than that; however, you never really quite know how long the plugs are going to last, or you may forget to replace them if you don't set up a yearly schedule.

With the introduction of the Boxster engine, Porsche eliminated the use of spark plug wires by integrating six small spark plug coils that sit on top of each spark plug. While this configuration may be a bit more expensive than the typical single coil, single capacitive discharge box configuration, it makes the car's ignition system more reliable by removing a component that constantly wears out and fails (spark plug wires). It's a pretty cool setup not commonly found on older cars. As manufacturing components have become increasingly inexpensive, ignition setups like these have become more common.

Begin by prepping the car. The only thing that you really need to do is make sure that the car is cold. If you try to remove or install spark plugs in a hot car, then you may encounter problems with the spark plugs gumming up or damaging the relatively delicate threads in the aluminum cylinder head. Make sure that the car is cold or, at the bare minimum, only slightly warm to the touch.

Jack up the car (Project 1). Access to the plugs may be easier if you remove the fender liners in front of each wheelwell, particularly on the passenger side. For each coil, remove the two bolts that attach it to the engine. Unplug the coil wire harness. Then simply remove the coil/plug assembly and place it off to the side. All of the coils are the same, so it doesn't matter which cylinder bank it came from, unless you are specifically trying to troubleshoot a bad coil fault code that was displayed by the main computer.

With the coil assembly removed, you should be able to look down the hole and see the spark plug hiding in there. If the tube has oil in it, it may have cracked or become contaminated. Replace it with a new one (see Photo 3 and also Photo 6 of Project 16).

Spark plug removal is easy. You just need the right spark plug wrench. I have one that I love—it's a spark plug socket with a rubber insert that catches the plug and also has a built-in swivel on the attachment end. These wrenches are readily available from the tools section of PelicanParts.com. This tool is especially useful when trying to remove plugs in hard-to-reach places.

Using a breaker bar, grip the plug and turn it counterclockwise until it is loose. Then pull out your tool and grab the plug. When the plug comes out, you may want to take a close look at it. The spark plug is really the best way to visually "see" what is going on inside your combustion chamber.

Install your new plugs using a torque wrench to measure the amount of torque applied to the plug. This is very important, as it is easy to over- or under-tighten spark plugs. Make sure that the plug is firmly seated in your spark plug socket, as it is very easy to insert the plug into the head and have it cross-thread. This means that the threads of the spark plug don't mesh properly with the ones in the head, instead choosing to "cut their own path." This damages the threads on the head, and in extreme cases, may destroy the threads in the cylinder head entirely. Trust me, you do not want this to happen. Proceed carefully and cautiously here.

Install each spark plug into the cylinder heads without using any anti-seize compound. Torque the spark plugs to 30 Nm (22 ft-lbs). I recently learned that Porsche published a bulletin indicating that it doesn't recommend using anti-seize compound on spark plugs for any of their engines (Porsche Technical Bulletin 9102, Group 2 identifier 2870). The bulletin applies retroactively to all models, and the theory is that the anti-seize compound tends to act as an electrical insulator between the plug and the cylinder head. This could have a detrimental effect on the firing of the spark due to the loss of a good, consistent ground connection.

With the new plugs installed and tightened to the correct torque, you can replace the coils and reattach the coil connectors. When you're done, your engine should look back to normal and run perfectly.

1 Each spark plug has its own individual coil. These are attached to the engine with two bolts (purple arrows). Remove each bolt and then disconnect the coil plug harness (green arrow). The coil should be able to be pulled from the engine once loose.

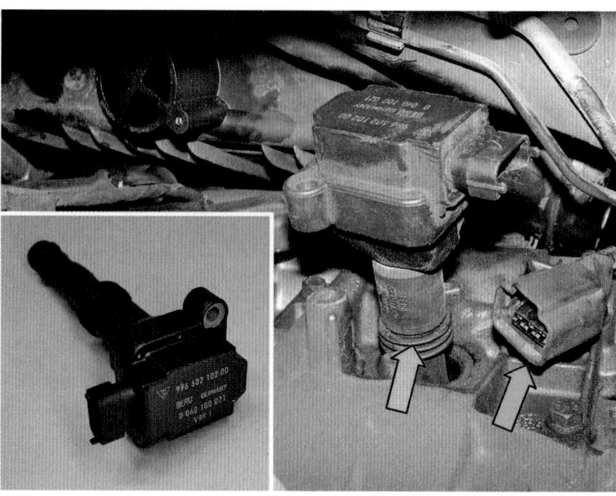

2 This particular photo shows an individual spark plug coil (inset). The blue arrow shows the plug that powers the coil, and the orange arrow shows the mini-bellows that is part of the coil that seals the chamber and keeps dirt and debris out. Be sure that you inspect the coil packs for cracks, particularly if the car has been driven on roads covered with salt. These coil packs can corrode, crack, and then cause misfires.

3 I like to use a swivel-socket spark plug removal tool from Craftsman. This tool is great for getting around bends and into hard-to-reach places. If you have a leaky seal on your valve cover, there is the opportunity for the spark plug holes to fill up with oil. When you pull out the spark plug connector/coil combo, you may find that it is contaminated with engine oil. If this is the case, then you should replace the spark plug tubes (yellow arrow, Boxster 1997–2004). These are plastic liners that seal the internals of the engine from the spark plug chamber. Use a pair of needle-nose pliers and simply grab the tube and pull it out of the hole. Later Boxsters and Caymans don't have tubes, but O-rings in the camshafts housings that should be inspected at this time.

4 In the photo inset, you can see an unusual spark plug with all four of its electrodes eaten away (red arrow). I would hazard a guess that this plug was improperly plated from the factory, and as it progressed through its life, the repeated sparking slowly ate away at the electrodes until they were gone. A plug in this condition would misfire often (if at all) and would generate poor performance for this particular cylinder. Surprisingly enough, none of the rest of the spark plugs in this set exhibited this type of damage. This is what leads me to believe it was defective from the manufacturer. On the right is shown a brand new Bosch Platinum spark plug. Spark plugs have varied over the years as engines have been changed slightly due to smog regulations. The important thing to remember is to get the proper ones for your car (they are scaled by both electrode type and also by heat range), otherwise you may encounter odd ignition problems. Spark plugs are cheap—I would go with a brand name like Bosch or NGK and avoid the no-name brands.

PROJECT 8
Boxster Engine Teardown

 **Time / Tab / Talent:** 6 hours / $0 /

 **Tools:** Camshaft holding tool

 **Applicable Years:** All

 **Parts:** None

 **More Info:** www.101projects.com/Boxster/8.htm

 **Tip:** Get two large folding tables to lay all of the parts out

 **Performance Gain:** Figure out what went wrong

 **Comp Modification:** Install a 996 engine

1 This project focuses on a brief overview of the Boxster engine and what it looks like inside. The engine featured here suffered a catastrophic failure, likely caused by a lack of oil to the main crankshaft. For the past 10 years, Porsche has offered an engine exchange program where you have to give back your old engine to Porsche when you get your replacement (known as a CORE charge). This means that very few of these engines have been floating around for people to disassemble, as we are doing here. We spent an entire two days at renowned Porsche workshop Callas Rennsport tearing down the engine and inspecting each component. For more detail on the teardown, I have made about 350 more photos of the disassembly process available with detailed captions on the 101Projects.com website.

2 Here's the camshaft cover coming off of the engine. It's always a good idea to mark parts so that you know where they go if you try to put them back together again. Here we have marked the camshaft oil scavenge pump so that we know exactly how to mount it again in the future (yellow arrow). It's important to note that the camshaft covers have an integrated camshaft bearing as well—the green arrow points to the section in the cover that holds the camshaft in place.

3 Here's a neat shot of the camshaft cover removed. The top camshaft is the intake camshaft, the lower one is the exhaust. On the earlier cars, they are tied together with a small chain that is attached to a tensioner/advance mechanism that slides back and forth and changes the relationship (in degrees) between both camshafts. This device is controlled by the solenoid in the center (yellow arrow). The green arrow shows the very useful camshaft holding tool that the fellows at Callas Rennsport designed to keep the camshafts in place when removing the side cover. As discussed previously, the camshaft covers contain the "bearing caps" that hold the camshaft to the heads, so when you remove the covers, the cams will pop out if they are not held in place.

4 The two camshafts are removed together. Yes, you can perform the camshaft removal and replacement with the engine in the car (the folks at Callas Rennsport have done that previously on a Boxster), but it's neither fun nor pretty. Lots of careful maneuvering is required. Four bolts hold the top and bottom camshaft end caps. Remove them, but remember which cap goes where. The tensioner/advance mechanism pulls off with both the intake and exhaust camshafts.

5 With the camshafts out of the way, you should be able to pluck the camshaft hydraulic followers out of the cam follower housing. Use your fingers or a suction cup to grab them out of there and be sure to place them in a tray, marking which valve they are matched to. The Porsche factory manuals recommend against using a magnetic tool to pluck out the lifters. Doing so may cause damage, presumably if part of the lifters become magnetized. When you reassemble the engine, you want to make sure that you reinstall the followers into the same exact bore that they came out of. This will reduce premature camshaft wear.

6 This photo shows removal of the cam follower housing. Removing this housing exposes the tips of the valves and each corresponding valve spring.

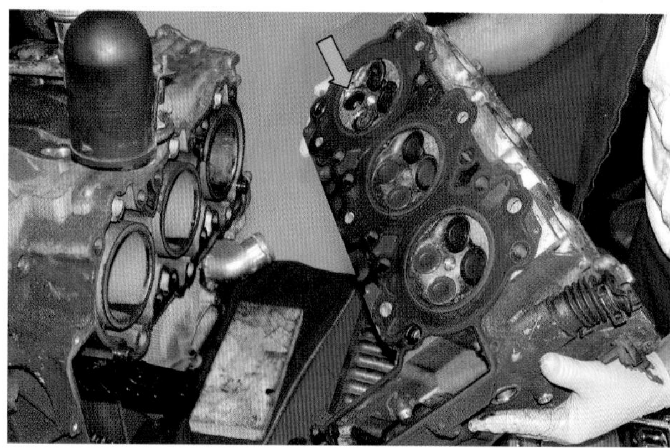

7 Remove the chain ramp bolts and then the chain ramps. Remove the head bolts and then gently tap the head with a hammer to release it from the case. It should slide right off. If it doesn't, you probably forgot a bolt somewhere. Here's a shot of the head coming off. Oops, looks like we're missing a valve (blue arrow)!

8 Yikes, there's that missing valve (blue arrow). It's quite obvious that we dropped a valve here, but it's not clear whether that happened before or after the rest of the damage to the engine occurred. Note the cracks in the cylinder walls of the case (red arrow). This is not what you would call a rebuildable core.

9 This photo shows the damaged cylinder head. The red arrow points to the valve where the head broke off. You can see that the oil from the engine is a light brownish color. This means that coolant and oil mixed together—it's typically a very bad sign if you see this when you change your oil.

10 Here's the oil pump removed from the engine. A few small bolts hold this in place. Remove them, and it should be simply plucked off.

11 We went to look at the piston, and, oops, it just slid out as there's no more rod attached!

12 Moving on, we now removed the front oil pump housing from the engine.

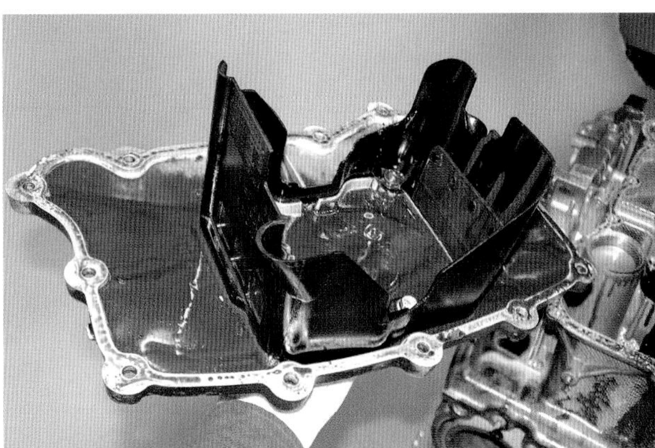

13 The oil pan on the bottom of the motor needs to be removed before splitting the case. These black plastic attachments are oil baffle plates, designed to channel and funnel oil in the sump of the engine.

14 Before splitting the case, we moved the arms on the engine stand so that we had three points of support instead of two. This engine stand is a generic one and thus doesn't support the engine as well as a Porsche factory tool. Make sure that you attach the stand to the half of the engine that has the water pump. This will allow you to easily lift the opposite side off of the engine. Rotate the engine so that the water pump side is facing down. With all of the bolts removed (see the 101Projects.com website for more info), you should be able to start prying the case to split the two halves apart. There are a few spots on the case where it's okay to pry them apart. Only use these areas, as you don't want to scratch the case surfaces. There's no seal or O-ring that goes in there—it's just metal-sealant-metal.

15 This appears to be where all the damage began. This bearing (#1) is cooked completely and burned into the crankshaft. This is symptomatic of a drop in oil pressure. The bearing becomes very hot and then basically fuses itself to the shaft. Then the rod seizes and completely breaks. The rod for this cylinder was completely missing. We found it in a half-dozen pieces at the bottom of the engine (more photos on the 101Projects.com website).

16 With a friend nearby, pry up the crankshaft bearing housing, and it should lift off of the engine with the intermediate shaft closely in tow. This is really a two-person job. I would not try to lift this yourself, as the angle is all wrong.

17 Remove the bolts that hold on the oil baffle/separator, and remove the guide for the main chain. You should then be able simply to pick the intermediate shaft up and off of the crankshaft bearing housing.

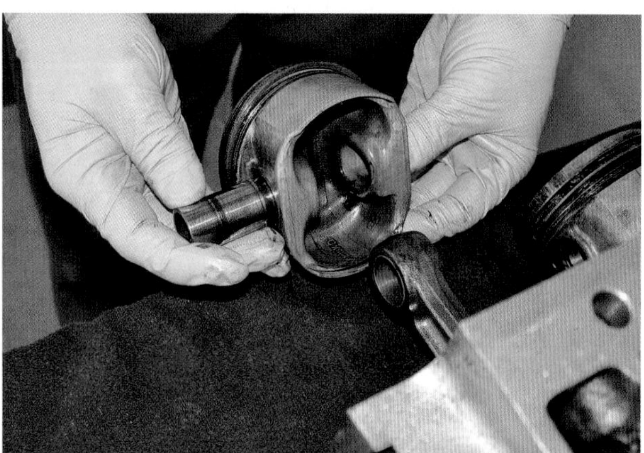

18 Here's one of the pistons with the piston circlip, which is very difficult to install in the engine when it's being rebuilt. You need a special Porsche tool—and lots of patience. I have heard it's like playing that childhood game Operation: one mistake and you can easily drop the circlip inside the engine.

19 This is something you only really see in modern cars—the bearing housing has a steel insert cast into the aluminum. This type of "insert molding" is presumably for strength around the bearing surfaces. After removing the bolts that hold the assembly together, gently pry it apart.

20 These engines use a cracked-rod design, where the rods are forged and machined, and then broken. Then the bearings are installed, and they are put back together again. This cracked-rod design is cheaper to manufacture, and the rod bolts don't need to have integrated "guide" pins as part of their design (like the rod bolts used on the older air-cooled engines). Unless you use some type of oversized bearing, you cannot rebuild or remachine these rods.

21 Here's another shot of that cooked rod bearing. Definitely caused by a lack of oil. Perhaps the previous owner forgot to check their oil level?

PROJECT 9
Replacing the Air-Oil Separator

Time / Tab / Talent: 2 hours / $110 /

Tools: None

Applicable Years: All

Parts: New air-oil separator

More Info: www.101projects.com/Boxster/9.htm

Tip: Check the oil cap for an unusual amount of crankcase vacuum

Performance Gain: No more oil screen behind you

Comp Modification: Change the oil

The engine air-oil separator is an emissions device located on the top-right rear corner of the engine. The separator is responsible for collecting residual gases and vapors contained inside the crankcase and funneling them back into the intake manifold where they can be burned in the combustion chamber. This reduces the overall emissions of the engine.

When the separator fails, you will begin to see a large increase in the overall vacuum in the engine crankcase. In the most extreme cases, the air-oil separator fails to separate the oil from the air, and oil is then sucked into the intake manifold. Oil in the intake system is not healthy for the engine, and it can foul spark plugs and destroy catalytic converters at the very least. The failure of the air-oil separator is often (but not always) accompanied by huge amounts of white smoke exiting the vehicle's exhaust and a generally poor running engine. You may experience a check engine light (CEL) as the oil being drawn into the intake can affect the mixture level.

The proper method to test for the failure of the unit is to measure the engine crankcase vacuum with a slack tube manometer. Normal crankcase pressure, measured at the oil filler cap, ranges from about 4 to 7 inches of water (drill a hole in the top of an old oil filler cap and attach the gauge there). When the air-oil separator fails, the intake manifold vacuum will draw into the crankcase, and the levels will reach 9–12 inches or more. If you don't have a slack tube manometer (most of us don't), then you can use a standard vacuum gauge and/or get a rough feel for the level of vacuum pulled by comparing it to a normal running car.

If you're still not sure, you can take a closer look at the hose that connects the air-oil separator to the intake manifold (yellow arrow, Photo 2). If the unit is failing, then there will be a significant amount of oil or residue in this tube. If the car is running rough, then removing this tube and blocking off both ends should disable the system and restore previous performance. This is not a long-term fix, but instead a short-term diagnostic step to use before you replace the air-oil separator.

There is also a motorsports air-oil separator available that you can use on dedicated track cars. This special separator is designed to work with the higher g forces that are exhibited with high-speed track driving. If your engine has a lot of blue smoke exiting the tailpipe after driving on the track, you may need this upgrade. See the 101Projects.com website for a copy of the Porsche bulletin explaining this upgrade.

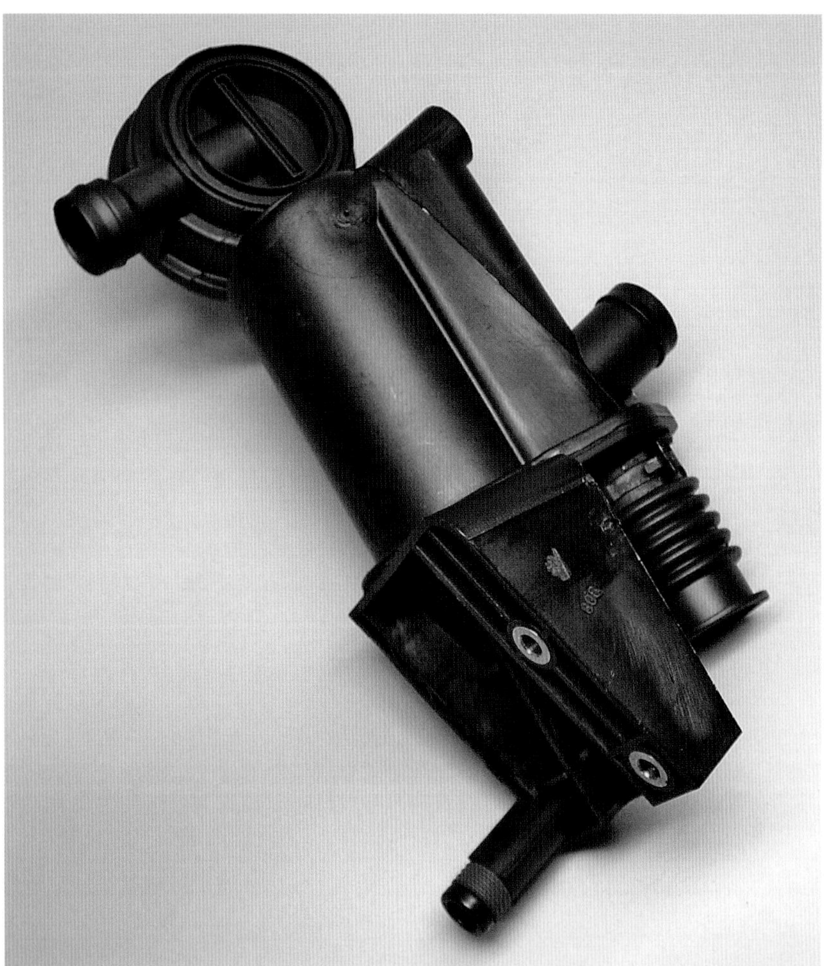

1 Shown here is a new air-oil separator unit for an early Boxster. The purpose of the separator is to separate fuel vapors from the crankcase and funnel them back into the intake. The air-oil separator is an emissions device, and although its presence doesn't hurt performance, if it fails or if one or more of the vacuum line connections develop a leak, it can negatively affect engine performance. There have been many updates to the unit over the years. The later-style units are a direct bolt-on replacement, but the hose that connects the air-oil separator to the throttle body has been updated as well (the old one is a little too short). If you are replacing your air-oil separator with a new one, be sure to install the updated connecting hose as well.

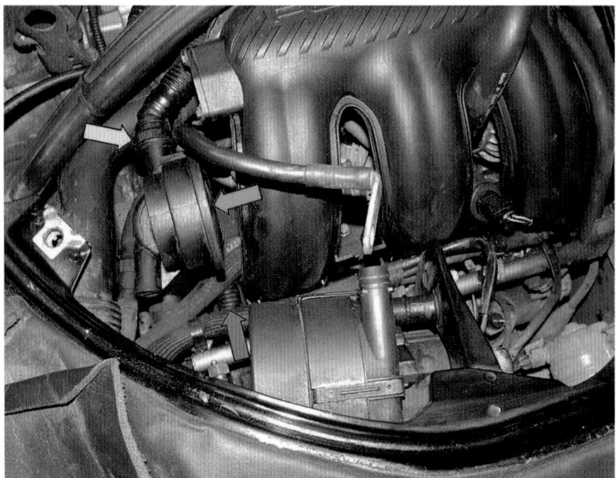

2 With the engine compartment lid open, it's fairly easy to gain access to the air-oil separator connections. The green arrow points to the separator. The yellow arrow points to the connection that leads to the intake. This is where vacuum is pulled from the intake manifold. Simply squeeze this connector and pull it off to disconnect it. The purple arrow points to the somewhat hidden flexible hose at the bottom of the separator. I found this connection easiest to disconnect from below (see Photo 3).

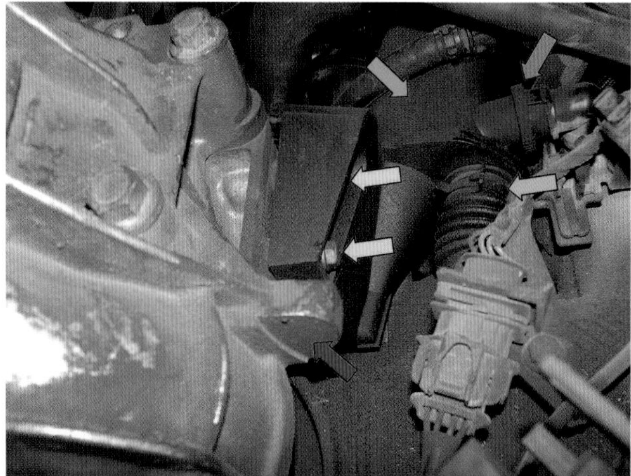

3 With the car on jack stands, you can poke your head up into the chassis and get a better view of the separator. The green arrow points to the separator itself. The purple arrow points to the quick-disconnect vacuum line that leads to the opposite camshaft housing. The red arrow shows the right side of the transmission. The blue arrow shows the flexible hose that connects the separator to the right-side cylinder head. I recommend replacing this hose along with the separator. Removing the little spring clamps that attach this hose is probably the most difficult part of the entire task. Use a set of special pliers specifically designed for the task. Finally, the whole unit is attached to the engine case using two bolts shown by the yellow arrows.

PROJECT 10
Motor Mount Replacement

 **Time / Tab / Talent:** 2 hours / $185 /

 **Tools:** Floor jack

 **Applicable Years:** All

 **Parts:** Motor mount

 **More Info:** www.101projects.com/Boxster/10.htm

 **Tip:** Remove the entire carrier and take it to your bench

 **Performance Gain:** Stiffer ride, better handling suspension

 **Comp Modification:** Replace transmission mounts

One of the most common parts to deteriorate on the Boxster cars is the engine mount. After years of use, the rubber that is contained within the mount becomes old and brittle and doesn't perform a good job of isolating the drivetrain from the rest of the chassis. The inside of the Boxster mount is hollow to help with reducing vibration. Unfortunately, this creates significant areas of structural stress and weakness, which can encourage cracks to appear in the mount.

Old, worn-out motor and transmission mounts can sometimes cause clunking and vibration problems because the drivetrain is no longer firmly held in its position. One sign of this failure mode is the gearshift knob jerking backwards under hard acceleration. A visible sign that the motor mounts need replacing is the appearance of cracks in the rubber of the mounts (impossible to see without actually removing the mount). The rubber will deteriorate over the years and needs to be replaced, even if the car has relatively few miles on it.

There have been many redesigns of the motor mount, and the latest one (PN: 987-375-023-04) is the strongest and should fit all Boxsters and Caymans. Early mounts (through 1998) were only attached to the engine via three bolts. You can use the later-style mount with four mounting holes to replace an early mount, but if you want to have it mount via four bolts to your early engine, you will need to upgrade/replace the oil pump housing (see Photo 17 and Photo 18 of Project 11).

There are alternative mounts you can use in place of the stock ones for your car. You can purchase a set of solid or performance mounts. I don't recommend these for street cars, as they may give you too harsh a ride. Stick with OEM mounts if you're going to be driving your car on the street most of the time.

Replacement of the mounts couldn't be easier. Simply jack up the car, and support it on jack stands (Project 1). Gently place the floor jack under the engine sump, taking care to only apply enough pressure to relieve tension on the front mount. Disconnect the engine carrier, and then disconnect the motor mount from the engine case. Take the assembly to your workbench and swap in the new mount. Bolt it back up, lower the car, and you're done!

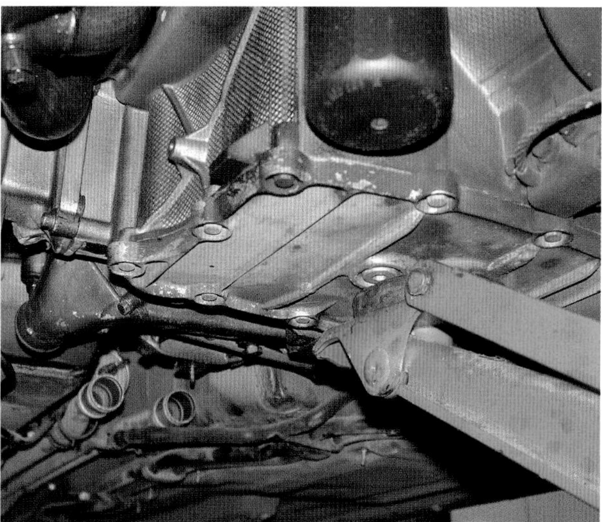

1 The first step is to jack up the car and support the weight of the engine with your floor jack. Don't actually lift the car or the engine, simply place the jack under the lower engine cover until it lightly makes contact. In general, you should never lift the engine from the bottom sump. But for the purposes of simply supporting the weight of the engine while replacing the engine mounts, the sump cover should suffice.

2 The engine carrier is attached to the chassis using four studs and nuts shown here (blue arrows). Carefully remove all four. There is a good chance that the entire stud will come out of the chassis. This is okay, as you can remove the nut and reinstall the stud later.

3 The engine mount is attached to the front of the engine case using four bolts (two shown with the purple arrows). Remove these four, and the engine mount should simply drop down.

4 With the engine mount assembly on your bench, disassemble the mount from the engine carrier. Two large bolts affix the two together (yellow arrows).

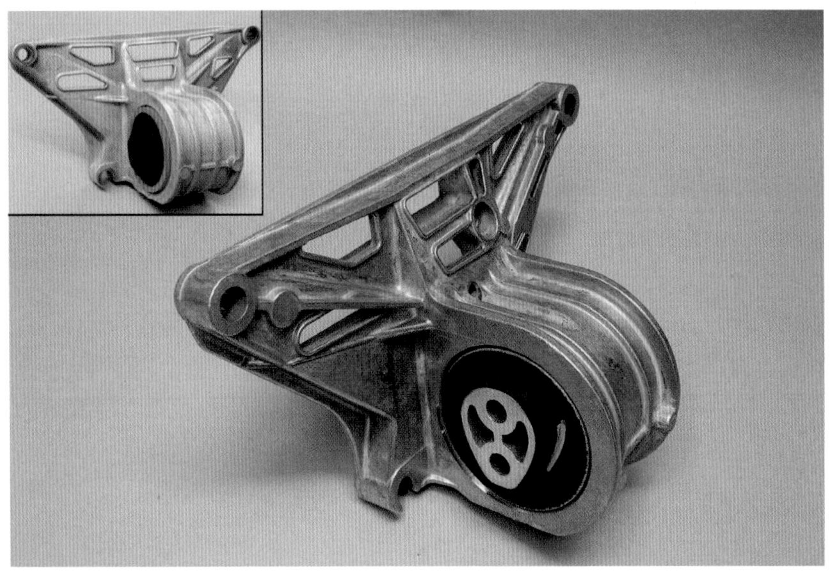

5 Shown here is a brand-new later-style engine mount, ready for installation. If you're looking for added performance, then I recommend going with a solid polyurethane mount like the one manufactured by WEVO and available through PelicanParts.com. This mount will translate more engine vibration into the chassis, but the ride will feel quite a bit more stable and stiff. Simply press out the old worn-out rubber from your old mount and install the polyurethane insert. I definitely recommend the polyurethane mounts if you're designing a track car. However, if you install the poly mount on the engine, I do not recommend installing solid transmission mounts. The resulting engine vibrations can cause lots of problems, such as knock sensor errors, which may actually result in a loss of horsepower.

PROJECT 11
Engine Swaps & Upgrades

Time / Tab / Talent: 150 hours / $10,000 /

Tools: All of them

Applicable Years: All

Parts: A bigger engine

More Info: www.101projects.com/Boxster/11.htm

Tip: Read this article carefully and ask specific questions on the Pelican Parts Boxster forum

Performance Gain: Gobs more horsepower

Comp Modification: Clutch replacement, suspension upgrade, brake upgrade

One of the great features about the Boxster is that it shares so many parts with its bigger brother, the Carrera. As Boxsters get more and more affordable, a growing number of owners are choosing to upgrade the engine in their Boxster with a bigger and more powerful unit from a Carrera. The Boxster engine and the Carrera engine are almost exactly the same—the Carrera is basically just a larger displacement version of the Boxster engine. As a result of these similarities, the conversion process is relatively easy to perform and is a very rewarding project for the do-it-yourselfer.

One of the toughest aspects of performing an engine conversion on the Boxster is figuring out which engines will fit into which chassis. There has been no definitive resource detailing this, so I decided to compile the information here. Working closely with Boxster conversion guru Todd Holyoak, I've managed to compile the following list of compatible engine/chassis combinations. Keep in mind that this is only an overview, and some additional research may be needed when installing an engine into your particular chassis. Information on these conversions is always evolving—be sure to check out the 101Projects.com website for updates on the latest conversion swap techniques.

I realize that an ideal engine swap would increase the displacement of the engine and increase power. However, it may be the case that you have a Boxster with a blown engine, and you find a used engine from a different year that may also fit. The following list also covers Boxster-to-Boxster engine swaps as well as the more popular Boxster-to-Carrera 996/997 engine swaps.

Almost all of the swaps require a remapping of the computer program inside the DME. DME is short for digital motor electronics and is the computer brain that controls the ignition and fuel injection system for the engine. The software that controls the DME is called Motronic, and each engine displacement has its own map—a set of instructions that tell the computer how to drive the engine. When performing a swap, you need to upgrade your map, either by using the factory PST-2 programming tool or by using laptop-based software from an aftermarket software company, such as Softronic (see Project 24).

BOXSTER 1997–1999 (2.5 LITER)

- The Boxster 1997–1999 chassis can accept any Carrera 996 3.4-liter engine or can use any Boxster engine from 1997–2002. In 2003, Porsche switched to a vane-cell adjuster mechanism to control the variable camshaft timing, and this system requires the later DME running Motronic version 7.8. Unless you upgrade the car to use the later DME (very difficult), you cannot use any 2002 or later 996 Carrera engine or any 2003 or later Boxster engine. You can swap in any replacement 2.5-liter engine from 1997–1999 without having to remap the DME.
- These cars ran the Bosch Motronic 5.2.2 system, which uses a cable-driven throttle body, similar to nearly all earlier Porsches. When installing an engine into one of these early cars, you need to use a cable-driven throttle body and corresponding crossover tube that matches that engine (for example, use the cable-driven throttle body from a 1999 996 Carrera when installing a 3.4 engine—the standard 2.5-liter throttle body is too small). The Boxster cable attaches directly to the 996 throttle body with no modifications necessary.
- Very early 1997 cars had non-programmable DMEs. If you have one of these cars, you might need to purchase a new DME and matching immobilizer to go along with it. Immobilizer codes for these early cars are not stored in the Porsche dealer information system, so there's no way of linking the existing immobilizer to a new DME.

Don't buy a 1997 if you are definitely planning on doing an upgrade, as you might get stuck with one of these non-programmable DMEs.

- Installing a 996/997 3.6 or 3.8 engine or 2003–2008 Boxster/Cayman engine is very difficult on these early cars, as you need to manually update many other systems in the car to get them to work properly. These later engines used VarioCam Plus, which is a system for controlling variable valve lift. You need to install a late-model DME and run Motronic 7.8 in order to control the variable valve lift properly. It is possible to run a piggyback computer that independently controls the variable valve lift, but this solution is not ideal and is complex to implement.
- Boxster engines from 2000–2002 and all 996 engines have an extra crossover tube with a variable resonance flap that is controlled by the DME. When you reflash your 5.2.2 DME to control the new engine, you also need to add some wires to the DME harness. The resonance flap is controlled by a solenoid switch that then applies vacuum to the flapper. You wire this solenoid by running one wire to a 12V source and the other wire to pin 59 on the DME (the DME controls the valve with a switchable ground).

BOXSTER 2000 (2.7 LITER AND 3.2 S)

- The Boxster 2000 chassis can accept any Carrera 996 3.4-liter engine or can use any Boxster engine from 1997–2002. In 2003, Porsche switched to a vane-cell adjuster mechanism to control the variable camshaft timing, and this system requires the later DME running Motronic 7.8. Unless you upgrade the car to use the later DME (very difficult), you cannot use any 2002 or later 996 Carrera engine or any 2003 or later Boxster engine. You can swap in any replacement engine of the same displacement from 2000–2002 without having to remap the DME (for example, a 2000 2.7-liter Boxster with a blown motor can accept a 2002 2.7-liter engine with no remapping needed). Installation of a 3.2 Boxster S engine would be an easy installation but would require an updated map for the DME.
- These cars ran the Bosch Motronic 7.2 system, which uses an electronic throttle body, linked to an electronic gas pedal (also known as drive-by-wire). When installing an engine into one of these cars, you need to use an electronic throttle body and corresponding crossover tube that matches that engine (for example, use the electronic throttle body from a 2000 or later 996 Carrera when installing a 3.4 engine).
- If for some reason, you want to backdate the engine to a smaller displacement 2.5-liter engine, then you will have to use the injection system and DME map from a 2.7-liter engine. The 2.5-liter engine injection doesn't have the extra crossover tube on the intake and also has the cable-driven throttle body, which is not compatible with the electronic throttle 7.2 DME.
- Installing a 996/997 3.6 or 3.8 engine or 2003–2008 Boxster/Cayman engine is very difficult on these cars, as you need to manually update many other systems in the car to get them to work properly. These later engines used VarioCam Plus, which is a system for controlling variable valve lift. You need to run Motronic 7.8 in order to control the variable valve lift properly. It is possible to run a piggyback computer that independently controls the variable valve lift, but this solution is not ideal and is complex to implement.

BOXSTER 2001 (2.7 LITER AND 3.2 S)

- The Boxster 2001 cars are by far the most flexible in which engine you can install in them. The 2001 cars still have the 7.2 DME installed, but most of the other systems of the car were upgraded in anticipation of moving toward the 2002 CAN bus system that integrates various electronic systems on the car. With the exception of the anti-lock braking system, the proper CAN bus systems are integrated into the 2001 chassis and allow the easy installation of the later 7.8 DME. As a result, you can install any 1997–2008 Boxster or 996 Carrera motor into these cars without too much difficulty. You can swap in any replacement engine of the same displacement from 2000–2002 without having to remap the DME (for example, a 2001 3.2-liter Boxster with a blown motor can accept a 2002 3.2-liter engine with no remapping needed).
- These cars ran the Bosch Motronic 7.2 system, which uses an electronic throttle body, linked to an electronic gas pedal (also known as drive-by-wire). When installing an engine into one of these cars, you need to use an electronic throttle body and corresponding crossover tube that matches that engine (for example, use the electronic throttle body from a 2000 or later 996 Carrera when installing a 3.4 engine).
- If for some reason, you want/need to backdate the engine to a smaller displacement 2.5-liter engine, then you will have to use the injection system and DME map from a 2.7-liter engine. The 2.5-liter engine injection doesn't have the extra crossover tube on the intake and also has the cable-driven throttle body, which is not compatible with the electronic throttle 7.2 DME.
- To install a Carrera 996/997 3.6/3.8 engine or a 2003–2008 Boxster/Cayman engine into one of these cars, you need to purchase a new 7.8 DME and then slightly modify the pinouts on the DME connector. In addition, you need to modify the Boxster engine wire harness, as the camshaft position sensors are located on the opposite ends of the engine than on the five-chain early motors. All of the systems on the car should work normally with one exception—the cruise control will not work properly with the later 7.8 DME unless you upgrade your ABS system as well (swap out the ABS controller and connector).

BOXSTER 2002 (2.7 LITER AND 3.2 S)

- The 2002 Boxster is somewhat unique in that it has an older-style 7.2 DME combined with the 2002 CAN BUS system that integrates various electronic systems on the car. As a result, if you wish to install a 3.4-liter Carrera 996 engine, you will need a custom DME remap from a third-party vendor, like Softronic (see Project 24). The best solution for these cars is to swap in a Carrera 996/997 3.6/3.8 engine or a 2002–2008 Boxster/Cayman engine. You can swap in any replacement engine of the same displacement from 2000–2002 without having to remap the DME (for example, a 2002 Boxster 2.7-liter with a blown motor can accept a 2000 2.7-liter engine with no remapping needed).

- To install a Carrera 996/997 3.6/3.8 engine or a 2003–2008 Boxster/Cayman engine into one of these cars, you need to purchase a new 7.8 DME and then slightly modify the pinouts on the DME connector. In addition, you need to modify/extend the Boxster engine wire harness, as the camshaft position sensors are located on the opposite ends of the engine than on the five-chain early motors (also the new camshaft adjusters have different connectors). All of the systems on the car should work normally with the later-style 7.8 DME (2002 has ABS version 5.7 so it does not have the same issues with the cruise control as the 2001 model). If you are installing an engine with VarioCam Plus (all Carrera 3.6/3.8 and Boxster 2007–2008), you will also need to add in the wiring to control the variable valve timing.
- If for some reason, you want/need to backdate the engine to a smaller displacement 2.5-liter engine, then you will have to use the injection system and DME map from a 2.7-liter engine. The 2.5-liter engine injection doesn't have the extra crossover tube on the intake and also has the cable-driven throttle body, which is not compatible with the electronic throttle 7.2 DME.

BOXSTER AND CAYMAN 2003–2008 (2.7 LITER/2.9 LITER/3.2 S)

- The 2003 and later Boxster and Cayman cars can accept any 996/997 3.6 Carrera engine and any Boxster or Cayman engine from 2003 and later. The best solution for more horsepower is to swap in a 3.6 or 3.8 996 or 997 engine. You can swap in any replacement engine of the same displacement from 2003–2008 without having to remap the DME (for example, a 2003 Boxster 2.7 liter with a blown motor can accept a 2005 2.7-liter engine with no remapping needed).
- On the 2004 and later cars with traction control, the installation of a more powerful engine into the drivetrain may cause the traction control system to become confused. You may need to upgrade some of the components of the system to the later 997 specification in order to achieve proper operation of the system with your new engine.
- The 2007–2008 Boxster engines were the first of the series to get VarioCam Plus (variable valve lift). The Carrera 996 had VarioCam Plus since the introduction of the 3.6-liter engine in 2002. The 7.8 DME used in the 2003–2006 Boxster didn't control variable valve lift, and there are no pins or wires in the engine harness to control the mechanism. Therefore, you need to add the wires into the engine harness when performing this installation. Pins A1 on both valve lift controllers connect to a 12V source in the harness—use the 12V supply for the variable valve timing solenoid. Pins A2 on the controllers connect to DME connector pin C1 for cylinders 1–3 and pin C26 for cylinders 4–6.

Fuel Return System: Starting in 2002, Porsche modified the fuel system in the Boxster to have a non-return type system. On 1997–2001 cars, the fuel was pumped from the tank to the engine and back in a circulating pattern. In 2002, the return line back to the tank was eliminated. When you install a non-return fuel system engine into a return system chassis, there are two different options you can take. The first option is to swap out the fuel pump and sending unit with one from a 2003 or later Boxster and use the system as a non-return system. In this scenario, you would use the existing fuel rails from the non-return engine.

For the second option, you can use the return system fuel rails and injectors and simply disconnect the vacuum line from the fuel pressure regulator. The base pressure for the return fuel system without the vacuum hooked up is the same as the fixed fuel pressure on the nonreturn systems. This second option is the least expensive of the two, but the better solution is the first option, as you can then run the later-style EV6 fuel injectors as they were intended to be run with your new engine.

Vacuum Pump: Starting in 2005, the Boxster was equipped with a vacuum pump that is powered off of the camshaft. This pump was added in order to provide the engine a more constant source of vacuum, which would be independent of the throttle position and other environmental conditions. When installing one of these vacuum-pump equipped engines into an earlier car, simply hook up the vacuum supply for the brake booster, and the secondary plenum resonance valve to this vacuum source.

Engine Oil Dipstick: 2005 and later Boxsters have no dipstick. Instead the oil level is monitored electronically. When installing one of the later-style M96 motors into an early car, there is typically a black plastic plug that covers the dipstick hole—install your old dipstick into this location. On the M97 motors, there is no mounting boss for the dipstick, so you will have to rely on the instrument gauge.

A/C Compressor: Since the air conditioning compressor stays with the chassis when performing an engine swap, it's important to note that all the A/C compressors from 1997–2008 appear to be compatible with all of the available engines. Some massaging of the A/C lines may be necessary to make them fit around the particular bosses and mounting points of some of the engines. In particular, the biggest hurdles are encountered when installing a three-chain vane cell engine into an early car. The three-chain engines have a different style casting around the end of the cylinder heads. This can be overcome if you use the parts from a three-chain motor when installing the engine into an earlier chassis (power steering supply and return lines).

Wayne's 3.4-liter Conversion: I took about 2,000 or so photos documenting the entire conversion process here—it was quite difficult to whittle them down to a mere 65 or so. However, I've archived all of the photos on the book's official website, 101Projects.com, so I advise you to point your computer there and browse through them so that you can learn more about the process and what's required to perform the swap. Keep in mind that I installed a 1999 3.4 factory rebuilt engine into a 2000 Boxster chassis. Your particular car and engine combination will most likely be different and will probably have some differences that are not captured here in these photos. The Boxster discussion forums on the PelicanParts.com website are an excellent place to ask specific questions regarding your particular installation—I'm there answering questions almost every day.

1 The Carrera 996 engine incorporates a completely different method of mounting and securing the exhaust system to the engine (yellow arrow). These large, heavy muffler brackets need to be removed from both sides of the engine—they are attached with bolts, three of which are shown by the green arrows.

2 With the large muffler bracket removed, there is a smaller bracket that needs to be removed from each side as well. This top bracket is difficult to remove because you need to loosen and/or remove the black plastic intake manifold and the aluminum intake manifold (green arrow) in order to remove the bolts (yellow arrow). This would probably be a good time to replace the seals that mate the aluminum intake manifold to the engine case. It's also a wise idea to stuff a few paper towels in the open intake pipes when you've reattached the manifold, just to make sure you don't drop any screws or washers down there while working on the engine.

3 There are a set of hoses that run across the top of the motor and connect to the air-oil separator that are not used with the Boxster. Disconnect the hoses attached to the air-oil separator (green arrows), disconnect the small water hose from the front (see next photo), and then lift up and remove the bundle from the engine (red arrow). You will not be using the smaller coolant hoses with the 996 air-oil separator—you can simply leave these small ports open or place some small plastic plugs on them.

4 Disconnect the coolant hose from the connection on the front of the engine (green arrow). If you are using an electronic throttle body (2000 and later Boxsters), you won't be using the air-oil separator hose that comes with the 996 engine, so disconnect it from the intake crossover tube as shown in the inset photo (red arrow).

5 When installing a Carrera 996 engine into the Boxster, you typically use the 996 intake manifold. However, you need to remove it from the engine and then reinstall it later on in the opposite direction. This is so the throttle body will face the rear of the car. I suggest that you take many photos as you remove the manifold, as the routing of the vacuum hoses can be tricky to decipher when you're reassembling the manifold back onto the engine.

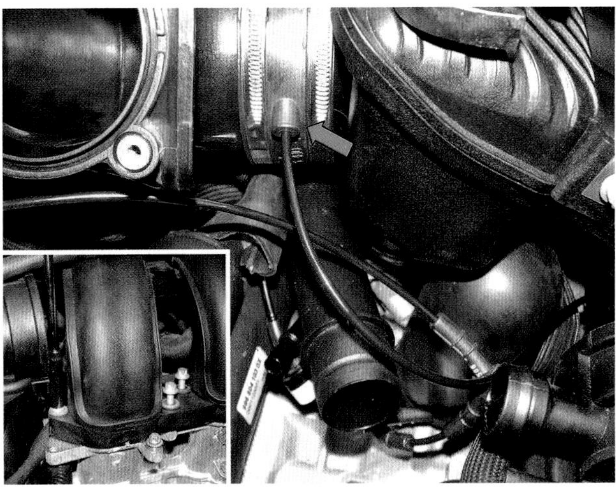

6 When you reinstall the manifold back onto the engine, you should point the throttle body toward the flywheel end. Also be sure that the intake boots with the small vacuum ports (green arrow) are located on either side of the throttle body and point downwards in the manner shown. The intake manifold is attached to the aluminum manifold via a number of small Torx bolts (inset photo).

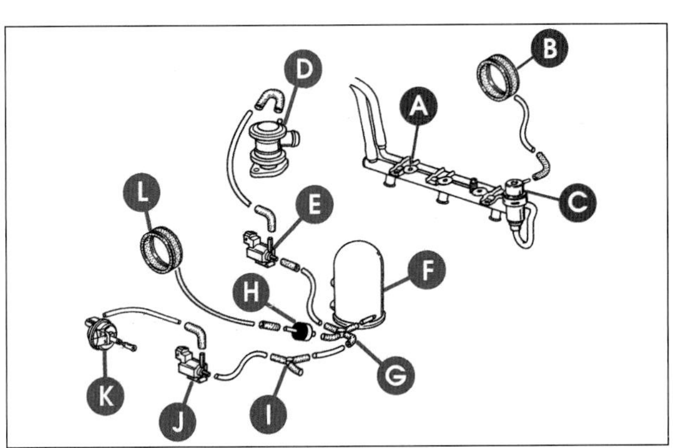

7 Figuring out where to plug in all of the little plastic vacuum hoses took quite a long time for me, so I decided to create this vacuum plug chart to assist during the reassembly process. Follow the diagram here when replumbing your engine. **A:** Fuel rail. **B:** Intake rubber sleeve with vacuum port (installed on right side of throttle body). **C:** Fuel pressure regulator on fuel rail. **D:** Air injection pump valve. **E:** Electronic vacuum solenoid valve for air injection pump valve. **F:** Vacuum reservoir. **G:** Four-way vacuum tee. **H:** Vacuum check valve (black side points toward the manifold). **I:** Three-way vacuum tee (one side is plugged). **J:** Electronic vacuum solenoid valve for resonance flap valve. **K:** Resonance flap valve. **L:** Intake rubber sleeve with vacuum port (installed on left side of throttle body).

8 You won't be using the Carrera 996 engine wire harness in your Boxster, so you will need to remove it from the engine (and later on, install your old Boxster harness; see Photo 39). Unplug all of the electrical connections from the various components and then pull it off of the engine.

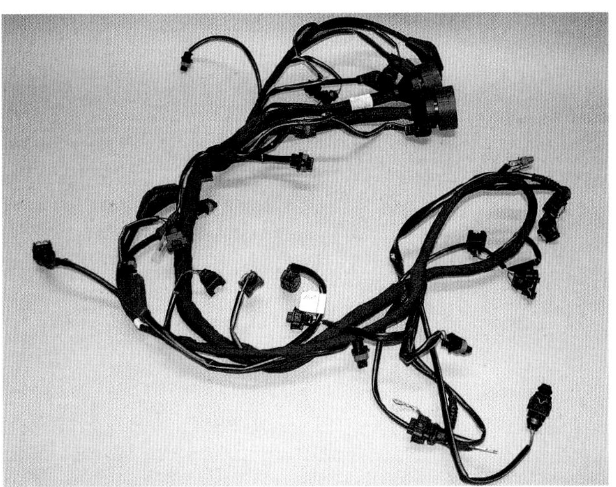

9 This photo shows the Carrera 996 wire harness that is no longer used. The Boxster harness is very similar, but it plugs directly into the DME in the rear trunk, instead of a set of connectors in the engine compartment like the 996.

10 The Carrera 996 engine has an electrical junction box (red arrow) that needs to be moved to the standard location on the Boxster (near the power steering pump; see next photo). I recommend that you use the starter harness from the 996, which is longer than the Boxster harness. I found that the junction box was a bit in the way on my installation, and I found that I had more clearance if I turned it around (see next photo). The inset photo shows the starter switch connection, which must be attached properly to the starter terminal.

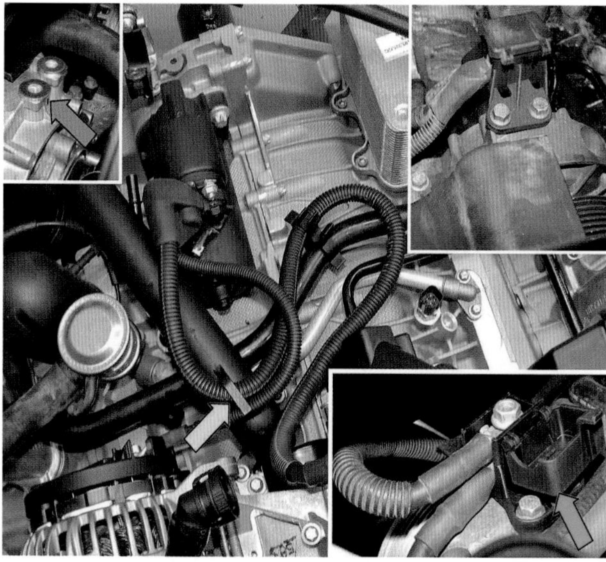

11 Shown here is the 996 starter/alternator harness (yellow arrow) and relocated electrical junction box (green arrow). Although the 996 harness is a bit longer, I simply tucked the extra wires up in a loop on top of the engine. The inset photo in the upper right shows the original junction box attached to the top of the Boxster engine. When installing the engine into the car, I actually found that the junction box had the potential to interfere with the resonance flapper valve, so I turned it around (inset lower right) and also had to add a few washers underneath (inset, upper left).

12 The Boxster uses an oil pressure switch to detect low oil pressure in the engine. The Carrera 996 engine uses a combination unit that senses pressure and also includes a low-pressure switch as well. The unit needs to be moved from one side of the 996 engine to the other side (the unit is installed on the right side of the engine when it is installed in the Boxster). Remove the plug from one side of the engine, and then swap places with the oil pressure sending unit as shown. Use new sealing rings to guard against oil leaks. Grab the sender by the base using a wrench—don't grab it by the canister, otherwise you may damage the unit and cause it to leak. In order to hook it up to your Boxster harness, install a spade tab on the unit if it doesn't already have one (shown in the upper inset photo). Even though the Boxster doesn't have a gauge in the dash to monitor oil pressure, you should utilize the 996 sender in case you ever decide to upgrade to the 996 gauge cluster (see Project 90).

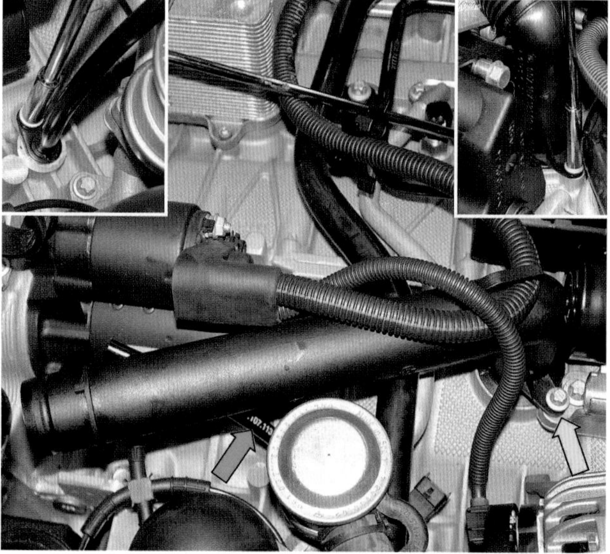

13 Both the oil filler tube and the oil dipstick tube are different on the 996 engine, so you need to swap them out with the ones from your Boxster engine. The photo shows the mounting bolt for the oil filler tube (yellow arrow) and the dipstick (green arrow)—install them as shown in the inset photos, and use new seals. Inspect the oil filler tube for cracks prior to installation—these can cause vacuum leaks that can affect engine performance.

14 There are a few items on the front of the engine that need to be swapped with pieces from your donor Boxster engine. The front water pipe connections are different on the two engines—the inset photo shows the 996 parts that need to be swapped out for the Boxster parts. Swap the 996 part shown by the green arrow with the cap (yellow arrow) from your Boxster engine. Swap the 996 part shown by the orange arrow with the pipe connector (blue arrow) from the Boxster engine. Use new gaskets to seal these two parts to the engine.

15 The front of the 996 engine has a water hose cap and connector piece that needs to be replaced with the one from the Boxster (red arrow). Begin by removing the idler pulley that blocks access to the lower bolt (yellow arrow and inset photo). Then, remove the cap by removing the bolts.

16 Here's the Boxster water cap installed in place (red arrow). The green arrow in the inset photo shows where it mounts to the engine—use a new gasket when transferring over the Boxster piece. Inspect the coolant hose that mounts to the Boxster piece as well, and replace it if it looks old. Don't forget to reinstall the idler pulley back onto its boss (purple arrow) when you are finished.

17 Except for some early cars, most Boxster and Carrera 996 engines have four mounting points for the engine mount. Although you can get by with three, I don't necessarily recommend it, especially when installing a higher-power engine. If your 996 Carrera engine does not have this fourth engine mounting boss (yellow arrow), then you need to remove the oil pump and housing from your Boxster engine and transfer it over to your 996 engine. If your original Boxster engine also doesn't have this fourth mounting boss, then I recommend you purchase the later-style oil pump with the boss integrated within the housing.

18 The Carrera 996 engines use studs to mount the front engine bar—the Boxster uses bolts. Therefore you need to remove the studs from the front of the engine with a good-quality stud remover (see inset photo). The yellow arrow in the main photo shows the fourth boss used for the engine mount. On my 1999 3.4 996 engine, this fourth boss was already installed because this was a brand new Porsche factory rebuilt motor that had all of the later upgrades installed on it.

19 Shown here is the Boxster mount test-fitted to the front of the 996 engine. I recommend removing the mount, mating it to the other half, and then installing it after the engine has been positioned into the car (see Project 10).

20 Converting over your engine is a somewhat lengthy process. I recommend doing it over several weeks—plan on spending an hour or two a night carefully cleaning up parts and swapping them over from the old engine. Even though I was writing this book and taking photos at the same time, I found it took me a lot longer than I expected to prep the engine. A glass of wine helps, and the oil cooler makes for a nice wine glass stand!

21 You need to swap out the power steering lines from the Boxster engine over to the 996 Carrera engine. The return line, shown here, can be somewhat difficult to remove. Using a wrench, carefully press in on the red plastic tab shown by the green arrow, and pull out the line from the rear. Use caution—if you damage the red connector, then you will need to replace the whole rear pump reservoir, which is not an easy task. Disconnect the line and then install the existing one from your donor Boxster engine.

22 Here's a photo showing the two Boxster power steering lines installed (pressure line = yellow arrow, return line = blue arrow). The pressure line is attached with a typical brake line-style fitting (inset photo). Use a flare-nut wrench (not shown) to remove the line to avoid damaging the fitting. Be sure to transfer over the proper mounting brackets for the lines as well (purple arrows).

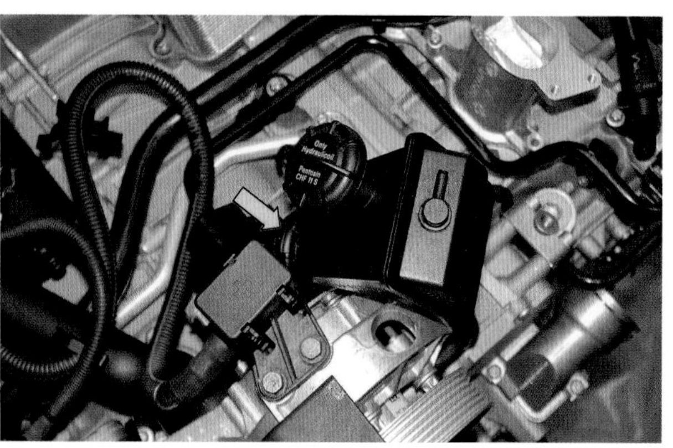

23 The top power steering reservoir is different on the Carrera 996 engine. Remove it from the motor by loosening up the locking dial shown by the yellow arrow. Don't install the Boxster unit just yet—leave it off until the engine is installed into the car. It's a smart idea to replace the O-ring that mates the reservoir with the pump at this time.

24 With the 996 engine on the stand, it's a good time to install the headers onto the engine. Shown here are some very nice looking stainless steel, large-diameter headers that match the original 3.4-liter exhaust system. Although I installed these with the engine on the stand, I ended up using a high-performance Fabspeed exhaust instead in the final assembly (see Project 47). Make sure that you use a new exhaust gasket (inset photo) and also use the proper exhaust hardware (blue arrow).

25 With the engine wire harness installed, you can also plug in the first set of oxygen sensors. I recommend only using Genuine Porsche or OEM Bosch sensors due to a problem with splicing in connectors—see Project 19 for more details.

26 This photo shows the auxiliary air valve that connects to the air pump located on the right side of the Boxster engine compartment. The valve is the same on the Boxster and 996 engines, but you need to transfer over the S-shaped hose from the Boxster engine to your 996 engine.

27 Shown here is the auxiliary air S hose installed along with the intake manifold. You need to install the hose first and then install the manifold, snaking the hose through the opening as shown. When the engine is installed in the car, connect this hose to the air pump located on the right side of the Boxster engine compartment.

28 The Carrera 996 engine has an oil cooler that is much taller than the Boxster one. As a result, you may have a difficult time fitting your air intake tube around it. If you do, then the solution is to swap it out with the shorter Boxster oil cooler (inset photo). However, I would keep the 996 one in place if at all possible, as more cooling is definitely better.

29 It's a smart idea to remove the cooler and install new oil cooler seals to assure a leak-free engine (yellow arrows).

30 The 996 engine has a resonance flapper valve installed in the rear intake manifold crossover tube. For the purposes of engine installation into the Boxster, I recommend that you point this valve up as high as it can go (inset photo) and also keep all of the intake tube connections loose so that you can rotate both the valve and the throttle body during the engine installation.

31 As mentioned previously, there are several miniature plastic vacuum hoses that need to be routed from the intake manifold. Two of the rubber boots will have plugs for the vacuum lines. Install and point them downwards as shown to ease installation (red arrow).

32 Here's a side view of a miniature plastic vacuum hose plugged into the rubber connection boot for the intake manifold. As you can see, the tube slightly sticks out of the boot as shown by the purple arrow. The inset photo shows the inside of the resonance flapper valve when it's fully opened. When the engine is installed in the car, you need to make sure that this valve has full freedom of motion and is not constrained by any hoses or wires.

33 Shown here is the stock configuration of the throttle body for the Carrera 996 cable-driven engine. The crossover piece (purple arrow) where the throttle body mount is different for the cable or electronic throttle bodies, so you need to obtain and use the proper one for your car. For the electronic throttle body, I was able to flip the crossover piece around (see the next photos). If you have a 1997–1999 Boxster with the cable-driven throttle body, you will need to install the throttle body in its standard position. In addition, you will need to use the stock Boxster air-oil separator connection piece and plug the tank vent hose into the nipple on the throttle body (1997–1999).

34 This photo shows me removing the crossover tube that is specific to the cable-driven throttle body. I replaced this with the crossover tube that is used with the electronic throttle body, and I installed it 180 degrees from normal in order to ease the connection to the air-oil separator (see Photo 37). The inset photo shows the engine compartment temperature sensor, which should be mounted on the manifold that is located on the right side of the engine compartment (when you flip around the 996 manifold, it should be on the correct side).

35 This photo shows the stock configuration of the Carrera 996 throttle body crossover tube and the air-oil separator. For installation in the Boxster, I removed the crossover tube, flipped it over, and then fabricated a simple connecting piece from an angled radiator hose I found at my local auto parts store (inset photo). I used the two connector pieces from the original plastic, semi-flexible air-oil separator hose used on the Boxster. The stock Boxster air-oil separator hose almost fit, but it was slightly cocked at an angle, which would have created a vacuum leak.

36 Shown here is the electronic throttle body installed on the flipped-over crossover tube. The green arrow points to the stock Boxster air-oil separator connection tube, which doesn't quite fit—a custom piece had to be fabricated (see Photo 35 and Photo 37). The inset photo shows the mounting point for the throttle body—use a new rubber gasket to prevent any vacuum leaks.

37 This photo shows the new air-oil separator hose installed. The green arrow shows the connector to the crossover pipe, the yellow arrow shows the connector to the air-oil separator unit. The red arrow points to the gas tank vent hose that connects to the valve shown in the next photo (Photo 38).

38 The gas tank vent valve is electronically controlled—the wire harness connection is shown by the yellow arrow and the blue arrow (inset photo). The vent tube hose (green arrow) leads back to a small port on the throttle body (see Photo 37). You need to make sure that you properly position and secure the vent valve prior to installing the engine, as it's very difficult to reach under the manifold with the engine installed in the car.

39 When installing the Boxster wire harness onto the 996 engine, you will most likely find that the lengths of some wires are not quite right. You will need to peel back the insulation on the wire harness and separate out the wires (blue arrow for the engine compartment temperature sensor in this case). Use some high-quality electrical tape to rewrap the wires that are exposed (inset photo). I also used some very small zip ties to keep the harness together, just in case the electrical tape started to lose its stickiness at some time in the future.

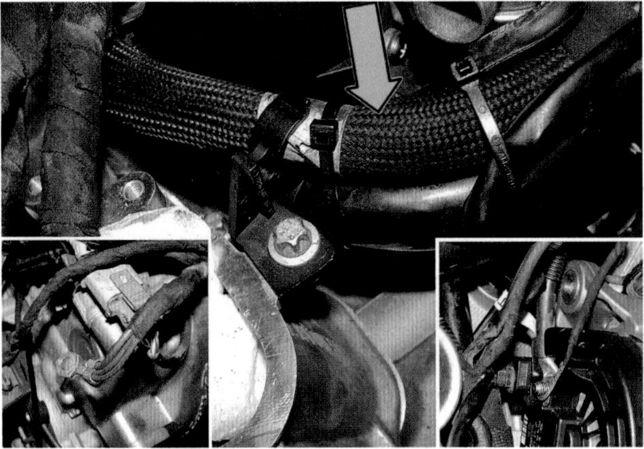

41 Install and route the engine wire harness following how it was installed on your Boxster motor. The 996 has different attachment and holding points for the harnesses, so use a generous amount of plastic zip ties to secure it in place. Don't forget to attach the very important ground points for the harness (inset photo, lower left). Also, take care when attaching the alternator harness—messing this up can literally cause a meltdown when you reconnect the battery (inset photo, lower right).

40 On the opposite side of the engine, I found that I had to separate the wires a bit for the connection to the solenoid that controls the resonance flapper valve (mounted on the end of the manifold, yellow arrow). Again, peel back the insulation (orange arrow), separate the wires (purple arrow), and then rewrap the harness with high-quality electrical tape. At this time, I also found it very useful to dig out my label printer and make some labels for each of the wires on the harness. This helps with routing and the reassembly process.

42 Figuring out what to do with the fuel rails was a challenging part of this conversion. While the process of adapting the fuel rails to the 996 engine is not difficult, there are several paths you can take. The path I chose here seemed to be the least complicated, but as I write about it, it would seem there might be an easier solution—I just haven't figured it out quite yet (check the 101Projects.com website for additional suggestions on how to handle the fuel rails). The first step I took was to completely remove the fuel rails from the 996 engine. This is accomplished by removing the bolts that hold the rails to the manifold and pulling both the rails and injectors from the engine. The inset photo shows the 996 injectors and rails removed. The red arrow points to the return line connection for the 996 engine.

43 The inset photo shows the Boxster rails lined up next to the 996 rails—they don't line up. In order to use the Boxster rails with the 996 manifold, you would need to grind off of the mounting tabs on the Boxster rails and then reweld them into the proper position for the 996 engine. I'm not a huge fan of welding fuel rails, so I decided I didn't care for this approach. Instead I modified the 996 rails and the chassis Boxster fuel lines instead. Shown here is the "left" side of the 996 fuel rail where I cut the secondary fuel rail off and also removed the second crossover fuel hose.

44 This photo shows the existing 996 fuel hose and the additional high pressure fuel hose that I ran across the top of the engine. When installing the engine into your engine bay, be sure that you confirm that the fuel hose is not rubbing on any other items or is coming in contact with any component that may cause it to wear. After installing the engine in the car, I went back and covered the fuel hose with a hard plastic sheath to protect it from any rubbing or vibration in the engine compartment. I used the flexible plastic conduit material that you commonly use to bundle and protect electrical wires in automotive applications (upper inset photo). The lower inset photo shows the 8×13mm high-pressure BMW fuel hose that I used to replumb the fuel lines.

45 Shown here is the "right" side of the engine as it is installed into the Boxster. I carefully trimmed off the prefabricated fuel line that was attached to the barb on the fuel rail (inset). Then I attached some of my own high-pressure fuel line to the barb and clamped it with a high-quality German hose clamp. This line I ran across the top of the engine to the opposite side and then down to the fuel line that runs down the center tunnel of the car.

ENGINE

46 The fuel return line that extends all the way over to the other side of the engine drops down on the left side for connection to the fuel hose that runs down the center of the car (green arrow). Unfortunately, I was not able to find an adapter that would allow easy connection of the hose to the right-angle fitting, so I had to fabricate the reducer shown here. Although this did work fine, there's probably a better solution out there (like a right-angle quick-connect that fits into the 8mm fuel hose), but I wasn't able to find it in time for this project. This photo shows me cutting the fuel line to length after the engine has been installed. The fuel line will connect to the top of the brass barb (purple arrow).

47 The pressure line that supplies the Boxster connects to the fuel rails at the rear right side of the engine. Since the 996 fuel rails have the pressure inlet located near the rear right side of the engine, I took a Dremel took and cut the aluminum fuel line just rearward of the air filter housing (yellow arrow, inset photo). Then I attached a piece of high-pressure fuel line along with two high-quality fuel line hose clamps in order to assure there would be no leaks. I ran about one foot of hose from this point to the connection point shown in the next photo.

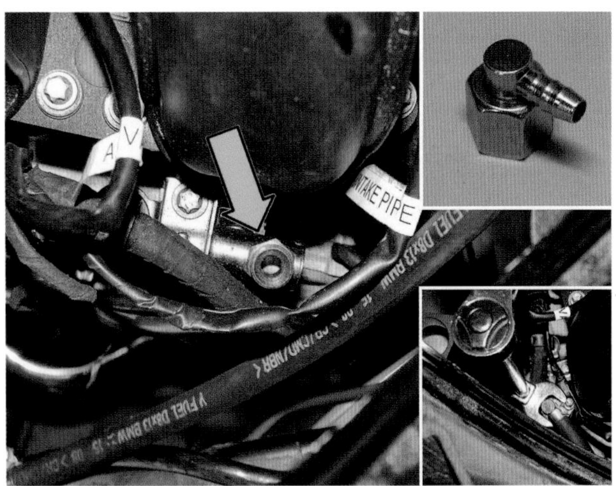

48 The 996 fuel rail has a larger connection fitting for the fuel pressure line, so you need to find an adapter (upper right inset photo) to fit. I took a piece of high-pressure fuel line and attached it to where I cut the main aluminum Boxster line. On the other end I attached this fitting and then fastened it to the 996 fuel rails using a crowfoot wrench (inset lower right).

49 The vacuum port for the brake booster is in the wrong spot on the 996 manifolds. I swapped the port to the front right side of the engine (as installed into the Boxster) and also modified the piece from the Boxster motor to create a right-angle adapter that plugs into the stock vacuum port (inset photo).

50 Here's the vacuum port installed on the right side of the engine (yellow arrow) with my modified adapter piece (green arrow). The 16mm hose shown in Photo 51 plugs into the aluminum adapter on the end of this piece. Clearance is very tight, so be sure that you hook up your vacuum line before you install the engine all the way in the car. In this photo, the engine has about 6 to 8 more inches to go before it's at its final height.

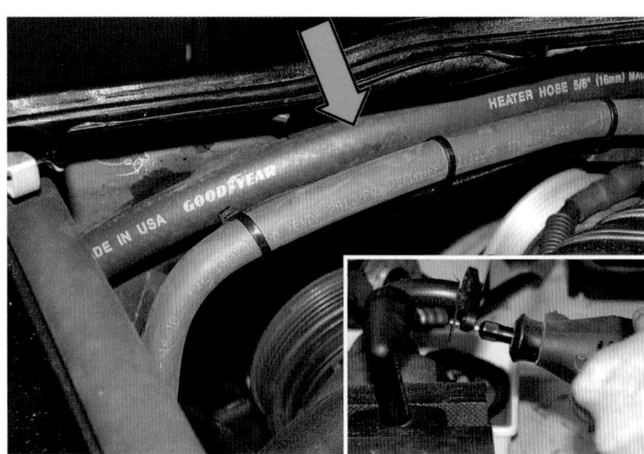

51 I was a bit uncertain whether or not the 16mm heater hose that I found at the local auto parts store would suffice for the brake booster vacuum. Sometimes hoses that are not designed for vacuum connections can collapse on themselves when there is a strong vacuum pulled. However, I did not find this to be the case with this hose, and it worked very well for this particular application. The inset photo shows me modifying the stock Boxster piece to create a right-angle adapter for the vacuum line.

52 Installation time! Install the engine, but stop about a foot or so before the final height and hook up the A/C compressor and lines. The outboard attachment bolt is difficult to get to, and you will need a swivel socket and some extensions to reach it through the spaces in the intake manifold.

53 The Carrera 996 intake manifold sits higher on the engine than the Boxster manifold, so you need to lower the entire drivetrain down slightly in order to make it all fit under the engine compartment lid. I used two ½-inch spacers and 100mm bolts placed between the mount and the chassis. These are standard steel spacers that you can find at any local hardware store. There shouldn't be any clearance problems lowering the drivetrain down, although you should be extra careful with steep driveways and speed bumps, particularly if you have lowered the car from its stock height (see Project 60).

54 For conversions, you need to use the Carrera 993 engine mounts (see Project 36) because they have longer studs exiting out of the bottom. The square boss on the bottom of the 993 transmission mounts fit into the transmission bracket. Therefore, simply adding a ½-inch spacer between the mount and the bracket will result in lowering the transmission down more than ½ inch. Instead, I simply used some steel washers carefully placed between the mount and the bracket. Total amount lowered was about ½ inch when measured. On this car, I later found out that there was an issue with the stud from the mount interfering with the upright located below (caused some odd vibrations on deceleration). The solution was to trim the very tip of the stud off with a saw.

55 Here's a shot of the engine almost fully installed into the Boxster engine bay. Although some people find it easier to install the engine and transmission together, I typically like to work with them separately—it gives you a lot more clearance and you also don't have to remove the rear chassis support bar (purple arrow). Shown here is also a brand new dual-mass flywheel, which I recommend with a new engine installation.

56 With the engine installed in the car, it's time to attach the oil filler tube. I like to use the improved-style OEM German hose clamps to secure the tube to its base. Clearance can be tight, and these clamps help out considerably by giving you greater access.

57 Securely attaching your ground strap is very important for the proper operation of the engine. The ground strap is attached to a bracket on the right side of the engine compartment, near the auxiliary air pump.

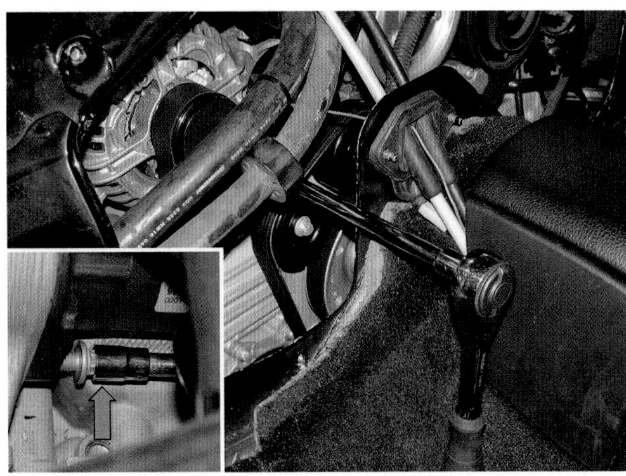

58 The ground strap is attached to one of the lower mounting bolts for the starter (purple arrow, inset photo). Loosen up this bolt by using a long extension accessed through the belt side of the engine. Although I didn't have a difficult time attaching it with the engine installed in the car, it probably would be easier to bolt this to the starter before engine installation.

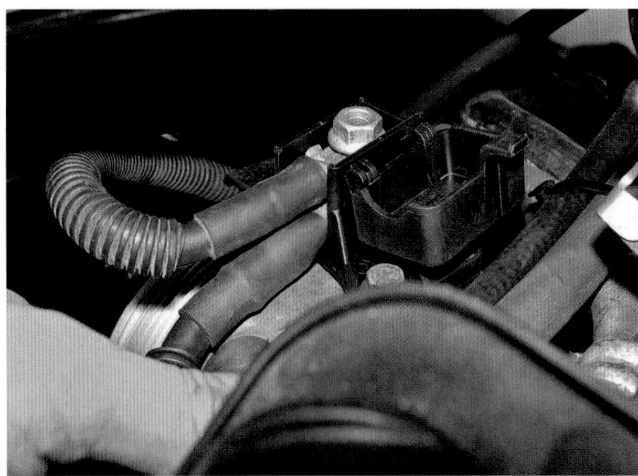

59 With the engine installed, hook up the electrical connections in the small junction box. Be sure that your battery is disconnected before you do this! As mentioned previously, I had to flip the orientation of the junction box around to make some extra room for the resonance flapper valve. The 996 cables are longer than the Boxster cables and can accommodate this alternative positioning quite easily. If clearance is really tight, you might want to hook this up prior to lifting the engine all the way to its final height.

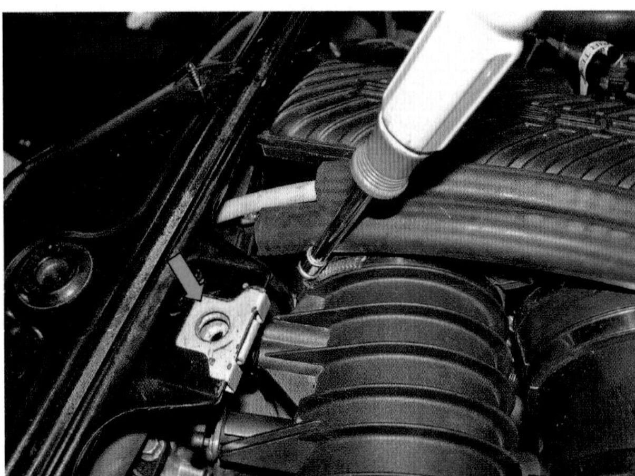

60 Clearance is tight for the resonance flapper valve (hidden under the engine lid attachment speed nut—green arrow). When you are raising the engine into place, continually monitor and adjust the position of the valve so that its proper operation isn't hindered by surrounding equipment. The fit is tight because the 996 manifold sits higher than the stock Boxster manifold.

61 This photo shows the engine properly placed into the engine bay. At this point, you still need to install the auxiliary air pump, install the power steering reservoir, install the transmission, hook up the shifter cables, and install the air intake.

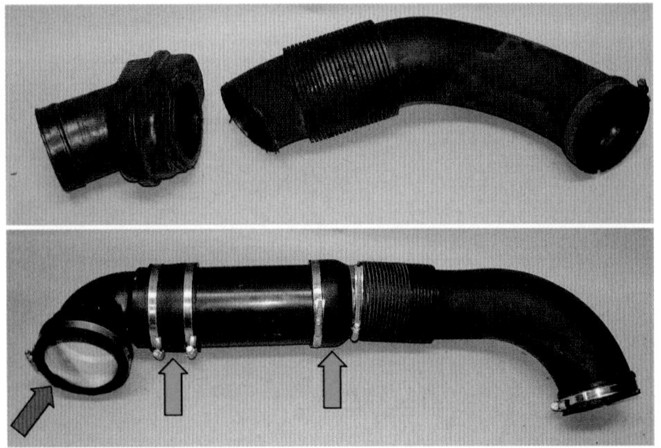

62 These two photos show how I put together the air intake for the new engine. I used the flexible right-angle piece from the stock Boxster air intake—the inside diameter was very similar to the one used on the 996. Then, I used a PVC right-angle piece combined with a length of straight PVC pipe that I cut to the proper size. All three pieces were then joined together with rubber boots (green arrows) and large hose clamps. Finally, I cut another rubber boot to attach the right-angle piece to the throttle body (red arrow). All of these pieces were easily available at my local hardware store and the resulting air intake worked very effectively. It's not an ideal solution from a fluid dynamics perspective, but there's only a limited amount of options that you have working in the tight confines of the Boxster engine compartment.

63 Here's a photo of me test-fitting the custom-made air intake in the engine compartment. The red arrow points to the outlet from the Evolution Motorsports air intake box. The green arrow points to the section of the stock Boxster air intake that I reused. Finally, the purple arrow points to the right-angle PVC piece (prior to me painting it black) that attaches to the throttle body. I test-fitted the air intake into the car in this manner so that I could measure the length of straight-pipe PVC that needed to be cut to fit between the right-angle piece and the remainder of the stock Boxster air intake.

64 Here's a photo of the completed air intake assembly, installed in the engine. The yellow arrow points to the section of straight-pipe PVC that needed to be cut to length in order to join the right-angle piece and the remainder of the Boxster air intake. When completed, I tested the entire assembly for air leaks and found none (see Project 21).

65 Here's another photo of the engine installed with the new air intake. Once you rotate down the throttle body, be sure that you remember to tighten up all of the rubber boots that connect the crossover pieces to the intake manifold.

66 Here's a photo of our new engine, fully installed. The shift cables have been attached, the front belt has been installed, the engine is full of coolant and oil, and we're ready to start it up. Don't forget that the cooling system needs to be bled (Project 29) prior to you driving away. I also recommend that you jumper the fuel pump relay (see Project 22) and test your fuel line connections before you start the engine. You want to find any fuel line leaks while the engine is off and cold.

67 As with any conversion project, there are going to be issues and problems. On this 3.4 engine, one of the oxygen sensors was not operating properly, and we traced this back to a pinched wire harness. Also, the fuel mixture was way off, causing the engine to run like it had a banana stuffed in the tailpipe. The solution (given to me by Boxster conversion guru Todd Holyoak) was that the 996 computer program map was expecting the mass airflow sensor to be mounted in a larger-diameter tube. This meant that the computer thought a lot more air was going into the engine than it really was. Our solution was to install a variable 0–1,000 ohm resistor (available at any electronics shop) and place it inline on pin 5 (white/blue) of the wire harness. This allowed us to use the PST-2 (or Durametric) tool to adjust the resistor value so that the fuel trim levels were properly set. You can also use a stock 987 MAF housing and position it approximately where the 996 MAF sensor is located in the 996 chassis (close to the throttle body). This is more of an issue with the later cars; the 5.2.2 (1997–1999) cars seem to deal better with the resistor trick, but the 2000 and later cars are less tolerant.

PROJECT 12
Installing a Deep-Sump Kit

Time / Tab / Talent: 3 hours / $300 /

Tools: Dremel tool

Applicable Years: All

Parts: Deep-sump kit, pickup tube extension

More Info: www.101projects.com/Boxster/12.htm

Tip: Add the pickup tube extension for maximum protection

Performance Gain: Better engine protection in high g-force cornering

Comp Modification: Change oil

The older Porsche 911 cars had what is known as a dry-sump oiling system. This meant that excess oil from the engine was removed (scavenged) from the bottom of the sump and stored in a separate oil tank. With a dry-sump system, a significant quantity of oil (approximately 12 quarts) is available to be supplied to the engine at all times. With a wet-sump system, the oil is stored in an area below the engine. A traditional wet sump, similar to the one used on the Boxster engine, doesn't hold as much oil as a dry sump and also may suffer from scavenging issues when the car corners and oil is sloshed from one side of the sump to the other.

As a result of the lower oil capacity of the wet-sump design, it's possible that the Boxster engine may exhibit oil scavenge problems under high-performance track driving. The engine is not likely to see these types of forces when driving on the street. One solution to help the problem is to lower the sump and increase its capacity. A deep-sump kit extends the bottom of the engine and adds about a half a quart to the total capacity. That half quart may be just what you need in order to save your engine if your Boxster is experiencing high g-forces on the racetrack. Installation is fairly easy and can be performed on the engine with it still installed in the car. Follow the instructions shown in the photos as well as the ones included with the kit.

1 After emptying the engine of oil, the first step is to remove the lower engine sump cover. A total of 13 bolts hold the sump cover to the engine (red arrow shows one). Remove all but two of these. Loosen the last two bolts but don't remove them. This is to keep the sump plate from falling on you when you pry it free. Have a large drip tray handy when you remove the sump cover, as there will some excess oil that will drip out of the engine. To remove the sump cover, use a pry bar between the two bosses located near the oil filter (yellow arrow). Some light tapping with a rubber mallet might help as well. Do not place any tools on the mounting surfaces of the sump plate or the engine. The deep sump plate sandwiches itself between the case and the stock lower sump as shown by the green arrow.

2 Remove the black plastic baffle from the bottom sump plate. The six "windows" on the baffle should be enlarged slightly in order to gain the maximum performance from your additional sump. Using a Dremel tool, carefully modify the baffle, removing about an ⅛ of an inch from the bottom of each window. The inset photo shows the first window modified (yellow arrow). Only take off a small amount of material here—you must leave enough material on the bottom so that the flaps will still seat on the raised bottom lip.

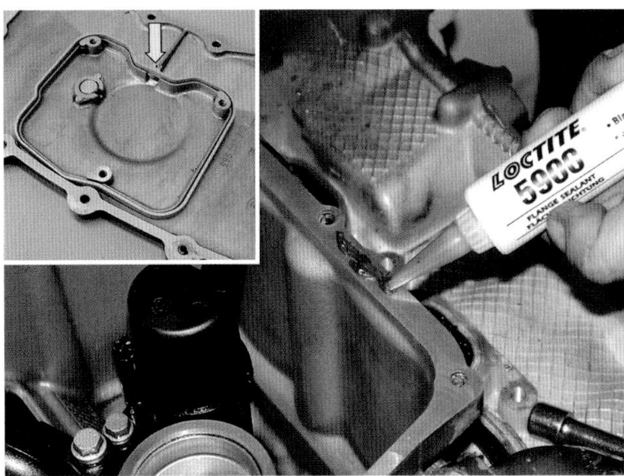

3 Install the baffle spacer onto the bottom of the sump plate. Make sure that the two small tabs line up with the fin that is cast into the bottom of the sump plate (yellow arrow). Install the plastic baffle onto the spacer using the bolts supplied with the kit. Use some Loctite threadlocker on the screws as you install them. Do not use any gasket sealant on the baffle extension. When you remove your old sump, be sure to carefully clean both the engine side and the sump plate so that you can reseal the sandwich plate upon installation. After meticulously cleaning the two mounting surfaces, I used Loctite 5900 to seal the flange surfaces.

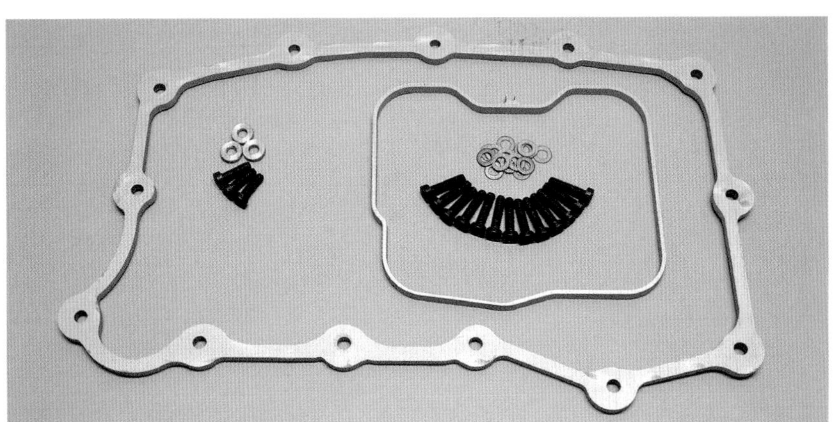

4 Shown here is the Brey-Krause deep-sump kit that we used for this project. This high-quality kit is available from PelicanParts.com and comes complete with the sump spacer, the baffle spacer, and the appropriate mounting hardware.

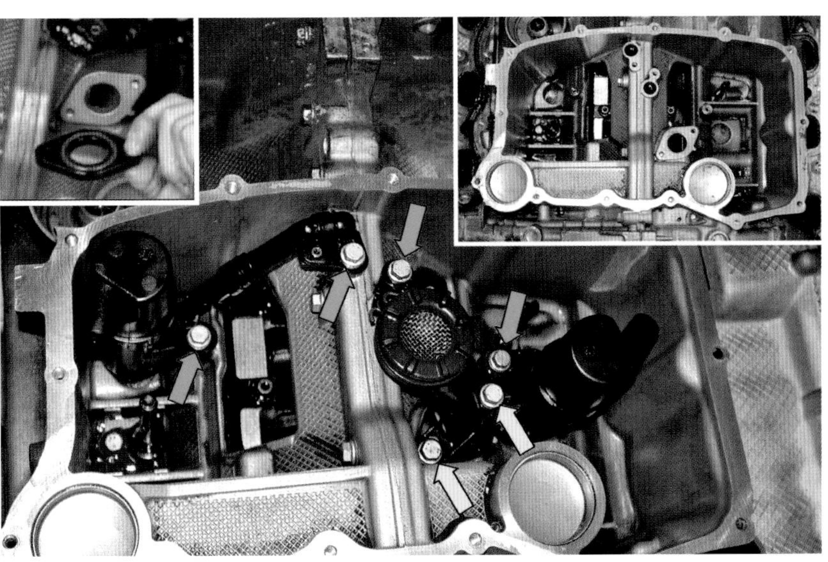

5 Shown here are the lower sump air-oil separators, which help to de-foam the oil in the bottom of the sump. They are held on with two bolts each (green arrows) but seldom need replacing. I would recommend that you replace them if you had some type of major engine failure at one time that might have contaminated them (inset photo shows them removed). For the installation of this kit, I chose to add the oil pickup tube spacer, manufactured by LN Engineering (inset photo). This spacer lowers the oil pickup tube all the way down to the bottom of the sump when the deep-sump kit is installed. This allows the maximum amount of oil to be sucked up by the oil pumps (cost is approximately $30). The yellow arrows point to the attachment points for the oil pickup tube.

PROJECT 13
Common Boxster Engine Problems

Time / Tab / Talent: As long as it takes / $0–$10,000 / 

Tools: Varies

Applicable Years: All

Parts: Replacement upgrades

More Info: www.101projects.com/Boxster/13.htm

Tip: Don't wait until your engine blows up to make some necessary upgrades

Performance Gain: Long, reliable engine life

Comp Modification: Clutch replacement

Using the expertise gained from years of designing and building engines, Porsche developed what is known as the M96 engine for the introduction of the Boxster in 1996. The horizontally opposed engine was developed with a throwback to the traditionally air-cooled motors, having kept the opposing cylinder or boxer layout. The engine was designed from the outset with the goal of providing a common platform for both the Boxster and the upcoming Porsche Carrera. The motor was indeed scalable, encompassing a displacement that ranged from 2.5 liters all the way up to 3.8 liters at the end of its production run.

The M96 (and subsequent similar M97) water-cooled engine is definitely a strong-performing engine, however along the stages of its development it has suffered from some design deficiencies that have been identified and corrected by Porsche over the 11-year lifespan of the engine. It's not uncommon to find a car listed for sale with "new factory engine recently installed" in the advertisement. No one but Porsche knows exactly how many engines were replaced under its recently discontinued engine exchange program. However, simply swapping out a broken engine for another one does not address known weaknesses in the engine due to design deficiencies. The purpose of this project is to identify some of the problem areas of the engine and offer up solutions on how to fix and/or prevent any damage from happening to your engine.

Rear Main Seal Leaks: When the M96 engine first came out, it was perhaps most known for its rear main seal (RMS) leaks. While some of the RMS problems were probably actually intermediate shaft cover leaks (see next section), there were definitely some problems with the seals on the early cars. For the most part this was a "cosmetic" issue, as the leaks did not tend to affect performance, unless they became so severe that they began to affect the proper operation of the clutch. But many engines were torn apart and/or replaced by Porsche under warranty due to this problem, because when you pay $75,000 for a high-performance sports car, you expect it not to leak.

It's not really 100 percent clear what causes the leaky rear main seals. One cause may be the fact that the crankshaft has insufficient support on the rear end. It also may be caused by the fact that the crankshaft carrier support is only pinned minimally in one plane to the outer case. This can lead to shuffling of the carrier—shuffle pinning the crankshaft carrier, as is commonly done when prepping an early 911 engine for the track, can help the problem.

The seal has been updated to a 997 "Cayenne-style" part number since the engine was originally introduced, and for the most part the engines no longer leak from this area when this new and improved seal is installed. If you find that your engine is leaking from the rear main seal (also known as the flywheel seal), then simply install a new one while adding a little bit of Curil-T sealant to help keep it dry (see Photo 10 of Project 44).

Intermediate Shaft Bearing Failures: The intermediate shaft bearing is probably the most troublesome of all of the M96/M97 engine problems. The intermediate shaft bearing (IMS bearing) supports the intermediate shaft on the flywheel end of the motor. Porsche designed these motors using a sealed ball bearing that is pressed into the intermediate shaft. These types of bearings are typically used in devices like copy machines and other machinery used in dry conditions. In theory, the area where Porsche designed the bearing to sit is supposed to be dry. However, after years of use within the engine, it would appear that oil and contaminants from the engine seep past the bearing seal, wash out the original lubricant, and become trapped inside. The result is that the bearing now operates in a less-than-ideal environment and begins to wear prematurely. When the bearing wears out, the timing chains on the engine may disengage, and the engine will quickly self-destruct. When the bearing does fail, foreign object debris from the bearing circulates throughout the engine, causing further damage to other areas in the engine.

On the early cars, Porsche also used a center bolt to secure the IMS bearing that was too weak and sometimes snapped. If this bolt breaks, then the intermediate shaft begins to float around in the bottom of the engine, and you can soon experience catastrophic engine failure.

This area is also highly prone to leaks. The seal around the intermediate shaft cover can leak, and it has since been updated and redesigned to prevent leakage. In addition, the three bolts that hold the intermediate shaft cover use through-holes that exit into the cavity of the engine case. You must coat these bolts when reinstalling them in order to prevent oil from leaking out through the bolt holes. In general, if this area is leaking, it may indeed be a sign that your intermediate shaft is failing and you should inspect it immediately.

The good news is that the IMS bearing problems are all fixable, thanks in part to a retrofit kit that can be installed with the engine still in the car. See Project 14 for full instructions on how to update your engine.

Cylinder Liner Cracks: In an effort to reduce costs during production, Porsche utilized a type of insert-mold casting process to directly incorporate Lokasil cylinder liners into the case. While this is a neat way to reduce the total number of parts used in the engine, this design basically casts a wearable part into the engine case. There is no factory replacement for the liners—when they wear, the factory expects you to buy a new engine case. In addition, the design of the cylinder liners allows them to "float" within an area filled with coolant.

Excess vibration and twisting from the normal operation of the engine appears to be causing some cracking in these liners, resulting in a small chunk of the liner breaking off. This "D-chunk" problem seems ironically to occur mostly in gently driven cars. Boxsters that are driven hard at the track or on the street do not tend to see this type of damage. At least with respect to the track cars, one theory is that these cars tend to have their oil changed much more often. The problem affects mostly the 2.5 and Carrera 3.4 engines—the 3.2 Boxster S engine appears to be unaffected because it has thicker cylinder walls than the 3.4 engine. When this failure happens, you will see oil and coolant begin to mix together or a slight unexplained coolant loss.

If your engine experiences this failure, it can be rebuilt using LN Engineering's Nickasil liners installed. They take your old case, machine out the cracked or damaged Lokasil liners, and install an aluminum Nickies insert, which is stronger and more reliable than the factory cast-in liner. In addition, with the installation of the liners it's fairly easy to increase the bore of the cylinders, which translates into increased displacement and more horsepower. If you go this route, you will also need to use some aftermarket pistons and perhaps update the software in your DME to accommodate the larger displacement.

Engine Casting Porosity: As mentioned in the previous section, Porsche used a new cost-effective method to cast most of the oil and water cooling passages directly into the engine case. This reduced the total part count for the engine and also helped reduce assembly time and production cost. Unfortunately, the advanced casting technique seems to have led to a number of engine cases experiencing what has been called "engine porosity." There is not a lot of information available on this problem, but it seems to be related to problems with the initial casting process.

In some cases, there appeared to have been a leak through the internal crankcase walls. The process of pouring the molten aluminum must be tightly controlled, otherwise pockets of air forming in the aluminum may result. Most of the time, post-casting inspections will reveal these flaws, but apparently some were still manufactured into running engines. The result is that oil and water became mixed within these engines. This resulted in coolant being found within the oil (turning it a milky brown color) or oil being found inside the coolant tank.

The expansion and contraction of the engine due to the heat of normal operation can expose this problem as well. I have also heard of engines that simply wept a slow bead of oil right through the walls of the engine case when running. Unfortunately, there's nothing that can be done to fix this problem, short of scrapping the engine. The good news is that most of these problems were discovered on the cars when they were new, and the engines were replaced under warranty.

Chain Tensioner Failures: There's been some chatter lately about chain tensioners failing on some of the M96 motors. If your car is noisy on startup and then suddenly quiets down, it may indicate a problem with your chain tensioners. Porsche updated the design of the tensioners in 2000 (TSB Group 1 NR 8/00) and replaced them with an improved design. I recommend that you replace your chain tensioners if they are noisy. See Project 16 for more information on how to identify and replace them.

Cylinder Head Cracks: In general, the cylinder heads are pretty well designed on the M96 engine. However, on some 3.2, 3.4, and 3.6 engines, small cracks can sometimes develop around the seats of exhaust valves and extend to the spark plug hole. The mounting point for the cam follower housing is also a weak point. Often these cracks can lead to coolant and oil mixing together. This is not an uncommon problem with automotive cylinder heads in general and can often be repaired by a skilled machine shop that can weld aluminum heads.

Oil System Inadequacy: The air-cooled predecessor to the M96 engine incorporated a dry-sump system that was designed to keep a significant amount of oil in reserve for extended performance driving. With the introduction of the M96 engine, Porsche moved away from that design, primarily due to the high cost of implementing a separate dry-sump system. The M96/M97 motors instead were designed with a compromise system, which has an oil sump built into the bottom of the engine—a kind of hybrid between a dedicated dry-sump system and a typical wet sump. As a result of the lower oil holding capacity and other factors, the M96/M97 engines tend to suffer more from oil starvation problems, particularly during high performance driving.

There are a few things you can do to protect against oil starvation problems. Firstly, be sure that your oil level is always at the high-level mark of your dipstick. The M96/M97 engine doesn't have a vast extra supply of oil, so if you're a quart low, it's a significant amount. You can also add in a deep-sump kit (see Project 12), which will expand the oil capacity of the sump by about a half a quart. Finally, you can install an Accusump oil accumulator system that will protect against unexpected oil pressure drops (see Photo 5 of Project 98).

In addition to the standard issues associated with the non-traditional sump system, the flapper windows on the bottom of the engine are manufactured out of plastic and can break off inside the sump and clog the oil pickup tube. This leads to oil starvation and complete engine failure. The solution is to remove the bottom sump and inspect the oil control windows (see Project 12) and replace them if they are missing or damaged. You can also add aftermarket stainless-steel windows for added protection.

As mentioned previously in Project 2, I do not care for Porsche's standard recommended oil change interval of 15,000 miles. The oil in engines tends to become contaminated with fuel and coolant, particularly as the cars age and seals and piston rings begin to wear. I generally like to run a thicker oil and change it every 3,000 to 5,000 miles. Keeping the oil fresh may help prevent some IMS bearing issues and generally prolong the life of your engine.

Connecting Rod Bolt Failures: The connecting rods that are used on the Boxster are forged out of steel and utilize what is known as a cracked-rod design. This means that the rods are forged and machined and then broken along pre-set stress points. Then the bearings are installed and the rods are put back together again. This cracked-rod design is cheaper to manufacture, and the rod bolts don't need to have integrated "guide" pins as part of their design (like the rod bolts used on the older air-cooled engines).

Unfortunately, it would appear that the rod bolt diameter may be too small for the large loads that these engines place on the rods. A number of recent failures in some early high-mileage engines have hinted that the rod bolts are too small and may be a failure point for the connecting rod.

The failure occurs when the engine is consistently revved at the high end of its rpm range. The stock rod bolts are designed to stretch and permanently deform when tightened down to their final torque values. At rpm's of 6,700 or higher, the rotating mass on the end of each rod (namely the piston and the mass of the rod itself) has a tendency to stretch the rod bolt further. Repeated stretching of the rod bolts causes them to deform and loosen up, which can result in rod separation and complete engine failure.

Unfortunately, due to the cracked-rod design, the connecting rods cannot easily be rebuilt. The solution is to install aftermarket connecting rods that can accommodate larger, race-proven fasteners like the ones available from ARP.

Variocam Solenoids: It's not uncommon for the variocam solenoids to fail on one side, which will result in a uneven or lopey idle. Moisture can get into the mechanism causing it to corrode and eventually fail. The DME computer should easily be able to detect this failure and trigger a check engine light (CEL).

Paper Oil Filters: The oil filter system on the Boxster is a bit lame in my opinion. Using the stock paper filter can

1 This photo shows the flywheel end of an M96 motor. This particular motor is a 3.4-liter crate motor from Porsche that has been updated with the latest and greatest improvements from the factory. The intermediate shaft has the updated bolt (yellow arrow), but the issue of the intermediate shaft failure has still not been completely addressed in this redesign. Although these updated engines tend to suffer from fewer problems than do the early ones, there is still a risk of IMS bearing failure. The rear main seal shown here is the updated and improved one that should not leak (green arrow).

lead to a disintegration of the filter, which can then clog the oil passages of the engine. Although this is a relatively rare problem, I have heard of it happening with cheaper-brand oil filters. Stick to the good-quality brands, and also consider upgrading to the LN Engineering screw-on oil filter upgrade (see Project 2).

Air-Oil Separator Failures: The air-oil separator is an emissions device that draws vapors from the engine crankcase and then sends them back into the intake manifold. When this unit fails, the result is oil sucked out of the engine and into the intake. While the air-oil separator will not cause immediate mechanical damage to your engine, it may smoke tremendously and/or run roughly (see Project 9).

Oil Change Intervals: The best recommendation to any Boxster owner is to change their oil more often, say every 5,000 miles, as well as use a minimum 5W40 viscosity oil. On cars not equipped with Variocam Plus (2006 and earlier), use of a 15W50 or 20W50 provides a much higher film strength, which will improve internal bearing life considerably.

Low-Temperature Theromostat: Also useful is the LN Engineering low-temperature thermostat (see Project 34). This specially designed thermostat starts to open at 160 degrees F instead of 187 degrees F for the factory unit. Keeping the oil cool is key to keeping it fresh, and the lower operating temperatures also help give you a bit more horsepower too.

3 Here is a fully repaired M96 engine with the LN Engineering Nickies liners installed. The case is prepared by machining out the old liner and completely removing the section that floats in the water jackets. Then, a Nikasil cylinder is press-fit into the case in its place. It's a clever solution to the irreplaceable case problem. The case itself must be a good rebuildable core and have no major issues (no major damage, no case porosity issues). In addition to replacing the liners with new and improved ones, the process allows you to increase the displacement of the engine at the same time. The 2.5 engines can be easily increased to 2.7, and the 3.4s can be pumped up to 3.6-liter displacement. There is even an option for 3.8-liter and beyond in current development.

2 This is the infamous "D-Chunk" problem that happens sometimes on these motors. Occurring almost exclusively with the two cylinders in the middle, it is theorized that excess twisting and vibration causes cracks to occur in the cylinder walls. Found mostly on the 2.5 and the 3.4 engines, this problem is almost non-existent on the 3.2-liter engines because the 3.2 has thicker cylinder walls. The solution is to machine the case to accept cylinder liners (next photo).

4 Although it may not look like much, this crack is enough to cause a lot of problems. Cracks like these can cause oil/coolant to mix, resulting in contamination of the coolant and/or oil. Cylinder head cracks are common among water-cooled cars and can sometimes be repaired by grinding down the head and then rewelding it.

PROJECT 14
Intermediate Shaft Bearing Upgrade

Time / Tab / Talent: 5 hours / $150–$600 /

Tools: Removal, installation, and camshaft timing tools

Applicable Years: 1997–2006

Parts: IMS bearing upgrade kit

More Info: www.101projects.com/Boxster/14.htm

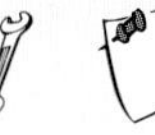

Tip: Perform this upgrade when doing a clutch job

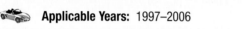

Performance Gain: Years of reliable running

Comp Modification: Clutch replacement

ENGINE

INTRODUCTION

The M96/M97 Boxster engine has had a checkered past when it comes to reliability (see Project 13). One of the weaknesses identified in recent years by Porsche has been the intermediate shaft bearing (IMS bearing), which supports the intermediate shaft on the flywheel end of the motor (see Photo 6). Porsche designed these motors using a sealed ball bearing that is pressed into the intermediate shaft (Photo 12). These types of bearings are typically used in devices like copy machines and other machinery used in dry conditions. In theory, the area where Porsche designed the bearing to sit is supposed to be dry. However, after years of use within the engine, it would appear that oil and contaminants from the engine seep past the bearing seal, wash out the original lubricant, and become trapped inside. The result is that the bearing now operates in a less-than-ideal environment and begins to wear prematurely. When the bearing wears out, the timing chains on the engine may disengage, and the engine will quickly self-destruct. When the bearing does begin to deteriorate, foreign object debris from the bearing circulates throughout the engine, causing damage to other areas in the engine. This appears to be one of the most common failure mechanisms present with the Boxster and 996 Carrera engine.

The center bolt that holds the entire assembly can also fail. If this bolt breaks, it will immediately allow the intermediate shaft to float, and the engine will skip timing. This will result in the complete destruction of the engine in a very short period of time (seconds). Typically, a deteriorating intermediate shaft bearing will also cause the center stud to weaken and break. The stud has a groove cut into it axially to allow for a sealing O-ring to seal to the outer cover. This groove causes a stress concentration to occur and promotes the failure of the stud. The solution is to pull out the bearing and replace the stud with a new one that is stronger and manufactured without any grooves (see a comparison of the old and new studs in Photo 5).

So how do you know if you have a problem? There are several warning signs. When you first start your car, you may hear a loud rattling noise that goes away after about 10 seconds or so. When you accelerate, you may also hear this noise too. This noise is the sound of the chains or the bearing rattling around in the engine because the bearing has deteriorated—the engine is soon on its way to skipping a tooth on the sprocket and costing you thousands of dollars. To detect the early stages of a failure, listen for a sound that is similar to what a throw-out bearing, water pump, or a belt idler pulley sounds like when the ball bearings begin to fail. If you have the car up in the air and running, you can listen carefully and you should be able to isolate the noise to the area of the IMS bearing (bottom rear of the engine, near where it mounts to the transmission), especially if you use a diagnostic stethoscope.

Signs of a failing IMS bearing can also be found by inspecting the oil filter. Shiny metallic debris from the balls used within the bearing itself may travel through the oil system and become trapped in the oil filter as well as small bits of black plastic from the seal on the bearing (see Photo 1). During a routine clutch job, you can also simply remove the IMS cover and take a closer look at the bearing itself (lock and check the camshafts prior to removing the cover though—see instructions below). If the center shaft is wobbly, or the center of the bearing doesn't spin freely, then it's probably on its way to failure.

Another way to check the engine is with the factory PST-2 tool, or the Durametric tool (see Project 20). You can compare the deviations in the timing between the two camshafts to see if they vary widely, particularly when revving the engine (see Photo 2). Sometimes a failing IMS bearing will also trigger a "check engine light" warning on your dash, as the car's computer realizes that there is a significant deviation between the timing of the two camshafts.

1 Here are the remains of a destroyed IMS bearing after we removed it from our M96 engine. It fell apart in my hand taking it out of the removal tool. We still didn't find the remains of one of the bearing rubber seals anywhere. Sometimes you can see the signs of an intermediate shaft bearing failure. The upper right inset shows what the oil filter looked like when we removed it from our engine. You can clearly see small flakes of metal in the filter. It looks like the filter did a pretty good job of blocking the particles—since this was caught in time, we anticipate that the engine should be fine. Lots of debris ended up getting caught in the oil sump and pickup screen, which is a good thing. If your bearing is trashed when you remove it, be sure to pull the sump off the bottom of the engine, clean it out thoroughly, and replace the two air-oil separators located in the sump area (see Project 12).

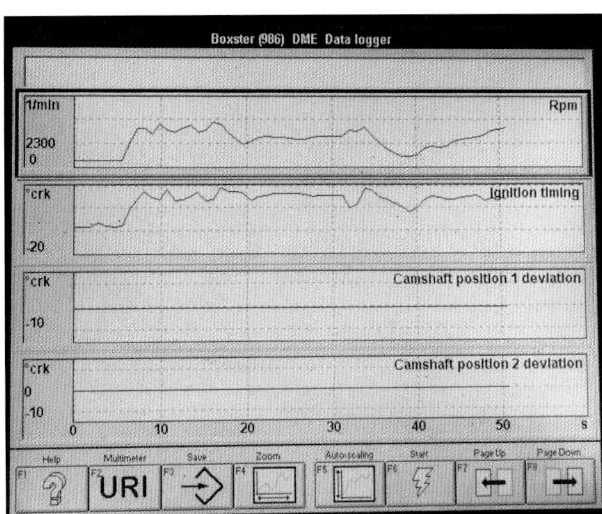

2 Sometimes you can detect a failing intermediate shaft bearing by running a test showing camshaft deviations. Using the Durametric tool, or a PST-2, you can set up the screen to log camshaft deviation as a function of ignition timing and rpm. Significant variations between the left and right camshaft banks can be an indicator of trouble with the bearing. In this graph, the deviation is zero, which is perfect and does not indicate a problem.

WHAT DOES A BEARING FAILURE LOOK LIKE?

If you take a look at Photo 1, you will see the remains of an intermediate shaft bearing from an engine with only 31,000 miles on it. Pulling off the intermediate shaft bearing cover revealed that the bearing had completely disintegrated and there wasn't much left. This engine was running and the car was driving, but every few seconds it would make a horrible screeching noise. Sometimes it would run for quite a few minutes with no sound at all. Hard to believe, considering that the bearing was completely destroyed.

So what can you do with an engine that has had this much bearing damage? The engine was still running when I took the bearing out, so I know there didn't appear to be any damage to the cylinder heads from the timing chains being out of sync. The oil filter appeared to do its job of blocking most of the bearing debris in the oil. The only thing that you can do when you have a situation like this is to clean everything out very carefully, replace the bearing, and button the engine back up.

WHAT CAN BE DONE TO FIX OR PREVENT A FAILURE?

Luckily, there are a few solutions available. Firstly, I recommend that you change your oil every 5,000 miles or sooner and use a higher viscosity motor oil that has additional anti-wear additives. Use Porsche approved 5W40 viscosity motor oils, preferably one that carries an API SJ-SL rating. Use of a 0W40 viscosity should be limited to colder climates in winter months, where cold starts are regularly below freezing, for added start up protection. Also consider using an oil with more anti-wear additives (like Zn, P, or moly extreme). Recent regulatory changes in the United States have caused oil companies to revise their formulations of oil and reduce the amount of anti-wear components in them. The reasoning behind this is the belief that these components contribute to premature deterioration of the catalytic converters. I'm not so sure I agree with that premise however. The solution to this problem is to make sure that you run motor oil with the proper anti-wear formulations and change your oil often.

Also curious is the fact that cars that are driven tamely seem to have more problems than cars that are driven aggressively. Boxster engines that are used at the track are known to have very few problems relating to the bearing, whereas Boxsters driven by "little old ladies" tend to show the most damage. The track-day Boxster bearing longevity may be explained by the fact that these cars often have their oil changed after every trip to the track.

The best solution to the problem is to replace the bearing prior to its failure. Porsche Club of America tech advisor Scott Slauson from Softronic (see Project 24) pioneered a procedure that allows you to replace the bearing with the engine still in the car. Building upon that procedure, LN Engineering and Pelican Parts have both developed bearing replacement kits to swap out the troublesome original bearing.

WHICH BEARING IS INSIDE YOUR ENGINE?

The first step in replacing the bearing is to figure out which one you have in your engine. There were three variations installed over the years. Early cars typically have a large double row bearing that has a snap clip inside the bearing. Porsche later went to a single-row bearing design when the timing chain design was modified (see Photo 7 for a comparison of the two). Then, around model year 2006, Porsche installed a third version that is not replaceable. The supposed cut-off on engine numbers is listed in the Porsche factory Technical Bulletins, but unfortunately, these numbers are not 100 percent accurate, so you need to look at the bearing housing on your engine in order to be 100 percent sure as to which bearing you have installed.

Porsche's electronic parts catalog lists the following engine numbers as the cut-offs for the various engines:

- Up to engine # M 651 12851, Boxster 2.7-liter M96.22
- Up to engine # M 671 11237, Boxster S 3.2-liter M96.21
- Up to engine # M 661 141164, Carrera 996 3.4-liter
- From engine # M 651 12852, Boxster 2.7-liter M96.22
- From engine # M 651 11238, Boxster S 3.2-liter M96.21
- From engine # M 661 141165, Carrera 996 3.4-liter
- All 2005 Boxster 987 (maybe some 2006 models)
- All 2005 Carrera 997 (maybe some 2006 models)
- Maybe some 2006 Cayman models

However, as mentioned previously, practical experience has determined that these numbers are not 100 percent correct. Porsche replaced and/or repaired a lot of engines over the years, and as a result there are a lot of engines out there where parts are mixed and matched. For example, the 3.4 Porsche factory motor that I installed in my 3.4-liter conversion has the very-late-style intermediate shaft bearing with the 22mm center nut (see Photo 15) but is missing some other upgrades that had been implemented over the years.

The only way to know for sure is to remove your transmission and look. The double-row version of the intermediate shaft was the first version used on these engines and will almost always be found on the early cars. The intermediate shaft cover for the double-row bearing is characterized by a shallow dish; the single-row bearings have a much deeper dish, as shown in Photo 7.

PELICAN PARTS REPLACEMENT KIT

The Pelican Parts intermediate shaft bearing replacement kit is shown in Photo 3 and contains everything that you need to perform the replacement in either a single-row or dual-row bearing engine. The Pelican kit uses the same bearing that Porsche used when originally building the engines, but the kit incorporates a stronger seal on the outside of the bearing. The kit is designed so that the bearing replacement can be performed during a routine clutch replacement (see Project 44). Changing out the bearing during each clutch job will ensure that the bearing is fresh and not wearing prematurely. As stated in the previous section, the failure mode of this bearing is not well known—if it's swapped out and replaced every 30,000–45,000 miles when the clutch is renewed, it should protect your engine from problems.

The kit uses a single-row bearing, just like the later-style Porsche design. For engines that originally had a double-row bearing installed, there are two spacers included with the kit (Photo 4). These spacers fill the space that was normally occupied by the double-row bearing. In addition to the bearing replacement, the kit also includes a stronger center stud. Instead of having the O-ring integrated into the stud, the O-ring is placed in a V-shaped sandwich on the outside surface of the bearing housing cover. The Pelican kit is still in the stages of prototype testing and will be available in the fall of 2010, most likely in the $165 price range.

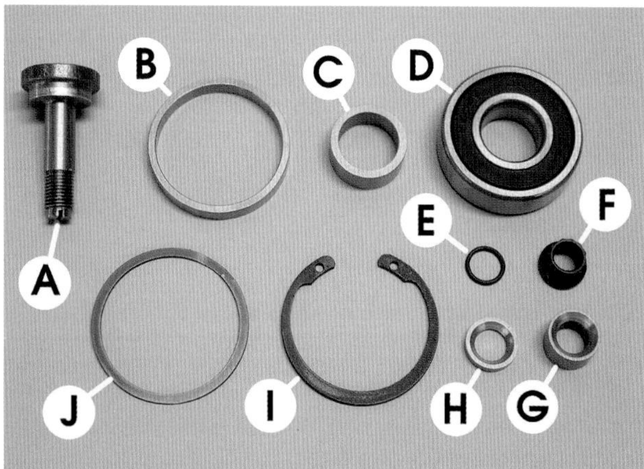

3 This photo shows some of the parts contained in the Pelican Parts intermediate shaft bearing replacement kit: **A:** Improved center bearing bolt, **B:** Outer race spacer (for engines with double-row bearings), **C:** Inner race spacer (for engines with double-row bearings), **D:** Replacement intermediate shaft bearing (NSK), **E:** Center bolt O-ring, **F:** Center bolt nut, **G:** Long center bolt spacer (for engines with single-row bearings), **H:** Short center bolt spacer (for engines with double-row bearings), **I:** Snap ring (for engines with single-row bearings), **J:** Spiroloc snap ring (for engines with double-row bearings). Not shown: three new micro-encapsulated cover bolts, three M6×25 installation helper bolts, and three M6×1×25mm set screws.

LN ENGINEERING RETROFIT KIT

The LN Engineering IMS Retrofit kit is also an easy-to-install upgrade kit that can be installed with the engine still in the car and provides almost bulletproof reliability to this critical component. This kit costs about $600 and is available online from PelicanParts.com. The upgrade kit incorporates a custom ceramic hybrid bearing (see Photo 5), featuring precision Japanese-made tool steel races and genuine USA-made Timken sintered silicon nitride ultra-low friction roller balls. This bearing, combined with a beefier center stud and a custom-machined housing, ensures that the IMS problems inherent in the stock design are mitigated. The engine can be upgraded during a routine clutch job and is fairly easy to install thanks to the installation tools designed by LN Engineering specifically for this task.

WHICH KIT TO USE?

I designed the Pelican Parts replacement bearing kit in order to fill a gap within the do-it-yourself (DIY) market. This kit is designed to replace the factory bearing with a very similarly manufactured bearing (with an improved seal and updated center bolt). I recommend that the bearing be swapped out each time a clutch replacement is performed (30,000–45,000 miles). The outer bearing seal is not removed on the kit,

4 Here are two sides view of the Pelican replacement kit—double-row configuration shown on the left with the spacers in place, single-row on the right. These covers have the updated brown seal (see Photo 8).

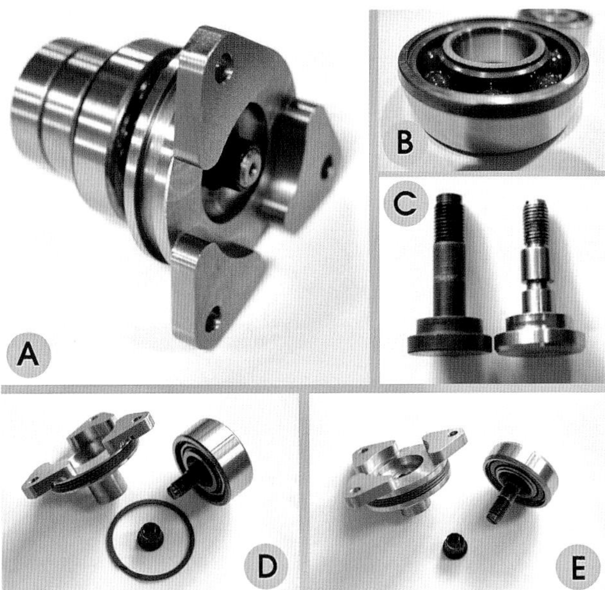

5 This photo array shows the various elements that comprise the LN Engineering upgrade kit for the intermediate shaft bearing. **A:** This is a version of the retrofit kit that is installed during the rebuild process and requires the engine be apart. **B:** The improved ceramic coated ball bearing. **C:** Stronger center bolt (left) when compared to the thinner and weaker OEM shoulder bolt (right). **D:** Upgrade kit for early engines with the double-row bearing. **E:** Upgrade kit for the later engines with the single row bearing.

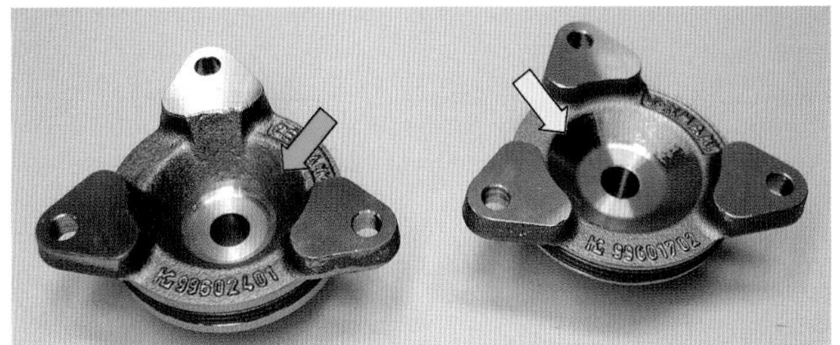

7 Shown here are two late-style intermediate shaft covers. The cover on the left has a deep dish and is used in engines that originally had a single-row bearing. The cover on the right is shallower and is used with engines that originally had a double-row bearing. Unfortunately, the records on which engine used which style of bearing are very spotty, so the only real way you can tell is by removing the transmission and seeing what you have installed in there.

6 Here's a neat side/cutaway view of the intermediate shaft and the LN Engineering IMS retrofit kit installed. This photo shows the intermediate shaft upgrade kit installed into a display Boxster engine with one half of the engine case missing. Shown here are the intermediate shaft timing chain (blue arrow), the intermediate shaft gear (yellow arrow), the intermediate shaft bearing cover/housing (red arrow), the housing-to-crankcase seal (orange arrow), one of the three bolts that attach the housing to the case (purple arrow), and the engine case (white arrow). The bearing stud and nut are also shown installed in the center of the housing. *Photo: Mike Seningen*

8 The top portion of this photo shows the troublesome O-ring that was found on the early intermediate shaft bearing covers. The bottom shows a close-up photograph of the improved three-ridge seal. If you pull off your intermediate shaft cover and you find that you have the early style, then I highly recommend that you upgrade to this later-style cover.

instead an improved seal is installed, which should offer longer life than the factory original. Replacement bearings, O-rings, and parts will be available for customers who have already performed the swap at least once and already have the tools, spacers, and the improved center bolt. The Pelican Parts kit uses the stock intermediate shaft bearing cover as a way to reduce the total cost of the kit.

The LN Engineering retrofit kit contains a stronger-than-stock center stud, a custom-machined intermediate shaft end cover, and a special, custom-manufactured ceramic bearing, which is very expensive but has a much longer life under harsh conditions. The LN Engineering kit is considered to be the more robust kit and is designed primarily for shops that are installing the retrofit and need that extra guarantee for their customers. The extended-life ceramic bearing (see Photo 5) is only available at this time with the LN Engineering kit, and its inclusion is responsible for a large portion of the cost difference between the two kits.

BEARING REMOVAL

The bearing is located behind the flywheel of the engine, so the first step that you need to do is jack up the car (see Project 1) and remove the transmission (see Project 37). Then, remove the clutch and flywheel from the engine (see Project 44). With the car elevated in the air, drain the oil out and remove and inspect the oil filter (see Project 1).

Before doing anything else, you want to remove the camshaft end plugs from your engine (see Photo 2 of Project 16). These plugs cover the camshaft timing marks—you will need to check the timing on the camshafts when you are done with your bearing replacement. If you have a pre-2003 Boxster engine (or pre-2002 for the Carrera 996), then you only need to remove the plugs on the exhaust camshafts (two plugs total). The exhaust camshafts are located on the bottom of the engine. If you have a 2003 or later Boxster engine (2002 or later for the 996 Carrera), then you need to remove all four plugs (intake and exhaust), because you will need to check all four camshafts when you are done. For the Boxster, the plugs for the camshafts that drive cylinders 4–6 should be easily accessible to the left of the flywheel area. The plugs for cylinders 1–3 need to be accessed through the panel in the passenger compartment that gives you access to the drive belts on the engine (see Project 5 for more information).

With the plugs removed, now remove the three bolts that hold on the intermediate shaft bearing cover (Photo 9). With the bolts removed, you should be able to shine a flashlight down the holes and see the intermediate shaft sprocket inside the engine (Photo 10). What you are looking at is the big sprocket for the intermediate shaft, as shown in Photo 5. What you want to do is rotate the engine clockwise until you can find three spots behind these through-holes where the metal surface of the sprocket is blocking the holes. You may find it easier to rotate the engine if you remove the spark plugs (Project 7). You will then insert set screws into these holes and push the screw into the sprocket in order to hold it in place while you're performing the bearing replacement (see Photo 12). Rotate the engine until you have found a spot where all three holes are blocked, then install the set screws. Tighten the screws down only hand-tight, but very snug, using a small tool or ratchet. Don't use the iron grip of death here, as you don't want to strip out the small M6 bolts. Just make them very snug and tight with your hand.

With the intermediate shaft sprocket locked in place by the set screws, now is the time that you want to mark the locations of your camshafts. Again, you only need to mark the two exhaust camshafts on the pre-2003 Boxster engines (pre-2002 on the Carrera 996). This is because the intake and exhaust camshafts are tied together with a chain of their own, and if one is properly set, then the other is properly set as well (see Photo 22 for more clarification). If you have a 2003 and later Boxster engine (or 2002 and later 996 Carrera engine), this particular design uses what are known as vane-cell adjusters and a single chain to link both the exhaust and intake camshafts together (see Photo 22). This design has a tendency to have the camshafts slip when performing the replacement, so you need to be vigilant in checking all four camshafts (see the section on checking camshafts at the end of this project).

Use some marking paint or a scribe to mark the locations of the camshaft with respect to the cylinder head (see Photo 13). Make sure that the marks are clear and visible—you will be rotating the engine 360 degrees when you are done to verify that all of the camshafts line up again with the marks that you created.

With the camshaft timing properly marked and the intermediate shaft secured, it's time to remove the two tensioners that pull on the flywheel-end sprockets of the intermediate shaft. The first one to remove is the tensioner for cylinders 1–3, which is located to the right of the flywheel area and is shown in Photo 14. Next, remove the tensioner that tightens the chain that connects the intermediate shaft to the crankshaft, located to the left of the flywheel area (Photo 14). Be sure to have an oil catch pan ready when you remove these two tensioners, as oil will spill out.

Next, remove the center nut from the bearing. I have found that these typically just come off with a 13mm socket, but you may have to use an open 13mm wrench and a screwdriver to hold the center of the bolt as you remove the nut. With the center nut removed, you should be able to slightly tap the cover counterclockwise so that you can get some pry bars underneath (Photo 15). You will need at least two of them to get the cover off (just one won't work), applying pressure in two places at the same time. There is a special tool available from Porsche to assist in removing the cover, but it's quite expensive and not really necessary.

With the cover removed, you should be able to see the bearing underneath. The inset of Photo 9 shows an example of a completely destroyed IMS bearing, and Photo 12 shows more of what a normal bearing should look like. If you accidentally drop the center bolt into the recesses of the intermediate shaft, then simply pluck it out with a magnetic tool. If you have a single-row bearing engine, at this point you will want to remove the large circlip that holds the bearing in place (see Photo 19). If you have a double-row bearing engine, then the internal snap ring will simply snap out automatically when you go to pull the bearing.

There is a specialized bearing removal tool that was developed by the folks at LN Engineering for this task (Photo 16). Thread the center bar of the tool onto the bearing stud and turn it so it threads all the way down to the base of the bearing (inset of Photo 16). Slide the removal tool canister over the threaded rod and then screw on the large nut that fits on the threaded rod. Apply some motor oil to the nut and the back surface of the tool to ease the removal process. With the tool in place, hold the threaded rod and turn the nut clockwise to remove the bearing. Be sure to wear safety glasses, as the tool applies a lot of force to pull the bearing out of the engine. Turn the wrench on the nut until the bearing slides out of the engine. For engines with a dual-row bearing, you will hear a loud pop when the internal snap ring pops out of its groove. Be sure to have an oil catch pan or a bucket handy, as a significant amount of oil will most likely exit out of the intermediate shaft bore when you remove the bearing.

Inside the intermediate shaft you will most likely find some oil and debris. Get some paper towels and tape them to the end of a stick and clean out the inside of the intermediate shaft. You can also attach a small rubber hose to the end of your shop vacuum and suck out any debris that might remain in there.

There's a small possibility that your bearing center stud may break when attempting to pull the bearing out of the engine. If this happens, then you need to remove the bearing using an internal bearing puller tool (like the Stahlwille puller shown in photo 8 of Project 44).

9 It all starts here with the intermediate shaft cover, located right under the rear main seal (located behind the clutch and flywheel). Using a 10mm socket, remove the three bolts that hold on the intermediate shaft cover. There's quite a bit of oil residue on the lower half of the cover, which seems to indicate that there is some leakage from the seal. The inset photo shows a completely destroyed intermediate shaft bearing (IMS). The outer seal and race are missing. The balls have fallen down in the bearing and are basically just sitting there. This engine was very close to self-destructing: it was wise for the owner to turn it off and not drive it any more. As a result, he may have saved the engine from complete destruction. However, the remains of the bearing have circulated out of this area and down to the engine sump: if any metallic particles got past the filter, then they would have caused damage to the rest of the engine (bearings, etc.).

10 The holes that hold on the intermediate shaft cover are through-holes, which means they exit out into the engine case. With the cover bolts removed, rotate the crankshaft until you see metal appear behind each of these holes. The intermediate shaft has some large relief holes cut in the big sprocket (see Photo 6). You want to rotate the engine until all of the small little holes here are blocked by metal on the sprocket. This way, none of the set screws will go into one of the larger holes on the sprocket. When you install the set screws, they should firm up just below the surface of the case. If they don't, then make sure you don't keep turning them: you may end up dropping them into your engine case, which will make them *very* difficult to retrieve later on.

11 After you've lined up the gear behind the cover, insert the set screws into the holes and tighten them down. Don't use the iron grip of death to tighten them down, they only need to be hand-tight. With the set screws in place, you should be able to tap the cover and rotate it back and forth in its bore a bit. The inset photo shows a close-up of the DIN916 M6 1.00×25 length set screws that fit perfectly for this task.

12 The yellow arrow shows how the set screw pushes against the sprocket surface and holds it in place. When you're rotating the engine, you want all three set screws to be pushing on the surface of the sprocket, not pushing through one of the open holes (green arrow). The screws act as a friction fit to keep the shaft from moving or rotating while you're working on it.

13 With the set screws in place, mark the camshafts with some marking ink or paint. Mark the two intake camshafts for pre-2003 engines, and mark all four for 2003 and later engines. The pre-2003 engines had the intake and exhaust camshafts tied together with a separate chain, so if one camshaft is properly timed, then the other one should be as well. You want to mark the camshafts to make sure that they do not move or rotate while you're doing the installation and alter the timing of the engine. When you're done with the installation, you will rotate the engine 360 degrees and double-check to make sure these marks all line up again perfectly.

14 You need to release a bit of the tension on the camshaft chains by unscrewing the tensioners out of their bore. Use a 32mm wrench or socket to release the primary chain tensioner located inside the engine block, next to the flywheel (shown on the left). This chain tensioner tightens the chain that connects the intermediate shaft to the crankshaft. In a similar manner, loosen up the chain tensioner for cylinders 1-3, which is located inside the bottom of the 1-3 cylinder head (shown on the right, and located on the right side of the car). The yellow arrow points to the aluminum sealing ring, which should be replaced when you reinstall the tensioner.

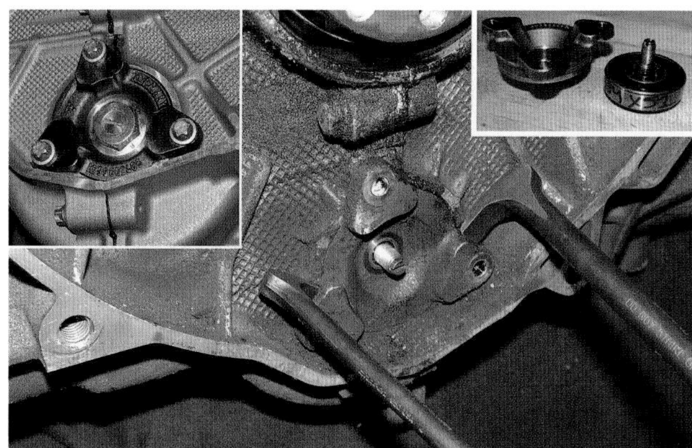

15 This photo shows the intermediate shaft cover/housing with the three bolts removed and the center nut disconnected. Use two small prybars to remove the cover from the engine. The cover shown installed in this engine is a shallow one, meaning that this engine has a double-row bearing inside. The inset photo in the upper right shows a stock cover for a single-row bearing—notice how the inside cone of the cover is deeper. The inset in the upper left shows the 2006-later-style intermediate shaft cover with the larger nut. The bearings behind this cover are nonreplaceable because the bearing is bigger than the hole in the engine case.

16 Install the bearing removal tool onto the center stud by threading the center rod piece onto the center bolt that holds the bearing and the cover plate together (inset photo). Make sure that you thread the hexagon-shaped piece down as far as it can go onto the bolt. Slide on the outer cylinder and spin on the nut to the threaded rod. I found it most useful to lubricate the back surface of the cylinder and the nut, too, in order to facilitate easier turning of the nut. With a 24mm wrench and a breaker bar/13mm socket combo, hold the center shaft in place (green arrow) while turning the wrench clockwise (yellow arrow). This will slowly pull the IMS bearing out of the bore of the intermediate shaft. For the double-row bearings, you will need to apply quite a lot of force. You will also hear a loud pop sound as the retaining ring snaps out of place. After this pop, the amount of force to remove and pull out the bearing should be moderate.

BEARING INSTALLATION

Begin by taking the bearing over to your table vice to press in the center stud. Press in the center stud, taking care only to apply pressing force to the inside bearing race. You can use a regular socket from your toolbox to accomplish this. It does not matter which side of the bearing faces the center stud. See the inset of Photo 17 for more details.

Prior to installing the new bearing, verify that your intermediate shaft bore is completely clean and free of debris. Using the bearing installation tool, place the new bearing/stud assembly into the end of the tool. The tool is designed to hold and constrain the bearing while you install it—you need to push the 12mm nut down the shaft of the tool and spin it onto the center stud's threads.

Prepare for the installation of the new bearing by placing it along with the installation tool in your freezer overnight. The cold temperatures will help shrink the bearing races and make it easier to install. This is an old trick that is commonly used when installing wheel bearings.

With the bearing and tool assembly combined tightly together, place the bearing into the bore on the intermediate shaft (Photo 17). Verify that the placement of the bearing is completely centered and square to the plane of the engine case (make sure it's not cocked off in any direction, even slightly). With a plastic hammer, carefully tap the bearing into place. It should go in relatively smoothly and without too much effort.

If you are performing the installation on an engine that uses a double-row bearing, install the outer spacer into the bore as is shown in Photo 18. Then, proceed to install the Spiroloc clip into the groove in the intermediate shaft (inset Photo 19). When the clip is completely installed into the engine, you can then install the intermediate shaft bearing cover in place. Take the smaller spacer and place it on the backside cover. Then place the cover on the engine and tap it into place using a small rubber hammer (Photo 20).

If you are performing the installation on an engine that uses a single-row bearing, then you don't need to install any spacers—just simply install the big circlip as shown in Photo 19, and then install the intermediate shaft cover as shown in Photo 20. With both single- and double-row installations, you will want to use a new seal on the cover. If your cover is the older-style one with the small black O-ring, you will want to upgrade to the newer-style cover and improved seal to guard against leaks. I also like to place a small bit of Curil-T sealant on this seal when I'm installing it, just as an added measure of oil-leak protection. The cover can only go on in one orientation—typically the numbers/writing on the later-style covers goes at the bottom. When installing the cover, be careful not to pinch or damage the seal, as it has a tendency to get caught sometimes during the installation process.

If for some reason you are having difficulty driving the intermediate shaft cover into place, then you can use the following procedure to assist you. Use three M6×25 bolts to help guide the cover into place. Place the cover into the bore and tap it down as far as it will go. Then, remove the set screws that you placed earlier (Photo 11). Install the bolts, and then crank each one down in an alternating pattern until the cover is flush with the engine case. When the cover is installed in place, then remove the three M6×25 bolts.

With the cover fully in place, you can now remove the set screws. Replace them with new micro-encapsulated bolts from Porsche (inset Photo 21). The phrase "micro-encapsulated" is a fancy word for bolts that have some sealant on them. It's okay to reuse your old bolts, but be sure that you coat the threads with a sealant like Curil-T or Loctite prior to installation or they will leak. Tighten the bolts down to 8 ft-lbs (11 Nm).

With the cover installed and the cover bolts tightened down and sealed, install the O-ring on the center shaft (Photo 20). I recommend putting a thin layer of Curil-T sealant around this O-ring in order to help seal against leaks. With the O-ring in place, now install the spacer. Finally, install the 12-point nut on the top, tightening it to a maximum of 24 ft-lbs. I also recommend placing a bit of Curil-T sealant underneath this nut.

If you are installing the LN Engineering retrofit kit, then the procedure is almost identical, if not simpler. Install the new intermediate shaft bearing cover in the same manner as described above. Prior to installation, verify that the O-ring that fits in the center of the shaft is in place and undamaged. Install the 12-point nut on the end using some green Loctite flange sealant as an added protection against leaks. Photo 21 shows the LN Engineering ceramic bearing installed in the case with the open no-seal side facing outwards, and the inset shows the retrofit kit intermediate shaft end cover installed in place.

At this time I also recommend that you replace your rear main seal (RMS) with the new, updated version. See Project 44 for more details.

17 If the center bolt is not pre-installed into the bearing, you need to gently press it in. Place an appropriately sized socket against the inner race of the bearing and then press the bolt in using a vice (upper right inset photo). Be sure that the socket only presses on the inner race of the bearing. This will assure when you press in the bearing that any force used is applied only to the inner race of the bearing. Applying force to the outside race of the bearing when pressing can damage the bearing and shorten its life. You can press in the center stud and then place the entire assembly into your freezer (inset upper left). This trick is commonly used with wheel bearings and shrinks the outer race just slightly when you install it, allowing you to use much less force during the installation. You want to place as little force as possible on the intermediate shaft because you don't want to knock it loose from where it's being held in place by the set screws. Using a hammer with a plastic head, carefully tap the end of the installation tool. With the bearing cold from the freezer, it should not require a tremendous amount of force to install. Tap the bearing in using the tool until it's seated against the back of its bore in the intermediate shaft.

18 Here's the bearing shown installed in the bore of the intermediate shaft with the outer spacer in place (yellow arrow). This is an engine that used the double-row bearing. The inset photo in the upper left shows the improved center bearing bolt. This bolt is much stronger than the original and does not suffer from any weak points like the original Porsche design. The lower left inset photo shows the long center bolt spacer for engines with single-row bearings. The secret to keeping oil from leaking out of the bearing assembly lies with the tapered groove precision-machined into the spacer. This design squeezes the O-ring tightly against the intermediate shaft cover plate and the bolt, creating a leak-resistance seal. This design element is very similar to the V-groove washers used on the case through-bolts that are installed in the 1965–1989 Porsche 911 air-cooled engines.

19 For engines with the single-row bearing, the bearing is held in place against the intermediate shaft by a big circlip. Using a set of circlip pliers, remove this clip before pulling the bearing, and place it back into its groove after the new bearing is installed. For engines that use the double-row bearing, you install the new bearing, the spacer, and then the Spiroloc circlip (inset photo). Thread the clip into the groove and then rotate it to install it in place.

21 This photo shows the LN Engineering ceramic bearing installed into the case. The engineers at LN Engineering have theorized that the removal of the seal will allow fresh motor oil to lubricate the ceramic bearing, thus they have removed the seal from the rear-facing side of the bearing. The upper left inset photo shows three brand-new Torx bolts from Porsche for the intermediate shaft cover. The bolts are "micro-encapsulated," which is a fancy word meaning that they simply have some sealant on the threads. I like to use new bolts to assure against leaks, but you can also reuse your old bolts if you liberally coat the threads with sealant prior to installation. The upper right inset photo shows the LN Engineering IMS retrofit kit installed. Use a small amount of Curil-T or similar flange sealant around the edge of the nut to insure against small leaks.

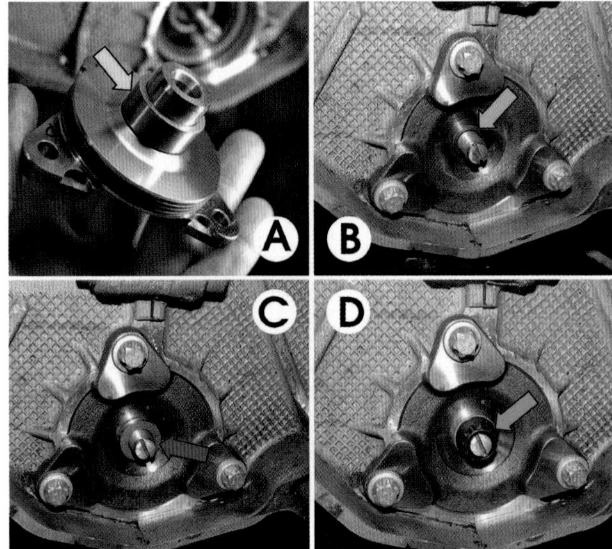

20 **A:** With the bearing, the large outer spacer, and the Spiroloc installed, it's time to install the bearing cover along with the smaller spacer (double-row only). Place the small spacer on the bearing cover as shown by the yellow arrow. If you are reinstalling the bearing cover with the later-style improved seal, I recommend using a new seal. **B:** Use the old bolts to tighten down the cover. Then remove the old bolts and use the new bolts to tighten down the cover. Torque to a maximum of 8 ft-lbs (11 Nm). If you're not using new bolts, then be sure that you coat the threads with a liberal amount of sealant so they won't leak. With the cover in place, slide on the O-ring as shown. I recommend coating the O-ring with a thin layer of Curil-T to guard against leaks (double-row shown). **C:** Install the spacer onto the bearing flange (double-row shown). **D:** Using a screwdriver to hold the center bolt in place, tighten down the 12-point nut to 24 ft-lbs maximum. I also like to add just a touch of Curil-T sealant between the spacer and the nut, just to make sure there is no oil leakage (double-row shown).

CHECKING CAMSHAFT TIMING

With the new bearing installed in place, you are basically done with the installation. However, it's very important that you check your camshaft timing prior to reinstalling the transmission and starting the engine. Photo 22 shows how the timing chains are oriented and setup on the five-chain (Boxster thru 2002, 996 Carrera thru 2001) and three-chain motors (Boxster 2003 and later, 996 Carrera 2002 and later). Particularly with the three-chain motors, you need to make sure that you check the exhaust camshaft for cylinders 1–3 (located to the right of the flywheel). This particular camshaft has the least amount of chain wrap, and removing the chain tensioner to perform the replacement has the potential to loosen the chain and allow the timing to skip a tooth on the sprocket.

To check the timing, simply take the crankshaft and rotate it 360 degrees from where you originally placed it when you installed the set screws. Then check the marks that you made on the camshafts (four marks on all four camshafts for the three-chain motors, two marks on the exhaust camshafts for the five-chain motors). If all of the marks line up perfectly, then you're golden, and you can continue on with finishing up the installation. If any of the marks are off, then there is the potential that the timing chain slipped off of the camshaft sprocket during the installation process. See Project 16 for more information on retiming the camshafts if this happens.

If you happen to have the P253 camshaft timing tool, you can use that to check the timing on the five-chain engines. Simply place the engine at top dead center (see Photo 1 of Project 16), remove all four green caps on the camshafts and install the tool on each side to check each pair of camshafts (see Photo 3 of Project 16). If the tool fits, then the timing is perfect. If it doesn't fit, then you will have to retime the cams (see Project 16). It's very good practice to check the timing on the five-chain motors, but in reality, very few of these have problems, unless the instructions were not followed correctly.

Still, I recommend checking the timing prior to reinstalling the transmission—it's cheap insurance.

When you're done, carefully rotate the engine a full 360 degrees and check the camshaft timing marks that you made before you started. If they all line up, then you're good to go. If they are off, then your timing chain skipped, and you need to retime your cams. See Project 16 for more details on this procedure.

After you're done checking the camshafts, install new camshaft end caps as shown in Photo 27 of Project 16. Although I like to use a bit of sealant everywhere, these end caps don't tend to leak.

Also important to note, if you have the camshaft tools handy, you might want to check your camshaft timing *prior* to beginning the installation of the bearing. If the timing is slightly off and the bearing appears fine, then you might have some additional problems in your camshaft timing chain mechanism (slipping sprockets on the intermediate shafts, worn pads on the camshaft solenoid mechanisms, etc.). I would advise investigating these problems prior to pulling out the bearing.

Don't forget to change the filter and add oil! See Project 2 for more details. If you pulled your bearing and found some major wear or damage, then you probably want to pull the bottom sump off and clean it out (see Project 12). Also think seriously about replacing your sump air-oil separators, as they tend to get contaminated, too, if you have bearing debris in your sump.

If you check the official website for the book, you will find more reference photos for this project, along with a complete list of part numbers of all of the parts used in this project (see www.101Projects.com/Boxster/14.htm).

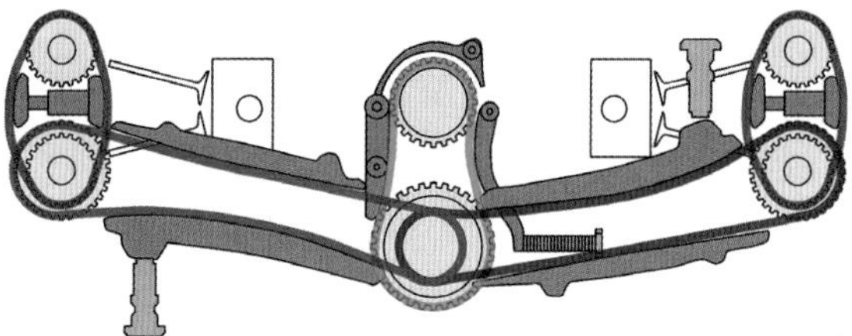

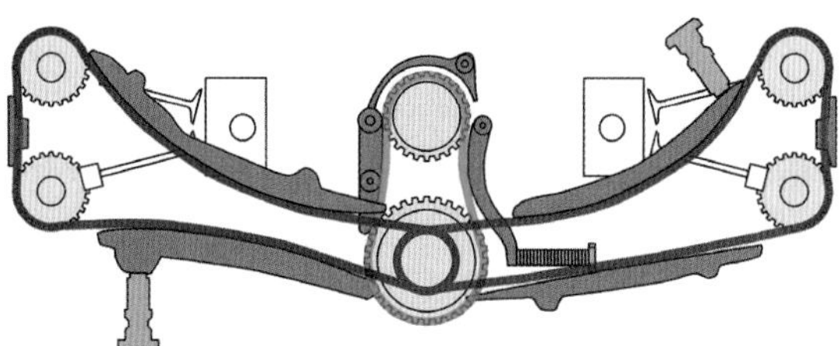

22 On pre-2003 Boxsters and Carrera 996s, the engines all had five chains: two linking each pair of camshafts to the intermediate shaft, one linking the intermediate shaft to the crankshaft, and two linking each camshaft together (top photo). I'm not sure why Porsche designed it this way: most modern cars don't have this many chains. The good news is that on these early five-chain cars, the timing chains almost never skip a tooth when performing the intermediate shaft bearing replacement. The chains are very tightly wrapped around each gear and as a result, when you loosen the tension from them, they tend to stay in place. Starting in 2003, Porsche went to a three-chain design, eliminating the chain that tied the two camshafts together (bottom photo). I can only speculate that this was done in order to simplify the construction of the motor (reduce cost and weight). This design works fine, except that there is more opportunity now for the chain to slip off the camshaft sprockets when replacing the intermediate shaft bearing. Specifically, the chain has a tendency to slip on the 1–3 exhaust camshaft when the chain is loosened. It is for this reason that it's very important to check the engine's static timing marks on all four camshafts to make sure that the chains did not skip a tooth. If you start up the motor and the chains are off by one tooth, then the valves can impact the pistons and the engine will self-destruct. It's not very difficult to check the timing; you just need to remember to do it.

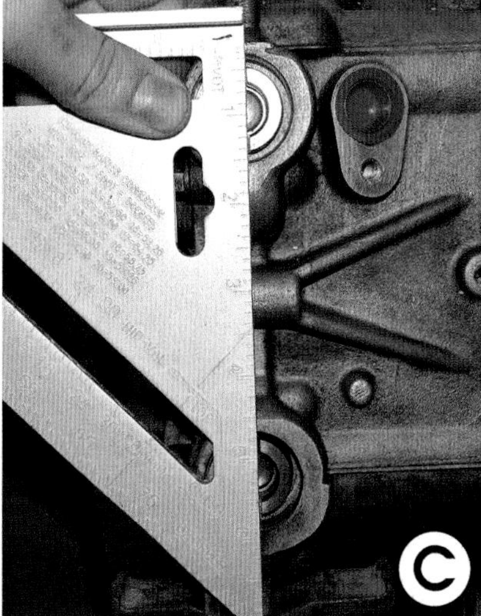

23 **A:** This photo shows the end of the intake and exhaust camshafts for cylinders 1–3 on the three-chain motor. Prior to removing the intermediate shaft bearing cover, you should have marked these camshafts. If you didn't mark them, you can set the motor to TDC and then visually inspect them to make sure that they are set to the proper timing. **B** With the later-style three-chain motors, the camshafts share a long chain that wraps around the outer edge of the camshaft gear. With these motors, you must check all four camshafts to make sure they are properly timed after installing your new bearing. The 9686 camshaft locking tool is shown here in this photo, locking camshafts 1–3 on this three-chain engine. The engine must be at top dead center for the tool to fit into the pair of camshafts. If it doesn't fit, then try rotating the crankshaft 360 degrees. With the locking tool in place, you can rest assured that your camshaft timing is set properly. I recommend that you check both sides, cylinders 1–3 and cylinders 4–6, although the 1–3 bank is the one most likely to skip a tooth. **C:** If you don't have the camshaft timing tool, you can use a straight edge to line it up against the edge of the camshaft and confirm that the timing is correct (as shown in the photo).

PROJECT 15
Boxster Engine Removal

Time / Tab / Talent: 10 hours / $200 /

Tools: Floor jack, furniture cart

Applicable Years: All

Parts: None

More Info: www.101projects.com/Boxster/15.htm

Tip: Remove transmission first so that you don't have to remove the chassis support bar

Performance Gain: Ability to perform engine repairs easily

Comp Modification: Swap in a 996 engine

The Boxster engine is not one of the easiest to perform repairs on. The tight enclosure of the engine compartment makes it pretty difficult to reach in and access a lot of the fuel injection components. There are indeed a lot of things that can be done with the engine in the car (fuel injection work, etc.), but many major operations need better access. In these cases, the only thing to do is to remove the engine—a task that many conceive to be very difficult. The reality is that the removal of the Boxster engine is not a difficult job—if you have the right tools and a little bit of the right knowledge, which I hope to provide here.

The car referenced in this project is my 2000 Boxster that I purchased with a broken engine. The engine was being dropped in preparation to install a brand-new 996 3.4-liter Porsche factory engine in its place (see Project 11). There were slight variations across the many years of Boxster production, but in general, the procedure for dropping the engine is almost the same for all the Boxsters. The following procedure checklist outlines what you need to do in order to drop the engine:

Preparation:
- Remove driver's seat (left side of the car, Project 73)
- Open the front and rear trunk lids
- Place the convertible top into service mode and remove the engine compartment cover (Project 3)
- Disconnect the battery (Project 81)
- Remove access panel behind rear seats (Project 5)
- Remove drive belt (Project 5)

Engine Compartment:
- Detach mass airflow sensor and loosen and remove the snorkel (Photo 1). Disconnect the air-oil separator hose from the intake and the separator if necessary (Project 9).
- Disconnect the brake booster vacuum line (Photo 2)
- Unplug the A/C compressor electrical connection
- Remove A/C compressor mounting bolts (Photo 4)
- Disconnect electrical junction box (Photo 2)
- Remove power steering reservoir (Photo 2)
- Disconnect ground strap cable (Photo 3), remove gas cap and disconnect air injection hoses, and remove secondary air pump (Photo 3).
- Loosen oil filler neck and coolant hose clamps (Photo 3)

Rear Trunk:
- In rear trunk, unplug engine harness from DME and other harness connectors (may require unbolting the DME from the firewall—Photo 5)
- Disconnect ground wire attached to the trunk wall (Photo 5)
- Pull dipstick out of reservoir tank holder (Project 33)
- Push the grommet in and feed harnesses into the engine compartment (Photo 5)

Underneath the car:
- Remove transmission (under trays, support braces, oxygen sensors and exhaust, muffler, Project 37)
- Remove safety cable (Photo 10)
- Empty coolant and remove all coolant hoses (Project 29)
- Disconnect power steering lines (Photo 8 and Photo 9)
- Remove power steering line from support bracket (Photo 9)
- Loosen power steering return line at junction in engine compartment (Photo 9)
- Remove accelerator cable linkage cover, disconnect cable and remove cable linkage assembly from chassis (1997–1999 only, Photo 11)

- Detach both supply and return fuel lines (return line was used only on early cars, see Photo 6)
- Pull engine oil filler neck off (Project 33)
- Position jack under engine, elevate
- Remove front motor mount (Project 10)
- Begin to lower engine (Photo 13)
- Guide A/C compressor out of the way (Photo 12)
- Lower engine down (Photo 13)
- Lower down onto cart and remove (Photo 14)

If you follow the procedure carefully and check/double-check to make sure that everything is disconnected, the actual process of lowering the engine is not difficult. Different years will vary in what you need to disconnect, but in general, the procedure outlined above and in the photo series should give a clear indication of the steps that need to be followed. The general rule of thumb is to carefully inspect all the areas and components (lines, vacuum hoses, and electrical connections) that connect the engine with the rest of the car. Cars equipped with Tiptronic transmissions have a few extra lines and hoses to worry about.

With this particular engine drop procedure, the transmission is removed first. You need to make sure that you support the engine with a jack stand after the transmission is removed from the car. It is possible to remove the engine and transmission together. Although I typically find this a bit unwieldy, mating the transmission with the engine installed can be a bit more difficult than when they are both on the ground. Also, if you lower the engine and the transmission separately, you do not need to remove the center chassis support bar, which holds the whole rear suspension alignment together.

When lowering the engine, it is very wise to have an assistant on hand. Not only can this person provide emergency assistance in case something goes wrong, but it's also important to have an extra set of eyes that can watch to see if anything was overlooked during the entire process. Make sure that your assistant is watching the surface where the engine and the rear axle support bar meet to keep tabs on the progress. When the engine case passes the support bar, the engine will become slightly unstable on the jack, so make sure that you have a hand free to steady it.

Keep in mind that you may need to jack up the car higher than you expected in order to remove the engine from underneath the car. It is quite common to lower the engine all the way down to the ground only to find that you need to raise the car much higher to pull it out from underneath. Use a high-lift jack on the rear axle support bar to raise the chassis higher. If you don't have enough clearance, you may need to remove the rear axle support bar and pull the engine out the back. It also may be useful to remove the rear bumper to gain additional clearance to pull the engine out from underneath. Either way, the amount of work needed is a direct function of the equipment that you have on hand. Regardless of how you raise the car, always practice extreme safety—stack your tires and wheels horizontally under the car just in case an emergency arises (the car will drop onto the tires and wheels).

Once you have the engine out of the car, it's really handy to have a furniture cart to place it on. Make sure that you don't crush any of the hoses, lines, or fixtures when you place it on the cart, and try not to let the engine rest on the exhaust headers. Use blocks of wood to make sure that the engine case actually rests on the cart.

There are a few things that you might want to consider doing to the engine while it's out of the car. It's a very wise idea to spend a little money now and do maintenance tasks that can only be performed when the engine is removed. Some of these include:

- Replace intake manifold hoses and seals. On older cars, these age and become brittle, which can then lead to vacuum leaks (Project 28).
- Replace the oil cooler seals. Although you can replace these with the engine still in the car, it is recommended that you tackle this job when access is much easier (Project 83).
- Update the intermediate shaft bearing and chain tensioners. The procedure for securing the camshafts and accessing the primary timing chain can be difficult with the engine installed. See Project 14 and Project 16.
- Replace the clutch and flywheel seal. I recommend that you inspect and replace the clutch disc when you have the engine out of the car. The flywheel seal, which can often leak, should be replaced as well (Project 44).
- Replace the spark plugs. Although you can access them underneath the car, it's much easier to do so with the engine out (Project 7).
- Check the air-oil separator hoses. These are made out of hard plastic, and although I haven't seen too many leak lately, I suspect they will begin to cause vacuum leaks as they get older and brittle (Project 9).

1 Disconnect the mass airflow sensor from the intake tube (yellow arrow), unplug it, and then place it off to the side in a plastic bag to prevent it from getting dirty. Disconnect the two hose clamps that hold on the intake tube (orange arrow) and then pull it back and remove it from the car.

2 This photo shows a variety of important items that need to be disconnected. The red arrow points to the electrical junction box. Snap up the black plastic cover (shown open here, blue arrow), and then disconnect the electrical cable underneath (red arrow). Make sure the battery is disconnected before you do this! The green arrow shows the power steering reservoir, which you need to disconnect and remove in order to maneuver the air conditioning hoses around the engine compartment. Pull off the cap and use a turkey baster or other suction device to siphon out the fluid in the reservoir. The inset photo (orange arrow) shows the thumbwheel on the lower part of the power steering reservoir—twist this counterclockwise to disconnect it and remove it from the engine. Believe it or not, the hose attached to the top of the reservoir doesn't actually connect to anything—it's an overflow hose that dumps excess fluid onto the top of the engine (I spent about two hours one day trying to research where this hose was supposed to plug into). Finally, the yellow arrow shows the power brake vacuum line—it's easiest just to remove the two screws and pull it off of the manifold.

3 Shown here is the secondary air injection pump. Disconnect the hose (green arrow), the electrical connection (blue arrow), and the bolts that mount it to its bracket. Remove it from the engine compartment. Also, disconnect the engine ground strap (red arrow). It's also a good time to disconnect the oil filler neck (yellow arrow). Loosen the clamp (purple arrow) and you should be able to pull the filler neck out. You can remove it completely by disconnecting it in the rear trunk after you get the transmission out (see Project 33).

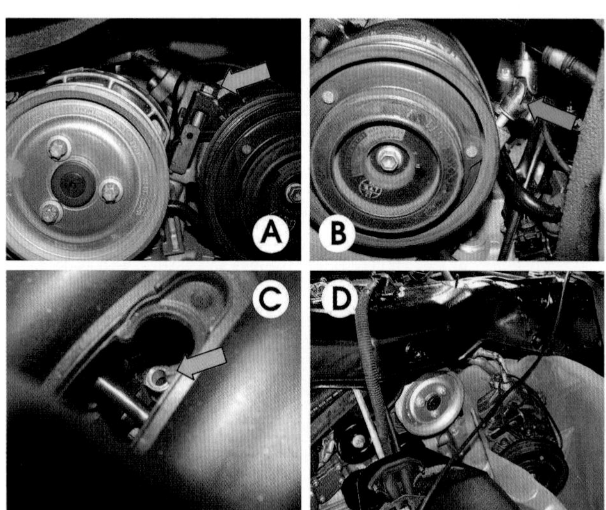

4 Removing the air conditioning compressor is one of the more difficult tasks. As on earlier Porsches, you leave the compressor in the car when removing the engine. This allows you to avoid emptying the system of A/C fluid, a task that requires specialized equipment. **A:** The compressor is held on by two bolts. The orange arrow shows the right-side compressor bolt. You can access and remove this bolt from the passenger compartment. **B:** The other bolt can be accessed by using a swivel socket (green arrow) through a gap in between the intake manifold (Photo **C**). **D:** Take some plastic wrap and lay it down in the back of your passenger compartment, and pull the compressor out of its mounting place on top of the engine. As the engine is lowered, you need to then route the hoses out of their channels and tuck them into the passenger compartment (see Photo 12).

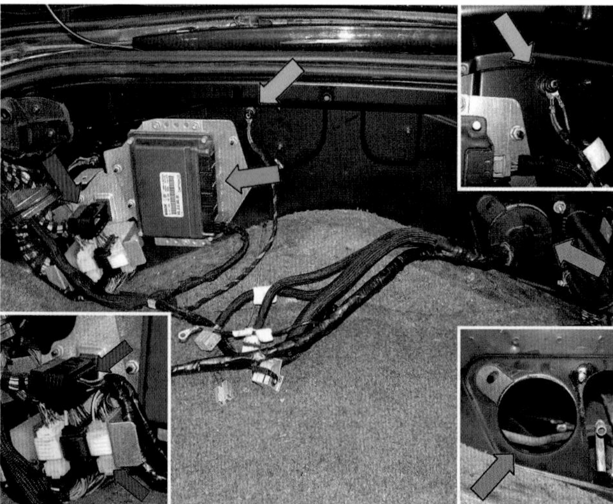

5 Shown here is the rear trunk with the carpet removed (see Project 33 for instructions on removing the carpet). You need to disconnect the engine wire harness from the DME (green arrow) and the chassis harness (red arrows). Also disconnect the engine wire harness ground point from its mounting point on the rear fire wall (blue arrow). Finally, push in the big grommet and stuff the entire wire harness through the big hole in the firewall (purple arrow) and place it neatly on top of the engine.

6 Shown here are the fuel line connections. Be sure to wear eye protection and have a small bucket handy when you unplug these. There may be a small amount of fuel still trapped in the system, and it will leak out onto you and your garage floor—be prepared. Disconnect these only when you have really good ventilation and are able to dissipate the fumes. The yellow arrow shows the power steering pressure line, which is lowered with the engine. The blue arrow shows the power steering return line, which is disconnected in the engine compartment, just above the blue arrow (see Photo 9).

7 This photo shows the engine compartment with the engine removed. If you are having difficulty getting the car high enough to pull out the engine, then you can remove the chassis support brace shown by the yellow arrows. Be sure to reinstall this support brace if you put the car back down on its wheels at some point thereafter (with or without the engine installed). I would also recommend getting the car's alignment checked when it's back on the road, as this brace is an important rear suspension piece and may affect the alignment settings when removed and then reinstalled.

8 This photo shows the disconnection of the power steering pressure line (yellow arrow). You only need to disconnect the pressure line—the return line (green arrow) is disconnected further up inside the engine compartment (see Photo 9). Be very careful not to lose the small pieces that are integral to this connection (inset photo). The only way to replace them is to purchase a new line, which is expensive and difficult to install into the back of the power steering pump. Exercise caution and remove the pieces carefully from the line and place them in a plastic bag. When I dropped the engine, I simply put a piece of tape over the end of the line, and the tape fell off months later, so I had to spend about 30 minutes scouring the garage floor for the small bits and pieces (which I found, luckily). I also found it useful to disconnect the brake booster vacuum line here and remove it from the car (blue). A small plastic circlip near the white connector attaches it to the other line.

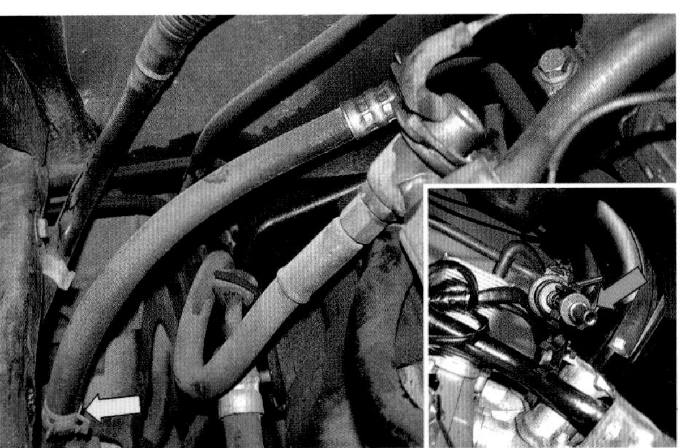

9 This photo shows two items that are a bit difficult to disconnect. The power steering return line has a rubber hose at this junction that mates into a barb attached to another hose. Remove the clamp and then pull off the hose. Do not cut this hose, as it is expensive and not easy to replace. If you can't get the hose off of the barb (it's very tight in there and you won't have much leverage), you can always disconnect the return line at the connection where you disconnected the supply line (see Photo 8). The inset shows the fuel tank vent line connection, which is mated underneath the manifold. This is also very difficult to get to—you'll have to reach in there and pull or disconnect the line further upstream.

10 Even though it looks a little bit like one, this is not a ground strap. It's a safety strap that attaches the engine to the chassis support brace that spans the center of the car. Disconnect it from the engine by removing the bolt shown (yellow arrow). If you have a zip tie handy, you might want to zip it to the support brace so that it doesn't get in the way when lowering the engine.

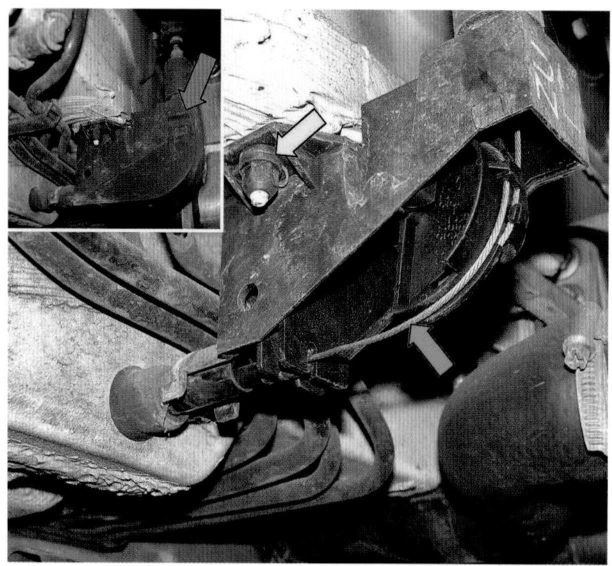

11 On the 1999 and earlier cars, the throttle was controlled by an actual cable. Remove the outer cover by releasing the tabs (purple arrow) and rotating the cover downwards. Then release the throttle cable that is connected to the main body of the car (green arrow). Finally, remove the two nuts that hold the cover to the chassis (yellow arrow) and disconnect the housing from the body. The housing remains with the engine when you lower it.

12 As you drop the engine, take the air conditioning hoses out of the plastic channel (green arrow), and carefully route them off to the side. Take care when lowering that they don't get crushed, scraped or damaged. You certainly don't want to be replacing the air conditioning hoses in your car because they accidentally got damaged during an engine drop. Also watch out for bad things happening, like what's shown in the inset photo. Here, one of the engine harness connectors is getting caught on the lip of the passenger compartment access hole as the engine is being lowered. If you don't check for items getting caught on the way down, then you will most likely damage something as the engine drops. Items getting caught happen almost 100 percent of the time—keep a close eye out for it.

13 This photo shows the engine about halfway out of the Boxster. The majority of the weight is supported by the floor jack—the jack stands are there for backup and for balancing (green arrows). In general, I don't suggest letting the engine weight rest entirely on the exhaust headers—the resulting force can put a lot of stress on the threads of the bolts that attach the headers to the cylinder head. To get the engine out, we put the engine down on a furniture cart, then jacked up the car very high in the air, pulled the engine out, and then lowered the car back down to a workable level. Using this method, we did not have to remove the chassis support brace (yellow arrow).

14 After all that hard work, you can claim your success here! This photo shows the Boxster engine successfully removed from the car and sitting on the engine cart. If you have a low-clearance jack (see Project 1), you can place your wooden furniture cart (yellow arrow) underneath the car. In this situation, we chose simply to drop the engine and exhaust together since the exhaust was filled with coolant and oil from this blown-up motor. You will find that you have to jack the car up really high to get the engine to clear the rear bumper and/or the chassis support brace when removing it from underneath the car. If you find that you have clearance problems that you cannot overcome easily, then you can remove the chassis support brace (see Photo 7), and you can also remove the intake manifold, working with the engine underneath the car. Removing the rear bumper cover can also gain you a few extra inches of working room as well.

PROJECT 16
Camshaft Swap and Valvetrain Repair

 **Time / Tab / Talent:** 10 hours / $100–$2,500 / 

 **Tools:** Camshaft timing tool, crankshaft locking tool

 **Applicable Years:** All

 **Parts:** New camshafts, lifters, solenoid, etc.

 **More Info:** www.101projects.com/Boxster/16.htm

Tip: All of these tasks should be able to be done with the engine in the car but are far easier with the engine removed

 **Performance Gain:** More horsepower

 **Comp Modification:** Replace intermediate shaft bearing

This project started out as a simple addendum to checking the camshaft timing when performing the intermediate shaft bearing replacement (see Project 14). However, after further consideration, I decided to expand it to include all of the items in your valvetrain that you might have problems with in the future. Specifically, this project covers the following tasks or potential problem areas you might encounter on your Boxster engine:

- Fixing camshaft cover leaks
- Replacing the VarioCam solenoid
- Swapping out your camshafts
- Checking the camshaft timing
- Replacing noisy lifters (tappets)
- Replacing the external chain tensioners
- Replacing the internal cam-to-cam chain tensioner
- Replacing chain ramps

For the purpose of illustration, the motor used in this project was out of the car on an engine stand. It's an old core motor that I purchased for demonstration purposes—it had been involved in a bad fire. The core motor is fine, but all of the injection and sensors were destroyed in the fire—perfect for rebuilding or for photos! This motor is a five-chain engine, which is significantly different than the later-style three-chain engines. See Project 14 for a description of the two types and how to tell the difference between the two. For those of you who have a three-chain engine, the procedures documented here are available on the official website for this book, refer to www.101Projects.com/Boxster/16.htm.

All of the tasks illustrated here should be able to be performed on the engine while it is still installed in the car, although clearance is tight and it's somewhat difficult to work under the car. I've broken the tasks up into photo captions—read along for the procedures detailing the tasks listed above.

1 Disassembly: The first step in this whole process is to set the crankshaft to top dead center (TDC) and lock it there. Turn the engine until the teardropped-shaped hole lines up with the hole in the case. Insert the way-overpriced factory knob in place, or simply use an appropriately sized drill bit (5/16 size worked well for me). Set the crankshaft at TDC now—the camshafts rotate at one-half the speed of the crankshaft, so the crankshaft is located either at TDC for cylinder 1 or TDC for cylinder 4. If need be in the next few steps, you might have to rotate it another 360 degrees if it's not at TDC for the cylinder bank you're working on. If you're performing these tasks with the engine in the car, then you need to access the crankshaft from behind the seats (see Project 5).

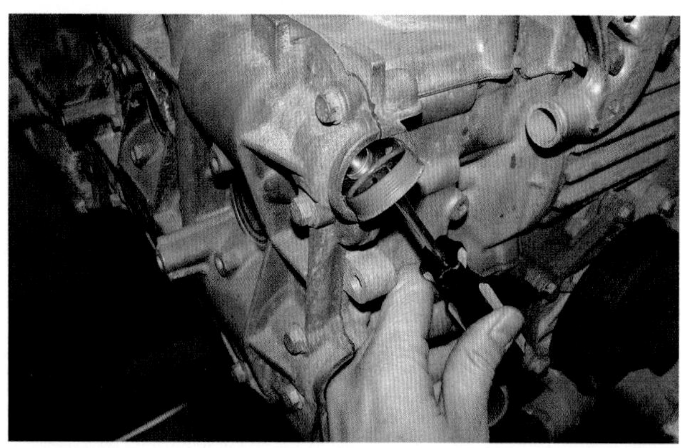

2 Now remove the two cam plugs that sit on the end of the two camshafts. You need to remove these green plugs to inspect/check the timing when performing the intermediate shaft upgrade. You basically poke a hole in the center of the shaft and then pull it out. Toss the old ones away, as you will not be reusing them. The engine uses a total of three per head, and the part number is 996-104-215-54.

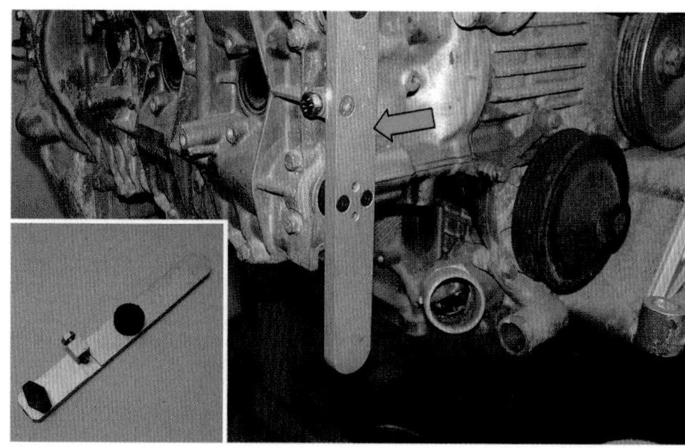

3 With the plugs removed, now install the camshaft timing tool, P253 onto the end of the camshaft. Normally, you would use Porsche tool 9624 to hold the camshafts onto the end of the motor (see Photo 3 of Project 8), but I found that the camshaft timing tool also pretty much did an adequate job of holding them in place as well. While I personally have most of the tools listed as required in the Porsche factory manuals, I like to try to recommend places where they may not be 100 percent absolutely necessary. This is one of those cases—use the P253 tool instead.

4 Remove the oil pump from the cylinder head. It's a wise idea to get a marking pen and mark the pump where it lines up with the engine case—it can be installed backwards by mistake. Remove the four bolts that hold the pump to the case (orange arrows), not the four Allen screws that are internal to the pump. Use two pry bars to simply pull the pump out of the end of the engine.

5 With the oil pump removed, remove all of the perimeter bolts from the camshaft cover. Also remove the two bolts that hold on the cover for the VarioCam solenoid (green arrow, lower right). With everything disconnected, use a few pry bars on the separation areas of the case and the cylinder head (yellow and red arrows) to pry the camshaft cover off of the head.

6 When you remove the camshaft cover, you should see the camshafts and the chains underneath. The top camshaft will want to move outwards when you remove the cover, but the force of the camshaft timing tool against its end should keep it relatively secured. It's okay if it pushes out by a few millimeters. I have heard from various sources that the camshaft can snap if there is enough force placed on it from the valve springs, so make sure that it doesn't move significantly out of its bore. The yellow arrow points to the spark plug tubes (found on early engines). Now would be a good time to replace them and the O-rings (found on all Boxsters/Caymans) that seal them to the cylinder head and camshaft cover.

7 Shown here is the solenoid that activates the valve that turns on the hydraulic oil pressure supply that advances the camshafts for the VarioCam operation. This solenoid has a habit of failing and needing replacement. Once you have the camshaft covers off, replacement is a snap. Simply unscrew the old one and install the new one in its place. At about $200 apiece, they are probably the world's most expensive solenoids.

8 Now, loosen and detach the camshaft sprocket from the exhaust camshaft. Four small bolts hold it on to the camshaft.

9 Carefully remove the leftmost camshaft-bearing caps on both of the camshafts (green arrow, inset photo). Then remove the three very long bolts that secure the VarioCam chain tensioner to the cylinder head.

10 Now, loosen up the chain tensioner on the head (refer to Photo 16 for cylinders 1–3 or Photo 17 for cylinders 4–6). With the chain tensioner loosened, the bearing caps removed, and the VarioCam tensioner disconnected from the head, you should be able to slide the gear off of the camshaft with your hand. A few gentle taps with a small rubber hammer can also help your cause if it's stuck. Let it sit next to the camshaft in the case. If you are performing this procedure with the engine in the car, be aware that once you remove the cam gear, the camshafts may slide out of the head—be ready to catch them. If you are performing this task on an engine stand, then simply rotate the engine at an angle, so that the camshafts won't fall out.

11 With everything disconnected, remove the camshaft timing tool from the engine. Remove the camshafts and move them over to your workbench.

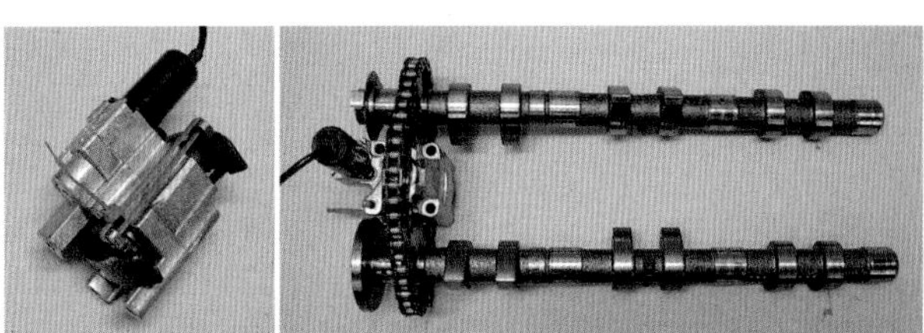

12 Shown here are the two camshafts, the small timing chain, and the VarioCam tensioner that ties them together. There is a special tool that is used to compress the tensioner together to make it easy to remove, but I just opted to use a zip tie instead. Works great, and when you're ready to expand it again, you just clip the zip tie.

13 With the camshafts removed, you can simply pluck out the lifters (tappets). Check both the lifters and the lifter guides for damage (pockets of wear greater than 1mm, fractures at the edges, irregular contact patterns on the running surfaces, grooves in the oil pockets for the cam lobes). Clean each lifter carefully with a lint-free cloth. I recommend using KimWipes, which I used all the time in the past when I was working in clean rooms building satellites. You can find these at PelicanParts.com—they are perfect for cleaning intricate engine parts where you don't want paper fibers or debris contaminating tiny oil passages. With the lifter clean, dip it in some fresh motor oil. Use whatever motor oil you're planning on using when you refill the car. Press down on the inside of the lifter while it's submerged so that you can clean out the internal passages as best as possible. It's particularly important to clean everything if your engine had its oil contaminated with coolant. Failure to clean and lubricate thoroughly may result in what is known as a noisy lifter—one that doesn't completely engage. This can lead to degradation in engine performance. The Porsche factory manuals recommend against using a magnet to pluck the lifters from their bores (use your fingers or a mini-suction-cup device instead).

14 This is one of the reasons why I don't care for Porsche's recommendation of going 15,000 miles between oil changes. This is an example of a camshaft bearing that is scratched and becoming worn. If this were on a 1965–1989 Porsche 911 engine, I would recommend replacing the bearing. However, the camshaft cover and cylinder head are matched pieces, and to replace this bearing, you basically need to replace the entire cylinder head! It's not worth the risk—change your oil every 3,000 to 5,000 miles with an oil that has a high content of anti-wear additives and keep bearing wear to a minimum.

15 There are three externally accessible chain tensioners on the Boxster motor. The one shown here tensions the chain for cylinders 4-6 and is by far the most difficult to reach. It's located underneath the air conditioning compressor, inside the cylinder head, and is accessible from inside the engine compartment. In order to loosen this tensioner, you need to remove the two screws that hold on the air conditioning compressor and nudge it out of the way. Then use a 32mm socket to loosen the tensioner as shown in the inset photo in the lower right.

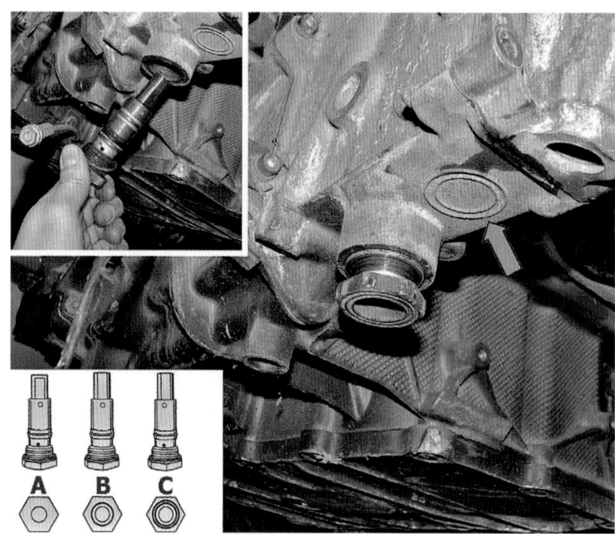

16 This photo shows the chain tensioner for cylinders 1–3, which is located inside the bottom of the cylinder head. The three tensioners are all different, but look remarkably similar. Porsche marked the top of each tensioner with different rings in order to help distinguish amongst them. **A:** The chain tensioner for cylinders 4-6 located under the air conditioning compressor. **B:** The main intermediate shaft tensioner, which fits inside the crankcase near the flywheel. **C:** The chain tensioner for cylinders 1–3, which fits into the bottom of the cylinder head. Note the handy marking on the head itself (purple arrow).

17 This photo shows the tensioner for the chain that runs between the crankshaft and the intermediate shaft, which is located on the left side of the engine case very close to the bottom of the flywheel. When replacing the intermediate shaft bearing (Project 14), loosen the tensioner as shown in the inset photo. If the tensioners are leaking, you should replace the metal sealing ring (orange arrow, PN: 900-123-147-30) and the small O-ring on the tensioner shaft (purple arrow, PN: 999-707-344-40).

18 **Reassembly:** Begin the process of reassembly by taking the two camshafts and lining them up on your bench. The cam-to-cam chain has two special links that are colored differently (green arrows). Align these links up with the divots that are located on each camshaft (yellow arrow). Keeping these two links lined up with the divots will keep the two camshafts timed with respect to each other.

19 Using care not to let the chain slip on the camshaft gears, install the tensioner in between the two sprockets. It's also a good time to replace your chain ramps if they appear worn (inset photo, lower right—they simply snap off). You will have to maneuver the tensioner and the camshafts back and forth to get the tensioner in there. Once installed, clip the zip tie and expand the tensioner—this should secure the chain, and the camshafts should be securely timed with respect to each other. Before going on to the next step, you should meticulously clean all of the mating surfaces of both the cylinder head and the camshaft cover (red arrows, inset photo) with gasket remover and a sharp razorblade. Remove all traces of sealant from both surfaces.

20 With all of the sealant material cleaned from the cylinder head, lay the camshaft assembly down into the cylinder head. Double-check that the light-colored chain links and the divots in the camshafts are still lined up properly. On the opposite side of the cylinder head, the lower camshaft should line up with the cylinder head/cover parting line, as shown in the inset photo.

21 Using your left hand, push the camshaft into place while affixing the camshaft bearing cap into place. Tighten down the bearing caps and also tighten down the tensioner housing. It's important to keep in mind that the German word for intake is *einlass*, which starts with the letter E, and the word for exhaust is *auspuff*, which starts with the letter A: E = intake, A = exhaust. The cylinder head, the camshaft cover, and these two little caps are all machined together and are labeled with the same number so that they won't be mixed up during the assembly process. Since the camshaft cover is machined and matched with the cylinder head, the cover is not available from Porsche as a separate, orderable part number. You must order a complete new cylinder head, which will include the head, the cover, and the caps all matched together. This makes rebuilding and repairing any damage due to camshaft bearing wear very difficult.

22 With the camshaft caps in place and the tensioner tightened down, affix the camshaft timing tool to the opposite end. There are a set of Porsche tools that are used to hold the camshaft in place while working on the engine at this stage. I found them unnecessary as the camshafts are held in place if you install the timing tool as shown.

23 Remove the chain tensioner for that bank—shown here is the tensioner for cylinder bank 1–3 (green arrow). With the tensioner removed, you should have enough slack to push on the chain sprocket (purple arrow) with your hand. Gently tap the sprocket on the rest of the way using a rubber mallet (inset photo). If you have the Porsche factory chain tensioner tool 9599, then install it into the bottom of the case. Tighten the tension screw until the small rod in the center is flush with the adjustment screw. If you do not have this extremely expensive tool (upper left inset of Photo 24), you can tighten up the tension on the chain using the regular chain tensioner. Reinstall the tensioner completely into the bottom of the case.

24 With the camshafts installed, the timing tool in place, the two bearing caps tightened down, the camshaft solenoid tensioner tightened down, and the primary tensioner reinstalled in the case, tighten down the four bolts that hold the camshaft sprocket to the camshaft. Double-check once again that the special colored links (green arrow) in the cam-to-cam chain are properly lined up with the divot mark in the camshaft (yellow arrow). Temporarily reinstall the camshaft cover using only a handful of bolts, lightly tightened down, and then remove the camshaft timing tool. At this point, spin the engine two full turns to recheck the camshaft timing by reinstalling the camshaft tool again. The upper left inset photo shows the very expensive Porsche chain tensioner tool in place (not required).

25 Next, reinstall the oil pump onto the exhaust camshaft using two of the four bolts to affix it to the cylinder head. Carefully line up the tab of the oil pump with the slot on the camshaft and make sure that it's inserted correctly. The two scavenge oil pumps are the same for either side, but they must be installed with the proper side facing up. There are markings for cylinders 4–6 (green arrow) and 1–3 (yellow arrow). The pump must be installed with the markings for the current cylinder bank closest to the crankcase. Sitting in the backseat of the Boxster, looking at the engine and the crankshaft pulley, cylinders 1–3 are on the left, and 4–6 are on the right. If you get confused, the basic rule is that the two pumps are installed opposite to each other. The oil pump for 1–3 is located on the flywheel side of the engine, and the oil pump for 4–6 is located on the drive belt side of the engine.

26 Perform a final cleansing of the surfaces with some isopropyl alcohol and let it evaporate fully before applying the sealant. Porsche recommends the use of Drei Bond silicone, type 1209, or Loctite 5900 flange sealant to seal the surface area of the head to the camshaft covers. Don't forget to apply a thin bead of sealant to the bearing saddle areas in the inner part of the head as well. With the sealant applied, tighten down all of the bolts on the camshaft cover in the order shown on this diagram. Carefully tighten each bolt to 10 ft-lbs (12 Nm), which is not a lot of force.

27 As a final step, insert the camshaft plugs into the end of the camshafts. Lightly tap them into place with a rubber mallet. Tighten down the two remaining bolts on the oil pump and also the two bolts that secure the cover for the solenoid. With one side of the engine complete, move onto the other side and repeat the process if necessary.

PROJECT 17
Replacing Belt Tensioners

Time / Tab / Talent: 1 hour / $150 /

Tools: 24mm wrench

Applicable Years: All

Parts: Three tensioner pulleys

More Info: www.101projects.com/Boxster/17.htm

Tip: The top and bottom pulleys are different, despite them looking the same

Performance Gain: Quiet-running engine

Comp Modification: Replace drive belt

The Boxster uses a complex belt path to drive all of the accessories of the engine off of a single belt. Even when I change the belt in my Boxster, the path is so difficult to remember off the top of my head that I have to refer to my own diagram in Photo 3 of Project 5 (belt replacement). The bottom line is that the three belt pulleys that are located on the crankshaft pulley side of the motor get a lot of wear and tear over their life. It's not uncommon for one or more of them to fail and begin to start squeaking.

When you get a high-pitched squeaking noise from your engine compartment, it's typically very difficult to diagnose where it's coming from. I like to run the engine and open the engine access lid while I'm carefully listening for the origin of the squeak. Be very careful of your hands and any items that might get stuck or caught in the engine if you're running it with the rear panel off. I often use a can of WD-40 with the spray nozzle extender attached to try to isolate which pulley or piece of equipment is making the noise. With the engine running, I typically soak the bearing shaft of each belt pulley, listening carefully for changes in the squeaking noise. Check every one, including the water pump, power steering pump, alternator, and the air conditioning compressor. Often, the noise will go away when the lubricant finds its way to the bearing. This works about 50 percent of the time to isolate the noise.

Another way to check the pulleys is to remove the drive belt and actually turn them with your hand. Sometimes you can feel significant resistance or hear a grinding noise as you turn each shaft by hand. Again, check each one, including the shafts of all of the accessories. All three of the idler pulleys should feel about the same. The accessories (alternator, water pump, etc.) will each feel different, so it's difficult to tell if there's anything wrong with the bearing unless you spin these on multiple cars every day.

Sometimes a squeaking noise may be caused by a belt that is deteriorating. As belts age they sometimes get worn out and smooth, and that may cause them to slip, which can result in a squeaking noise. If you suspect the belt may be the problem, then I recommend you replace it first. Or, you can try out some of the spray-on belt dressing that is available at your local auto parts store. The belt dressing is a temporary fix that makes the belt a little stickier and less prone to slipping.

Fortunately, the tensioners are very easy to replace. Simply remove the back panel behind the seats (as detailed in Project 5). Then remove the drive belt from the engine. Removal of the two idler pulleys is as simple as unbolting them and replacing them with a new one. Be careful not to drop the large washer that is on the front of the two idlers and the spacers in back either. Although they look almost identical, the top and bottom idler pulleys have two different part numbers, so be careful not to mix them up if you are replacing them both at the same time. Reinstallation is a snap; simply install the bolts and tighten. The bolts that are used on the pulleys originally had self-locking compound on them when they were new, so if you are reusing them again, simply add a little bit of blue Loctite 242 to the threads prior to installing them.

The tensioner pulley is a little bit different. It is attached to a spring-loaded arm via a single bolt that is backwards in orientation from the other two idler pulleys. You need to get a 15mm wrench on the head of the bolt behind the pulley and then loosen the pulley with a 24mm wrench on the front. Be careful not to drop the spacer located behind the pulley when you pull it off. Reinstall the new pulley in the same manner, using a small bed of blue Loctite 242. Tighten the assembly to 44 ft-lb (60 Nm).

1 This photo shows the front of the engine and the three pulleys discussed in the text. The yellow arrow points to the top idler pulley, and the green arrow points to the lower idler pulley. Although they look the same visually, there are two different part numbers for these two rollers. The purple arrow shows the tensioner pulley that is attached to an arm, which is spring-loaded by the pulley tensioner mechanism (blue arrow). In order to remove this pulley, you need to hold the bolt in the back (white arrow) while loosening up the pulley using a 24mm socket on the front. In order to fully remove the bolt that holds in the top idler pulley, you may have to loosen up the alternator attachment points (see project 82).

PROJECT 18
Turbos & Superchargers

Time / Tab / Talent: 30 hours / $3,000–$10,000 /

Tools: All of them

Applicable Years: All

Parts: Supercharger kit

More Info: www.101projects.com/Boxster/18.htm

Tip: Plan ahead and purchase a kit that fits your personal desires

Performance Gain: Gobs of horsepower and huge bragging rights

Comp Modification: Replace your head gasket, install new pistons

A lot of people think that turbo and supercharging are the Holy Grail of power increases. While indeed you can extract a large amount of power from them, people incorrectly assume that any aftermarket supercharger tossed on an engine will instantly generate gobs of horsepower. As with any good, reliable means of generating horsepower, the addition of a turbo or supercharger needs to be carefully coordinated with your engine's design—all the while keeping in mind your desired performance characteristics.

It's important to take a few moments here to talk about turbo and supercharging, or "forced induction," as it is known. A forced-induction engine has some "assistance" when filling the combustion chamber with air/fuel mixture. On a normally aspirated engine, the maximum manifold pressure is atmospheric pressure (14.7 psi). On a forced-induction engine, manifold pressure is increased by the supercharger (or turbocharger) to a level above 14.7 psi. The result is that a greater mass of air and fuel is injected into the combustion chamber, resulting in more power.

Both a turbocharger and supercharger are very similar in principle. Both use a compressor/blower to increase the overall pressure of gasses inserted into the combustion chamber (cold side). This increase in pressure results in an air/fuel mixture that is compressed greater than normal. The result is that the denser mixture generates a more powerful stroke. Because of the higher density of the mixture, with forced induction you can create an engine with a smaller displacement that has the same energy output as you would have with a larger displacement engine (more power).

What about reliability? Factory-designed forced-induction engines (like the Porsche 911 Turbo) are specially designed to accommodate the additional stresses placed on them by the added boost. Engines like these are designed from the ground up and usually have very low compression ratios to compensate for the added pressures when the car is operating under full boost. Bolting on a turbocharger or supercharger to a stock engine will result in more wear and tear on the engine. If you are planning on installing a forced-induction system on your stock engine, you must plan on purchasing only high-octane fuel. The increased compression in the cylinders will increase the likelihood of detonation, which can destroy your engine very quickly.

HOW THEY WORK

The supercharger is powered by a pulley that attaches to the crankshaft. As the engine's rpm increases, outside air is compressed and mixed with fuel and discharged into the intake system. There are three common types of superchargers: impeller (centrifugal), twin rotating screws (screw-type), and counter-rotating rotors (roots-type). As the engine spins faster, the boost from the supercharger will increase. Typical boost levels for a street Boxster range from 4 to 6 psi. Boost is the measurement of the increase in pressure in the intake charge over normal outside atmospheric levels.

The turbocharger unit drives its compressor from the excess exhaust given off by the engine. Although the backpressure on the exhaust may rob a small amount of power from the engine, the boost from the turbo is generally thought of as free boost. The turbocharger unit is very similar in operation to the centrifugal supercharger, with the exception that it is driven off of the exhaust gases, versus a pulley attached to the crankshaft. Typical peak revolutions of turbos can range anywhere from 75,000 all the way up to 150,000.

HEAD-TO-HEAD COMPARISON

Power and Efficiency: Whereas the turbo runs off of the exhaust system, a supercharger takes power from the engine crankshaft to run the blower. All things being equal, superchargers sap more power overhead (40–50 horsepower to spin the blower at full boost) from the engine to run the compressor than do turbochargers. Turbos are not without horsepower cost—the backpressure from the turbo and restrictions due to the convoluted exhaust piping act to reduce horsepower. However, these losses are minimal when compared to the horsepower cost of driving a supercharger off of the crankshaft. The bottom line is if you're looking to squeeze the maximum amount of power out of a specific displacement (as you would if you were running in certain club racer classes), then the turbocharger systems win hands down over the supercharger.

Power Lag: Reduction of lag is a top reason why superchargers are preferred over turbochargers for street cars. Since the turbocharger is spooled up by the exhaust gases from the engine, it doesn't achieve significant boost levels until the engine's rpm reaches a certain level. This results in little or no boost in the lower rpm range. When the boost finally kicks in, it can be an unsettling experience, as the car rockets off as soon as you reach an rpm level that produces boost. This power surge can also place additional stresses on stock drivetrain and suspension components. There are several things you can do to reduce turbo lag (described further in this project), but these "fixes" sacrifice top-end power. A supercharger, on the other hand, is connected directly to the crankshaft and is spinning and creating boost at all times. Superchargers are able to create significant boost levels at low rpm, so there's typically not much lag. Whereas a turbocharger has power that instantly comes online at about 3,000–4,000 rpm, the supercharger has a nice, even boost curve that generates excellent power off of the line.

Reliability: Turbocharger systems are somewhat complex and thus are considered less reliable than superchargers. In addition, all of the turbo system components work with exhaust gases, which further create additional heat stress and wear on the system. When you first shut off your car with a turbo system, the temperatures can spike inside the turbo and you can experience problems with the impeller bearings being cooked by this high heat (some people install what are known as turbo timers, which let the engine run at idle and cool down for a minute or so before shutting off). Turbochargers spin at much higher rpm than superchargers, and thus the bearings inside have a tendency to wear out much faster. Many turbo system exhaust components are handmade, and often welds in the seams crack with age.

Heat: The turbocharger system is powered by hot exhaust gases that have a tendency to inadvertently heat up the intake mixture charge. Hot air expands and becomes less dense, so this heating effect works against the compressing action of the turbocharger. Cooler air means a higher density air/fuel mixture, which is the whole point of the installation of a forced-induction system. To solve this problem, most turbo systems require an intercooler, which increases the complexity and cost of the system. This hot air is cycled through a large intercooler that cools the air before it is injected into the intake manifold. The cooler air helps to reduce detonation and also increases the density of the air/fuel mixture. In addition to the heat gathered from the exhaust gases, the intake air temperature increases as well when the air is compressed. All turbochargers should be run with an intercooler, and most superchargers can also see benefits from the use of an intercooler.

Installation and Tuning: Superchargers in general are pretty easy to install. Many bolt-on kits exist that can be installed over a long weekend. The supercharger kits require only a few modifications to the fuel system mostly provided in the form of a new software map for the DME to get the engine up and running well. On the other hand, most turbo installations involve complex routing of exhaust pipes, oil lines, and other components—many of which must be modified to fit. Intercoolers are typically a difficult item to fit into the tight space available with the Boxster engine compartment. Although turbo systems can be made to run with the stock fuel and ignition systems (DME), in order to extract the most power out of a turbocharger system, you should probably run the engine using a dedicated and custom engine management system like Tec-3 or Motec.

Cost: In general, both types of systems can be expensive, costing anywhere from $6,000 for a basic kit up to $10,000 for a complete setup installed. In general, since the turbo systems are more complicated, they tend to be slightly more expensive, particularly when you add in the modification costs associated with an intercooler. Another consideration is the cost of installation. Most supercharger setups are relatively straightforward installations, as you only need to modify one side of the engine bay and the intake system. Installation of a turbo setup is much trickier (and a bit more expensive) due to all of the effort involved with the routing and installation of the exhaust pipes. Despite what many manufacturers may say, turbo kits are almost never a straight bolt-on installation. The pipes and brackets are almost always handmade and often require some tweaking to fit.

Power Output and Streetability: Both turbochargers and superchargers can produce significant power gains, although turbochargers can squeeze more total power out of the system due to the fact that they are run off of the "free energy" from the exhaust system. Because the turbocharger units operate at very high rpm, they can produce very high levels of boost in the upper rpm range and deliver much more peak horsepower at these levels. However, most people don't drive their cars at peak rpm all the time on the street. Most of the driving is done in the lower rpm bands, where superchargers have their power advantage. If you want to drive around town with more power off of the line, then a supercharger kit is probably the best choice. If you are going to be racing the car on a track or you want maximum top-end power on the highway, then a turbocharger will allow you to squeeze the most power out of your engine.

Superchargers: In general, the most common type of supercharger installed into the Boxster is the centrifugal type. The centrifugal supercharger is most similar to a turbocharger, with the exception that it is driven off of a belt that is connected to the engine's crankshaft. The centrifugal superchargers compress air using a spun impeller. The advantage to these units is that you can often swap out impeller sizes and change the drive pulley to customize the boost curve for your particular needs. Centrifugal superchargers are typically set to generate their peak boost at or near the redline of the engine. In general, they develop more of their boost at higher rpm and offer less boost on the low end of the rpm range. Paxton, Powerdyne, ProCharger, and Vortech are all good-quality manufacturers of centrifugal superchargers.

TURBOCHARGER SYSTEMS

Many people incorrectly think that a larger turbocharger will generate more boost and horsepower. In reality, this is not necessarily true. Installation of a larger forced-induction unit must also accompany other important changes in the engine. Maximum boost pressure is limited by a pressure relief valve called the wastegate. The wastegate acts to release excess exhaust gas pressure, slowing the turbine so that the engine doesn't suffer from too much boost being applied. Installing a larger turbocharger without making adjustments to the wastegate will result in no increase in maximum boost levels.

How does the size of the turbocharger affect performance? The numeric digits used to describe the turbocharger (K24, K26, K27, etc.) usually correspond to the actual size of the turbo exhaust fan wheel inside the turbocharger (called the hot side). In addition, there is the wheel on the intake (cold side) that compresses the air to create the actual boost. Changing the sizes of the two wheels can alter the overall personality of the turbocharger and can be used to tailor the turbo response to your specific application.

For example, a small turbine wheel in the exhaust combined with a small impeller wheel on the compressor side will spin the turbo up quickly and generate a quick throttle response, but will also tend to drop off power on the top end. A small turbine in the exhaust with a large blower will generate a good compromise between throttle response and top-end power. To obtain the best top-end performance, a large turbo wheel combined with a large blower wheel can be used together. The downside is that throttle-response will suffer in the lower rpm range.

Installing a smaller turbine wheel in the exhaust means that it will spin up much faster than a larger one. The ideal turbo configuration for everyday street driving is to have a smaller turbine on the hot side and a larger blower turbine on the cold side. This particular configuration is a good compromise between low-end throttle response and high-end power. The downside to this configuration is that it takes a certain level of exhaust pressure at a minimum rpm to spin up the exhaust (hot-side) turbine to the point where it can begin to have an effect on the intake pressures. This is what is commonly known as turbo lag. In a race engine, turbo-lag is typically not a major issue, since the transmission gearing and overall setup of the engine is usually designed to operate within a narrow powerband in the high rpm range.

How do you improve performance? Swapping the turbocharger with one that has a different ratio between the wheels can change your turbo engine's characteristics. There are numerous options for turbochargers—each one changes the performance characteristics slightly differently from the next. Perform some research and ask others who have installed various units on their Boxsters before you spend a large amount of money on a new turbocharger. Adding an intercooler or upgrading your existing one will also increase your overall performance. Simply dialing in more boost from the turbocharger (by changing the wastegate relief valve setting) can give you an immediate performance improvement. Also, increasing the compression in your engine will give you more low-end power. However, these approaches can be extremely hazardous to your engine. Severe detonation from poor quality gas can cause pistons to overheat, and the engine can literally blow itself apart. For more information on turbocharging, see the book *Turbochargers* by Hugh MacInnes or *Maximum Boost* by Corky Bell.

HOW MUCH BOOST?

This is an age-old question that is answered with the old saying, "There's no such thing as a free lunch." How much boost you run on your forced-induction system depends upon a wide variety of factors.

What type of induction is it? As mentioned previously, turbo systems come to full boost capability and then bleed off excess with a wastegate. While this creates great power in the upper rpm range, it also means that you're running at highly boosted levels for extended periods of time. With a centrifugal supercharger, it only reaches maximum boost at the highest rpm, and then only for a few seconds. So you can run much higher peak boost levels on a centrifugal supercharger than you can with a turbo setup.

Which fuel octane? Running a boosted engine puts a lot of stress on the internals of the engine, as you are pushing more and more power through the drivetrain. However, the real killer for these engines is detonation. If the octane is too low and the compression of the engine too high, then the fuel will explode prematurely, resulting in what is commonly known as engine knocking, or detonation. When the mixture in the combustion chamber explodes, it increases the pressure in the cylinder and pushes down on the piston. When detonation occurs, the piston is still rising and still compressing the mixture. Thus, when ignition occurs, the pressure builds and has no release. The pressure is pushing down on the piston as it's rising, creating a tremendous amount of pressure that has nowhere to go. Unchecked, detonation will destroy pistons and blow out head gaskets. It's the number-one killer of forced-induction engines. The solution is to reduce your boost levels so that the engine no longer detonates. The engine management system (DME) normally adjusts timing and ignition in response to signals received from the knock sensor to reduce detonation in the cylinders. However, running really high amounts of boost with lower octane fuel can overwhelm and confuse the stock system. The bottom line is that the higher boost you wish to run, the higher the octane of fuel you will have to buy. If you want to head to the drag strip and run all-out with as much boost as you possibly can, be prepared to buy some race fuel with octane ratings in the 105–110 range.

What is the air/fuel mixture? When you install a forced-induction system onto an engine, you are increasing the amount of air that is injected into the combustion chamber. Most of the time, this will cause the air/fuel mixture to become lean. You must compensate for this by increasing the amount of fuel that is combined with the air mixture, since that mixture is now compressed and thus denser. According to modern fuel injection theory, fuel and air combustion achieves its maximum efficiency at a ratio of 14.67:1. Although this ratio may be optimum for good fuel economy, it's not best for maximizing power. On a normally aspirated engine at full throttle, maximum power is achieved with an air/fuel ratio set at about 14.2:1 to 14.3:1. On boosted engines this maximum power ratio is more in the range of 12.2 to 12.4. If your boosted engine is running too lean, this will increase the likelihood of detonation and also will increase the operating temperature of the cylinder head. It's very important to make sure that your engine is running on the rich side. I recommend running an aftermarket air/fuel mixture gauge to monitor and protect against the engine running lean.

What modifications have been done to the DME? The DME (Digital Motor Electronics) controls the ignition and air/fuel ratio injected into the engine. Installing a forced-induction system is such a major change to the engine that it's difficult to adapt the computer to correctly compensate for the compressed intake charge without performing a complete remapping of the air/fuel mixture program (see Project 24).

What is the compression ratio? Engines that start out with a high compression ratio (like the 2000 Boxster at 11:1) cannot be boosted as much as engines with lower ratios. To properly integrate forced induction into any engine, it should be designed from the ground up with forced induction in mind. The higher compression ratios of the Boxster and 996 Carrera engines don't naturally lend themselves to forced-induction kits. In general, forced-induction engines are blueprinted to have a very low compression ratio (like the venerable Porsche 911 Turbo with 7.0:1). The bottom line is that you can generate more horsepower from maximizing the boost from the turbo than you can with higher compression. If you run higher compression, then you will be forced to run with less boost at the higher end to avoid destroying your engine. You want to design your engine to have low compression so that you can run higher boost at higher rpm's, and generate more horsepower. You can lower the compression ratio by a variety of methods—adding a thicker head gasket, installing lower compression custom-made pistons, etc.

How old is the engine? Bearings and clearances wear over years of use. Most companies that sell superchargers don't recommend installing them on a tired engine. The chances that you will blow out your head gasket are quite high as the engine gets older.

Boost Level	Compression Ratio
8 psi	10.5:1
9–10 psi	10.0:1
11–12 psi	9.5:1
13–14 psi	9.0:1
15–18 psi	8.5:1

*running on 91 octane

1 Here's a shot of the supercharger kit developed by Stephen Kaspar for Imagine Auto, installed on a Boxster 2.5. These compact cars are very light and very nimble and create quite a performance machine when you bump up the horsepower with one of these kits. Because of the lack of room in the engine compartment, this supercharger kit requires the use of a lot of custom parts, including a whole set of new intake plenums. It's a tough squeeze, but the centrifugal supercharger fits quite nicely tacked onto the side of the camshaft cover. The engine compartment retains its "stock look," and the kit simply bolts into place under the car. A new belt is required, of course, as well as a complete remapping of the DME.

2 Here are the main contents of the supercharger kit described in the previous photo. Although it takes thousands of hours and testing to successfully design and implement a good bolt-on kit, the actual installation and assembly process can be completed typically over a long weekend by a semi-experienced do-it-yourselfer.

Increasing the overall compression inside the combustion chamber increases the wear and tear on all the parts in the drivetrain.

The bottom line? There are a few rules of thumb when it comes to running forced-induction engines. The following table gives you a broad outline of what boost levels you can run for a variety of compression ratios:

CONCLUSIONS

Which forced-induction unit to install really depends upon your overall goals, which includes ease of installation and budget limitations. If you ask 10 different enthusiasts out there what their preferences are, you will get 10 completely different answers. There are people who are turbo fans and there are people who are die-hard supercharger recruits. Obviously, this project can only scratch the surface of what's involved in designing and implementing a turbocharger or supercharger system.

There are some generalizations that you can make, though, regarding the relative performance of these two systems. If you want a drag car with lots of power off of the line, then you should probably go with a supercharger system. This will give you boost at low rpm and a predictable power curve. If you're looking for top speed on the autobahn where you want to squeeze out all the power you can, then I recommend a turbocharger system. It will give you maximum power at the higher end of your rpm range. With most supercharger systems, you will achieve maximum boost when you're at redline. With a turbocharger, you will have nearly full boost all the way from about 3,000–4,000 rpm to redline. If you like the feel of a rush of power and the ability to create gobs of peak horsepower, go with a turbocharger. Turbo systems are also considered to be more flexible in that they can often be designed to fit most owners' requirements—superchargers can be a bit more limited. If you want your car to feel somewhat stock with a big push on the high end, then go with a centrifugal supercharger. Of course, if you want more overall power without the hassle of forced induction, then just put a 996 Carrera engine in your Boxster (see Project 11).

In terms of installation ease, the supercharger systems win overwhelmingly. Turbocharger systems can be made to be better performers, but they generally require more time, money, and installation effort to achieve this.

ENGINE

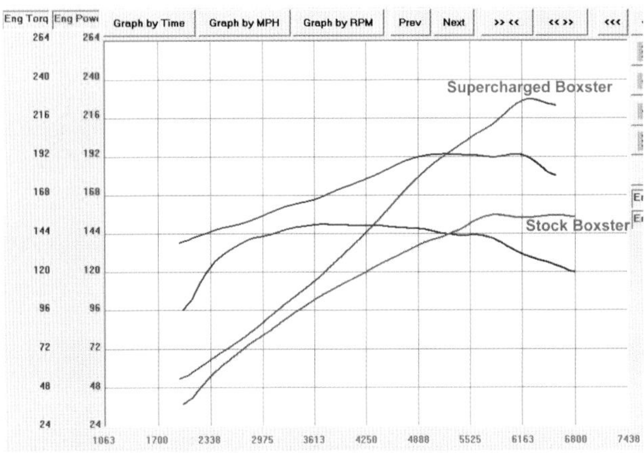

3 This graph shows clearly why Imagine Auto's supercharger kits are so popular. They take the mild-mannered Boxster 2.5-liter engines and turn them into monsters. When combined with a lightweight chassis like the Boxster, the combination makes for a powerful and nimble track car with performance exceeding that of a Boxster S.

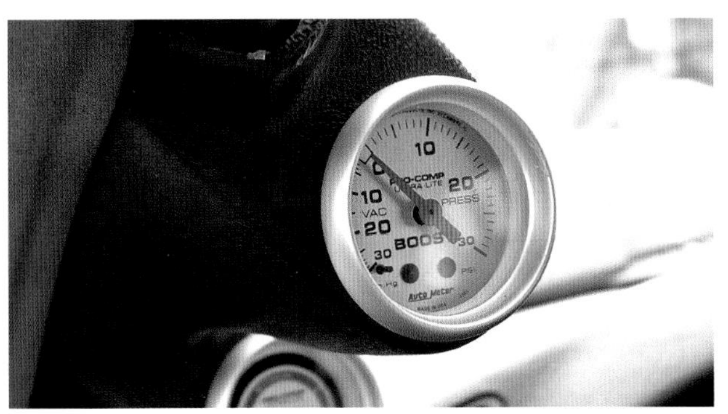

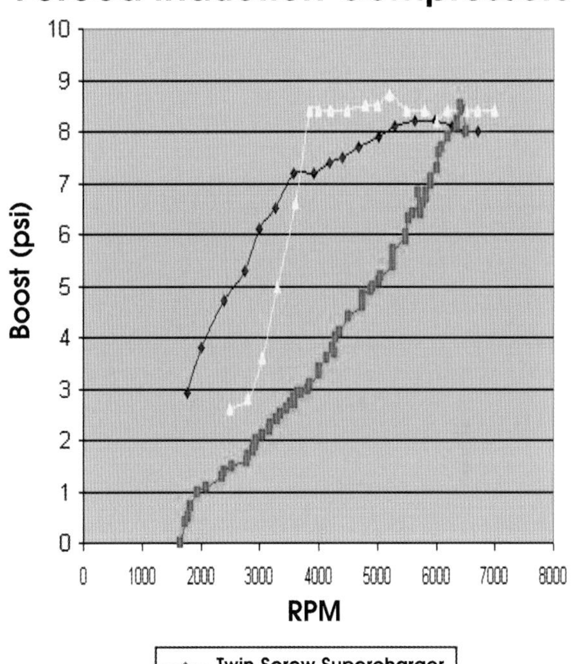

4 This chart shows the different boost levels between a centrifugal supercharger, a twin-screw supercharger, and a turbocharger system. As you can see, the twin-screw generates more boost per rpm than does the centrifugal unit. The turbocharger graph shows low boost levels until about 3,500, where it rockets up to full boost in a hurry. *Steve Anderson*

5 Shown here is a boost gauge mounted on the driver's side A-pillar. I recommend installing one of these in your car if you're running a forced-induction system. A boost gauge will give you a snapshot of the health of your induction system and will also alert you to boost levels that may be too high.

SECTION 3
FUEL

Without a doubt, the fuel injection system on your Boxster can be one of the most finicky systems to diagnose and troubleshoot. While one can write volumes simply on fuel injection systems, this section focuses both on introducing the Motronic engine management system, and also on identifying common problems and potential pitfalls. Reading through these projects will help you identify and solve problems with your own fuel injection system.

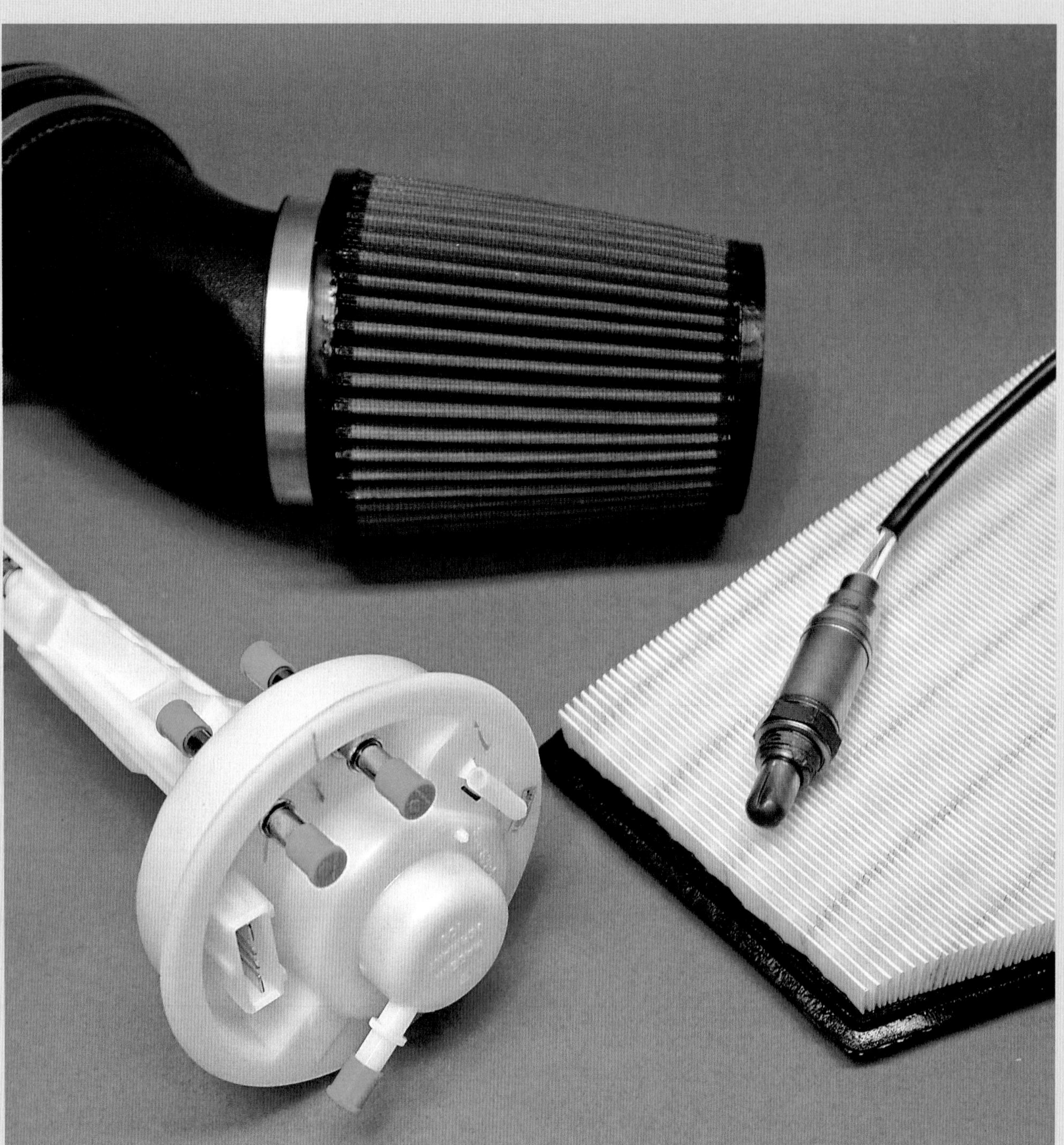

PROJECT 19
Replacing Your Oxygen Sensor

 **Time / Tab / Talent:** 1 hour / $100–$400 / 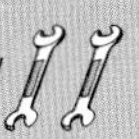

 **Tools:** Floor jack and jack stands, 22mm wrench

 **Applicable Years:** All

Parts: New oxygen sensor

More Info: www.101projects.com/Boxster/19.htm

 **Tip:** Use anti-seize compound on the threads of the sensor to make it easier to replace it next time

 **Performance Gain:** More accurate air/fuel mixture and better-running engine

Comp Modification: Install an aftermarket exhaust system or replace old exhaust gaskets

The oxygen sensor (also called an O_2 sensor) is one of the most important elements of the modern fuel injection systems. A finely tuned fuel injection system with an oxygen sensor can maintain an air/fuel ratio within a close tolerance of 0.02 percent. Keeping the engine at the stoichiometric level (14.6:1 air/fuel ratio) helps the engine generate the most power with the least amount of emissions.

The oxygen sensors are located in the exhaust system of the engine, and they sense the oxygen content of the exhaust gases. There are a total of four on most Boxsters—two for each catalytic converter on each side of the car. The sensor located just in front of the catalytic converter measures the mixture of the exhaust gases exiting the engine. The sensor located after the catalytic converter is used to measure the performance of the converter by comparing the O_2 levels before and after. The amount of oxygen in the exhaust varies according to the air/fuel ratio of the fuel injection system. The oxygen sensor produces a small voltage signal that is interpreted by the electronic control unit (ECU) of the fuel injection system. The ECU makes constant adjustments in fuel delivery according to the signal generated by the oxygen sensor in order to maintain the optimum air/fuel ratio.

There are a few signs that your oxygen sensor may be failing. In general, it is difficult to diagnose problems with the sensor, unless all of the other components in the fuel injection system have been checked and determined to be operating correctly. Some of the symptoms of a failed oxygen sensor system are:

- Irregular idle during warm-up
- Irregular idle with warm engine
- Engine will not accelerate and backfires
- Poor engine performance
- Fuel consumption is high
- Driving performance is weak
- CO concentration at idle is too high or too low
- Check engine light is illuminated

In general, if the oxygen sensor is not working, the car may be running very poorly and may also be outputting a lot of harmful emissions. If the signal received by the computer is out of its normal range, the Boxster's computer will almost always give a warning signal that lights up the check engine lamp. Sometimes the computer may output an error code stating that the oxygen sensor is reading out of range, when in reality the values are out of range because there is something else wrong with the fuel injection system. Prior to replacing the oxygen sensors, make sure there are no other codes being recorded that may affect the O_2 sensor readings. For more info on reading these fuel injection codes, see Project 20.

If you disconnect the oxygen sensor and ground the signal wire to the chassis, the ECU will think that the car is running lean (not enough fuel), and will try to richen the mixture. At the other extreme, if you disconnect the oxygen sensor, and replace it with a small AA battery that supplies 1.5 volts, the ECU will think that the car is running really rich and attempt to adjust the mixture to be leaner.

Needless to say, troubleshooting the complete fuel injection system is beyond this project's scope. If you think that the oxygen sensors may be causing some of your fuel injection problems, they should be replaced. In general, I recommend that you do this every 30,000 miles. You have to jack up the car to gain access to the sensors (see Project 1).

Using a 22mm wrench, simply remove the sensor from the exhaust pipe. On the Boxster, the sensors are very easy to reach. On many other cars, you would need a special deep socket with a slit cut in the side to remove it. The electrical plug for the O_2 sensor simply unplugs from the chassis plug. New O_2 sensors should have the same exact plug—ready to attach to your car. When you remove the O_2 sensor, you will probably find that it is coated with black soot. This is normal for an old, worn-out O_2 sensor. On our project car here, the O_2 sensor was covered in motor oil and coolant. This is a bad sign that corresponded with the seized engine in my project car (I bought it that way). See Project 13 for more details on the problems sometimes found with these late-model Porsche engines.

Install your new sensor snug-tight, or if you have the proper slit-tool and a handy torque wrench then tighten it to 40 ft-lbs (55 N-m). It's also a smart idea to add some anti-seize compound to the threads of the plug before you install it, but make sure the anti-seize doesn't get into any of the slits on the head of the sensor. Check the sensor first though, as new ones sometimes come with anti-seize already on the threads.

There are two different types of sensors you can purchase—generic ones that allow you to snip the connector off of the old sensor and put it on the new one, and original OEM sensors with the correct connector. On older cars, I used to use the generic sensors, but I've had problems with using them on these newer cars. Researching further, I discovered that the wires and connectors are very important on these O_2 sensors. The Porsche factory workshop manuals state the following:

> 911 Carrera 4 has a new, water-proof oxygen sensor. Water-proof means that the upper sensor section and housing are connected leak-proof with a later welded seam and previous reference air openings are omitted. Reference air is now taken via the connecting lead and plug connection. For this reason it is important to keep contact solutions, lubricants, liquids or similar products out of the 3-pin plug, since they would lead to sensor failure

Soldering wires together can interrupt the reference air signal and lead to problems with the sensor. I've also had problems with the Bosch factory Posi-Lock connectors that are supposed to work with these newer sensors. Because the relationship between the connector and the O_2 sensor is so vital to the proper reference signal, I recommend that you only use the correct sensors with the proper plug.

FUEL

1 Shown here is the catalytic converter and its two oxygen sensors (red arrow shows the front, yellow shows the rear). The small black connector, shown by the green arrow, attaches the sensor to the wire harness and can easily be removed by pushing the release tab. I have often found that the new O_2 sensors come with the correct plug, but sometimes the cable is way too long. If this is the case, then secure the cable with a nylon zip tie. Make sure that the cable is not located anywhere near any exhaust components—you don't want the heat melting the cable to the O_2 sensor. The photo inset shows the special tool that is sometimes required to remove O_2 sensors in hard-to-reach places (available from PelicanParts.com).

PROJECT 20

Reading Fuel Injection Fault Codes

Time / Tab / Talent: 30 minutes / $300 /

Tools: Durametric Software

Applicable Years: All

Parts: None

More Info: www.101projects.com/Boxster/20.htm

Tip: The Durametric software is essential to diagnosing problems

Performance Gain: Better-running engine when the problems are fixed

Comp Modification: Replace O_2 sensor—the computer often shows this error code

Almost all Porsches from about 1984 use a sophisticated Bosch engine management system called Motronic. The Motronic system (also called the Digital Motor Electronics, or DME) is hands down the best overall fuel injection system that you can use when you consider price and performance. Ignition timing and fuel delivery are all controlled by a digital map that is recorded in a removable chip within the main fuel injection (DME) computer. The computer takes input from a variety of sensors that are located on the engine—engine coolant temperature, crank angle, throttle position, exhaust gas oxygen (mixture), ambient air temperature, and mass airflow. The DME flash memory chip is programmed from the factory with certain performance characteristics (mostly conservative) so that the engine will react well under a host of varying conditions.

As with any electronic device, components can fail, triggering problems with the system. The Porsche Motronic system is designed to react to these failures and indicate them to the driver so that they can be fixed. If one of the computer's sensors is not working properly, then the computer may not be able to successfully identify the current state of the engine and choose the appropriate fuel mixture or timing advance level. When this happens, the fuel mileage drops, engine performance suffers, emissions increase, and the car typically illuminates the check engine light.

Pre-1995 Porsches were equipped with what is known as OBD I (On-Board Diagnostics Level I). Starting in 1996, they were equipped with a more advanced version called OBD II, which was mandated by the U.S. government in order to standardize automotive repair and diagnostics. The OBD system is responsible for monitoring and checking all of the fuel injection sensors and systems in the vehicle, and turns on the check engine lamp if it finds a problem or irregularity with one of them. If there is a problem with a sensor or component, the computer lodges a Diagnostic Trouble Code (DTC) in the main computer until it is read and reset.

In order to accurately find the sensor and fix the problem, you will need to find out which error code is being triggered by the computer. There is no method to pull these codes out of your Porsche without the use of a computer tool. The factory has produced a version of this tool for use by Porsche dealers called the Porsche System Tester 2 (PST2). Unfortunately, finding one of these is next to impossible, and they cost about $4,000 used anyway. There's a newer version of the PST2 called the PIWIS, but getting your hands on one of those costs about $20,000 with a monthly $1,000 maintenance contract from Porsche. You can indeed use a standard off-the-shelf OBD II reader available at any auto parts store, but it will only give you the standard read-out codes for the fuel injection system—you will not be able to do any extra diagnostics on any other area of the car.

Thankfully though, there is aftermarket software available produced by Durametric that performs almost all of the important reading functions that the PST2 does. It runs on a Windows laptop computer, and the cost is about $300 for the home-based version that will allow you to read codes on up to three cars. If you're planning on working on your Boxster at all, I suggest that you pick up this essential tool.

With a standard ODB II code reader, you can access and reset the codes on the car that are related only to the fuel injection system. The PST2 and Durametric software allow you to dig deep into the various systems of the car and read values from the various systems of the car (air bag, ABS, Tiptronic transmission, alarm, seat memory, heating and A/C). The current version of the Durametric tool does not program the computer though—you are still at the mercy of the dealer when it comes to making changes to any of the non–fuel injection settings on your car.

When you obtain the trouble codes output by the PST2, you can look them up in the Porsche ODB II factory diagnostic book (expensive) or refer to the Bentley Workshop Manual for additional details. Both manuals have extensive sections describing the various faults and what is needed to fix them.

Tip: Wire harnesses are a major cause of fault code problems. As the cars get older, the wiring harnesses have a habit of becoming what is commonly known as "work-hardened." This causes the wiring to become brittle and often break inside of its plastic sheath. Only by testing the continuity of the wires end-for-end will you be able to determine whether the wire is broken or not.

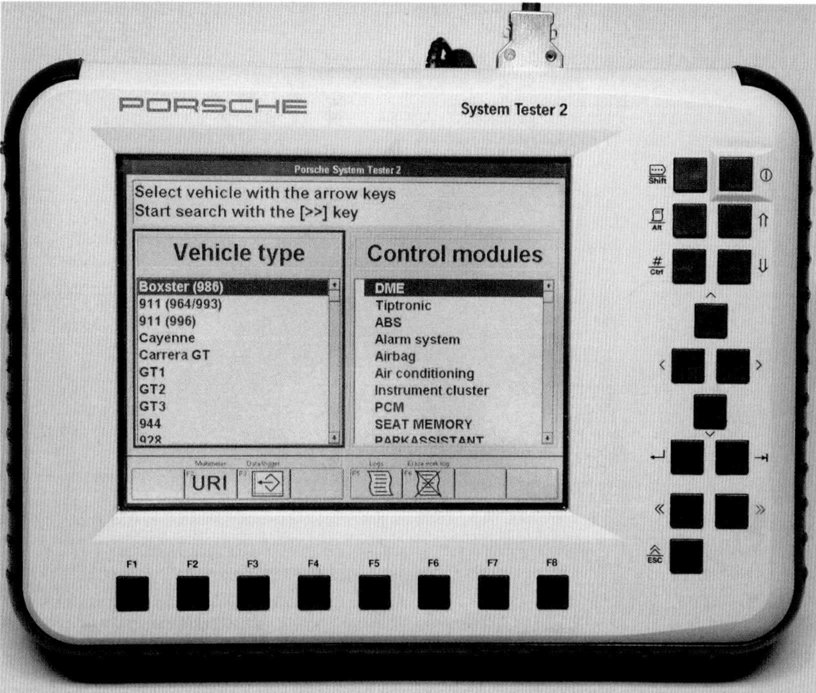

1 Here it is, the Holy Grail of Porsche code reading. The Porsche System Tester 2 (PST2) is a rare and expensive tool that can be used to diagnose multiple car systems on a variety of Porsches. Every dealer has one of these, or the later-model PIWIS tester, so that the dealer can quickly diagnose problems and change settings on the various computer systems within the car.

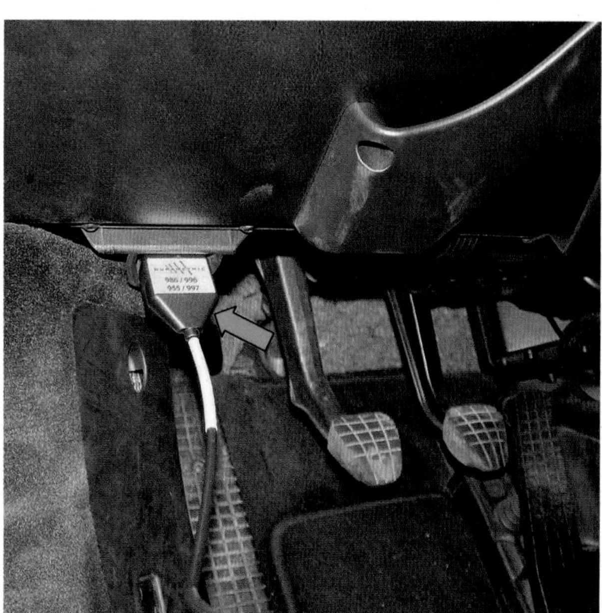

2 Both the PST2 and the Durametric software interface with the car through the OBD II port located beneath the steering wheel on the lower left-hand side of the car. Make sure that the plug is firmly seated, as it has a tendency to occasionally fall out.

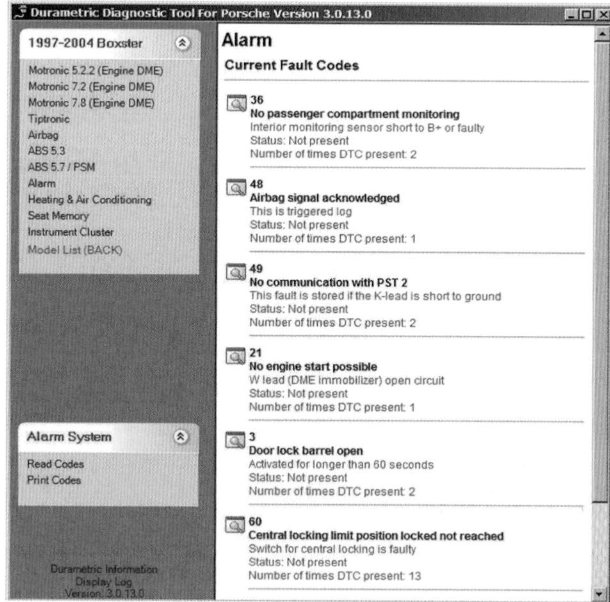

3 Shown here is a screenshot of the Durametric software available for diagnosing various system problems. The software is nearly as powerful as the reading functions on the original Porsche PST2 and is a required diagnostic tool for the do-it-yourself enthusiast.

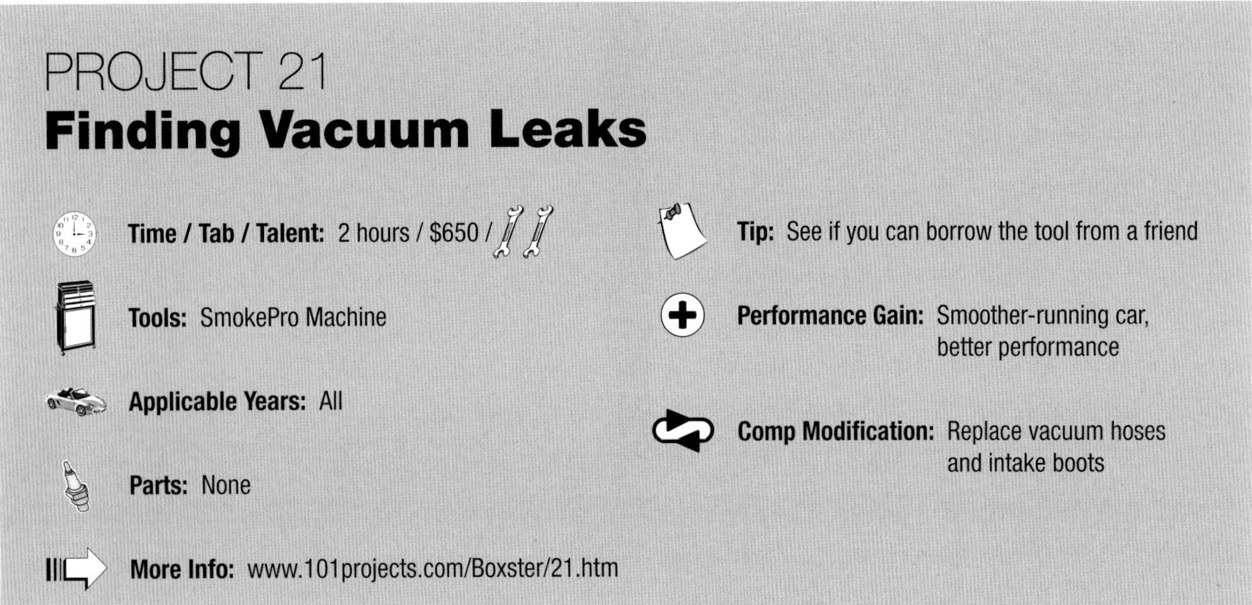

PROJECT 21

Finding Vacuum Leaks

Time / Tab / Talent: 2 hours / $650 /

Tools: SmokePro Machine

Applicable Years: All

Parts: None

More Info: www.101projects.com/Boxster/21.htm

Tip: See if you can borrow the tool from a friend

Performance Gain: Smoother-running car, better performance

Comp Modification: Replace vacuum hoses and intake boots

Today's modern cars have a tremendous number of vacuum hoses and boots contained with the engine compartment. To the uneducated eye, the engine compartment can easily look like the insides of an oil refinery with all the hoses running in and out. As these hoses and boots age and are constantly exposed to hot and cold temperatures, they tend to break down and develop cracks, which can then cause vacuum leaks. Unfortunately, when the fuel injection system develops a vacuum leak, it will tend to confuse the fuel injection computer's sensors, and the car will cease to run properly. You may get decreased gas mileage, rough idling, misfires, and sometimes a check engine light (CEL) on the dashboard.

Whenever someone contacts me and indicates that their car is running rough, I almost always tell them to check the entire system carefully for vacuum leaks. Without the proper tools, this can sometimes be very difficult. Old rubber boots have a tendency to crack and leak in spots that are not visible to the naked eye. Sometimes squeezing them will show a crack that you can't normally see when the boot is in its initial resting position.

One poor-man's way to check for vacuum leaks is to artificially create a leak and see how the engine reacts. There are two primary vacuum systems on the Boxster engine—crankcase vacuum and intake manifold vacuum. You can test for proper crankcase vacuum by removing the oil cap while the car is idling. The engine should change idle and begin to run a bit rougher with the oil cap off. If there is no change in the running of the engine, then you might have a crankcase vacuum leak somewhere (sometimes caused by a failing air-oil separator—see Project 9). To induce a vacuum leak into the intake manifold, you can disconnect one or more of the hoses that connect to the intake. One example would be the hose that connects to the air-oil separator. If you crack one of these hoses open just a bit and the engine rpm doesn't change, then you might have an intake vacuum leak somewhere.

By far, the best way to test for vacuum leaks is with a smoke machine. Although these are somewhat expensive at about $650, you can rent and/or borrow them from some shops. The machine generates smoke and then blows it through your engine's intake and crankcase. All you need to do is sit back and watch for little puffs of smoke where there is a leak in the system. This can save many, many hours of random troubleshooting and guesswork. For the project car for this book, I wanted to make sure all of my custom-made hoses that were required for the installation of the 3.4 engine into the Boxster were leak-free. I ran the car through the smoke machine and confirmed that everything was airtight and there were no troublesome leaks.

The smoke machine runs on standard household baby oil and generates smoke by heating the oil. The smoke generated is very similar to the type created in model railroad steam engines. The machine also needs to be connected to a shop air compressor. The compressed air is mixed with the smoke and then funneled through the intake system of the engine. In the case of the Boxster, I removed the intake air filter and used a cone adapter that comes with the machine to seal the smoke hose to the intake pipe. The car should be completely cold when you are testing it for leaks, as the rubber hoses and boots are most likely to leak when they are cold and contracted. You should also remove the mass airflow sensor from the system so that the smoke doesn't build up on the sensor and affect its operation. Plug the hole for the sensor with some masking tape.

After you power up the smoke machine, it will take a minute or two to fully smoke out the car. If your car is completely airtight (a good thing), then you might not see any smoke. You can check to see if the smoke machine is operating correctly by removing the oil cap in the rear trunk. You should see a steady plume of smoke exiting out of the oil filler (this is normal). On the Boxster, you may also see some very tiny plumes of smoke exiting out of the resonance flapper bearings—this is also normal and doesn't affect the operation of the car or indicate a major vacuum leak. If you do see steady plumes of smoke exiting out of the engine compartment, then investigate further. On the 3.4 conversion engine, there weren't any major leaks, but there were a few minor ones that were found (one of the breather hoses that connected to the radiator tank needed to be tightened).

Although you might think a smoke machine is a limited-use tool, it's highly versatile for solving other problems as well. Basically, any system that contains air can be tested. You can use the system to check climate control systems, leaky headlamp housings, exhaust systems, and A/C lines and compressors (although most A/C leaks are very small and difficult to detect with just a smoke machine). You can also bench test components, such as radiators, prior to installation to make sure that they are factory perfect.

You can even use the smoke machine to detect leaks from door and window seals. First, roll up all windows and seal the car. Then turn on the fresh-air fan motor to the maximum setting (do not set the system to recirculate). Using the smoke machine with a diffuser (a wider nozzle that will slow down the flow of smoke), move around the outside of the car and blow the smoke onto the area you think might have a leak. The fresh-air fans inside the car will create a positive pressure environment that will push air out through any leaks. By slowly blowing smoke on these suspected areas, you can see the smoke pattern become disturbed by the leaking air. This test, of course, requires that you do it inside your garage in an environment where there is very still air.

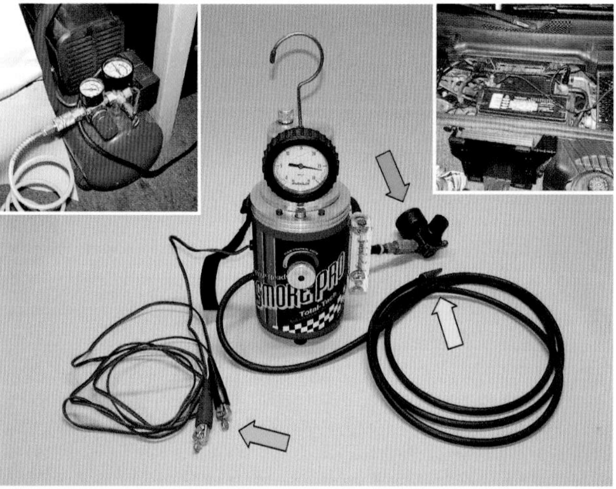

1 Shown here is the Redline Smoke Pro machine. This extremely useful tool is invaluable for finding vacuum leaks within your fuel injection system. The machine's air supply is provided by an air compressor (upper left) that is plugged into a pressure regulator (green arrow). The heater is powered by your car battery (upper right and blue arrow). The compressed air is combined with smoke and then pushed out through the nozzle (yellow arrow).

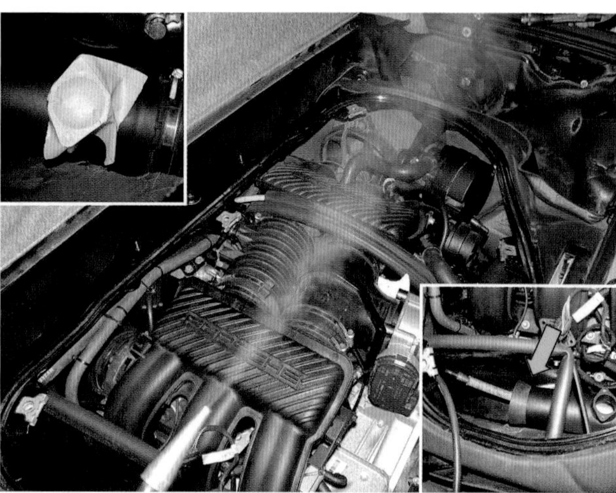

2 With the smoke machine turned on, you can see the trail of smoke that exits out of the nozzle. You don't want to "smoke out" your mass airflow sensor (MAF), so be sure that you remove it and tape off or plug the hole prior to pressurizing the system (upper left). The Smoke Pro comes with a whole set of adapters that you can use to plug into the intake system. On the Boxster here, we removed the aftermarket cone filter and plugged the intake with the rubber cone adapter that comes with the Smoke Pro (blue arrow).

3 With the system pressurized, you can check to see if your engine is "fully smoked out" by removing the oil filler cap. A steady stream of smoke should exit the filler hole. This means that smoke is going from the intake, through the air-oil separator, and into the crankcase. At this point, replace the cap and carefully examine your intake for smoke trails that will indicate vacuum leaks.

PROJECT 22
Replacing the Fuel Pump

 **Time / Tab / Talent:** 2 hours / $300 / 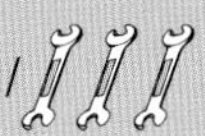

 **Tools:** Oil filter wrench, battery charger

 **Applicable Years:** All

 **Parts:** Fuel pump, O-ring, sending unit

More Info: www.101projects.com/Boxster/22.htm

Tip: Jumper the relay to empty the tank

 **Performance Gain:** More reliable fuel system

 **Comp Modification:** Replace battery

Some common fuel injection problems can be traced back to a faulty or non-operational fuel pump. If your pump is noisy and loud or the fuel pressure in the engine compartment is below what is needed for proper fuel injection operation, then it's probably time to replace it. The fuel pump is a not as simple a device as one might think. The fuel actually runs through the pump and acts as a coolant and lubricant for the entire assembly. Therefore, if you let your car run out of gas, make sure that you turn off the pump immediately or you might damage the internal components of the pump. Trust me—not much is worse than a broken or faulty pump leaving you stranded on the side of the road.

Typical fuel pump problems can sometimes be headed off in advance. If the pump is noisy and making loud clicking noises, then chances are that the bearings inside are worn and should be replaced. If the pump continues to make noise even after the ignition is shut off, internal check-valves in the pump may be showing signs of failure. The pump could seize up at some time, or the pressure to the fuel injection system could drop. Either way, the car will not be performing at its peak. Another symptom of failure is the pump getting stuck and then finally kicking in after turning the ignition on and off a couple of times. This could be a clear sign that you are living on borrowed time and that you should replace the pump immediately. Check the electrical connections to the pump before you replace it to make sure that it's not an electrical problem.

The first step in replacement is to prep the car. Remove as much gasoline out of the car as possible (see photos). Some other tips:

- Always have a fire extinguisher handy in case an emergency arises.
- Gasoline is highly flammable. When working around fuel and fuel line connections, don't disconnect any wires or electrical connections that may cause electrical sparks.
- Always remove the gas cap to relieve any pressure in the tank prior to working on the fuel system.
- Do not use a work lamp when working near fuel or fuel tanks. If you need some light, use a cool fluorescent lamp and keep it far away from the tank.
- Gasoline vapors are strong and harmful, and they can cause you to become drowsy and not think straight. Always perform work in a well-ventilated area with plenty of fresh air blowing through.
- Always disconnect the battery when working on the fuel system. Leave it disconnected for at least 30 minutes to allow any residual electrical charge in components to dissipate.
- Keep plenty of paper towels on hand, and wear rubber gloves to prevent spilling gasoline on your hands
- Be well grounded—don't do anything that will create static electricity. Keep all cell phones and pagers a safe distance away.
- Run the car so that the gas tank is near empty, and then remove the remaining fuel as detailed in Photo 1.

The first step is to remove the battery from the car (see Project 81). The lower battery tray acts as both a retaining platform for the battery and a cover for the fuel pump area. Underneath this tray, you will see the top of the fuel tank sending unit. Disconnect the connector that mates with the sender. Now, squeeze and disconnect the fuel lines and breather hose that feed into the top of the unit. There might be some small gas spillage here—have a roll of absorbent paper towels on hand. You might want to find an old pen to carefully plug the lines to prevent further leaks. If there is any fuel in your tank, now would be an excellent time to empty it. (See Photo 1 and Photo 2.)

The sender is held in place by the big circular disc with the risers on it. There is a special tool that is used to remove and tighten this black plastic ring. However, with a large flathead screwdriver or chisel and a small hammer, you can easily tap the plastic ring loose. Carefully remove the ring from the top of the sender.

Now comes the fun part. Make sure that you are prepared at this stage—in a heavily ventilated garage and with rubber gloves and plenty of paper towels. Pull up on the top of the sender, and the entire assembly should come right out of the tank (Photo 3). There is a big, thick O-ring that seals the pump to the tank—grab it and put it off to the side. See Photo 4 and Photo 5 for instructions on removal of the pump.

When reinstalling the pump into the car, make sure that the fuel hoses inside the tank don't interfere with the proper operation of the fuel tank sender. I found that my sender was getting stuck and the problem was the hoses. The solution was to open the tank up again and zip-tie the hoses out of the way. I would verify that they don't interfere with the movement of the sender before you button everything back up.

I recommend that you replace the large sealing ring with a new one. If you do opt to reuse the old one and it doesn't seal well, you might be plagued with a fuel smell in the car from that point on. Make sure that the big O-ring is properly sealed around the outside of the pump and will seal with the opening of the tank. Spin on the large circular ring and use the hammer/screwdriver tapping procedure to tighten it. I tightened mine about as tight as I could get it without feeling that I would break the ring. Reconnect the fuel hoses and the electrical connector.

Reinstall and connect the battery after all fumes have subsided. Then crank the car over and see if it starts. If the car starts and runs for any length of time then the pump is working fine.

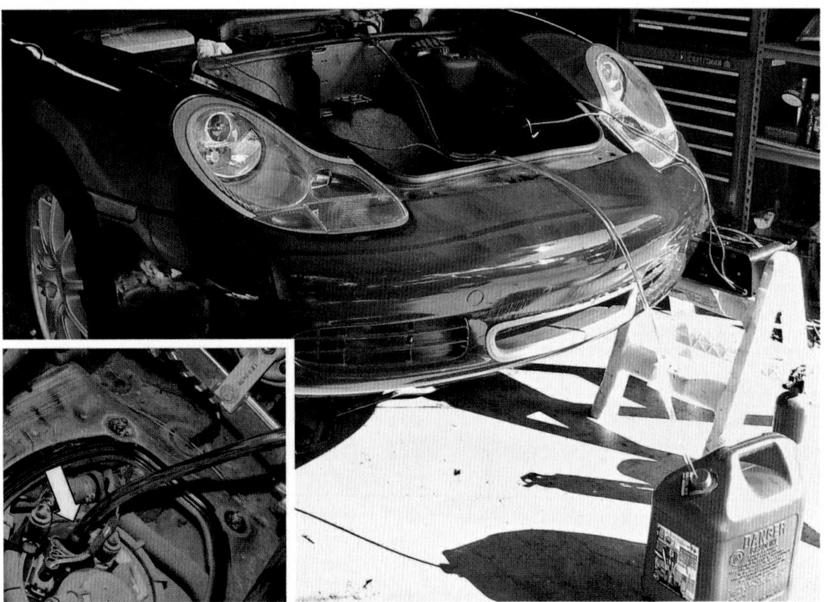

1 This photo shows a safe method for emptying the gas out of the tank in your Boxster. Disconnect the pressure side hose from the top of the pump and connect some clear plastic tubing to the barb (yellow arrow). Carefully connect the car's battery terminals up to a 12-volt supply, making sure that you wrap and insulate both terminals carefully. Jumper the relay in the driver's side footwell (see Photo 2) and turn on the ignition, and the pump should turn on and begin to pump fuel into your gas can. Watch the level carefully, and shut the pump off when the external gas can fills up or when the Boxster's fuel tank runs dry. If the pump in your Boxster is non-operational, then you will have to rig up a small electrical fuel pump to siphon the fuel out of the tank and into your external gas can.

2 This photo shows the relay panel under the driver's side footwell. The fuel pump is not normally turned on unless the engine is running, but you can remove the relay and bypass it using a simple jumper wire as shown here. Remove the fuel pump relay (shown in the inset) and then jumper pins 30 and 87 (typically labeled 3 and 5 on the relay panel). This will cause the fuel pump to turn on automatically when you turn the key in the ignition.

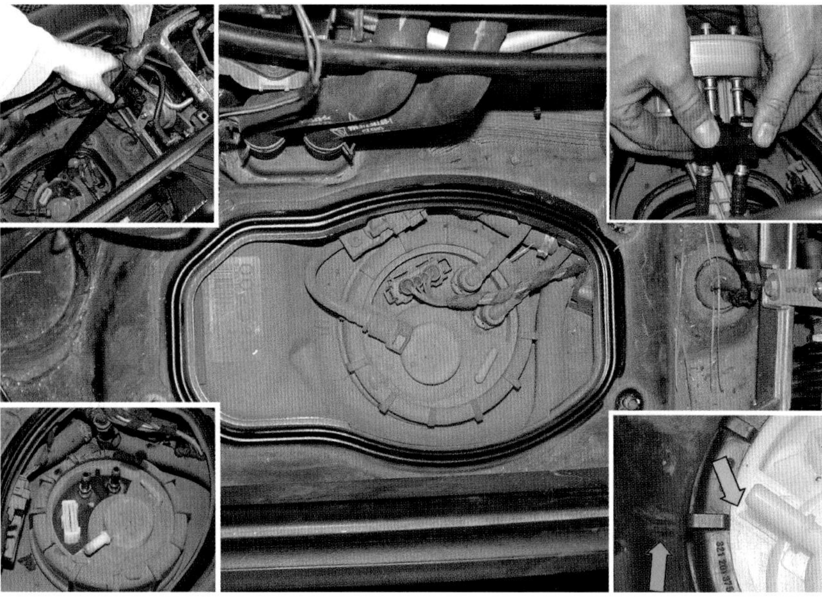

3 Once you remove the battery and the lower tray/cover, you will see the top of the tank and the fuel sender. Squeeze the fuel line connectors and remove them along with the vent hose and the electrical connections (lower left). Use a large chisel and a medium-sized hammer to carefully tap on the outer ring that holds the fuel pump in place (upper left). It should turn and loosen up with a few taps. With the ring loose, pull out the fuel tank sending unit, and you should be able to carefully squeeze and remove the fuel supply hoses that attach to the bottom. When you reinstall the sending unit, be sure to line up the big arrow (blue arrow) with the three lines on the tank (green arrow).

4 The upper left inset shows the fuel pump sitting inside the empty fuel tank. I had a really difficult time removing the pump from the bottom of the tank. Supposedly you should be able to simply turn it with your hands and unlock it from the bottom, but my grip wasn't strong enough. Instead, I used a rubber oil-filter wrench to carefully wrap around the circumference of the pump. One solid twist of the tool, and the pump came free of its locking site on the bottom of the tank.

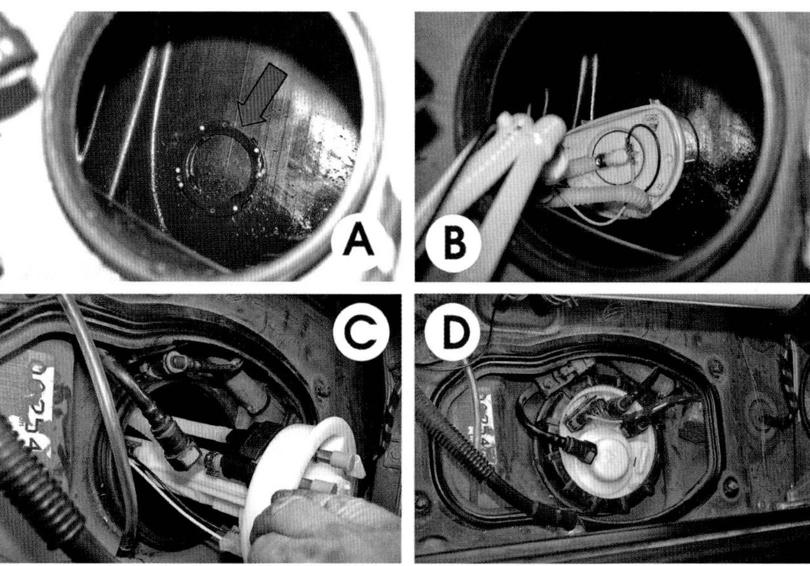

5 Installation is pretty straightforward. **A:** The red arrow shows the circular locking ring that the bottom of the fuel pump snaps into with a twist. This secures the pump to the bottom of the fuel tank. **B:** Shown here is the new pump installed. It looks slightly different than the original, but it's functionally equivalent. **C:** With the new pump in place, install the fuel tank sending unit into the top of the tank. Be sure to connect the hoses from the pump to the bottom of the unit. **D:** Shown here is the new pump installed with the new sending unit all buttoned up and ready for testing. Be sure to put some fuel back into the tank prior to starting the fuel pump up.

PROJECT 23
Installing a High-Performance Air Intake

Time / Tab / Talent: 8 hours / $400 / 4 wrenches

Tools: Torx anti-tamper screwdriver

Applicable Years: 1997–2004

Parts: Cold air intake kit

More Info: www.101projects.com/Boxster/23.htm

Tip: Plan for this to take longer than you expected

Performance Gain: Freer-breathing engine

Comp Modification: DME software upgrade

There's been a lot of talk on Internet chat boards lately about cold air intake (CAI) systems. Some manufacturers will swear up and down that there's hidden horsepower in the intake system. Other "experts" claim that it's total bunk—a myth that has easily circulated in the age of the Internet. I personally believe that the truth is located somewhere in between. On some models, a properly engineered cold air intake kit can effectively cool the intake charge entering into the cylinders. Cooler, denser air will further decrease engine detonation and will also deliver a denser air charge, which theoretically corresponds to an increase in horsepower.

First of all, the stock Boxster intake system is indeed already a cold air intake system. It sucks air from the outside and insulates this intake from the heat generated by the engine. Where it doesn't work too well is in the area of airflow restriction. The stock system is somewhat restrictive and makes the air work its way around in order to enter the engine. Aftermarket performance intakes serve two purposes: to better inject colder air directly into the intake system and also to reduce the restrictions that are inherent in the stock system.

Just how much horsepower can you expect to gain? It all depends on which model kit you use. It is possible that a poorly designed kit used with an aftermarket air filter will actually create more restriction in the intake and cause a decrease in horsepower. In addition, a poorly installed intake system with leaks will also decrease performance. I have seen dyno tests where the installation of an intake system has done nothing or has even reduced horsepower. Then again, I have seen other tests where significant gains of about 10 horsepower were recorded.

The bottom line is that a performance intake system is (typically) an expensive aftermarket add-on that may increase your horsepower only slightly. Some kits cost over $500, which translates into a very high dollar-per-horsepower ratio. Some other kits are less expensive and incorporate reusable aftermarket filters. While I'm not a huge fan of these filters, as they tend to filter less than the stock ones (see Project 3), there can be some costs savings in the long run from not having to buy multiple stock air filters.

Perhaps the only thing that most people agree on is that a performance intake system will often give you a much better engine growl at higher revs. I'm personally a huge fan of growling noises, so this would certainly be a plus for me if I were making the decision to install one of these systems. For those of you who prefer a quieter engine, you might be slightly annoyed at the new music your engine is playing.

There are literally hundreds of manufacturers of these products, from the large tuning companies to people selling homemade kits on eBay. If you are going to install one of these on your car, I would do your research first and stick with a well-known manufacturer. For this project, I decided to install the intake system manufactured by well-known and reputable Evolution Motorsports. It replaces the stock air cleaner with a high-flow cone filter and a special tube to house the mass airflow sensor (MAF). The result is a freer-flowing intake with no headaches caused by check engine lights (CEL). The air intake housing is sealed off from the engine compartment and is designed to only funnel airflow from outside the car into the intake system. It was also a very good choice for installation with the 3.4 engine upgrade (see Project 11).

The installation of the system is not as easy as you would think—plan to spend an entire day wrestling with getting the old intake out and the new one in. Follow the photo array in this article for details on the installation for Boxsters up through 2004.

1 Here's the EVO Fresh Air Induction System for the Porsche Boxster as supplied by Evolution Motorsports. The kit consists of a housing that is molded from crosslink polyethylene, which has a very low thermal conductivity to keep engine compartment heat away from the cold air side of the intake. The reusable cone filter is freer-flowing than the original stock filter. The MAF intake tube is manufactured to OEM diameter specifications to avoid CEL problems.

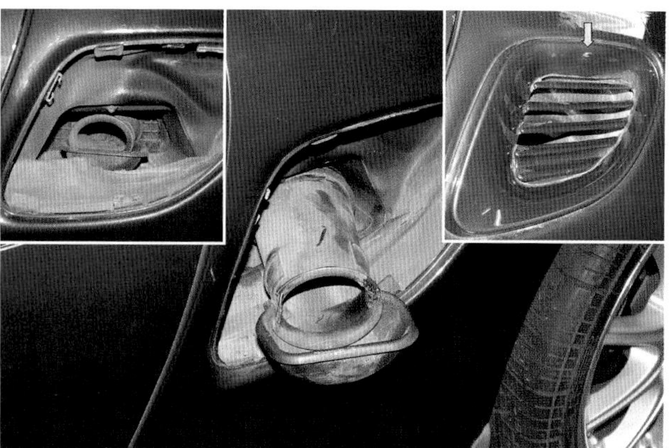

2 The first step is to remove the left-side fresh-air grille. A single screw (yellow arrow) attaches the grille in place, along with a set of plastic snaps. Use a plastic spatula to carefully work around the outside of the grille and pry it out of the clips. Remove the air intake snorkel by pushing it up and down and then out toward you. It is on tight and will require some force to remove.

3 Carefully remove the mass airflow sensor (MAF) using a T20 tamper-proof Torx driver and install it into the new metal tube provided in the kit while the tube is on your workbench. Handle the sensor with care and make sure that no dirt gets into it as you are moving it around. The sensor requires a tamper-proof Torx screwdriver to remove, which EVO provides in the kit. It's also a good time to clean the MAF (see Project 27).

4 Disconnect the two clamps (one at each end) that hold the stock air intake tube to the throttle body (green arrow). Remove this C-shaped tube from the car and put it off to the side.

5 Loosen the clamps at the top of the intake manifold. The next few steps are required in order to gain enough access to remove the really large stock air intake box. Also disconnect the 10mm nut that mounts down the throttle body housing (see Photo 2 of Project 83: Starter Replacement, for a photo of this nut).

6 Loosen the intake manifold screws. You will need a Torx socket set for these. Also remove the vacuum hose right-angle connection from the manifold (yellow arrow). You will be lifting up the intake manifold slightly in order to gain access to remove the stock airbox.

7 Now it's time to detach the stock airbox. There are three bolts that attach the assembly to the car. Two can be accessed from the top of the car, the third must be removed from below (you need to jack up the car, see Project 1). With the airbox loose, it's time to remove it from the car. Have an assistant pull the intake manifold toward the left side of the car in order to give you the room you need to pull out the airbox. Removing it by pulling out the MAF tube first is easiest way to get it out. This is by far the most difficult and frustrating part of the installation and the removal of the airbox will require quite a bit of wiggling and quite a bit of force to remove from the car.

8 Installation of the new fresh-air-box is a snap. Simply install it into the car where the old airbox was located. Insert the MAF pipe, and then install the top bracket in place.

9 Clamp the cone filter onto the end of the MAF pipe. Install the OEM air intake tube that you removed previously (yellow arrow). With the new air intake in place, reassemble the intake manifold, taking care to reconnect any vacuum lines you may have disconnected.

PROJECT 24
Updating Your DME with Performance Software

Time / Tab / Talent: 1 hour / $700 /

Tools: Windows computer

Applicable Years: All

Parts: Softronic cable and software

More Info: www.101projects.com/Boxster/24.htm

Tip: Required if making any significant changes to the drivetrain

Performance Gain: 10–15 percent more horsepower

Comp Modification: Install a 996 engine!

When you consider price and performance, the Motronic system (also called the Digital Motor Electronics, or DME) is hands down the best overall fuel injection system to use. Ignition timing and fuel delivery are all controlled by a digital map that is recorded in a flash memory chip located within the main fuel injection (DME) computer. The computer takes input from a variety of sensors that are located on the engine: cylinder head temperature, crank angle, throttle position, exhaust gas oxygen (mixture), ambient air temperature, and mass airflow. The DME is programmed from the factory with certain performance characteristics (mostly conservative) so that the engine will react well under a host of varying conditions. Major changes to the engine (increased displacement, the addition of different camshafts, etc.) require an updated map to take full advantage of these modifications. Failure to update the Motronic system may actually result in a decrease in performance, as the original system is finely tuned to supply the correct timing and fuel injection values for a stock engine configuration. To gain the maximum benefit from engine modifications, you need to either update the flash software in your DME (easy) or install a programmable aftermarket engine management system (not so easy).

The Motronic system is generally very reliable. Its main failure points are the sensors that send data back to the DME computer. Although I haven't seen it on the Boxsters just yet, another odd failure point on other older Porsches appears to be the DME relay. Corroded contacts appear to cause this mission-critical part to fail somewhat intermittently. I have had many customers claim that their cars run much better right after they have replaced the DME relay. While I don't have any empirical data to back this up, there are a lot of people who will swear by replacing their DME relay once every two years. I do recommend that you carry a spare one, as a failure can potentially leave you stranded on the side of the road. On the Boxster, there are two DME relays in the trunk, in slot number one (DME) and slot number two (Ignition). Also vulnerable is the fuel pump relay above the front fuse panel (see Photo 2 of Project 22).

If you are running a stock engine with the Motronic injection, one of the best upgrades you can perform is the installation of aftermarket performance software. As stated previously, the factory programmed the original software to compensate for a wide variety of driving characteristics. These days, you can find software maps that will elevate the rev-limiter, advance your timing, and generally run the engine with less conservatism than the factory programs. The only downside to running a more aggressive map is that sometimes the timing curves are a bit too advanced and may cause detonation on low-octane pump gas (as it is here in California). The Boxsters have a knock sensor that will reduce detonation if the timing is too far advanced, and you can also get maps that are specifically tailored to your region if lower octane fuel is the only type available.

One downside to installing a performance software map is that you basically need to run premium fuel with the chip installed. Whereas the stock chip is designed and mapped to provide good performance across a wide variety of operating conditions, the performance chips are typically mapped to assume that you are running high-octane gasoline. If you run low-octane fuel, the knock sensor will generally prevent detonation, but in general you will not fully utilize the performance improvements of the chip.

There are many manufacturers out there selling various variations of performance software for the Boxster. One company that has differentiated itself from the pack is Softronic, founded by former PCA tech guru Scott Slauson. The Softronic software upgrade kit has a few innovative features not found in other DME programming products. The software upgrade is installed using a Softronic cable attached to a typical Windows computer (others often require you to ship them your DME for programming). The DME is updated and reprogrammed using the OBD II port (see Project 20), which allows you the freedom to update your software and then also convert it back to stock when needed. This is particularly useful when you need to bring your car in for emissions testing and the updated software in the computer might make it difficult to pass. The Softronic software makes an exact backup copy of the software on your DME prior to installing the updated maps.

Installation of the software is a snap. Simply install the Softronic software onto your computer and then connect it via the supplied cable to the ODB II port on your Boxster. The software will perform a variety of pre-programming checks, create a full backup on your hard drive, and then install the performance software into your car. Just sit back, drink your coffee, and let the computer do all the work. The total programming time is about five minutes or so.

Performance software is required if you are upgrading your engine to a 3.4 liter, as was done in Project 11. I used the Softronic performance software to install a higher output Porsche 996 program into the 3.4-liter engine after the installation. The increase in horsepower went from 300 to 322, and torque increased from 258 to 271—quite an improvement. In addition, Softronic was able to custom design our program to fit our particular Boxster engine conversion profile (engine/intake/exhaust).

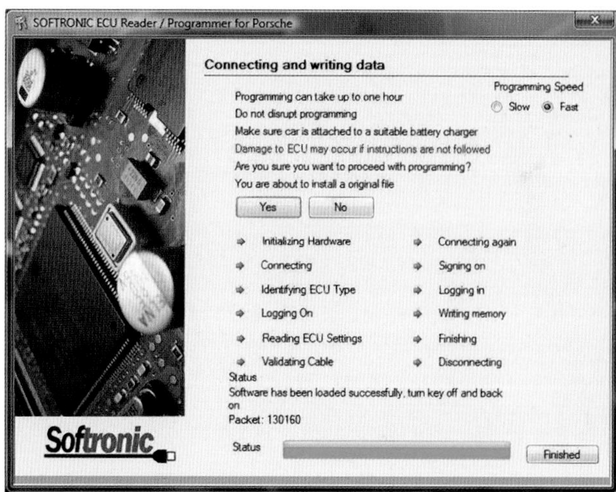

1 It really is as easy as it looks. Here is a screenshot from Softronic's software. Simply plug the cable into the OBD II port on the Boxster and run the software. It will create a full backup of your existing configuration and install the performance software update in less time than it takes to brew a cup of coffee.

2 It really is as simple as it looks. All you need is a laptop, or a desktop computer with a long USB extension cable. Plug the connector into the ODB-II access port (green arrow), start the software, and in about five minutes your Boxster's software will be upgraded.

PROJECT 25
Fuel Injector Replacement

Time / Tab / Talent: 2 hours / $20–$600 /

Tip: Be extra careful of the plastic injector tips

Tools: 8mm or 9mm crescent wrench

Performance Gain: Cleaner, better-running fuel injection system

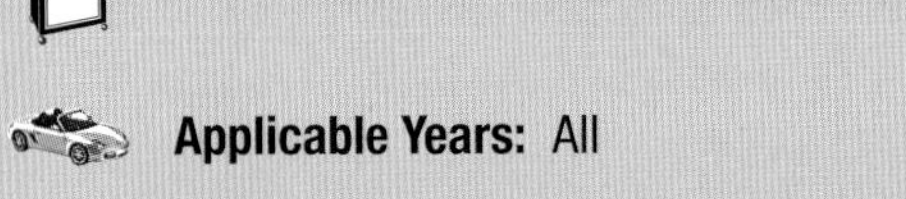

Applicable Years: All

Comp Modification: Replace your fuel filter

Parts: Injector O-rings, new injectors, white lithium grease

More Info: www.101projects.com/Boxster/25.htm

In this project, I'll walk you through the process of replacing your fuel injectors. Before we begin, a good question to ask would be why would you want to replace them to begin with. There are several myths and misunderstandings regarding fuel injectors. The first one is "bigger injectors will give you more power." This statement is completely false. It's the equivalent of saying that adding more lights to your already brightly lit living room will make you see better.

The fuel injectors that are in your Boxster are more than adequate for stock engines and supply more than enough fuel for maximum power and open throttle. For your engine to achieve maximum power, it must have an air/fuel ratio maintained within a certain range. Adding more fuel to the mixture makes it richer and won't necessarily give you any more power. In fact, it is typically the opposite—a richer mixture will foul plugs and won't ignite as easily. The goal of any good fuel injection system (whether it be carburetors or electronic fuel injection) is to maintain the air/fuel ratio (typically about 14.67:1) for ideal combustion and power. Adding higher flow or larger injectors disrupts the balance of the engine, makes the engine's fuel management system run richer, and generally decreases power from ideal levels. It's the same principle as adding more high-powered lights to your living room—if the room was adequately lit to begin with, then you won't see better—you'll see worse, because it will be too bright for your eyes.

So what are the exceptions to this rule? There are a few. Major changes in the displacement or flow of the engine can cause the engine to run lean. Examples would include increasing the displacement of your engine, changing your camshafts, or adding a turbo or supercharger. The supercharger compresses the air/fuel mixture and allows more of it to exist within the same size combustion chamber. Therefore, ideally there should be more fuel injected into the combustion chamber when compressed with a supercharger than is normally injected on a normally aspirated engine. For owners who add a supercharger or turbo to their car, they need to be especially concerned about keeping the engine's mixture correct—the tendency is for these cars to run too lean, which can lead to destructive problems, such as detonation or overheating (see Project 18).

In general, you should not upgrade or replace your injectors with larger ones unless you have made a significant engine modification that would cause the engine to run lean. If you are replacing injectors, then make sure that you use ones that have stock flow rates for your engine—don't buy ones that have higher flow rates thinking that they will give you more power. They won't.

So why would you want to replace your injectors? Well, as the engines get old, the injectors tend to fail and leak. If you pull fault codes out of your computer, it may tell you that you have a faulty or leaking fuel injector. See Project 20 for more details on how to pull these codes. You may also find that you can see or smell a particular injector leaking. If this is the case, you may not have to replace the injector itself but may only need to replace the injector O-rings.

The first step is to prep the car. I like to tell people to pull out the fuse for the fuel pump (see Project 4) and then try to start the car. The car will turn over and then die. Do this about 2–3 times—it will help drain excess fuel out of your system. Then, make sure that the car has cooled down—you don't want to be working with gasoline when the car is hot. Have a fire extinguisher handy, as there will be some spillage of fuel—it's nearly impossible to prevent. Also, wear chemical resistant gloves if you don't want to get any gasoline on your hands, and make sure that you have plenty of paper towels or rags on hand to help you clean up. Perform the injector removal in a clear, open, and well-ventilated space, and it may not hurt to have an assistant around in case there are any problems.

Begin by removing the top engine cover (see Project 3) and disconnect the battery (Project 81). On the 2005 and later cars, if you wish to remove the injectors on the left side of the car, then you'll probably want to remove the air cleaner to give yourself more working room (Project 23).

Now, loosen the clamp that holds the fuel line to the top center of the motor. Remove the connectors from each of the fuel injectors (see Photo 1). With the clips disconnected, you should be able to remove the wire harness from the tops of the fuel rail and move it out of the way. Now you should have much better access to the injectors—it's time to remove them from the fuel rail. The fuel rail is the long, round metal bar that runs along the top of the injectors and is held onto the manifold with a few bolts (see Photo 1). Depending upon the configuration in your car, and which side you are working on, you may have to disconnect the main fuel lines to the rails in order to give yourself more working room. It may also be useful to remove the front panel to assist in the disconnection of these lines.

At this point you should be able to pull off the fuel rail from the top of the injectors. Use caution and work from the front of the car to the rear—pulling and making progress slowly. The injectors have big fat O-rings that are pressed into bores in the fuel rail—you are battling these O-rings as you lift up on it and pull it out.

When you have lifted up your fuel rail (expect some fuel spillage from the rail), you should be able to push it out of the way enough to be able to pull out the injectors. With the injectors no longer attached to the fuel rail, you can now pull them out of the manifold. They are held in place using the same type of big fat O-ring at the tip of the injector. Simply pull straight up on the injector, and it should come out of the manifold. You may have to tug a little bit to get it out, but don't use excessive force. Sometimes repeated wiggling helps. Be careful of the injector tips—they are made of plastic. Do not damage them.

With the injectors out of the manifold, you can now take them to be cleaned and calibrated. Over the years, the injectors become dirty and may also not distribute flow evenly amongst all six. It costs about $150 for all six to be cleaned, tested, and calibrated. New injectors cost anywhere from $150 to $200 a piece, making their replacement a somewhat pricey endeavor.

There are three types of injector leaks—they can leak fuel into the manifold from the nozzle, they can leak fuel into the engine compartment from the fuel rail, and they can leak air (vacuum leak) from the manifold. The first leak cannot be fixed at home—you need to have the injector repaired or replaced (I recommend replacement, as it will probably be pretty old anyway). The fuel rail leak is easy to contend with—simply replace the old, fat O-ring that seals the injector to the fuel rail (PN: 944-110-901-01). This should be done anytime the injectors are out of the car.

The third leakage area is a bit of a Catch-22. On some of the early cars (through 2000), the tip of the injector needs to be removed from the injector. While this seems easy, and indeed it is easy to remove, it is just as easy to damage the tip when you remove it. The method that I used to replace one of the seals in the tip works well, but it also slightly dinged and damaged the fragile green plastic tip of the injector (see Photo 3). The 2001 and later injector O-rings can be easily removed without damaging the injector.

If you are replacing all your injectors or the O-rings, make sure that you place a very tiny, tiny bit of white lithium grease, or the Porsche-recommended Optimol MP3, on the edges that will be pressed into the fuel rail and the manifold. This will aid in the insertion of the injector and the reassembly of the fuel rail. It will also help to prevent the O-ring from pinching and will guard against tiny leaks as well.

Installation is basically the reverse of removal. You may find it easier to insert the injectors into the manifold first if you have enough room (instead of into the fuel rail first). Double-check to make sure that all of the fat O-rings are securely seated when you reattach the fuel rail. When you are ready to fire up the car, have an assistant on hand in case there is a fuel leak. Have them watch the injectors and the fuel lines to make sure that there are no leaks.

Porsche has made a few changes to the fuel injectors for the early cars. The early fuel injectors used through 1999 have a blue top on them (PN 996-606-120-00) and are still available to be replaced individually if one goes bad. However, if you are replacing all six of your injectors, you should upgrade to the year-2000 ones with the green top (PN 996-606-120-01). For 2001-2004 cars, use the later-style injectors with the white top (996-606-122-00).

1 Unplug the wire harness from each injector (yellow arrow). Unclip the harness from the fuel rail (blue arrows), and place it off to the side. Then unbolt the fuel rail from the manifold (green arrows) and lift the rail upward. You may also want to pull off the rubber U-hose that connects to the pressure regulator. Shown here is the Porsche 996 Carrera motor that was transplanted into the Boxster. As you pull up on the fuel rail, some may stick in the manifold, or some may come out with the fuel rail—it all depends upon a variety of factors.

2 Release the fuel rail from the tops of the injectors by removing the small, square retaining clips that fasten and secure the injectors to the fuel rail (blue arrow). Use a pair of needle-nose pliers to pull this clip off. It pulls off from the front (it's C-shaped) and should slide off with a reasonable amount of force. This task is performed with the rail still installed on the engine, but is shown out of the car here in this photo for clarity. The inset photo in the upper left shows the fuel pressure regulator removed from its housing (simply slide off the clip holding it in place). The inset photo in the lower right shows the injector once you remove it from the fuel rail. The big, fat O-ring will offer quite a bit of resistance (yellow arrow). The same O-ring that holds the injector into the fuel rail (red arrow) is also the same type that is used to hold the injector into the manifold.

3 To remove the nozzle O-ring, first cut it off carefully with a razorblade. Be careful not to damage the green plastic tip when you cut through the O-ring. Then, remove the O-ring with a pick, again taking care with the tip. Finally, to get the new O-ring on, you will need to remove the tip. The best method I figured out for removing the tip was to get a small 8–9mm crescent wrench and apply uniform pressure against the tip. However, this still results in some of the plastic on the tip becoming marred. Pressing up with the wrench using a surprisingly large amount of force will make the tip pop off of the injector. At this point, you can attach the new O-ring and snap the tip back on.

PROJECT 26
Replacing Engine Sensors

Time / Tab / Talent: 1–3 hours / $300–$900 /

Tools: None

Applicable Years: All

Parts: Engine sensors

More Info: www.101projects.com/Boxster/26.htm

Tip: Check the codes first prior to replacing sensors

Performance Gain: Optimal-running engine

Comp Modification: Replace oxygen sensors

1 I've split this article up into various photos of the sensors and their locations on the engine so that you can easily find them when you need to replace them. The ambient air temperature sensor measures the air temperature in the engine compartment. This tells the DME computer how hot it is inside the engine compartment so that the engine compartment fan can be turned on or off. This sensor is simply held in place by a rubber grommet that is attached to the intake manifold on the right side of the engine near the air pump.

2 The coolant temperature sensor is located on the pulley side of the engine off to the left side of the car near the cylinder head. This sensor measures the temperature of the coolant and is used to adjust mixture levels as the engine begins to heat up to optimum operating temperature.

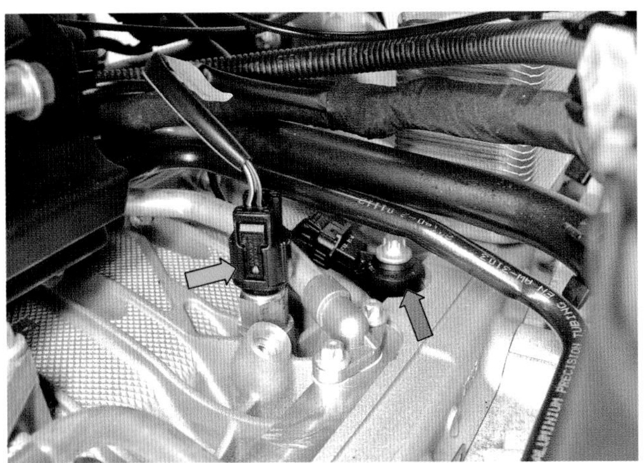

3 Shown by the blue arrow is the oil level sensor/oil temperature sensor. This is a somewhat unique sensor in that it contains both oil level and temperature sensing functions within a single unit. Next to it is the knock sensor (purple arrow). There is one installed on both the left and right side of the engine block. Located under the intake manifold, both of these sensors are relatively difficult to get to (you need to remove the intake tubes to access them—see Project 83).

4 This photo shows the group of sensors located on the right rear of the engine. The purple arrow shows the crank angle sensor, or flywheel sensor, which reads the toothed flywheel as it rotates past the sensor (harness plug shown by yellow arrow). The orange arrow shows the camshaft timing advance solenoid (red arrow is the connector). You can access the sensor/solenoid from underneath the car and the electrical connections from the engine compartment.

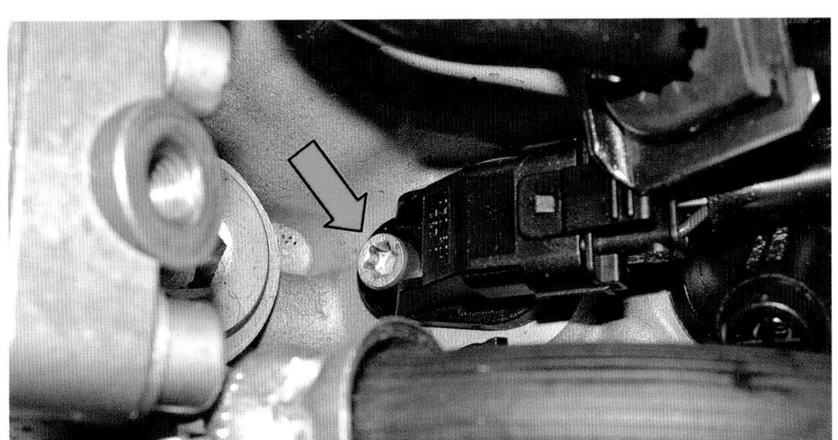

5 Shown here is the camshaft position sensor. There is one located on the top of the left cylinder head toward the front and one on the right cylinder head toward the rear for the five-chain motors used up to about 2001. For 2003 and later three-chain motors, the sensor is located on the top of the left cylinder head toward the rear and on the right cylinder head toward the front.

6 This photo shows the oil pressure sender/switch. Located on the right-side cylinder head, the oil pressure sender is installed if you are upgrading your instrument cluster to the 996 Carrera one (see Project 90). Normally, a simple emergency switch is installed in this location (inset photo, upper right). Use a new sealing ring if you replace this part.

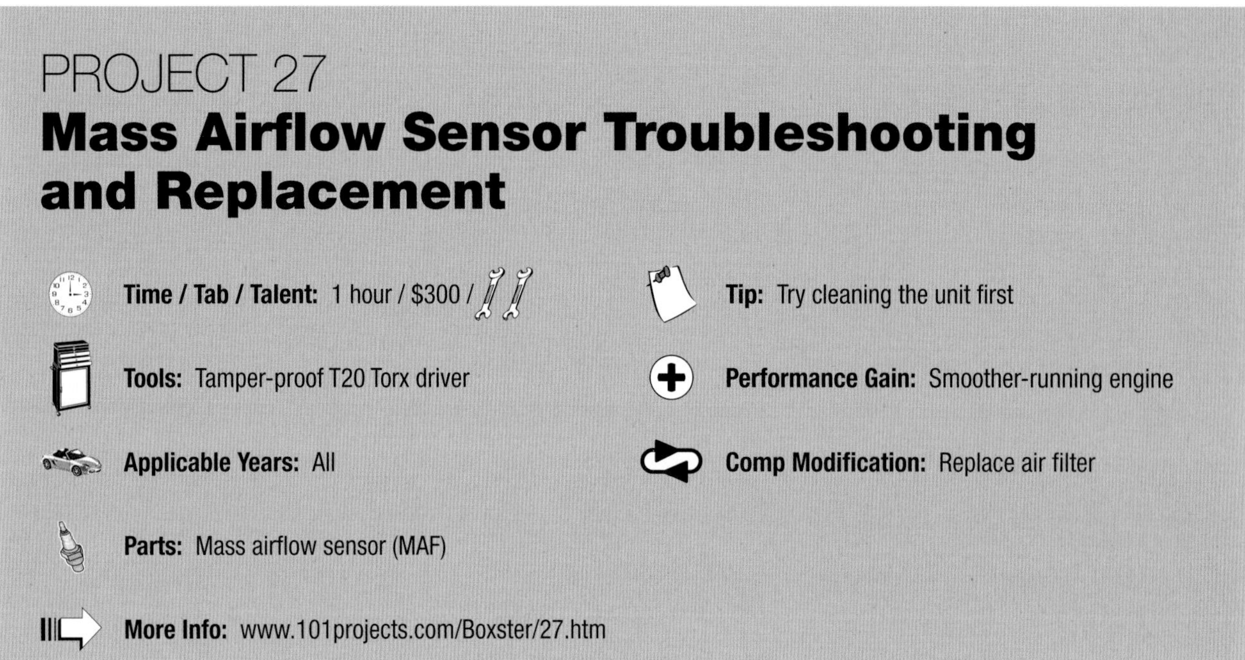

PROJECT 27

Mass Airflow Sensor Troubleshooting and Replacement

Time / Tab / Talent: 1 hour / $300 /

Tip: Try cleaning the unit first

Tools: Tamper-proof T20 Torx driver

Performance Gain: Smoother-running engine

Applicable Years: All

Comp Modification: Replace air filter

Parts: Mass airflow sensor (MAF)

More Info: www.101projects.com/Boxster/27.htm

The mass airflow sensor (MAF) is located inside the engine compartment and is used to measure the amount and temperature of air that is entering the engine at any one time. Older-style meters used on fuel injection systems in the 1980s measured air volumetric flow, which worked fine, but then you also needed a separate sensor to figure out how cold or dense the air was. The mass airflow sensor senses the total amount of air passing the sensor and allows the fuel injection system to adjust the fuel mixture to compensate for cold weather and/or high altitude conditions. The MAF also incorporates an internal intake air temperature sensor that measures the temperature of the intake air.

The first indication that you might have a problem with the MAF is the presence of a check engine light (CEL) on your dashboard. The check engine lamp can be caused by a wide variety of problems with the engine—you need to read the codes from the computer to get a starting clue as to what the problem is (see Project 20 for details on reading the codes). It's perfectly safe to continue to drive the car while the CEL is on, as long as it is not flashing. However, the engine will not be operating at peak efficiency, and you will most likely experience a loss in power and a decrease in gas mileage as a result. It's best to get the problem taken care of relatively quickly, as running the engine in this condition can potentially cause damage to other components, such as the catalytic converters.

The computer will know if something is wrong with the MAF because it will compare the values being output by the sensor to "expected" values that it should be receiving. This commonsense check by the computer helps diagnose problems with every component in the system. If the MAF becomes dirty and is falsely indicating to the engine that the car is receiving very little air while at full throttle, then the computer will most likely kick back an error code.

To gain more information about the problem, you can try disconnecting the sensor completely and take the car for a drive. If you take short drives (30 minutes or less) with the sensor disconnected, it shouldn't cause any major damage to your car. The engine management system (DME) will enter into a type of "limp mode" that will compensate for the missing MAF. If engine performance improves dramatically when disconnecting the MAF, then the problem quite likely lies with the MAF.

Vacuum leaks and other air leaks in the system can cause MAF sensor errors. If you have a crack or leak in your air intake downstream of the sensor, then the MAF will be sensing less air than the engine is actually receiving. If the clamp on the throttle body happens to come loose and fall off, then the MAF will indicate almost no air being sucked through the intake, yet the engine will be sucking air directly from the engine compartment into the throttle body. The bottom line is that you should carefully inspect all of your hoses, clamps, and intake tubes for air leaks prior to replacing the sensor (see Project 21).

The MAF is located on the left side of the engine compartment, just behind the air filter (see Project 3 for access to the engine compartment). For some reason, Porsche made it unusually difficult to remove the MAF by securing it with a T20 tamper-proof Torx screw. You need the special tamper-proof Torx drivers, which are not typically found in everyone's toolbox, but usually can be purchased at a good local auto parts store. Although the holes on the MAF look symmetrical, they are not, and the unit can only be installed in one direction. See Photo 1 for a close-up of the MAF. Removal is easy once you have the tool. Simply remove both screws holding it in place and pull it out. Boxsters from 2005 and later have a MAF with an integrated housing—simply unclamp the housing from the intake tube and remove it.

It's very important to keep the sensor clean. If the air cleaner isn't working too well, it could allow dust and debris to collect on the MAF. If you've had a problem with your air-oil separator, it may have contaminated the sensor as well. Oil sucked into the engine intake from a defective separator can easily find its way back to the intake tube. If you have had major engine problems (like our project car with the blown-up engine), then you may find a ruined MAF. On our donor car, the MAF was soaked in oil and coolant residue that had found its way all over the inside of the engine. If you have an aftermarket reusable air filter, beware of how much cleaning and filtering oil you use on it. Excess oil may get sucked into the intake and find its way onto the MAF. To keep your MAF healthy, I recommend changing or cleaning your air filter often (see Project 3).

If you are replacing your sensor, it is extremely important that you get the proper one for your car. There are two basic types, one for the cars that use a traditional throttle cable (up to 1999) and one for cars with an E-gas electronic throttle (2000 and later). In addition, the later-style E-gas sensor has been updated at least twice as of this writing. Porsche updated the sensors in the Boxster in mid-2000 and also released a new version of the DME software that is a required update if you are going to use this new and improved sensor (see Porsche Tech Bulletin Boxster 1a/00 2445). Here is a chart that shows the differences between all of the sensors:

If you own a 2000 Boxster or 2000 Boxster S, then you need to make sure that you have the proper sensor installed. Much confusion lies in the fact that most people don't know if their car has been updated by Porsche or not. If the old sensor that you removed is 996.606.124.00, then you need to replace it with the same part number (or have Porsche update your DME software to accommodate the newer-style sensor—see Technical Service Bulletin 1/00 2445 Air Flow Sensor, dated 4-18-00). If the old sensor you're removing ends in 125.00 or 125.01, then replace it with 986.606.125.01 (the latest version available).

After reinstallation, reset your CEL using your code reader (see Project 20). You can also disconnect the battery for a short while to reset the lamp, but I don't really recommend this approach (see Project 20). On 1997–2002 Boxsters, you can disconnect the battery for more than 20 seconds, but less than 50 seconds, to clear the trouble codes without having to enter your code back into your radio. On pre-2003 cars, the computer's CEL memory is cleared after being disconnected for 20 seconds, but the radio code is needed after 50 seconds disconnected.

After you have replaced or cleaned the sensor and cleared the code, you need to go drive the car and see if the code returns. If the same error code appears, then the problem probably lies elsewhere. Most of the time when you have an error code indicating a problem with the mass airflow sensor, it is usually solved by the installation of a new sensor. However, the computer can become confused sometimes and give misleading error messages. Wire harness issues, DME problems, and secondary air injection equipment problems may all give false MAF error codes. At this point, it's best to dive into the factory manuals and start going through the laborious test procedures contained in there.

Porsche Part #	BOSCH Part #	Application	Notes
996.606.123.00	0-280-217-007	1997–1999 All Boxsters	Sensor for use with cable throttle cars
996.606.124.00	0-280-218-009	Early 2000 Boxster/Boxster S	Original sensor for E-gas cars (thru Boxster 2.7L Chassis #98 6YS 62 0414 and #98 0YU 62 5099) (thru Boxster S 3.2L Chassis #98 0YS 66 0257 and #98 3YU 66 2413)
996.606.125.00	0-261-231-148	Mid-2000–2004 Boxster/Boxster S	First updated sensor for E-gas cars (discontinued and replaced with version 125.01 below)
986.606.125.01	0-280-218-055	Mid-2000–2004 Boxster/Boxster S	Latest updated sensor
987.606.125.00	0-280-218-145	2005– All Boxster/Cayman	Integrated housing design

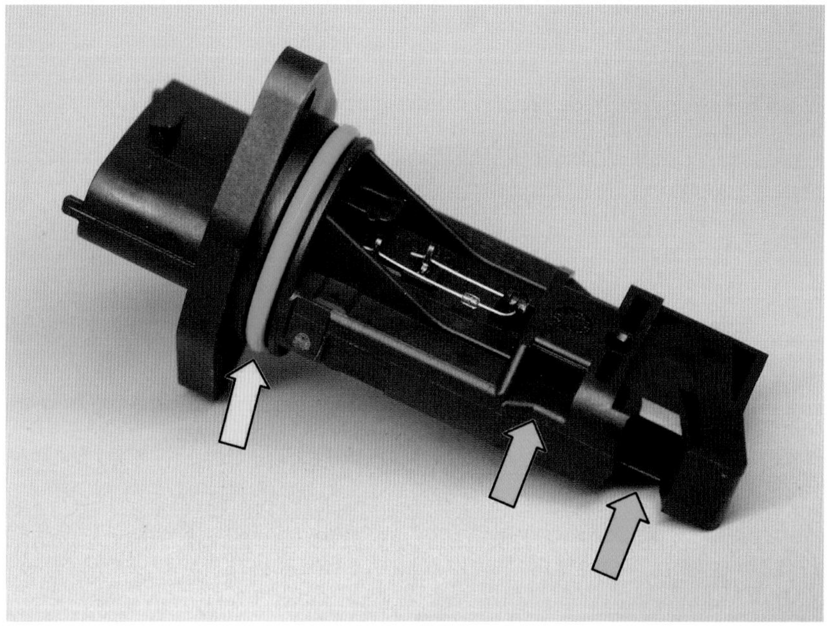

1 Shown here is the mass airflow sensor (MAF). The main sensor fits in a hole in the air intake right downstream of the air filter. The green O-ring seals the sensor to the intake tube (yellow arrow). If you're having trouble with your MAF, you can try to resurrect it by cleaning it. Lightly spray the areas shown with the blue arrow with electrical contact cleaner—the one that I recommend is CRC Mass Air Flow Sensor Cleaner. Spray it and then shake the sensor so that any dirt or debris is washed away. Don't touch any of the sensor elements with anything (like your finger or a brush), as this will damage them almost immediately. Let it dry completely prior to reinstallation.

2 You need a T20 tamper-proof Torx bit (inset upper left and lower left) to remove the mass airflow sensor from its home in the intake pipe (yellow arrow). It's typically easier to pull the sensor out of the intake tube first, and then disconnect the electrical harness. Be sure not to touch any of the sensor elements that are exposed (red arrow). Clean the entire housing area prior to installing your new sensor.

PROJECT 28
Throttle Body Cleaning/Intake Plenum Replacement

Time / Tab / Talent: 3 hours / $15 /

Tools: Torx driver set

Applicable Years: All

Parts: New O-ring or idle control valve gasket

More Info: www.101projects.com/Boxster/28.htm

Tip: Remove the throttle body and let it soak in carburetor cleaner overnight

Performance Gain: Smoother-running engine

Comp Modification: Replace intake plenum boots

FUEL

1 The Boxster throttle body is a precision piece of equipment that is subject to a rather harsh environment. After years of reliable service, the throttle body may become dirty or clogged, which may result in lowered performance. You may find that there is a lot of built-up dirt, particularly if a previous owner didn't change the air filter too often (Project 3). Instructions on how to access the throttle body are detailed in Project 83 (starter replacement). Remove the throttle body (yellow arrow) from the intake plenum and then take it over to your workbench and clean it out using some carburetor cleaner. Run lint-free cloths through all of the passages and make sure all the dirt and debris is removed. The blue arrow shows the intake plenum boots that should be checked for cracks and/or replaced after many years of use.

2 This is what your throttle body should look like after you've finished cleaning it. Shown here is the early-style cable throttle with the idle control valve (green arrow). This valve controls the air that passes by the throttle. If it's clogged you will get erratic idle and warm-up problems. Be sure to use a new gasket when you remount the idle control valve to the throttle body. With the throttle body completely clean, remount it to the intake plenum using a new rubber gasket (yellow arrow, inset photo).

3 Clean out any oil and debris from the inside of your intake plenum, and replace the rubber hoses/boots if they are old or cracking. This photo shows the inside of the intake plenum on my Boxster project car, which had a disastrous engine failure. Those small pieces of metal that you see there are leftover piston rings! Normally, you will only find oil and gas residue in the intake plenum. If your air-oil separator has failed, then you will indeed find plenty of excess oil in here and also coating the throttle body.

SECTION 4
WATER

Porsche built some great engines with these Boxsters. However, the mid-engine design made for some tricky routing of water hoses, and some creative solutions were developed. As a result, there are issues that are unique to these cars. Failures in the water-cooling system can account for a significant portion of overall engine failures and breakdowns. Fortunately, the engine's reliability can be significantly increased by paying careful attention to the maintenance of the cooling system.

PROJECT 29
Coolant Flush/Replacement

Time / Tab / Talent: 2 hours / $120 /

Tools: Large bucket, socket set

Applicable Years: All

Parts: 6–12 quarts of coolant

More Info: www.101projects.com/Boxster/29.htm

Tip: Make sure your bucket is big and wide to catch the coolant stream

Performance Gain: Prevents electrolysis in your engine

Comp Modification: Water pump and hose replacement

One often neglected task on many cars is the maintenance of the cooling system. In general, Porsche recommends that you flush and clean out your cooling system once every 36 months, or approximately every three years. I like to perform this task on my own cars about once a year, or if I let it slip, once every two years. The reason for this is that old, exhausted coolant can actually cause irreversible damage to your engine components—I found this out firsthand when I recently replaced the head gasket on one of my older BMWs. It looked like the previous owner hadn't changed the fluid once in the past 10 years. As a result, there were many parts of the engine that were corroded and showing severe signs of wear.

A properly maintained cooling system must have a few things in order: adequate supply of coolant, a radiator that acts as a heat exchanger with the outside air, a fan or airflow source, a water pump to keep the coolant circulating, and a thermostat to regulate the engine at its optimum operating temperature. The coolant must also have the correct mixture and chemical compounds to promote heat transfer, protect against freezing, and also inhibit corrosion. To keep your Boxster operating correctly, it's important to check the level, strength, and overall condition of the coolant on a regular basis. You also need to change the coolant before it degrades to the point where it doesn't perform its job adequately.

A fact that I keep hearing kicked around revolves around the reported findings of the U.S. Department of Transportation, which states that cooling system failures are the leading cause of mechanical breakdowns on the highway—not exactly surprising, since proper cooling maintenance is one of the most neglected areas of most cars.

Electrolysis: One failure mode associated with dirty coolant is known as electrolysis. Electrolysis occurs when stray electrical current routes itself through the engine coolant. The electricity attempts to find the shortest path, and impurities in the coolant often generate a path of least resistance that the electricity travels across. The source of this stray electricity is often from electrical engine accessories that have not been properly grounded. A missing engine or transmission ground strap can also cause the coolant to become electrified. Sometimes the path of least resistance becomes a radiator, a heater hose, or even the heater core. These components are often well grounded and offer a ground path from the engine to the chassis by means of the semi-conductive path of the coolant.

Electrolysis can destroy your engine quickly. Although it's semi-normal to have very small amounts of voltage potential in your coolant system, values greater than about a tenth of a volt can start reactions between the coolant and the metal in your engine. In particular, electrolysis affects primarily aluminum engine components, resulting in pitting and scaring of the aluminum surface. This eating away of the metal can cause coolant system leaks and, in particular, radiator leaks around aluminum welds. Cast-iron components are also vulnerable, but typically the aluminum metal parts fail first. Often, electrolysis can be easily seen attacking aluminum cylinder heads (see Photo 1).

How can you test for electrolysis? Other than actually seeing visible signs of erosion, you can perform a current flow test. Connect the negative terminal of a voltmeter to the chassis ground. Test for adequate continuity by touching another point on the chassis—the resistance should be near to zero. With the engine cold and running, submerge the positive probe into the coolant tank, making sure that the probe does not touch any metal parts. The voltage should be less than 0.10 volts. If not, methodically turn off or unplug each electrical accessory until the reading reads below 0.10 volts.

Have an assistant switch accessories (like the A/C compressor, heater blower, etc.) while you measure the voltage.

If an accessory doesn't have an on/off switch, test it by temporarily running a ground from the housing of the accessory to the chassis. Ground each component and check the voltmeter. If the wire restores a missing ground connection to the accessory, then you've found a component with a faulty ground.

During this test, be sure to check the starter. Not only will a poorly grounded starter struggle to turn over the engine, it will also zap away tremendous amounts of metal in your cooling system components. Watch the meter carefully when starting the engine. Any voltage spike will indicate a faulty ground connection.

Coolant System Additives: Many people are rightly skeptical of coolant system additives—there are a lot of myths in the automotive industry. Luckily, the coolant system additives are in the category of good practice, for reasons I'll explain here. It all begins with chemistry. Like today's modern oils, many of today's modern coolants incorporate some of the chemicals that help cooling and increase heat flow around your cooling system components. As more and more automotive components are made out of aluminum and radiators become smaller, the use of these additives becomes more advantageous.

Aftermarket coolant system additives are known as surfactants. What is a surfactant? A surfactant, or surface active agent, is a molecule that has a water-loving end (hydrophilic) and a water-fearing end (hydrophobic). Localized boiling of coolant in the cylinder head can create large shock waves that can wreck havoc on your engine, particularly on aluminum components. Without going into too much boring detail, these surfactants also help reduce the amount of air in the cooling system and also control the amount of foam within the system.

In general, there are three main reasons why using these additives is beneficial to your cooling system. Firstly, they reduce harmful cavitations and foaming that may occur when your water pump is kicking out fluid at a rapid pace. This reduced foaming helps to prevent damage to aluminum surfaces. Secondly, the use of these additives aid in the transmission of heat from the coolant to the radiating surfaces within the radiator. Even if your car runs very cool, these additives add an extra level of protection in case a thermostat or similar component fails. Thirdly, the additives contain corrosion inhibitors. Most cars on the road have cooling systems that do not contain the ideal 50/50 water/antifreeze ratio that the antifreeze manufacturers design for. The additives help minimize potential corrosion by maintaining adequate pH levels. Even if your antifreeze already contains surfactant additives, the use of these additional additives is typically beneficial because most cars are shortchanged on the 50/50 coolant/water mix.

In general, the benefits of additives, such as Water Wetter, are that they:

- Reduce corrosion due to rust and electrolysis
- Increase the "wetting ability" of water and improve heat transfer, thus reducing cylinder head temperatures
- Clean and lubricate coolant system seals like those found in the water pump
- Reduce the formation of foam and cavitations, which can cause corrosion
- Reduce the effects of "hard water" in the cooling system

In general, the addition of these additives is cheap, and it's a proven benefit too—no snake oil here. Using the additives on a perfectly maintained car can also provide a significant margin of error in case something goes wrong. Porsches are not generally known for cooling system failures, but keeping the odds on your side can prevent a costly head gasket replacement.

It's important to keep your cooling system at the correct pH as well. Water has a pH of 7 and is considered neutral. Battery acid is highly corrosive and has a pH of about 2–3, whereas baking soda is very alkaline and has a pH of about 10–11. In general, you want to make sure that your coolant has a pH greater than 7. Any pH less than that will result in an acidic mixture, which will start to corrode your engine. The corrosion inhibitors in additives and antifreeze are added specifically to keep the pH above 7. A properly mixed 50/50 split between water and antifreeze will yield a pH of about 8–9. Over time, the glycol (one of the main components of antifreeze) will break down and degrade, creating acidic compounds. The alkaline corrosion inhibitors must be adequate enough to neutralize these acidic byproducts over the life of the coolant. Minerals in the water, heat, dissolved oxygen, and other factors gradually deplete the coolant of its corrosion inhibitors. Once gone, the mixture will become acidic and will begin to eat away at your engine.

Cooling System Maintenance—Checking the Level: It's very important to check your coolant level regularly, as this will help detect leaks that can siphon off coolant and cause overheating in your engine. You should regularly check the coolant level in your coolant reservoir, making sure that it is within the prescribed high/low marks. These marks are printed on the side of the coolant container, located in the rear trunk. The container is slightly transparent, and you can see through it slightly to see the current coolant level.

Your Boxster will lose a little bit of coolant here and there over time due to evaporation and/or sporadic leakage. However, a significant loss of coolant over a very short period of time almost certainly signifies a leak in the system. Sometimes a leak can be seen when you park the car overnight. Often the coolant leaks out and then evaporates while you're driving, leaving no telltale mark of coolant on the pavement. If you suspect a coolant leak, visually inspect all of the hoses, the water pump, the reservoir, and the radiator for seepage or the "weeping" of coolant out of seams and gaskets. Check the seal on the radiator cap. Check that the radiator cap is fastened securely. If you suspect a leak that you cannot see, a pressure test from a professional mechanic can verify the integrity of your system. If your coolant leaks out and the level becomes low, the low-coolant sensor in the tank will trigger an alert that will show up as a blinking coolant temp lamp on the dashboard coolant gauge.

If you can't find any visible leaks and the system appears to hold pressure, then check to make sure that the cap is good and is rated for the proper pressure. Verify that the cap you have for your Boxster is the proper one for your engine. If you look inside the coolant tank and the coolant is muddy or cloudy, then you may have a serious head gasket problem. Oil may be leaking past the gasket and mixing with the coolant. This typically means that the engine needs to come apart and the head gaskets resealed, which is a complex and expensive repair as you might imagine.

If the system does not hold pressure, and you're still at a loss where coolant might be disappearing to, then you might want to start looking in the oil. A faulty head gasket will often cause coolant to leak into the oil. If you remove your oil cap and find a yellow murky substance, then you probably have a faulty head gasket. The oil level may be elevated and you will be able to see droplets of coolant inside the oil filler hole. If coolant is leaking past the gasket into a combustion chamber, you will see steam exiting out of the tailpipe, and the spark plugs will foul easily. In addition, the exhaust will be contaminated with the silicate corrosion inhibitors found in the coolant, and your oxygen sensor will be destroyed—plan on replacing it if you have experienced this problem.

If you can't discover what has happened to the coolant, it may be because there was a temporary overheating problem and some of the coolant boiled over. In this case, top off the coolant and keep a very close eye on it. It's not uncommon for overheating issues to suddenly destroy a head gasket.

Checking Coolant Strength and Condition: You should periodically test the strength and condition of your coolant to assure that you have achieved the optimum balance for your Boxster. This is just as important for protection against heat as it is for protection against freezing. An imbalance between water and antifreeze levels will change the boiling point and/or freezing point of the mixture. A 50/50 mixture of water and ethylene glycol (EG) antifreeze will provide protection against boiling up to approximately 255 degrees Fahrenheit (with a 15 psi radiator cap). This mixture will protect against freezing to a chilly -34 degrees Fahrenheit. On the other hand, a similar 50/50 mixture of propylene glycol (PG) antifreeze and water will give you protection from -26 degrees Fahrenheit to about 257 degrees Fahrenheit.

If you increase the concentration of antifreeze in your coolant, you will raise the effective boiling point and lower the freezing point. While this may seem beneficial on the surface, having an antifreeze content of greater than 65–70 percent will significantly reduce the ability of the coolant to transmit and transfer heat. This increases the chances of overheating. As with most things in life, it's a good thing to maintain a healthy balance.

Beware: You cannot accurately determine the condition of your coolant simply by looking at it. The chemical composition and concentrations in the coolant are very important—if the chemistry is off, then your coolant may be harming your engine.

As mentioned previously, it is important to keep the coolant fresh. The main ingredient in antifreeze, ethylene glycol, typically accounts for 95 percent of antifreeze by weight. It does not typically wear out, but the corrosion inhibitors that comprise the remaining 5 percent typically do degrade and wear out over time. Keeping the coolant fresh is especially important with engines that have both aluminum heads and cast-iron blocks.

I recommend that the coolant be changed at least every two years, or every 25,000 miles. I'm not a huge fan of long-life antifreeze—if these longer-life fluids are mixed with conventional antifreeze (a very easy mistake to make), the corrosion inhibitors react and reduce the effective protection of the long-life fluid. If you do have this long-life fluid installed in your car, only add the same type of antifreeze to the car. Don't mix and match regular and long-life fluid.

Unfortunately, it's tough to determine if your long-life coolant has been mixed or topped off with ordinary antifreeze. Although some coolants are dyed a separate color (like Dex-Cool in GM vehicles), when mixed with standard antifreeze, it typically isn't enough to overpower the bright green color. In general, unless you know the entire service history of your Boxster, it's a wise idea to err on the side of caution and use a shorter service interval for changing your coolant.

Okay, so how do you check the coolant in your system? I recommend using little chemical strip tests that measure how much reserve alkalinity is left within the coolant. The test strip changes color when immersed in the coolant. You can then compare the final color change to a reference chart in order to determine the condition of the coolant. Obviously, if the coolant tests poorly or is borderline, you should plan on replacing your coolant very soon.

An additional note—ethylene glycol (EG) and propylene glycol (PG) antifreeze have differing specific gravities, so make sure that you use the correct type of test strip when testing your coolant. Otherwise, you may end up with false readings. EG antifreeze is very toxic to pets and small animals yet smells and tastes pretty good to them, so make sure that you keep old coolant away from them.

CHANGING THE COOLANT IN YOUR BOXSTER

Okay, so I've convinced you that your coolant needs changing. The good news is that it's relatively straightforward on the Boxster. Begin by getting a large drip pan to place underneath your car. My favorite choice is kitty litter boxes, as they are large, are made of plastic, and will hold a lot of coolant. The Boxster six-cylinder engines will hold about 4–6 gallons, so make sure that whatever container you use is capable of holding all of that coolant.

With your Boxster cold, elevate it on jack stands (see Project 1) and remove the plastic protective panels that cover the radiator hoses on the underside of the car. Place the heater temp controls all the way to high, turn the ignition to the on position, and turn on the passenger compartment fan to its lowest setting. Do not start the car. By turning the heater on, you are opening the valves to the heater core, which will allow you to drain the coolant located in the core. Move to the rear trunk and slowly remove the radiator cap inside the trunk to allow any coolant system pressure to vent out.

Now it's time to empty the coolant—refer to Photo 2 for the location of the drain plug and the hoses that need to be disconnected. At the bottom of the engine, open the drain plug and let the coolant empty into your large bucket. When the flow has stopped, replace the plug using a new O-ring and torque to 7–11 ft-lbs (10–15 Nm). Next disconnect the two large radiator hoses that feed the supply and return coolant lines to the front of the car. I also like to disconnect the front lower hoses from the radiators as well, but this requires removing the front bumper cover (see Project 68 and Project 32).

Reconnect the hoses when all of the coolant has drained using new hose clamps. I used to only recommend the use of good quality German screw-type clamps, but I'm slowly coming around to the annoying spring-clip type that were used in the initial assembly of the car. These clips have an advantage over the clamp type in that they apply constant pressure when the hose expands or contracts as the car heats and cools.

Next, disconnect and empty the coolant from the two heater hoses. Reattach with new hose clamps. Now it's time to refill the coolant and bleed the system. In the trunk, remove the oil cap, lift up the "trap door" panel (Photo 3), and then screw the oil cap back on. Flip up the metal clip that opens the bleeder valve (Photo 4). If you have an automatic transmission car, then you need to remove fuse B1, which is located in the fuse panel near the driver's side footwell (see Photo 5 of Project 95). This will disable the ATF cooler shut-off valve temporarily. Now, fill the car up with coolant until the coolant level is visible at the bottom edge of the coolant tank. Start the car and run it at idle, topping off the coolant to the maximum level, until no more coolant can be added. Rev the engine, let it settle down, and top it off again if the level decreases. Be sure during the whole process that the car does not exceed 176 degrees Fahrenheit (80 degrees Celsius) while bleeding the system—if the car gets too hot, it will interfere with your ability to fill and bleed the system to the proper level.

Now, reinstall the reservoir cap and let the car continue to warm up at about 2,500 rpm for 10 minutes or until the thermostat for the front radiators opens up. When the thermostat opens and coolant starts flowing forward, the electrical radiator fans should turn on. Now allow the car to continue to warm up a bit more, revving the car to about 5,000 rpm every 30 seconds or so. Remove the reservoir cap slowly, letting any built up pressure dissipate. There should not be any tremendous pressure built up because the bleeder valve is still open at this time. Top off the coolant in the tank to the maximum level, reinstall the cap, and repeat the process of revving the engine to about 5,000 rpm for another five minutes.

Now, allow the engine to idle for a few minutes until you hear the radiator fans cycle on and off at least once. Turn off the engine, and slowly remove the reservoir cap again, relieving any pressure that might have built up there. Top off the coolant until it reaches the MAX level indicated on the coolant tank gauge, located on the side of the tank. Flip down the metal clip to close the bleeder valve and replace the "trap door" panel on top of the tank. If you have an automatic transmission car, then replace fuse B1 in the driver's side door kick panel.

I'm sure one question you're about to ask is "What type of coolant should I use?" The Porsche factory manuals indicate that the coolant used inside the Boxster engines should be considered a "lifetime" fluid, and mixing regular fluid with this life-time fluid is not recommended. I prefer to use the Porsche factory coolant in my cars. At $35 a gallon, it can be somewhat more expensive than generic coolant, but the Porsche coolant is not premixed so one gallon becomes two when mixed with distilled water. Plan on using about 19 liters (5 gallons) of coolant for cars without a center radiator (all 1997–2004 Boxsters). The 2005–2008 cars and the Boxster S take about 22 liters (6 gallons) of coolant. Add one more liter as well if you have an automatic transmission. If ordering coolant for your flush job, I would be sure to order an extra gallon—you might need them to top off down the road, and the Porsche OEM coolant can be difficult to find in a pinch. The part number for a 1-gallon (3.79-liter) container is 000-043-301-05-M100, and it costs about $35 per gallon from PelicanParts.com.

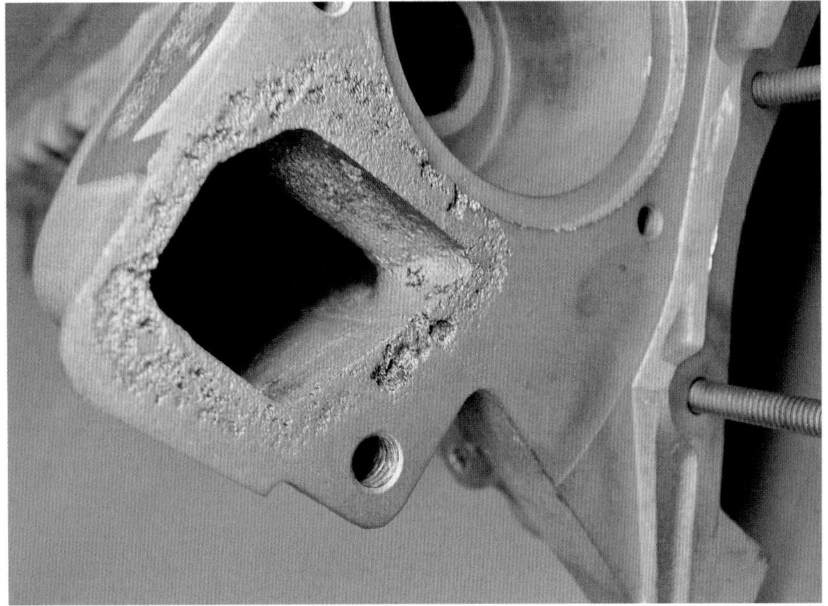

1 This photo shows a picture of the thermostat area of a BMW cylinder head that has been partially damaged by electrolysis. Notice how the aluminum has been eaten away and eroded by the chemical/electrical reactions. The process works somewhat like electrical discharge machines (EDM). These machines work by passing a large electrical current through metal, literally zapping away bits of material until nothing remains. Unfortunately, the electrolysis process works in a similar manner, zapping bits of metal in proportion to the amount of electrical current passing through the coolant. A poorly grounded starter can literally destroy a radiator or head within a matter of weeks, depending upon how often the car is started. A smaller current drain, like an electric cooling fan, may slowly erode components over many months.

2 This photo shows the coolant drain plug (yellow arrow) and the hoses that need to be disconnected in order to empty the coolant from the system. Green arrow: Return hose from the front radiators. Orange arrow: Thermostat housing and hose that supplies coolant to the front radiators. Red and purple arrows: Heater supply/return lines. The white arrow shows the radiator vent hose, which should not need to be disconnected.

3 I personally like to use the Porsche factory coolant, which is a bit more expensive, but specially formulated for the cars. However, if you use a standard off-the-shelf coolant that meets or exceeds the factory's specifications, then that should suffice as well. The red arrow points to the coolant level indicator on the side of the tank. The photo inset shows the "trap door" panel that hides the bleeder valve underneath.

4 The coolant bleeder valve has a small metal clip on it. Flip the clip upward to open the valve so that you can bleed the coolant system.

PROJECT 30
Coolant Hose Replacement

Time / Tab / Talent: 1–8 hours / $20–$400 /

Tools: Knife, handheld hex tool set

Applicable Years: All

Parts: Water hoses, coolant

More Info: www.101projects.com/Boxster/30.htm

Tip: Use the better-quality German squeeze clamps

Performance Gain: Prevent catastrophic hose breakdown

Comp Modification: Replace radiator, bleed coolant system

I've owned a lot of cars over the past several years, and the Boxster by far has the most radiator hoses of all of them. When Porsche designed this car, they really didn't try to reduce the amount of rubber used in the assembly. As a result, the task of replacing all of the radiator hoses on the car is a really big chore. One of the more difficult parts is actually figuring out where they are all located! For that purpose, I've created a table of hoses and general locations to help you check your hoses and replace them if necessary. Please keep in mind that slight variations in hoses and locations have occurred over the length of production of the Boxster.

I recommend inspecting your rubber hoses every two years or so. As they age, they have a tendency to get hard and brittle. When you gently squeeze a hose, it should be relatively soft and easy to indent with your hand. It shouldn't feel like it's brittle or crunching when you squeeze it. It should spring back to its original shape pretty quickly after being compressed. If it feels very hard, then it might be time to replace it. If there is a bulge in the hose, or any type of crack in the surface of the hose, then you should replace it as well. Also check for wetness or leaks around where the hoses create their connections—that is a sign that the hose should be replaced. Some hoses may be coated with some leftover cosmoline from the factory—don't mistake these for bad radiator hoses.

Unfortunately, there's no exact milestone on when to replace your radiator hoses. The recommended automotive industry standard is about four years or 60,000–80,000 miles. On some cars, they may last 10 years or longer depending upon how the car is driven or how it's stored during winter or summer months. Since there are so many hoses on the Boxster, I suspect that many of these cars will have many of their original hoses still installed many years down the line.

Front Hoses (connect to radiators):
- Bottom Radiator Hoses (left and right, yellow arrow, Photo 1 of Project 32)
- Top Radiator Hoses (left and right, green arrow of Photo 3 of Project 32) or Top Radiator three-way hose (left and right) if center radiator is installed (see Photo 2 of Project 31)
- Radiator Vent Hoses (small, left and right, blue arrows, Photo 3 of Project 32)

Intermediate Hoses (connect to metal pipes in front wheelwells—see Photo 7 of Project 31):
- Upper "S" Hoses (left and right, orange arrow)
- Lower "S" Hoses (left and right, blue arrow)
- Vent Hoses (left and right, purple arrow)

Rear Hoses (see Photo 2 of Project 29):
- Thermostat housing to pipe that connects to front radiators (red arrow)
- Return hose that connects to pipe that feeds front radiators (green arrow)
- Hose that connects to pipe that runs down the center of the car and is the radiator vent hose/pipe (white arrow)
- Three-way coolant hose near thermostat (purple arrow)
- Heater core hoses (red arrow)

Radiator Tank Hoses (see Photo2 of Project 33):
- Oil cooler to coolant tank (green arrow)
- Radiator vent hose (blue arrow)
- Coolant filler hose (yellow arrow)
- Coolant overflow hose (shown removed, mates to the nipple shown by the red arrow).
- Three right-angle hoses located internal to the coolant tank, visible from the trunk (see Photo 4 of Project 33)

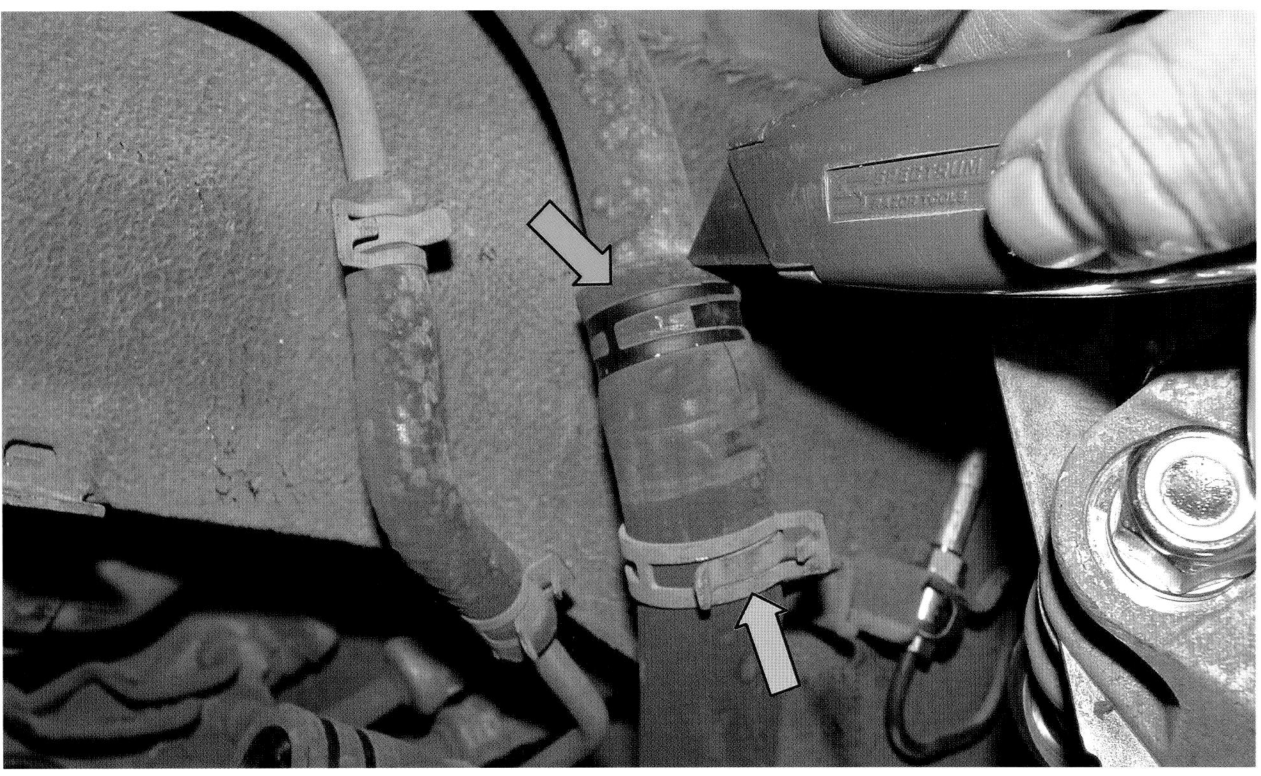

1 Use some pliers or channel locks to release the clamp and slide it down the hose (orange arrow). Then, use a razor knife to cut a slit in the hose along the length of the hose (green arrow). This will allow you to peel back the hose and easily remove it from the metal pipe.

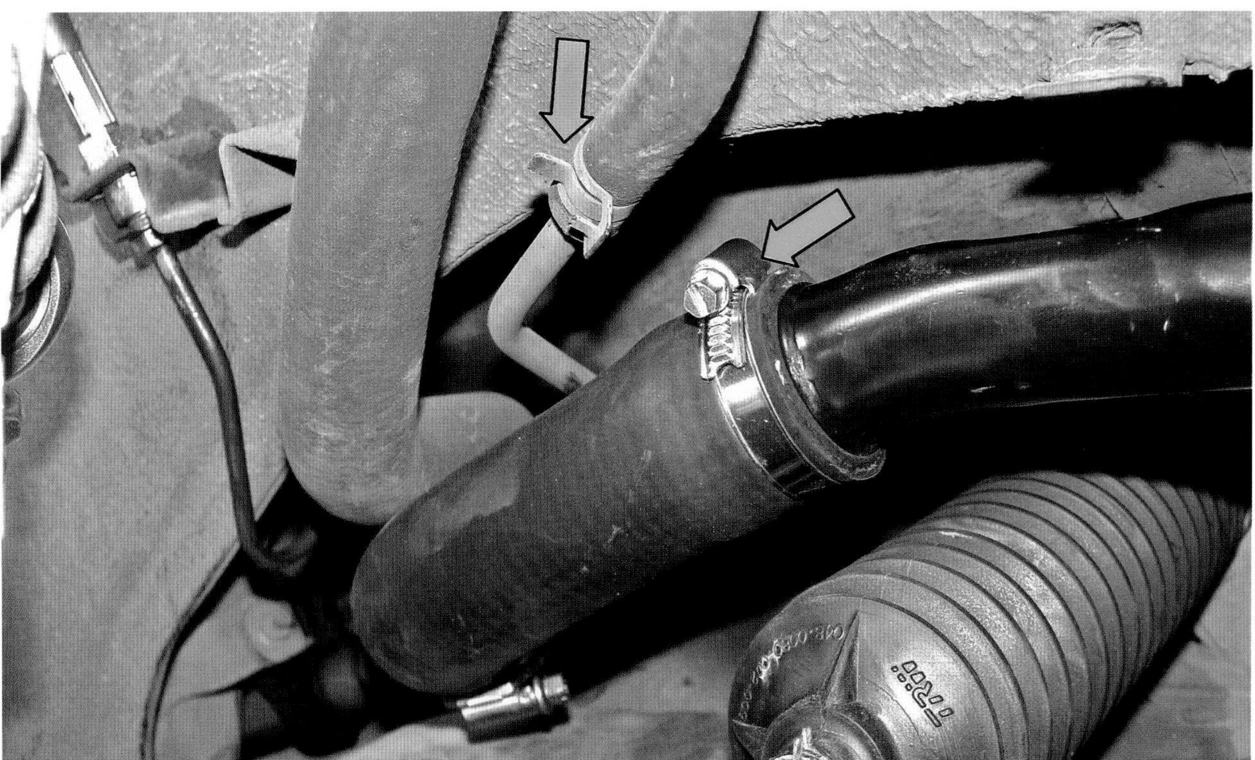

2 The standard hose clamps used on the car when new are difficult to attach properly (orange arrow). The nice advantage to these clamps is that they supply constant pressure around the hose even when it expands or contracts. For ease of installation, I often use German OEM screw-type hose clamps that will not loosen up or fail over time (green arrow).

PROJECT 31

Installing a Center Radiator

Time / Tab / Talent: 8 hours / $550 /

Tools: None

Applicable Years: All non-S cars

Parts: Center radiator, brackets, hoses

More Info: www.101projects.com/Boxster/31.htm

Tip: Cut your front bumper instead of buying a new one

Performance Gain: Cooler-running engine

Comp Modification: Replace side radiators and hoses

The 2000 Boxster S design included the front-mounted radiator used on the Porsche 996 and the venerable GT3, as well as some Tiptronic-equipped cars. The larger, more powerful engine dictated the use of the front-mounted radiator in addition to the two standard side radiators. Adding the front-mounted radiator is a good upgrade for cars that will be driven in hot weather or have undergone some performance modifications. In particular, if you're going to be taking your Boxster out to the track someday, I indeed recommend the installation of the additional radiator. It will provide some significant added protection against overheating, as it typically reduces the highest operating temperatures by about 10–20 degrees Fahrenheit (7–12 degrees Celsius) after installation.

The first step is to gather all your needed parts and pre-assemble the radiator assembly on your bench (see Photo 2 and Photo 3). Pay careful attention to the radiator inlets and outlets as well as the frame tab locations, as it's very easy to assemble this backwards the first time. Lay out all your parts and make sure that you have everything that you need prior to tearing apart the car. This project details the installation on a 1997–2004 Boxster, but the upgrade kit for the 2005 and later cars is very similar (different part numbers).

Next, jack up the car, remove the two front wheels and remove the front bumper cover and the lower part of the inner wheelwell liners (see Project 68 for instructions on the bumper cover removal). Next, remove the air scoops, detach the air conditioning condensers, empty the coolant, and loosen the radiator assembly so that you can drop down the whole assembly (see Project 32 for instructions on these tasks).

Replace the lower hose on the passenger side with the new three-way hose that will feed the radiator. Use new adjustable hose clamps, as shown in the bottom of Photo 2. Rotate the hose so that the small section of the hose is properly oriented to mate with the top of the center radiator port. Now, replace the hose on the upper left side, again positioning the small portion of the hose so that it will mate with the top of the center radiator when installed. This left-side hose twists and bends in a crazy pattern—use Photo 5 as a guide on how to properly route it.

You may find that when installing the new three-way hoses into your Boxster, the diameter of the hoses are larger than the input pipes. This is because the standard Boxster pipes that feed coolant to the front of the car are smaller than the ones used on the Boxster S or the 996 (which use the center radiator). The solution is to replace the standard pipes with the 996/Boxster S pipes for the left upper side of the car and the lower right side of the car (see Photo 7). In order to mate these larger pipes with the smaller pipes that run down the center of the car, I used a Boxster S hose and a standard Boxster hose, cut them in two, and installed a reduction fitting in between (see Photo 6). There may be other ways of accomplishing the same task, but this seemed to be the easiest at the time.

Now attach the center radiator to its position in the center of the car. Loosely attach the radiator using the two top M8 bolts and the corresponding speed nuts that clip into place on the chassis (see Photo 4). Attach and clamp the left and right hoses to the radiator—loosen and remove one of the M8 bolts if you need to gain enough room to secure the hose. When the hoses are secure, attach the remaining M8 bolts and speed nuts and secure the radiator to the chassis.

When installing this center radiator into my Boxster, I encountered some interference between the air conditioning hoses and the bracket for the center radiator. Your car may or may not have the same problem, as the hoses are somewhat flexible and tend to be in slightly different places on different cars. To protect the air conditioning hoses from damage, I used some rubber hose as insulation and wrapped the air conditioning hoses as a precaution (see Photo 4 and Photo 8).

To finish, reattach the radiators and air conditioning condensers and tighten up all of the hardware that holds them in place. Refill the car with the coolant you removed, or use a new quantity of coolant equal to what came out when you disconnected the radiator hoses. Start the car up and let it run for a few minutes to check for leaks.

After confirming that the car is leak-free, attach the rubber surround onto the center radiator, install the left and right rubber air guides, and reinstall the wheelwells and the bumper cover. You have a few options for modifying the bumper cover. You can purchase a cover with the center radiator hole already pre-drilled, which is a very expensive option, considering that you also have to paint it. You can also use a bumper cover from an early 996. Or you can cut your own insert out as per the instructions I provide with Photo 9.

When everything is buttoned up properly, bleed the entire cooling system as described in Project 29. Over the next few days, check the coolant level regularly, and also check for coolant leaks when you park the car.

The factory thermostat starts to open at about 187 degrees Fahrenheit (86 degrees Celsius) and only fully opens at almost 210 degrees Fahrenheit (99 degrees Celsius). This means that the effects of the front-mounted radiators are limited until the engine gets very hot. For this reason, I recommend installing a low-temp thermostat in conjunction with the center-mounted radiator upgrade. See Project 34 for more details.

1 Here's a photo of a Boxster S with the center radiator installed from the factory. The rubber air guide inside connects to the inner retaining piece and channels air through the center radiator.

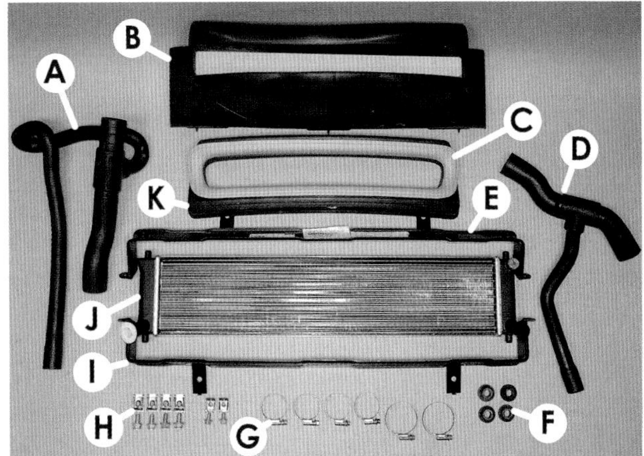

2 Here are most of the parts that you will need for your center radiator installation. The parts are available from PelicanParts.com as complete kits for either the early (1997–2004) or late (2005–2008) Boxsters: **A:** Left side radiator hose (996-106-665-57). **B:** Front rubber air guide (996-575-141-02). **C:** Front bumper cover trim piece (986-505-551-00). **D:** Right side radiator hose (996-106-666-55). **E:** Upper radiator bracket (996-504-487-02). **F:** Radiator spacers (Qty 4- 930-113-430-00). **G:** Hose clamps (Qty 2 999-512-666-09, Qty 4 999-512-551-00). **H:** Mounting hardware (Qty 4 - Hex Bolt M6×12 - 900-378-036-09, Qty 4 - Speed Nut M6 - 999-507-550-02, Qty 2 - Hex Bolt M8×16 - 900-378-074-09, Qty 2 - Speed Nut M8 - 999-591-869-02). **I:** Lower radiator bracket (996-504-485-02). **J:** Center radiator (996-106-037-51). **K:** Front bumper cover inner retainer (986-505-555-00).

3 This photo shows the new center radiator with the upper and lower mounting brackets installed. This side of the radiator faces the rear of the car. Pay close attention to the tabs on the radiator brackets—the top tab attaches near the front, the bottom tab attaches near the rear of the bracket. When installed, the radiator will be facing slightly upwards at an angle. As shown in this photo, the surface of the radiator shown here faces the rear of the car.

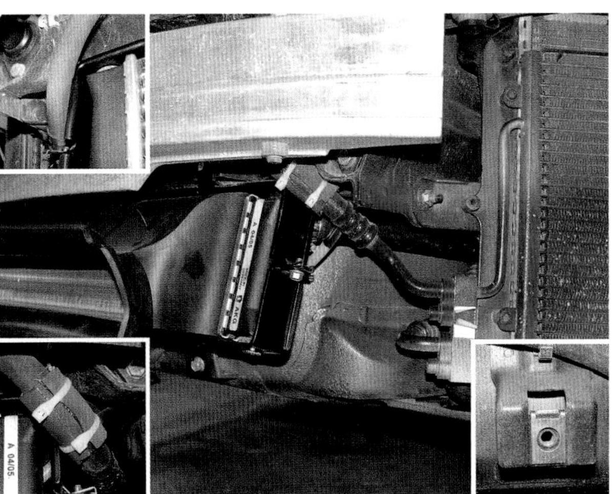

4 Here are some installation details for mounting the front radiator. Upper left: I found that the radiator bracket leaned against the air conditioning hose and would probably damage it if it wasn't protected. So, I used a small section of old radiator hose and zip-tied it around the air conditioning hoses to protect them from wear (lower left). The lower right inset photo shows the proper orientation of the speed nut fasteners—the chassis should already have the small mounting brackets built in.

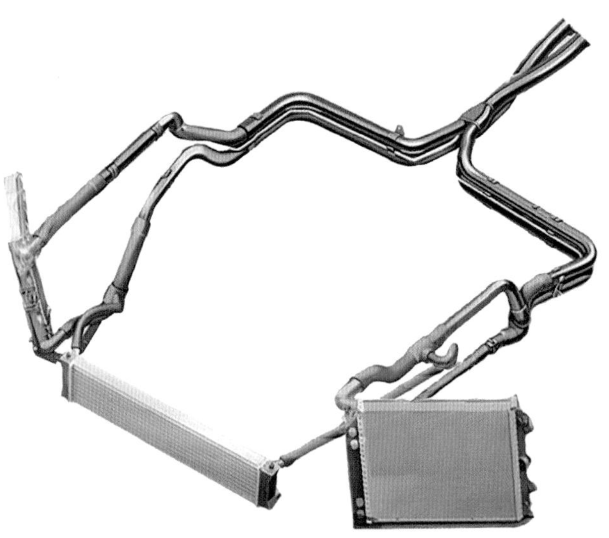

5 Here's a useful diagram showing the routing of the hoses for the three radiator setup. As shown in the photo, you need to replace the lower radiator hose on the right side of the car and the upper radiator hose on the left side of the car. The center radiator "taps" into the hoses for the left and right radiators and provides additional cooling.

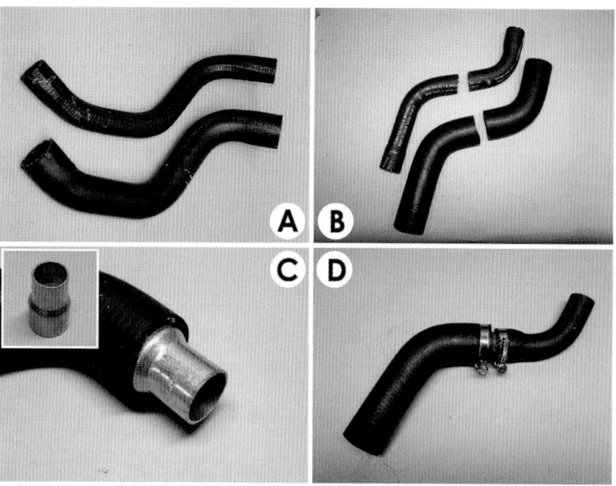

6 One of the problems with the upgrade kit is that the pipes on the regular Boxster are smaller than those on the Boxster S. The trick is to cut the hoses and create a step-down hose using a copper pipe reducer available at any good hardware store (outside diameter 1.25×0.875 inches). **A:** The regular hose and the larger Boxster S hose are shown side by side. **B:** Cut both hoses at similar points. **C:** Insert the reducer into the larger-diameter hose. **D:** Join the two pieces together and secure with hose clamps.

7 These two photos show the left and right side of the inner wheelwells with the larger radiator pipes installed (yellow arrows). In addition to the larger-diameter pipes, you also need to install the plastic larger-diameter pipe retainers (green arrows). One end of the pipe attaches to the new three-way radiator hose (red arrow), and the other end of the pipe attaches to your custom-made hose with the reducer piece installed (blue arrows).

8 Shown here is the center radiator installed just prior to putting the front bumper cover back on. Note how the air conditioning hoses have been wrapped with protective rubber (old radiator hoses) since the upper center radiator bracket tends to wear into them.

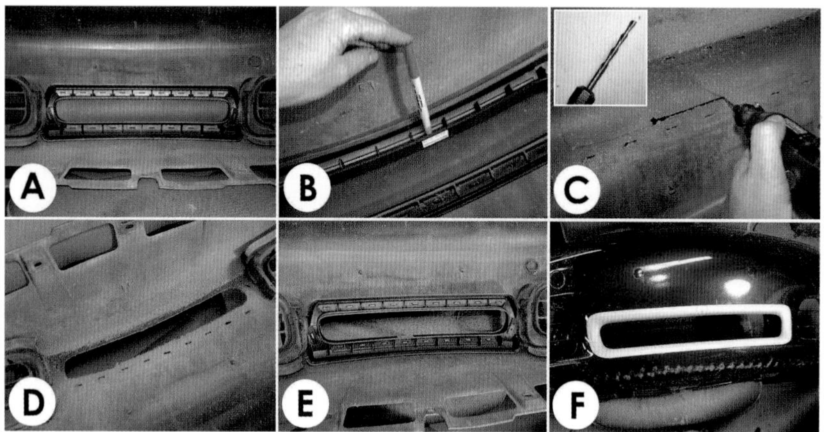

9 If you wish to save some money, you can drill out the opening for the front radiator yourself and reuse your old bumper cover. **A:** Line up the retaining piece with the inside of your front bumper cover. It should be centered between the left and right openings and fit flush against the curve of the bottom of the cover. **B:** Using a marker, trace the outline of the opening and the slots for the retainer as well. **C:** Using a Dremel tool and a milling bit, carefully make your cuts in the cover. It's okay if you're not 100 percent accurate, as there is a front trim piece that fits over the opening and frames it. **D:** This shows the opening cut out along with all of the small slits needed for the retaining piece. **E:** Test-fit the outer trim piece and the inside retainer to make sure that they fit together well. **F:** Here's what the final assembly will look like before it's painted.

PROJECT 32
Radiator & Fan Replacement

 **Time / Tab / Talent:** 4 hours / $180 / 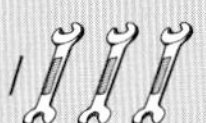

 **Tools:** Torx driver set

 **Applicable Years:** All

 **Parts:** Radiator, hoses, coolant

 **More Info:** www.101projects.com/Boxster/32.htm

 **Tip:** Install the center radiator for improved cooling

 **Performance Gain:** Cooler-running engine

 **Comp Modification:** Replace hoses, repaint front bumper

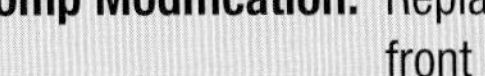

Proper maintenance of your coolant will go a long way toward extending the life of your radiator. The cooling systems on most cars are often very neglected, as most owners don't know much about them (see Project 29 for more information). The most vulnerable components in the entire system are the radiator and the heater core, as they tend to be damaged by corrosion and electrolysis. Poor maintenance of the system can result in the buildup of corrosion elements in both the radiator and heater core, creating clogs and leaks that decrease cooling performance. If the engine overheats, the additional heat from the coolant can also damage sensitive plastic attachments and components.

When replacing your radiator, you want to make sure that you replace it with one that meets or exceeds the OEM cooling standards. Although Porsche cooling systems don't typically fail very often, age and neglect may lead to overheating problems. Therefore, it may be a wise idea to install a center-mounted radiator that performs a better job of cooling than the standard pair (see Project 31). I also recommend replacing your water pump, radiator hoses, thermostat, and any hose clamps too (PelicanParts.com sells complete kits for this replacement). All of these components can be damaged by a cooling system that has overheated. It's also a good time to swap out your old belt.

The first step in replacing your radiator is to remove all of the coolant from the system (see Project 29). Now, you need to gain access to the radiator. Remove the front bumper cover and pull back the front part of the inner wheelwell liners (see Project 68). It is possible to remove the radiators without removing the front bumper cover, but it takes only a few minutes to remove it and it makes the job a whole lot easier in my opinion. Follow the removal procedure detailed in the photos to remove the radiator/fan assembly. Shown here are photos from the 1997–2004 Boxster, but the 2005–2008 models are very similar in nature.

The installation is basically the reverse of removal. Use new clamps on your new radiator hoses. Top off and bleed your coolant system as detailed in Project 29. Keep an eye on the front of your car for coolant leaks for about a week after the installation and tighten up any hoses that show any signs of leakage or weeping.

It's a good idea to use these instructions to clean out the radiators every spring, as they tend to collect a lot of debris, which decreases their cooling efficiency over time. This can also lead to moisture collection and premature corrosion of the radiator.

It's also a good idea to check the proper operation of the radiator fans while you have access to them, as the resistor packs that help to power them tend to fail. You can turn on and test the fan speeds using the Porsche PST-2 tool, or you can simply turn on the air conditioning system, and that should trigger the high-speed level of the fans. If you start the car and let it warm up, it should start the fans in low speed mode before graduating to the higher speed mode.

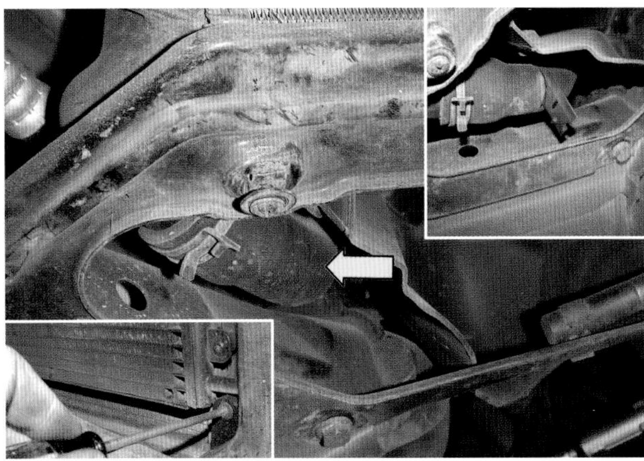

1 With the front bumper removed (Project 68), you should have easy access to both the right and left radiators. Begin by removing the large rubber air funnel that is located in front of each radiator—it is held on with five screws (lower left). Then, cut a slit in the lower radiator hose and allow the coolant to empty out of the radiator and hoses (upper right).

2 Detach the air conditioning condenser from the front by removing the two bolts (green arrows) and sliding it out of its mounting tab (red arrow). Using a zip tie, secure the air conditioning condenser to the chassis. This is to assure that the condenser pipes do not become damaged while you're working on the radiator (upper left inset). The lower left inset photo shows the rubber air funnel for the right side of the car—the temperature sensor boot must be carefully threaded out of this boot upon removal.

3 This photo shows the backside of the radiator and fan assembly with the inner fender liners removed (see Project 68). In order to remove the radiator and fan assembly, you need to disconnect the small radiator vent hose (red arrow). I recommend replacing this hose during this procedure, so you might save some time and effort by just clipping it off. Unclip the vent hose from the radiator bracket (blue arrows). The green arrow shows the upper radiator hose. In a similar manner, I also recommend just cutting it, since you will be replacing it anyways. Sometimes it can be nearly impossible to remove the hose from the radiator, and you will need to cut it off to remove it (inset photo). If you decide not to remove the front bumper cover, then you will need to remove the fender brace (white arrow), and detach the headlamp vent hose as well.

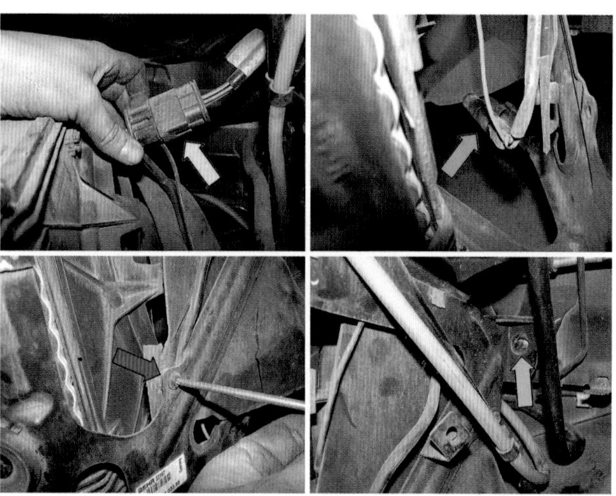

4 The yellow arrow shows the electrical connection to the fan that must be disconnected. Pull out the resistor pack from its bracket and loosen the wire harness (green arrow). Disconnect the rear radiator air guide from the metal radiator bracket (red arrow). Finally, disconnect the bracket from the chassis by removing the nuts that hold it in place (blue arrow).

5 Here is a shot of the radiator area after the radiator has been removed. The radiator-like unit on the left is the air conditioning condenser.

6 On the left is shown a brand-new OEM replacement radiator. If you are merely replacing the radiator fan and are reinstalling the old radiator, be sure to blow out the dirt and debris with some compressed air (right).

7 The radiator fan assembly is clipped to the rear of the radiator using metal snap clips (inset photo). Remove these snaps, and the fan assembly should lift right off. The fan is attached to the fan housing via three mounting screws located on the backside. A new fan is shown in the lower right.

PROJECT 33

Coolant Tank Replacement

 **Time / Tab / Talent:** 4 hours / $350 / 

 **Tools:** None

 **Applicable Years:** All

 **Parts:** Coolant tank, level sensor, coolant tank cap

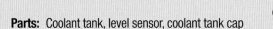

More Info: www.101projects.com/Boxster/33.htm

 **Tip:** Replace the tank when you have the transmission out

 **Performance Gain:** No more coolant in the trunk

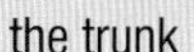 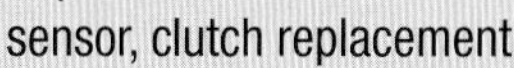 **Comp Modification:** Replace coolant level sensor, clutch replacement

Replacing the Boxster coolant tank is probably one of the top ten jobs that typically needs to be done on an older Boxster. The coolant tank is one of the worst designs I have seen ever come out of an automotive company. Six separate coolant hoses feed into the tank, with three of them internal to the tank mechanism itself. The hoses from the tank feed into an integrated manifold on the engine bulkhead that is manufactured out of plastic and is prone to breaking. In addition, the plastic tank itself often cracks with age and leaks coolant in the trunk compartment. Porsche had redesigned this part several times over the past decade, and to this day, there are still problems with the tanks.

When should you replace your tank? If your tank is looking old or yellow, or if you are finding a pool of coolant in your trunk area, then it's probably time to replace your tank. Lift up the carpet in the rear of your trunk to check. I also recommend replacing the coolant tank when it's really old, particularly if you have your transmission out for a clutch job. The hoses inside the engine compartment can be difficult to reach, and having the transmission out of the car makes a very difficult job a lot easier.

If you are losing coolant from your engine, and you're not sure where it's going, then you can perform a few relatively simple tests to check. First, get an air pressure adapter that will allow you to hook up a shop compressor to your coolant tank cap. Then, pressurize the system to about 13–15 psi. Let it sit and see if you can hear or see any coolant escaping. If the coolant is getting past the head gasket into the crankcase, it will mix with the oil, and you will be able to see that easily when you empty the oil (Photo 1). If the head gasket is leaking coolant into the cylinders, then they will begin to fill up with coolant, and you can see this when you remove the spark plugs.

The first step in replacing the tank is to drain the coolant. I recommend replacing all of the coolant if you are swapping out the tank—refer to Project 29 for complete instructions on how to empty the coolant from the car.

The most difficult part of this project is the disconnection of the existing hoses from the back of the radiator tank manifold. With the car completely assembled, it can be very difficult to reach these hoses. It is possible to reach them from inside the engine compartment, but you may not be able to get tools onto the clamps that hold the hoses. It's also possible to reach them from below, but you need to remove the lower suspension support bars and the transmission cover plate (see Project 35). Photo 2 shows the hoses that you need to disconnect from the engine compartment side of the radiator tank.

Once the hoses are disconnected, move to the rear trunk and pull back the carpet and flooring that surrounds the coolant reservoir. Remove the electrical sender plug in the bottom of the tank, and gently pull out the dipstick tube from the top of the coolant tank. Four screws hold the tank to the chassis—remove them as shown in Photo 4. Remove the oil cap and coolant tank caps. You should be able to remove the tank at this point from the car.

With the tank out of the car, transfer the coolant level sender, the large top tank seal, the bulkhead manifold/oil filler, and the three right-angle hoses to the new tank (or install new ones if you wish to replace everything with new parts). Don't reuse the spring-type clamps—use new ones or clamp-style hose clamps instead. Installation is pretty much the opposite of removal. With everything back in place, refill and bleed your cooling system as per the instructions in Project 33.

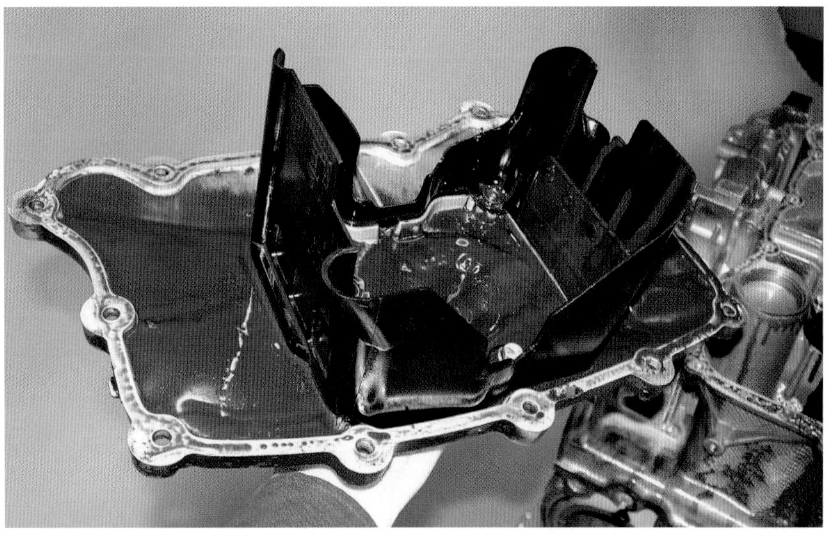

1 Shown here is the lower engine sump plate removed from an engine where coolant and oil mixed heavily. The oil will turn a light brownish color with streaks of light brown running through it. If you see this or anything similar to this when you empty your oil, then you most likely have a head gasket leak or other severe engine problem that needs to be addressed right away. When coolant mixes with engine oil in this fashion, the oil looses its ability to function as a lubricant for the engine bearings, and you can damage the crankshaft and rods.

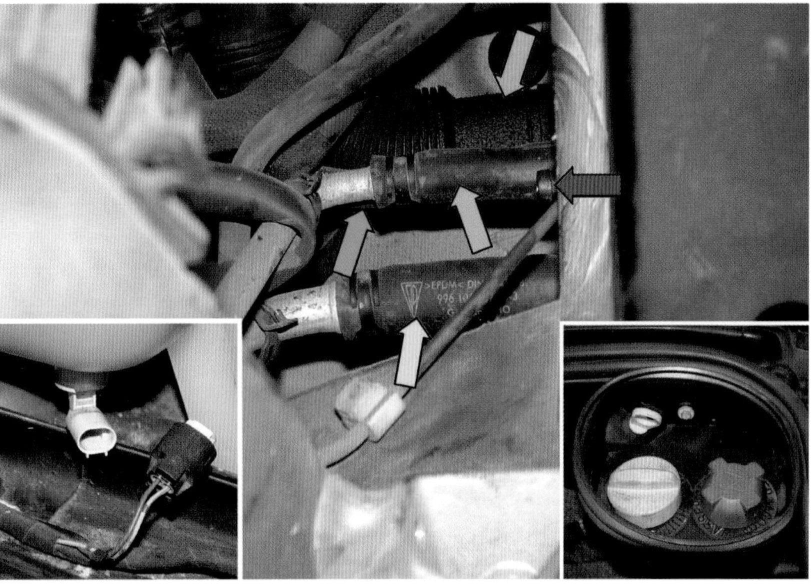

2 Here's the best photo I could take of the hoses in the engine compartment. They are so difficult to reach that it's very tough even to get a good accurate photo of them. This photo was taken with the transmission out of the car, which is indeed the best time to replace the coolant tank. The arrows point to the hoses that need to be disconnected: oil filler hose (orange), oil cooler hose (green), radiator vent hose (blue), coolant filler hose (yellow), and coolant overflow hose (shown removed, mates to the nipple shown by the red arrow). The lower left inset photo shows the coolant level sensor unplugged. The lower right inset photo shows the top of the tank.

3 If you're having difficulty reaching some of the hoses from underneath, you may be able to gain some additional access by pulling out the tank and loosening the hose clamps through the rear trunk compartment. For this photo, I was able first to disconnect the filler hose, and then I had enough room to pull the tank out to reach some of the other hoses. You can also push the DME wire harness grommet into the engine compartment and gain some additional access that way (see Photo 5 of Project 15).

4 Shown here are the screws that attach the coolant tank to the chassis. The blue arrows point to the nuts that hold the plastic manifold to the chassis. The yellow arrow points to the coolant sensor. The green arrow shows another mounting point for the bottom of the tank. In the inset photo, the red arrow points to a bolt that holds the top of the tank to the chassis, and the purple arrow shows the oil dipstick tube pulled away from the top of the tank housing.

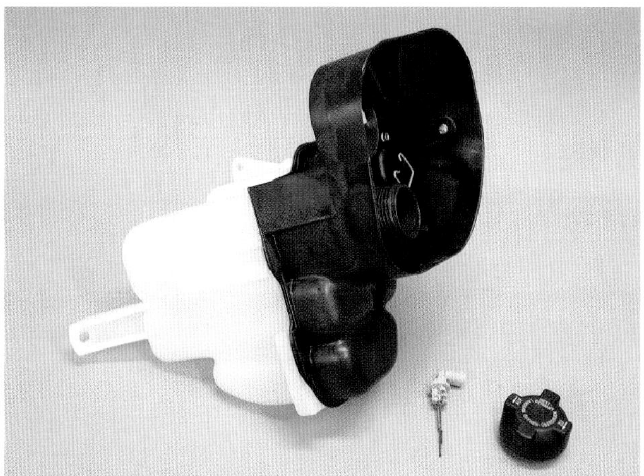

5 Shown here is the new tank, along with a brand new coolant level sender and a new expansion tank cap.

6 The oil filler tube/bulkhead manifold is one of the goofiest designs I've seen in a long time. On our project car, just as we started up the 3.4 engine transplant, coolant started spilling all over the place from a broken plastic nipple on this manifold. After staring at the puddle on the ground for several minutes, I "fixed" the design of the manifold by simply cutting a hole in the manifold and running a hose directly from the engine compartment to the bottom of the tank. This was designed to be a temporary fix until I was able to replace the entire piece, but frankly, it's worked flawlessly and is still installed in this configuration today.

PROJECT 34
Water Pump and Thermostat Replacement

 **Time / Tab / Talent:** 2 hours / $450 /

 **Tools:** Swivel socket set

 **Applicable Years:** All

 **Parts:** Water pump, thermostat, and gaskets

 **More Info:** www.101projects.com/Boxster/34.htm

 **Tip:** Install the low-temp thermostat for better performance

 **Performance Gain:** Protects your engine against overheating

 **Comp Modification:** Replace radiator hoses

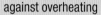

WATER

The modern water-cooled Porsches have been known to have troublesome problems with their cooling systems. Two of the principle areas of failure are the thermostat and water pump.

Begin the replacement process by jacking up the car (Project 1) and removing the lower plastic tray that covers the front part of the engine and the coolant hoses. Disconnect the lower hose that is attached to the water pump (see Photo 4), and let the coolant empty into a five-gallon or larger bucket. If you are replacing your thermostat, too, then now would be a good time to disconnect the hose attached to it as well.

The next step is to gain access to your water pump. This requires the removal of the main belt (see Project 5). You may also want to remove the right-side (passenger) seat as well, in order to give you more room to work. With the belt removed, the front of your engine should be relatively accessible. Seven bolts attach the water pump to the engine, and access to some of them may only be achieved from underneath the car. I recommend using a flex 10mm socket to get into the tight spots.

When the engine was assembled, Porsche installed the coolant manifold and the water pump together. Therefore, they use a shared gasket, which you must cut apart in order to remove it from the engine. Photo 2 shows the gasket removed from the water pump housing on the engine, and Photo 3 shows where you must clip it in order to remove it. The new gasket must also be modified prior to installation (see Photo 3). With the pump removed, check the inside bore where the water pump fits for debris or corrosion. With a wire brush, remove any corrosion or debris that may have built up there. Clean off the water pump mounting surface on the engine and install the water pump with the new gasket. Tighten down the bolts to 10 Nm (7 ft-lbs).

At this time, I also recommend that you remove the thermostat housing (located below the water pump) and replace the thermostat as well. The thermostat is a relatively cheap part that can fail quite easily, which can lead to your engine overheating. Simply disconnect the thermostat hose if you haven't already, and unbolt the thermostat from the engine. The thermostat used to be sold separately from the thermostat housing, but now Porsche and the aftermarket suppliers simply sell the whole assembly as one integrated unit.

The factory thermostat starts to open at about 187 degrees F (86 degrees C) and only fully opens at almost 210 degrees F (99 degrees C). This means that the engine needs to get very hot before it starts sending its coolant to the front radiators. For this reason, I recommend installing a low-temperature thermostat in place of the factory one. LN Engineering has developed a thermostat that starts opening at 160 degrees F (71 degrees C) and is fully open at about 180 degrees F (82 degrees C). Lower coolant temperatures translate into lower oil temperatures, and the dyno tests that LN Engineering has performed on the cars with the low-temp thermostat installed have revealed a small increase in horsepower (typically about 5 horsepower). It is my guess that Porsche designed the thermostat to open a bit later in order to help the cars run a bit hotter, which typically helps with emissions testing and the burning off of water out of the oil, which can then lead to longer oil change intervals. Installing the low-temp thermostat is a smart idea for engine longevity—it's available for about $175 from PelicanParts.com.

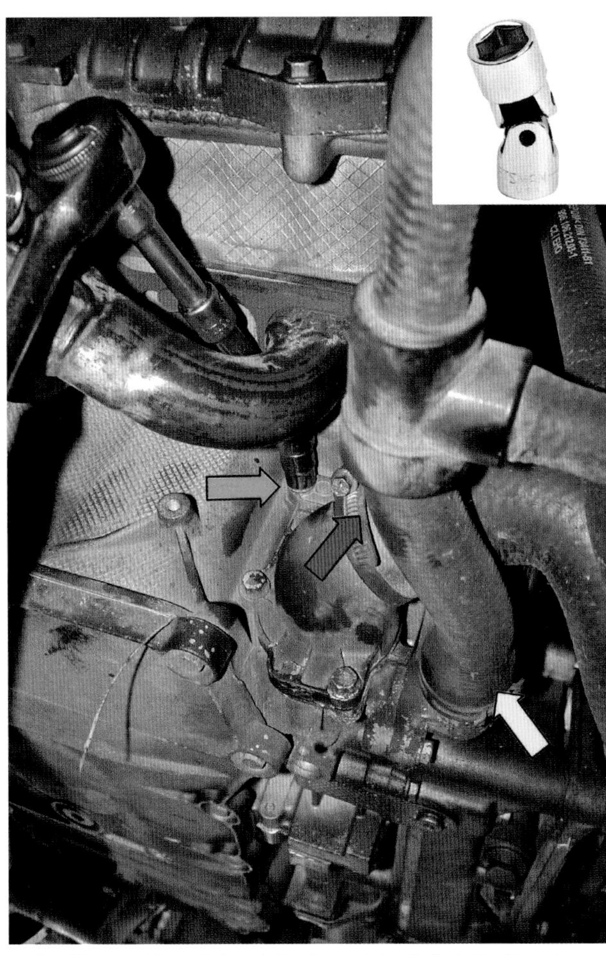

1 Disconnect the main hose to the thermostat, as indicated by the red arrow. In order to gain enough clearance to remove the thermostat, you typically need to disconnect the water pump hose shown by the yellow arrow. For the tight spaces near the thermostat, I recommend using a swivel-foot socket (green arrow and upper right inset photo).

2 Here's what the engine looks like with the water pump removed. For the 1997–2004 Boxsters, you need to cut the old metal seal in order to get it off, as part of it is still trapped in the engine off to the right (it's a dual-purpose gasket). With the new gasket properly trimmed, it should fit into place (lower left).

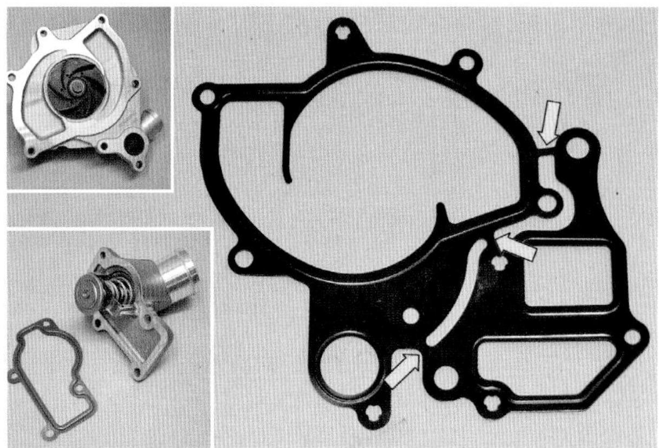

3 The water pump seal needs to be trimmed prior to installation (1997–2004 only). The part off to the right is separate from the water pump and is typically only used when rebuilding an engine. Trim the seal at the yellow marks and use the part on the left. The upper left photo shows a brand-new water pump. The lower left shows a new thermostat and seal. The newer-style Boxster thermostat is integrated into its aluminum housing.

4 The water pump is located next to the crankshaft on the right side of the car. Access to the pump is obtained through the access panel behind the seats and from below.

5 Install the new thermostat in place using a new gasket (lower left).

SECTION 5
TRANSMISSION

Projects focusing on the transmission, cluth, and axles have been combined into this section because they are all interrelated and linked together. The transmission and clutch can be a mysterious setup, leading many owners to ignore and neglect its maintenance until it's too late. This section aims to demystify the transmission, clutch, and rear axle assemblies; it also provides some upgrades and improvements for performance.

PROJECT 35
Replacing Your Automatic Transmission Fluid

 **Time / Tab / Talent:** 3 hours / $150 / 

 **Tools:** Transmission fluid pump, 17mm hex tool, 8mm hex tool, T-30 male Torx driver, infrared thermometer

 **Applicable Years:** All

 **Parts:** Automatic transmission filter, gasket kit

 **More Info:** www.101projects.com/Boxster/35.htm

Tip: Don't neglect this maintenance—transmissions are expensive to replace

 **Performance Gain:** Long-life transmission

 **Comp Modification:** Oil change

TRANSMISSION

Replacing your oil is easy. Porsche knows that this needs to be performed once about every 3,000–5,000 miles and designed the car that way. On the other hand, changing the tranny fluid is not an easy task, and you can probably bet that the previous owner of your car did not perform this task as often as they should have when they owned it.

What are the symptoms of low automatic transmission fluid? I experienced this when I purchased a car with a known transmission problem. When the car was stopped suddenly via the brakes and then the accelerator was immediately pressed, the transmission would slip, and then slam into gear, lurching the car forward. I had a strong suspicion that the transmission was low on fluid. A thorough inspection of the car showed the remnants of significant leakage of transmission fluid.

What causes this symptom with the transmission? Well, when you slam on the brakes, all of the fluid in the transmission flows to the front of the car and away from the fluid pickup, which is located toward the rear of the transmission. With the fluid at the front of the car, the transmission loses fluid for a very short while. Automatic transmissions use the fluid both as a hydraulic fluid and a coolant—they won't work if there isn't any fluid running through them. After the car has stopped and the fluid has moved back toward the pickup, the transmission began to work normally. If the transmission had the proper levels of fluid, then this condition would not occur. Needless to say, after I replaced the transmission fluid and checked the levels, the problem disappeared. The previous owner had let it run down about two quarts low (the Boxster transmission takes about nine quarts with about four quarts replaceable during each fluid change). Driving for any more time with the transmission in this state would have led to substantial damage and could have resulted in a wrecked tranny (replacement cost: $2,500 or so).

Okay, enough background on the automatic transmission. The first step in replacing your fluid is to jack up your car so that you can reach the underside of the transmission (see Project 1). It is very important that the car be level—don't jack up just the front or rear of the car, make sure that it is as level in the air as it is on the ground. The reason for this is that you will be checking the transmission fluid by removing a drain plug and checking the fluid level. If the car is not level, then you will not achieve an accurate reading. Also elevate the car with the rear tailpipe sticking way outside the entrance of your garage—you will be running the car while it's on the jack stands in order to top off the fluid.

With the car elevated in the air, you should be able to see the rear transmission pan cover (see Photo 1). You need to remove this cover and the two aluminum support bars on either side of the car. You may also have to remove the plastic cover toward the front of the car in order to remove the two aluminum support bars. Wear safety glasses when you're under the car, as you never know what small piece of dirt may fall into your eye.

The next step is to remove all of the existing fluid from the main transmission sump. There is a drain plug on the bottom of the sump that can be used to empty most of the fluid contained inside. Remove the drain plug and let the fluid flow out into a container. Your container should be able to hold at least three gallons (about 12 liters) of fluid. Once the fluid is empty, replace the drain plug. This plug should be tightened to 40 Nm (29 ft-lb).

Now you will proceed to remove the sump from the bottom of the transmission. You need to remove the sump so that you can replace the transmission filter, clean the sump magnet, and also remove the extra fluid that may be trapped inside. You remove the sump by removing each of the small Torx bolts that attach it to the bottom of the transmission. Once those are out, you should be able simply to pull on the sump cover and it should fall off. Be aware that there will still be some transmission fluid in the sump that can spill out if you're not careful.

Plastic cat litter boxes make excellent containers for catching fluid in these types of situations. They are wide and large enough to prevent you from making quite a mess on your garage floor. Turn your attention now to the sump and clean it out. Then, remove the transmission filter from the bottom of the transmission.

What type of fluid do you use in your automatic transmission? The Boxster requires a special type of fluid that you cannot easily find in most auto parts stores. The Porsche part number for the transmission fluid is 999-917-545-00, but is almost $35 a liter. The Boxster also can use off-the-shelf Esso LT 71141, or Pentosin ATF-1, both available along with gasket/filter kits from PelicanParts.com. I would avoid using any other type of fluid in your transmission. Also, use the same fluid for the entire replacement process—mixing and matching different types of transmission fluid can cause your transmission to fail.

With the new filter in place, you will now reinstall the lower sump. No need to fill it with fluid—simply bolt it up into place. Torque each bolt to 11 Nm (8 ft-lb), and use a crisscross pattern as shown in Photo 6. Now it's time to fill the sump with fluid. Using a hand pump attached to the bottle of transmission fluid, thread the hose up into the filler hole and through one of the access holes in the side of the filler baffle (Photo 5). Fill up the transmission sump until fluid starts to significantly run out of the filler hole. A few drips can be expected when the fluid runs down the side of the hose—when the fluid level is at the top of the filler, it will start to exit the filler hole rapidly. Replace the filler plug and tighten it hand-tight.

At this point, you are ready to start the car. Keep in mind that the transmission fluid can only be checked when the transmission temperature is within a semi-narrow range. This temperature range is 85–100 degrees F (30–40 degrees C). You will need to start the car and let it warm up before you can check the levels. Depending upon the outside temperature, it may take up to 45 minutes for it to reach this temperature. Check the temperature of the fluid by using one of those handy infrared laser thermometers. Years ago, these used to cost thousands of dollars, but nowadays, you can pick one up for about $50.

You will be running the car while it is up and on jack stands. This can be dangerous if the car is not secure on the jack stands—check them again before you continue. You will also be running the car for an extended length of time while it warms up and you will need to make sure that you perform this outside (on level ground), or funnel the exhaust gases out of the tailpipe and out of your garage. I used a long, flexible aluminum tube that I purchased from the hardware store that is typically used for venting gas dryers out to the atmosphere (see Photo 8). If you clamp this tightly to the end of your tailpipe and run the other end out of your garage with the garage door open, you should be able to safely have the car idle inside the garage. Also make sure that you use an electronic carbon monoxide monitor inside your garage (also available from most hardware stores) as an added measure for safety.

Climb into the car, place your foot on the brake, and start it. If you hear anything amiss, or encounter any unusual problems, then shut off the car immediately. It should start and idle normally. You will need to let the transmission warm up until it is in the operating range indicated above. Note that this will make the bottom of the sump feel warm to the touch, not hot. Use your infrared thermometer to periodically check the temperature. Again, it should take 10–45 minutes depending upon the outside temperature to heat the transmission to this level, if the car is simply idling.

With the car at the proper temperature, remove the filler plug, and begin filling the transmission again. It's okay to use your finger to gently stick the hose attached to your pump up inside the transmission. At this time, the fluid should be warm to the touch. But be careful not to burn yourself on the catalytic converters, headers, or the muffler that is merely inches away. When the fluid begins to empty out of the filler hole, replace the filler plug again, and tighten it hand-tight.

Now, sit inside the car, apply the brake pedal, and slowly shift the transmission through reverse, and first and second gear, using the manual shift lever. Leave the car in each gear for about 10 seconds. Repeat this twice, move underneath the car again, and remove the fill plug from the side of the transmission. With the engine still running, top off the transmission once more until fluid comes out of the fill hole. Replace the fill plug, using a new sealing O-ring. This plug should be torqued to 80 Nm (59 ft-lb).

That's about all there is to it. When you've topped off the fluid, lower the car down off of the jack stands and take it for a short drive. If all is well, you shouldn't notice any difference in performance or operation. If you were having problems with the transmission slamming into gear, then these issues should be gone by now. One last thing to note: The automatic transmission also has a built-in differential that requires standard gear oil. Check and fill your gear oil as per the instructions in Project 38.

1 In order to gain access to the bottom transmission sump, you will need to remove the rear transmission pan cover and the aluminum support bars on either side. The pan cover is held on with two screws in the rear (green arrows) and two more up front (yellow arrow) and also shares some screws with the aluminum support bars (red arrows). Once the cover and bars are removed, then you will need to drop down the rear sway bar. Simply remove the bolts that fasten the sway bar and bushing to the chassis (blue arrows in inset photo).

2 I recommend that you start the draining process only when the car is cold. When the car is warm, a lot of the transmission fluid will be trapped within the transmission itself. When the car is cold, almost all of the transmission fluid has seeped out and is trapped in the lower sump. Note that this is opposite from the procedure for changing the oil—where you should empty it when the engine is hot. That is because the engine oil is thinnest and flows best when it's hot. The transmission fluid has a totally different viscosity. Working on the car when it's cold also assures that you will not be burned by hot exhaust, transmission, or engine parts. The green arrow shows the transmission filler plug, and the inset photo shows the 8mm hex socket required to remove the transmission drain plug.

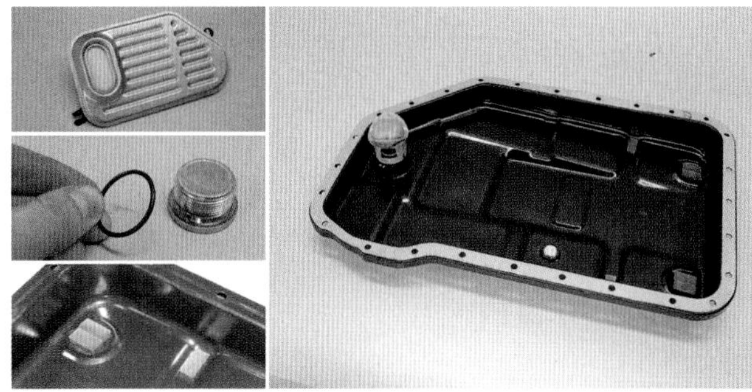

3 Using a lint-free cloth, carefully wipe down the inside of the sump (I used lint-free KimWipes, available from PelicanParts.com). You want to use a lint-free cloth, because tiny cloth fibers left in your transmission sump can clog the transmission and filter. The sump needs to be clean, spotless, and look brand-new, as shown on the right. Make sure that you remove any remaining gasket material from the edge of the sump cover. A new transmission sump gasket has been lined up with the holes, and the assembly is ready for installation back onto the transmission. In the upper left, the new transmission filter is displayed. You should always use a new O-ring on the transmission filler plug, as shown in the middle left photo. Pay close attention to the magnet in the bottom of the sump (shown on the lower left). You should be able simply to pluck this magnet from the bottom of the sump and clean it.

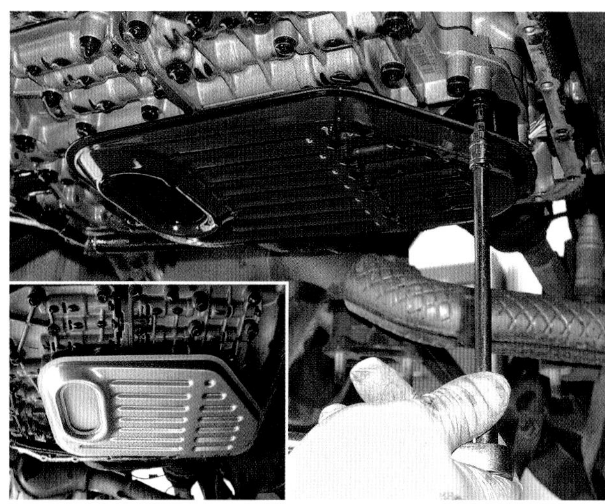

4 The transmission fluid filter is a large canister that is attached to the bottom of the transmission and needs to be removed and replaced. Remove the bolts that attach it to the bottom of the transmission and carefully pull off the filter. Discard it in the trash. Check the mounting surfaces where the sumps attach to the transmission, and remove any excess gasket material that may have been left there. When you reinstall the filter into the transmission, use the same bolts that you just removed. These bolts should be torqued to a very light 6 Nm (4.5 ft-lb). The inset photo shows the new filter installed in place.

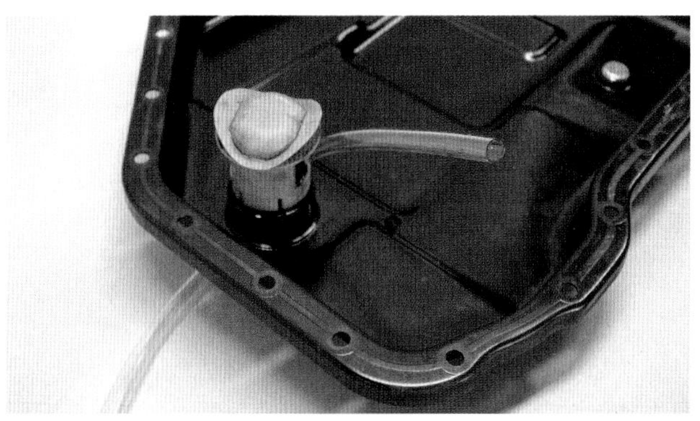

5 Getting the hose into the sump area so that you can fill the transmission can be a bit tricky if you're not aware of where the hose is supposed to go. This photo shows the hose threaded up the bottom of the filler hole and sticking out into the transmission sump. When the sump is installed back onto the transmission, you will need to feed the hose up the filler hole and through the openings in this baffle attachment.

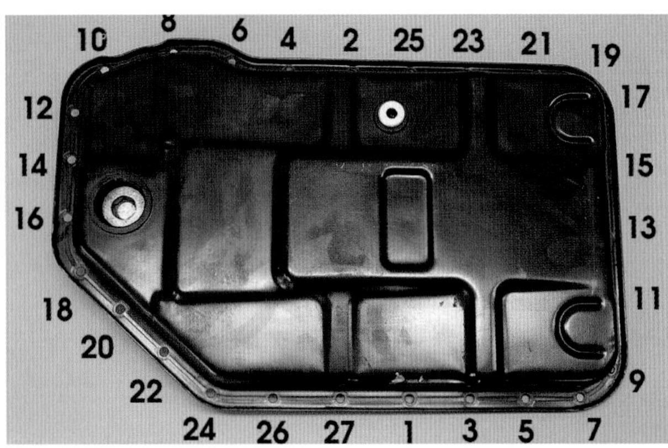

6 With the sump installed, tighten the bolts according to the following pattern. These bolts require very little torque—only 11 Nm (8 ft-lbs). Be sure to clean off any dirt or debris that may be on the screws prior to reinstalling them.

8 Carbon monoxide is dangerous, and although today's modern cars don't emit too much of it, you can still kill off some brain cells by breathing it in. Play it safe and route the exhaust from your tailpipe out of your garage area, or perform the job outdoors on level ground. Use a standard dryer vent hose and plug the sides of the tailpipe if you happen to feel exhaust escaping.

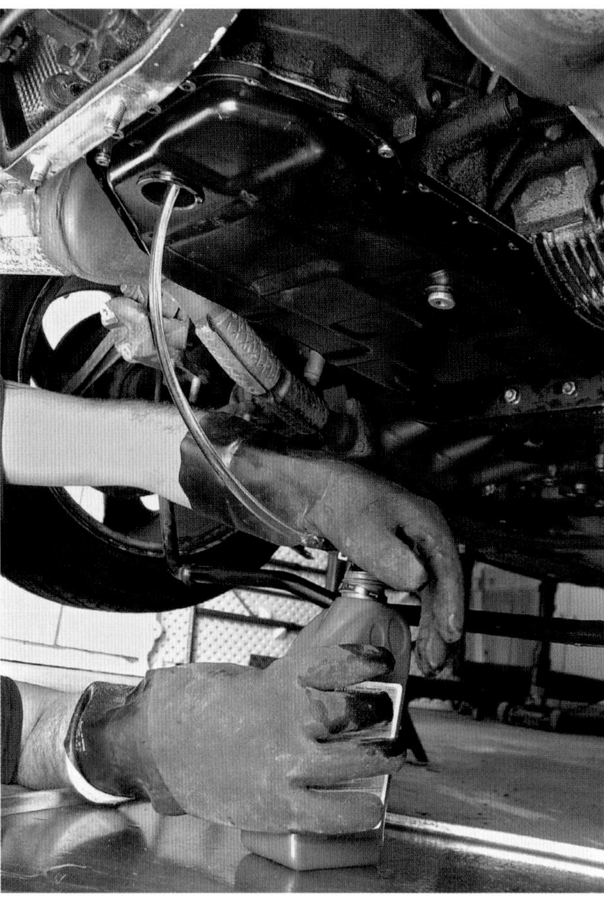

7 You will need to use a transmission fluid pump, which you can find at almost any local auto parts store, in order to fill the sump. The pump works just like a liquid soap pump in your bathroom. The transmission fluid should be pumped into the bottom of the sump through the transmission fill hole. Remove the plug, place one end of the pump into a bottle of transmission fluid, and start pumping. Pump fluid into the filler hole until fluid begins to run out rapidly. Clean up the small spill (be sure to use a large oil drip tray during this process), then replace the fill plug, only slightly tighter than hand-tight (you will be removing it again shortly when you recheck the levels).

9 The infrared thermometer is one of those whiz-bang devices that never ceases to amaze me. Years ago, these used to cost thousands of dollars, but nowadays, you can pick one up for a mere $50. Monitor the temperature of the transmission sump by pointing the thermometer at the bottom of the metal sump in the center. Don't take the measurements from the sides, as the catalytic converter is nearby and will tend to heat the sump a bit more in that area, leading to false readings.

PROJECT 36
Replacing Transmission Mounts

 **Time / Tab / Talent:** 2 hours / $300 / 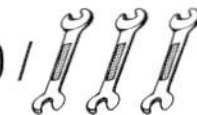

 **Tools:** Torx socket set

 **Applicable Years:** All

 **Parts:** Pair of transmission mounts

 **More Info:** www.101projects.com/Boxster/36.htm

Tip: Use the 993 mounts and save some money

 **Performance Gain:** Reduced drivetrain vibration

 **Comp Modification:** Replace front engine mount

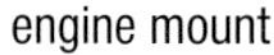

Some of the most common parts to deteriorate on older cars are the engine and transmission mounts. After many years, the rubber that is contained within the mounts becomes old and brittle and doesn't perform a good job of isolating the drivetrain from the rest of the chassis. Old, worn-out motor and transmission mounts can cause shifting problems because the drivetrain is no longer firmly held in its position. A visible sign that the transmission mounts need replacing is the appearance of cracks in the rubber of the mounts. The rubber will deteriorate over the years and need to be replaced, even if the car has relatively few miles on it. These mounts are also hydraulic, so if you see fluid leaking out of them, then that is also a sure-fire way to know that they have failed.

The transmission mounts are fairly easy to replace. Replace them one at a time (remove and replace on one side and then remove and replace on the other side). Begin by jacking up your car and placing it on jack stands (Project 1). Remove the pan that covers the transmission (Project 35). Now, place a jack under the transmission to support the weight (Photo 1). Then, carefully remove the transmission mount nuts from under the car (Photo 2). You may have to use some swivel extensions to access the nuts, as the exhaust components will be slightly in your way and you will have to hold the bolts from turning at the top of the mount.

With the two bolts disconnected from the chassis, you can then remove the two bolts that hold the mount bracket to the transmission (Photo 2). These bolts thread directly into bosses on the transmission. With the bolts removed, you should simply be able to pull the mount off of the car. Installation of the new mount is as simple as bolting it back in place.

Replacement Boxster transmission mounts include the triangle-shaped bracket. At about $250 each, they're pretty expensive. While performing the installation of the Porsche 996 engine into the Boxster (see Project 11), I discovered that the engine mounts from the 993 are functionally equivalent and are sold without the triangle bracket for about one-half the cost of the Boxster mounts. You will have to carefully remove your old triangle bracket off of your old mount and install it on the new one if you decide to go this route. The stock 993 transmission mount part number is 993-375-049-05.

At the same time that you're replacing your transmission mounts, I recommend replacing the front motor mount (Project 10). This will ensure that your entire drivetrain is stiff and firm at all times.

1 With the car raised up on jack stands, take your floor jack and support the transmission from underneath. Just push up very slightly on the bottom of the transmission so that you can support the weight of the drivetrain when you disconnect one of the transmission mounts.

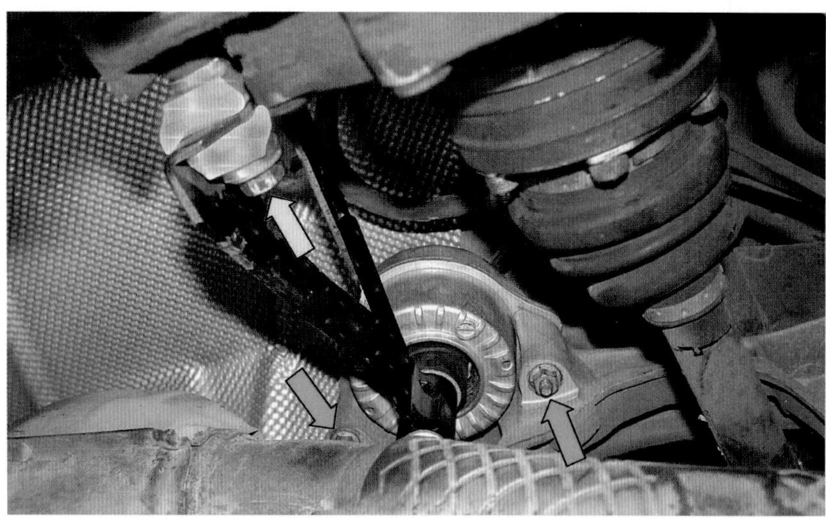

2 With the transmission supported by your floor jack, carefully remove the nuts that attach the mounts to the chassis (green arrow). You will also have to hold the bolt head on the opposite/top side of the mount using a wrench. The yellow arrow shows the bolts that hold the triangle bracket to the transmission.

3 Here's a side view of the triangle bracket. The two orange arrows show the two bolts that attach the bracket to the transmission.

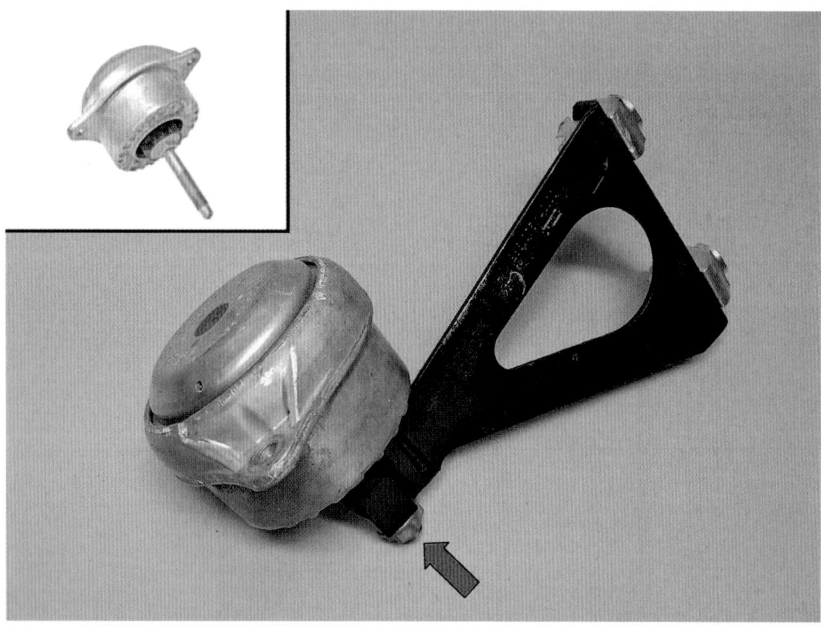

4 Here's a photo of the stock Boxster transmission mount. The Porsche 993 transmission mount is nearly the same, but minus the triangle bracket (inset). If you wish to use the 993 ones instead, then remove the nut that attaches the old mounts to the triangle bracket and move the bracket to the new 993 mount.

PROJECT 37
Transmission Removal

Time / Tab / Talent: 3 hours / $0 /

Tools: Torx socket set, jack, and jackstands

Applicable Years: All

Parts: None

More Info: www.101projects.com/Boxster/37.htm

Tip: Have a buddy help you when you're ready to drop the unit

Performance Gain: Ability to access engine

Comp Modification: Clutch replacement, replace transmission mounts

One really nice feature of working on the Boxster is that you can drop the transmission out of the car without dropping the entire engine. This allows the potential for you to complete many different projects that would have taken a lot more time and had been a lot more difficult to perform. As a result of this design, a clutch job on the Boxster is a fairly straightforward task and is not too terribly daunting. The first step of course, is to remove the transmission from the car. Follow the list of steps below:

- Jack up the car (see Project 1).
- Remove the lower plastic covers that protect the front part of the engine.
- Remove the two diagonal aluminum braces under the transmission and the aluminum transmission cover (see Project 35).
- Disconnect and remove the rear sway bar (see Project 11).
- Remove the rear muffler (see Project 46) and the muffler heat shield (see Photo 1).
- Remove the reinforcement bracket and muffler bracket (see Photo 2).
- Disconnect the axles from the transmission (see Project 41). Tie them up out of the way so that they don't interfere when you drop the transmission.
- Disconnect the backup lamp switch on the transmission (see Photo 3 of Project 45).
- Disconnect the clutch slave cylinder from the side of the transmission (see Project 45).
- Disconnect the hydraulic line bracket from the transmission if there is one. Suspend the slave cylinder from the chassis so that it won't hang from the hydraulic fluid line.
- Disconnect the shifter cables (see Photo 3). Very early cars have a slightly different cable setup that is attached with multiple cotter pins that need to be removed.
- Install a jack stand below the engine (see Photo 5 and 6).
- Support the weight of the transmission using the floor jack (see Photo 6).
- Disconnect and remove transmission mounts from both chassis and transmission (see Project 36).
- Disconnect, remove, and label each bolt that holds the engine and transmission together using Photo 4 as a guide. It's very important that you make sure you don't mix up the hardware and where it goes—use a plastic storage bag for each bolt and label it with the letter corresponding to Photo 4. When I first removed the transmission, I mistakenly mixed up all the hardware, and it took nearly two hours of looking at the Porsche factory diagrams to figure out what bolt went where.
- Using a buddy, slide the transmission back and lower to the ground.

The transmission weighs more than 100 pounds, so make sure that you are prepared when you pull it out and lower it. I recommend placing the transmission on a rolling furniture cart so that you can easily move it around and work on it.

Installation is pretty much the reverse of disassembly. See Project 45 for the proper installation of the slave cylinder. When attaching the transmission to the engine, tighten all of the M12 bolts down to 63 ft-lbs (85 Nm) and all of the M10 fasteners down to 33 ft-lbs (45 Nm).

The procedure is a bit more complicated for removal of the automatic transmission. You need to order some special tools in order to secure the torque converter when separating the transmission from the engine. You also need to disconnect the vacuum lines, the shift selector mechanism, and the coolant lines prior to removal. Due to space limitations here, I am not able to go over all of the details, but fortunately, most automatic transmissions do not need to be removed very often. The Bentley manual has a detailed section on the automatic transmission removal process.

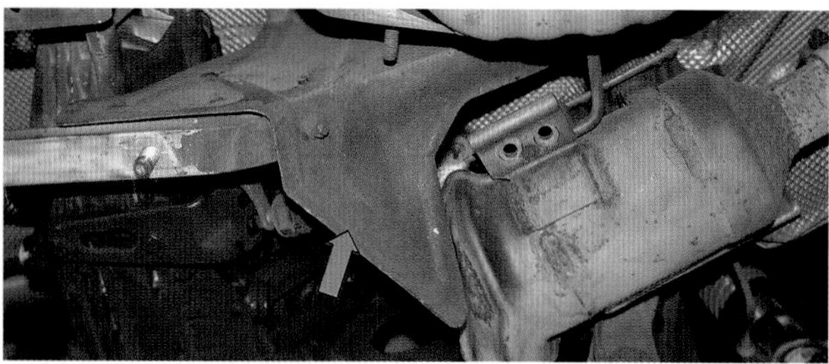

1 Remove the right-side heat shield from the support bracket. Do not forget to reinstall this when you put the transmission back into the car, as it protects the shifter cables and mechanism from the extreme heat of the exhaust system.

2 With the muffler removed from the car, remove the aluminum reinforcement bar from underneath the car (attached with bolts indicated by green arrows). Detach the muffler support bracket from the end of the transmission (orange arrow).

3 This photo shows the process of disconnecting the shifter cables. Using two screwdrivers placed on either side of the ball, pull up and snap each shifter cable end (orange arrow) off of its ball mount (yellow arrows). Detach the shifter cable sheath from its bracket by removing the small spring clips and prying them out of their bracket (inset photo, upper left). Inspect the inside of the cables carefully, as you may find that they are cracked and need replacement (red arrow). Unfortunately, at this time, you cannot replace just the bushing in this cable, but only the cable itself. I am currently working on having repair kits made for these cables, however—check the website link at the beginning of this project for details.

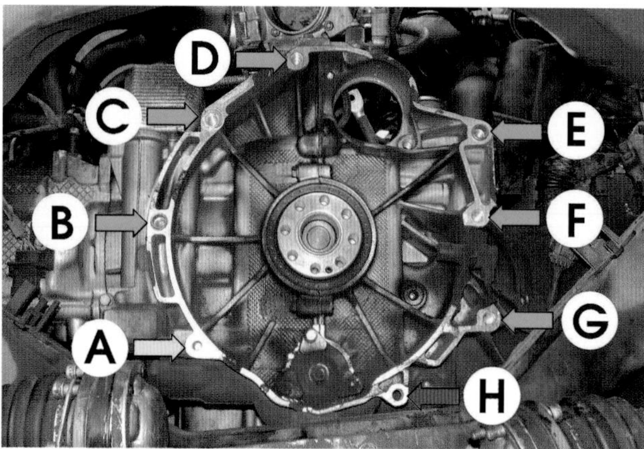

4 This photo of the engine with the transmission removed shows location and type of the fasteners that attach the transmission. The location and orientation of the hardware can be very confusing, and it's not well documented in the Porsche factory diagrams, so I've provided a legend with part numbers for all Boxsters 1997–2008 here: **A:** M10×40mm triplesquare (999-073-118-09). **B:** M12×1.5×100mm (999-072-010-09). **C:** M12×1.5×100mm (999-072-010-09) with 15×28×3.5 washer (N-905-028-02). **D/G:** M12×1.5×70mm (999-072-008-09). **E/F:** M12×1.5×90mm (999-072-009-09). **H:** M10 hex nut (900-377-011-09) attached to M10×30mm stud in transmission case (999-218-088-09).

5 This photo shows the bottom of the transmission as we are pulling it away from the engine. The engine weight is supported by a jack stand (white arrow). Place the jack stand on the boss of the engine case where the green arrow is pointing. As you pull away the transmission from the engine, you will see a small gap begin to appear (yellow arrow). This indicates that you are proceeding correctly and the transmission is beginning to come out.

6 Although you can do it yourself, I recommend having a transmission-drop buddy around to help you. Using your jack, carefully line up the bottom of the jack with the bottom of the transmission as shown. If you position it just right, you will be able to balance the transmission perfectly on the jack. Don't put your arms, legs, or face underneath the transmission as you are pulling it out—once the mainshaft disconnects from the center of the clutch, it will become really wobbly on your jack. Lower it to the floor carefully and pull it out from under the car. Also useful is a transmission jack made specifically for this purpose.

PROJECT 38
Replacing Transmission Fluid

 **Time / Tab / Talent:** 1 hour / $25 /

 **Tools:** 16mm triple-square tool, 17mm hex socket (five-speed), 10mm hex socket (six-speed)

 **Applicable Years:** All

 **Parts:** Transmission fluid

 **More Info:** www.101projects.com/Boxster/38.htm

 **Tip:** Make sure that you have a 4-quart drip pan and plenty of paper towels

 **Performance Gain:** Longer life for your transmission

 **Comp Modification:** Use Swepco 201 transmission fluid for better shifting

One of the easiest tasks to perform on your manual transmission Boxster is to change the transmission oil. The Boxster transmission is what is known as a transaxle. It includes all the standard components of a normal transmission, plus an integrated differential. This design is possible because of the mid-engine design of the Boxster. The transaxle design is more compact and theoretically lighter in weight since you don't need a dedicated differential.

The differential and the transmission both share the same lubricating fluid. It's very important to make sure that the fluid in your transmission is at the proper level, otherwise your transmission will experience significant wear. The synchro rings and sliders all depend on a slick surface in order to match speeds when shifting. If your transmission is low on oil, the wear on these components will accelerate significantly. In addition, shifting the car will be more difficult. One of the first things that you should check with a Boxster that is having problems shifting is the level of the transmission oil. Keeping the differential and all the associated gears well lubricated should also help increase your fuel mileage.

The transmission oil also helps to keep temperatures down inside your transmission. The engine is one of the primary sources of heat for the transmission as it conducts and radiates through and around the points where the engine and transmission are mounted. The transmission also creates heat itself as the gears and synchros turn within its case. Keeping the transmission fluid at its proper level helps to mitigate heat problems. Having a large reservoir of oil to spread the heat throughout the transmission helps to keep temperatures down. On some of the higher-performance Porsche transmissions, there is even an external transmission cooler that operates similar to the engine cooler.

I recommend that your transmission fluid be changed every 30,000 miles or about once every two years. This number is a rough estimate and may vary depending upon your use of your Boxster (track versus street). There are many moving parts in the transmission, and they have a tendency to drop small microscopic metal particles into the oil. Specifically, the synchro rings wear down slowly over time, each time you shift. While the transmission bearings are not as sensitive to oil contaminants as the engine bearings, they can still exhibit wear from these particles in the oil.

The Boxster transmissions have two plugs for filling and emptying the transmission oil, located on the side and the bottom of the case. The five-speed transmission requires a 17mm hex socket to remove the filler plug and a 16mm triple-square anti-tamper socket (Hazet 2567-16) to drain the fluid. Both are available in the online catalog at PelicanParts.com. The six-speed plugs are a bit more generic—a 10mm hex socket is all that is required to remove both the drain plug and the filler plug.

The first step in checking or filling your transmission is to gain access to the plugs. Jack up all four corners of the car (Project 1), making sure that the car is perfectly level with respect to the ground. Then remove the front plastic engine covers, the lower diagonal aluminum braces, and the metal transmission cover (Project 35).

If you are simply checking the level of oil in your transmission, start by removing the filler plug on the side of the transmission. This is the plug that you add fluid to. For the five-speed transmission, take a large paper clip bent at a right angle, stick it inside the hole pointing toward the ground, and measure the fluid level on the paper clip. This "mini-dipstick" should register transmission fluid at about 11mm below the lowest edge of the filler hole. Make sure you do this when the car is cold and parked on level ground. If the level is lower than 11mm, then you will need to add some fluid. For the six-speed transmissions, it's a bit easier. Simply stick your finger in the hole and see if you can feel fluid at the bottom level of the hole. If you can feel the fluid level with your finger, then your fluid level is about right or perhaps will need only a little topping off.

If you cannot feel the fluid level, then you will need to add transmission oil to the case. If you are planning on changing the oil, then remove the plug on the bottom of the transmission case. It's a wise idea to try to empty the transmission oil when the car is warm, as this will make the oil more viscous and it will flow out easier. Make sure that you have a drain pan capable of handling at least four quarts of transmission oil. Check the fluid in the pan to see if you see any unusual metal pieces, or grit in the oil. The five-speed transmission holds about 2.25 liters (2.4 quarts), and the six-speed transmission holds 2.8 liters (3.0 quarts).

While the fluid is emptying out, you can use this time to clean out the drain and filler plugs. The bottom drain plug should have an integrated magnet in it that traps metal debris. Using a cotton swab or a paper towel, carefully clean out all of the black debris and particles that may have found their way in there.

Replace the bottom plug on the transmission, but don't tighten it too tightly (18 ft-lbs, or 25 Nm, maximum). These plugs do not have a tendency to leak (transmission oil is thicker than engine oil). If it does leak later on, you can always tighten it a little more. Now, add transmission oil to the case. The best method for this is with a hand-operated oil pump. These are available from most auto parts stores and attach to the top of the plastic transmission oil bottle. They work very similar to the liquid soap dispensers you find in most bathrooms. Pump the transmission case full of fluid until it just starts to run out the filler hole. Replace the filler plug and clean up the few drips that might have run out of the hole. Tighten down the filler plug in a similar manner to the drain plug.

The automatic transmission cars also have a differential built-in to the transaxle. This differential uses the same type of fluid as the manual transmission and must be checked and filled in addition to the automatic transmission fluid. On the automatic cars, there is no drain plug, however, so the gear oil must be drained by loosening the outer differential cover (see Project 39 and Photo 5). Or, you can possibly get around this by inserting a fluid vacuum pump into the fluid fill hole and sucking out all of the old fluid. You top off the fluid and fill the differential in a similar manner to the six-speed transmission. Simply unscrew the plug and fill until the fluid starts flowing out of the hole. The automatic transmission uses the same differential fluid as the manual transmissions and takes about 0.8 liter (0.85 quart). Tighten up the drain plug to 22 ft-lb (30 Nm).

In many cases, generic transmission gear oil that meets or exceeds SAE 75W-90 will suffice perfectly fine. Also very effective are the Porsche factory lubricants (typically manufactured by Shell Oil) or Mobil Delvac Synthetic Gear Oil 75W-90. In addition, if you have a limited slip differential (LSD), be sure that you get transmission fluid that is appropriate—using a fluid that is too slippery can reduce the torque bias effects of the differential and make it less effective at distributing torque (see Project 39).

1 This photo shows a typical five-speed Boxster transmission that has been removed from the car. You need a special hex socket in order to remove the filler plug located on the side (17mm for the five-speed and 10mm for the six-speed). The inset photo shows the 17mm hex socket tool along with the special 16mm triple-square anti-tamper drain plug removal tool required for the five-speed transmission. The six-speed requires only a 10mm hex socket. The lower inset photo shows the transmission being filled using a hand pump.

2 Here's a photo of the five-speed transmission from my Boxster being reinstalled. With all of the exhaust components out of the way, it shows a clear view of where the drain plug is located in relation to the rest of the transmission (yellow arrow). The inset photo shows a close-up of the wacky plug that requires the triple-square removal tool. I'm not sure what the motivation was for Porsche to use such a specialized plug here, but it's available at PelicanParts.com.

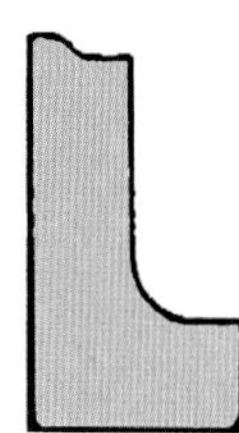

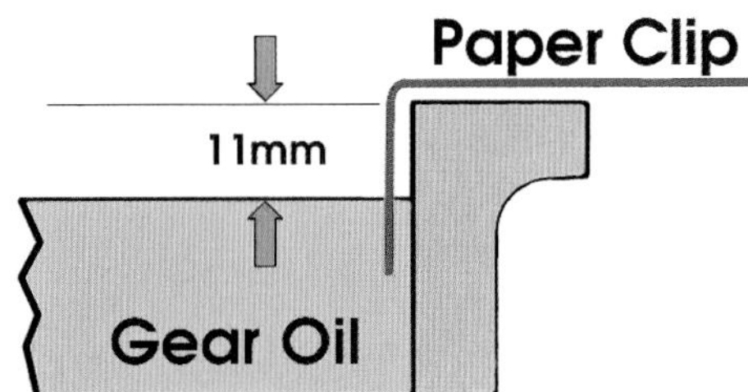

3 The five-speed transmission should be filled approximately 11mm below the bottom edge of the fill plug in the side of the transmission. Use a paper clip as a mini-dipstick to measure the level inside the transmission, as shown here in this diagram.

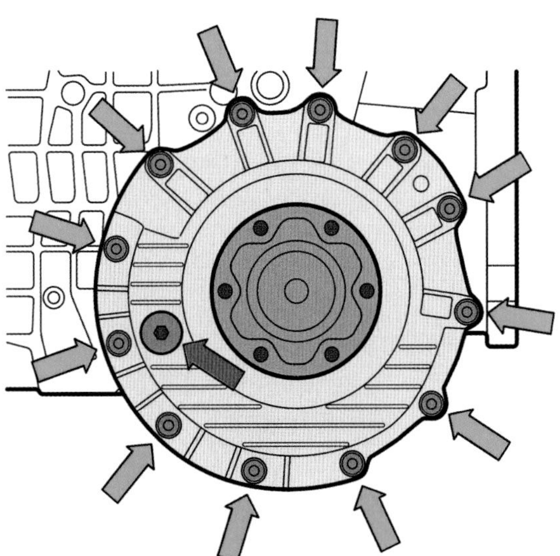

4 Shown here is the side of the automatic, Tiptronic transmission for the Boxster. The green arrows point to the differential cover bolts that need to be removed in order to loosen the cover and drain the differential gear oil. If you can't empty the differential by simply loosening the cover bolts, then you need to remove the center bolt and pull out the stub axle. The red arrow points to the fill plug. Top off the fluid to the edge of the bottom of the fill plug, just like on the six-speed transmission.

PROJECT 39

Limited Slip Differential/Carrier Bearings & Seals

 **Time / Tab / Talent:** 8 hours / $2,500 / 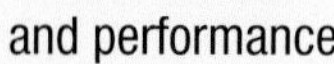

 **Tools:** Torx set, slide hammer, gear puller

 **Applicable Years:** All

 **Parts:** LSD, differential carrier bearings, seals

 **More Info:** www.101projects.com/Boxster/39.htm

 **Tip:** It's best to perform this installation with the transmission out of the car, during a clutch job

 **Performance Gain:** Better traction and performance

 **Comp Modification:** Clutch replacement

While there certainly isn't enough space in this book to cover a complete transmission rebuild, there are a few tasks that can be performed to upgrade and restore the differential portion of your transmission.

Transmission Internals: If your transmission is leaking from the driveshaft area, your differential seals are probably shot. The photo array in this project shows you how to pull your axles and replace these seals. At the same time, you can replace your differential carrier bearings. These are the bearings that support the output flanges in the transmission. Sometimes when you have a grinding noise or high-pitched whine that you cannot locate, it can be your differential carrier bearings. Often when you've replaced your wheel bearings (Project 40) and your CV joints (Project 41) and you still have a whining noise, it's the carrier bearings that are worn.

The best time to perform this work on your transmission is when you have it out of the car for a clutch job or engine work. You can perform these tasks with the transmission still installed in the car, but it makes life much more difficult if you do so.

When you install a new differential into your transmission, you need to make sure that you have the proper shims for the differential carrier bearings. In 1999, there was a change from two 46mm inner diameter differential bearings to one 46mm and one 50mm. When you install your new differential, you will need to provide a measurement to the shop that provided the differential so that they can provide you with the appropriate shim set.

Limited Slip Differentials (LSD): Gears in the differential allow the axles to rotate at different speeds, but supply torque (rotational force) to each wheel equally. If one wheel is on ice and another wheel is mounted firmly on pavement, the wheel on ice will spin at twice the speed of the ring gear, while the wheel on the ground will not spin at all. Each wheel gets the same amount of torque, and since the wheel on the ice requires very little torque to spin, the wheel on the ground also receives very little torque. Likewise, in performance driving, when turning around a corner, the weight shift due to cornering forces may increase or reduce the effective weight placed on each drive wheel. If, for example, during cornering, the inside drive wheel comes completely off the ground (unlikely, but let's assume it does for demonstration purposes), then the situation becomes very similar to the case where one wheel was on ice and the other was on the ground. The differential will supply less torque (power) to the outside wheel as the inside wheel begins to slip. This is the primary argument for using a limited slip differential on the track. It's important to note that under normal, everyday street driving, you will almost never encounter this situation. Thus, the installation of an LSD is often overkill for street-only cars.

An LSD contains small plates inside called clutches that limit and constrain the movement of the side gears. Springs or spring plates inside the LSD force the gears outward against the clutch plates, which in turn forces them outward against the differential housing. The friction between the plates causes the side gears and housing to rotate at the same speed. However, the springs and clutch plates are not strong enough to prevent normal differential rotation of the wheels on curves. When one wheel loses traction, the clutches will limit the "slip" and provide some additional torque to the non-spinning wheel. The amount of torque provided is determined by the clutch plates and the springs and is called the torque bias.

Torque bias indicates the ratio of the torque that can be transmitted to the high-torque (high-grip or ground) axle, divided by the low-torque (low-grip or ice) axle. A standard open differential often has a built-in torque bias ratio of about 1 to 1.3. A limited slip differential can provide almost any torque-bias level depending upon the arrangement of the clutch discs and strength of the springs inside. Stronger springs means a higher torque bias.

A torque bias of about 1.4 (40 percent) is best suitable for mid-performance street cars that will inhabit the occasional autocross or cars that will be driven on the track with stock engines and suspension. A more aggressive bias of 1.6 (60 percent) is best for modified street/track cars that have stiffer suspension and perhaps an upgraded or larger engine. Track-only cars that are not going to see any street time often run LSDs with torque bias levels of 1.8 (80 percent).

Clutch-type LSDs provide excellent lock-up on both acceleration and deceleration, and the units can be customized by changing the sequence of the internal clutch plates and springs. Differential lock-up on deceleration allows for late braking and very aggressive driving into high-speed turns.

You also need to make sure that you fill your transmission with fluid that is compatible with your differential. Typically a manufacturer will have some recommendations for transmission gear oil that works well with their particular differential. If you use oil that is too slippery, you may reduce your torque bias and render the LSD less effective. If you use oil that is not slippery enough, you may increase the bias and encourage premature wear of the clutch discs inside of the LSD.

As stated previously, limited slip differentials are not necessarily ideal for street driving. The clutch-pack limited slip unit can have a nasty habit of locking up the rear differential at inopportune times, like when you are cornering a road in the rain or on slick surfaces like ice. The reason for this is that sometimes these surfaces don't provide enough friction to provide for the normal differential action that allows slip between the two wheels. Limited slip differentials also have other drawbacks. They tend to be noisier than open differentials, the clutch discs wear out because they are friction components, you need to use special transmission lubricants, tire wear is increased, and overall fuel economy is reduced. They also exhibit a slight time lag between when the clutch springs compress and when the torque is transferred. For these reasons, I primarily recommend that people avoid traditional limited slip differentials in street cars.

If you're looking for an alternative to an LSD for your street car, then I recommend looking at what is known as a torque biasing differential (TSB). These are differentials that are similar to conventional open differentials, but can lock up if a torque imbalance occurs. Through a complex arrangement of gears, the TSB units provide some biasing of torque toward an unloaded axle, but only if that particular axle remains planted firmly on the ground. TSB differentials are a good choice for street cars because they act mostly like an open differential, except when cornering begins to skew the traction between both wheels. TSB units, such as the differentials manufactured by Quaife, only provide lock-up on acceleration though, which makes these units better suited for slower-speed turns like you would find during an autocross. Using a high-bias clutch-type LSD in an autocross would likely cause a significant amount of unwanted understeer.

Transmission Gear Ratios: Another thought to consider is your choice of transmission gears. A poorly matched transmission can make the most powerful engine seem sluggish. Nearly all of the Boxster and 996/997 Carrera engines have a somewhat high-rpm powerband (like the early 911 S). Because of this, you will probably want a transmission with very close ratio gears. This will allow you to maintain your optimum powerband and maximize the power output to the wheels. The six-speed Boxster transmission is ideal for this purpose. It's not uncommon to find Porsche race cars specifically designed for long tracks and rolling starts that have a "tall" first gear. This basically allows the racers to use first gear for actual track use, which effectively creates a true five-speed transmission for racing. Such a car would be very difficult to drive on the street, because "off-the-line" performance would be quite sluggish. However, on the track in the narrow powerband is where the drivetrain would shine, delivering peak power in a powerband closely matched to the transmission and the type of racetrack. For more information on choosing gear ratios, see chapter nine in the book *Gearing and Differentials in Race Car Engineering & Mechanics* by Paul Van Valkenburgh.

Another option may be the installation of the Boxster S six-speed transmission into a Boxster that normally had a five-speed. The proper gear ratios can make a world of difference—taller gears in the five-speed tend to make the car feel slower, even if the same engine is installed. If I compare the five-speed Boxster with the 3.4 engine to my six-speed 996 with the same 3.4 engine, the Boxster seems slower, because the gear ratios are taller. If you wish to install the Boxster six-speed transmission into your five-speed Boxster, the swap is pretty straightforward but time consuming and expensive to acquire all the parts. You need the six-speed transmission, a six-speed clutch slave cylinder, the 3.2 clutch package and flywheel, the six-speed shifter and shift cables, a set of 3.2 axles, the updated transmission mounts and brackets, and a handful of other small odds and ends.

1 The first step is to remove the half shafts from the transmission. Begin by removing the center bolt that fastens the half shaft to the transmission. To pull out the half shaft, I used a slide hammer, combined with an old CV joint, as shown. Place the end of the slide hammer shaft against the half-shaft flange and then fasten it down with two CV bolts. Tap the hammer along the shaft and the half shaft should slide out of the transmission. Another method you can use involves placing two bolts into the half-shaft flange and then using them to wedge the half shaft out of the transmission (inset photo). This is the method documented in the Porsche factory manuals.

2 Here's a photo of the half shaft after it has been pulled out of the transmission. Although it's more difficult in the tight space, you can remove the half shaft while the transmission is still in the car. For clarity in the photos, these tasks were performed on a transmission that was out of the car and on my bench.

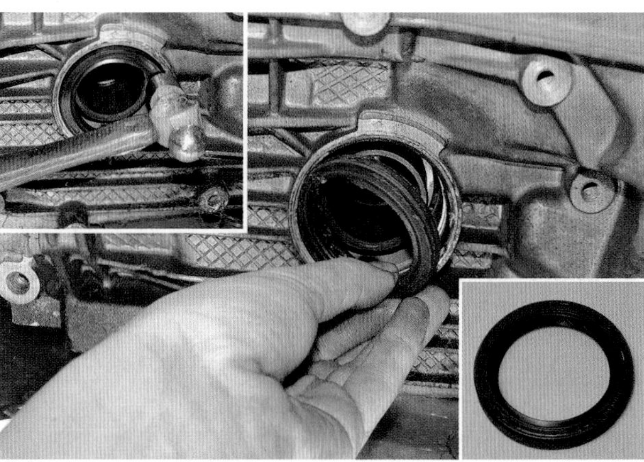

3 After you have the half shafts removed, you can replace the differential shaft seals. There is one on each side of the transmission, and these seal the driveshaft flanges to the transmission case. If they are old and leaking, then you will see transmission fluid leaking around your axles. Pull out the old seal, and then gently tap in the new one.

4 With the half shafts removed, you can then pull off the differential cover. Use a Torx socket tool to remove the screws on the outside of the cover (inset photo). Removing the cover will expose the differential inside the transmission. Be sure that you have emptied all of the transmission fluid out of the unit before you remove the cover—otherwise you will have a big mess on your hands. Be prepared for some residual fluid to leak out when you remove the cover. The six-speed transmission has a large O-ring on the differential cover that I recommend replacing when you reseal it.

5 With the cover removed, you should be able simply to pull out the differential. This is what an open differential looks like. It has planetary gears that distribute and provide equal torque to each wheel. This type of differential allows for both wheels to rotate and spin at different rates of speed, such as when the car is going around a corner or turn.

6 Here's the view inside the transmission case. The curved gear on the right (yellow arrow) is attached to the pinion shaft and mates with the ring gear that is attached to the differential. On some transmisions, there is a magnet in the case that attracts debris and metallic parts that have worn in the transmission (blue arrow). Take a paper towel and thoroughly clean this magnet, removing any grit or grime attached to it.

7 If you are replacing the differential carrier bearings, then use a bearing puller to remove the old ones off of the transmission. If they are difficult to pull off, then you might try lightly heating the bearing with a propane torch to loosen it up.

8 New bearings need to be pressed on the shafts. If you heat them in an oven or on a hot plate beforehand, it can make their installation much easier (obviously don't pick them up with your bare hands as shown in this photo if they are hot). The open differential is shown here with new carrier bearings installed. Don't forget the spacer and any shims that you may have taken off when you disassembled the unit. If you are installing a new differential, then you will need to obtain new shims that are matched to your transmission.

9 Shown here is a limited slip differential from Guard Transmission. GT is one of the leading providers of LDS differentials to the Porsche market, having earned their stripes designing race transmission components for the cars that competed in the GT class of the American Le Mans series. In addition, GT is an OEM supplier to Porsche AG with components used in the factory race cars on a regular basis. The unit I chose here is a street/track version with 60/40 biasing, which is ideal for a Boxster with a stiffer suspension and higher-power engines.

10 Here is the GT LSD installed onto the ring gear and fitted with new bearings. As mentioned previously, be sure to confirm that you install the correctly sized shims with the new differential, as there have been some changes over the years (see text for details).

11 Here's a side shot of the GT LSD installed back into the transmission. The inset photo shows how the half shafts sit inside the differential (shown without the differential cover installed).

12 When reinstalling your half shafts, be sure to use a new circlip on the end as mentioned in the Porsche factory manuals. The part number for all Boxsters (1997–2008) is 012-409-413.

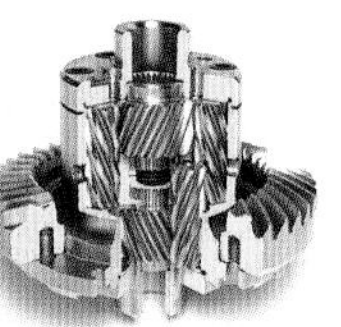

13 Shown here is a Quaife Automatic Torque Biasing Differential. This is a slightly different type of limited slip differential that is often a good compromise between street and track use for everyday drivers. Geared LSDs, such as the Quaife units, provide friction through the gears and their supports rather than the clutch plates found in typical LSDs. However, both output shafts must be loaded in order to maintain the proper torque distribution within the unit. If one shaft of the differential becomes free, then no torque is transmitted to that shaft, and the differential behaves very much like an open differential at that point.

PROJECT 40
Replacing Wheel Bearings

Time / Tab / Talent: 4 hours / $120 / 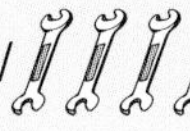

Tools: Wheel bearing puller, breaker bar, or torque wrench

Applicable Years: All

Parts: Wheel bearing

More Info: www.101projects.com/Boxster/40.htm

Tip: Put the bearing in the freezer prior to installation

Performance Gain: Smooth driving, no wheel noise

Comp Modification: Replace CV joints and boots

1 Wheel bearing replacement has always been one of those tasks that I have found very difficult to explain in text. So, for this project, I have simply arranged them in order with captions. This first photo shows the wheel hub after the car has been raised (Project 1), the caliper removed, and the brake disc removed as well (Project 55). Also, before you raise the car off the ground, remove the center wheel hubcap (see Photo 3 of Project 100) and loosen the axle nut (blue arrow) with a very long breaker bar while the tire is still on the ground and the car is in gear with the parking brake on. The photos for this project are of a front wheel bearing for a four-wheel-drive 996 Turbo, but the whole assembly is very similar to the Boxster setup.

2 We're going to be removing the whole wheel bearing carrier here, so we need to disconnect everything that is connected to it. Disconnect the tie rod from the wheel bearing carrier (inset photo—see Project 59), and also loosen the clamp nut (green arrow) that holds the shock (see Project 63). Disconnect the sway bar drop link (Project 59). Disconnect the wheel speed sensor at its connector.

3 If you didn't loosen up the axle nut while the car was still on the ground, you can use an impact tool to remove the nut (inset photo). This nut is on very tight, and you might have to work at it with the impact wrench in order to get the nut off.

4 Use a high-quality ball joint removal tool (yellow arrow) to separate the ball joint from the wheel bearing carrier. When the joint is loose, use a pry bar (blue arrow) to push the control arm (green arrow) down while you lift up the carrier. Push the control arm out of the way and then you should be able to slide the carrier off of the shock. If you can't deflect the control arm enough, then loosen the bolt at the other end of the control arm and you should be able to drop it down further. Don't retighten this bolt until the car is back on the ground in its fully weighted position. Remove the wheel speed sensor from the carrier when you have it on your bench.

5 Here's the axle with the carrier removed. Again, this is from a 4WD 996 Turbo, so there's a drive axle attached to this particular carrier. This design is very similar to the front and rear Boxster wheel carrier though. The toothed section of the axle generates a signal that is read by the wheel speed sensor that is mounted inside the carrier. If your CV joints need attention or your rubber boot is ripped or damaged, now would be the ideal time to replace them (see Project 41).

6 The problem with this car was suspected to lie within the wheel bearing, but we weren't 100 percent sure. With the carrier out and on the bench, a simple spin of the bearing gave the answer—the bearing was toast. It felt like there was sand or something in the bearing and its rotation was rough, not smooth.

7 Positioning the wheel bearing carrier in Callas Rennsport's hydraulic press, we pushed out the inner hub (the part that the brake disc and wheel attaches to). As is common with wheel bearing replacements, the bearing itself fell apart and half of it remained attached to the hub (inset).

8 To clean up the hub, we used a standard bearing puller to remove the remains of the wheel bearing off of the hub. The inset photo shows the hub all cleaned up with all remnants of the old bearing removed.

9 When the hub was removed from the wheel bearing carrier, the bearing split into two parts—one that was stuck on the hub and the remainder that was stuck inside the carrier. We went back to the press to remove the remains of the bearing. Remove the bearing retainer plate first (inset, lower right). With the bearing completely pressed out of the carrier, it should look like the inset photo in the lower left.

10 Here's a neat photo showing the physical damage on the worn-out wheel bearing. The blue arrow shows pitting of the bearing surface—once this starts in a section of the bearing, it tends to continue and get worse. The bearing should be smooth like the section indicated by the purple arrow. The other half of the bearing is also showing the same deterioration and pitting. Although the seal on the bearing looked intact, this amount of damage leads me to believe there had been some type of contamination issue at play here.

11 Using the hydraulic press, you can easily install the new bearing. New bearings should be kept in the freezer right up until they are installed in the car (inset). If they are very cold, it will make pressing them into the wheel carrier much easier. During installation, press on the outer race of the bearing only—don't place any force on the inner race, as this can damage the bearing. Install the bearing with the numbers facing toward the wheel hub. Typically the red/orange seal goes toward the inside of the car.

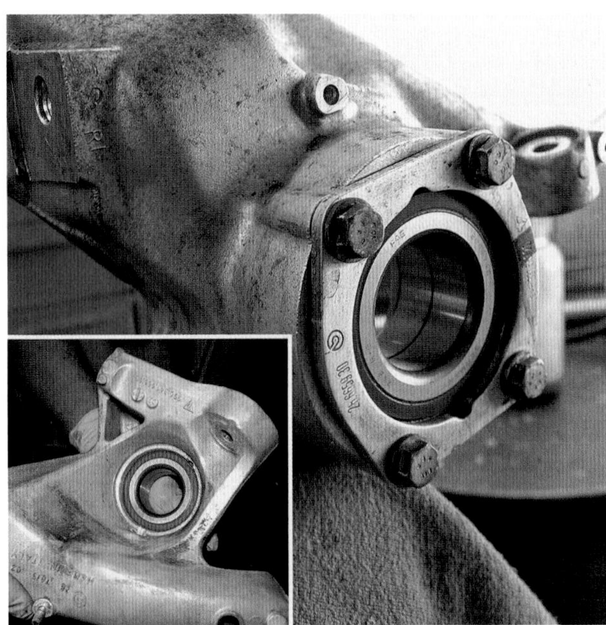

12 Shown here is the wheel bearing carrier from both sides with the new bearing installed and the bearing retainer plate in place.

13 With the new bearing installed in the wheel bearing carrier, it's time now to install the hub back into the inside race of the bearing. This is performed using a wheel bearing installation tool (blue arrow). Using a circular backing plate that is the same size as the inner race (yellow arrow), the tool pushes the hub inward while compressing on the inner race. Crank down the bearing installation tool until the inside surface of the hub rests against the surface of the inner race of the bearing (green arrow). The inset photo in the lower left shows what the backside of the installed bearing/hub assembly should look like when the hub is fully installed. Test the hub on the bearing with a few test spins. Don't be alarmed if it doesn't spin too freely—new bearings are generally pretty stiff at first.

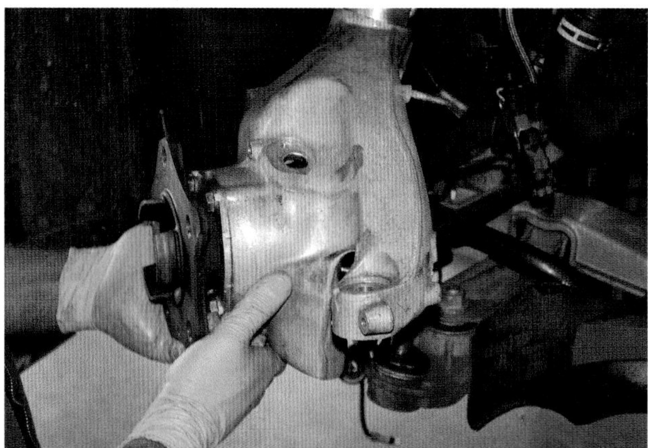

14 Reinstall the wheel bearing carrier back onto the car securing the ball joint, shock tower, sway bar, tie rod, speed sensor connection, brake disc, brake caliper, and anything else you disconnected in the process. Tighten up the axle using a brand new nut.

15 With the car back on the ground, use a really big torque wrench to tighten up the axle nut. If you don't have a really big torque wrench, you can use a long breaker bar and your bodyweight to apply the torque. The torque value for this nut is 340 ft-lbs, so if you divide 340 by your weight (for example 200 pounds), you will need to stand on your breaker bar with your full weight, 1.7 feet (1 foot 8 inches) away from the center of the wheel. Do this with the breaker bar perfectly parallel with the floor.

16 It's important to note that you do not always need to remove the wheel bearing carrier from the car in order to remove the wheel bearings. In the case of the 4WD Turbo, it was necessary because the axle was inserted in the inside of the carrier, and it was not possible to remove it without removing the carrier. In some cases, you can replace the wheel bearing with the carrier still installed in the car and avoid using the hydraulic press altogether. In this photo (and Photos 17 and 18 as well), you can see part one of a bench demonstration of the process of pulling out the wheel hub using the tool. Put a backing plate on the inner race and use the tool to pull the hub out of the bearing (the bearing will break apart at this point).

17 Here's part two of the process of pulling the bearing using the tool. With a backing plate covering the diameter of the outer race on the back side, the tool can simply pull the rest of the bearing out of the bore using the long center screw.

18 Part three of the process involves using the tool to press in the new bearing. Using a really big backing plate that compresses against the back of the aluminum wheel bearing carrier, the front part of the tool compresses the wheel bearing into place. Finally, the installation of the hub into the carrier is performed in the exact same manner as shown in Photo 13.

PROJECT 41
Replacing CV Joints, Boots, & Axles

Time / Tab / Talent: 4 hours / $350 /

Tools: Hex socket tool set

Applicable Years: All

Parts: CV Joints or complete axles, CV joint grease, gaskets, CV boots

More Info: www.101projects.com/Boxster/41.htm

Tip: Use the weight of the car to hold the axle while you loosen the axle nut

Performance Gain: Smoother drivetrain

Comp Modification: Replace your rear wheel bearings

One of the most common suspension items to replace or service on the Boxster are the constant velocity (CV) joints that connect the wheels to the transmission. These bearings, packed in grease, experience a tremendous amount of abuse throughout the years and thus have a tendency to wear out after about 100,000 miles or so. One of the clear signs that the joints need replacing is the distinct sound of a clunk, clunk, clunk coming from the rear axle when the car is in motion.

In some cases, the boots that cover and protect the CV joints will be torn and will need replacing. The procedure for replacing the boots is very similar to the procedure for replacing the entire joint. New boots should be installed each time a CV joint is replaced.

For the Boxster, Porsche sells only the inner CV joints or a complete replaceable axle. The new axle contains both the inner and outer CV joints, as well as the boots that cover and protect them. Although the inner Boxster CV joints are available separately, I typically recommend installing the complete axle. All you need to do is bolt it up to the car, and you don't have to mess with disassembly or CV joint grease.

If you are going to be replacing the entire axle, then you first need to loosen up the big axle nut. With the car on the ground, in gear, and the emergency brake on, remove the center hubcap (see Photo 3 of Project 100), and use a long breaker bar to loosen up the driveshaft flange axle nut. This nut is tightened to more than 460 Nm (340 ft-lbs)—it will take quite a bit of force to loosen it up. If you are going to be replacing the inner CV joint only, then you can leave this nut alone.

The next step in replacement of boots, joints, or the axle is to jack up and raise the car off of the ground and remove the road wheels (see Project 1). Then, remove the diagonal braces and the aluminum transmission cover (see Project 35). Now remove the bolts from the inner CV joint using a hex socket (see Photo 2). In order to gain access to the CV bolts, rotate the wheel of the car until you can clearly get your hex socket on the bolts. Then, pull the emergency brake and place the transmission into first gear. This will allow you to loosen the bolts without having the axle spin. When you have removed all the bolts that you can from this angle, release the brake, take the car out of gear, and rotate the wheel until you can reach the next set of bolts. When all of the bolts are removed, pull the axle out of the flange and suspend the end of the drive axle with some rope or wire.

With the CV joint disconnected from the transmission, you can work on replacing either one of the CV boots or the inner CV joint. If you're replacing the entire axle, then you can skip these steps, as the axles come complete with new joints and boots. Remove the six bolts and the half-moon washers from the joint and pry off the dust cap (blue arrow, Photo 2). Then remove the circlip that holds the CV joint onto the axle (Photo 3). Cut or disconnect the clamp that holds the boot to the shaft, and the old CV and boot should simply slide off of the shaft. In general, it's a really bad sign if large balls from the bearing start falling out. That's a clear indicator that you need to replace the joint. If you are reusing the joint again, make sure that you carefully place it in a plastic bag and avoid getting any dirt or grime in it. Even a crystal of sand or two accidentally placed in the CV joint can help it wear out prematurely. Inspect both CV joints for any wear prior to installing them back into the car. If you are simply replacing the boots, then carefully pry the old boot off of the joint. It is pressed onto to the end of the joint in a similar manner as the dust boot.

With the inner CV joint and boot completely removed, your axle should resemble the inset of Photo 4. If you are replacing the boot on the outer joint, undo the clamp, and remove the boot and cover. Replacement boots aren't typically sold with the metal mounting plate attached, so you'll have to pull the old boot off of the plate and transfer the new one to it. Reinstall using a new pinch clamp, but don't tighten it quite yet. Reassemble your old CV joint or a new one onto the axle. With the new boot attached, rotate the joint through its entire motion before tightening the small, inner boot clamp—you don't want it to be too tight.

Whether you're reinstalling your old CV or using a new one, I recommend repacking the joint with grease. Also make sure that you place plenty of grease in and around the boot. Move the joint in and out as you insert the grease to make sure that you get it well lubricated, as the new CV joints do not come pre-greased. My preferred choice of lube is Swepco 101—a $12 tube should be good for about four joints total. When reinstalling the bolts into the transmission flange, make sure that the bolt threads are free of grease. Any grease on the threads can cause the bolts to come loose and create a dangerous situation. Also, all your CV bolts should be checked after about 500 miles of driving.

If you are replacing the entire axle, then there are two different methods you can use. You can remove the entire wheel bearing carrier (detailed in Project 40), or you can simply slide the axle out of the hub if you have enough clearance. Very often, the axle will get stuck in the wheel hub due to corrosion or rust—it may need some encouragement with a big hammer to be removed. You will need to remove the exhaust and the rear sway bar once you have the axle nut removed in order to gain enough clearance to drop the axle down (see Photo 6).

Once you have the entire assembly back together, take the car out for a drive, and check the rear for noises. All should be smooth and quiet, and the boots should no longer leak.

1 Shown here is an inner CV joint replacement kit. The kit comes complete with the joint, the boot, a new boot clamp, new bolts, a new circlip, and enough CV joint grease to lubricate the joint. If you are planning to remove the whole axle, be sure to order a replacement axle nut as well (shown in photo). On the Boxster, the outer CV joint is not available separately, but must be purchased as part of a complete axle. This is because the joint is integrated into the stub axle and cannot be separated. If the boots are damaged and leaking, then you should replace them, because dirt and debris can find their way inside.

2 This photo shows the process of disconnecting the inner CV joint from the transmission. Use a really long extension and a hex socket tool to easily remove each of the six bolts that secure the joint to the transmission (inset). With the joint disconnected, remove the bolts and the half-moon washers. There is a dust cap (blue arrow) that protects the CV joint. Carefully pry this dust cap off to access the circlip underneath.

3 The CV joint is held onto the axle by a circlip, which is very difficult to see in this photo. The two orange arrows point to the ends of the circlip that must be removed by using a set of special circlip pliers designed specifically for the task (inset).

4 The four CV joints are located in the rear of the car, attached to both the transmission flanges and the stub axles on the wheel carriers. I recommend that you replace the joints in pairs—either both of the inside ones or both of the axles. Chances are if one of the joints is showing signs of wear and deterioration, then the other three will not be far behind. This photo shows the new CV joint installed with a new boot and boot clamp (purple arrow). The inset photo shows the axle with the boot and CV removed. You need to remove everything off of the inside end of the axle as shown, in order to slide on new boots for both the inner and outer joints.

5 If you are replacing the entire axle, then you need to remove the outer axle nut (yellow arrow). This is best done with the car on the ground by placing a long breaker bar on the nut while the wheel holds it steady. Pry off the small inner hubcap to gain access to this nut while the wheel is still on the car (see Photo 3 of Project 100).

6 There are two methods you can use to remove the axle from the car. You can remove the wheel bearing carrier as detailed in Project 40, or you can drop down the rear sway bar and exhaust to gain enough clearance to remove the axle. Unless I'm planning on doing some major work on the brake calipers or the wheel bearing, I typically prefer to drop down the exhaust to gain enough clearance. As you can see in this photo, the exhaust pipe (blue arrow) is getting in the way of dropping down the axle (red arrow). The axle flange on the transmission is shown by the orange arrow.

PROJECT 42
Installing a Short Shift Kit/Shifting Improvements

Time / Tab / Talent: 3 hours / $150–$350 /

Tools: None

Applicable Years: All

Parts: Short shift kit (SSK)

More Info: www.101projects.com/Boxster/42.htm

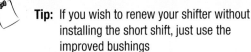

Tip: If you wish to renew your shifter without installing the short shift, just use the improved bushings

Performance Gain: Shorter shift throws

Comp Modification: Replace your shifter cables

One of the most popular additions to the Boxster is the installation of a short shift kit. The kit shortens the length of throw on the stock shifter, theoretically giving you the ability to shift faster. Installation is a moderate task and should only take the better part of an afternoon.

For the purpose of this project, I chose the Porsche factory short shift kit, which is nearly identical to others on the market (B&M supposedly manufactures the kit for Porsche). Both are available from PelicanParts.com.

The factory kit is shown in Photo 2. It comes complete with everything that you need to replace your shift lever and replace many of the shift bushings that have a tendency to wear out. Specifically, this kit contains Delrin bushings for the shifter arm and shift lever. The kit is very well constructed, and all of the parts fit together with very tight tolerances.

The process of installing the short shift kit involves basically swapping out the shift lever with the old one and installing the new bushings. Follow the steps shown in Photos 1 through 10 to remove the shifter and install the kit. When you have reinstalled the kit into the car and reattached the cables, be sure to test the shifter through all gears. Only when you have confirmed the shifter is working properly should you reinstall the center console.

It took a short while (no pun intended) for me to get used to the new short shift kit. At first, I didn't really care for it, but after driving the car with it installed, I didn't want to go back to the standard shifter. If you're not sure about whether you'll like the short feel, I suggest that you drive someone else's car that has a short shifter installed. The procedure to remove the kit takes as long as the one to install it, so if you're not sure, try it out beforehand.

On a side note, many people install short shift kits in their cars thinking that it will fix problems that they are having with their transmission. This will not solve any problems and will in most cases make a poorly shifting car shift even worse. The reason for this is that with the short shift kit, the torque arm on the shift lever is much shorter, giving you much less "resolution" on your shifter. It's similar to having a gas pedal that only travels 1 inch over its range instead of 2–3 inches (see Project 94). You have less precision in how much throttle you want to give the car. In a similar manner, with the short shift kit you will have less precision on where the shift rod is placed. It's a wise idea to tackle the core problems with your transmission (synchros, shift bushings) prior to the installation of the short shift kit (see the other transmission projects in this book).

Shifting Improvements: There may come a time in the ownership of your Boxster when you feel that the shifting performance of the car is not quite what it's supposed to be. Renewing the shifter bushings and the cable ends as detailed in this project are a good first step in ensuring crisp shifting. The other end of the shifter cable can wear too (see Photo 3 of Project 37). Unfortunately, at this time the only way to renew the transmission-end bushings is to replace the entire cable. Replacement is pretty straightforward—it involves disconnecting the cable from the shifter and then feeding it through the engine compartment to the transmission. On some cars, excessive deterioration of the engine or transmission mounts can cause erratic shifting. This is less of an issue with a cable-driven shifter like the Boxster, but crisp, firm mounts do help overall performance. See Project 10 and Project 36 for complete instructions on replacing the engine and transmission mounts.

1 Begin by unclipping the shifter boot from the rear and lift it up (inset). To remove the shifter knob, some cars use a set screw and some require you to twist the lower collar 90 degrees and then lift to remove. Remove your old knob by simply pulling upward on it—be careful not to smack yourself in the face accidentally!

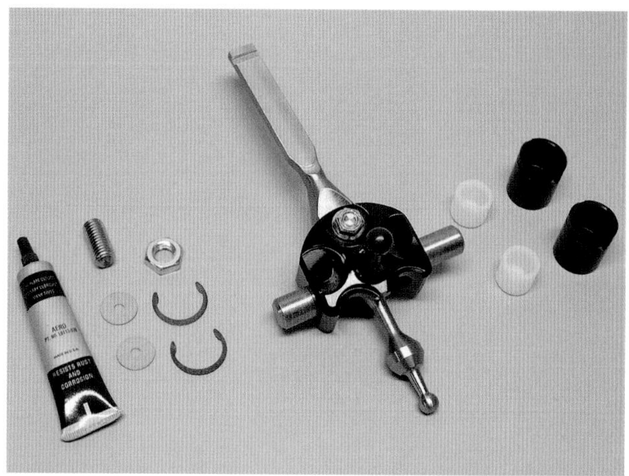

2 Shown here is the Porsche factory short shift kit. The kit consists of a metal shifter, a set of improved bushings and aluminum bushing carriers, and associated mounting hardware.

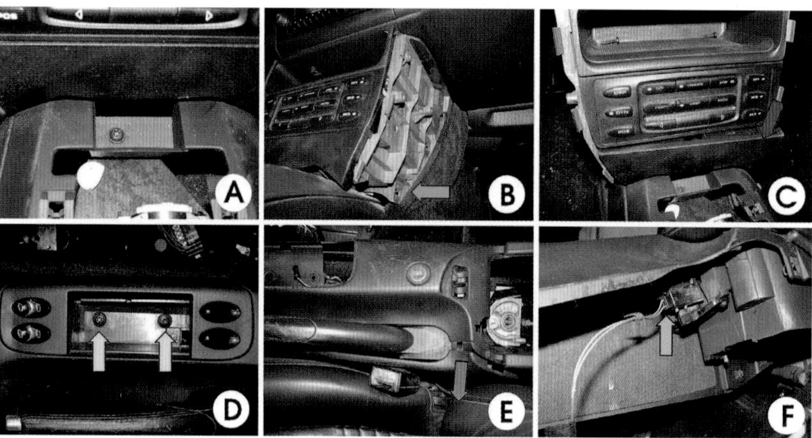

3 Shown here are the various steps required to remove the center console. **A:** Remove front retaining screw, located under the shifter boot. **B:** Pull off side cover (it snaps off) and remove lower screw (green arrow). **C:** Pull off the front lower console cover (red arrow). **D:** Remove the coin tray insert, remove the two screws (yellow arrows), unplug and remove window switch assembly, and remove the additional screw found underneath. **E:** Pull back e-brake side cover and remove (pull in the direction of the purple arrow). Also remove the rear storage compartment—there is a screw hidden underneath the small rubber mat inside the compartment, and another screw hidden under the small coin holder (three total in the rear). **F:** Unplug any remaining harnesses still attached to the console.

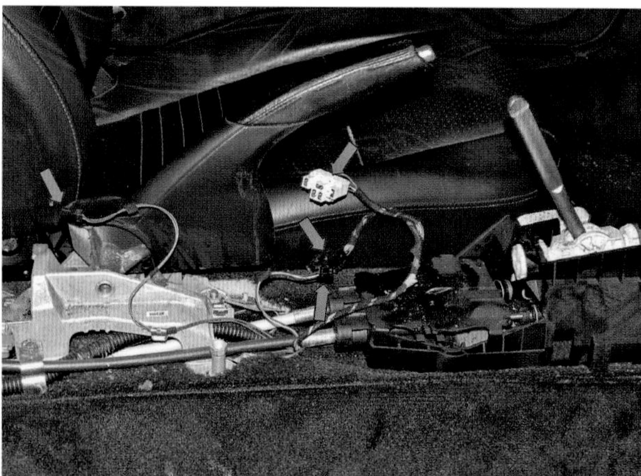

4 This photo shows the center console removed. The purple arrows point to wire harnesses that need to be unplugged prior to pulling the console from the car.

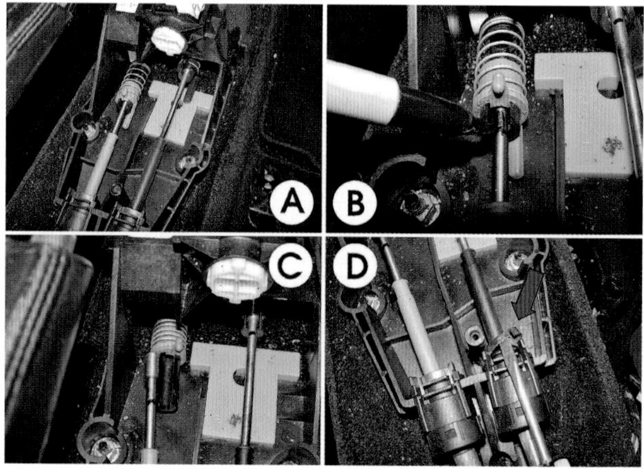

5 With the center console removed, you can now work on disconnecting the cables from the shifter. **A:** Remove the plastic shifter cover and you will see the cables underneath. **B:** Mark the existing position of the cables with a permanent marker so that you can assemble them back together in the same position as when they came apart. **C:** Slide the spring-loaded retainers toward the front of the car and release the cable from its holder. **D:** Unclip the shift cables from the rear of the shifter housing and place them off to the side. Finally, unscrew the shifter housing from the floor and remove from the car.

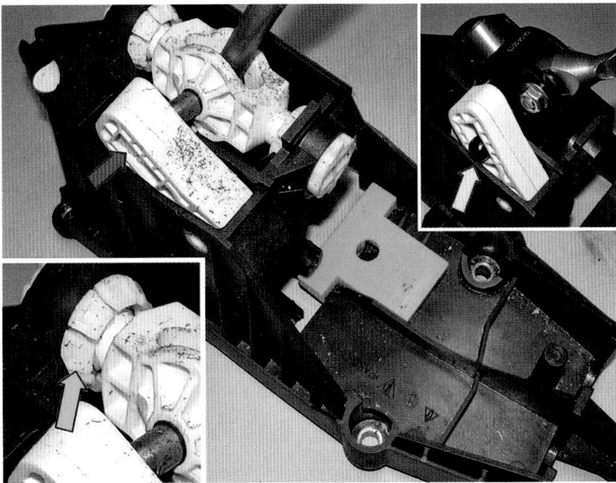

6 The stock shifter uses a square bushing that rides in the side cam piece (red arrow). The new short shifter uses a metal ball instead—lubricate this ball prior to assembling it into the shifter (yellow arrow). To remove the old stock bushings, use a razorblade and chip away at the edges of the bushings (blue arrow). When the edges have been removed, slide the bushing out of the bore and remove the stock shifter. If you are reusing the cable end, pop it off of the old shifter and install it onto the new one (see Photo 9).

7 The new bushings are installed onto the aluminum cylinders located on either side of the shifter. Place the washer in-between the bushing and the bottom of the cylinder. Place the bushing on the shifter shaft, push it in toward the shifter (the direction of the purple arrow), and then fasten it in place using the circlip (yellow arrow, lower left). The circlip goes on the inside of the shifter housing to hold the metal housing from falling out in the direction opposite of the purple arrow (see Photo 10). Be sure to pre-lubricate the bushing prior to assembly (upper left).

8 Reduce the end play in the shifter by turning the set screw with a hex driver. Turn the set screw until it's tight, and then back it off about ¼ to ½ turn. Lock it in place with the jam nut to secure the assembly. The set screw and jam nut can be installed on either side of the shifter.

9 I recommend using new cable ends (yellow arrow) when refurbishing your shifter—they will aid in keeping a crisp, reliable feel in your shifter. Lubricate the ball end of the shifter with some white lithium grease prior to installing the cable end. You may have to use some significant force to get the cable end attached—use a hammer to tap it on if necessary.

10 Here is the shifter assembly, completely upgraded with the new factory short shift kit and the improved bushings. The two purple arrows point to the location of the two installed circlips. Reinstall the kit back into the car, reversing what you had done previously. Use plenty of grease on all the bushings and pivot points.

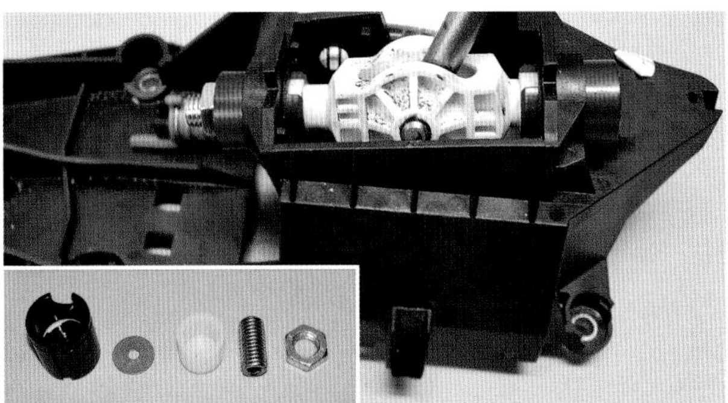

11 Replacement bushings for the stock shifter are not available separately—you have to purchase a whole new shifter, at a cost of about $200! Fortunately, the short shift kit contains a set of improved bushings that can also be used with the stock shifter. If you wish to keep your stock shifter and renew the feel in your shifter, then I recommend picking up a set of these improved bushings. One bushing kit is shown in the inset (two required).

PROJECT 43
Installing an Aftermarket Shift Knob

Time / Tab / Talent: 2 hours / $50–$200 /

Tools: Bench grinder

Applicable Years: All

Parts: Shift knob, boot, finishing ring

More Info: www.101projects.com/Boxster/43.htm

Tip: Be careful not to smack yourself in the face removing the old knob

Performance Gain: Cooler shifts

Comp Modification: Install short shift kit

One of the most popular and easiest upgrades for your car is the addition of an aftermarket shift knob. Let's face it, the steering wheel, gauges, and shift knob are the three main items on the car that you have a personal interaction with. Why not spruce them up a bit?—I personally find the Boxster OEM shift knob in particular to be quite boring. The shift knob I chose for this article is the MOMO Shadow carbon fiber, available for about $90 from PelicanParts.com. I also used a black MOMO Endurance shift boot and the Endurance finishing knob that attaches to the bottom of the shifter. Installation takes about two hours, as you need to remove the shifter from the car (unless you have the short shift kit installed). Some slight modifications are needed to the shifter handle to make the aftermarket knobs fit, but this is relatively easy to do.

Begin by removing the existing shift knob off of your shifter (see Project 42 for instructions). If you have the factory short shift kit installed, then all you need to do is unbolt the shifter handle from the inside of the shifter (see the inset of Photo 3). If you have the standard shifter in your car, then you will have to remove it (see instructions in Project 42). With the shifter removed, lightly grind down the edges of the shift handle, as detailed in Photo 1. You only need to remove a very small amount of material. Measure and test fit the knob to make sure it fits on the shaft, and then install the shifter and console back into the car. You also might be able to use sandpaper and/or files to modify the shifter while it's still installed in the car, but that seems like it would be a lot of work and would create a bit of a mess in your interior.

Attach the boot to the retaining frame as detailed in Photo 2. Install the boot, place the finishing ring on the shaft, and then install and tighten the knob using the three set screws at the bottom of the knob. Finally, screw on the finishing ring, and then attach the top of the boot to the finishing ring by stretching the top of the boot over the bottom of the ring. The final result is very professional-looking and looks better than stock!

1 The factory shaft is just a little too wide to accommodate most of the aftermarket shift knobs. Using a common bench grinder, simply grind a bit of the handle down on each side until the width is about 13.75mm. Bevel the edges of the handle so that it will easily fit inside of the shift knob, and test fit the knob on the end of the handle (short shift kit shown in the inset photo). Wear gloves while grinding the handle down—it will easily become hot to the touch.

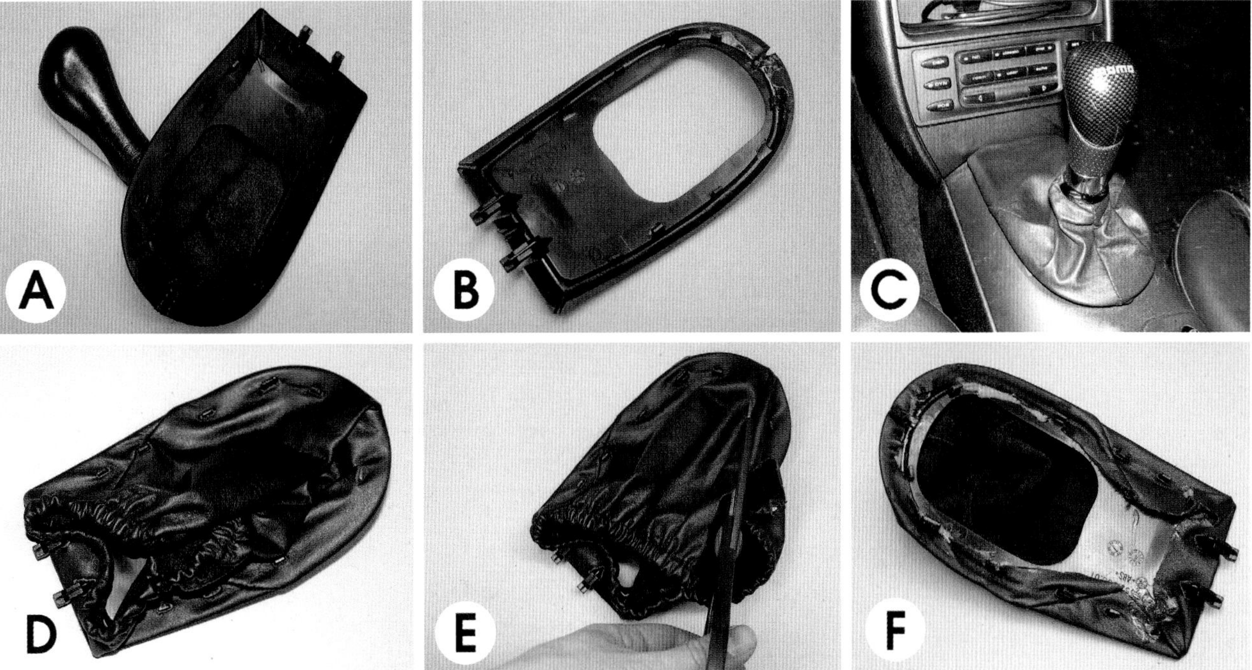

2 **A:** Remove the shift boot retaining frame from the existing shifter. **B:** If you don't want to destroy your existing shifter, then you can simply order the retaining frame, PN: 996-552-655-01 (cost about $8). **C:** Wrap the new boot around the frame and test fit it in on top of your shifter. Move the shifter into all of the gear positions 1-2-3-4-5-R and make sure you have enough slack in the boot. **D:** Poke holes in the boot for the tabs on the back of the retaining frame. **E:** Carefully cut the excess material on the boot using a pair of scissors. **F:** Finally, using some 3M or Permatex Super Weatherstrip adhesive, glue the edges of the leather to the retaining frame.

3 Here's the finished product. The shift boot finisher shown in the photo is chrome, but it's also available in black and silver as well. The final installation looks very professional—as good or better than stock! The inset photo shows a shortcut that you can use if you have the short shift kit installed. Simply unbolt the center shifter from the metal housing and remove it so that you can easily modify it on your workbench.

PROJECT 44
Clutch Replacement

 **Time / Tab / Talent:** 12 hours / $750 / 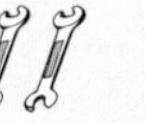

 **Tools:** Torx socket set, clutch alignment tool, flywheel lock, torque wrench

 **Applicable Years:** All

Parts: Complete clutch kit

 **More Info:** www.101projects.com/Boxster/44.htm

Tip: Purchase a kit with everything in it, not some simple version

 **Performance Gain:** Smoother shifting, no power loss

 **Comp Modification:** Replace intermediate shaft bearing, replace coolant tank, install lightweight flywheel

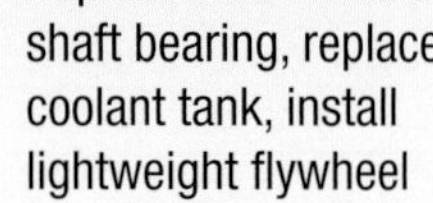

One of the most common repair procedures for the manual transmission Boxster is the replacement of the clutch assembly. Unfortunately, it is a rather big process involving the removal of the transmission. The good news is that it's really not a super-difficult job if you have some information and a few hints and tips.

How do you know if your clutch is beginning to fail? There are a few ways to tell. First, you should figure out how old your current clutch is. If your car is driven with mostly highway miles, then clutches can last almost forever. However, if you often drive around town somewhat aggressively, then you will probably have to replace your clutch at about 30,000 miles or so. With a hydraulic clutch system like the one on the Boxster, it can be a bit more difficult to determine the exact problem than with an older-style cable clutch system. Spongy pedals, excessive free play, and grinding noises all indicate problems with the clutch or hydraulic system. Strange noises that change when you push in the clutch pedal can indicate a pilot bearing or throw-out bearing beginning to fail. Finally, if your clutch begins to slip when the pedal is not depressed, then chances are your clutch disc is worn or the spring plates in your pressure plate have worn out.

The first step is to remove your transmission from the car. See Project 37 for detailed instructions on this procedure. Once the transmission has been removed, you will want to remove the pressure plate. On this particular car, I found that some of the pressure plate bolts had problems rounding out when I went to remove them. If this happens, then dig out your trusty Dremel tool and cut them off in about 1 minute. Don't waste your time trying vice grips or other foolish methods—you can cut them off, and you don't need to worry about damaging the pressure plate because you're going to be replacing it anyways. When you're ready to remove the last bolt, grab the pressure plate with one hand—it's easy for it to fall off when the last bolt is removed. The disc should also pop out when you remove the pressure plate.

With the pressure plate removed, you should be able to see the flywheel. The Boxster uses a dual-mass flywheel, which is a two-piece component that is bonded together. This changes the natural frequency of the flywheel and reduces vibrations in the engine. Unfortunately, this flywheel can be expensive to replace. Porsche has released a Technical Service Bulletin on checking the dual-mass flywheel (TSB 911 8/02 1360), which I have placed on the 101Projects.com website for reference. Basically, the test procedure is to twist the pressure plate surface of the flywheel about 15mm to both the left and the right and check to see if it returns to approximately its original position. If the flywheel cannot be twisted at all, or if the flywheel can be twisted beyond the 15mm without a noticeable increase in the spring force, then the flywheel is likely to be faulty. Typically it's a wise idea to replace your dual-mass flywheel every 100,000 miles or every other clutch replacement.

The next step here is to remove the flywheel bolts. You can use a socket and breaker bar along with your flywheel lock (Photo 2). With the bolts removed, your flywheel should be able to be tugged off of the crankshaft.

At this point, you'll want to turn your attention to the transmission and refurbish the throw-out bearing and arm. Start with the throw-out bearing guide tube. This is the small tube that the throw-out bearing rides on when the clutch is disengaged. As the throw-out bearing slides back and forth on the tube, the tube has a tendency to wear out. Remove the bolts that hold the guide tube to the transmission. Remove the guide tube, and inside you will find the mainshaft seal. Using a small screwdriver, punch a small hole in one of the indents in the surface of the seal, and pick out the old seal and remove it (see Photo 5). Clean out the inside of the bore where the seal fits, and install the new one. Tap it in lightly with the end of a socket extension, taking care to make sure it doesn't go in half-cocked. Install the seal so that it is flush with the flange. Now install the new throw-out bearing guide tube, using a new O-ring. Although the factory manuals state to install the guide tube without any grease, I like to apply a light coat of white lithium grease to help things along. Check the small retainer clip, the pivot pins, and the throw-out arm pivot piece (see Photo 6). Lubricate the two pivots with white lithium grease. Take the new throw-out bearing, snap it on the throw-out arm, and attach the arm to the transmission. Your throw-out arm is now ready for assembly back into the car.

Now would also be an excellent time to replace your coolant tank if you've been having problems with it. Access is very easy at this point—the removal process is very difficult when the transmission is installed in the car (see Project 33). I also recommend that you replace your intermediate shaft bearing at this time. This bearing has been responsible for more than its share of Boxster engine failures over the years (see Project 14).

Now, it's time to turn our attention back to the flywheel end of the engine. Porsche Tech Bulletin 8/02 1360 says to check the dual-mass flywheel by twisting it approximately 15mm to both the left and the right, checking to make sure that it returns to its approximate starting position. If the flywheel can be twisted beyond about 15mm with no noticeable increase in spring force or if it cannot be twisted at all, then it probably needs replacement. If the flywheel checks out okay, then replace the flywheel pilot bearing and the flywheel seal as shown in Photo 9 and Photo 10.

Now you're ready to reinstall the flywheel onto the engine. Always use new flywheel bolts, as they are only meant to be tightened and stretched once. Install your new or reconditioned flywheel onto the engine, then install the new flywheel bolts and torque them down. You must use a torque wrench and a flywheel lock to tighten the flywheel (See Photo 11 and Photo 12).

With the flywheel mounted, now take your clutch alignment tool and place it in the center of the pilot bearing. Install the clutch disc onto the flywheel (see Photo 13). Then install the pressure plate onto the flywheel, compressing the clutch disc. Use new pressure plate bolts to keep everything fresh. When the pressure plate is tightened down to its proper torque, remove the alignment tool. The disc, pilot bearing, and pressure plate should all be aligned (Photo 14).

Reinstall your transmission as per the instructions in Project 37. Reattach your slave cylinder, the backup lamp switch, the driveshafts, and the exhaust. At this time, I also recommend that you bleed your clutch system (see Project 45).

I wish I could say this was an easy job, but it's not. It's not impossible, but there's a lot of stuff to remove and a lot of tricky spots. One of the things that you want to do is purchase a complete kit that contains everything that you need for the job—all of the nuts, bolts, and bushings, as this will be a huge timesaver. The only place that currently sells such a kit is PelicanParts.com.

Lightweight Flywheel: While reducing this weight will not buy you any more horsepower, it can increase your engine's response and acceleration. The reasoning behind this is that the rotational mass of the engine takes time to "spin up" when you accelerate. Decreasing the rotational mass of the engine allows for quicker response times when accelerating. This is because more energy from the engine is being used to accelerate the mass of the car, instead of accelerating the mass of the engine components. In addition, reducing the mass of rotating engine components has a two-fold result on performance—you not only make the engine quicker, but you are also reducing the total weight of the car. This is discussed further in this book under "Weight Reduction" in Project 98. The flywheel and other rotational components serve to raise the rotational or angular momentum of the engine so that the engine will continue to rotate smoothly until the next compression stroke. Adding a lightweight flywheel or other lightweight components allows you to adjust engine rpm's much quicker. However, it will also drop down in rpm much quicker as well when you let off of the throttle. This often makes the car difficult to drive on the street in day-to-day traffic conditions. Also be sure to only use a spring-centered clutch disc with a non-dual-mass flywheel (see Photo 5).

If you are looking for an easy performance upgrade for your 1997–2004 Boxster, you can install the 987 Boxster/Cayman clutch package instead of the stock setup. The later-style clutch package will give you a better disc with more clamping force from the pressure plate. Just make sure that you order the 987 Boxster/Cayman clutch that matches your transmission (five-speed 987 clutch works with the five-speed 986 Boxster, and the six-speed 987 "S" clutch works with the six-speed 986 Boxster S).

1 Here's what your engine will look like after you have removed your transmission. Shown here is the pressure plate (blue arrow). There is a jack stand underneath the engine supporting the weight that is normally supported by the transmission.

2 Attach your flywheel lock (see Photo 11) and constrain the flywheel in position as you remove the flywheel bolts. With the flywheel off, remove the flywheel seal underneath. Using a screwdriver, puncture and remove the seal. Be careful not to damage any of the side surfaces where the seal mates to the engine case.

3 The first step is to make sure that you gather all the required parts for the job before you begin. It is very frustrating to get halfway through a replacement job only to find out that you need a part or a tool that you don't have. Here is photo of the PelicanParts.com clutch SuperKit that contains a comprehensive set of clutch replacement parts for a Boxster: **A:** Pressure plate. **B:** Throw-out arm pivot piece. **C:** Throw-out bearing. **D:** Pivot ball pin for pivot piece (B). **E:** Dual-mass flywheel. **F:** O-ring for guide tube. **G:** Pilot bearing (shown already installed in flywheel E). **H:** Throw-out bearing guide tube. **J:** Engine flywheel seal. **K:** Pressure plate bolts. **L:** Clutch disc. **M:** Transmission mainshaft seal. **N:** Flywheel bolts. **O:** Retaining spring for pivot piece (B). **P:** Clutch release lever.

4 Shown here is a lightened flywheel. The main advantage to using the lighter-weight flywheel is that it reduces the weight of the rotational elements in the engine. However, the installation of the lightened flywheel may make the car difficult to drive, particularly in traffic. In addition, if you install a lightened flywheel, make sure you install a spring clutch disc along with it (inset photo). Don't use the stock clutch disc. If you use the stock disc there will be nothing to absorb driveline shock and vibrations, and you might damage your engine and/or cause the engine to trigger false misfire faults.

5 This photo shows the steps associated with replacing the transmission mainshaft seal. Pluck the old seal out of the guide tube and tap in a new one. Replace the O-ring with a new one and then install back onto the transmission.

6 The throw-out fork (inset) is attached at one end with a small metal clip (yellow arrow). Remove the fork from the transmission by pulling out on the fork and unhooking the clip from its catch on the bottom. Clean the entire assembly and then lubricate everything with white lithium grease, including the throw-out bearing guide tube (green arrow). Make sure that the parts are assembled correctly, as per the photo. The throw-out bearing clips onto the throw-out arm as shown in the inset photo. Pay special attention to the orientation of the pivot piece and pin (red arrow).

7 If your backup lamp switch is giving you trouble, now is the perfect time to replace it. The switch is located on the top of the transmission (non-S models). Replacement is as simple as removing it from the top of the transmission case. The inset photo shows the plug for the switch.

9 **A:** The pilot bearing holds the transmission input shaft in place and aligns the transmission up with the crankshaft. **B:** To remove the flywheel pilot bearing, use an appropriately sized socket and gently tap it with a hammer. **C:** The new bearing should fit easily inside the hole in the crankshaft. **D:** Use a deep socket to evenly tap in the bearing so that it's flush with the surface of the flywheel (inset).

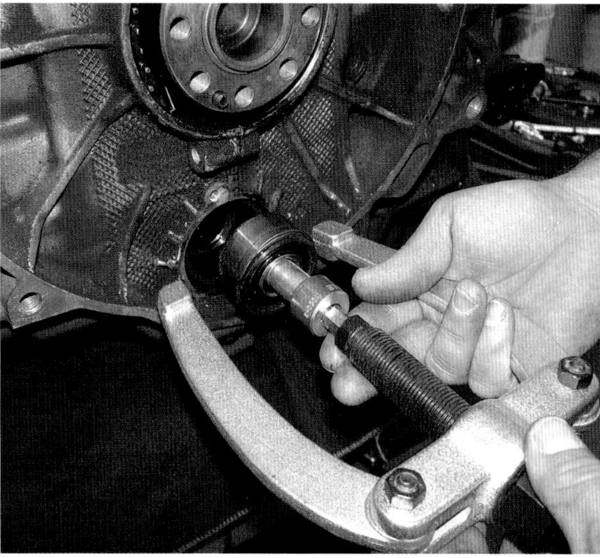

8 Shown here is the infamous intermediate shaft bearing that is responsible for so many engine failures on both the Boxster and the 996. Recent advances from crafty engineers in the aftermarket have developed a solution to remove and repair this bearing while performing a clutch replacement. To ignore this bearing while performing your clutch replacement is somewhat foolhardy—the majority of engines that have blown up in recent years have been attributed to the failure of this bearing. For more information, see Project 14.

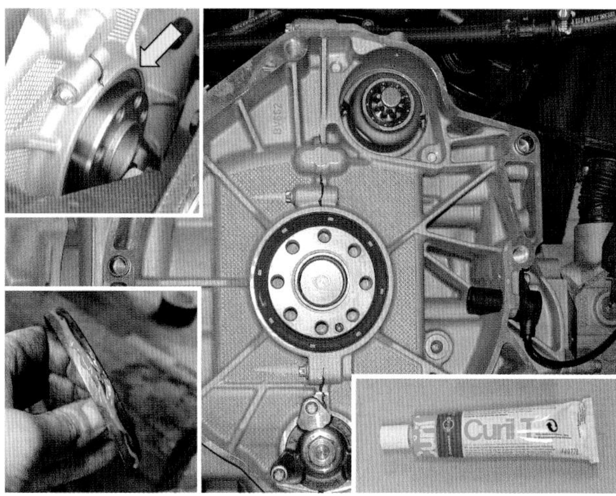

10 Take your new flywheel seal and coat it with a light touch of Curil-T. Then install it onto the engine, tapping lightly around the edge. The newer-style seal is supposed to be seated about 14mm or so below the end of the crankshaft. This means that the seal will sit about 3mm or so recessed beyond the edge of the case (yellow arrow). There is a special Porsche tool designed for the installation of this seal, but I simply made my own using some plastic pipe from the local hardware store that was the same diameter of the seal. Tap lightly and carefully—make sure that the seal doesn't become cocked in its bore. Clean up any leftover sealant that squeezes out.

11 I use a simple flywheel lock that is basically a strip of metal with two large slots in it (arrow, right). This allows you to attach the lock to a bolt affixed to the engine case, and one affixed to the flywheel, where the pressure plate bolts normally mount. This inexpensive lock works great on almost any car. With the lock in place, torque the bolts, working in a crisscross pattern. Start by tightening all the bolts to 50 percent of their final value, and then go around again and tighten them to the final value. Then crank them another 90 degrees as shown in the next photo.

12 Shown here is a simple degree wheel that I made for tightening flywheel bolts. Download and print out the wheel on a thick piece of paper. Then, get some 3M tack adhesive and spray the back, so it sticks to the flywheel like a Post-It note. Then, crank each bolt 120 degrees clockwise to achieve the proper tightness/stretch of the flywheel bolts. You can download and print out the template of the degree wheel from the 101Projects.com website.

13 The clutch alignment tool (green arrow) is used to align the clutch disc (red arrow) with the pilot bearing, pressure plate, and flywheel (blue arrow).

14 Without the alignment tool (blue arrow), it would be nearly impossible to insert the transmission input shaft into the pilot bearing when mating the engine and the transmission back together. When the pressure plate bolts are all tightened down, you should be able to easily pull out the alignment tool, and the pressure plate and clutch disc should be centered with respect to the pilot bearing (photo inset). I recommend using new pressure plate bolts when performing a clutch replacement project.

PROJECT 45
Replacing Clutch Hydraulics

Time / Tab / Talent: 2 hours / $150 /

Tools: Socket set

Applicable Years: All

Parts: Clutch slave cylinder

More Info: www.101projects.com/Boxster/45.htm

Tip: Replace when performing a clutch job

Performance Gain: Reliable shifting and clutch operation

Comp Modification: Bleed brake system

The Boxsters have a hydraulic clutch engagement system—there are no cables involved with the actuation of the clutch. Although this actually creates a more reliable clutch system over time, there can be a failure or breakdown of the system if the slave or master cylinder get old and begin to leak or fail. A spongy feel to the clutch pedal, grinding of gears when shifting, long pedal travel, and hydraulic leaks under the car are all signs that one or more components of the system have failed. The first place I like to start is the clutch slave cylinder, as it is easy and inexpensive to replace.

Replacement of the slave cylinder is also pretty easy. Its location is easy to get to from underneath the car. Start by jacking up the car (Project 1). The slave cylinder is located on the left side of the transmission—a single nut fastens it to the transmission. Begin by disconnecting the hydraulic line from the cylinder. Make sure you use a flare-nut wrench to remove the hose. These hydraulic fittings have a tendency to strip if you use a regular wrench. Also, inspect the clutch slave line—you might want to replace it if it's bulging or shows signs of cracking in the rubber. Before you disconnect the line, make sure that you have a drip pan to catch the fluid that will leak out.

Now, remove the 13mm head bolt that holds the cylinder to the transmission. The slave cylinder should remove easily. Install the new one and reattach the clutch fluid line. Place a little bit of white lithium grease on the tip of the slave cylinder prior to installation.

Replacement of the clutch master cylinder is fairly straightforward. Begin by removing the plastic cover to the left of the battery in the front trunk. Using a turkey baster, remove enough brake fluid to lower the level in the reservoir below the fill hole for the clutch master cylinder. Then disconnect both the supply line and the slave cylinder line (see Photo 1). Next, from underneath the dash, disconnect the master cylinder from the pedal and unbolt it from the car (Photo 2). Have a whole bunch of paper towels handy to wipe up any spilled brake fluid—the stuff is very hazardous to your car's paint.

The system now needs to be bled. I like to use the Motive Products Power Bleeder (available from PelicanParts.com) for this task. For more information on using the Power Bleeder, see Project 48 on Bleeding Brakes. Fill up the brake fluid reservoir to the MAX level, and attach the power bleeder to the top of the master cylinder reservoir. Press in the clutch pedal. Pump up the pressure in the bleeder to about 22 psi. Move to underneath the car and attach your bleeder hose to the bleed nipple on the slave cylinder. Open the bleeder valve by turning it counterclockwise and let the system bleed out until no more bubbles appear.

When finished, remove the bleeder system, lower the car, and try the clutch again. The pedal should have a good feel to it, and the clutch should engage normally. If you are still having problems, you should try replacing your clutch master cylinder next.

1 In the front trunk under the plastic cover, you will find the clutch master cylinder. Empty the fluid reservoir below the clutch fill hole, and then disconnect both the filler hose (red arrow) and the hydraulic line that leads to the slave cylinder (pry out the locking clip—yellow arrow).

2 From underneath the dash, remove the clevis pin (yellow arrow) and circlip that attaches the clutch master cylinder to the clutch pedal. Unbolt the two attachment bolts (green arrows) and slide the master cylinder out. The inset photo shows a brand new clutch master cylinder.

3 Shown here are the various components associated with the slave cylinder. The yellow arrow points to the slave cylinder and the green arrow is pointing to the bolt that attaches the slave cylinder to the transmission. The blue arrow shows the transmission backup lamp switch.

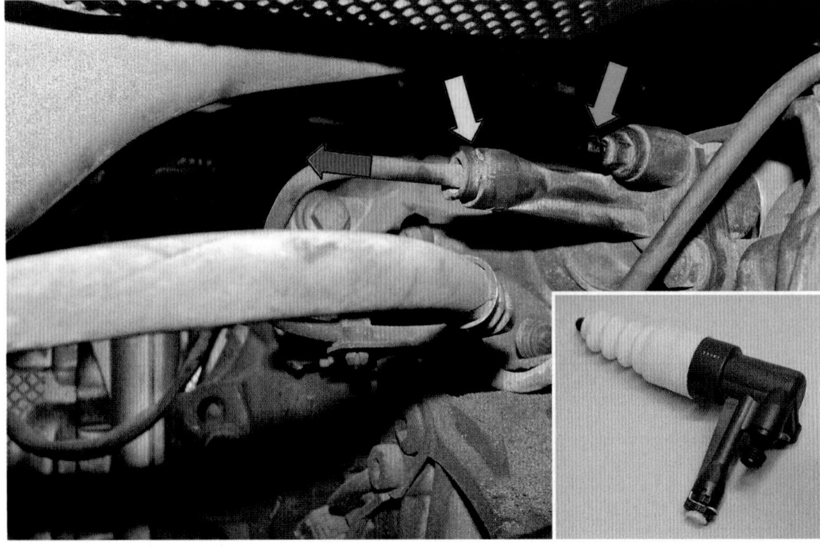

4 Here's a shot of the slave cylinder installed in the car. To disconnect the fluid line, simply remove the metal clip (yellow arrow) and pull the red line out of the bore. The green arrow points to the bleed nipple, which is required for bleeding air out of the clutch system.

SECTION 6
EXHAUST

Fortunately, Boxster exhaust systems are relatively simple, and upgrading and/or replacing components is fairly easy. This section shows you how to swap out mufflers, and also how to install a performance exhaust system.

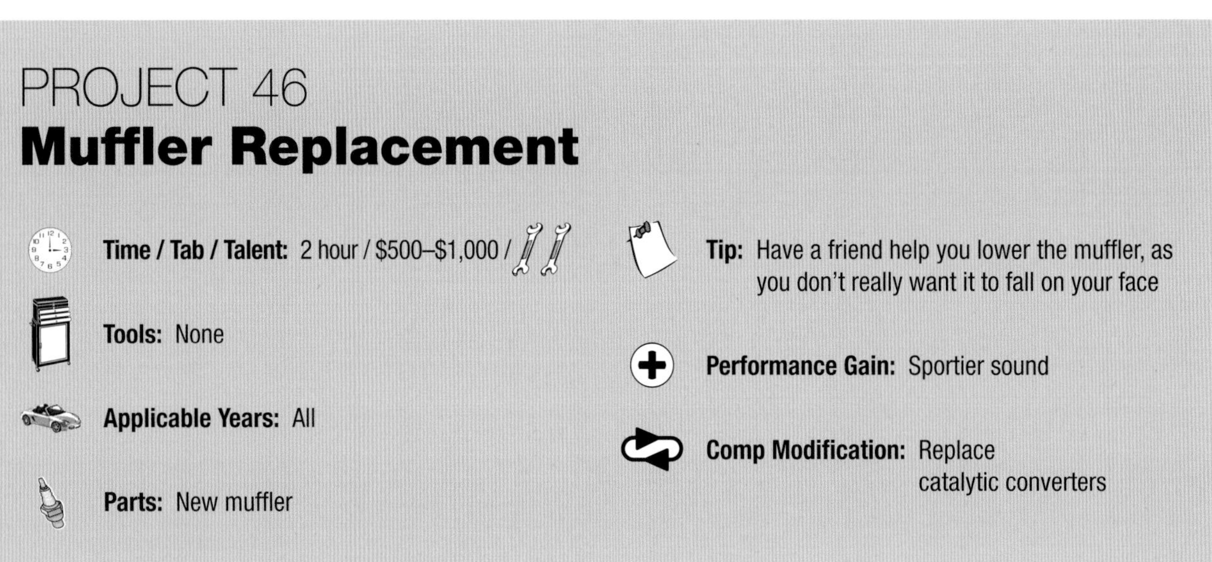

PROJECT 46
Muffler Replacement

Time / Tab / Talent: 2 hour / $500–$1,000 /

Tools: None

Applicable Years: All

Parts: New muffler

More Info: www.101projects.com/Boxster/46.htm

Tip: Have a friend help you lower the muffler, as you don't really want it to fall on your face

Performance Gain: Sportier sound

Comp Modification: Replace catalytic converters

One of the easiest and rewarding upgrades you can perform on your Boxster is to upgrade your muffler. Today's modern sports cars have exhaust systems that don't wear out as much as in the past, but there's still a definite need to upgrade to that "sporty sound." Luckily, on the 1997–2004, you can upgrade to a sport muffler pretty easily.

The process is quite simple—jack up the car, undo the brackets and pipes, and then drop down the muffler. I would definitely recommend having a buddy help you with the process—these mufflers are heavy and can be unwieldy, particularly underneath the car. Have a friend hold the muffler up into the car when you disconnect the brackets. Also, the removal of the muffler is made easier if you remove the rear bumper first, as you will have easier access to all of the mounting brackets.

The Dansk stainless steel sport muffler shown here is a great addition to your Boxster. Similar, if not identical to the sport muffler option provided on the Boxster S, the Dansk system is designed to give a sportier exhaust sound, all the while reducing backpressure and increasing horsepower. I have not personally tested its performance on the dyno (Project 101), but it certainly sounds great and is pretty easy to install. For a higher-performance system that includes high-flow catalytic converters, see Project 47.

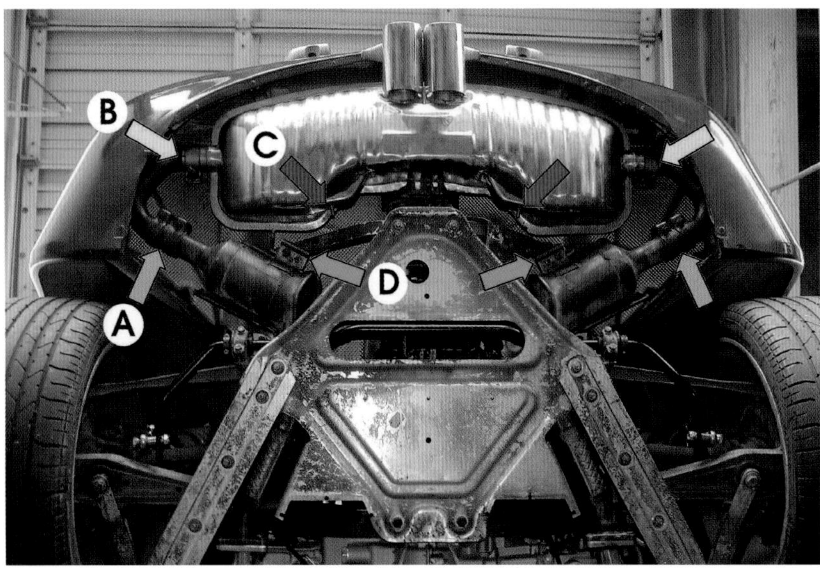

1 Shown here is the very cool-looking underside of the Boxster (1997–2004). There are a few pipes and brackets that need to be disconnected in order to remove the muffler. Items A/B/C/D correspond to the close-up shots in Photo 2.

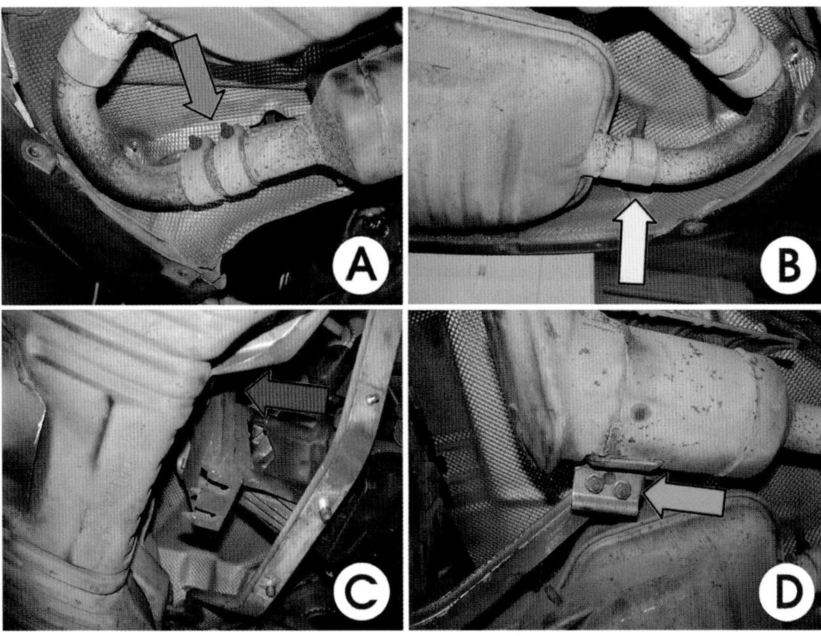

2 **A:** This is the catalytic converter side of the U-shaped pipe. Two clamps hold this connection together. **B:** The other side of the U-shaped pipe is clamped to the muffler. **C:** The topside of the muffler is bolted to the bracket on the back of the transmission. See the blue arrows in Photo 3 for details on the studs that connect to this bracket. **D:** The rear catalytic converters are supported by a small bracket shown here, which is attached to the muffler.

3 Here's a shot of the top of a Dansk sport muffler. The top muffler bracket that spans the length of the muffler is attached to studs welded onto the muffler (orange arrow). The bracket has studs that then mate with the bracket that is affixed to the transmission. The whole goofy setup seems way too complicated to me, but it appears to work fine.

4 In 2005, Porsche redesigned the whole exhaust system and made it a lot simpler. The muffler now has a built-in catalytic converter. It's attached at the rear of the car (yellow arrows) and is also supported by clamps in the middle (red arrow). A bracket in the center provides additional support (green arrow). The mufflers are attached to the exhaust manifolds all the way on the other side of the axles (orange arrows).

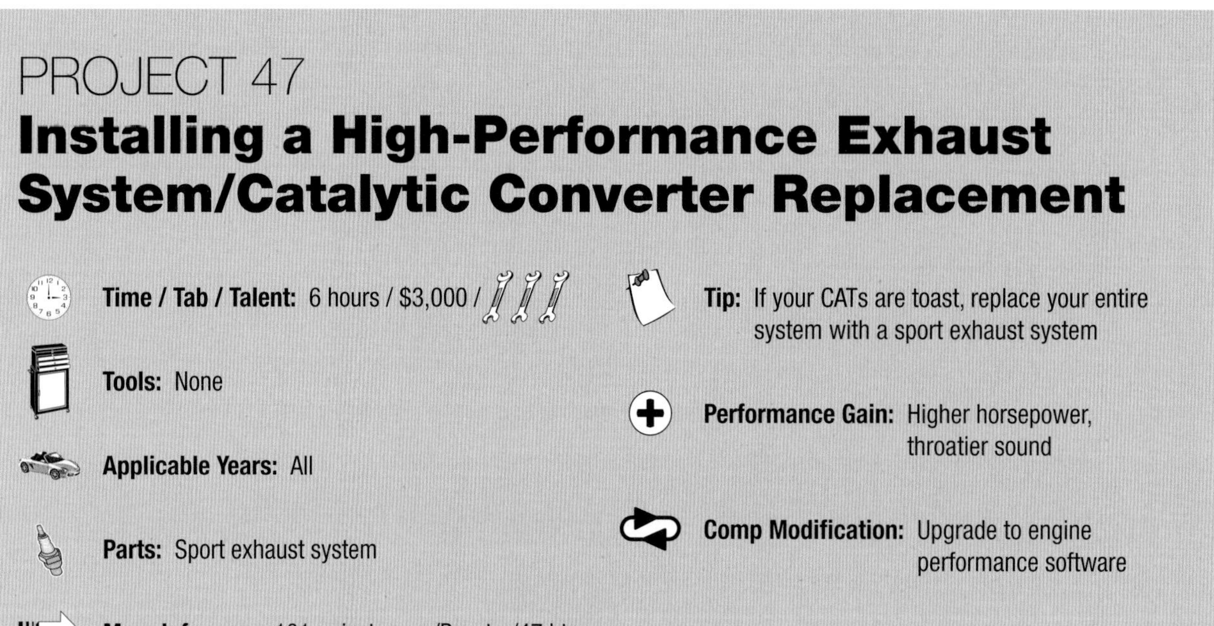

PROJECT 47

Installing a High-Performance Exhaust System/Catalytic Converter Replacement

Time / Tab / Talent: 6 hours / $3,000 /

Tools: None

Applicable Years: All

Parts: Sport exhaust system

More Info: www.101projects.com/Boxster/47.htm

Tip: If your CATs are toast, replace your entire system with a sport exhaust system

Performance Gain: Higher horsepower, throatier sound

Comp Modification: Upgrade to engine performance software

One of the most important emissions devices ever invented is the catalytic converter. The converter works by altering harmful exhaust gases into more environmentally friendly byproducts. The first converters used a platinum-coated ceramic honeycomb or aluminum-oxide pellets coated with platinum to convert HC and CO into water vapor (H_2O) and carbon dioxide (CO_2).

Starting in 1980, a new type of converter design was introduced. These new three-way catalytic converters control HC, CO, and NO_x emissions only when the air/fuel mixture is exactly set to 14.6:1. Without going into too much detail about fuel injection design theory, this air/fuel mixture is the absolute ideal for running the engine and is the overall goal of almost all fuel injection systems. With the installation of these new catalytic converters, the addition of an oxygen sensor is required. The oxygen sensor (Lambda or O_2 sensor) is connected to a computer that meters and controls the system to maintain, as best as possible, this 14.6:1 ratio. When the car is running at this level, also called the stoichiometric mixture, it has reached a high level of efficiency, and the catalytic converter is also working at its best.

Problems can occur for a number of reasons. If the oxygen sensor becomes disconnected or stops working, then the fuel control system can become confused and have difficulty metering the system. Usually this will cause the car to run richer than normal. Running the car in a rich mode instead of at its normal level can cause the catalytic converter to become clogged with soot from the exhaust system. As the converter, or CAT as it's sometimes called, becomes clogged, it can severely affect engine performance.

When you have catastrophic engine problems, you can sometimes damage your catalytic converters as well. With my 2.7-liter project car, the engine experienced a catastrophic failure, where coolant and oil mixed and were dumped into the exhaust system. There the mix sat for months or years. Very often, the remains of this stuff will burn off when you start your new engine, and many times the catalytic converters will recover. However, since this was a highly modified car with a 3.4 engine trying to pass California smog check, we decided not to take any chances and instead installed the high-performance system prior to taking it in for its smog check. Some components of coolant and engine oil are catalyst poisons—they coat the surface of the catalytic converter and render it less efficient or useless. Silicon and phosphorus, commonly found in coolant, and zinc additives, found in oil lubrication additives, are all detrimental to catalytic converters. When head gaskets fail, coolant mixes with engine oil and is often deposited into the exhaust (as was the case with our project car's original engine). The result is that the catalytic converters can become poisoned and permanently damaged.

Most Boxsters have a total of four catalytic converters, which makes replacing them extremely expensive (early 2.5-liter cars only have two). The primary converters are monitored by the Motronic engine management system via the signals output by the O_2 sensors. If one of your two primary converters is starting to go bad, then the Motronic computer (DME) will be able to figure this out and alert you with a check engine light (CEL) on the dashboard. Each one from Porsche costs about $1,000–$1,500, which makes replacing them extremely expensive (aftermarket ones are available, although are still expensive at about $300 each). You can find plenty of used ones on the market, but there's no guarantee that a used one is any good, and it's difficult to near impossible to test them prior to installation. The solution I recommend is to install a high-performance exhaust system like the one I put on my project Boxster here. See the photo array for installation instructions.

Another alternative is to bypass the converter completely. While this will generate less restriction than a CAT, the tailpipe emissions will basically go through the roof. If you decide that you wish to remove the CATs from your Boxster and replace them with headers, then you will find that your DME will generate secondary O_2 sensor errors. This is because the system will see no difference between the readings of the primary and secondary O_2 sensors. Using CAT bypass headers and pipes in most states is legal only for off-road use and should only be used for racing purposes. Removing the catalytic converter from your car will make it output significantly more emissions than today's new cars. Doing so is not really worth the few extra horsepower that you will gain from polluting the air.

Troubleshooting CAT problems can be a bit frustrating. Some clues that the car may have a CAT problem include loss of power at higher rpm's and speed even though the car idles perfectly fine. Many mechanics troubleshoot the fuel injection system first (indeed a smart place to start) but never really think that the problem might be a clogged CAT. If you remove the CAT, you should be able to clearly see through it. Chances are if you shine a bright light on one end, and you can't see any light through the other end, then it's clogged. The Boxster CAT has a right angle built in, so you can't really see directly through regardless, but some reflected light should be able to shine through. Cars that have recently had their oxygen sensor replaced are ideal candidates for CAT problems. If you purchase a car that has receipts that include an oxygen sensor replacement, be aware that the previous owner might have possibly driven the car many miles in a rich condition, thus damaging the CAT. If your car is having problems passing an emissions test, it may be a sign that your CAT is worn out and needs to be replaced. You may also be surprised at the additional horsepower that you might gain when replacing the CAT. Any clogs in the CAT will directly affect the efficiency and power of the engine.

It is very common for the nuts and bolts on older cars to rust and make exhaust components very difficult to remove. This very well may be the case with your CAT. If so, then you might need to grind off the nuts and/or heads of the bolts to get the CAT off of the car. It's not an easy job, and it is complicated by the lack of room underneath the car. If you have extreme difficulty, then take the car to your local mechanic. The header bolts are very prone to breaking and if they are highly rusted, they should be heated up red-hot with an oxy-acetylene torch to assist in their removal.

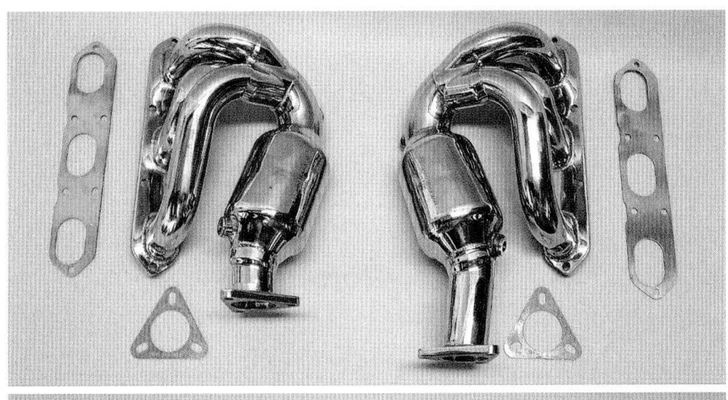

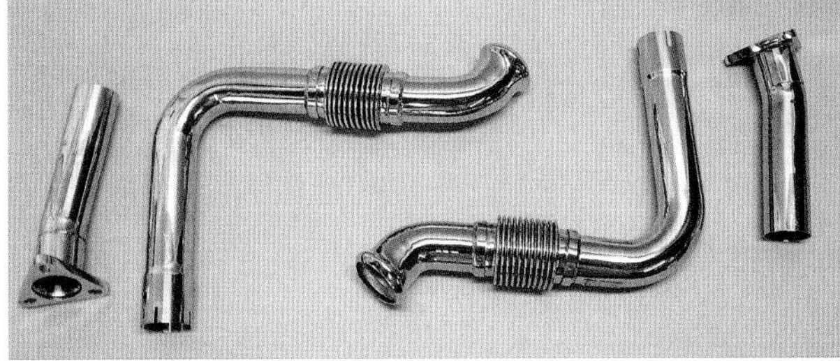

1 Shown here is the Boxster Maxflo Exhaust manufactured by Fabspeed Motorsport and available from PelicanParts.com. This finely crafted setup is manufactured out of high-performance T304 stainless steel and is CNC mandrel bent for optimum flow and fewer restrictions than Porsche factory exhaust systems. The Maxflo header systems feature 2-inch (50mm) pipes that connect to a dedicated true 2.25-inch dual muffler system (only one shown in the photo). The dual canister Maxflo exhaust system is low profile and utilizes secondary CAT bypass pipes to save 30 pounds of weight compared with the Porsche factory system. Plus, the whole sound of the system is way cooler than the wimpy stock factory muffler.

2 The two mufflers are joined together to reduce resonance and balance the exhaust on both sides.

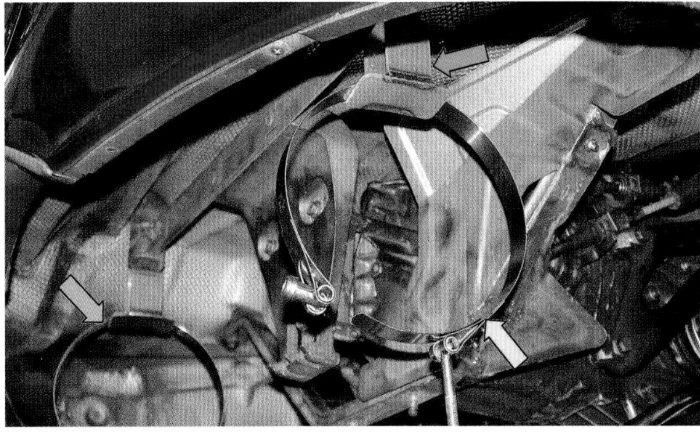

3 The system utilizes the long stock muffler mounting bracket that normally is attached to the top of the stock muffler. Custom brackets attach to the existing mounting holes on the bracket (green arrow). A large stainless steel clamp is used to support the weight of each muffler from the bracket (yellow arrow). There are two brackets, one on each side (blue arrow, opposite side).

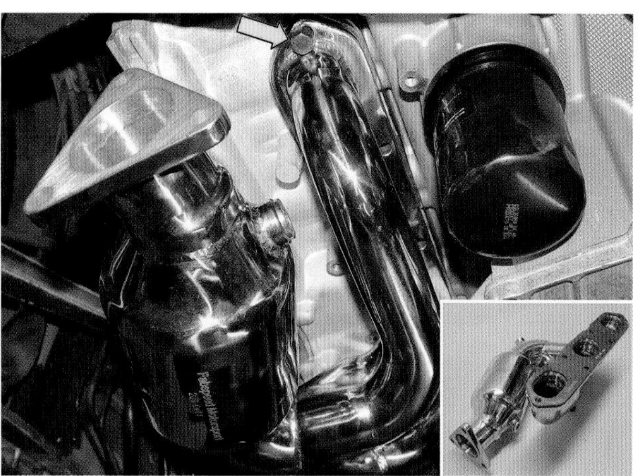

4 This system includes a pair of high-flow catalytic converters. As mentioned in the text, these converters are lighter weight and also are more efficient than the stock dual units designed over a decade ago. Use the stock manifold hardware (yellow arrow) to mount the header/CAT unit with the supplied copper gasket (inset).

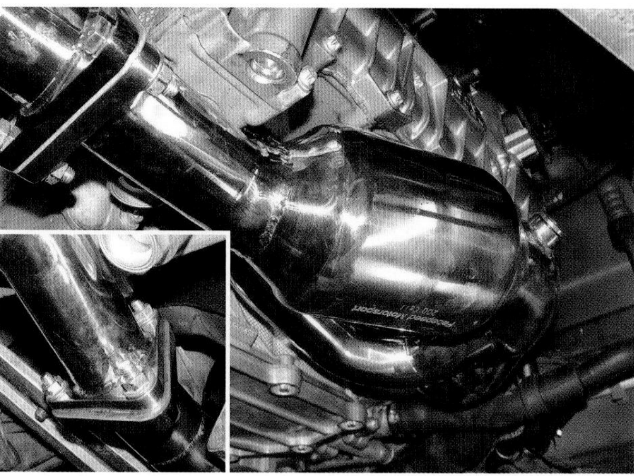

5 Here's a side shot of the new catalytic converter unit installed. These things look so good, it's a shame they are hidden underneath the engine. Connect the joints together using the supplied thick copper gaskets and self-locking copper nuts.

6 The crossover pipes are attached to the ends of the catalytic converter/ header assembly and joined with a clamp (inset). This allows some flexibility when installing the system. All cars are made slightly differently, and sometimes rigid pieces of exhaust pipe will not fit perfectly without some give and take.

7 The secondary pipes that connect to each muffler have a built-in flexible joint. This allows vibration and chassis flex to be transmitted through the exhaust system without weakening the joints or causing annoying exhaust leaks. The secondary pipe is attached directly to the muffler via a heavy-duty exhaust clamp (yellow arrow).

8 On the Maxflo system, an additional support bracket attaches to the lower part of the original muffler bracket on the transmission (yellow arrow). This helps support and retain the two mufflers via a set of brackets that attach to the large stainless steel muffler clamps (red arrow). The clamps are also supported by the original muffler hanger (blue arrow).

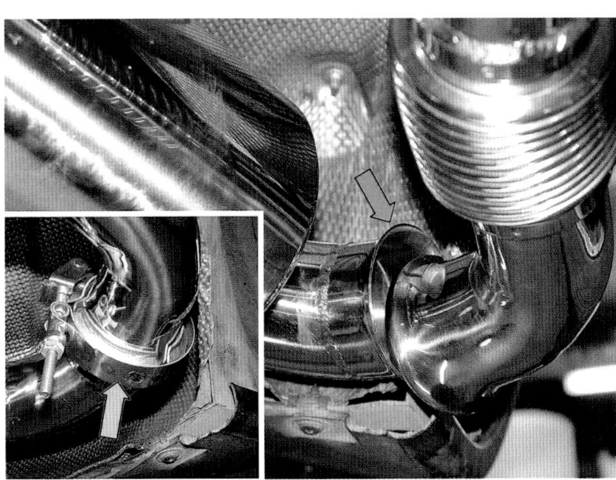

9 There's not much chance of these joints leaking. Instead of using an exhaust gasket here, Fabspeed uses a high-quality clamp that both joins the pipes together and seals the connection. The inherent spring in the clamp assures that the connection will be tight regardless of temperature or vibration.

10 With the whole system connected, the final step is to install your oxygen sensors (O_2 sensors). The stock sensors should fit, and the cables should be the proper lengths—just like the stock units.

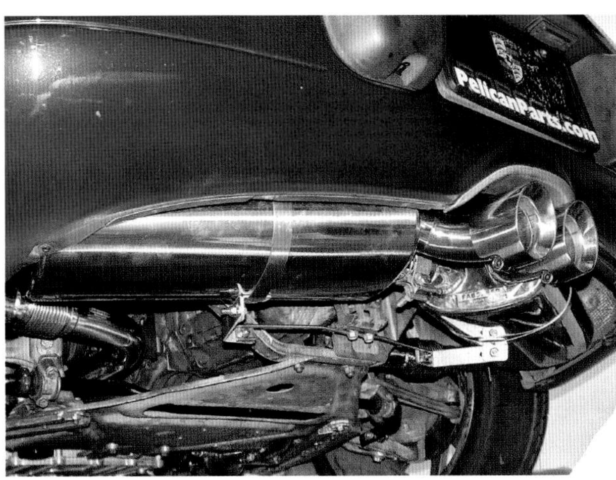

11 Here's a rear shot of the completed unit with all of the brackets installed.

12 The rear tailpipes are dramatically different from the stock muffler, and the sound that comes out matches the look. It's a deep, throaty, performance-type sound that's not "annoyingly loud," but makes you think, "Why didn't they design the stock system to sound like this?" Actually, Porsche probably toned down the stock system to appeal to "sensitive" initial buyers and also to encourage buyers to pay more to upgrade to one of their premium exhaust packages at the time of purchase.

13 Yikes! This is what our project Boxster looked like when we went to start it for the first time with the new engine. We had temporarily used the old exhaust system from the 2.7 motor, and all four catalytic converters were full of oil and coolant when we initially started it up. The mix of coolant and oil in the converters from the engine failure most likely rendered them inoperative.

SECTION 7
BRAKES

Your brakes are probably the most important system on your Porsche. No matter how fast you go, you will always need to stop, and sometimes rather quickly. It's of paramount importance to keep your brakes in top condition. The stock Boxster braking system is a very capable setup if properly maintained. The projects in this section detail the troubleshooting, restoration, upgrades, and maintenance of your all-important brake system.

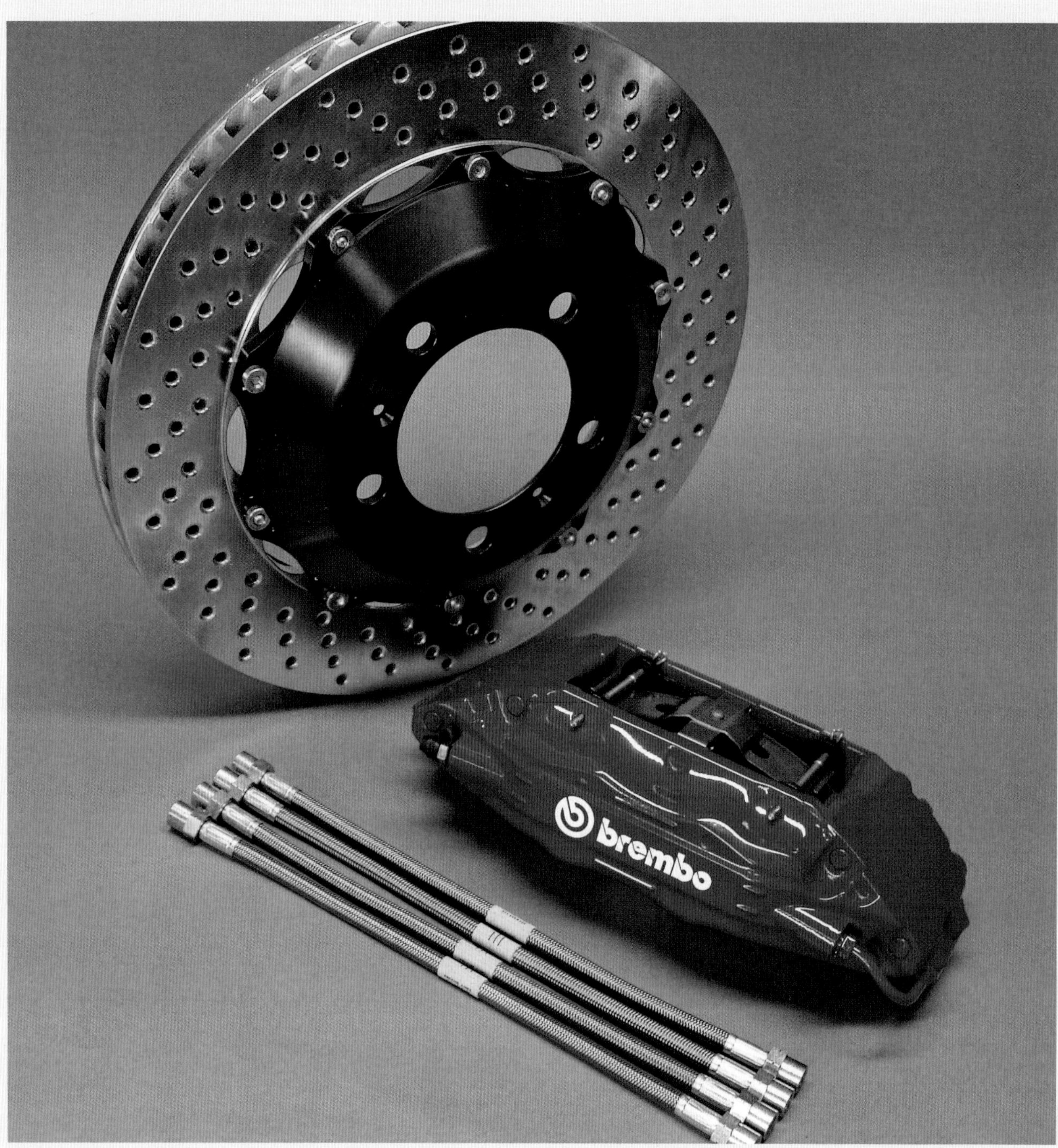

PROJECT 48
Bleeding Brakes

Time / Tab / Talent: 2 hours / $20 /

Tools: Power Bleeder, 11mm wrench, floor jack, jack stands

Applicable Years: All

Parts: 3-plus quarts of brake fluid

More Info: www.101projects.com/Boxster/48.htm

Tip: Use different-colored brake fluid so that you know when your system is flushed

Performance Gain: Quicker, firmer stopping

Comp Modification: Rebuild brake calipers

Bleeding brakes is not one of my personal favorite jobs. There seems to be a bit of black magic involved with the bleeding process. Sometimes it will work perfectly, and then other times it seems like you end up with a lot of air in your system. The best strategy to follow when bleeding your brakes is to repeat the procedure several times in order to make sure that you have removed all the trapped air from the system.

The basic Boxster brake system with anti-lock brakes (ABS 5.3 and 5.7 without PSM) can be bled using traditional methods. For cars with traction control or Porsche Stability Management (PSM), you need to use the Porsche System Tester 2 (PST2) in order to activate the valves in the hydraulic unit during the bleeding process. If your car has a "PSM off" switch on the dashboard, then you will need to go to a shop that has a PST2 so that the brake system can be bled properly.

There are currently two popular methods of bleeding the brake system: pressure bleeding and vacuum bleeding. Pressure bleeding uses a reservoir of brake fluid that has a positive air pressure force placed on the opposite side of the fluid, which forces it into the brake system. Vacuum bleeding is where you fill the reservoir and then apply a vacuum at the bleeder nipple to pull fluid through the system.

The method that I've come up with combines the first method described above and yet another third finishing method. Basically, I advocate bleeding the system with the pressure bleeder and then using a family member to stomp on the pedal to free up any trapped air in the system. If the family member really owes you big-time, you will be the one stomping on the pedal, and they can spill brake fluid all over themselves while working near the calipers.

The first step in bleeding your brakes is to jack up the car and remove all four wheels (see Project 1). The next step is to fill the system with brake fluid. I recommend using colored brake fluid, such as ATE SuperBlue, in order to determine when fresh fluid has been flushed through the entire system. One of my favorite tools for pressure bleeding is the Motive Products Bleeder. The system has a hand pump that you can use to pressurize the brake fluid to just about any pressure. A small gauge on the front of the brake fluid reservoir indicates the pressure of the brake fluid inside. The very large reservoir can hold about two quarts of brake fluid—more than enough for most brake flushing and bleeding jobs. Retailing for about $50 online from PelicanParts.com, the bleeder kit is a very useful and cost-effective tool to have in your collection.

The system bleeds by pressurizing a bottle filled with brake fluid from air from an internal hand pump. The procedure is to add fluid, attach the bleeder to the top of the reservoir cap, and pump up the bleeder bottle to about 25 psi using the hand pump. This will pressurize the system. Check to make sure that there are no leaks around the bleeder or where it attaches to the top of the master cylinder reservoir.

Now start bleeding the system. Start with the right rear caliper, the one that's located furthest away from the master cylinder. Bleed the right rear caliper by attaching a hose to the bleed nipple, placing it in a jar, and then opening the valve by turning the bleeder nipple counter-clockwise with an 11mm wrench. Let the fluid flow out until there are no more bubbles. If you don't have a pressure bleeder system, you need to find someone to press on the pedal repeatedly to force fluid through the system. Another solution is to get a check valve and place it on the nipple while you stomp on the pedal (see Photo 3). This will work for getting fluid into the system, but you will still need a second person for the final step to make sure you have bled the system completely. The Boxster calipers have two bleed nipples—bleed the outer ones first.

When no more air bubbles come out, then move to the next caliper. Bleed them in this order: right rear caliper, left rear caliper, right front caliper, left front caliper. Bleeding in this order will minimize the amount of air that gets into the system.

Repeat the process until you can no longer see any air bubbles coming out of any of the calipers. Make sure that you don't run out of brake fluid in your reservoir or you will have to start over again. It is wise to start out with about a ½ gallon of brake fluid in the pressure bleeder and another ½ gallon on the shelf in reserve. Depending upon your car, and the mistakes you may make, I recommend having an ample supply. Also, only use new brake fluid from a sealed can. Brake fluid is hydroscopic, meaning that it attracts water and water vapor, which diminishes its performance. Brake fluid containers left exposed to air will have the fluid inside compromised after a short period of time.

If you had to replace the master cylinder, or if the system needs a large amount of fluid, then supplement the bleeding process by opening up the right rear nipple and then pressing down on the brake pedal two or three times. Slowly release the pedal. Repeat for the other three corners of the car.

During the bleeding process, it's very easy to forget to check your master cylinder reservoir. As you are removing fluid from the calipers, it will be emptying the master cylinder reservoir. If the reservoir goes empty, then you will most certainly add some air bubbles in to the system, and you will have to start all over. Keep an eye on the fluid level and don't forget to refill it. Make sure that you always put the cap back on the reservoir. If the cap is off, then brake fluid may splash out and damage your paint when the brake pedal is released. If you are using a pressure bleeder system, make sure that you often check the level of brake fluid in the bleeder reservoir so that it doesn't accidentally run dry.

If you are installing a new master cylinder, it's probably a wise idea to perform what is called a dry bleed on the workbench. This is simply the process of getting the master cylinder full of brake fluid and "wet." Simply add some brake fluid to both chambers of the master cylinder and pump it a few times. This will save you a few moments when bleeding the brakes.

Now, make sure that all the bleeder valves are closed tightly. Disconnect the pressure system from the reservoir. Now, get your family member to press down repeatedly on the brake pedal at least five times, and then hold it down. Then open the bleeder valve on the right rear caliper. The system should lose pressure, and the pedal should sink to the floor. When the fluid stops coming out of the bleeder valve, close the valve, and then tell your family member to let their foot off of the pedal. Do not let them take their foot off until you have completely closed the valve. Repeat this motion for each bleeder valve on each caliper at least three times. Repeat this entire procedure for all the valves in the same order as described previously.

I recommend that you use this procedure as a final step, even if you are vacuum or pressure bleeding. The high force associated with the pressure from the brake pedal can help free air and debris in the lines. If the brake fluid doesn't exit the nipple quickly, then you might have a clog in your lines. Brake fluid that simply oozes out of the lines slowly is a clear indication that your rubber lines might be clogged and constricted. Don't ignore these warning signs—check out the brake lines while you are working in this area (see Project 54).

Now, let the car sit for about 10 minutes. Repeat the bleeding process at each corner. The pedal should now feel pretty stiff. If the pedal still feels spongy, make sure that you have the proper adjustment on your rear calipers or parking brake drum shoes. Also, you may need a new master cylinder, have a leaky caliper, or have old spongy flexible brake lines.

For cars with the standard ABS 5.3, the bleeding method detailed here works very well. If you find that your ABS-equipped car feels spongy on the brake pedal, take the car to a deserted parking lot and engage the ABS system by stopping short a few times. Then go back and re-bleed the system—it should take care of the spongy pedal.

Another important thing to remember is that brake fluid kills—paint jobs, that is. Brake fluid spilled on paint will permanently mar the surface, so be very careful not to touch the car if you have it on your hands and clothing. This, of course, is easier said than done—don't bleed the system in a tight garage. The probability of spilling on yourself and then leaning against your car is too great. Rubber gloves help protect you from getting it on your hands and your paint. If you do get a spot on your paint, make sure that you blot it with a paper towel—don't wipe or smear it. It's also important not to try to clean it off with any chemical or other cleaning solutions.

1 There are few little tricks that you can use when changing your brake fluid. The company ATE makes a brake fluid called SuperBlue that comes in two different colors. It's a smart idea to fill your reservoir (green arrow) with a different-colored fluid and then bleed the brakes. When the new-colored fluid exits out of the caliper, you will know that you have fresh fluid in your system. Make sure that you use DOT 4 brake fluid in your car. The use of silicone DOT 5 fluid is not recommended for street use, and never mix DOT 4 and DOT 5 fluid together or severe component corrosion can occur. Shown here is the Motive Products Power Bleeder. Available for about $50 from PelicanParts.com, it is a huge timesaver when it comes to bleeding your brakes.

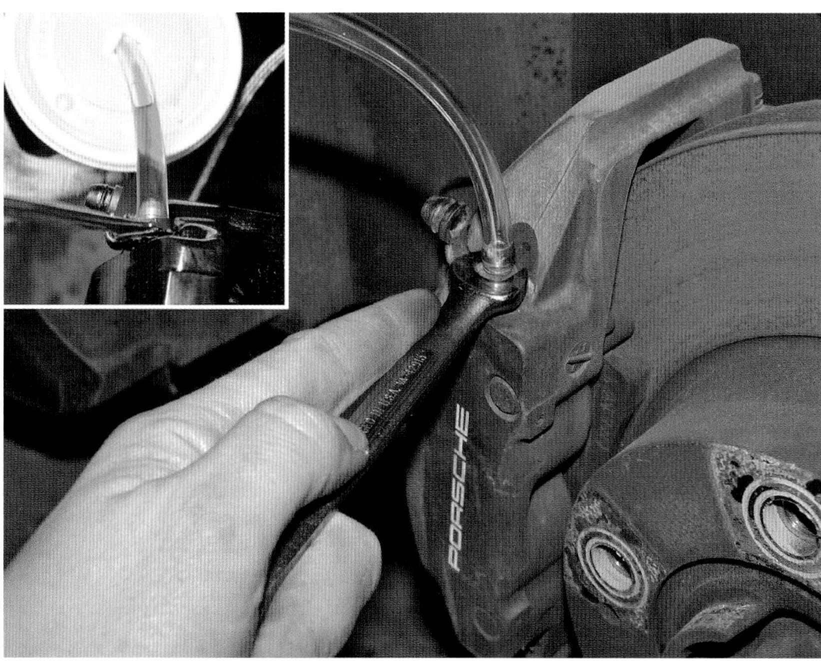

2 Open the bleed nipple by loosening it in the caliper by about a quarter of a turn. If you can fit a flare-nut wrench over the bleed nipple, then I recommend using one, to help avoid rounding out the nipple. Let the brake fluid run out of the caliper until no more bubbles appear (inset). You should also routinely flush and replace your brake fluid every two years. Deposits and debris can build up in the lines over time and decrease the efficiency of your brakes. Regular bleeding of your system can also help you spot brake problems that you wouldn't necessarily notice simply by driving the car. Also, never reuse brake fluid—always use new, fresh fluid. In addition, don't use brake fluid that has come from an empty can that has been sitting on the shelf or sitting in your Power Bleeder for a while. The brake fluid has a tendency to absorb moisture when sitting on the shelf. This moisture "boils" out of the brake fluid when you start using the brakes and can result in a spongy pedal.

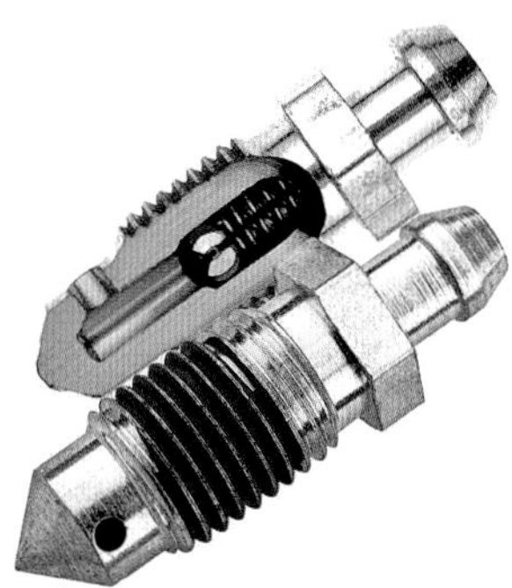

3 There is a relatively new product out called Speed Bleeders. These small caps replace the standard bleeder valves located on your calipers. The Speed Bleeder has a built-in check valve that eliminates the need for a second person when pedal bleeding the brakes. Simply open the bleeder valve for a particular caliper and step on the brake pedal. The Speed Bleeder will allow brake fluid to cleanly bleed out of the system without sucking air back in. When used in conjunction with a pressure bleeder system, you can achieve a pretty firm pedal bleeding the brakes by yourself. I still recommend using the two-person pedal-stepping method as a final procedure, simply because the high pressure from this method can help unclog trapped air bubbles.

PROJECT 49
Replacing Brake Pads

Time / Tab / Talent: 2 hours / $150 /

Tools: Screwdriver, isopropyl alcohol, wooden block

Applicable Years: All

Parts: Brake pads

More Info: www.101projects.com/Boxster/49.htm

Tip: Check your brake discs when replacing your pads in case they have worn too thin

Performance Gain: Better braking

Comp Modification: Caliper rebuild, brake disc replacement, install stainless steel brake lines

Replacing your brake pads is one of the easiest jobs to perform on your Boxster. In general, you should inspect your brake pads about every 10,000 miles and replace them if the material lining of the pad is worn down enough to trigger the pad replacement sensor. In reality, most people don't inspect their pads very often and usually wait until they see the little brake-warning lamp appear on the dashboard. It's a wise idea to replace the pads and inspect your discs as soon as you see that warning lamp go on.

If you ignore the warning lamp, you may indeed get to the point of metal-on-metal contact, where the metal backing of the pads may be contacting the brake discs. Using the brakes during this condition will not only give you inadequate braking, but will also begin to wear grooves in your brake discs. Once the discs are grooved, they are damaged, and there is often no way to repair them. Resurfacing will sometimes work, but often the groove that is cut will be deeper than is allowed by the Porsche specifications. The smart thing to do is to replace your pads right away.

Brake pads should only be replaced in pairs—replace both front pads or both rear pads at a time. The same rule applies to the brake discs that should be checked each time you replace your brake pads.

The procedure for replacing pads on all the wheels is basically the same. There are slight configuration differences between front and rear brakes, but in general the procedure for replacement is similar. The first step is to jack up the car and remove the road wheel (slightly loosen the lug nuts before you lift the car off of the ground). This will expose the brake caliper that presses the pads against the disc. Make sure that the parking brake is off when you start to work on the pads.

Begin by using a pair of needle-nose pliers to remove the brake pad sensor (see Photo 1). The pads are held within the caliper by two retaining pins. There are also small retaining clips that hold these two retaining pins in the caliper. Start by removing the small retaining clips, and then tap out the retaining pins using a small screwdriver and a hammer (see Photo 2). When the two retaining pins are removed, the cross spring that holds the pads in place will fall out. Now the pads can be pried out with a screwdriver (Photo 3). Use the small holes on the pads that normally surround the retaining pin as a leverage point for removing them. They may require some wiggling to remove, as it is sometimes a tight fit. It is important to keep in mind that the caliper piston is also probably pressing against the pads slightly and will add to the difficulty in removing them.

Once you have the pads removed, inspect the inside of the caliper. You should clean this area with some compressed air and isopropyl alcohol. Make sure that the dust boots and the clamping rings inside the caliper are not ripped or damaged. If they are, then the caliper may need to be rebuilt (see Project 50).

At this point, you should inspect the brake discs carefully. Using a micrometer, take a measurement of the disc thickness. If the disc is worn beyond its specifications, then it's time to replace it along with the one on the opposite side. See Project 55 for more information.

The installation of the new brake pads is quite easy. You will need to take a small piece of wood or plastic and push the caliper piston back into the caliper. This is because the new pads are going to be quite a bit thicker than the old ones, and the piston is set in the old pad's position. Pry back the piston using the wood, being careful not to use too much force (see Photo 4). Using a screwdriver here is not recommended as it can accidentally damage the dust boots and seals inside the caliper. Make sure that you push both pistons (inside and outside) back in the caliper.

Be aware that as you push back the pistons in the calipers, you will cause the level of the brake reservoir to rise. Make sure that you don't have too much fluid in your reservoir. If the level is high, you may have to siphon out a bit from the reservoir to prevent it from overflowing. Also make sure that you have the cap securely fastened to the top of reservoir. Failure to do this may result in brake fluid accidentally getting on your paint.

When the piston is pushed all the way back, you should then be able to insert the pad into the caliper. If you encounter resistance, double check to make sure that the inside of the caliper is clean. You can use a small hammer to tap it in, but don't use too much force. When the pads are in place, insert the retaining pins and spring clip back into place. It's wise to use a new set of pins and clips when replacing your pads. Make sure that you replace the pin retaining clips inside the small holes in the retaining pins.

In general, I recommend removing and replacing the brake pads one side at a time. When the piston is pushed back into the caliper, it will try to push out the piston on the opposite side of the caliper. Leaving the brake pad installed on one side keeps the piston from being pushed out too far.

You also may want to spray the back of the brake pads with some anti-squeal glue. This glue basically keeps the pads and the pistons glued together and prevents noisy vibration. Some brands of pads may come with anti-squeal pads already attached to the rear surface. Anti-squeal pads can also be purchased separately as sheets that are peeled off and stuck on the rear of the pads.

When finished with both sides, press on the brake pedal repeatedly to make sure that the pads and the pistons seat properly. Also make sure that you top off the master cylinder brake fluid reservoir if necessary. Brake pads typically take between 100 and 200 miles to completely break in. It's typical for braking performance to suffer slightly as the pads begin their wear-in period. Make sure that you avoid any heavy braking during this period.

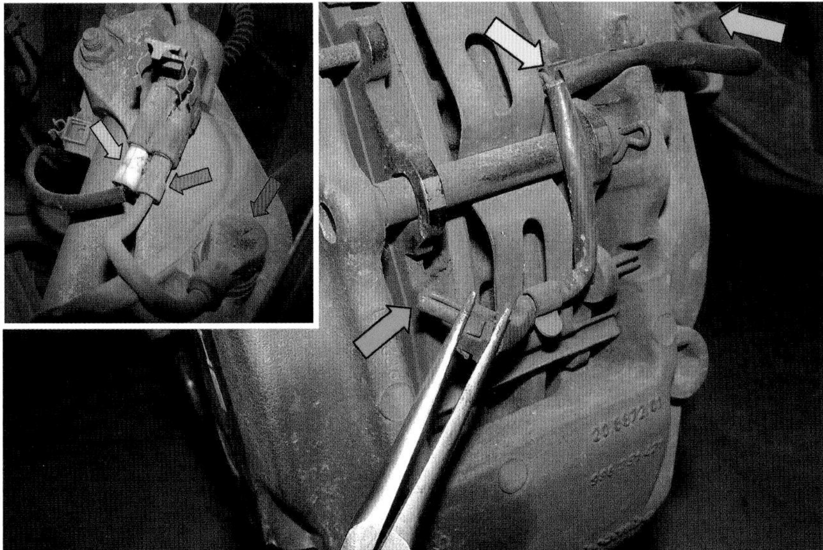

1 Grab the brake pad sensor (yellow and green arrows) with a pair of needle-nose pliers. If your brake sensors activated the lamp on your dashboard, they should be replaced with new ones. Disconnect the sensor, and plug in the new one—the plug for the sensor is located in the top of the wheelwell (orange arrow). This photo also shows the wheel speed sensor and plug (red arrow and purple arrow), which is used with the anti-lock braking system (ABS)

2 To remove the old pads, pull out the small pin retainers (blue arrow, inset), and tap out the retaining pins (green arrow) with a screwdriver and a small hammer. They should slide out pretty easily, as there is usually no load on them. If there is much difficulty encountered during the removal process, then tap on the pads slightly to remove pressure from the pins. The yellow points to the electrical cable clip for the brake pad sensor.

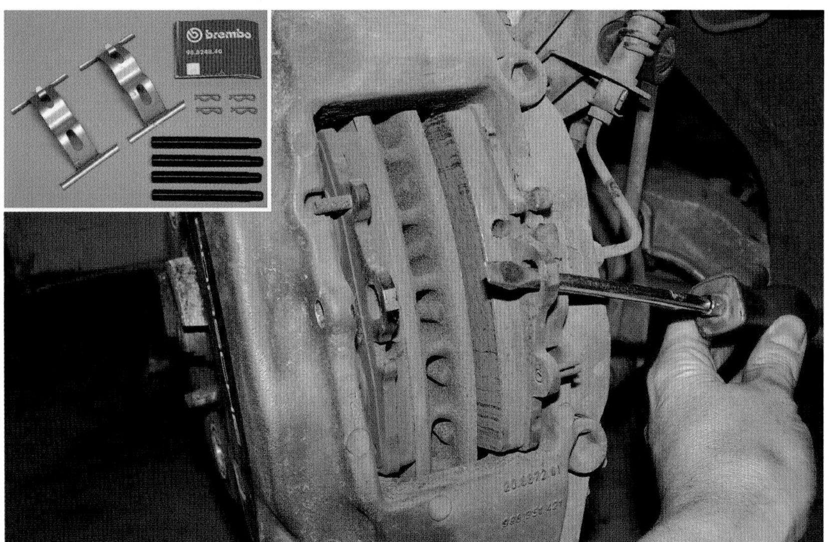

3 Pulling out the pads usually involves the use of a screwdriver for leverage. The pads are loose in the caliper, but it's a pretty tight fit, and there is usually lots of dust and debris in the caliper. Wiggle the pads back and forth in order to pry them free. Although these parts usually can be reused, some people prefer to install new retainer kits. The kits include two new retainer springs, four pin clips, and four pins that are used to hold the pads into the caliper.

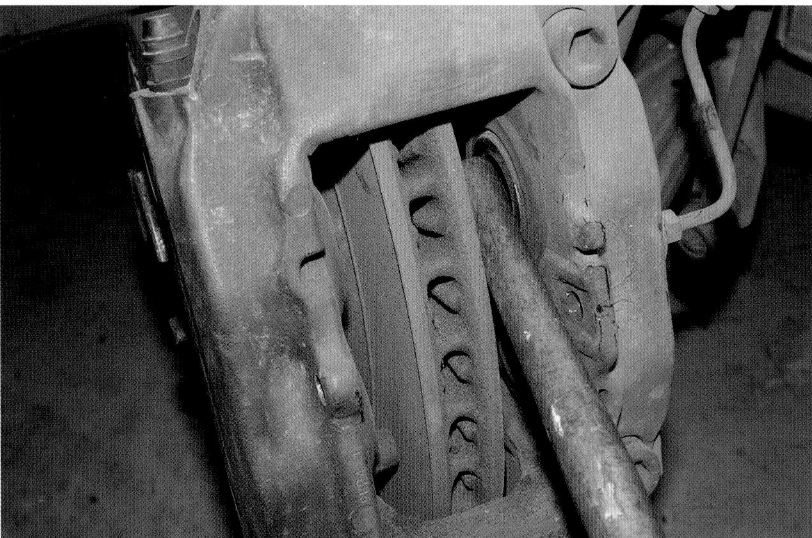

4 When you are ready to install the pads back into the caliper, use a wooden or plastic handle to push back the caliper pistons. Don't use a screwdriver, as you might damage some of the piston seals. Keep your eye on the fluid level in the master cylinder reservoir—it can overflow when you push back on the pistons.

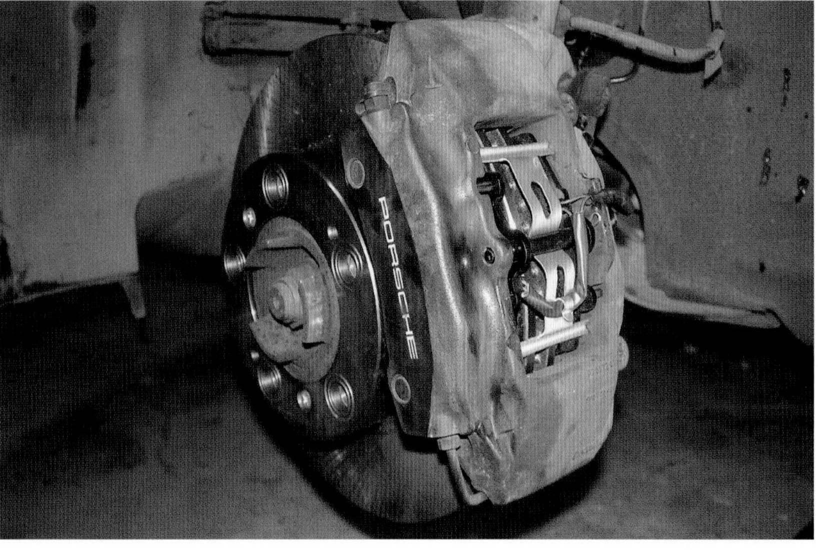

5 Don't forget to reinstall the small retaining clips for the pad retaining pins. The completed assembly should be carefully tested before you do any performance driving. Brake pads can also take several hundred miles to fully break themselves in. Exercise care when driving with brand new brake pads.

PROJECT 50
Rebuilding Your Brake Calipers

Time / Tab / Talent: 6 hours / $60 /

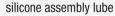

Tools: Flared-end wrench to remove brake lines

Applicable Years: All

Parts: Brake caliper rebuild kits, brake fluid, silicone assembly lube

More Info: www.101projects.com/Boxster/50.htm

Tip: Soak the caliper in parts cleaner overnight if possible

Performance Gain: Better braking—no more sticking calipers

Comp Modification: Replace the flexible brake lines, replace brake pads and discs

If your car is pulling to one side when braking, then there is a good chance that you might have a sticky caliper that needs rebuilding. The rebuilding process is actually a lot simpler than most people think. It basically involves removing the caliper, cleaning it, and then reinstalling all of the components with new seals. Very often, the most difficult part of the task is the process of actually removing the caliper from the car.

The first step is to jack up the car and remove the caliper. Refer to Project 55 for details on removing the caliper from around the brake disc. Refer to Project 54 for more details on disconnecting the brake line from the caliper.

Once you have the caliper free and clear from the car, take it over to your workbench and begin the disassembly process.

The first step is to remove each of the four pistons from the calipers. One method of removal is to use compressed air to blow out the piston. Using a small screwdriver, remove the dust boot that surrounds the piston. Place a small block of wood in the center of the caliper to prevent the pistons from flying out of the caliper. Blow compressed air through the caliper bleeder hole to force the piston out of its chamber. Start slowly and gradually increase pressure until the piston reaches the block of wood. Make sure that the piston doesn't come all the way out of its chamber. After the piston is far enough out, you should be able to get a grip on it with your fingers. Be careful when working with the compressed air, as it is more powerful than it appears and can make the pistons suddenly fly out of the caliper unexpectedly.

Using a rag to protect the sides of each piston, carefully remove all of them from the caliper using either your hands or a large pair of vise grips. Make sure that you don't touch the sides of the pistons with any metal tools, as you don't want to scratch this surface.

If the piston is frozen, then more radical methods of removal may be necessary. Using a block of wood, you can try pounding the half of the caliper on the block of wood until the piston begins to fall out. If the piston starts to come out and then gets stuck, push it back in all the way and try again. Eventually, the piston should come out of the caliper half. Another method is to use the car's braking system to release the pistons. Reconnect the caliper to the car and have an assistant pump the brakes to force out the piston.

Once the pistons have been removed from the caliper, carefully clean both the inside and outside of the caliper using brake cleaner or another appropriate solvent. All of the passages should be blown out with compressed air, and it's a good idea to let the whole assembly sit in some parts cleaner overnight. If the piston or the inside of the caliper is badly corroded or pitted, then the caliper should be replaced. A little bit of surface rust is okay—this should be polished off using a coarse cloth or some Scotch-Brite. Make sure that you thoroughly scrub out the entire inside of the caliper and the piston so that they are perfectly clean.

After the caliper and piston have been cleaned and are dry, coat the caliper and piston with silicone assembly lube. If you don't have this silicone assembly lube handy (it's available from PelicanParts.com), then make sure you coat the entire assembly with clean brake fluid. Do not get any lube or brake fluid on the dust boot.

Insert the new piston seal into the inside of the caliper piston groove. It should fit smoothly in the groove, yet stick out only slightly. Make sure that you wet the seal with a little brake fluid prior to installation. Now install the dust boot onto the piston so that the edge of the boot fits into the inside groove of the piston. Then, insert the piston slightly into the caliper. It should slide in easily—make sure that it doesn't get cocked. Push the piston all the way into the caliper. As the piston reaches the internal O-ring, you will encounter some resistance. Make sure that the piston doesn't become cocked as you insert it. If you have trouble inserting the piston into the caliper, you may want to softly tap it with a plastic hammer or use a small piece of wood to compress the piston into its home position in the caliper housing. Finally, make sure the outer rim of the seal mates properly with its groove in the caliper housing.

Install the brake pads (Project 49), and remount the caliper back onto the car. Bleed the brake system (Project 48), and you should be good to go. Make sure that you carefully check the brakes on the car before you do any significant driving.

1 Remove the outer seal by simply prying it out of the caliper housing. The new seals are installed in reverse fashion but may require some finesse work to get them properly seated in their grooves.

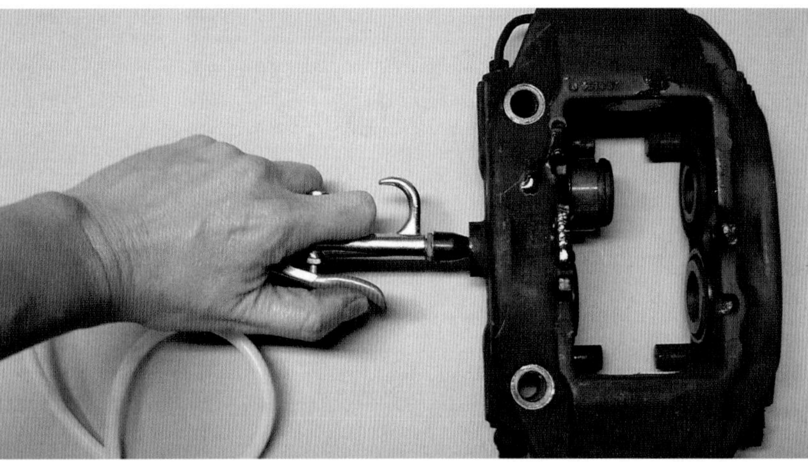

2 The best method I've found for removing the caliper pistons is to use compressed air to blow them out. Beware though—start with low pressure and then increase it if it's not enough. It's easier than you might think to send your pistons flying across the room with 100 psi of air pressure!

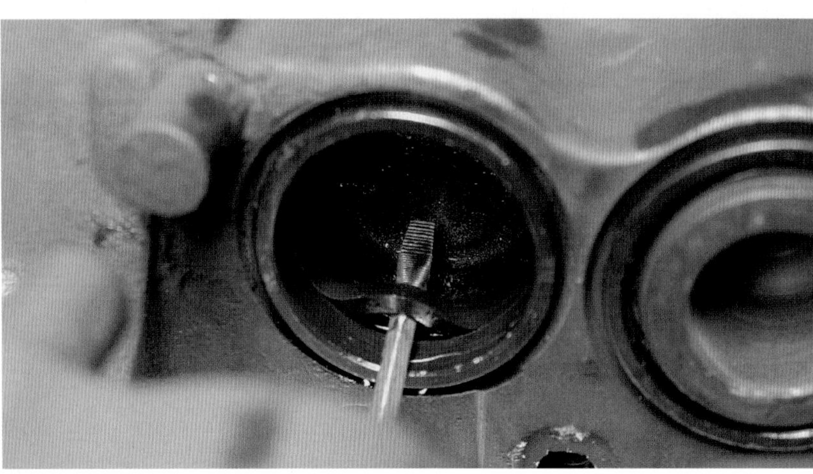

3 Make sure that you replace the inner piston seal. This seal is what keeps brake fluid from leaking out past the cylinder. Also be sure that you clean the entire inner cylinder for dirt, debris, and corrosion. Don't scratch the inside of the caliper cylinder while you are working on it or you may have problems with the caliper leaking when you reassemble it.

PROJECT 51
Parking Brake Adjustment

Time / Tab / Talent: 1 hour /

Tools: Long screwdriver, 13mm wrench, flashlight

Applicable Years: All

Parts: None

More Info: www.101projects.com/Boxster/51.htm

Tip: Properly adjusting your parking brake can reduce the amount of drag on your road wheels

Performance Gain: Better parking brake performance

Comp Modification: Replace brake pads or discs

Over the years, the parking brake on your Boxster may become unadjusted and fail to perform properly. The adjustment of the brake shoes that control the parking brake is an easy process, and shouldn't take you more than an hour to accomplish.

The first step is to raise the rear of the car and remove the two road wheels. This will allow you access to the rear calipers. Make sure that the parking brake lever is released and the car is in neutral. Using a screwdriver, push back slightly on the brake pads until the brake disc is allowed to turn freely on its spindle. Be careful to check the fluid level in the master cylinder reservoir, as pushing the pads back will make the fluid level rise and may cause it to overflow.

Once the brake disc can be moved easily, move to the cockpit of the car. Underneath the rear cover on the center console, you will see a rubber insert with a plastic panel underneath. Remove the rubber insert and the Torx screw underneath, and pry up the plastic panel. Now loosen the two nuts that attach the handbrake turnbuckle so that the two cables become slack. If there is any tension on these cables, then it will be difficult to adjust the handbrake.

The adjustment of the parking brake shoes is accomplished by turning a small gear or sprocket with a screwdriver. Unfortunately, this sprocket can only be reached through one of the lug nut holes in the brake disc.

Rotate the brake disc until you can see the small adjusting sprocket through the lug nut hole (see Photo 1). You may need a flashlight for this procedure. Reaching in through the hole, use a screwdriver to rotate the cog until the parking brake shoe is tight and the rotor can no longer be rotated. It's probable that the cog assembly got turned around at one point when the shoes were replaced, so you will have to play with the mechanism a little bit to see if you need to turn the cog up or down to tighten. If you are turning the sprocket a lot, and the brake disc isn't tightening up, then you are probably turning it in the wrong direction. Repeat this procedure for the opposite side of the car. After you have the sprockets adjusted so that the brake shoes have just pressed up against the inside of the disc, and you can no longer turn the disc, back them off nine notches, making sure that the disc can spin after the ninth notch.

Now move back to the cockpit of the car, and pull up on the hand brake several times to help seat the cables. Finally, pull up on the hand brake so that the ratchet clicks through two notches. Now, tighten up the cables using the nuts at the bottom of the handbrake lever. Tighten each of these nuts to the point where there is just a bit of slight resistance on each of the two rear wheels. Now, release the lever and verify that the wheels turn freely. The brake discs should be free to rotate with the handle in the down position but fully locked by the time that the handbrake is pulled up a few notches past the two clicks.

When you are finished, recheck the master cylinder reservoir and also step on the brake pedal a few times in order to make sure that the pistons have repositioned themselves properly against the brake pads. Also verify that the parking brake lamp on the dashboard illuminates as soon as the handle is pulled up (there's a switch near the base of the handle that triggers this lamp).

1 Removing the rotor reveals the mechanism for the parking brake adjustment. As the small cog is turned, the parking brake shoes are pushed outwards toward the inside of the disc. The proper adjustment of the shoes exists when the shoes are just about to touch the inside of the disc. The photo inset identifies the location of the sprocket when you are trying to look through the access hole in the brake disc – removal of the brake disc is not necessary for adjustment.

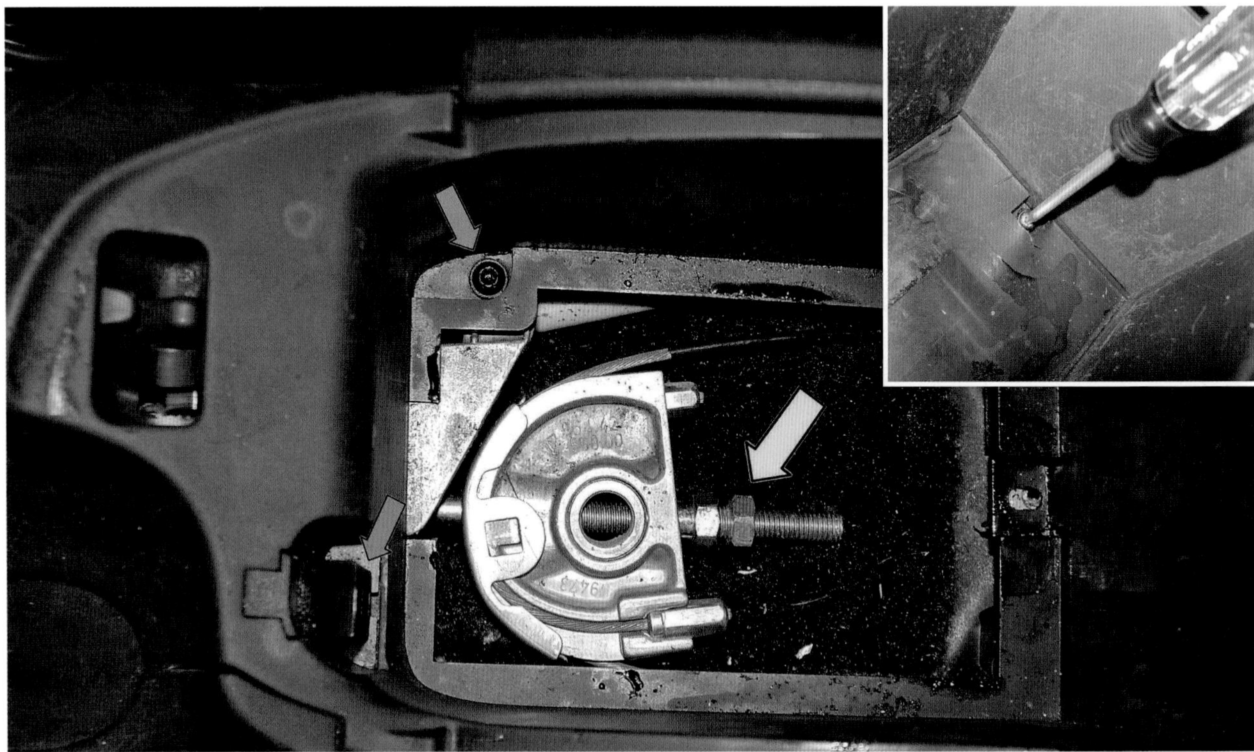

2 Shown here are the ends of the two parking brake cables wrapped around the turnbuckle. The two nuts that lock together need to be loosened (yellow arrow) prior to your adjustment process, and then tightened up later on. The two purple arrows show two screws needed to remove the entire console (required for Project 42). The inset photo shows the screw that holds the panel covering this area.

PROJECT 52
Big Brake Upgrade

Time / Tab / Talent: 12 hours / $1,500–$3,000 / 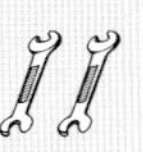

Tools: Flare-nut wrench

Applicable Years: All

Parts: Brembo big brake kit, brake fluid

More Info: www.101projects.com/Boxster/52.htm

Tip: Check the fit of your wheels after you mount the caliper

Performance Gain: Shorter stopping distances and reduced brake fade

Comp Modification: Replace rear pads, discs, and e-brake shoes

The standard Boxster braking systems have always been good, but I've often thought that the stock systems could be better. If you're going to be doing any significant performance driving, it's a very wise investment to upgrade your brakes.

High-performance kits aren't cheap—they range in price from about $1,500 to $3,000, with the top end of the dollar range belonging to the premium brand kits from Brembo. Some may find this an expensive price to pay, but when you figure that it includes the cost of a caliper rebuild, new discs, and new brake lines, the cost becomes a bit more reasonable. In addition, you can expect the following from your upgrade:

- **Shorter stopping distances.** Depending upon the application and road conditions, you can experience up to 20–30 percent shorter distances. The faster you are traveling, the greater the improvement.
- **Repeatability.** Even the simplest brake systems can stop a car very well once or twice. However, as the brake fluid and pads heat up, performance decreases, and each stop gets longer and longer. Installing a big brake kit will give you remarkably shorter stops consistently.
- **Reduce or eliminate brake fade.** The larger brake discs on the big brake systems are able to dissipate heat that causes brake fade and failure. Each component in the big brake system is designed for performance braking, which includes the proper cooling of the system. Whether you're coming down a steep mountain or blasting from turn to turn on a racetrack, the bigger brake systems are better equipped to prevent overheating than the stock system.
- **Better control and modulation.** With a performance brake setup, you achieve a better pedal feel, brake harder, and still maintain control. The big brake systems work flawlessly with the Boxster's anti-lock braking system (ABS).

The big brake kits typically only come with equipment to replace your front brakes. This is because the front brakes typically perform 80 percent or more of the stopping—sometimes more during panic stops. I don't recommend putting a high-performance big brake system on the rear, because this can cause the rear brakes to lock up prematurely. This can actually cause increased stopping distances and a loss of control—exactly what you're trying to avoid! For cars that have performance systems on the rear, they are often coupled with anti-lock controllers or proportioning valves to prevent rear brake lockup.

The big brake setup that we chose for this project is manufactured by Brembo and was supplied to us by PelicanParts.com. Brembo is one of the leading brake system manufacturers and an OEM supplier to world-class sports car manufacturers, such as Porsche and Ferrari. The Brembo "Big Red" kit we used for this upgrade is widely considered to be one of the best you can buy for the Boxster. The car that this was mounted on was our 2000 "Boxster Carrera" that had a few "other performance mods" to match (3.4-liter engine, Bilstein PSS9 suspension, etc.).

The only real requirement for the kit is that you have 17-inch or larger wheels on your car. The stock Boxster wheels will fit and were installed on this car at the time of the upgrade. Not all 17-inch wheels will allow the huge calipers to fit, so make sure that you plan in advance and verify that your wheel combination will work with the larger brake systems. Some thin spacers may be necessary for some wheels.

The first step is to loosen the lug nuts on your wheels and then raise the front of the car (see Project 1). You might want to raise the rear of the car as well, as I recommend that you inspect and refurbish your rear brakes at the same time so that you have fresh components on all four corners of the car. For example, on this particular car, I installed new rear rotors, new rear brake pads, and new parking brake shoes to match.

With the car up in the air, remove the two road wheels and disconnect the brake pad sensor. Then unbolt and disconnect the brake caliper from the car (see Project 55 for detailed instructions on removing the caliper, and brake disc). Tie the caliper up out of the way and do not disconnect the brake line at this time. Make sure that there is no tension on the brake line—even though we will be replacing it, you don't want to make a habit of hanging the caliper by the brake hose.

Now, remove the small screw that holds the brake disc to the hub. The brake disc should simply lift off. If not, then you may need to tap it with a rubber mallet. If there is any dust or debris in this area, be sure to clean it out thoroughly.

Now place the new rotor on the spindle. There is a left and right rotor—they usually have a sticker on them, but you can also tell the difference by the way that the internal fins are cast into the disc (see inset of Photo 2). Use the brake disc locating and mounting bolt to secure and correctly register the brake disc with respect to the hub. The holes for the wheel studs should be correctly lined up with both the brake disc and the spindle. Use a spare wheel lug nut to help secure the disc to the spindle if needed.

The pads should be preassembled in the caliper, but if they're not, now is the time to insert them into the caliper. Remove the two retaining pins by tapping them out with a small hammer and the end of a punch or small screwdriver. Insert the pads and replace the pins. Take the new Brembo caliper mounting adapter and place it on the strut assembly (Photo 3). Now, mount the new, huge caliper to the strut with the adapter sandwiched in between. Tighten the bolts to the values detailed in the installation instructions and use a dab of Loctite 271 on the threads to make sure they don't come loose. There should be an embossed arrow on the front

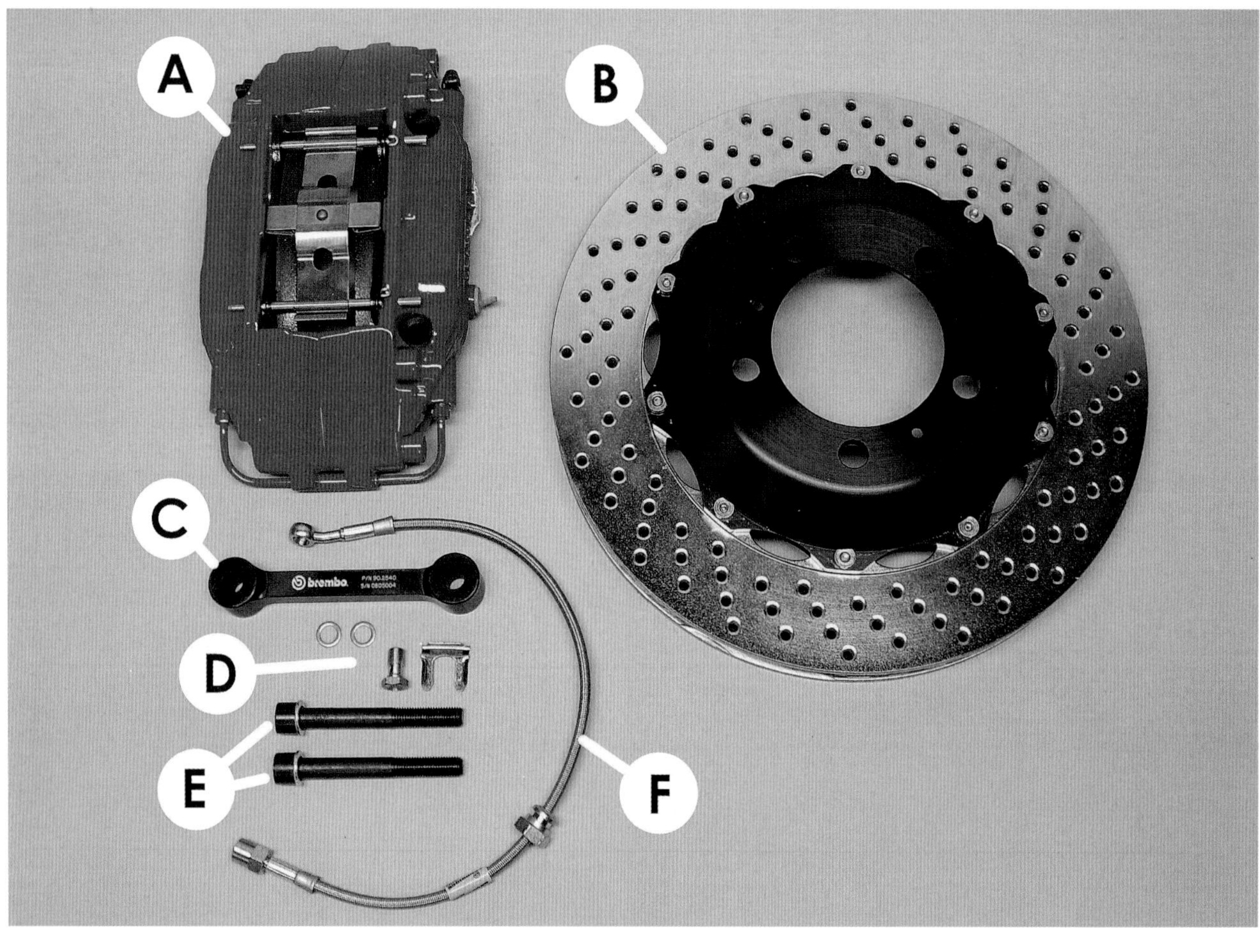

1 Shown here is one half of the Brembo big brake upgrade kit as purchased from PelicanParts.com. The kit includes everything that you need for the installation: two calipers, two rotors, two brake lines, two brackets, and two sets of pads and retaining clips. Truly a sight to be seen, it's unfortunate that all of this braking beauty has to be hidden behind the wheels. **A:** Brembo caliper **B:** Brembo brake disc **C:** Caliper adapter **D:** Brake line hardware **E:** Caliper mounting bolts and washers **F:** Stainless steel brake line with metal grommet.

2 Mount the disc to the hub and temporarily fasten it with the brake disc locating screw (red arrow). Verify that the disc turns freely and doesn't hang up on any part of the strut or hub assembly. The discs are specific to each side of the car—verify from the diagram that the proper one is mounted according to how the wheel turns when the car is moving forwards.

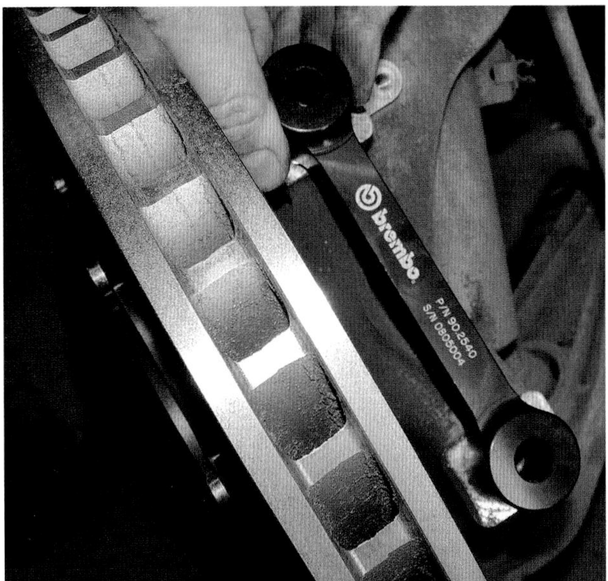

3 The caliper is mounted in a similar position as the factory one, using the same original bolt holes as mounting points. The spacer is sandwiched between the caliper and the mounting surface.

of the caliper that indicates the direction of the disc rotation. When mounting the calipers on the spindle, this arrow should always point up (see Photo 4).

At this point (before you disconnect the brake line to your old caliper) I suggest that you perform a test fit of your wheel to your spindle. You want to make sure that there are no interference problems when the wheel is fully mounted. Cover the caliper first with a piece of tape to protect the paint in case the wheel happens to scrape the caliper. Put the wheel on the spindle and tighten it down with two lug nuts. Then give the wheel a spin and make sure that it turns freely without rubbing or scraping on the caliper or any other brake system component. If there is a clearance problem, you may have to use a spacer and longer wheel bolts (see Photo 6).

When you have verified that the wheel turns freely, remove it and set it aside. Now attach your new braided brake hose to the brake caliper. There should be a small copper washer that will seal the line fitting to the caliper. Route the brake line through the small bracket that secures it to the strut (see Photo 7).

Now, using a flare-nut wrench, quickly disconnect the old rubber hose from the steel hard-line that connects the hose to the main brake system (at the top of the inner wheelwell). Don't use a regular wrench on the hard line—only use a flare-nut wrench, as is explained in Project 54. Reconnect the new line quickly, minimizing the amount of brake fluid that leaks out of the system.

With the brake line attached, now clean up any spilled brake fluid (beware—it is very harmful to paint). Now, repeat the process for the opposite side. When you have completed the install, you will need to bleed the brake system—see Project 48 for more information. After the brakes have been bled, reattach the road wheels, lower the car, and tighten the lug nuts to 74 ft-lb (100 Nm).

The brake system needs to be broken in before you can really test its performance. First, you should make sure that your emergency brake system is working properly. This is just in case anything went wrong, and you need to pull that lever to stop the car. Before you drive the car, pump the pedal and make sure that you have firm pressure. Have an assistant push the car while you have your foot on the brake—just to test that the system is working.

Drive the car slowly to a nearby parking lot or deserted area. Now, perform about 15–20 stops from 55 miles per hour to 10 miles per hour using light pressure on the pedal. This will increase the temperature on the pads, the caliper, and the rotors and will help mate the pad and the disc's friction surface together. After these repeated stops, drive the car around town for a few miles and try to avoid using the brakes. This will allow the components to cool back down. Now park the car and look at the brake discs. They should be a grayish-blue color consistently across the surface of the disc. If this color is not consistent, then repeat the 15–20-stop-heating-and-cooling procedure.

An additional easy update is the installation of the GT3 brake duct spoilers. They replace the existing plastic inserts that are attached to the front suspension and funnel more air to help cool the brakes. The left and right part numbers are 996-341-117-91 and 996-341-118-91.

4 Shown here is the caliper mounted to the strut assembly. The embossed arrow on the caliper should always point upwards (green arrow). The brake pads should be installed in the caliper from the factory.

5 Perform a test fit of the road wheel to the hub to make sure that there are no interference problems. Place some tape on the painted surface of the caliper, just to make sure that the inside of the wheel doesn't accidentally scratch the surface of the caliper. The 18-inch Porsche OEM SportDesign wheels shown in the photo work very well with the Brembo kit. Clearance is very tight, but with the addition of a spacer, the wheel fits as if the kit was tailor-made for this particular wheel.

6 After checking the clearance of the caliper with the SportDesign wheels, I discovered that I needed some thin spacers because the caliper was contacting the inside of the wheel. The solution is easy—a set of 4mm spacers and 38mm-long lug bolts from PelicanParts.com. It's very important not to forget to use the longer lug bolts when you add the spacers to your hub.

7 This photo shows the attachment of the new stainless steel brake line. The fitting on the chassis side fit well with the new line (inset photo, upper left), but the small bracket that holds the line and clamp (green arrow) to the strut had to be slightly modified with a Dremel tool. The center hole needed to be opened up to accommodate the larger brake line fitting (see inset, lower right).

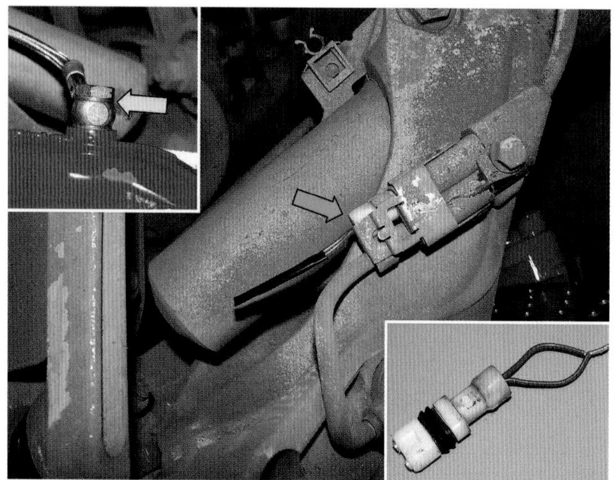

8 The Brembo system does not have an accommodation for the brake pad wear sensors, so you will need to trick the system into thinking the pads are within spec. This is easy—simply take an old sensor, clip its wires, and connect the two together. Cover the ends with some electrical tape, and insert the connector back into the strut housing. Be sure to inspect your pads for wear periodically since the brake pad wear system is now disabled. In the upper left inset photo, you will see the point where the brake line enters the brake caliper (yellow arrow). This line attaches to the lower part of the caliper, and the bleed nipple should be on top of the caliper.

PROJECT 53
Parking Brake Shoe Replacement

 **Time / Tab / Talent:** 3 hours / $110 /

 **Tools:** Rubber mallet, screwdriver, small pliers

 **Applicable Years:** All

 **Parts:** New parking brake shoes, springs

More Info: www.101projects.com/Boxster/53.htm

 **Tip:** Wear safety glasses when working around the spring-loaded mechanisms

 **Performance Gain:** Better parking brake performance

 **Comp Modification:** Replace the brake pads, brake discs

If your parking brake is not functioning properly, then perhaps it's time that you replaced your parking brake shoes. The first step in the process is to make sure that your parking brake cables and handle are adjusted properly. Refer to Project 51 for details on this procedure.

The parking brake shoes can only be inspected after the removal of the rear brake discs. Refer to Project 55 for the procedure for this removal. After you have the brake discs off, you can visually inspect the shoes for wear. The shoes should have some brake lining along the top and should not have any heavy grooves cut into them. Compare your brake shoes to the new shoes in the pictures in this project to determine if you need to replace yours.

After the brake disc has been removed from the brake assembly, remove the small parking brake adjuster by prying it out from between the left and right parking brake shoe. Make sure that the parking brake handle is all the way down for this procedure. Be careful while you are performing this removal, as the adjuster is spring-loaded and the springs may fly out when you are prying it out.

When you have removed the adjuster, take a set of needle-nose pliers and remove the long spring that that holds the left and right shoes together near where the adjuster was mounted. Again, be careful of the spring, as it may fly off unexpectedly. Make sure that you wear safety glasses during this entire procedure.

Now remove the conical spring-retaining mechanisms at the far left and right of the assembly. Press in the spring, and then rotate the spring so that you can slide it out of its slot in the back. You made need to stick your head around the backside of the axle carrier in order to see how to remove the hook on the end of the spring. Make sure that you don't lose the parts if they happen to fly out.

Now remove the long spring from the bottom of the two brake shoes. Use the needle-nose pliers again, and be careful not to catch your fingers in the process.

After the springs have been removed from the parking brake assembly, both the top and the bottom shoes should simply lift off of the assembly. The new shoe should be installed in an opposite manner to the removal process. Reassemble the parking brake by attaching the lower spring first, then the two conical springs, and then the spring toward the top. It's important to note that this reassembly involves quite a bit of maneuvering with your pliers and is not an easy task—you'll probably swear at the car a couple dozen times.

When you are finished, test the assembly by operating the emergency brake handle a few times. Carefully check the springs and make sure that they are properly seated in the restraining holes in the brake shoes. Loosen up the parking brake cables before you reinstall the brake disc and make sure that you recheck and adjust the parking brake mechanism (Project 51) before you reinstall the caliper and the brake pads.

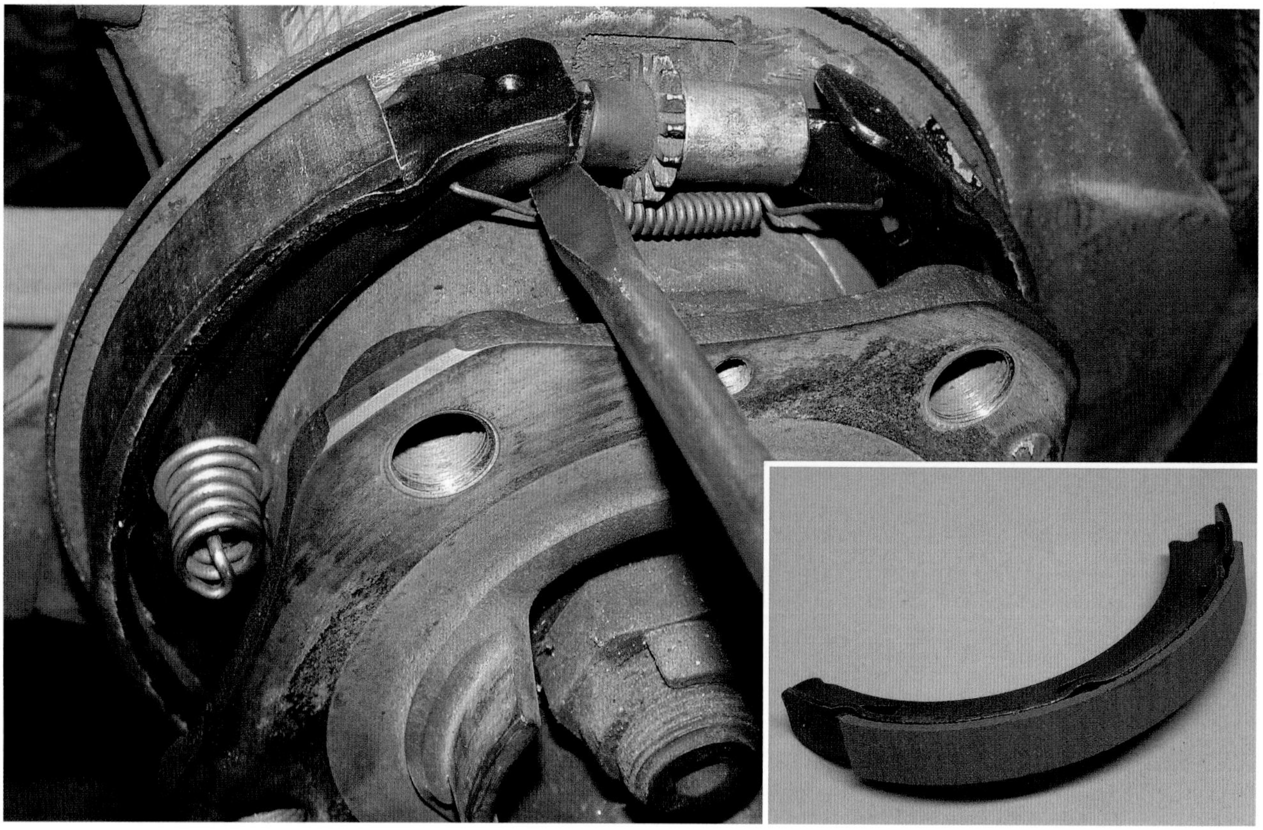

1 Remove the small adjusting cog assembly by using a large screwdriver to push it out from between the two parking brake shoes. With some effort, the cog assembly should pop out, leaving a little bit of slack between the two parking brake shoes. Be very careful when installing the new shoe, as the retaining springs have a tendency to snap out of place and fly out. Make sure that you keep your hands out of the way, and use safety glasses when installing or removing the springs. The inset photo shows a brand new parking brake shoe. Compare your old one to this one here in the photo to see if it needs replacement.

2 Using a pair of pliers, grab and unhook the parking brake spring from the brake shoes (green arrow). Be careful of the spring, as it is under a lot of tension at this point. Use a pair of vise grips and a pair of needle-nose pliers to twist the spring and unlatch it from the assembly. Also undo the small spring retainer (inset) that secures the brake shoes to the rear suspension assembly. If you're not sure if your parking brake shoes are worn, take a close look at these (red arrow). The brake lining on this particular shoe actually looks pretty good and probably wouldn't warrant replacing.

PROJECT 54
Brake Line Replacement

Time / Tab / Talent: 4 hours / $95 /

Tools: 10mm/11mm crescent flare-nut wrench

Applicable Years: All

Parts: New brake lines or stainless-steel brake lines

More Info: www.101projects.com/Boxster/54.htm

Tip: Make sure that corroded rubber from old lines didn't end up in your caliper

Performance Gain: Better braking performance

Comp Modification: Rebuild calipers, replace brake pads, flush brake system, replace master cylinder

One of the most popular projects for the Boxster is the replacement of the flexible brake lines that connect from the main chassis of the car to the brake calipers. These lines are made out of rubber and have a tendency to break down and corrode over many years. The rubber lines should be carefully inspected every 10,000 miles or so. They can exhibit strange characteristics, such as bubbling and expanding, prior to actually bursting. Needless to say, failure of these lines is a very bad thing, as you will instantly lose pressure in one half of your brake system.

Faulty brake lines in the front of your Porsche can cause all sorts of steering problems when braking. It is common for bad hoses to cause a car to dart from side to side to when braking. Bad hoses allow pressure to build up in the caliper but sometimes do not release this pressure properly when the pedal is depressed.

The first step in replacing your lines is to elevate the car. Remove the wheels from each side of the car, as this will make it much easier to access the brake lines. To prevent a large amount of brake fluid from leaking out, I recommend pushing the brake pedal down just to the point of engagement and blocking it there. If you do this, you will lose less brake fluid, and also less air will enter into the system.

Now it's time to disconnect the brake lines. Make sure that you have some paper towels handy, as there will be some brake fluid that will leak out of the lines. Brake fluid is perhaps the most dangerous fluid to your car, as any amount spilled on the paint will permanently mar it. If you do get some on the paint, make sure that you blot it and don't wipe it off. Be aware that your hands may contain some brake fluid; don't even touch anything near the paint on the car with your hands.

The brake lines themselves can be very difficult to remove. The goal of this job is to remove the lines without damaging anything else. In this case, the easiest thing to damage (besides your paint) is the hard steel brake lines that connect to the flexible rubber lines. These lines have relatively soft fittings on each end and often become deformed and stripped when removed. The key to success is to use a flare-nut wrench. This wrench is basically designed for jobs like this one where the fittings are soft and might be heavily corroded. The flared end of the wrench hugs the fitting and prevents it from stripping. It is very important to use only one of these wrenches, as it is very easy to damage the fittings using a regular crescent wrench.

The other disastrous thing that can happen is that the fitting can get stuck to the rest of the hard line. The fitting is supposed to turn and rotate on the end of the line, but sometimes it becomes too corroded to break free. When this happens, the fitting and the line will usually twist together, and it will break the line in half. Be careful when you are removing this fitting to make sure that you are not twisting the line.

If you do damage the hard line or strip the fitting, then the replacement line might be a special order part that will have to be shipped in from Germany. You can usually find the correct length line at your local auto parts store, but then you will have to bend it into shape, and most of the time, this is a very difficult process that requires a few special tools. The moral of this story, and this entire book, is that you should use the right tool for the job (the flare-nut wrench).

After you have disconnected the hard metal line, you can now remove the flexible lines from the car. At both ends, the lines are attached using spring clips. Use a good pair of vise grips to pull them off of the car.

Installation of the new lines is straightforward and the easy part of the job. Before you start attaching the lines, make sure that you have the correct ones for your car. There are a few different types and a few different lengths, so make sure that the ones that you are putting on are the same length and have the same fittings as the ones that you are removing. If the line you install is too short, then when your car goes over a bump, it may stretch and break the line.

When it comes to replacing brake lines, many people install stainless steel braided lines on their car. The rumor has it that the stainless steel sheath keeps the rubber line from expanding under pressure and actually delivers better performance than do the standard lines. While this reasoning sounds good at first, it's mostly hype. The stainless steel braided lines are often made of the same rubber underneath and are simply protected by the outside sheath. Even if the sheath were tight enough and strong enough to prevent the lines from expanding, it really wouldn't make a difference in braking. Even if the lines expand a little, the resulting pressure that is exerted at the caliper will be almost the same.

Regardless of the rumor mill, I will recommend that you place the stainless steel lines on your car because the outside sheath protects the lines from dirt, grime, rocks, small animals, and other things you might run over with your car. The stock lines already have a metal "spring" that insulates them, so the gain is minimal.

The other thing that might warrant your consideration is the label of DOT (Department of Transportation) certification. With the original rubber lines, they were required to be certified under a certain set of specifications dictated by the DOT for use on U.S. highways. Often, the stainless steel lines are aftermarket components that are not DOT certified and are subsequently listed for "off-road use only." In reality, these lines are more than adequate for use on your car, and any concern over the use of them is not really necessary. However, for those who want to be absolutely sure and certified, there are manufacturers who will make DOT-certified stainless steel lines, but they are usually more expensive than the non-certified ones (DOT lines are available at PelicanParts.com).

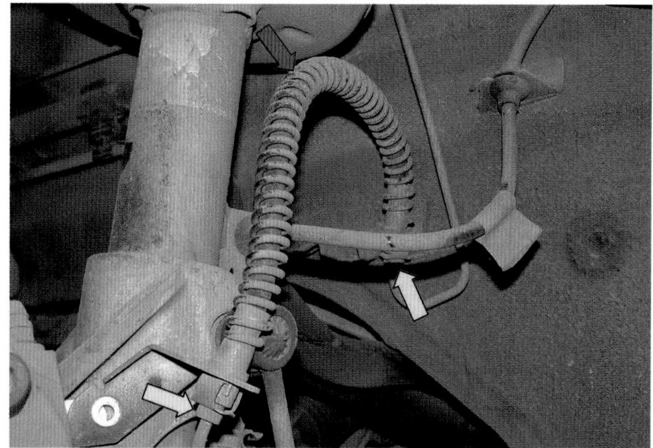

1 Old rubber brake lines are often responsible for poor brake performance. As the car ages, the rubber begins to break down and can clog the lines, leading to very little pressure getting to the calipers. The brake lines should be renewed if they are old or if you are having problems with your brakes. The red arrow points to the flexible brake line on the front of the car that needs to be replaced. The yellow arrows point to the fittings on the hard brake lines that need to be released using a flare-nut wrench.

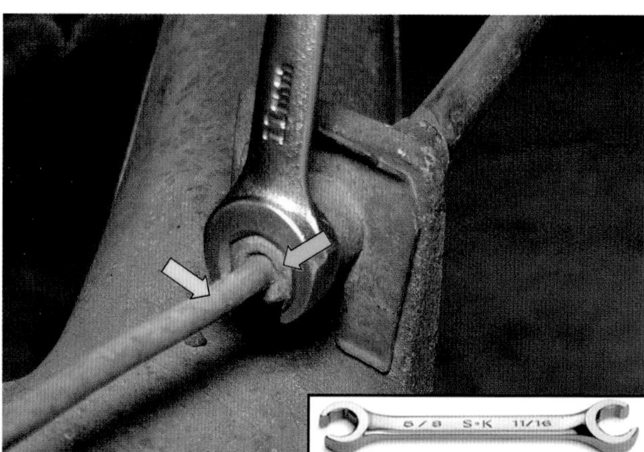

2 A required tool is the flare-nut wrench that fully wraps around the brake line. If you use a standard wrench, then there is a high chance of rounding off the corners and permanently damaging the hard brake lines. These fittings are not very strong and will become stripped if you don't use one of these wrenches. Once the fitting becomes stripped, the line needs to be replaced (usually a special order part from Germany). Also make sure that the fitting is turning (blue arrow), not the line itself (yellow arrow). It is very easy to twist off the ends of the hard lines when the fitting binds.

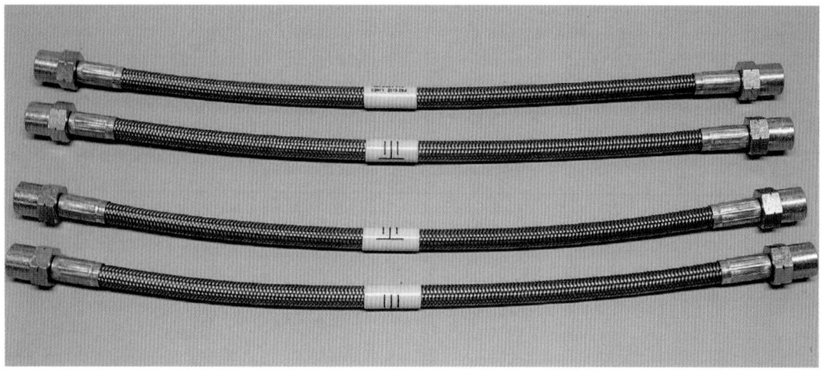

3 New stainless steel lines are identical in size and length to the original ones that shipped with the car. The advantage to the stainless steel lines is that they have a protective coating on the outside that prevents the elements from attacking them as easily. There is a downside though. The stainless steel sheath doesn't allow you to inspect the rubber inside to see if there is any significant deterioration. Some of the aftermarket lines are made out of Teflon or have Teflon components to help increase their durability.

PROJECT 55
Replacing Brake Discs

Time / Tab / Talent: 3 hours / $600 / 

Tools: Phillips head socket tool, rubber mallet, socket set, micrometer

Applicable Years: All

Parts: Brake discs, new pads, new emergency brake shoes (if required)

More Info: www.101projects.com/Boxster/55.htm

Tip: Adjust your emergency brake while you have access

Performance Gain: Better, safer braking

Comp Modification: Replace brake pads, emergency brake shoes, install stainless-steel brake lines, install new wheel bearings

Brake discs (or rotors as they are often called) are a very important part of the braking system. The brake pads rub against the discs to create a friction force that is responsible for slowing the car down. If the rotors become too thin or develop grooves in them, then their ability to stop the car decreases.

When replacing your brake pads, you should always measure the thickness of your brake discs. If they fall below the specified value for your car, then they should be replaced with new ones. Check for grooves in the rotor, and make sure that you take several measurements of the disc in several different places. This will guarantee that you get an accurate reading. If the brake disc has a groove in it, then it should most certainly be removed and resurfaced by a machine shop or simply replaced with a new one. Discs with grooves not only brake less efficiently, but they also heat up to higher temperatures and reduce your overall braking ability.

The measurements that you take with your micrometer should be made from the center of the disc. It is common for OEM rotors to have the minimum thickness stamped on the rotor hub (as is the case with the ceramic PCCB brake option). If you can't find this information, use the following chart to determine if your rotors need to be replaced.

Type and Year	Min Thickness
Front Vented Steel Rotor (Boxster 1997–2004)	22.6mm
Rear Vented Steel Rotor (Boxster 1997–2004)	18.6mm
Front Vented Steel Rotor (Boxster/Cayman 2005–)	26.0mm
Rear Vented Steel Rotor (Boxster/Cayman 2005–)	22.0mm

If you do find that you need to replace your rotors, the process is a relatively simple one. The procedure for the front or the rear rotors is very similar, but for the sake of this project, we'll look at replacing the rears, which is slightly more complicated due to the addition of the rear parking/emergency brake. With the rear rotors, if the parking brake shoes are very worn, then you may need to back off the adjustment sprocket in order to be able to remove the rear disc (see Project 51 for more details).

The first step is to jack up the car and remove the road wheel. If you haven't already, remove the brake pads from the caliper. Refer to Project 49 on replacing brake pads for more details. The flexible rubber brake hose is attached to the wheel carrier assembly of the car via a large clip. This clip retains both the flexible line and the hard line that connects to the rear caliper. Remove this clip so that you will be able to remove the caliper without bending the hard metal brake line.

Now, unbolt the caliper from the wheel carrier assembly where it is mounted. There should be two bolts that mount the caliper and hold it in place. After you remove these two bolts, you should be able to slightly move the caliper out of the way of the disc. Exercise caution when moving the caliper around—make sure that you do not let the caliper hang from the rubber brake line, as this will most certainly damage the line.

Once you have the caliper out of the way, remove the small screw that holds on the brake disc. You will need a Phillips head socket tool for this task (you can try using a big screwdriver, but odds are the screw will be on too tight and you may end up stripping it). At this point, make sure that the parking brake is off. You should now be able to pull the disc off of the hub. If there is any resistance, use a rubber mallet to tap the brake disc off. Sometimes the disc will require some heavy smacks with your rubber mallet to get it off.

If you are having a difficult time getting the disc off, it's probably because the parking brake shoes are stuck on the back of the disc. You might need to adjust the parking brake so that it's not gripping the disc. For more information on this process, see Project 51.

Installation of the new brake disc is a snap; simply push it onto the hub. Before you install the new disc, take a close look at your parking brake shoes and see if they warrant replacing. If you can see metal on the shoes, or if the previous owner had a hard time remembering to remove the emergency brake, then it might be a good time to replace these. After you install the new discs on both sides, you should test your parking brake and adjust it if necessary. Refer to Project 53 and Project 51 for more details.

After the new disc is installed, replace the retaining screw, reattach the caliper, and install new brake pads. Your new rotors should last a long time, and you should see an improvement in your braking after the wear-in period for your new brake pads.

1 The front and rear brake discs look almost identical. The rear brake discs have an inner "drum" area that acts as the surface for the emergency brake to press against. While the Boxster and Cayman both have disc brakes at all wheels, the rear parking brake mechanism is most similar to a drum brake system. You may want to paint the inner hats and edges of the discs with some high-temp paint. This will keep them from rusting after you install them.

2 Before you remove your brake discs, it is important to first measure them to see if they need to be replaced. Use a micrometer to perform the measurement. If you use a dial caliper, then you might get a false reading because the disc wears on the area where the pads make contact, not on the edges of the disc. Make sure that you take several measurements in a few different places on the disc in order to compensate for potential low or high spots.

3 Removal of the caliper is accomplished by unbolting the two hex bolts that mount it to the arm (yellow arrow). The caliper (green arrow) can be pushed out of the away and doesn't need to be physically disconnected from the brake line. Hang the caliper from a string or coat hanger (blue arrows) so that you don't put unnecessary tension on the rubber brake line (orange arrow).

4 There are two small locator screws that hold the brake disc in place. Use a big screwdriver or a Phillips head socket tool to remove these screws, and the brake disc should slide off of the hub. Keep in mind that the lug nuts that hold on the wheel apply the majority of the force that constrains the disc to the hub—not this screw.

5 The new disc can be tapped on with a rubber mallet. If installing the rear discs, make sure that you have your parking brake shoes adjusted away from the inside drum, or they might interfere with the installation of the disc. New discs may not be perfectly flat and may take a few hundred miles of break-in to achieve their maximum braking efficiency.

PROJECT 56
Master Cylinder Replacement

Time / Tab / Talent: 3 hours / $100–$300 / 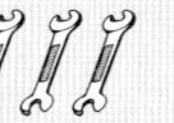

Tools: Brake bleeder, torque wrench

Applicable Years: All

Parts: Master cylinder, brake fluid

More Info: www.101projects.com/Boxster/56.htm

Tip: Make sure that you keep all brake fluid away from your paint

Performance Gain: Better braking, no more leaky master cylinders

Comp Modification: Replace brake booster, install stainless-steel brake lines

Without a doubt, your brakes are one of the most important systems on the car. The heart of the brake system is the master cylinder, which controls the hydraulic pressure of the entire system. Unfortunately, over many years, the master cylinder has a tendency to wear out and leak. The leakage can occur internally or externally, resulting in a weakened braking system. If you have any problems with your brakes, and you think that it's related to the master cylinder, you should probably replace it.

The master cylinder is located in the front trunk area, on the driver's side, under a large plastic panel. To gain access to the master cylinder, you need to remove this panel. Begin by pulling up the hood seal and removing the three Phillips head screws located on the top of the panel. Rotate the slotted plug on the lower front corner of the panel and remove it, disconnecting the trunk lamp harness as you go. Now, remove the strainer from the brake fluid reservoir and then remove brake fluid using a turkey baster or a suction device. Or, you can also bleed the entire system of fluid by emptying the brake fluid out of one of the caliper bleed screws (see Project 48). Be aware that some residual fluid will remain inside of the master cylinder and that brake fluid is very damaging to paint. Disconnect the brake fluid level sensor from the reservoir.

Now you need to remove the reservoir. Disconnect the clutch master cylinder supply line—you will need to push in the press-fit connector with a small wrench carefully as you pull on the line. If you are not replacing the reservoir, then I recommend just leaving it connected and pushing the reservoir off to the side. Simply pull up on the reservoir to remove it from the O-rings that seal it to the master cylinder.

With the reservoir disconnected, place a towel under the master cylinder and disconnect the two brake line fittings. As with the installation of new flexible brake lines, it is very important not to strip out the fittings on the lines. You should always use a flare-nut wrench to remove the fittings from the master cylinder. See Project 54 for more details. It's also a wise idea to spray the area with some WD-40 or other lubricant if the lines seem to be heavily corroded. Cap the open brake lines with plastic covers to prevent brake fluid leakage. Remove the two nuts that attach the master cylinder to the brake booster, and you should be able to remove the master cylinder.

Installation is basically the reverse of removal. If you are replacing your ABS control unit or your brake booster, then at this point, see Project 57 for instructions on how to accomplish that task.

When the master cylinder is reinstalled, it's time to bleed your brake system. You may want to dry bleed the master cylinder on the bench in order to prime it before you start the install. For more information on bleeding your brakes, see Project 48. Following the bleeding of the brakes, reassemble all the surrounding parts in the trunk that you have disassembled and make sure that everything is tightened. Reinstall all the carpets and fasteners.

When you are ready to drive the car, make sure that you test the brakes beforehand. Don't drive near other cars, and prepare to use the emergency brake if necessary. It's probably a wise idea to bleed the brakes again a few days after you install the new master cylinder to make sure that you have gotten all of the air out of the brake system.

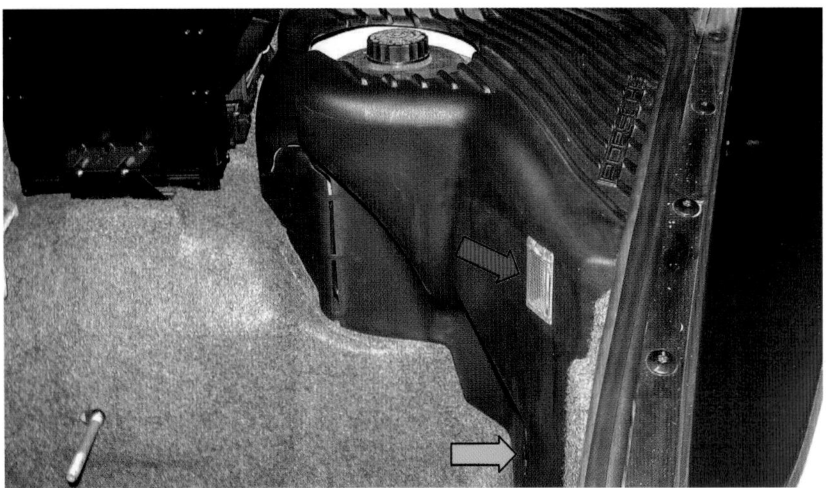

1 The master cylinder is hidden behind a plastic panel located in the front trunk. Remove the plastic screws that hold the trunk liner down (blue arrow), and pull the liner out. There is a front trunk lamp (red arrow) embedded in the liner—remember to unplug the harness connected to this lamp.

2 Here's what you will see when you remove the front trunk liner. The purple arrow shows the vacuum-powered brake booster, which is the muscle behind the power-brake system. The orange arrow shows the brake fluid reservoir, which supplies hydraulic fluid to both the brake and clutch systems. The red arrow shows the ABS hydraulic control unit. The white arrow points to the master cylinder. The yellow arrow indicates the connection for the reservoir level sensor, and the green arrow shows the vacuum line that powers the brake booster. Finally, the blue arrow shows the electrical connector that plugs into the front trunk lamp.

3 Shown here is a close-up of the master cylinder connections. First, empty out the reservoir, and then disconnect the clutch system supply tube (green arrow). Then, disconnect the two brake lines attached to the side of the master cylinder (yellow arrows). Only use a flare-nut wrench (blue arrow, inset) as you otherwise may end up damaging the connectors on the lines.

4 With the brake lines disconnected and the reservoir removed from the top of the master cylinder, remove the two nuts that fasten the master cylinder to the brake booster (yellow arrows).

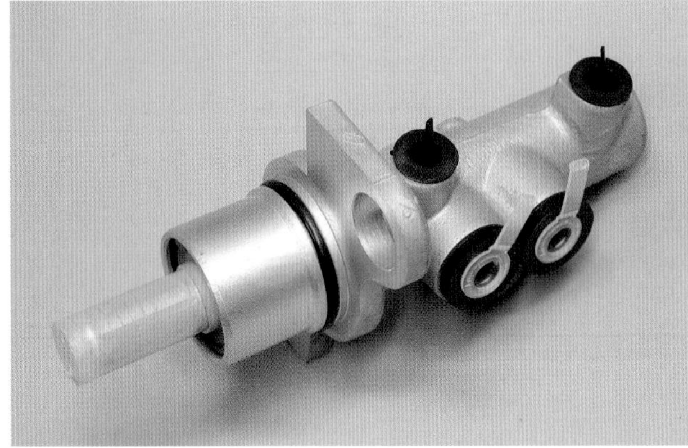

5 Shown here is a brand new master cylinder with five protective caps attached. Carefully remove the caps right before you are ready to install the unit and/or the brake lines.

PROJECT 57

Brake Booster & ABS Control Unit Replacement

Time / Tab / Talent: 3 hours / $250 /

Tools: Brake bleeder, torque wrench

Applicable Years: All

Parts: Master cylinder, brake fluid

More Info: www.101projects.com/Boxster/57.htm

Tip: Make sure that you keep all brake fluid away from your paint

Performance Gain: Better braking assist

Comp Modification: Replace master cylinder, install stainless-steel brake lines

The Boxster is equipped with power brakes that utilize excess vacuum from the engine in order to assist with the pressure needed to apply the brakes. The vacuum is routed from the engine via a long plastic hose that runs up the side of the car, into the front trunk area, and plugs into a large circular brake boost canister that the master cylinder attaches to. After years of use, the rubber diaphragm inside the booster may leak or fail, causing the power assist function to lose its efficiency. In addition, this may cause an engine vacuum leak, which can affect the proper metering of the fuel injection system. Before you replace your brake booster, though, be sure that you check the vacuum hose connections that run to the engine to see if there are any leaks there (see Project 21).

The first step in removing the booster is to remove the master cylinder (see Project 56). With the master cylinder removed, disconnect the three fittings from the top ABS control unit that were not attached to the master cylinder. Remove the ABS controller harness plug—the plastic tab on the side slides outward to allow the plug to pull up and off. Pull the brake line pressure regulator out of its clip. Loosen the two nuts on either side of the ABS controller and lift the controller out of the retaining bracket, maneuvering around the existing brake lines.

Now move to the other side of the booster, near the front firewall. Remove the clip that secures the brake booster actuation rod to the brake pedal rod and separate the two (see Photo 2). New boosters have an updated design that includes an integrated boot and an internal screw. This change was put into place for cars manufactured after September 13, 1999, and to use the newer-style booster with the older cars, you need to update the brake pushrod and the hardware associated with it. The process of updating the older cars is a bit of a pain, but instructions are documented in a 16-page Porsche Tech Bulletin Boxster 6/01 4770 031 (Brake Booster Seal at the Firewall Changed). See the 101Projects.com website for more information on this update.

With the booster rod disconnected, now disconnect the vacuum line on the front of the booster. Remove the two very long Torx T-45 bolts that secure the brake booster to the firewall. These bolts are the same ones that the master cylinder nuts attach to. With the bolts off, the booster should simply separate from the wall.

Installation of the new booster is basically the reverse of disassembly. With the new brake hardware in place, carefully bleed the brakes according to the instructions found in Project 48.

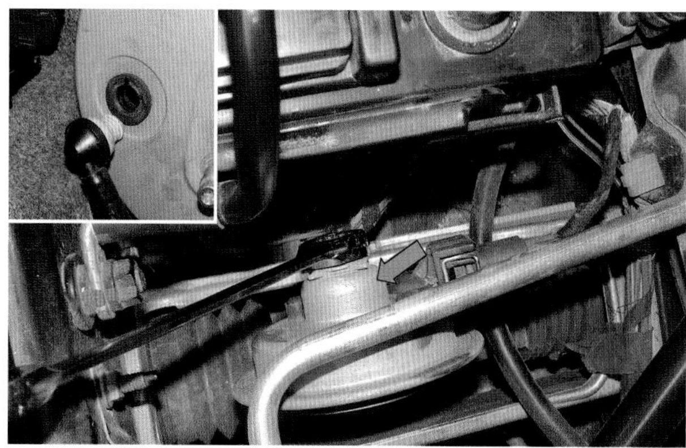

1 In order to gain access to the linkage that connects the brake pedal to the booster actuator, you need to remove the alarm horn (purple arrow). The upper right inset photo shows the vacuum hose plug that connects the engine vacuum line to the booster. Tug on this gently to remove it from the booster housing.

2 Use a set of wrenches to loosen up the connection between the booster actuator and the pedal cluster rod. This photo shows an early 2000 Boxster—later cars have a booster with a longer bellows. The photo in the upper right shows the booster and pedal cluster disconnected. The pedal cluster rod (upper left) must be changed if the booster is replaced with a newer-style one.

3 This photo shows what needs to be disconnected in order to remove the ABS control unit. Using a flare-nut wrench, disconnect the main brake lines (yellow arrow). Then release the ABS electrical connection by pulling the connector release handle in the direction of the red arrows. Finally, unbolt the ABS unit from its bracket (purple arrow shows one of the mounting points).

4 Shown here is the front trunk with the master cylinder and ABS control unit and bracket removed. At this point, the bolts that hold the booster to the firewall have been removed, and the unit is ready to be removed from the car. The photo in the lower right shows the ABS control unit mounting bracket that needs to be removed so that you have enough clearance to pull the booster out (remove nuts—yellow arrows).

5 Here's the new booster and master cylinder installed. At this point, simply remove the protective caps from all of the openings, install the ABS unit, reconnect the vacuum line, and reconnect the brake lines. Don't forget to bleed the entire brake and clutch system (Project 48).

SECTION 8
SUSPENSION

As cars get up there in age, one thing is almost always certain—suspension components will begin to wear out. This creates a sloppy feel to the car—exactly the opposite of what the original Porsche designers intended. Fixing and repairing the effects of age is straightforward—in most cases, suspension components need to be disassembled, evaluated, and possibly replaced. This section details the overhaul of the Boxster suspension, and also offers some projects for suspension upgrades that you can perform along the way.

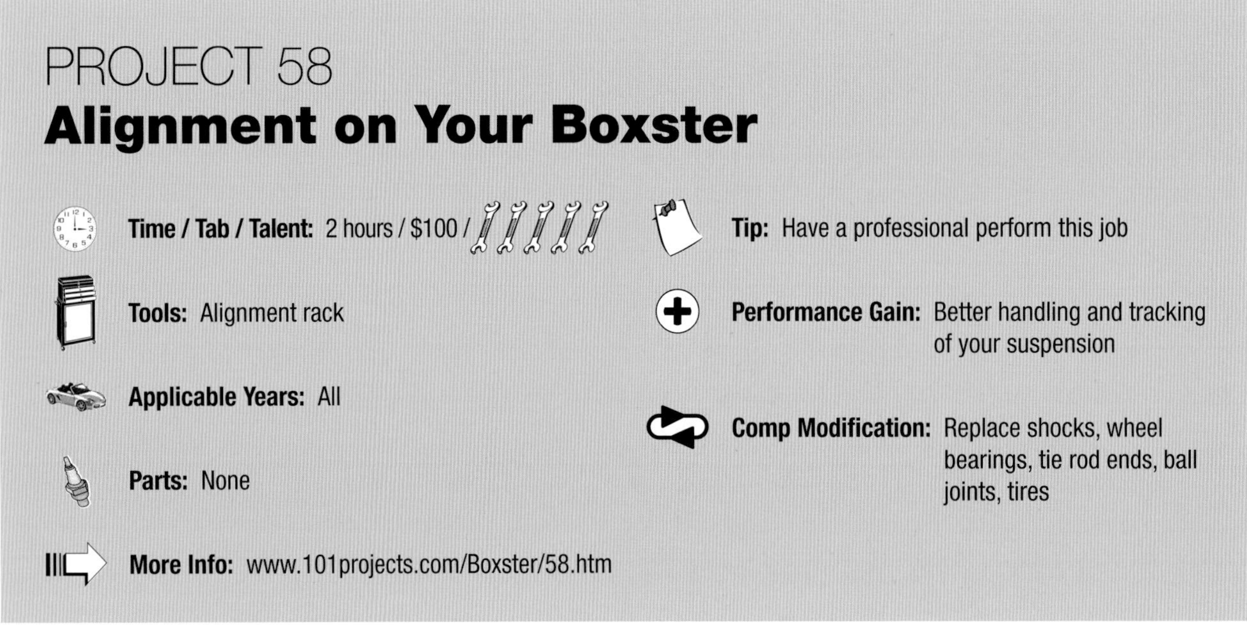

PROJECT 58
Alignment on Your Boxster

Time / Tab / Talent: 2 hours / $100 /

Tools: Alignment rack

Applicable Years: All

Parts: None

More Info: www.101projects.com/Boxster/58.htm

Tip: Have a professional perform this job

Performance Gain: Better handling and tracking of your suspension

Comp Modification: Replace shocks, wheel bearings, tie rod ends, ball joints, tires

The Porsche Boxster is known for its good handling and excellent suspension system. Of course, precise handling and cornering are nonexistent if the car is not aligned properly. There are five different specifications that must be within spec to properly align the chassis. These are front-end caster, camber, toe, and rear-end camber and toe. On the stock Boxster, the settings that you can easily change are for camber and toe on the front and rear suspension. Caster is adjustable if you replace your suspension control arms with ones used on some of the GT racing cars. Also, unlike the earlier Porsche 911, the ride height is not adjustable using the factory suspension components. To change the ride height, you need to upgrade your front and rear suspension to a fully adjustable coil-over system or install lowering springs (see Project 60).

If the alignment of the suspension is slightly off, then you might get some significant tire wear and a loss of power and fuel economy. The most common sign of a misaligned front suspension is the car pulling to one side of the road when driving straight. Although the home mechanic can perform the basic front-end toe-in setting, I suggest that you allow a trained professional with an alignment rack make the other adjustments. It's nearly impossible to determine the correct angles and settings for your car without the use of an alignment rack.

Camber refers to the tilt of the wheel, as measured in degrees of variation between the tire centerline and the vertical plane of the car. If the top of the wheel tilts inward, the camber is negative. If the top of the wheel tilts outward, the camber is positive. On the Porsche Boxster, the camber should be slightly negative for Euro-spec cars and slightly positive for the U.S.-spec cars. On some older cars, chassis deformation due to rust and age can sometimes lead to the camber adjustments and measurements being slightly off. If the car has been in an accident, then oftentimes the resulting chassis damage will show up in an alignment that indicates values not within spec.

The front stock Boxster suspension has a limited range to which the camber setting can be adjusted. If you wish to run more negative camber (useful for racing purposes), then you can install aftermarket upper strut mounts that allow you to dial in more than one whole degree of additional negative camber (see Project 60 for more details). Installing aftermarket strut mounts can also be used to correct the chassis camber when it falls out of factory specifications. In addition, you can install the 996 GT3 lower control arms, which are a two-piece unit that allow you to shim the arm for additional camber adjustments (see Photo 8).

Worn suspension bushings may also add to odd alignment measurements. As the bushings and suspension mounts age, they have a tendency to introduce some slop into the suspension system, which can result in poor alignment readings. Lowering your Boxster (through an aftermarket strut swap) will also change your alignment specifications from the factory defaults. If your alignment specialist tells you that your fixed specifications are outside the factory ranges and your car has not been in any accidents, then it's likely that some of your suspension components are worn and need replacement (see Project 59). Lowering your Boxster beyond about 1 inch or so may result in an inability to set the proper toe on the rear suspension without the use of adjustable rear toe links. The stock adjustment does not have enough flexibility to accommodate the proper toe and correct camber with a ride height change greater than 1 inch or so.

The rear wheels should be set from the factory for a slight negative camber (about -1.5 degrees), as the suspension arms tend to bend slightly outward as the car accelerates under power. Since one half of the wheel is mounted firmly on the ground, the top of the wheel has a tendency to twist outward when power is applied. Setting the rear wheels to have a slight negative camber means that under power they will be mostly neutral.

Caster is the angle that the steering axis is offset from the vertical plane. On the Boxster, the strut points toward the rear of the car, resulting in a positive caster angle. From the factory, the default caster angle should be about 5 degrees. The amount of caster in the suspension directly influences the control and stability of the wheels when traveling in a straight line. Since the Porsche rear suspension utilizes a multi-link design, which has a tremendous amount of built-in caster, there is no specification for the rear caster. Front suspension caster is very good for high-speed stability—it helps to keep the wheels aligned and straight. If you wish to reduce the amount of front caster, you will need to install the GT3-style front control arms that allow you to vary the caster angle for the car (see Photo 9).

Toe refers to the angle of the two wheels with respect to each other. If a car has toe-in, it means that the front edges of the wheels are closer to each other than the rear edges. Toe-in is adjustable by changing the length of the tie rods (see Project 59). With rear-wheel-drive cars like the Boxster, sometimes the front wheels try to move toward a toe-out position under power. Setting the wheels to have very slight toe-in can help neutralize this effect. Toe-out occurs when the front edges of the wheels are farther apart than thc inncr edges. Some toe-out is necessary when turning, since the angle of inclination of the inner wheel must be tighter than the outer wheel. The rear toe should be set as close to neutral as possible.

So how should your Porsche be set up? If you are planning to race your car, then you need non-stock suspension components, and you will probably want as much negative camber as allowed by the racing rules. This is because the car will have a tendency to straighten out in turns, and you want the maximum tire patch on the road when you are cornering. Setting the camber to a negative value means that when the camber starts to change to slightly positive through turns, the negative setting will help neutralize this effect. There's also a misnomer that a lot of caster is good for racing. While adding more caster to your suspension can indeed make it handle better, the reality is that introducing too much caster into the suspension can reduce your track times. On a perfectly balanced rear-wheel-drive car, adding too much caster can have a tendency to transfer loading from the outside front and inside rear tires to the opposite corners. This can upset the balance and cause a corner entry push. The bottom line here is to seek professional help for alignment specifications and any answers to questions that you might have, and don't accept the common misnomers about suspension upgrades—do your own independent research. Two books that I refer to on these topics are *Race Car Engineering* by Paul Van Valkenburgh and *How to Make Your Car Handle* by Fred Puhn.

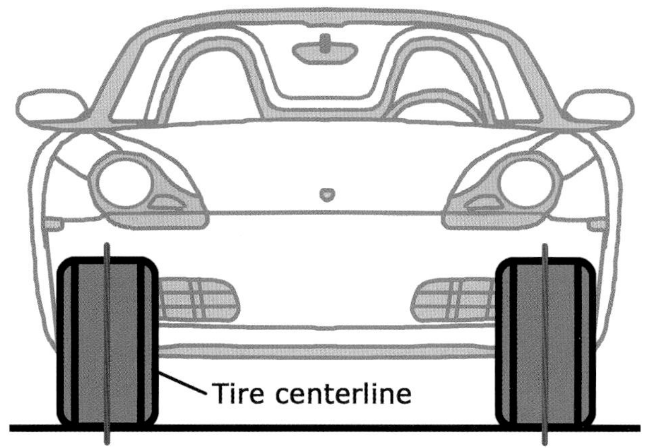

1 **Zero Camber.** When the car is aligned with zero camber, it means that the wheels are directly perpendicular to the ground. The tires make even contact with the road and exhibit a minimal amount of wear and friction when turning. The weight of the car is distributed evenly across the tire tread, but the steering control can be a bit heavy. Tire sizes are shown smaller than scale and camber angles are exaggerated for ease of illustration in these diagrams.

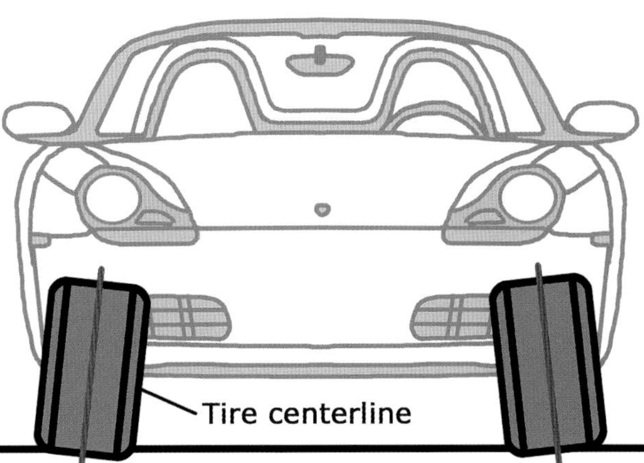

2 **Negative Camber.** The lower parts of the tires are angled outward, causing tires to wear more on the inside edges. The Boxster has an independent front suspension, which creates a slight negative camber when traveling over bumps. As the suspension compresses upward, the wheel tilts in slightly to avoid changing the track (distance between left and right wheels). Although this momentarily changes the camber of the wheel, it prevents the tires from scrubbing and wearing every time that the car travels over a bump.

3 **Positive Camber.** This can cause the outer edges of the tires to wear more quickly than the inside. Positive camber is sometimes designed into the suspension to provide increased stability when traveling over bumpy roads or through turns on the typical high-crowned roads.

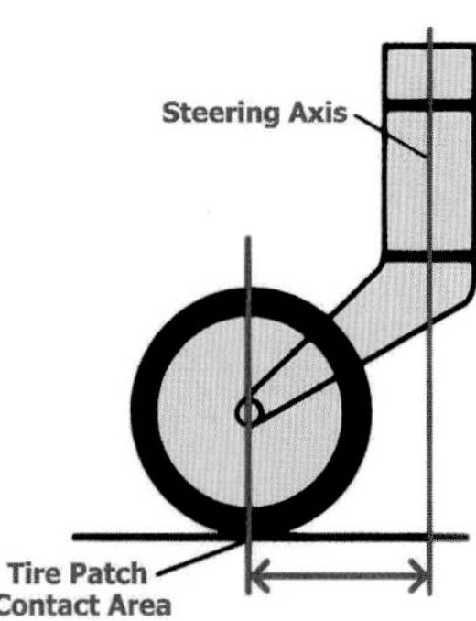

4 **Positive Caster.** The concept of positive caster is best demonstrated by the wheels of a shopping cart. The steering axis of each wheel is located in front of the point where the wheel touches the ground. The load of the cart is in front of the wheels, and as the cart moves forward, the wheels rotate on their axis to follow the cart's direction. This creates an inherent stability that tends to keep the wheels straight, unless they are forcibly steered in a different direction.

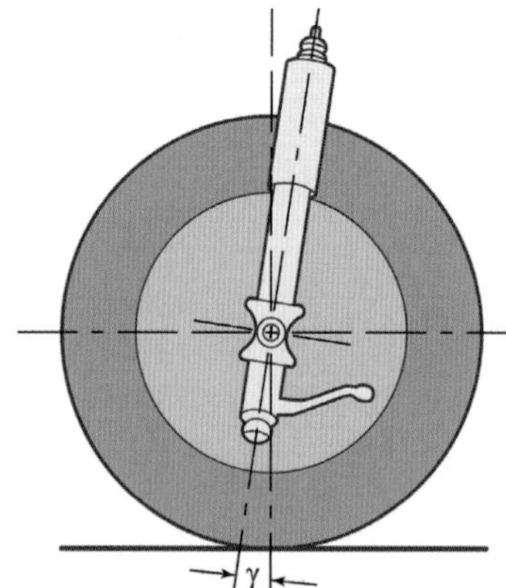

5 **Positive Caster.** All Boxsters have slight positive caster, which creates an inherent stability when the car is moving in a straight line. With the angle of the strut tilted back, it places the steering axis and the load in front of the contact patch where the tire meets the pavement. Like the shopping cart example in the previous illustration, the car tends to move forward in a stable, straight line until the wheels are turned in a different direction. The rear multi-link suspension components of the Boxster, by their design, have extensive positive caster built in.

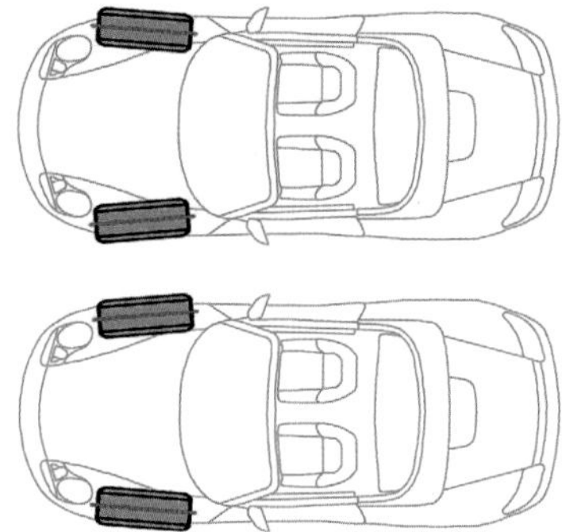

6 **Toe-In and Toe-Out.** The toe of the front suspension refers to the angle of the two wheels with respect to each other. Significant toe-in or toe-out will cause extreme tire wear, as the wheels constantly try to move toward each other (toe-in) or move away from each other (toe-out). The result is that severe friction is created on the tires, and at highway speeds, the tires will wear significantly and power/fuel economy will suffer.

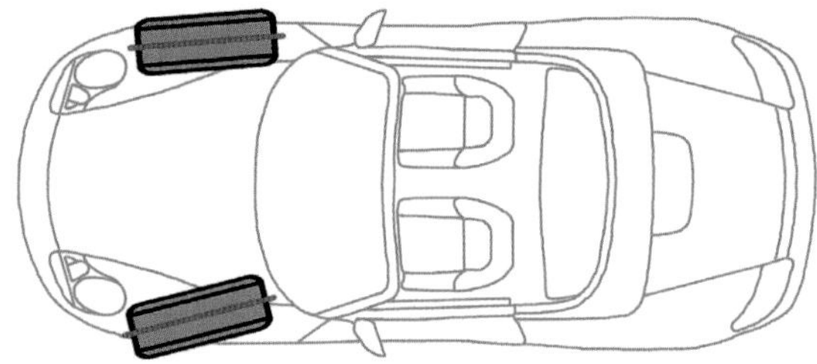

7 **Toe-Out through Turns.** When going around a turn, the inner wheels will turn at a tighter radius than the outer ones. This is so that both wheels will be able to turn around the same point without any tire wear. The outer wheel turns at an angle less sharp than the inner wheel. This minimizes the amount of "scrub" of the tires on the pavement as the car turns.

8 The only way to get the proper measurements for aligning your car is to have it professionally done on an alignment rack. The proper alignment of your Porsche is not something the home mechanic can reliably perform. Don't cheap out either—the Boxster has a lot of adjustment that needs to be set and measured, so be sure you take your car to an expert who has done plenty of them previously. The inset photo shows our project Boxster being corner balanced on top of four scales. Corning balancing is the process of shifting weight from one corner of the car to another in order to achieve an optimum balance. Changes to the balance is typically achieved by raising and/or lowering the suspension spring height by very slight amounts.

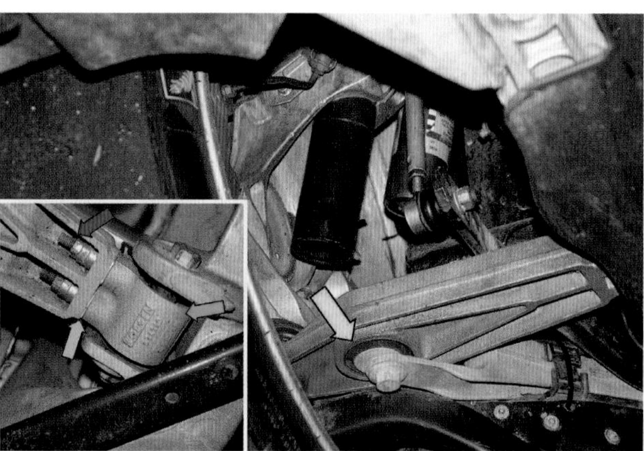

9 This photo shows the underside of a Porsche Cup racing car with fully adjustable suspension. Specifically, this photo shows the GT3 adjustable control arms. The caster can be adjusted using an eccentric bolt that mates with the control arm (yellow arrow). The inset photo shows the opposite side of the control arm, which is a two-piece design that can be shortened or lengthened depending using shims, based upon the amount of additional camber required (blue arrow). The green arrow shows the smaller inside part of the control arm—the red arrow shows the studs that mount into the outer part of the control arm. Add or subtract shims between the two in order to increase or decrease the camber.

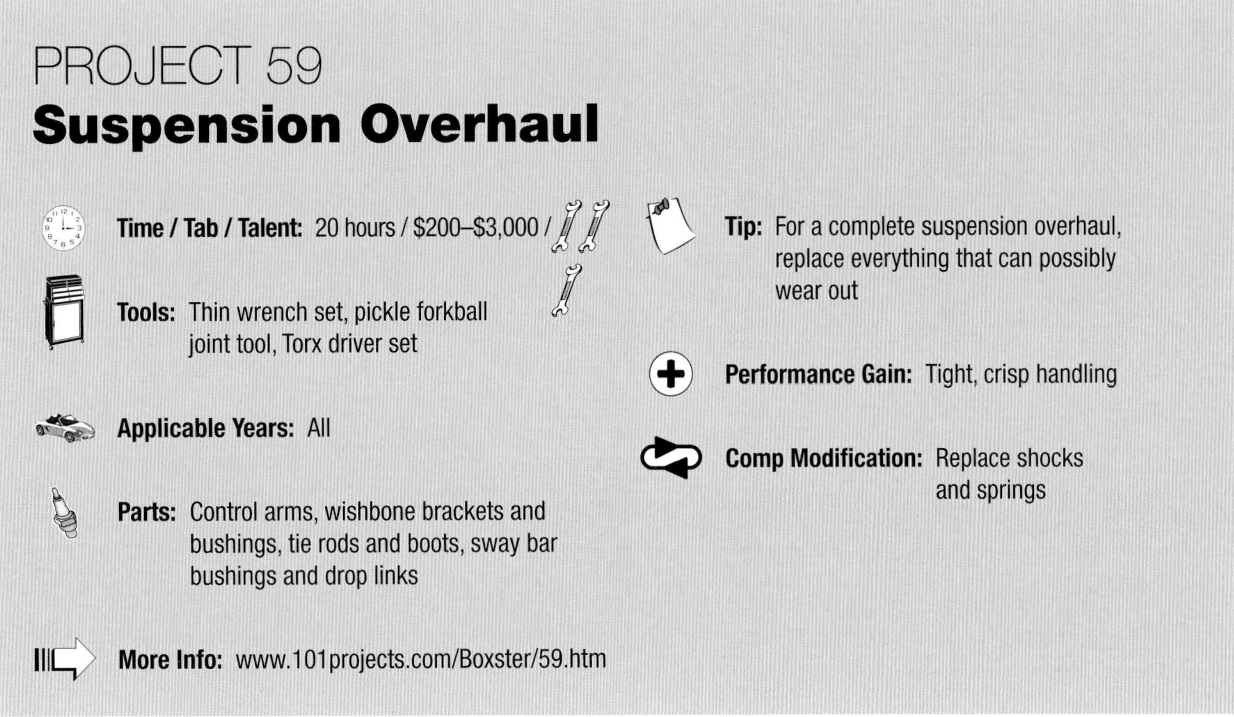

PROJECT 59
Suspension Overhaul

Time / Tab / Talent: 20 hours / $200–$3,000 /

Tools: Thin wrench set, pickle forkball joint tool, Torx driver set

Applicable Years: All

Parts: Control arms, wishbone brackets and bushings, tie rods and boots, sway bar bushings and drop links

More Info: www.101projects.com/Boxster/59.htm

Tip: For a complete suspension overhaul, replace everything that can possibly wear out

Performance Gain: Tight, crisp handling

Comp Modification: Replace shocks and springs

There are lots of bushings and joints on the Boxster suspension that can wear and become loose after many miles of driving. If your car's steering wheel vibrates when traveling on the highway, then there are most likely components in your front suspension that need replacement. In general, I recommend replacing every wearable part in the suspension every 80,000–100,000 miles. This will assure you a crisp, firm-handling ride. There are four main components that need attention when you overhaul your front suspension: control arms, ball joints, sway bar bushings, and tie rods. On the Boxster, the rear suspension is a very similar, yet simpler version of the front—replacement procedures are almost identical. The PelicanParts.com online catalog has complete replacement kits with everything you need for your overhaul, making the job of acquiring the parts substantially easier.

Tie Rods: One of the most common parts to replace are the tie rods. These rods have two universal joints on each end and control the angular position of each front wheel when the car is steered. If the tie rod's joints are worn, then precise steering is impossible, and the car will also have wobbly front wheels and a possible alignment problem. Sometimes vibrations in the steering wheel can be caused by worn out tie rods too.

Replacement of each tie rod is relatively simple—if you have the proper tools. Each tie rod is attached to the wheel bearing carrier with a beveled fit. This means that the tie rod is securely pressed into the spindle arm and cannot be removed without a special tool. The best tool for removal is an angled pitchfork tool, called a pickle fork, that is designed specifically for this task. Do not attempt to hit the top of the rod end with a large hammer, as this will only serve to bend or damage your strut. Place the pickle fork tool in between the strut and the rod end and then hit the tool repeatedly with a large hammer. The wedge in the pickle fork tool will drive the rod end out of the arm. You may have to hit the pickle fork tool quite a few times before the rod end will pop out of its location.

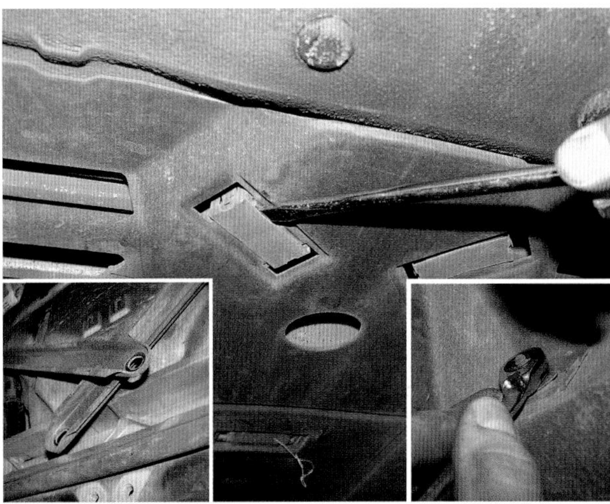

1 A large portion of the front suspension is covered by a large plastic tray. Remove this tray prior to working on the front suspension. The tray is held on with small metal clips that need to be pried off and also a few plastic nuts that need to be removed (lower right). The lower left shows the two crossbraces that need to be loosened and moved out of the way if you are removing the sway bar.

2 Removal/installation of the outer tie rod is started by holding the inner ball joint with a Torx T30 driver and turning the nut. Once the nut is off, then you can use a pickle fork tool to pop the ball joint out of the wheel carrier (see Photo 3).

3 The steering tie rods are removed in a similar manner to the ball joints. The pickle fork tool is essential for popping the tie rod ends out of the end of the strut. Proceed cautiously, as the rubber boot can easily be damaged when you remove the tie rod end. However, if you are replacing the tie rod end anyways, then this shouldn't be a concern. You can also use a clamping tool like the one shown in Photo 4 of Project 40.

Start by removing the top self-locking nut with a Torx socket wrench (Photo 2). Place the pickle fork tool in between the spindle arm and the rod end and then hit the tool repeatedly with a large hammer (Photo 3). The wedge in the pitchfork tool will drive the rod end out of the arm. You may have to hit the pitchfork tool quite a few times before the rod end will pop out of its location.

Once you have the outer rod ends disconnected, remove the boot clamps that attach and secure each end of the rubber boot (bellows) to the tie rod and the steering rack. You will see the exposed metal shaft of the steering rack. Make sure that you don't get any dirt or debris on the rack while you are working on it. Now, it's time to unscrew the old tie rod from the rack. This sounds easier than it really is. The old tie rod may be quite snuggly secured to the rack and could require significant force to remove it. There are a few specialty wrenches designed for this purpose, but I've always had good luck with channel locks and/or a plumber's wrench.

Before the final install of the new tie rod, place the new one and the old one side by side on a workbench, and adjust the new tie rod so that the length from the rod end to the rack-mating surface is the same. You want to set the two lengths of the tie rods to be equal so that you can minimize the change in alignment of the car (Photo 4). You will have to get the car realigned regardless, but it's a good practice to get the alignment close so that you can safely drive to the alignment shop. Mark the final position of the tie rod end on the new tie rod (white paper correction fluid comes in handy here), and then remove it. Don't install the new rod end yet.

Before you screw the tie rod into the rack, make sure that you spread a few drops of Loctite or Permatex Threadlocker onto the threads. After you insert the tie rod into the rack, use a pair of large vise grips or channel locks to tighten it down. There really isn't too much to grab onto with a regular wrench, and chances are you won't have the special thin wrench that is required to tighten the tie rod. The torque specification for the tie rod to the rack is 59 ft-lbs (80 Nm).

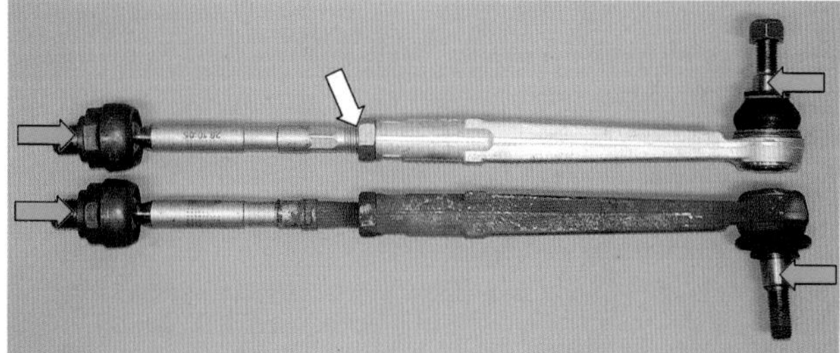

4 Before you install the new tie rods, you should attempt to get each one as close as possible in length to the originals (the distance between the green arrows should be the same). Place them on your bench and compare the lengths, then mark the position of the tie rod end using some white correction fluid (small white arrow). Adjust the new ones as necessary to the lengths of the old ones. This will enable you to get as close as possible to the toe-in alignment adjustment. You will still need to take the car in for an alignment, but you want to get as close as possible to minimize tire wear while you're driving to the alignment shop.

Once the tie rod is tight, then place the rubber boot over the tie rod and onto the steering rack. You will have to remove the rod end on the end of the tie rod in order to make the boot fit. Use pliers and screwdrivers to stretch the boot over each end. Once the boot is in position, install two new clamps over the two ends of the boot to secure it to the rack housing.

After the boot is installed, reattach the tie rod end. Make sure that the length of the tie rod is the same as the measurement of the old one. Adjust the position of the rod end to match up with the mark that you previously made when you compared it to the original tie rod. The torque specification for the tie rod end to the wheel bearing carrier is 37 ft-lb (50 Nm).

To complete the job, install the new rod end into the front control arm. Perform the same procedure for the opposite side. The car should be taken straight to an alignment shop, as it is very easy to mess up the toe-in of the front suspension when you are replacing the tie rods. If you are planning on performing any other front suspension work that might affect the alignment, it would be advisable to do it now, since you will have to realign the car anyway.

Wishbone/Control Arms: The Boxster uses two separate components to create a virtual A-arm suspension that integrates four joints—two ball joints, one center connection, and one rear rubber bushing. Many suspension problems can be traced back to worn out control arm/wishbone ball joints or bushings. Shaking of the steering wheel at high speeds is a good indicator that the control arm/wishbone bushings are worn, the ball joints are worn, or the control arm itself has become bent.

The ball joints, located at the bottom of the strut and attached to the chassis end of the control arm, help the entire assembly pivot and rotate as the control arm turns and pivots and the suspension rides up and down. Needless to say, these critical components can wear out over time and should be replaced every 100,000 miles or so or if the front suspension is beginning to feel a little wobbly.

Both ball joints are integrated into the two assemblies and are not replaceable (you must replace the entire control arm and/or wishbone). Removal of the control arm involves the following steps: disconnect the inner ball joint and disconnect the attachment point to the wishbone (see photos).

The wishbone removal requires that you disconnect the wheel bearing carrier from the wishbone (attached with the outer ball joint) and the control arm. For the outer ball joint, the nut is easily accessible on the lower part of the strut. The ball joint is attached with a beveled fit, similar to the tie rod ends. This means that the ball joint end is securely pressed into the spindle arm and cannot be removed without a special tool. The best tool for removal is the angled pickle fork tool discussed previously. Installation of the new ball joint on the wishbone is easy—simply insert it into its hole and tighten down the nut on top. Follow the photo array in this project for guidance on which components need to be disconnected for replacement.

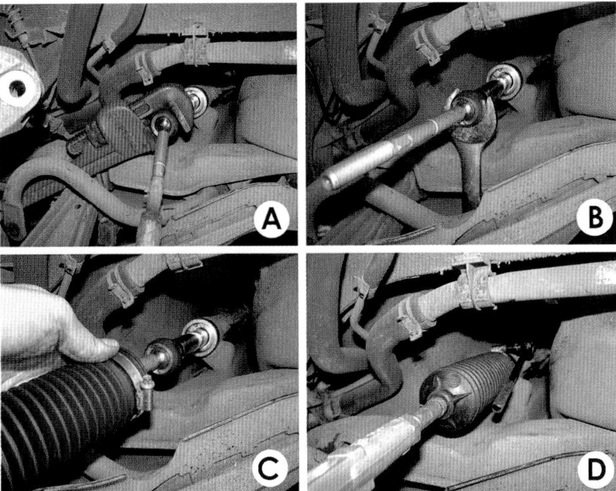

5 Shown here are several steps in the tie rod installation process. **A:** A good tool I've found to remove tie rod ends is a plumber's wrench. I've had good luck removing the tie rod ends with this tool, especially when access to the area is tight, as it is on the Boxster. **B:** The new tie rods are screwed into the ends of the steering rack. Although there is a torque specification for this, it's nearly impossible to measure without the use of a special installation tool. I typically tighten it as tight as I can using the plumber's wrench. Add some Loctite or Permatex Threadlocker to the assembly as well, as shown in Photo 6. **C:** Pre-fit the boot and clamps, and slide them onto the tie rod. **D:** It's an understatement to say that the OEM clamps are a bit difficult to work with. I believe that they are meant to be used during the car's assembly when good access can be had to all areas. So instead, I typically use standard hose clamps, which I feel are better constructed and easier to install.

6 On just about every other car I've worked on, there are locking tabs that act as a stopgap measure to prevent the tie rods from backing out of the steering rack. Surprisingly, the Boxster lacks these, so I prefer to apply some Loctite or Permatex Threadlocker compound to ensure that the tie rods stay in place. Carefully clean out the inside of the steering rack prior to screwing on the tie rods with the Threadlocker applied to the threads.

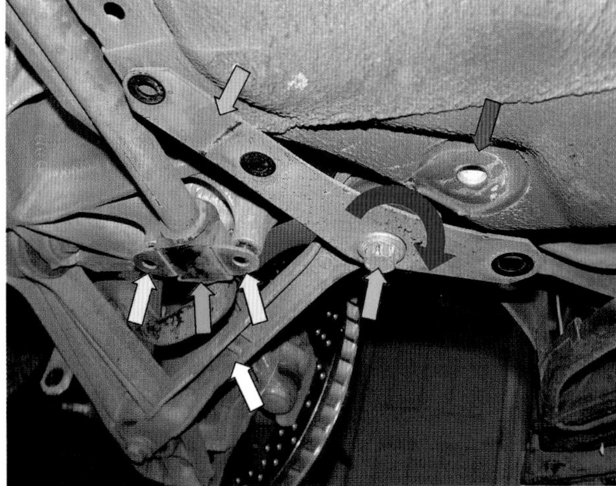

7 The front control arm (white arrow) is attached to a boomerang-shaped plate (orange arrow) that is bolted to the bottom of the chassis. In order to loosen the control arm connection and remove the sway bar bushing (green arrow), remove the two bolts on either side of the sway bar bushing (yellow arrows) and the large bolt at the rear (red arrow). You do not need to remove the bolt indicated by the light blue arrow. Finally, rotate the boomerang out of the way (dark blue arrow).

Sway Bar Bushings: As Boxsters age, the tendency is to find them with worn-out bushings, particularly the sway bar bushings. The first step in replacing your bushings is to figure out if they need to be replaced. Carefully inspect them for cracking, and also check to make sure that their inner diameter hugs the sway bar tightly. If they do not appear to be worn, then simply apply a little bit of lithium grease inside the bushing. If they are worn, then they will need to be replaced.

Replacing the bushings is very easy. With the car elevated and the front wheels removed, simply disconnect the bracket that holds on the sway bar bushing (see Photo 7). The bar and bushing together should drop down slightly if you release both sides at the same time.

The new replacement bushings are split down the middle, so they should easily slide onto the bar and into the bracket (see Photo 9). Remove the old bushings and insert the new ones, making sure that you coat the bushings with some white lithium grease on the inside.

The sway bar drop links are an easy replacement too. Both the top and bottom parts of the drop link contain small ball joints that attach to the strut tower and the sway bar. Remove the nut from each of the two mini ball joints on each end of the drop link. The small ball joint may present a bit of a challenge—you may need a special thin wrench to remove the retaining nut (see Photo 8). Installation of the new drop links involves simply bolting them into place while holding the ball joint from spinning using your thin wrench. The replacement of the rear sway bar bushings is nearly identical to the front.

It's important to note that you should always use brand new factory hardware when replacing your suspension components. Most of the nuts and bolts used in the front suspension have self-locking compounds impregnated into their threads. Reusing old hardware can result in nuts or bolts coming loose and causing a dangerous situation.

8 The drop links (green arrow) may present a challenge to remove, as the ball joint integral to the link may spin when you try to remove the outer nut. If this happens, you will need to use a thin wrench (yellow arrow) to hold the ball joint in place while you loosen the nut. You can purchase a set of these wrenches that are specifically designed to fit into places where a normal, thick wrench will not (available in the tools section of the PelicanParts.com online catalog). They are typically about an ⅛ of an inch thick and are a very useful tool to add to your arsenal.

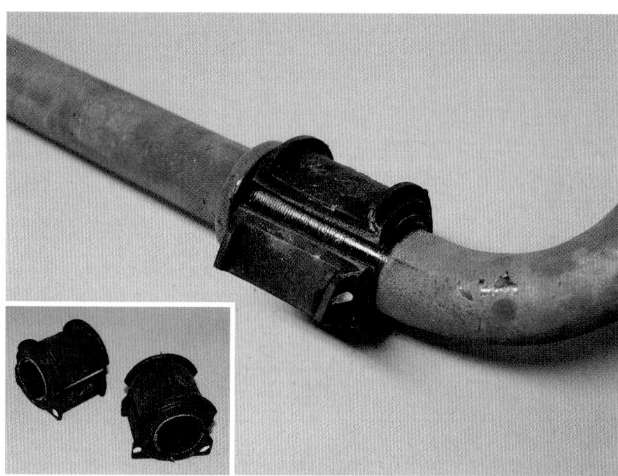

9 Solid sway bar bushings are essential to good handling. To perform a complete renewal of your suspension, you should replace the sway bar bushings and drop links as well. The bushings have a slit down the center so that you can easily pry them on and off the sway bar.

10 Shown here is the top view of the front suspension. Since the front shock has been removed, the assembly must be supported by the floor jack (blue arrow). The brake caliper is tied up and hung from wire on the left (purple arrow). The tie rod is connected to the wheel carrier as shown by the orange arrow. When removing the shocks, you need to loosen the main bolt that attaches the wishbone to the chassis (yellow arrow). Don't remove it; only loosen it, as this will give you enough free play to drop the assembly down and remove the front shocks. The control arm is connected to the center of the wishbone (red arrow), and the boomerang-shaped plate shown in Photo 7 (green arrow). Finally, this photo also shows the sway bar (white), which has been disconnected from its drop links (not shown). Reminder: Don't tighten up the wishbone bolt (yellow arrows) until the car is back down on the ground. Tightening it prematurely will place a preload on the bushing and cause it to fail in a short period of time.

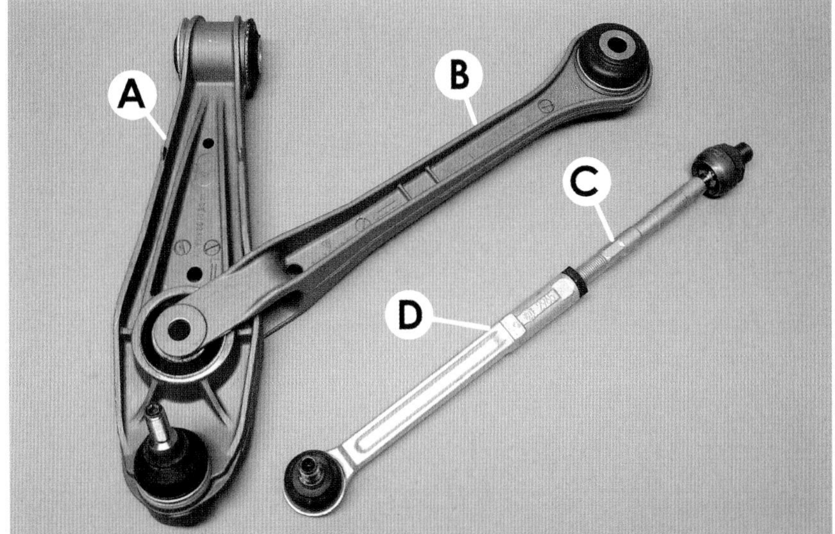

11 This photo shows the main components of the front suspension on the Boxster. **A:** This is the wishbone, and it supports the wheel carrier, which wraps around the shock and contains the wheel bearing. **B:** The control arm constrains the movement of the wishbone so that it travels in a mostly up and down manner. **C:** The inner tie rod attaches to the steering rack and is mated with the outer tie rod (D). Changing the effective length of the tie rod assembly (C and D together) changes the toe-in alignment specification for that side of the car (see Project 58). **D:** The outer tie rod attaches to the wheel carriers and transmits steering input from the rack to the carrier.

12 Although I haven't quite seen it yet on the Boxster, this steering column rubber coupling tends to age and wear out on other cars. At this time (2010), the only way to replace this coupling is to replace the entire steering column. At $1,600 or so, that's a bit cost prohibitive. I suspect that as the Boxster and 996 age, an aftermarket replacement part will become available.

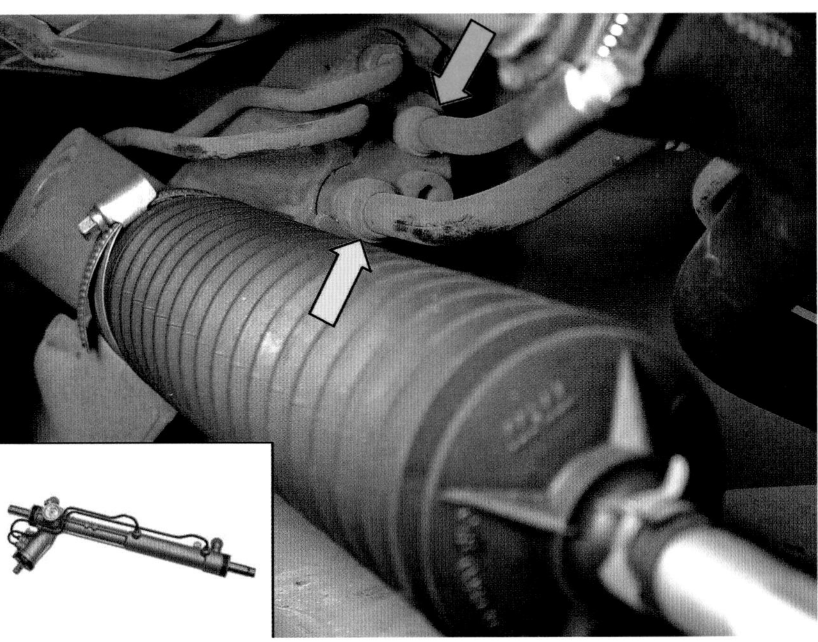

13 There's a night-and-day difference between a new and used rack. The inset photo shows a Genuine Porsche rebuilt power steering rack-and-pinion assembly. If the rack wears out, then you will find that your steering will be sloppy. Also common are leaky racks that deposit power steering fluid on the floor of your garage. Be aware though—sometimes it may only be the power steering lines that are leaking and need to be replaced—not an expensive rack (green arrow = pressure line; yellow arrow = return line). Carefully check the rack and lines first, prior to spending your money on a rebuilt rack. The most common leakage point for the rack is out the ends. If you cut open your tie rod boot and a lot of power steering fluid starts flowing out, then chances are that the seals in the ends of your rack are worn, and it needs to be rebuilt or replaced. Unfortunately, there are no individual repair parts available for you to fix the rack yourself—it must be sent back to the manufacturer.

PROJECT 60
Performance Suspension/ Lowering Your Boxster

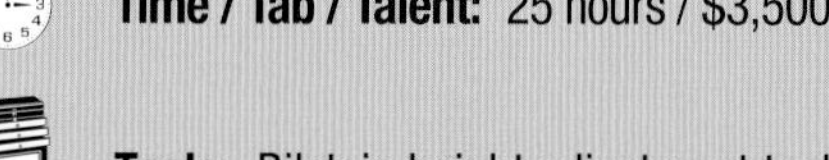

Time / Tab / Talent: 25 hours / $3,500 /

Tools: Bilstein height adjustment tool

Applicable Years: All

Parts: PSS or PSS 9 Performance suspension kit

More Info: www.101projects.com/Boxster/60.htm

Tip: The PSS kit is a good value if you want a sporty suspension and a lower ride height

Performance Gain: Stiffer suspension, firmer ride

Comp Modification: Replace suspension bushings

Shocks and Springs: The PSS performance suspension kit from Bilstein is the one of the top performing kits available for the Boxster. The system includes two front coil-over spring/shock setups and two rear coil-over spring/shock assemblies. Both the front and rear springs are easily adjustable for tweaking the exact ride height that you're looking for. The kit is a bolt-in replacement available for all Boxsters and comes in two varieties. The PSS kit incorporates adjustable spring perches for both front and rear height adjustment. The PSS 9 kit is identical to the PSS kit, with the added feature of four easily adjustable spring-rate shock absorbers. Installation of the kit is no more difficult than installing stock shock absorbers and new springs (see Project 63). At the time of this writing, Bilstein is gradually replacing the PSS 9 kits with the more advanced PSS 10 kits. Although they are not available yet for the Boxster, the features and performance of the PSS 10 kit will be similar to the PSS 9 kit. Also recently made available for the Boxster is the Bilstein Damptronic kit, which has electronically controlled dampening settings.

After you have installed the PSS kit, you need to have the car realigned. Due to the design of the front suspension, the alignment specs will change when you lower the car from the stock height. See Project 58 for more details. In addition, lowering your Boxster can cause issues with clearance of wider wheels and tires. Before you test the suspension to the max, make sure your tire and wheel clearances are okay.

Sway Bars: For the Boxster project car, I chose to use upgraded sway bars, drop links, and strut mounts manufactured by Tarett Engineering. The sway bars are lightweight, hollow, and 26.8mm in diameter, and they weigh about one-half the weight of the stock solid bar with equivalent stiffness. These sway bars are also fully adjustable with multiple mounting holes located on each end so that you can increase or decrease stiffness by moving the drop links in or out.

Many times owners will want to upgrade their sway bars to larger units with more torsional stiffness. If you install a larger engine, or are planning on creating a dedicated track car, then adding a stiffer bar will give you a flatter ride and help with cornering. As with anything in this world though, there is a tradeoff. Stiffer sway bars may result in a rougher ride around town, particularly on bumpy pavement. Installing too stiff a sway bar may actually decrease performance if one of your front wheels begins to lift during hard cornering. It's best to speak with someone who has run a particular sized bar in their car and see how it performed for them on the street and on the track.

Adjustable Drop Links: The best way to set the drop link preload is with the car on flat ground after it's been aligned and corner balanced. After the car is balanced, it will have the correct theoretical weight on each wheel so that handling will be the same going into left or right hand turns. It will also help to minimize the chances of a wheel locking up under hard braking. You want to set the drop links so that there is no sway bar preload that can affect this balance. It may be possible to get the preload close with the car up on jack stands and the suspension hanging, but it is far more accurate to set it with the suspension loaded (car on the ground).

To remove the sway bar preload, you only need to adjust one drop link on each sway bar. With the drop links connected on both ends and the center jamb nuts loose, rotate the center link in either direction to lengthen or shorten the link. If you're rotating it the correct direction (reducing preload), it will begin to feel easier to turn. Conversely, the drop link will become more difficult to rotate if you're turning it in the wrong direction. Once you get to the point where you reach neutral preload, the drop link will be very easy to turn and then will start to become more difficult to turn as you pass the optimum setting. Rotate the drop link back to the neutral point and lock the center jamb nuts.

With the Boxster, the front preload should be set with the wheels pointing straight—if the wheels are turned, it will slightly preload the sway bar. Additionally, the rear drop link preload should be set with the front wheels facing straight—turning the wheels will tip the car slightly, causing the rear sway bar to preload as well. Since the front drop link also connects to the strut, it needs to accommodate the strut turning when the wheels are turned with steering input. Therefore, the drop link rod ends need to be phased relative to each other such that they don't bind when the wheels are turned. The specially machined spacers installed on each side of the drop link rod ends are designed to roll into the rod end housing and provide an appropriate amount of clearance needed to accommodate the wheels turning lock to lock.

Even with these special spacers, proper rod end phasing is still required. To accomplish this, first adjust the preload as described previously. Lock only one jamb nut on each of the drop links. Next, rotate the wheels to full lock in one direction. Working on one side at a time, rotate the upper and lower rod ends in the same direction until they bind and will not rotate further. Then tighten the loose jamb nut. The rod ends should now be phased properly. If it's set properly, there should be no binding and you should be able to rotate the entire link slightly between bind points. Next rotate the steering to opposite lock and check the opposite side to see if the link will still rotate slightly. If there is more free rotation of the link with the steering at full lock in one direction, make an adjustment to get it close to being equal for both sides. Then repeat for the other drop link.

Front Strut Mounts/Camber Plates: The camber plates are a bolt-in replacement for the factory strut mounts. They eliminate the compliant factory rubber bushing and replace them with a precision Teflon-lined spherical bearing for a tighter front suspension and quicker steering response. The increased precision reduces front wheel camber changes during hard cornering, which maintains the optimum tire contact patch for improved traction and better handling. Two sets of mounting holes allow for more than 1.1 degree of extra negative camber.

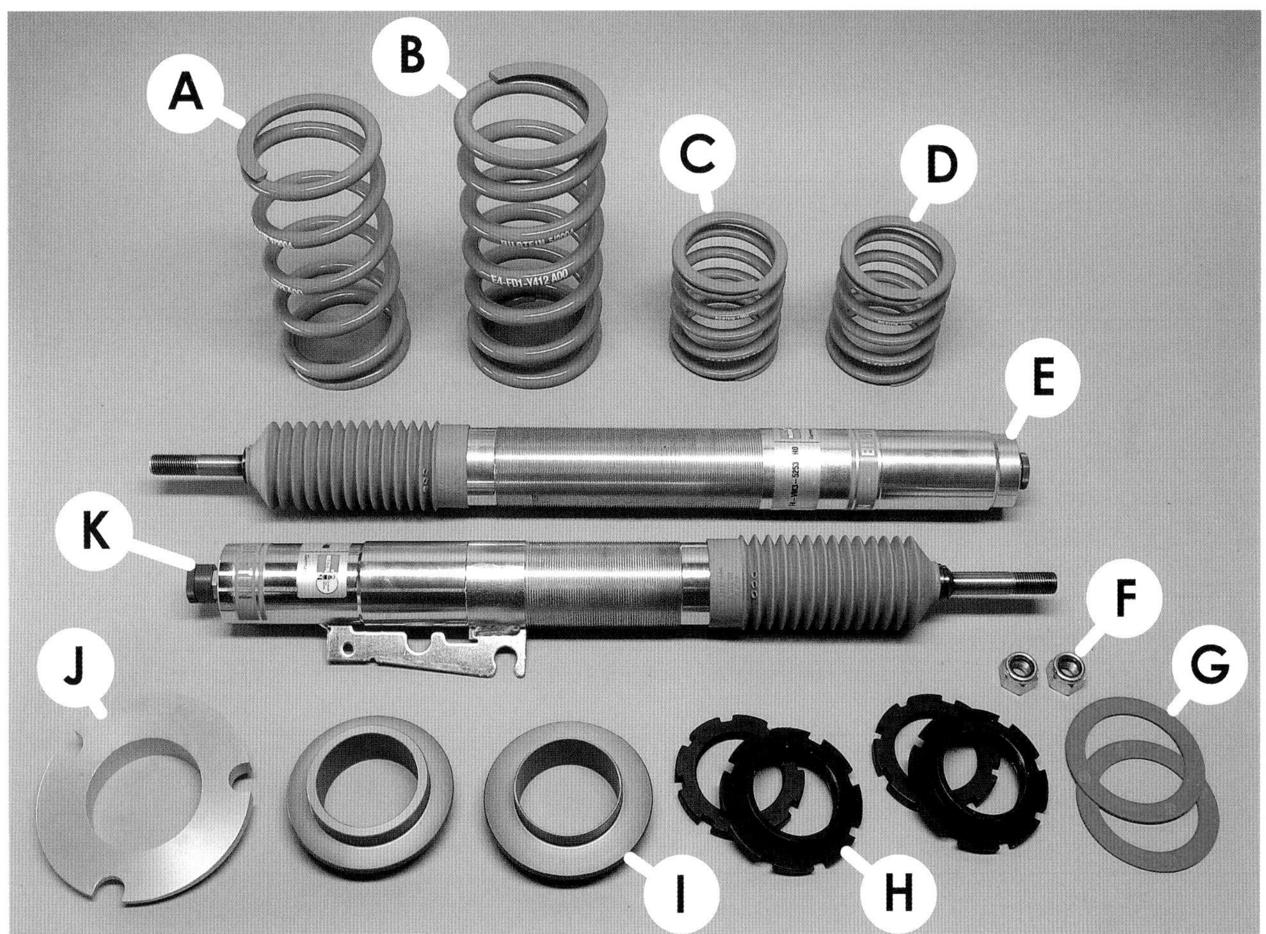

1 Shown here is one-half of the Bilstein PSS 9 kit. **A:** Front upper spring. **B:** Rear upper spring. **C:** Front lower spring. **D:** Rear lower spring. **E:** Fully adjustable rear shock absorber. **F:** Lock nuts for shock absorber. **G:** Slip inserts for front spring retainer. **H:** Spring perch support. **I:** Upper/lower spring retainer. **J:** Rear spring top plate. **K:** Adjustment knob for front shock absorber.

2 Shown here is a close-up of the front PSS 9 shock. The upper and lower springs are separated by the spring retainer and two blue plastic slip inserts (inset photo, upper left). The adjustment knob is located at the bottom of the shock for easy adjustment (inset, lower right). Turn the knob to 9 for a softer ride, or turn it to 1 for a stiffer performance feel. The adjustment of the ride height is accomplished by rotating the spring perch and retainer (red arrow) up or down the length of the shock.

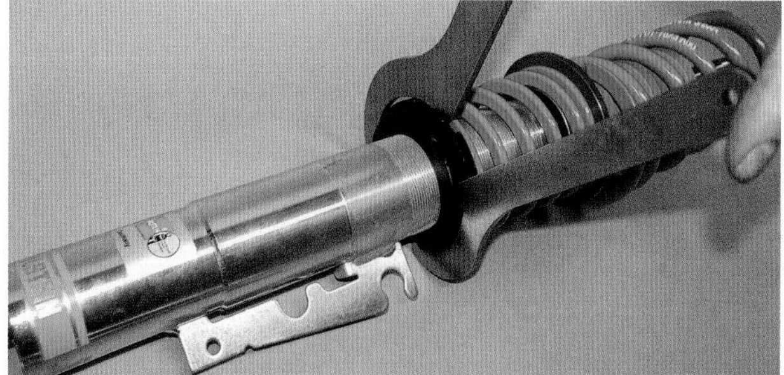

3 The ride height of the suspension is adjusted by changing the location of the lower spring perches on the shock housing. Using the two special Bilstein adjustment tools, you can lower or raise the perches. Lock them together when you've achieved the proper height.

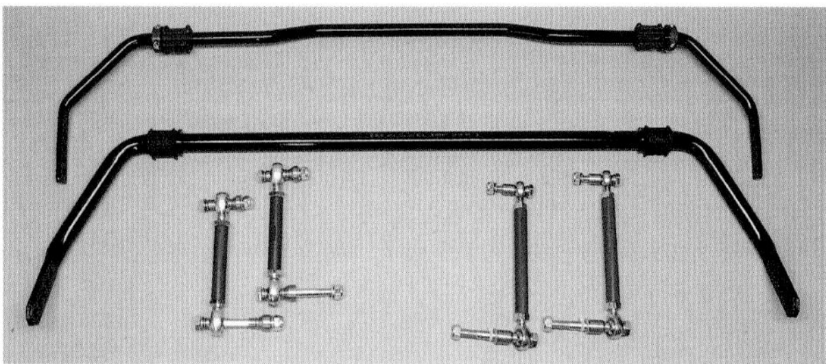

4 Shown here are aftermarket front and rear sway bar kits from Tarett Engineering. This performance kit is specifically designed to work with the Boxster and includes new bushings and drop links. The bar has multiple adjustment settings. Bolting the drop links to the outer holes produces a softer ride, whereas using the inner holes results in a stiffer suspension.

5 This photo is quite possibly my favorite in this entire book. With one shot, it shows the PSS 9 system, the Tarett Engineering drop links, adjustable sway bars, upper camber plate strut mount, and the Brembo big brake kit (Project 52). The yellow arrow shows the adjustable drop links, which need to be dialed in along with the rest of your suspension components.

6 This photo shows the Tarett Engineering front upper strut mount attached to the PSS 9 kit. The upper right inset photo shows the bottom side of the bearing assembly. The lower right inset photo shows how the strut mount moves the top of the shocks inward to achieve the maximum amount of negative camber.

7 The rear shocks are set up very similarly to the front ones, except for the top shock mount, which is attached against an angled upper aluminum plate. This allows the shock to mate at the correct angle to the chassis.

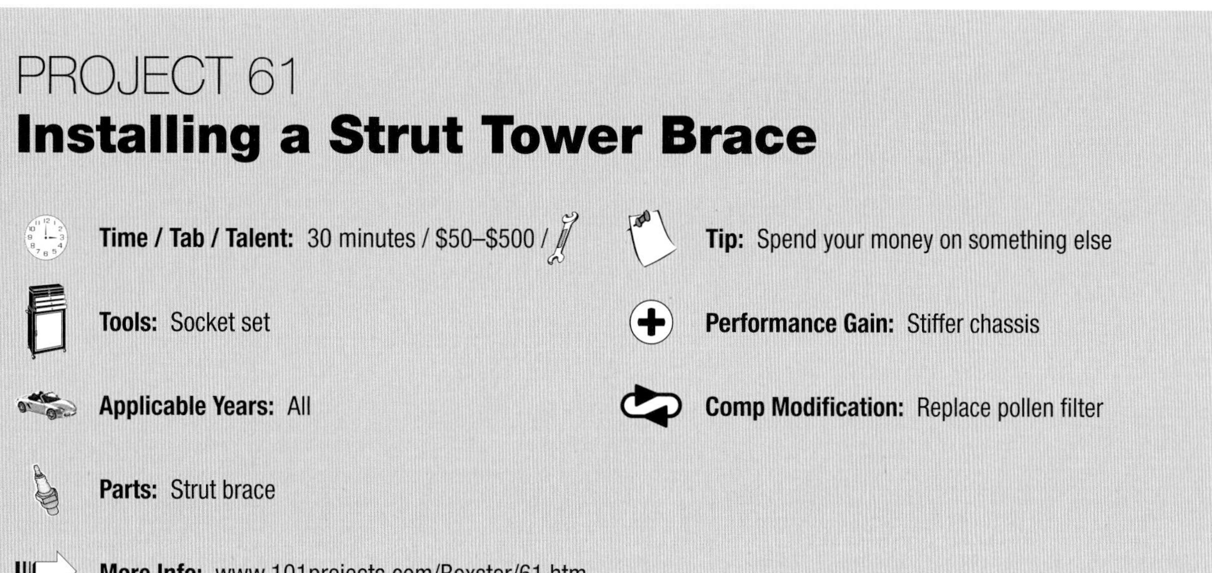

PROJECT 61

Installing a Strut Tower Brace

Time / Tab / Talent: 30 minutes / $50–$500 /

Tools: Socket set

Applicable Years: All

Parts: Strut brace

More Info: www.101projects.com/Boxster/61.htm

Tip: Spend your money on something else

Performance Gain: Stiffer chassis

Comp Modification: Replace pollen filter

"*The Porsche Boxsters are well known for their agility and superb performance in handling. However, because of the design of the chassis, there exists a weakness in the handling of the cars. The front shock towers are not well supported in the Boxster chassis—they are somewhat isolated and unsupported. As a result, the towers can bend and flex under heavy cornering. This flexing can cause detrimental changes in the handling of your car, because in general, the stiffer the chassis, the better the handling of the car. Camber strut braces are designed to maintain the distance between the shocks under heavy cornering. A bar linking the top of the shock towers insures that the towers do not bend when the chassis is flexing.*"

Well, that's what the marketers say when selling these bars. The strut bars are yet another controversial product that many people feel the need to install on their cars. On some cars, the early Porsche 911s, for example, the installation of the strut bar is an important chassis stiffening device. Because of their rear engine design, the front chassis can be decidedly weak, particularly when rust has started to affect the chassis stiffness. But the Boxster mid-engined chassis is different—it's supported by a much more rigid frame, which includes a very strong sheet metal structure that runs the width of the car. Included in this are two welded strut braces that can be seen in Photo 1.

Which strut bars are most effective? First of all, I have little faith in the strut bars that are manufactured out of aluminum. Aluminum is not a very strong metal—you can often bend aluminum pipes with your hands. Add to that the fact that most of the strut bars must have some type of angle in them in order to fit neatly around the engine and under the hood—there's no straight shot across the engine bay. This combination creates a very weak support when you think of the forces you're trying to counteract. In my opinion, the aluminum strut braces are merely window dressing for the engine compartment.

I'm also not fond of bars with hinges built into the strut mounts. If they move at all, the shock towers are likely to see movement that would place the strut brace in both compression and tension. This means that a stiff connection between the strut towers is vital to proper operation of any strut bar. Any time you place a fastener in the assembly, you will introduce backlash and slop in at least one direction (compression or tension). This results in the bar becoming ineffective in at least one direction (compression or tension).

The best strut tower braces are the one-piece units manufactured out of thick steel pipe welded together. These will offer the best protection against any chassis flex when installed between the two strut towers. Unfortunately, I can't say that I've seen one installed in a Boxster that I actually thought would provide additional stiffness.

I also find it surprising that if you ask die-hard racers who drive their Boxster cars on the track, most of them don't run with a strut brace and can't even feel the difference even when pulling some significant side loads (1.4G) out of the corners. For dedicated track cars, the strut towers are often reinforced with steel pipe that is welded diagonally across the front trunk compartment. Another problem I see is that the Boxster already has reinforcement bars bolted from the shock towers to the chassis. These already provide a tremendous amount of structural support for the towers.

The bottom line? If you believe that a strut bar will do you some benefit, or if you are looking to spruce up your engine compartment, then adding one to your car is a relatively simply task—simply bolt it on top of your strut towers. If your goal is increased performance, then I would probably spend your money elsewhere.

1 Shown here is a great-looking carbon-fiber strut bar that extends across the rear of the battery. This bar in particular is only really good for show, in my opinion. The aluminum brackets that these bars are manufactured out of are relatively weak, are designed with multiple fasteners, and also have their strength weakened by the angled bracket design. Ironically, the entire strut brace is hidden by the side plastic covers, thus diminishing its visual appeal as well.

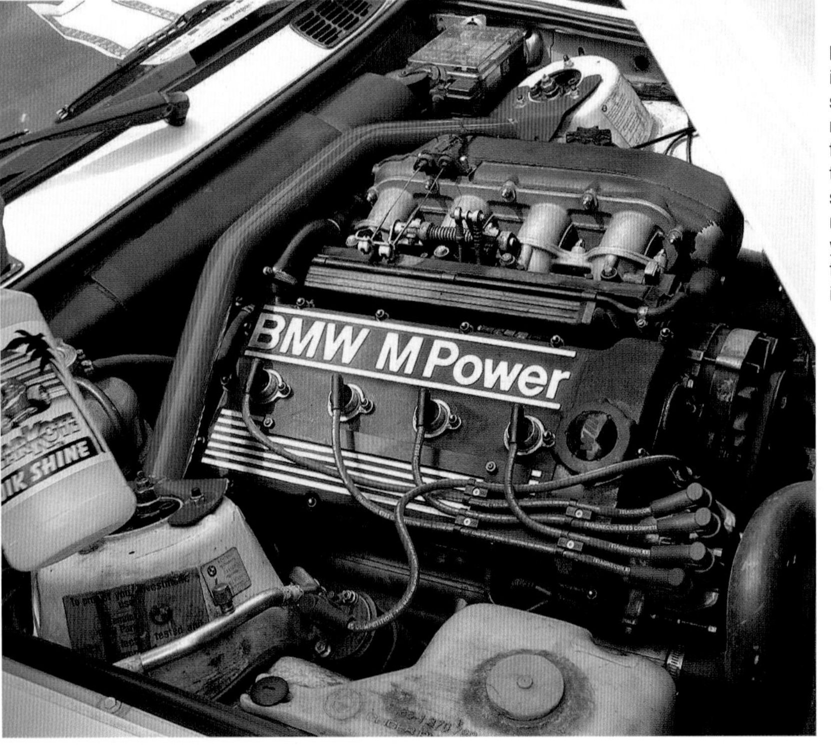

2 I included this photo of an E30 BMW M3 to illustrate what I feel a good strut brace should look like. Although not as attractive, the brace shown in this photo is probably one of the most effective I've seen. It's a thick, large-diameter steel pipe that directly reinforces the shock towers and requires significant forces to deflect and bend. Despite the fact that there are two rather large angles in the brace, the strength of the steel pipe should more than compensate for the reduced rigidity. These are the types of bars that I recommend if you're going to be installing one in your car. Unfortunately, the lack of room in the Boxster's front trunk makes the installation of this style somewhat prohibitive.

PROJECT 62
Steering Wheel Replacement

 **Time / Tab / Talent:** 1 hour / $150–$1,000 / 

 **Tools:** Torx driver set

 **Applicable Years:** All

 **Parts:** Steering wheel and hub adapter

More Info: www.101projects.com/Boxster/62.htm

 **Tip:** Use a steering lock bar to help loosen the wheel

 **Performance Gain:** Good improvement in driving feel—much improved looks

 **Comp Modification:** Upgrade your dashboard information computer

One of the most exciting and rewarding projects that you can perform on your Boxster is the replacement of the standard four-spoke steering wheel. In addition to the gorgeous factory three-spoke wheel, there are a wide variety of aftermarket wheels to choose from. Let's face it—the stock Boxster wheel is not something that many people can get too excited about. Installing a wheel of your choosing cures all that.

It's important to mention a word about safety here. All the later-model Boxsters came from the factory equipped with driver's side air bags built into the steering wheel. Air bags are important pieces of safety equipment, and I fully recommend keeping them in place. That said, you cannot install a nonfactory aftermarket steering wheel and also keep your air bag in place, unless you purchase an aftermarket wheel specifically made for the Boxster with an integrated air bag (Aitwe manufactures one such wheel). With that in mind, I recommend that you install an aftermarket wheel only if your car originally didn't come with an air bag when you purchased it or if you are converting your car into a club racer or weekend track car. You can still choose to install the wheel into your street car, but be forewarned—air bags are probably the best protection you will have in a crash. Also, state and local regulations may legally restrict what you can do with your air bag.

That said, I recommend upgrading to the factory three-spoke wheel with the integrated air bag. The wheel is a bolt-on upgrade, and it looks very good too—particularly the gold crest in the center of the air bag.

The first step is to disconnect the battery and wait at least 15 minutes (see Project 81 for details). This is very important, as the air bag itself is a dangerous explosive package and can be accidentally set off by a variety of factors. Also, the air bag control system is designed to remain operational for up to 15 minutes after the battery has been disconnected. The next step is to remove the air bag from the steering wheel by disconnecting the two T27 Torx screws that attach it to the front of the wheel (see the insets in Photo 2). Extend the steering wheel as far toward the rear of the car as you can go to afford yourself the maximum amount of room to get your Torx tool in there. With the screws loosened (they do not come out of the steering wheel), the air bag should be loose from the wheel—disconnect the small harness, remove it, and place it aside.

The next step is to remove the wheel itself. If you don't happen to own an impact wrench, there is another neat trick that I developed for removing the steering wheel. First, take one of those obnoxiously large, red steering wheel locks and clamp it onto the steering wheel. The long handle on the lock will allow you to gain a significant amount of leverage on the wheel. Then insert the deep socket onto the center steering wheel nut. Compressing together the steering wheel lock handle and the long handle attached to the socket will enable you to loosen up the steering wheel nut. Under no circumstances should you ever turn the steering wheel all the way to the end of the rack and use the end stop to hold the wheel while you remove the nut. The steering wheel has a lot of leverage, and you can easily damage your rack and pinion if you apply a large amount of torque to the wheel.

Once you have the nut off of the wheel, take some white correction fluid or a marker pen and mark the steering wheel and the shaft so that you know which spline to place it back on. Then simply pull the wheel off of the steering column. If the wheel is stuck on the splines and doesn't want to come off, then take a rubber mallet and gently tap the rear of the wheel until it begins to move. If you are installing an aftermarket wheel, place the new wheel onto the included steering wheel hub and then onto the car. Be sure that you properly hook up the horn and test it before you tighten the wheel down again. For the Porsche three-spoke wheel, the installation of the new wheel is basically the reverse of the removal process.

1 Shown here is one of my favorite steering wheels of all-time, the Porsche factory three-spoke wheel. Available as an option on the cars when they were new, this upgrade is pretty spendy, but in my opinion, definitely worth it. Remember, you can recover the cost of your new wheel by selling your old air bag on eBay or the classifieds section of PelicanParts.com. The part number for the wheel in black is 996-347-804-54-A28, and the part number for the air bag with the gold crest is 996-803-089-02-A28.

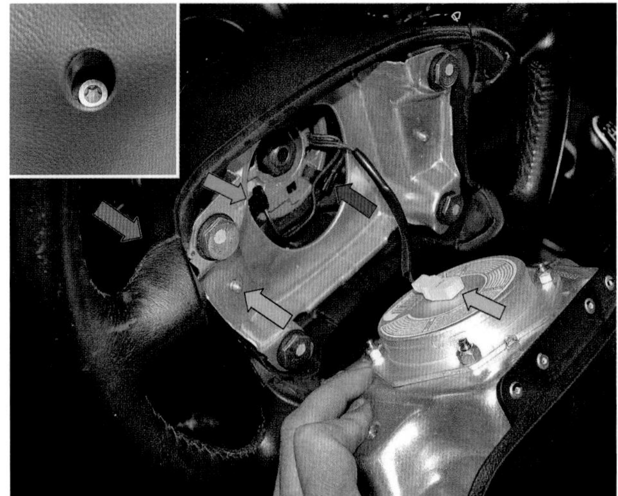

2 Removal of the air bag itself is pretty easy. Remove the two screws on either side of the back of the steering wheel column by using a T27 Torx driver (upper left photo). These holes are somewhat hidden from view and have tiny access holes in the backside of the steering wheel. The purple arrow shows you where you need to insert the Torx driver, and the orange arrow indicates the tail end of the Torx bolt. With these two screws loosened, the air bag should simply pop out of the center of the wheel. Disconnect the wire harness to the air bag (blue arrow shows where it plugs into the air bag), and place it aside. Also disconnect the horn wires (green and red arrows). Make sure you disconnect the battery and wait at least 15 minutes before attempting to remove the air bag.

3 A trick that I developed for removing steering wheels involves locking the wheel with one of those steering wheel locking devices like the Club. Don't allow the steering wheel to lock against the mechanism in the lock cylinder, and don't let it bottom out against the steering rack. Using a breaker bar and the Club in this fashion, you can easily remove the steering center nut.

4 Before you remove the wheel, mark its position on the shaft with a permanent marker (inset). With the wheel retaining nut removed and the wire harnesses disconnected, you should be able to pull the steering wheel off of the splined hub in the center. Thread the wires through the hole in the wheel as you remove it from the steering shaft.

5 Although you lose the safety of the air bag, the new steering wheel really spices up the interior of the car and gives your Porsche that motorsport feel. If you are removing the air bag, you need to "trick" the air bag computer into thinking that it's still connected. Placing a 0.3 ohm resistor across the two terminals of the connector will indicate to the computer that the air bag is still in place, and it won't trigger your air bag lamp. This should allow your system to continue to properly control and operate the passenger side air bag. The installation of a MOMO aftermarket wheel requires the use of a ½-inch washer under the steering wheel nut because the shaft is not threaded deep enough for the aftermarket hub adapters.

PROJECT 63
Replacing Shocks and Springs

Time / Tab / Talent: 8 hours / $1,200 /

Tools: Spring compressor, floor jack, jack stands

Applicable Years: All

Parts: Shocks, springs, and hardware

More Info: www.101projects.com/Boxster/63.htm

Tip: Purchase an electric or air impact wrench for this task

Performance Gain: Smoother, crisper handling

Comp Modification: Install performance springs and lower your suspension

One of the most popular projects to perform on the Boxster is the replacement of the front and rear shocks. I usually recommend that you replace both the front and the rear at the same time, as they take roughly similar abuse over their lifetime, and the fronts or rears are not likely to be more or less worn than the other ones. As a rule, the shocks should always be replaced in pairs (left and right together). The replacement procedures for the front and rear shocks are very similar.

I recommend that you replace your shocks every 50,000 miles or so or if they start to show signs of fading or wearing out. If you push down on a corner of the car, it should spring back with almost no oscillation up and down. If the car bounces up and down, then you probably need new shocks. Different driving patterns may also affect the life of shock absorbers. Cars that are raced or often driven on windy roads may need to have their shocks replaced more often than street cars. It is also important to remember to have the car realigned if you install performance springs into your car that lower it from its stock level. Changing the height of the suspension changes the values of the alignment/suspension settings.

With the car elevated in the air and the wheels removed, start with one strut, and remove the brake caliper (see Project 55). Unplug any brake sensors that may be connected to the caliper and disconnect them from the strut (see Photo 1). Use some rope or wire to tie the brake caliper aside so that it doesn't hang by its rubber hose. Now, disconnect the sway bar drop link from the wheel bearing carrier (see Photo 2). In the front trunk compartment, mark the location of the three nuts that hold the shock to the tower and then remove them (Photo 3). Finally, loosen but do not remove the bolt that attaches the wishbone to the chassis (see Photo 4). This will allow us to drop the strut downward to its lowest point so that we may pull it out from the car after we remove the shock insert and spring.

With the strut assembly and wheel bearing carrier loose, you should be able to push down on the wishbone and maneuver the shock down over the top of the fender. If your car has been lowered or has had some other suspension changes made from the stock configuration, you may need some extra wiggle room. In this case, use your spring compressors to compress the spring and remove it while the strut is still under the fender. Then you should be able to compress the shock further and remove it from the bottom of the fender. When working close to the fender here, be careful that you don't scratch your paint—lay out a moving blanket or something similarly soft to protect the paint finish.

With your strut assembly off and on your workbench, install your spring compressor onto the spring and compress it until it no longer is tight in the strut assembly. While compressing the spring, be sure that you wear safety goggles—these springs are under a lot of pressure, and it is possible that the spring compressor may slip off suddenly. Place the two halves of the compressor on exactly opposite sides of the spring. I have found it very useful to use two ratcheting wrenches (I prefer the ones manufactured by GearWrench and available at PelicanParts.com) on each side of the compressor to assure that I achieve even and equal compression on both sides. Failure to maintain even compression when compressing the springs can make the compressor slip off.

With the spring compression removed from the strut assembly and the springs loose on their perches, remove the center nut that is attached to the top of the shock (see Photo 6). The reassembly process on the Boxster doesn't necessarily require an impact wrench, but it can sometimes make the job easier. So if you don't have one, now is a great time to buy one. I recommend an electric one—no air compressor is required (see Tools of the Trade in the front of this book).

With the upper strut mount removed, you should simply be able to lift the old spring off of the bottom spring perch. If you are reusing your old springs, then simply place them back onto the top of the lower spring perches. If you are replacing your springs with new ones, then move the spring to your workbench and slowly release the spring compressor on your old springs. Compress the new springs in a similar manner. You can use stiffer springs like Eibach Performance Springs, which serve to create a stiffer suspension and lower the car a little more than an inch in both the front and the rear.

Install the compressed spring assembly back onto the lower spring perch and reassemble the assembly as per Photo 8. Reinstall the dust boot/rubber bumper assembly over the shock to protect it from road debris and grime. Reinstall the upper spring plate and spring pad, taking care to verify that the plate is nestled correctly against the top of the spring. Inspect your upper strut mount and bearing carefully prior to assembly. The mount is manufactured out of rubber—both the rubber mount and the bearing will wear over time. I recommend replacing both of them if they look old or if they haven't been replaced previously. Reinstall the upper strut mount on top of the spring plate, and tighten up the retaining nut. Always use new hardware when replacing your shocks—all of the nuts are self-locking and will loose some of that self-securing ability if they are reused.

Reinstall the shock assembly into the wheel carrier, and attach the lower sway bar drop link (which also functions as the pinch bolt for squeezing the shock assembly). Install the assembly back into the top of the shock tower. The upper strut mount may have to be rotated a couple of times in order for you to properly line up the studs integrated into the mount with the holes in the chassis tower. Attach the three nuts at the top of the tower, lining them up with the marks you made when you removed them. Reinstall the brake caliper (Project 55) and any other components you may have disconnected. Plug in the sensor connectors that you may have disconnected, and route the wires and hoses back through the tabs in the strut.

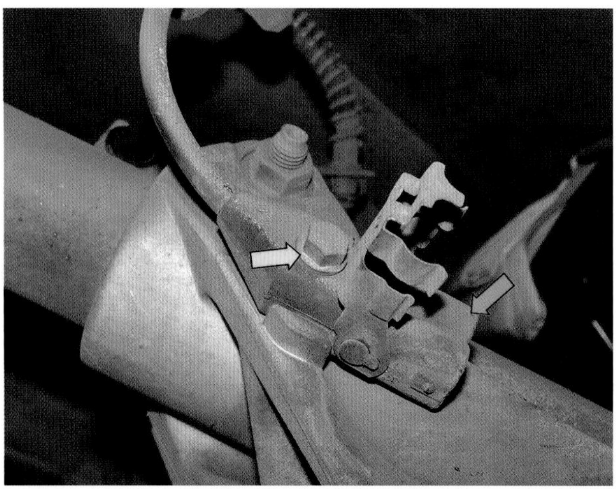

1 With the cable disconnected from its holder, make sure the wheel speed sensor and brake pad sensors are unplugged from their connector (green arrow). Then remove the bracket entirely by unbolting it (yellow arrow).

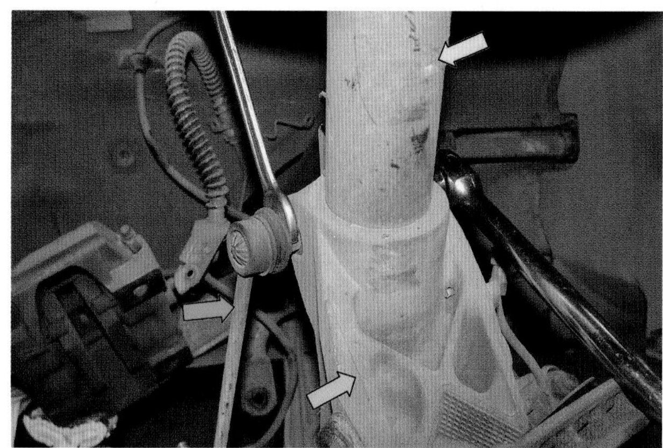

2 The shock (yellow arrow) is held onto the wheel carrier (blue arrow) by a long bolt that is integrated into the sway bar drop link (green arrow). Remove the bolt/sway bar link, and then the shock should be free to be pulled out of the wheel carrier.

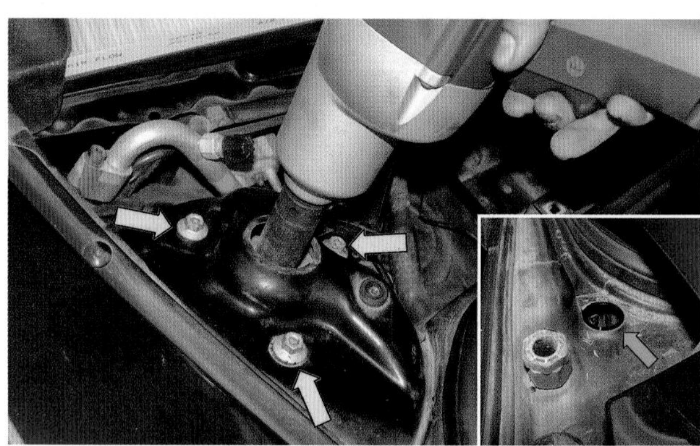

3 An electric impact wrench is a very handy tool for both removing and installing new shocks. The tool allows you to tighten nuts without having the shock shaft rotate. The three nuts that hold the front shock to the tower are shown by the yellow arrows. The three nuts that secure the rear shock mount to the chassis are hidden from view—two are located near the rear of the engine compartment, and the third is accessible only through an access hole in the sheet metal in between the trunk and the engine compartment (inset photo). Mark the position of these nuts prior to removal—you want them to be in the same spot when you put them back on.

4 The yellow arrows in the photo show the bolt that needs to be loosened in order to gain enough clearance to lower the shock and clear the edge of the fender. You don't need to remove the bolt—simply loosen it so that the arm can rotate a bit more than is possible through the deflection of the rubber bushing. Don't retighten this bolt until the car's tires are back on level ground and the suspension is fully loaded. In the lower right is shown a new bearing installed in a new front strut mount.

5 With the wheel carrier supported by your jack, lower it down so that you have enough clearance to rotate the assembly out from under the fender. Then, pull on the shock to remove it from the wheel carrier (green arrow). Watch out that you don't accidentally scratch your paint.

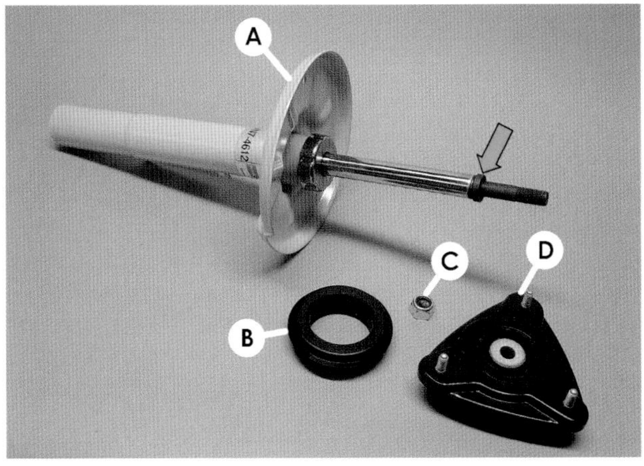

7 When replacing shocks, I recommend installing new parts. Shown here is a new front shock **(A)**, a new strut bearing **(B)**, a new lock-nut **(C)**, and a new front strut mount **(D)**. Your Bilstein shocks should come with a beveled washer on the shaft (green arrow).

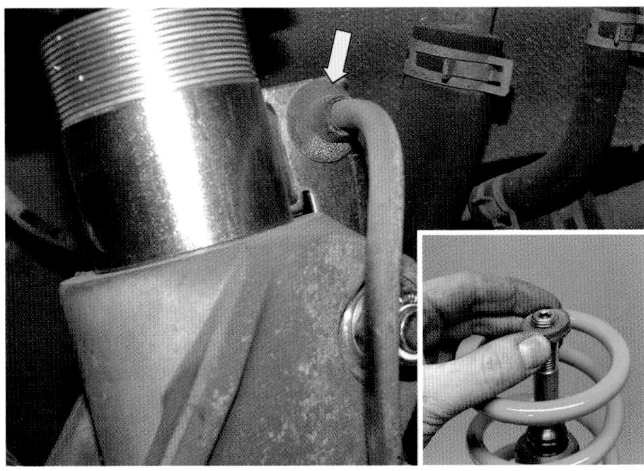

9 When removing or installing the shock, be sure to remove and replace the wire harness for the brake pad and wheel speed sensors. Don't forget the beveled washer when installing the new shocks (inset).

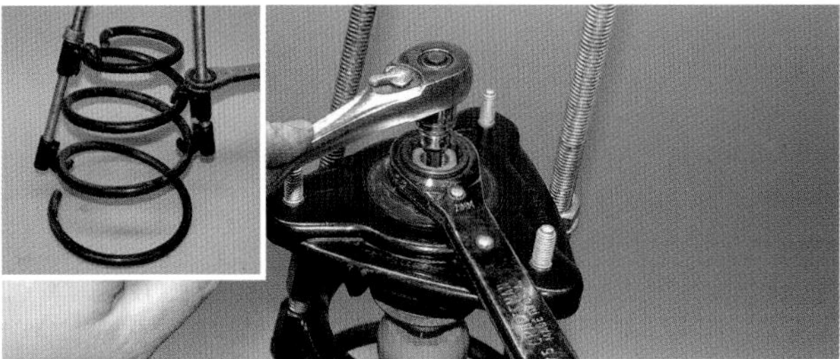

6 Use a hex socket to hold the shaft of the shock as you tighten the nut and clamp down the entire assembly. In order to get the springs compressed enough to be placed on the shock, you will need a spring compressor like the one shown in the upper left. When the assembly is clamped down with the locking nut, then carefully release tension on the spring compressors and remove them.

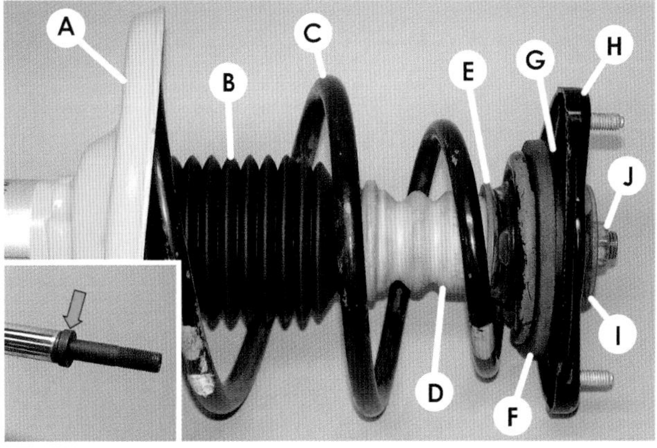

8 This diagram shows the installation of a new front shock and how all the bits and pieces fit together. These new Bilstein shocks came with a tapered washer that needs to be fit to the shaft prior to assembly (see Photo 7). **A:** Shock. **B:** Bellows. **C:** Spring. **D:** Bumper stop. **E:** Cup washer. **F:** Foam insulator. **G:** Upper strut bearing. **H:** Upper strut mount. **I:** Cup washer. **J:** Nut.

10 Replacement of the rear shocks is quite a bit more difficult than the front because you need to disconnect more parts on the suspension. Replacement of the rear shocks require removal of the axle nut (hard) or disconnection of the CV joints from the transmission (easier). The green arrow shows the CV joint/axle disconnected from the transmission—with the axles disconnected, you can rotate the shocks out under the edge of the fender. The yellow arrow shows the track rod disconnected from the wheel carrier. The purple arrow shows the wishbone disconnected from the chassis mount. The orange arrow shows the control arm disconnected from the wish bone. The red arrow shows the rear chassis reinforcement bar disconnected. In this photo, the shock has been already removed from the wheel carrier (white arrow). See Project 41 for more information on the CV joints.

PROJECT 64
Rear Suspension Support Brace

Time / Tab / Talent: 1 hour / $100 /

Tools: Hammer

Applicable Years: All

Parts: TechnoBrace kit

More Info: www.101projects.com/Boxster/64.htm

Tip: Be sure to order the correct brace for your car

Performance Gain: Stiffer rear suspension

Comp Modification: Replace suspension bushings

The TechnoBrace is a precisely machined bar that fits across the rear aluminum suspension mounts and creates a stronger, boxed structure that reduces flexing under load. Manufactured from strong and lightweight 6061 aluminum, the bar reduces rear lower suspension flex, allowing for static camber settings to be maintained through sharp turns and cornering. Installation is a snap and can be done in about an hour.

Be sure to order the correct brace for your car—Technolab manufactures four different versions. There's a version for manual transmission cars and one for automatic (Tiptronic) cars. In addition, each of those bars is available in a slightly longer version for cars that have had their engines lowered (as is necessary for the installation of the 996 engine—see Project 11).

The first step is to raise the car off of the ground (see Project 1). Then loosen the two nuts that hold on the ends of the aluminum crossbars (see Photo 1 and 2). Using a hammer, tap out the two studs. Then, install the brace in place using the hardware included with the kit. I recommend using a new nut on each of the bolts (PN: 999-076-053-09). Sometimes the brace will not slide in easily without first disconnecting and loosening one or both sides of the sway bar mounts (see Photo 1).

1 The TechnoBrace installs across the rear suspension of the Boxster. Begin the installation process by removing the nuts that hold in the last mounting point of the aluminum crossbars (green arrows). The rear sway bar mounts are shown in the lower right inset—if you loosen these, it may make the installation process easier.

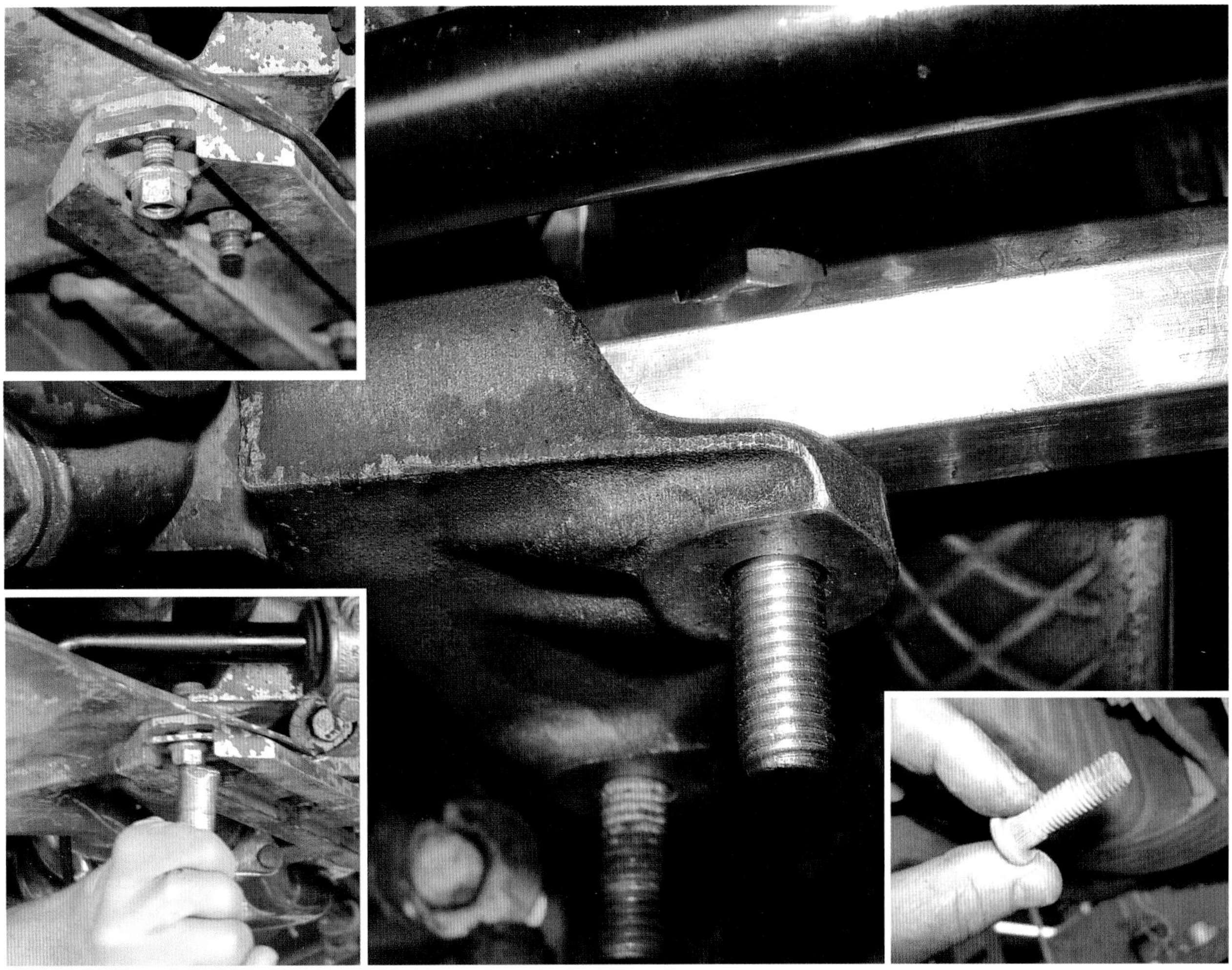

2 Loosen the nut but leave it on the pressed-in stud, as shown in the upper left inset photo. Tap the nut with a hammer to knock the stud out of its bore (lower left inset). The stud that you are removing is shown in the lower right inset photo. Finally, the main photo shows the TechnoBrace installed with the recessed bolt in place. The bolt is held in place by the slot that is cut within the brace—no wrench is needed to hold it when tightening. Install a new nut and torque to 48 ft-lbs (65 Nm).

3 This photo shows the TechnoBrace installed in a Boxster without the aluminum protection plate installed. As you can see, other than the thin aluminum plate, there is no longitudinal support for the suspension components that support the rear suspension mounts. The TechnoBrace solves this problem by creating a boxed structure that prevents the mounts from flexing under load.

SECTION 9
BODY

You spend a lot of time inside your car, so why not have it look good on the inside as well the outside? A great looking interior improves the overall appearance of your Boxster, and also makes it more fun to drive. In a similar manner, a few moments spent on small exterior items can simply wipe away the effects of aging on your car. This particular section is a grab bag of projects that deal with everything from headlamp upgrades to door equipment repair. Whether you're planning to replace your hood shocks or install a rear spoiler on your car, the projects in this section will help you improve the overall performance and looks of your Boxster.

PROJECT 65

Replacing Lenses and Bulbs

Time / Tab / Talent: 30 minutes / $15–$250 /

Tools: None

Applicable Years: All

Parts: New lenses, bulbs

More Info: www.101projects.com/Boxster/65.htm

Tip: Don't tug heavily on the lenses when removing them—they may break

Performance Gain: Better-looking exterior, clearer lamps

Comp Modification: Upgrade to clear corners and clear/smoked rear lenses

There are few projects that are as easy as lens replacement, yet improve the look of your car so significantly. Replacing old, faded lenses not only improves your Boxster's overall appearance, it also increases its safety as well. Faded lenses tend to be harder to see and block much more light than brand-new ones. On the front of the Boxster, the side marker lenses are removed by simply pulling on them. A snap-tab holds them in place.

The rear lenses are very easy too—they are simply held on with screws that you can access in the rear trunk. Pull back the trunk lining and you should have easy access to the screws and the bulbs. The third brake light is easily accessible from the rear trunk when the roof is lowered into the service position (see Photo 6 and Project 3).

If you are replacing bulbs, make sure that you replace your old bulbs with the same exact style and wattage as the originals. Swapping in higher wattage bulbs could damage your wiring and possibly melt your lens and bulb holder.

The photos show the replacement process on the 1997–2004 Boxster—the 2005–2008 is very similar.

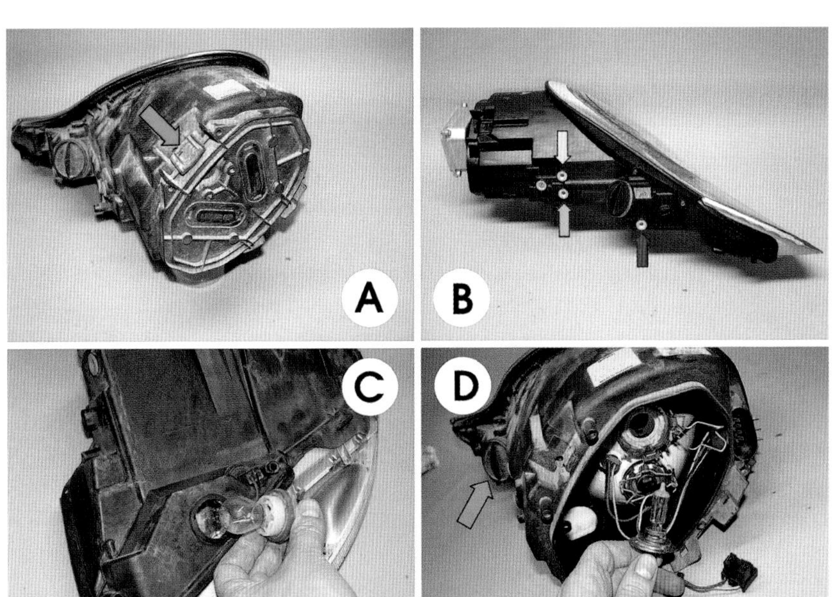

1 The Boxster headlamp is a somewhat complicated piece of equipment. **A:** To replace bulbs inside the assembly, first detach the end cover by squeezing the tabs on both sides (one side shown with green arrow). **B:** These are the adjustment wheels and can be turned by inserting a 5mm hex head tool through access holes located in the chassis. Red = fog lamp adjustment; yellow = left/right adjustment; blue = up/down adjustment. **C:** The turn signal/parking lamp bulb is accessed through the bottom of the assembly. **D:** The two halogen bulbs are clipped into the rear of the lamp and are easily accessible once you remove the end cover. Don't touch the bulb with your fingers, as the oils in your hand will damage it. The purple arrow points to the access hole you use to replace the fog lamp bulb.

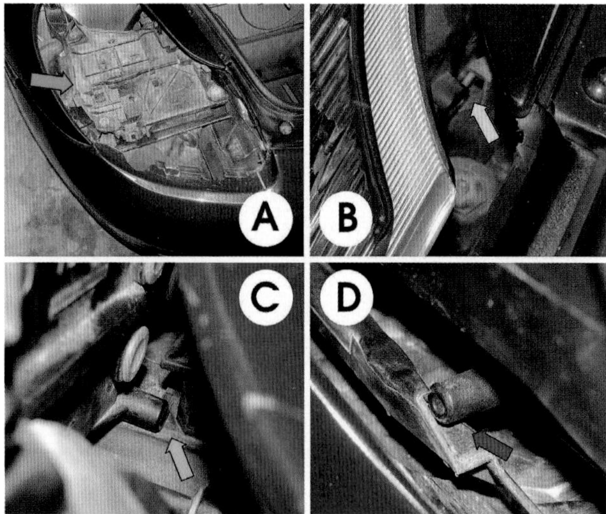

2 Installing the headlamp back into the car can be a bit tricky. **A:** The headlamp mates with the carrier plate (green arrow) and harness connector. A bar integrated within the carrier plate locks the headlamp assembly into place. **B/C/D:** Three circular tabs on the headlamp assembly fit into three channels located on the carrier plate. It's important to look carefully as you install the headlamp to make sure that these tabs are properly aligned in the channels.

3 With the assembly pushed back into the fender, use the headlamp tool from your Boxster tool kit to lock it into place. If you don't have this tool, you can also use a 5mm socket. With the tool facing upward, rotate it toward the rear of the car to lock it into place, or rotate it toward the front of the car to unlock.

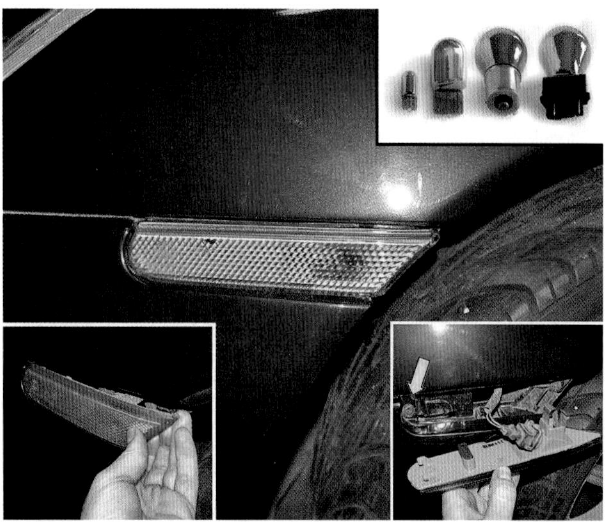

4 New side marker lenses take about one minute to install. I prefer the clear ones with orange bulbs. Simply reach in and pull on them to remove the lenses, then unclip the harness by pressing on the thin metal clip. For some reason, the amber U.S. lenses that are stock equipment just don't cut it. In order to maintain legal standards, you must run orange bulbs inside the lenses. This can cause the lens to take on an orange hue. There's a product out there that I recommend called Stealth Bulbs (inset) that is available online at PelicanParts.com. These bulbs are silver coated on the outside, but glow bright orange when electricity is applied. They look clear when installed in the clear lenses, but retain the orange illumination required for U.S. roads.

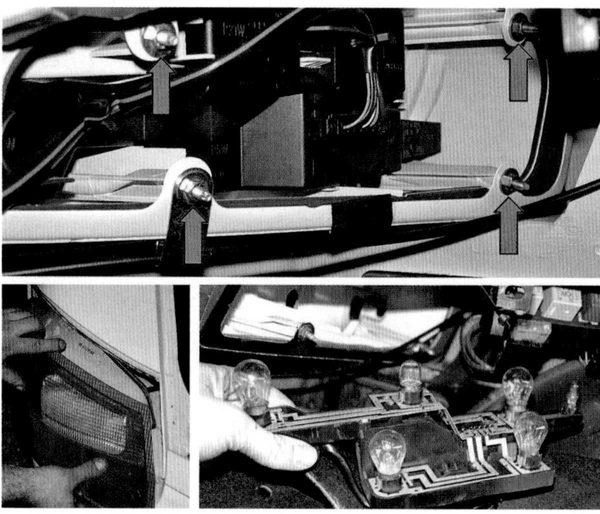

5 Removal of the rear taillamp is easy. Simply remove the four nuts that hold on the rear assembly (purple arrows). Then push out the assembly and pull from the opposite side (lower left). If all you need to do is change bulbs, then press the lock tab and remove the bulb carrier from the back of the taillamp assembly (lower right).

6 To change the bulbs in the third brake lamp, put the roof into the service position (see Project 3) and release the two screws on either side of the lamp. Unplug the harness connector, and then you should be able to unsnap the bulb carrier from the rear of the lamp. Be careful not to break any of the delicate plastic tabs on the bulb carrier. Also, when reinstalling the lamp, pay close attention to the two screws—they have a unique system for securing the lamp to the chassis. Push the screws and their rubber washers into the holes in the chassis, and then tighten them only slightly to make the screws expand the rubber and become snug in their holes.

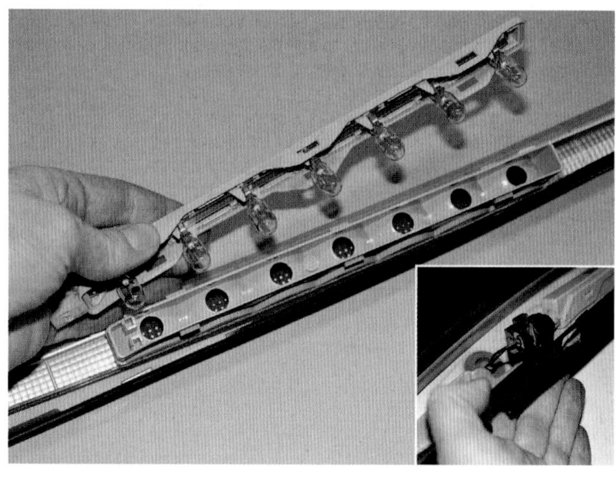

PROJECT 66
Installing a New Hood Crest and Emblems

Time / Tab / Talent: 30 minutes / $60 /

Tools: None

Applicable Years: All

Parts: Hood crest, seal, two speed nuts

More Info: www.101projects.com/Boxster/66.htm

Tip: Don't tighten the crest too tightly, or you might crack the gels on the front

Performance Gain: Sharper looking hood

Comp Modification: Replace rear emblem

Over many years, the Porsche crest located on your front hood can take a beating. Rocks, gravel, soot, rain, snow, sleet, and other debris can scratch and dull the finish of the crest so that it no longer shines the way it should. The good news is that the replacement of the crest is one of the easiest projects that you can do, and it significantly improves the looks of your car.

It is important to note that you should only use the original Porsche crests manufactured under license from Porsche. In past years, there have been some counterfeit crests available for about half the cost, but the OEM ones from Porsche are typically of a much higher quality.

Over the years, there have been several different styles of the crest, so if you are looking for 100 percent originality, you may want to look for a crest that is new old stock (NOS). It is also important to replace the rubber seal that mates the crest flush with the hood.

The crest is attached using two small self-threading nuts that Porsche calls "speed nuts." The speed nut is a small aluminum disk with a putty-like insert that allows it to hold the emblem snug without the danger of denting or damaging the hood of the car. The speed nut also stops water from leaking into the inside of the sheet metal.

The crest is attached to the car and held on with the speed nuts on the inside of the hood. To remove the old crest, simply open the hood, and unscrew the nuts using a small 8mm socket and extension. Be careful that the speed nuts don't fall into the recesses of the hood. When installing the new crest, place the rubber gasket around the crest and test fit it against the hood. Sometimes the small prongs on the crest may need to be bent slightly in order to make them fit the holes. Be sure not to bend them too much, or they will break off.

It's also a wise idea to get a small piece of masking tape, and tape the crest and seal to the hood before you install it. The speed nuts are meant to be attached once, and removing and reinstalling them can damage the small studs on the crest. Use a small dental pick to fit the gasket around the crest before it's completely tightened down. Tape the crest to the hood to make sure that the rubber seal doesn't slip out of position while you are tightening the speed nuts. Proceed slowly, and check the seal before you tighten up the nuts. This is a very simple job that can be messed up if you don't keep a watch on the seal.

1 This before (right) and after photo (left) really shows the difference that a new crest can make. As with the lenses on the car, it is difficult to tell how tarnished and old the hood crest has become without looking at a brand new one. With such an easy installation, it is perhaps the quickest method of instantly improving the exterior looks of your 911. The new crest is so shiny, it's hard to take a good picture of it!

2 The inside of the hood is manufactured with access holes so that you can remove and replace the crest. Make sure that you don't tighten the two speed nuts too much, or you can crack some of the plastic gels embedded into the front of the crest or damage your hood. The inset shows a complete Genuine Porsche crest with the crest seal and two speed nuts.

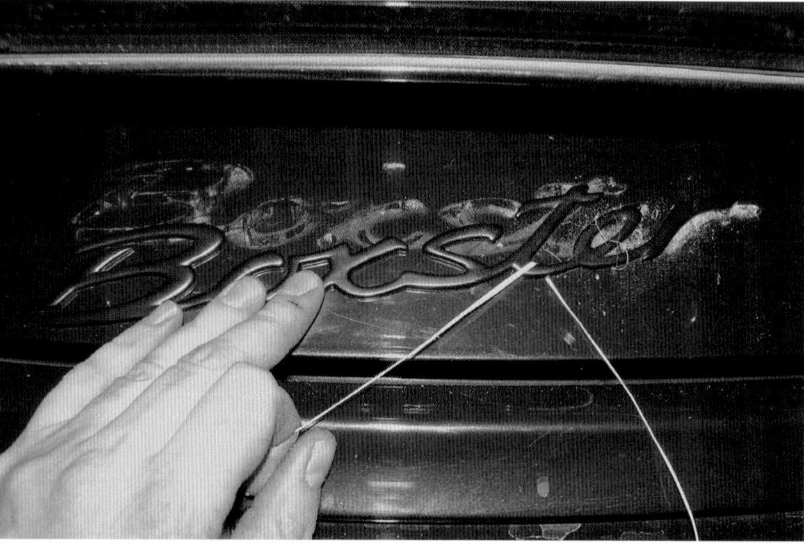

3 Replacement of the rear plastic emblem is relatively easy. New emblems come with a pre-applied adhesive that's similar to double-sided sticky-tape. A trick to removing the old emblem is to use dental floss. Get a few strips and work them under the emblem, cutting away the old adhesive. When the emblem is off, carefully clean the area with some isopropyl alcohol, and then apply the new emblem.

PROJECT 67
Installing the Das Schild Protector

 **Time / Tab / Talent:** 30 minutes / $300 /

Tip: Install both the front and rear liners

 **Tools:** None

Performance Gain: Protect your trunk lid

 **Applicable Years:** All

Comp Modification: Replace your hood crest

 **Parts:** Das Schild protector set

 **More Info:** www.101projects.com/Boxster/67.htm

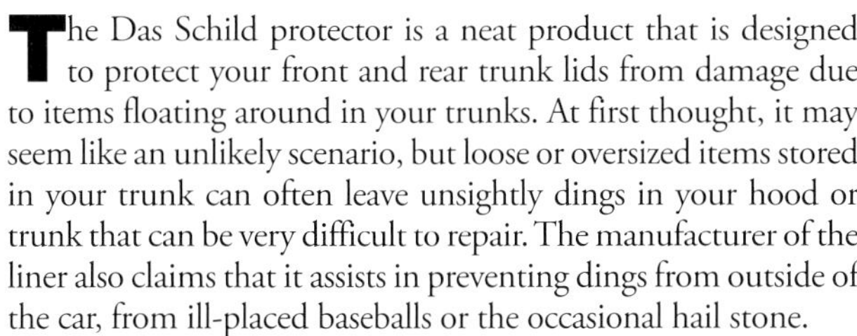

The Das Schild protector is a neat product that is designed to protect your front and rear trunk lids from damage due to items floating around in your trunks. At first thought, it may seem like an unlikely scenario, but loose or oversized items stored in your trunk can often leave unsightly dings in your hood or trunk that can be very difficult to repair. The manufacturer of the liner also claims that it assists in preventing dings from outside of the car, from ill-placed baseballs or the occasional hail stone.

The liner is manufactured out of thermoformed, lightweight ABS plastic and exudes a very high quality finish. The cost for a front and rear set is about $300 from PelicanParts.com. Installation is very simple—place the liner into the recesses of the front or rear trunk lid and attach it into the factory lid bracing with the included plastic snaps.

1 Shown here is the front hood with the Das Schild protector installed. The liner is manufactured out of lightweight ABS plastic and easily installs in minutes. With the protective lining in place, it looks like it's a Genuine Porsche factory part.

2 Installation is literally a snap. Simply take the liner and place it against the rear of the trunk lid. The liner is held in place using small plastic push clips that fit inside the slots that are already in place in the front and rear trunks (inset).

PROJECT 68

Front Bumper/Wheelwell Removal/Replacement

Time / Tab / Talent: 30 minutes / $850 /

Tools: None

Applicable Years: All

Parts: Front bumper cover

More Info: www.101projects.com/Boxster/68.htm

Tip: See if a good body shop can repair your front cover

Performance Gain: Cleaner-looking car

Comp Modification: Replace shocks, install center radiator

Unless your Boxster was stored in a time capsule when it was purchased new, it's highly likely that you will have at least some type of cosmetic damage to your front bumper cover. The amount and depth of the damage is, of course, completely dependent upon the care of the driver. The Boxster that I picked up as the project car for this book was cheap and had been abused, and the front bumper cover wore all the scars of the car's previous life. That said, the inner wheelwells of the car were damaged even further—I was able to save and repair the front bumper cover, but the wheelwells required complete replacement.

The first step is to jack up the front of the car. Loosen the lug nuts on your wheels prior to jacking if you are planning on removing the wheelwell liners. The next step in removing the front bumper cover is to remove the screws that attach it to the top of the chassis (see Photo 1 and Photo 2). To remove the trim panel and expose the actual screws holding the top of the bumper to the chassis, turn the plastic screws (Photo 1) a half turn and remove them. The plastic trim panel can then be removed, exposing the screws securing the bumper (Photo 2). Next, you need to pull out the side marker lamps. Behind the side markers you will see the small screw that needs to be removed (see yellow arrow, inset of Photo 5). There is also another screw that needs to be removed that is located right next to this one, near the edge of the wheelwell that screws upwards to the sky (red arrow, Photo 5). Then, disconnect the temperature sensor that sits in a small hole near the front grille on the right side of the car. The temperature sensor is a small device with a wire attached to it that looks a bit like a very short pencil (see Photo 1). Finally, remove the screws that attach the bottom of the bumper cover to the car (Photo 3 and Photo 4). With all of the hardware disconnected, the bumper cover should slide right off with a few strong pulls.

The front bumper cover is an insanely expensive part ($600–$950 depending upon whether you have a regular or S model). As an additional tip, I found that the Boxster S bumper was virtually identical to the normal car except for the cutout for the center radiator. If you wish to save several hundred dollars on a replacement bumper cover, see if you can find a non-S version, and then cut out the insert yourself, as I did in Project 31.

Removal of the wheelwell liners is not quite as easy as pulling off the front bumper cover. First, remove the two road wheels. The wheelwell liners are attached using plastic rivets that must be pried out one by one. Photo 4 and Photo 5 show the location of these rivets. It is not necessary to remove the suspension strut in order to replace the liners, but if you're planning on replacing your shocks anyway, then now would be a good time to do it.

When installing your new wheelwell liners, be sure to purchase the small little mud flaps that attach to the front ends (1997–2004, PN 996-504-503-00 and 996-504-503-00). These are often missing from years of abuse. The 2005 and later Boxsters have a different wheelwell design that is actually three pieces instead of two, making for a much easier installation.

1 Start in the front trunk by removing the black plastic cover piece near the front hood latch. Four small fasteners hold this piece in place. Simply rotate them a half turn or so to loosen them up and remove them. The inset photo shows the temperature sensor that you need to remove from the grille.

2 With the front black plastic cover piece removed, you can see some of the screws that hold the front bumper cover onto the chassis.

3 Underneath there are a few more screws that attach the bumper cover to the chassis.

4 This section of our project car was really ugly. It's difficult to tell from this particular photo, but the damaged piece hanging down (yellow arrow) is actually part of the inner wheelwell liner (see next photo). A poorly executed paint job resulted in the wheelwell liner being painted body color—it's normally black. The bottom left photo shows one of the plastic rivets that are used to attach the wheelwell liner to the chassis. The photo in the upper left shows a new wheelwell liner with the small rubber lip/flap attached. These flaps typically get a lot of abuse and are often missing entirely from the car.

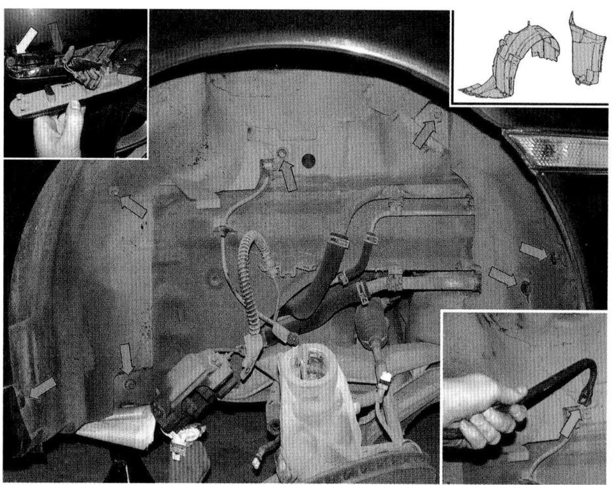

5 This photo shows some of the various fasteners that are used to attach the inner wheelwell liner. The brakes and shocks have been removed for clarity but are not required to be removed in order to replace the liner. Some are plastic rivets that are easily removed with a crowbar (green arrow, lower right). Others are plastic nuts that simply require a socket to remove. The photo in the upper right shows the two wheelwell liner pieces and their shapes. The photo on the upper left shows the screw behind the side marker that must be removed in order to remove the front bumper cover (yellow arrow) and the receptacle for the screw that must be removed from inside the wheelwell (red arrow).

PROJECT 69
Hardtop Installation

 **Time / Tab / Talent:** 1 hour / $1,100 / 

 **Tools:** Hex socket kit

 **Applicable Years:** All

 **Parts:** Hardtop and installation kit

More Info: www.101projects.com/Boxster/69.htm

 **Tip:** Check your local classifieds or Craigslist for good used tops

 **Performance Gain:** Quieter cabin

 **Comp Modification:** The speedster humps use the same spin clips

One of the neat must-have accessories for the Boxster is the hardtop. This roof attaches to the car and insulates the inside from both road noise and cold weather. If you've never driven a car with the hardtop installed, then you will be in for a surprise—the road noise is cut down tremendously. It really works very well. The roof has a lot of sound padding to assist in keeping things quiet inside, and the addition of a big, glass rear window is certainly welcome in place of the annoyingly small plastic one.

I believe that Porsche still has new tops available for purchase, however, they are a little less than $3,000, and then you will have to pay for shipping from your dealer. I've found that the best place to find hardtops is in your local classifieds or on Craigslist. People tend to get stuck with these in their garages after they sell their car, and they are incredibly difficult to ship as well. Plus, you have to find a seller who has the same color car that you had too. The bottom line is that you can typically pick up good used tops for about $1,000 or so.

When you purchase your hardtop, it's almost always missing the front and side cover trim pieces which snap on to cover up the latch mechanisms. The part number for the top piece is 986-563-551-00 (1997–2004), 987-563-551-00 (2005–2008) and it costs about $17. The part numbers for the two side pieces for the 1997–2004 cars are 986-563-553-00 and 986-563-554-00 and cost about $13 each (987-563-553-00-A03 and 987-563-554-00-A03 for 2005–2008).

In addition, if you are going to be using your car for track racing, many of the racing clubs and circuits require both a hardtop and roll bar extensions to protect you in the unlikely case of a rollover. The roll bar extensions are required because if you're wearing a helmet, then the top of your helmet will stick out above the normal, stock roll bar (see Project 98).

Prepping your car for the hardtop is easy—just install the insert kit as per Photo 2. Actually installing the top is relatively easy too if you have two people. Simply lower the top into the insert holes and then pull the handles to clamp down the top and seal it with the car. The top is not an item that you will want to take on and off every day, but if you want to be able to install it yourself, I suggest you purchase one of the custom-made ceiling-mounted winches designed specifically for lifting and lowering the top.

1 Shown here is the hardtop installed on my Boxster. I've always thought that the hardtop was a neat option for the Boxster. I was lucky enough to find one that was almost the exact color as our project Boxster, however, I have also used this particular blue hardtop on my wife's white-colored Boxster, and it actually looks pretty cool with the two-tone color scheme. I guess you need the right color combination to pull that off. You can install the hardtop yourself, but I wouldn't terribly recommend it—it's too easy to drop it and scratch your paint.

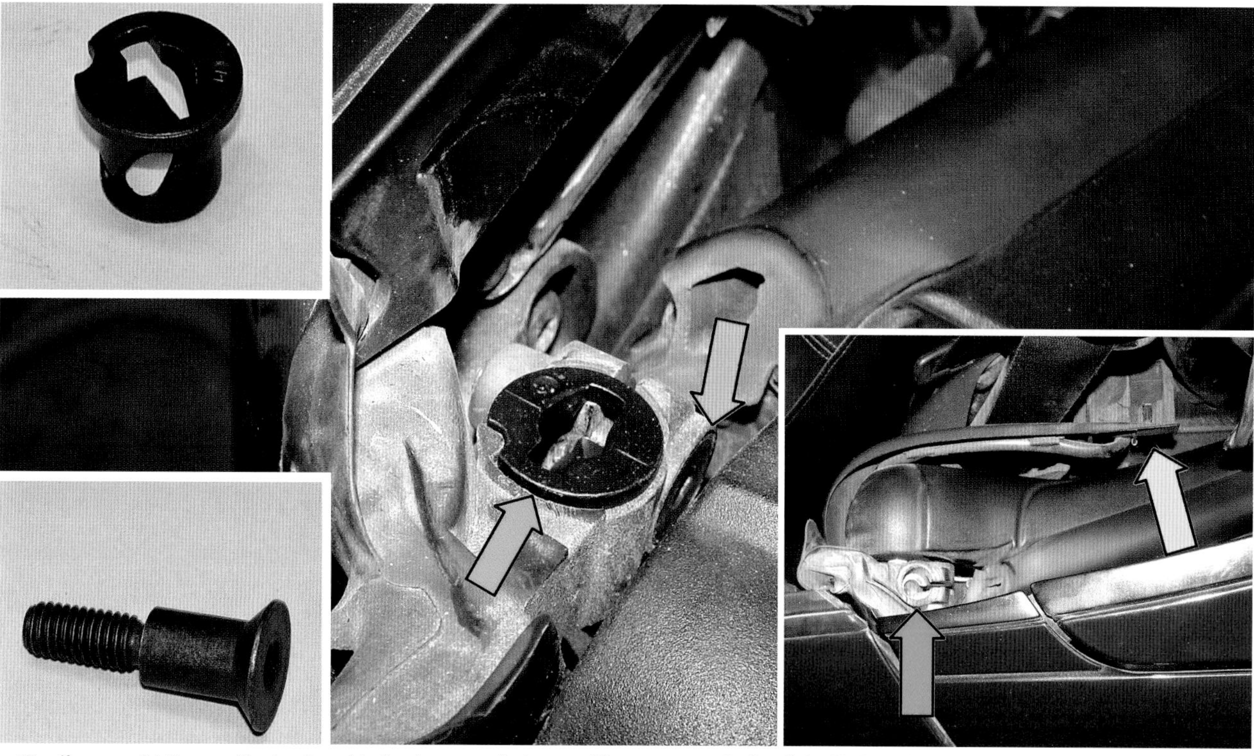

2 If your car didn't come with a hardtop originally, chances are that you need the super-expensive installation kit. These four parts might qualify for the most overpriced Porsche parts on the car. The spin-lock inserts shown in the upper left (Left PN: 986-563-713-03, Right PN: 986-563-713-03) are about $40 each. The two shoulder bolts are $14 for the pair. They fit into a slit in the chassis, pointed to by the green arrow. There is usually a plastic cap covering this area—remove the cap to see if the inserts are already installed. If not, then simply slide the insert into each side, and tighten down the pinch clamp with the shoulder bolt (orange arrow). Once you place the hardtop on the car, you can plug in the rear windscreen defroster near where the yellow arrow is pointing.

3 No discussion of hardtops would be complete without mentioning the Zeintop. Designed by an innovative company in South Africa, the Zeintop is an alternative to the Boxster hardtop and is designed to replicate the look and feel of the Porsche Cayman (the 2006 and later Boxster coupe). The top installs very similarly to the hardtop, although with a few more intermediate steps—you need to remove the rear trunk lid and wire up a separate brake lamp. It's designed to be installed for a season of winter driving and then removed in the springtime. With a cost of about $3,000, it's definitely cost competitive with a new factory hardtop and a lot better looking as well.

PROJECT 70
Replacing the Convertible Top

Time / Tab / Talent: 16 hours / $650 / 🔧🔧🔧🔧🔧

Tools: Torx driver set

Applicable Years: All

Parts: New roof liner, weather stripping

More Info: www.101projects.com/Boxster/70.htm

Tip: Install a new roof with the glass window upgrade

Performance Gain: Ability to see out back

Comp Modification: Replace weather stripping on roof

One of the common complaints of convertible owners is the condition of the rear window. It's manufactured out of a clear plastic, and as such, it does not have the longevity of a clear glass window. Over time and exposure to the elements, the window can become scratched, damaged, or faded. Unfortunately, on the Boxster, the window is sewn in as part of the roof, and there is no way to replace it short of cutting it out and re-sewing a new one in or replacing the entire roof. There is a new technique that I've been working on that would make the window replacement easier, but I'm not done testing it at this time—check the 101Projects.com website for more information on this in the future.

The original Boxsters came with a plastic window—later ones were upgraded to include a real glass one. You can purchase a new roof that has a built-in glass rear window instead of the rear plastic window. I chose this route for my wife's Boxster (shown here in this project) because this car is kept outside almost all of the time, and sun exposure is terrible for the rear plastic windows. The glass window is fantastic, has perfect clarity, has the option for the rear defroster, and doesn't scratch like the plastic ones. The only downsides are that the actual window area is quite a bit smaller and the glass window slightly restricts access to the engine compartment when the convertible top is in the service position. These are two distractions I don't really notice very much.

Replacing the roof is not an easy task—most roof manufacturers will not even sell the roofs to do-it-yourselfers. For this article I've divided up the process into a large picture array to try to give a better understanding of the steps involved. We took over 500 photos of the process—see the 101Projects.com website for the additional bonus photos not displayed here. The car shown here is a 1999 Boxster—other years are similar, but may have slight differences here and there.

1 Shown here is the glass rear roof upgrade for the early Boxsters that only had the plastic rear window. As you can see, the window is a bit smaller than the plastic version.

2 Begin by placing the roof into the service position (see Project 3 for instructions).

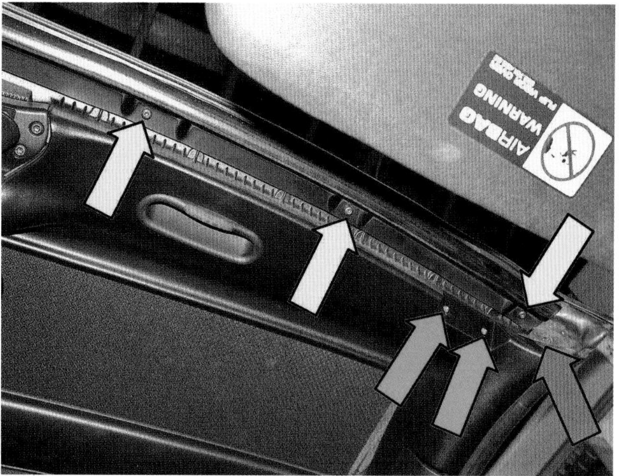

3 Remove the two front latches (green arrows), the screw that holds on the side seal (purple arrow), and the front retaining rail (yellow arrows).

4 With the attachment screws removed, pull down and remove the front convertible top seal. Inspect this seal carefully—you might want to replace it if it's old or damaged.

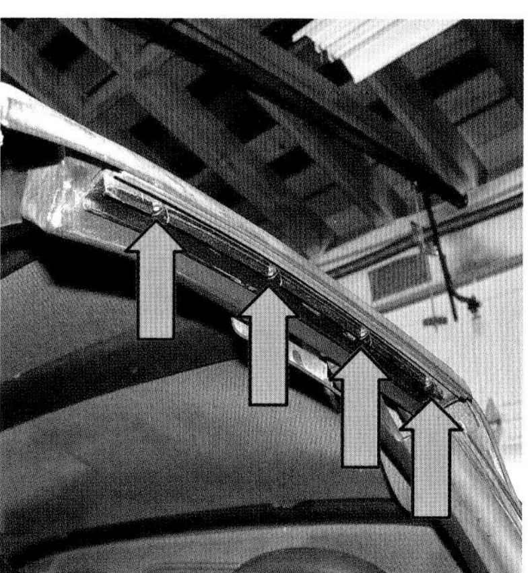

5 Remove the seal retainer by removing the four screws shown here.

6 With the seal channel removed, you can access the support underneath. Remove these small Phillips screws.

7 With the screws removed, you should be able to lift up the front part of the convertible top. Much of it will be stuck to the frame with double-sided adhesive—peel it back slowly and carefully to avoid damaging the frame.

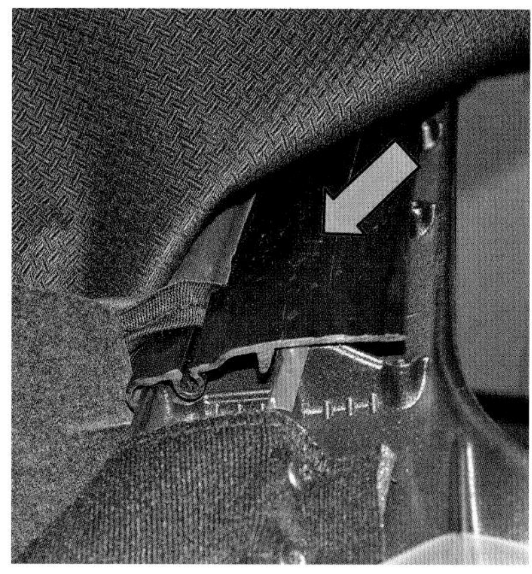

8 The top is attached to a plastic channel piece that runs down the center of the car. Remove the metal clip in the center that affixes the channel to the top.

9 Pull back the top, and then you should be able to slide this channel piece off of the top (pull in the direction of the red arrow).

10 On the top of the roof will be two aluminum pieces with a cable and spring attached. Cut away the plastic shrink wrapping and disconnect the cable from the end of the spring.

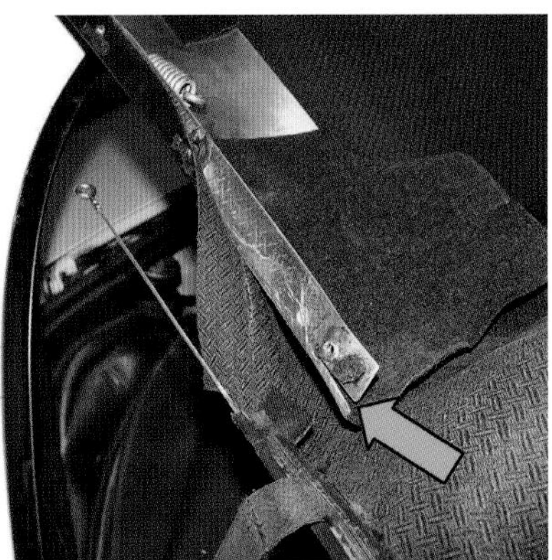

11 With the cable removed from the spring, remove it from the end of the aluminum channel. This cable is used to guide the top around the window frames when raising or lowering the roof and is integrated/sewn into the roof lining.

12 Taking caution not to damage the aluminum panels, cut them out from the old roof and place them on your workbench. You will be reusing these on the new top.

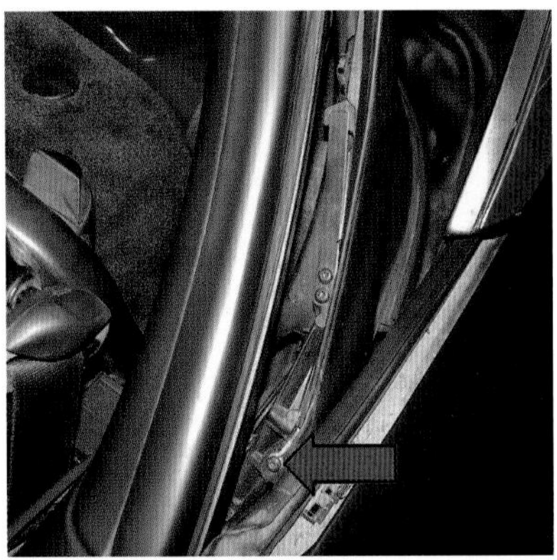

13 Turn on the ignition and carefully lower the roof so that it's about 75 percent down. Remove the screw that holds the other end of the tensioning cable. This screw also secures a flap on the top and the plastic slider. Be careful not to drop it into the recesses of the roof compartment, as it can be difficult to retrieve.

14 There is a plastic slider piece that is attached to the top liner and held onto the frame with two plastic rivets. Using care, remove the rivets and squeeze the prongs from behind and pull the piece out of the frame.

15 This photo shows the backside of the slider piece with the plastic rivet broken. It's very easy to damage this piece when removing it, but new ones are inexpensive at about $10.

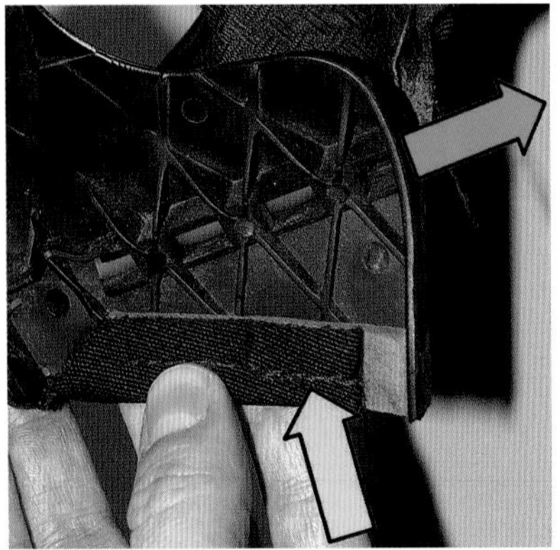

16 With the rivets detached from the frame, the slider piece can be removed from the top by peeling back the top material (yellow arrow) and sliding its groove out of the plastic retainer that is sewn into the top liner (green arrow).

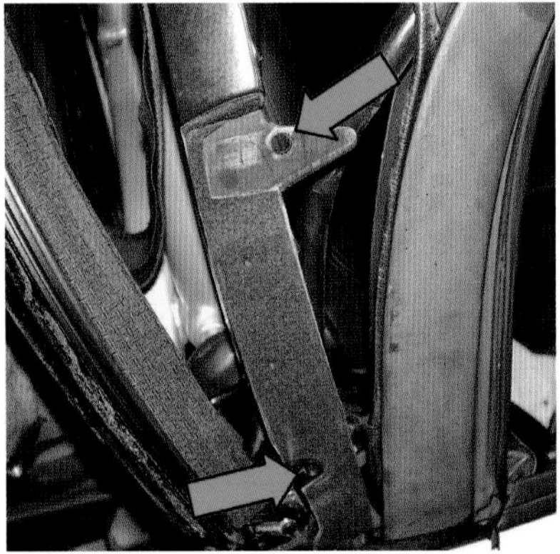

17 Here's what the frame looks like after you have pulled out the plastic slider piece (arrows show the two pivot holes).

18 There are two Velcro straps (one on each side) that need to be loosened/disconnected.

19 Move the top back to its original position of about 18 inches open, and be sure that the ball-joint cable is disconnected (see Project 3, Photo 2B). Lift up the rear of the top, and there will be a thick piece of weather stripping that seals the trunk to the top. Carefully remove this seal, taking care not to rip it.

20 Pull up on the weather stripping channel located in the middle of the channel and remove it.

21 Pull back the roof material from the channel. You may find it easier to remove the locking strip first (see next photo).

22 The yellow arrow points to the locking strip that holds the roof fabric to the channel. Remove this strip.

23 The last and final step in the removal of the roof is to slide it out of the channel that is attached to the middle bar of the roof frame.

24 Go over the Boxster frame carefully and remove all traces of double-sided tape and residue with a mild degreaser and isopropyl alcohol. Also clean the two aluminum pieces that you removed from the original roof.

25 Apply new tape to the aluminum pieces (3M 06384 recommended).

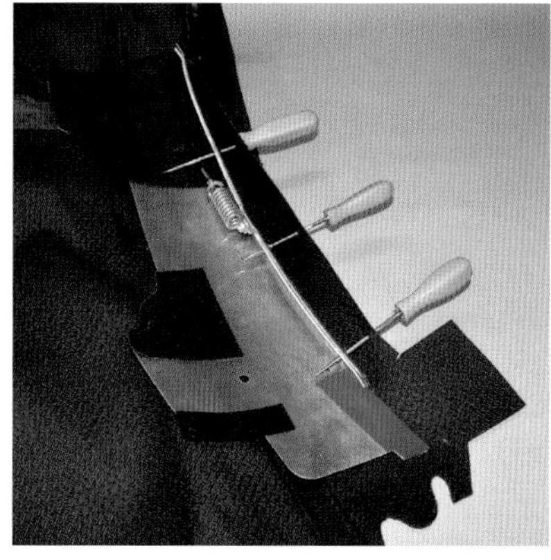

26 Poke holes in the new fabric (for the screws) and then affix the new fabric using the double-sided tape. Attach the cable to the spring, and wrap it with some tape or heat-shrink tubing.

27 Cut and bend the flaps into place as shown and affix them with double-sided tape (arrow).

28 Take the two plastic sliders removed in Photo 16 and transfer them to the new roof liner. Push each slider onto the liner in the direction indicated by the arrow.

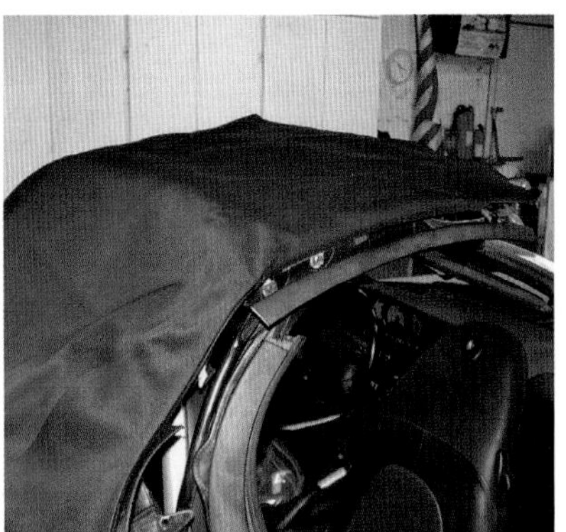

29 Install the new roof onto the frame, first sliding the middle part into the rear channel (as shown in Photo 23). I suggest covering the rear window with some paper and tape to avoid accidentally scratching it during the installation process.

30 Slide the middle plastic channel into the new roof liner. Use a light bit of silicone spray on the plastic piece if you're having a tough time getting it threaded.

31 Affix the middle plastic channel to the frame using the metal clip.

32 Apply some 3M Super Weatherstrip Adhesive to the channel, and then screw down the top liner using the sheet metal screws.

33 With the roof about 75 percent open, snap the slider pieces back into place on both the left and right sides, and reinstall the plastic rivet. On the roof that we installed, the new liner included a set of "helper straps" that needed to be affixed to this rivet. After the slider pieces are installed, reattach the roof cable using the screw removed in Photo 13.

34 Move the roof back to about 18 inches open. At the rear of the car, measure the center of the window and the center of the rear channel and mark the liner and the channel so that you can line them up during the next steps.

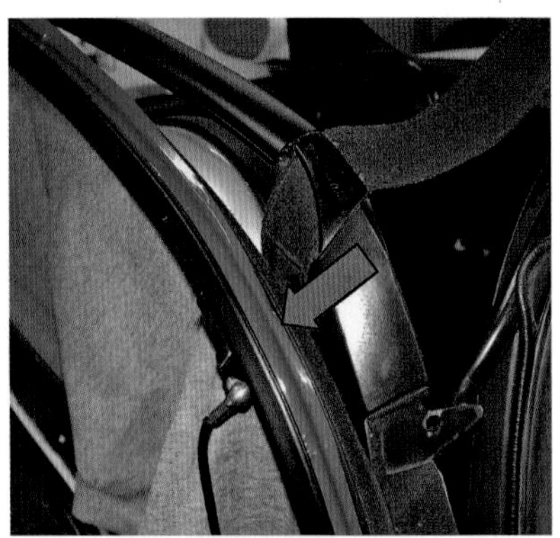

35 Apply double-sided adhesive tape to the rear channel in the same manner as it was when you removed the old top.

36 Lining up the rear and making sure it's centered, feed the top material into the top of the rear channel. Keep the seam aligned slightly low along the edge of the rail, otherwise, the seam may be visible when the top is closed. Use a small rubber hammer to tap in the locking strip (shown with orange arrow).

37 Reinstall the rear weather stripping into the middle channel.

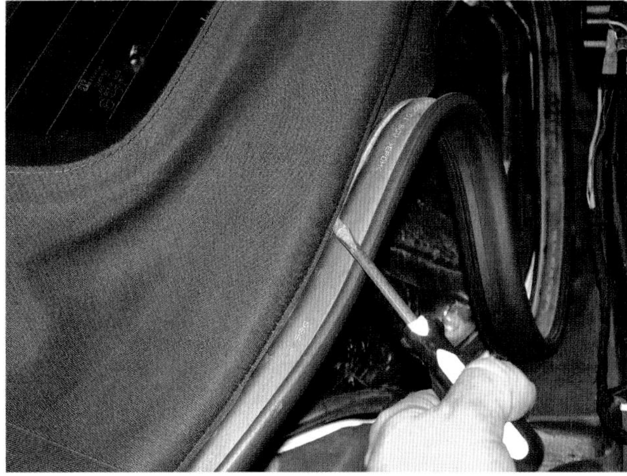

38 Reinstall the thicker seal into the lower channel. We used double-sided tape for this, but the seal repeatedly fell out when the roof was raised and lowered. Consider using the 3M Super Weatherstrip Adhesive instead if this happens.

39 Apply more tape to the front edge of the material, in the same places where it was on the old roof liner.

40 Pull the roof material tight and affix the front channel and seal into place. Pull and affix evenly to avoid getting wrinkles in the top. If you installed a roof with the defroster capability, then plug in the connection as detailed in Photo 2 of Project 69. It may take a few days for all of the wrinkles to disappear. Leaving the car out in the hot sun may also help to ease the top fabric into the frame.

PROJECT 71

Convertible Top Mechanism Repair

Time / Tab / Talent: 8 hours / $100–$1,000 / 3 wrenches

Tools: Power drill

Applicable Years: All

Parts: Various components, depending upon what is damaged

More Info: www.101projects.com/Boxster/71.htm

Tip: Check over all components carefully—there may be some damage that is hidden

Performance Gain: Properly functioning top

Comp Modification: Replace rear window, upgrade top to glass window

The Boxster convertible top mechanism is used a lot and is often exposed to a lot of stress and strain as a result. It's very likely that you will experience a problem with the opening or closing of your top somewhere along the line—knowing what to replace and fix is valuable information.

One of the first things I installed in my wife's Boxster was the SmartTOP controller that allows you to open and close the roof with one-touch operation (see Project 72). This is a neat feature, except that there are no safeguards built into the unit. So, if the top latch is not fully released and the roof catches on it as it is being automatically lowered, you can seriously damage your roof. I accidentally did this one day, and the resulting damage ended up including about 20 hours of work along with $1,200 worth of parts (see the photos in this project). If you install one of those automatic controllers in your Boxster, just beware of the potential damage from the one-touch operation button.

When compared to other convertible cars (like the BMW 3-Series), I find the design of the Boxster roof to be relatively simple. A single motor connects to two cables and drives a leveraged gear mechanism that raises the rear of the roof, then raises the rear convertible lid, and then folds and tucks the top away. When your roof is not opening or closing correctly, then one or more of the components in the mechanism are probably worn out or damaged. Follow the photo array in this article to learn about each of these components and how to replace them.

The early-style convertible top transmissions have been replaced with a more reliable later-style one. This can be installed in place of the early one, but you need to also replace the three standoff bolts/spacers with different ones specific to the late-style assembly (see F in Photo 1).

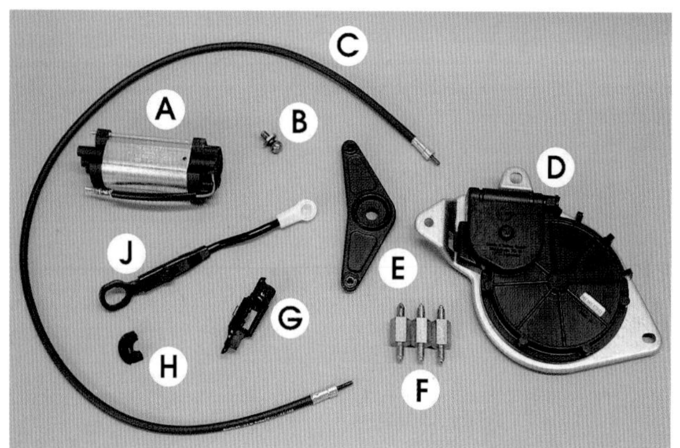

1 This photo shows some of the parts that you might need to repair your convertible top. **A:** Convertible top motor (powers both left and right sides at the same time) **B:** Ball pivot pin (2 required) **C:** Control cable **D:** Improved transmission assembly (increases the leverage of the motor to lift the top), left and right required **E:** Control lever (attaches to the opposite side of the transmission assembly, 2 required) **F:** Improved transmission assembly standoffs (required in order to bolt the transmission assembly in the same place that the old one fit; 2 required) **G:** Switch to detect closed position of the top handle **H:** Bushing for convertible top push rod (item J, 2 required) **J:** Convertible top push rod (pulls and pushes the top open and closed; 2 required).

2 This photo shows tremendous destruction on the left side of the convertible top motor assembly. The blue arrow shows the red plastic ball socket for the top assembly that has completely broken away. This normally would connect a pivot ball pin that is located out of view near the green arrow. In addition, the mechanism for lifting the rear metal cover has completely sheared off as well. The pivot ball pin (shown in inset) would normally be attached to end of the control lever (yellow arrow), but due to the top getting stuck, it has been broken off. In this case, the top transmission, the lever, and the convertible top pushrod needed to be replaced with new parts.

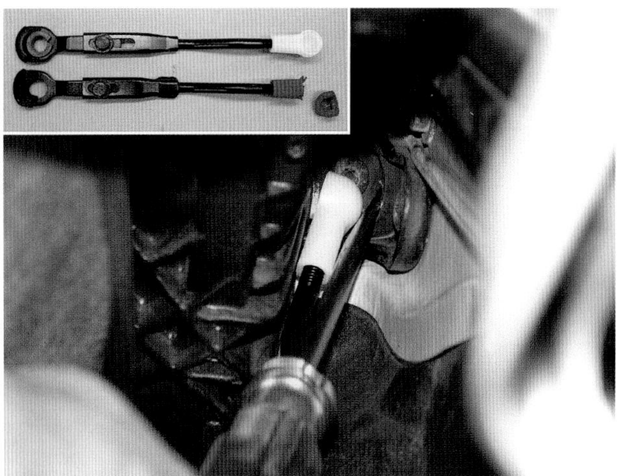

3 If your convertible top pushrod has broken, then you will need to replace it with a new one. Unfortunately, at the time of this writing, a new plastic ball cup end is only available by purchasing an entirely new rod (about $75). When you get the new rod, line it up to the old one, and make sure that the two are exactly the same length. Alter the two adjustment points on the rod if necessary. To install the rod back onto the convertible top linkage, use a screwdriver wedged up inside the mechanism to obtain the necessary leverage to snap it on.

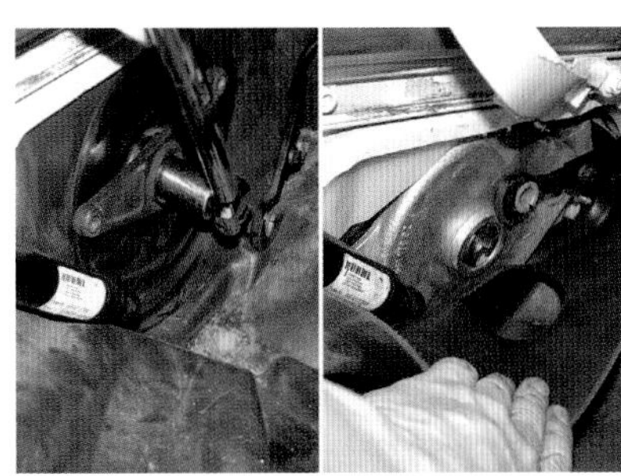

4 To remove the convertible top transmission, begin by removing the boomerang-shaped lever (left photo). Using a 19mm socket and a breaker bar, you should be able to loosen the bolt and remove it from the transmission. In this particular case, the lever arm had bent and the transmission had also broken. Pull back on the foam sound-deadening material to reveal the convertible top transmission (right photo). Three nuts attached to standoffs hold the transmission in place.

5 This photo shows the various steps involved with removing the transmission and disconnecting the cable. **A:** With the three nuts removed, pull back on the transmission and separate it from the side of the car. **B:** Loosen up the four nuts on the back side of the transmission housing, but do not remove them. **C:** With enough slack in the mechanism, carefully pull out the cable. **D:** The green arrow shows one of the three standoffs that need to be replaced if you upgrade to the later-style convertible transmission. **E:** The later-style transmission allows you to simply snap the cable in place without removing any screws. **F:** Shown here is the replacement, later-style transmission installed in place with the new longer standoffs.

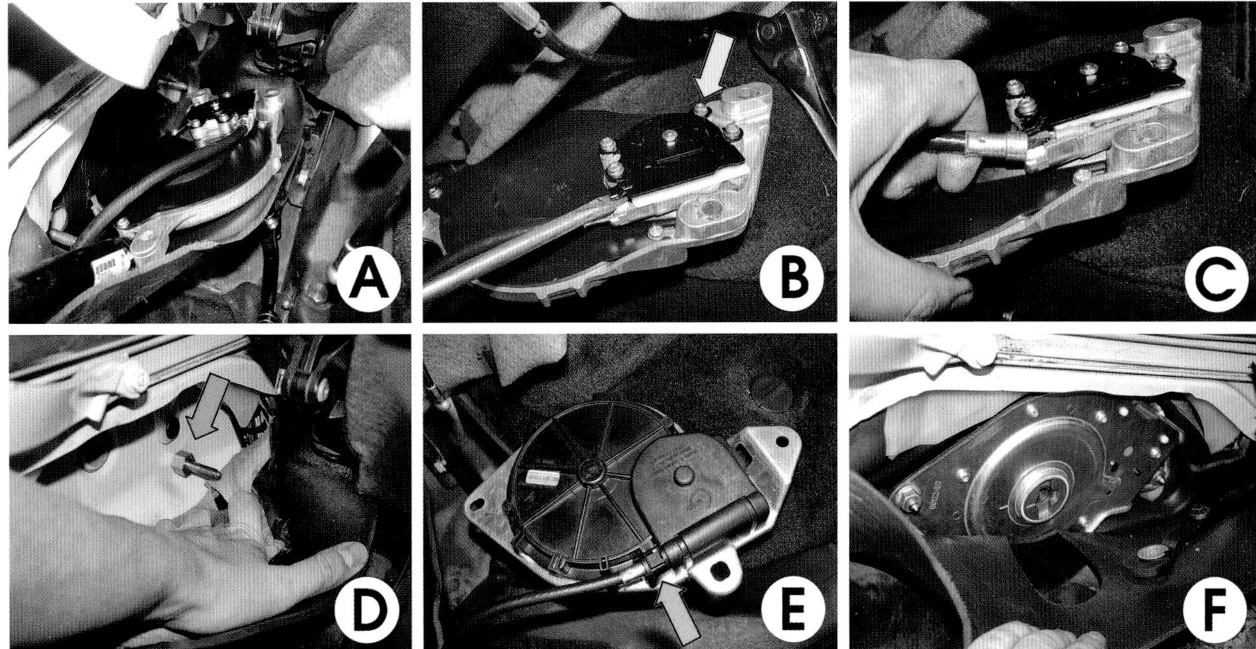

6 To disconnect the cable from the motor assembly at the rear of the compartment, simply remove the circlip (yellow arrow), and pull out the cable. Replacement of the motor and/or switch are fairly easy too—simply remove both cables, unplug the electrical connection, and unbolt the motor assembly. Unfortunately, at the time of this writing, the only way to replace this microswitch is to purchase the entire bracket assembly (about $130 from Porsche).

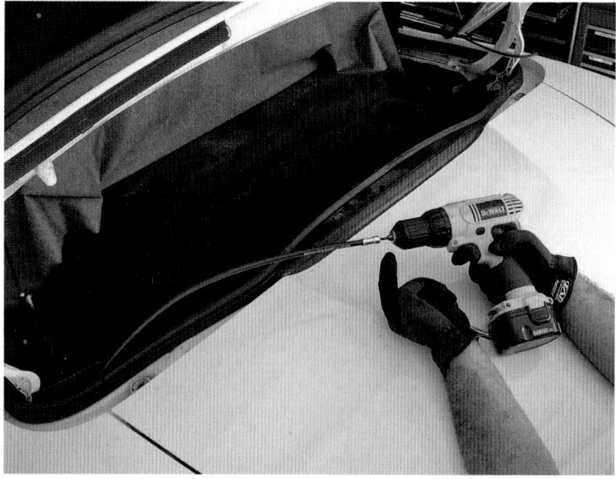

7 The factory manuals recommend using a drill to move the cables while aligning the left and right side, however, after repeatedly doing this many times, I discovered a shortcut. If you disconnect one side of the cable to the motor, you can then press the roof up/down button for short bursts of time. This will move one side of the roof mechanism, but not the other side, allowing you to align one side with the other. For extensive movement of the convertible top transmission, I recommend using the cordless drill.

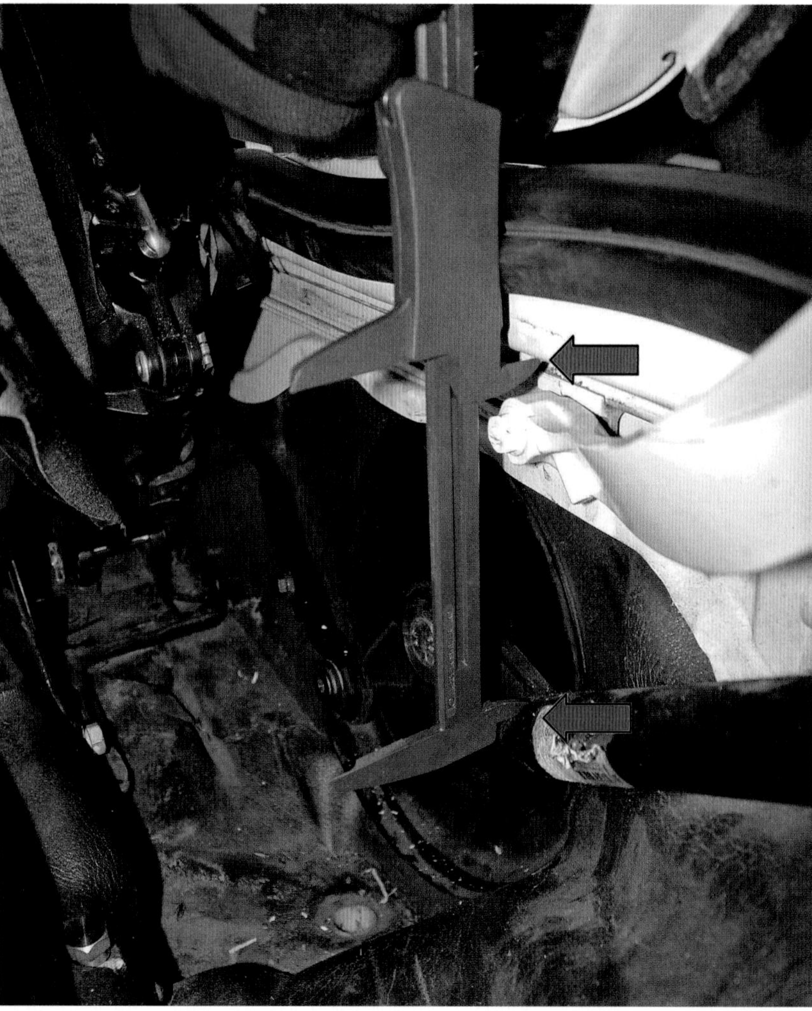

8 When all of your parts have been replaced, you need to align the left and right assemblies together. Keep in mind that if something broke on your roof, then you might have bent some of the tracks for the rear cover or other important components of the mechanism. In other words, you may not be able to get the top aligned completely perfectly. The goal is to get the lever arms on both sides in the same position at the same time. Measure the length from the lever arm to a reference point on the top of the car and compare it to the opposite side. Adjust one side of the mechanism by using the technique described in Photo 7 to match both the left and right side.

PROJECT 72
SmartTOP/Rolling Top Override

 **Time / Tab / Talent:** 15 minutes / $250 /

 **Tools:** None

 **Applicable Years:** 1997–2004

 **Parts:** SmartTOP control module

 **More Info:** www.101projects.com/Boxster/72.htm

 **Tip:** Operate the automatic feature with extreme caution

 **Performance Gain:** Open the top while driving less than 15 miles per hour

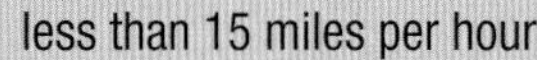

 **Comp Modification:** Check your fusebox for blown fuses

The Boxster roof controller is somewhat bothersome in that you need to bring the car to a full stop and apply the emergency brake in order to raise or lower the roof. This can be annoying to both you and other drivers if you're trying to raise or lower the roof at a stoplight. This restriction is designed to protect the roof so that you don't damage it while driving and exposing it to large wind forces.

Fortunately, there are a few ways around this restriction. You can purchase an aftermarket module that plugs into your car. The SmartTOP, designed and manufactured by Mods4cars and available at PelicanParts.com, is one of these replacement relay/controller modules for your Boxster. This module allows you to raise and lower the roof while the car is cruising at speeds under 25 miles per hour (40 km/h). In addition, the roof can be raised and lowered with one-touch operation—simply press the button once and the roof will completely raise or lower itself without you having to hold down the button. But beware: If the roof catches on something or someone sticks their hands in the roof during this one-touch operation, the results can be ugly (see Project 71).

Installation is a snap. Simply put the roof down, turn off the ignition, pull out the old controller relay from your relay panel and install the SmartTOP unit in its place (see Photo 1).

There is also a "poor man's" version of this feature override. By removing one of the pins on the factory convertible top relay, you can override the speed control limiter and open the roof while driving. You will also need to pull up on the emergency brake one click in order to activate the switch. Of course, this will allow you to open the roof when the car is going 60 miles per hour—which can be dangerous and will certainly damage your roof. Exercise caution when you have these overrides installed.

Adding this is a snap—simply remove the relay and bend pin No.18 down toward the center of the relay so that it won't be inserted into the relay socket any more. The pin numbers are written down on the back of the relay. You can also override the emergency brake switch too by simply grounding pin No. 15. You can do this by bending the pin over pin No. 15 and soldering a wire to it and then connecting that wire to a chassis ground. Or, you can remove the wire that goes to pin No. 15 in the relay socket, put it off to the side, and install a ground wire in its place.

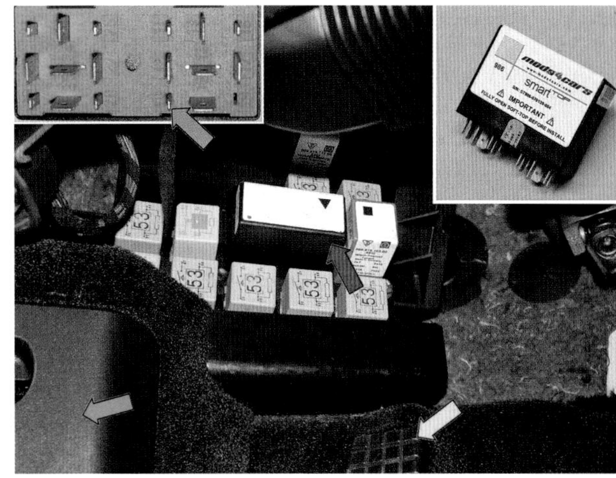

1 This photo shows the location where the SmartTOP module is installed. This relay panel is located above where your left foot rests while driving. The yellow arrow shows the foot rest, while the green arrow shows the location of the panel that covers the fusebox. The SmartTOP module replaces the factory control module located in the center of the relay panel (red arrow). The inset photo in the upper left shows the back of the relay with all of the pins labeled (pin No. 18 indicated by the purple arrow).

PROJECT 73
Installing Performance Seats

Time / Tab / Talent: 1 hour / $2,500 /

Tools: None

Applicable Years: All

Parts: GT3 seats

More Info: www.101projects.com/Boxster/73.htm

Tip: Good pairs can be found on eBay relatively easily

Performance Gain: Tight, snug seat performance

Comp Modification: Install a racing harness and bar

Having the right seats really make a huge difference in any car. The good news is that the seats that are used on the venerable Porsche GT3 or even sport seats from a regular 996 can be easily fitted into the Boxster. The GT3 seats are sportier, are more supportive, and have the appropriate cutouts in order to accommodate an appropriate multi-point racing harness. The GT3 mounting brackets also have a lower bar to accommodate a sub-belt too. Stock seats, particularly the power ones, weigh a ton, and the GT3 seats typically save about 30 pounds of weight or more over the stock seats. At about $3,000 each, genuine Porsche ones (with the Porsche crest embossed on them) are not cheap, but they are definitely the coolest seat around. Aftermarket ones and OEM Recaro seats can be had for less—replicas tend to run around $1,500 a pair.

In order to mount the seats to your car, you need a set of seat mount brackets. Brey-Krause manufactures a dizzying array of brackets and adapters for race seats and is the obvious choice when selecting a seat bracket. The parts required for installation depend upon the seat, the year of your Boxster, and whether you plan to mount the seat to the floor or to sliders. In general, I recommend the adapters that allow you to mount the seat to the stock non-power seat sliders. The GT3 seats also tend to sit lower in the car than stock seats or aftermarket race seats, which is great if you're tall and your helmet tends to stick up too much in the car. The GT3 seats should be a direct swap into the 1997–2004 Boxsters with no air bag computer programming required.

If you install an aftermarket seat in your car, you will initially have a problem with the air bag computer giving you errors. You need to reprogram the computer (using the Porsche factory PST-2 or PIWIS) to ignore the error signals. The late-model cars with side air bags in the seat also need to be disabled. If you use a five-point harness with your seats, then you will need to disable the seat belt sensors. Finally, you need to turn off the Automatic Weight Sensor (AWS) for the passenger seat. If you take your car to the Porsche dealer or an independent with the PIWIS tool, then it should take about 20–30 minutes for them to reprogram the air bag controller for you.

1 Here's what the Genuine Porsche GT3 seats look like in a highly modified Boxster (this is the Boxster on the front cover of this book). The customer who designed this highly modified Boxster Speedster wanted the ultimate in high performance seats.

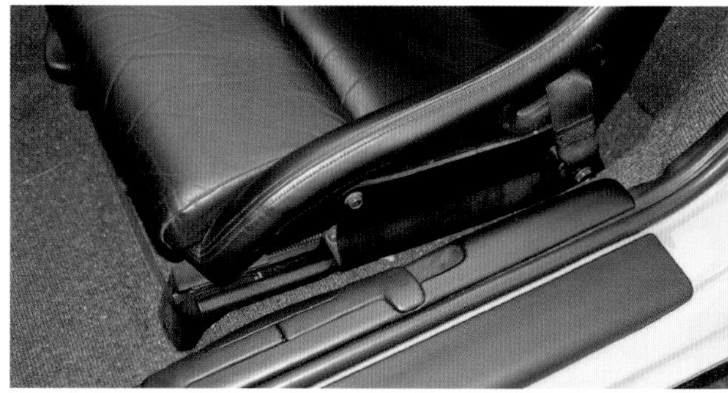

2 This photo shows a close-up shot of the GT3 seats mounted in the Boxster. These seats are adapted to a set of manual seat adjusters and maintain the functionality of adjustable seats while offering a super-easy bolt-in solution.

PROJECT 74
Headlamp Protection Film

Time / Tab / Talent: 1 hour / $70 /

Tools: Squeegee, hair dryer

Applicable Years: All

Parts: Headlamp film kit

More Info: www.101projects.com/Boxster/74.htm

Tip: Take your time—don't rush

Performance Gain: Protection for your headlamps

Comp Modification: Litronic headlamp kit

If you install new headlamps on your Boxster, you may be concerned with keeping rock chips and other debris from damaging them. Replacing a broken headlamp assembly can be very expensive, particularly if you have the Litronic headlamps ($750 each). One solution that I typically like to deploy on each car I own is the application of headlamp protection film. The film I typically use is manufactured by 3M and is a few millimeters thick. According to the specifications, the film can supposedly protect against 1-inch rocks travelling at 120 miles per hour. Film kits are available for the Boxster headlamps in pre-cut shapes, which makes installation very easy. The film is also available in different colors like yellow, which may be cool for track cars. The kit used for this project was manufactured by Xpel, using 3M film, and is available from PelicanParts.com for about $70.

You can install the film dry or wet. In general, you typically get better results with a wet installation, although I have personally done it both ways with similar results. For a dry installation, carefully clean the surface of the headlamp to remove any grease, tar, dirt, bug residue, etc. I like to use a glass cleaner like Windex to start, then use a de-greaser like Simple Green, and then go over it again with Windex. For a final wipe, I use isopropyl alcohol and some lint-free KimWipes, but that may be overkill for most applications. Be sure the headlamp is completely dry. Perform the installation of the film with the car at room temperature—you don't want it to be too cold. In colder environments, you can turn on the headlamps to warm them up prior to installation.

Prior to removing the paper backing off of the film, test-fit the film to the headlamp—it can sometimes be easy to confuse the left and right sides, as they are cut differently but look the same if they are accidentally flipped upside down. When ready, remove the paper backing from the film, taking care not to touch the adhesive side. As many times as I have done this, I have learned that it's helpful to have an assistant peel the backing while you hold the film. The film is a bit expensive, and you don't want to make any mistakes or drop it while you're pulling off the backing paper.

With the adhesive exposed, simply line up and place the film on the headlamp starting with the lower inside corner, making sure the top part is properly aligned. Press the film down on the headlamp from the inside to the outside. Use the squeegee that comes with the film kit to press it down on the headlamp. If there are any significant bubbles on the film, simply lift it up and reapply it to the lamp. Since the film is clear, small bubbles don't show up unless you look at the lamp very, very carefully. It takes about two days for the adhesive to fully cure, so don't wash your car or let it get wet for about 48 hours after.

For wet installation, you need a spray bottle, a hair dryer, 70 percent isopropyl rubbing alcohol, and some ordinary tap water. Thoroughly clean the headlamp as described in the previous section on dry installation. Mix about 25 percent of alcohol and 75 percent of water into the spray bottle. For the wet installation, the temperature should be above room temperature. Turn on the high beams and let the lamp housings get warm to the touch. Also warm up the film pieces using a heat gun or hair dryer. Test-fit each piece to the headlamp prior to removing the paper backing. Wet your fingers completely with the water/alcohol solution, and then have your assistant help you by removing the paper backing from the film. With you holding the film, have your assistant spray the adhesive side of the film. Do not touch the film with dry fingers, as this will leave marks that will not go away when the film is installed. Now spray the warmed up headlamp with the water/alcohol solution. Apply the film to the headlamp and use your hand to smooth the piece onto the lamp from the inside out. Using the squeegee supplied in the kit, press down on the film and from the center out squeeze out any of the water/alcohol solution toward the sides of the headlamp. Use firm continuous strokes to achieve the best results.

The Boxster headlamp is slightly contoured, which means that the adhesive may not stick to the lens immediately. If this is the case, then simply use the hair dryer to heat the film and smooth it out. The heat will soften up the film and also help to evaporate some of the solution to allow for a better fit. It's important not to overheat the film—you just need to get it warm and compliant. There may be a hazy appearance in the film after installation—this is caused by excess moisture trapped between the headlamp and the film. This is typical and should disappear within a week or so. The application of heat helps to dissipate the moisture, so I recommend that you drive with your headlamps on at all times for about a week. As with the dry installation, avoid letting the car get wet for about 48 hours after installation.

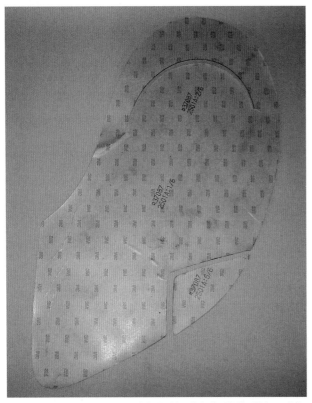

1 This photo shows one side of the Xpel headlight film kit. The kit is specially cut for the Boxster headlamp pattern from 3M film and contains two separate pieces. The film is available in various colors, which allows you to color your headlamp, as is shown in Photo 3.

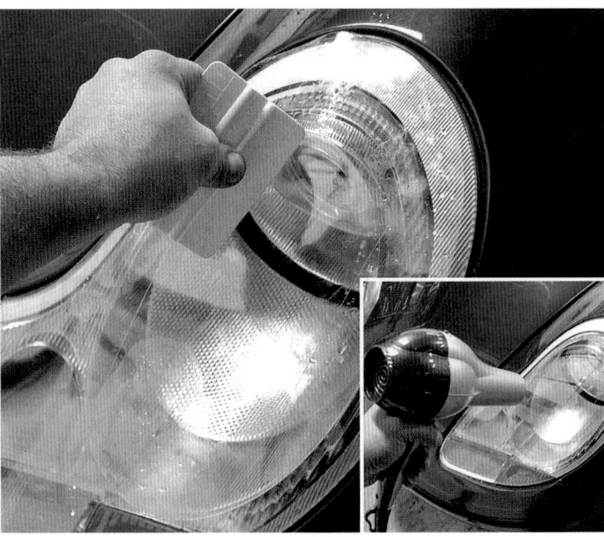

2 For the wet installation, apply firm pressure from the center of the headlamp working your way to the outer edges. Squeeze out as much residual moisture from the water/alcohol solution. If the film isn't adhering completely to the headlamp, then heat the film up with a hairdryer (inset), being careful not to apply too much heat to the film.

3 The installation of the film allows you the freedom to change the color of your headlamps (the headlamp and fog lamp are both tinted yellow). Check with your local vehicle codes to determine if this is legal in your area.

PROJECT 75
GT3 Center Console Delete

 **Time / Tab / Talent:** 2 hours / $175 / 

 **Tools:** Torx driver

 **Applicable Years:** 1997–2004

 **Parts:** GT3 console and trim cover

 **More Info:** www.101projects.com/Boxster/75.htm

Tip: Great upgrade for tall people

 **Performance Gain:** More comfortable driving

 **Comp Modification:** Install short shift kit

1 The Boxster is one of the worst cars to drive if you're just a bit taller than normal. If your legs are just a little bit too long, you can remove the not-so-useful center console bins and install the GT3 cover in its place. The two parts that you need are 986-552-113-02-A10 (A10 is black, many other colors are available) and 986-552-241-02-A03 (plastic trim piece, black). At $175 for the pair, they are a bit expensive, but if it makes the car more drivable, then it's probably worth it. Begin the process by removing the two side trim panels—they simply pull off with a bit of force (green arrows). Also, pry out the plastic trim piece located under the center console tray (yellow arrow).

BODY

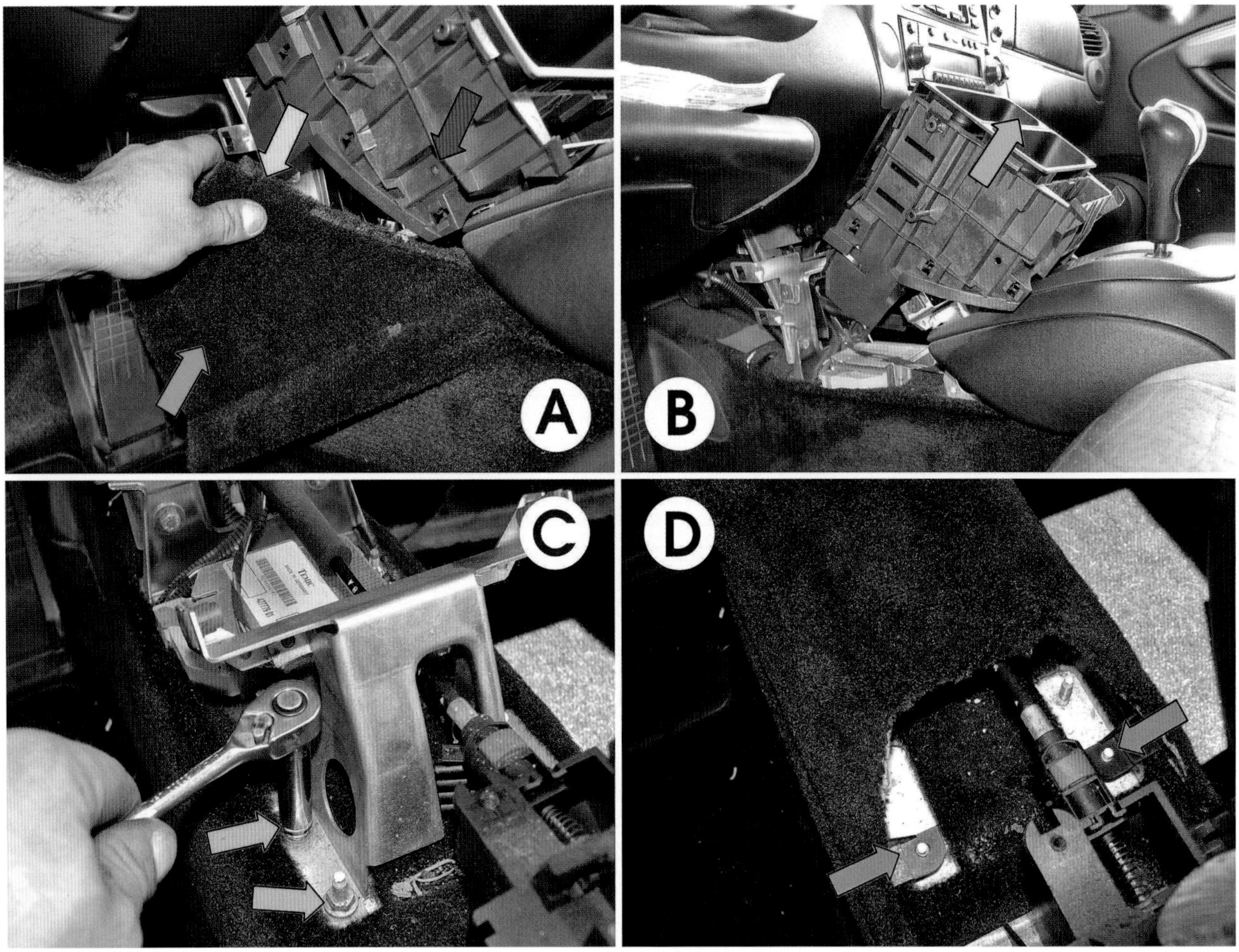

2 **A:** Next, pull away the carpet trim that is located on both sides of the console (green arrow). Remove the screws that hold the center console to the chassis (red arrow and yellow arrow, two screws on each side of the console). **B:** With the screws disconnected, pull the console up and out of the car. You will have to shift the car into second gear or put it in drive (Tiptronic transmission shown here) in order to gain enough clearance to remove the console. **C:** At this point, you need to remove the bracket that holds the center console to the chassis. Remove the shift knob and remove or lift up the entire center console—see Project 42 for instructions on how to accomplish this. You don't need to completely remove the entire center console, simply give yourself enough wiggle room to remove the bracket and install the new GT3 piece. With the console removed, remove the four nuts that hold the bracket to the center tunnel. **D:** Install the GT3 center console cover in place using two of the studs that formerly held in the console bracket. Reinstall the center console when you're done.

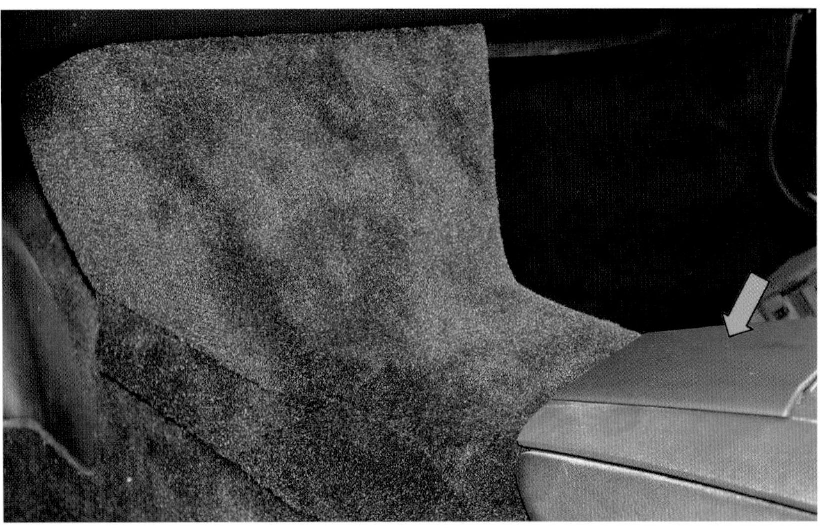

3 Shown here is the completed installation with lots of extra side legroom for you. The final step is to snap the plastic trim piece onto the center console (blue arrow).

PROJECT 76
Door Panel Removal

 **Time / Tab / Talent:** 1–5 hours / 0 / 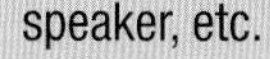

 **Tools:** Torx driver set

 **Applicable Years:** All

 **Parts:** Door handle, door stay, mirror switch, speaker, etc.

 **More Info:** www.101projects.com/Boxster/76.htm

 **Tip:** Don't pull too hard on the foam moisture barrier

 **Performance Gain:** Working door equipment

 **Comp Modification:** Repair your window regulator

If you are not the original owner of your Boxster, then chances are that there are quite a few things wrong with your car and you wonder how they got broken. There probably isn't a place on the car with more gadgets and devices that break than inside or on the door. Not only do you have window glass and seals that leak water, but you have door handles, mirror switches, window regulators, door stays, and door panels—all of which are very susceptible to damage and breakage. Even if you work on your car only moderately, there is a very high chance that you will need to dive into the door to fix something that has broken. This project shows you how to remove the door panel, specifically so that you can get to the door lock assembly and the window regulator (see Project 78 and Project 77), but because there are so many moving parts on the door, I'll discuss just about everything else as well.

The first step in working on just about anything on the door is the removal of the door panel. Photos 1, 2, and 3 detail the process of the door panel removal. The toughest part is pulling the panel out from the door—it is attached with nine plastic clips that can be difficult to snap out of their home in the frame of the door. With the door panel removed, you should see a foam covering that is "glued" onto the backside of the door. A black, sticky goo is what attaches this to the door—it can be removed and reused again if the gooey material is still pliable. Be careful not to tear the foam covering when you remove it.

With the panel removed, you have access to a whole lot of items inside the door. The door stay can be simply unbolted from the door frame and removed. The plastic door handle can easily be swapped out. The window regulator can be removed or repaired (see Project 77). Any door seals or channel guides that need renewing are available to you as well. If one of your door-mounted speakers is broken, don't forget to replace it while you have the chance.

Closing up the door panel is straightforward. I always like to use new plastic door panel clips because new ones are cheap, and the old ones get brittle and may break in the very near future, causing an annoying rattle. Don't forget to install the foam covering—it's common to accidentally leave this on your workbench, only to discover it later on when you're putting your tools away!

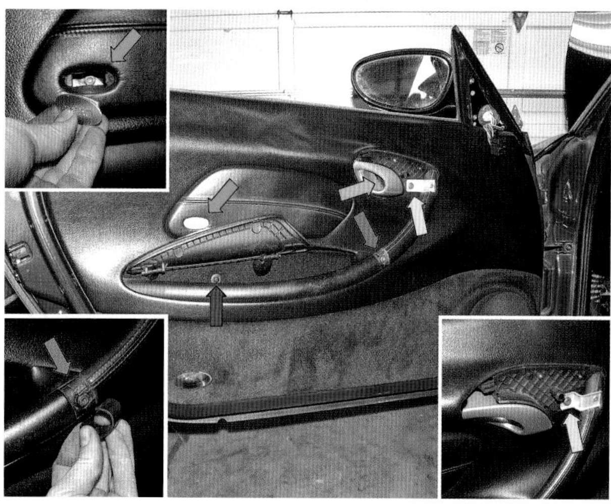

1 Shown here are the fasteners that hold on the door panel. Pluck out the small air bag emblem and remove the screw underneath (green arrow). Remove the small screw underneath the trim clip on the pull handle (purple arrow). Under the plastic trim that surrounds the door handle there is a screw that needs to be removed (yellow arrow). Remove the screw inside the door pocket (red arrow) and the one behind the inside of the door handle pull (orange arrow).

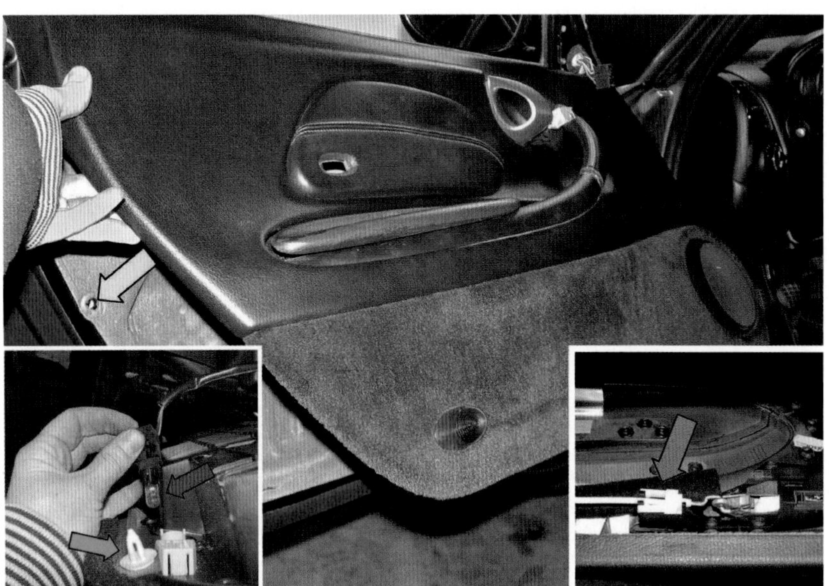

2 The Boxster panel is attached to the door using plastic clips (green arrow). To remove the door panel, simply pull on the panel near where the plastic clips are located, and they should pop right out of the holes in the door (one shown by the yellow arrow). Use Photo 3 for guidance on where the clips are located around the outer edges of the door panel. With the door panel loose, pull it out from the bottom, and release the door lamp bulb from its holder (red arrow). Pull the panel off of the door and then reach around the rear to disconnect the door handle cable (purple arrow). You may have to clip a zip tie in order to disconnect the cable.

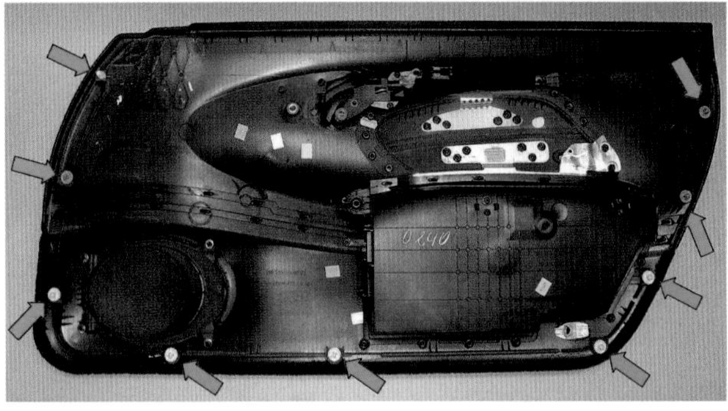

3 Shown here is the back side of the left driver's side door panel. There are nine plastic clips that attach the panel to the door. You need to remove each of these clips from the holes in the door prior to removing the door panel. It will feel like you're breaking the door panel, but you will need to apply significant force to pull off each of the plastic clips. Use a stiff plastic spatula to wedge the door panel out without scratching the paint on the door.

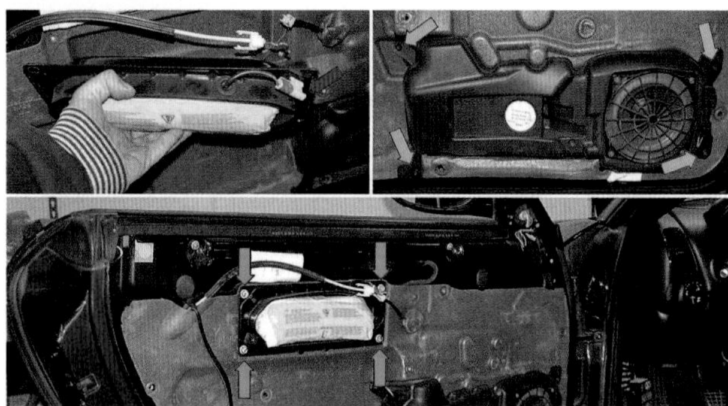

4 With the door panel off, disconnect and remove the air bag. Be sure that you disconnect the battery and wait about 15 minutes prior to disconnecting the air bag (see Project 81). The air bag is simply attached to the door using four screws (green arrows). The speaker located in the lower corner is attached to the door with four screws (blue arrows). Remove the screws and then unplug the speaker connection. All that remains is the foam moisture barrier, which is removed in the next photo.

5 The pre-molded foam moisture barrier is glued onto the door with a gum-like adhesive. You should be able to carefully pull it back without damaging it. Use a plastic spatula and take your time—it's very easy to rip or tear it and a new one costs about $70. As you can see, with the moisture barrier removed, you can access all of the door components underneath (see Project 78 for the door locks; see Project 77 for the window regulator).

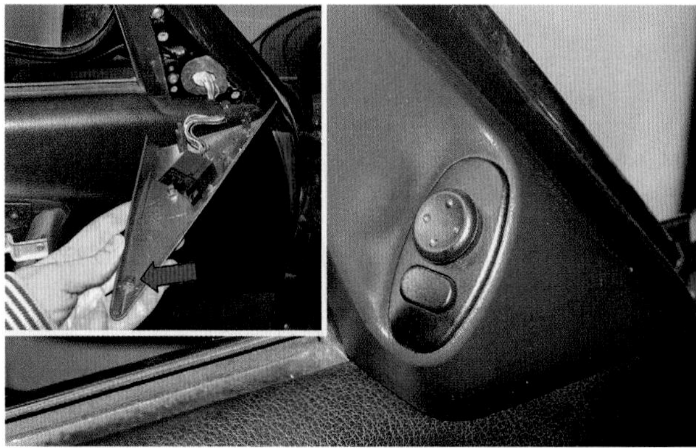

6 The mirror switch simply pops out of the door panel plastic trim piece. If you need to replace this switch, pry it up out of the door and unplug it. Be sure to install it with the left/right switch on the bottom—it's very easy to install it upside down. If you need to pull off the triangular panel, pull on it from the bottom and slide it up. There's a small tab on the top that breaks very easily (red arrow). The good news is that a new piece is only about $10 if/when you break it.

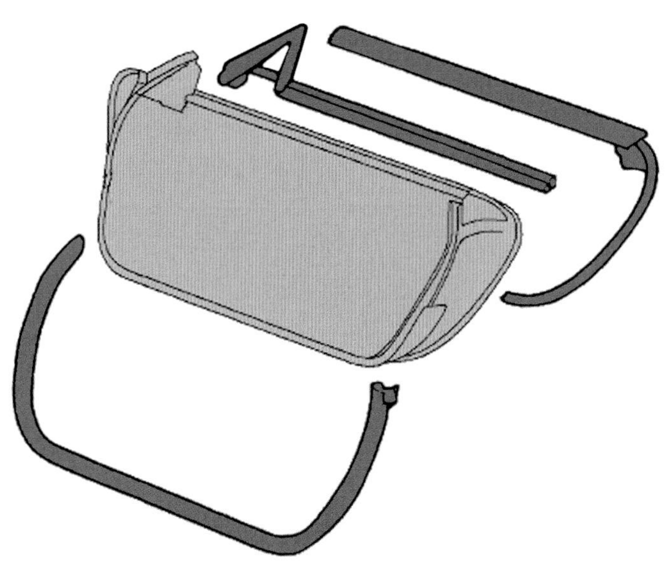

7 With the door apart, it might be a good time to think about replacing your door seals. At the time of this writing, the door seals are super expensive (over $200 each). However, I expect the costs of these to come down as more and more of them start to wear out and the aftermarket manufacturers start making replacement reproduction rubber available.

8 The door stay is another item that you can replace with the door panel removed. Disconnect the stay from the body by removing the pin that holds the stay to the body (red arrow). Then remove the two bolts that attach the stay to the door. Finally, remove the stay from the inside of the door by reaching into the forward access panel in the door.

9 The procedure for removing later-style door panels is significantly different than for the early ones. Begin by prying out the mirror triangle piece and unplugging the harness (yellow arrow) and removing the door panel screw behind it. Then remove the screw inside the door handle pull and remove the handle piece (green arrow). Behind the door handle, there is an oval trim piece—gently pry this off and then remove the screw behind it. The red arrow shows the handle trim—gently pry this off and remove the two screws underneath. The orange arrow points to the end trim that must be gently pried off—remove the screw underneath. With all six screws removed (including the one holding on the door handle), you should be able to pull off the door panel.

PROJECT 77
Replacing Your Window Regulator and Motor

Time / Tab / Talent: 1 hour / $235 / 3 wrenches

Tools: Torx driver set

Applicable Years: All

Parts: New window regulator and motor

More Info: www.101projects.com/Boxster/77.htm

Tip: Clean the window and regulator channels carefully prior to the reinstallation

Performance Gain: Smooth, reliable window operation

Comp Modification: Replace lock assembly, mirror switch

Have you gotten tired of having to open your door and get out to retrieve your burger at the drive thru window? Is your roof stuck up because the window is broken and the car won't let you open the roof without the window rolling down? Perhaps it's time to replace or clean your window regulator or install a new power window motor. Nothing's better than driving in your Boxster with the roof and windows down on a nice sunny day. Having a broken window regulator can surely put a damper on that.

The first step in replacing either the regulator or the power window motor is to remove the door panel (see Project 76). Make sure that you eliminate the power window switch as a potential problem before you start tearing into your door (see Photo 1). Double-check all the fuses that control the power windows, and swap out the relays to make sure that there isn't a problem with them. If one of the windows works and the other doesn't, then chances are that it's the window motor or the window switch. The switches themselves are often faulty, which can sometimes make this an easy fix. Test the switch by removing it from the center console, and swap it with one that is working. If there is any noise coming from the door (clicks and whines) and the window isn't moving, then it's quite obvious that the motor is fine, but the regulator needs to be repaired. If your window is not dropping down when you pull open the door handle, then you probably have an issue with the electrical switch that is integrated into the handle or door lock. See Project 78 for more details on replacing the handle and door lock.

For details on removing the door panel, see Project 76. When you have the door panel removed, you can view the regulator. With your fingers clearly out of the way, roll down the window until it's about 75 percent of the way down. Observe what is happening—the goal here is to figure out if the motor or the regulator needs replacing. If there is no movement, then the motor is suspect. If the motor moves or clicks, then your regulator probably needs to be replaced. Remove the motor (Photo 4) and then the regulator (Photo 5).

With the regulator detached from the door frame and the window, you should test the motor. With your hands out of the way of the motor, carefully press lightly on the window switch and see if the motor moves properly. If the motor doesn't move at all, then it probably is worn out, assuming that you've checked the window switch (check the voltage to the motor when you press the window switch to see if it's getting 12V).

Before you reinstall the window, I recommend that you inspect and replace the front window channel guide if it's worn. This is the channel that guides the front of the window as it is raised and lowered by the regulator. Also worth replacing are the window slot seals if they are worn out. These inner and outer "window scrapers" keep water from dripping down into the recesses of the door. You should also grease all of the moving parts of the regulator: the slides, the motor, the gears, etc.

Before you close everything up inside your door, it's a wise idea to test the proper operation of the window. With your fingers clearly out of the way, hook up the power connections to the window motor, and try to raise and lower the window. Also verify and adjust the stop positions of the window once you have reinstalled the regulator (see Photo 6). There are screws located on the regulator that control these stop positions. If the power is disconnected from the car, the power windows lose their reference point for the closed position and need to be re-initialized. With the convertible top fully closed and windows up, press the up button on each window and then continue pressing the switch for about five more seconds.

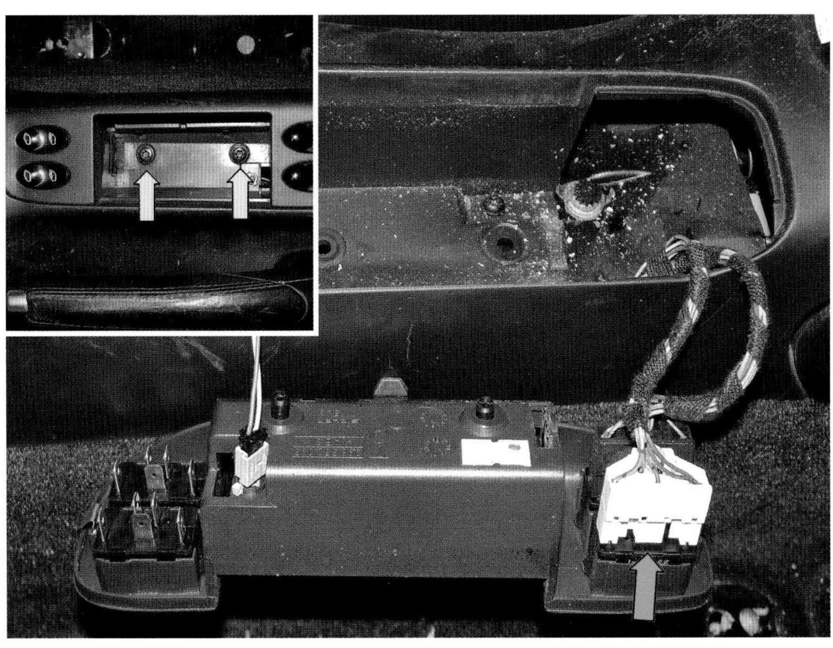

1 The first step in checking the proper operation of your window is to verify that the window switches are working. Remove the two screws in the coin tray (inset), and then pull out the assembly. If one window works and the other does not, try swapping the switches with each other. Replacement is easy, they snap out the back (in the direction of the green arrow) after releasing the tab inside with a small screwdriver.

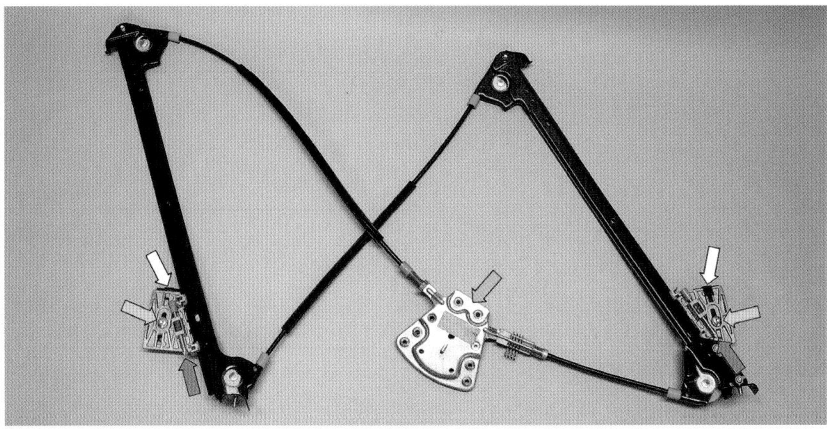

2 Here's a photo of a brand new regulator. Compared to the "old days," modern window regulators are an advanced design, incorporating the cables, gears, and rails into a single assembly. The blue arrow shows where the motor bolts to the regulator. The white arrows point to where the lower edge of the window mounts to the regulator. The orange arrows show the adjustment/tightening screws for the window clamps. The purple arrows show the height adjustment points for the window (see Photo 6).

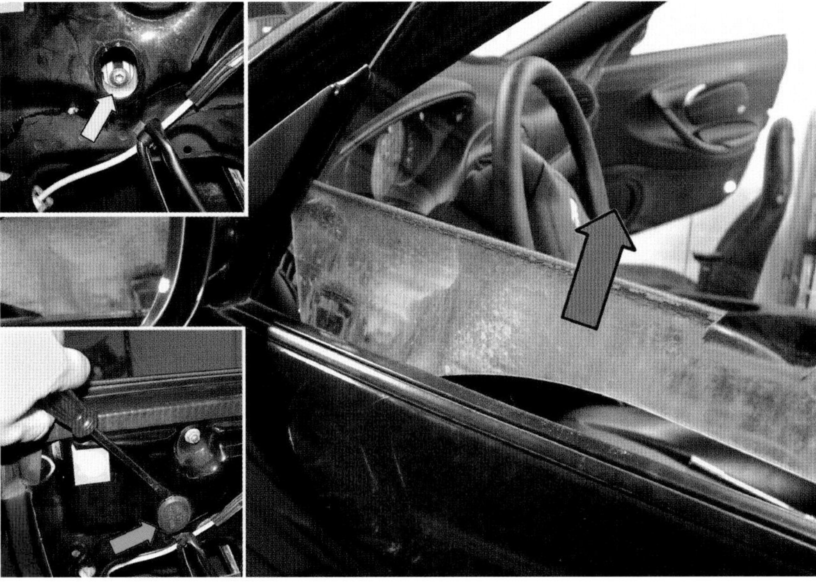

3 Shown here is the procedure for window removal. Raise the window all the way up and stick a screwdriver in the door latch mechanism to trick the car into thinking the door is fully closed. This will keep the window in the top elevated position (see Frame A of Photo 6). Pry off the rubber plugs that cover the access holes (green arrow). Loosen but do not remove the two window clamping screws (yellow arrow). Finally, pull the window up out of the door (purple arrow).

4 Removal of the window motor is fairly easy. Disconnect the electrical harness connection (blue arrow). Then remove the three nuts that hold the motor to the door. Push the motor into the door and pull it down so that you can access the studs that you just took the nuts off of. Remove the three studs (purple arrow shows one of them)—they are what hold the motor and the regulator together. Finally, pull the motor off of the regulator (inset photo, upper left).

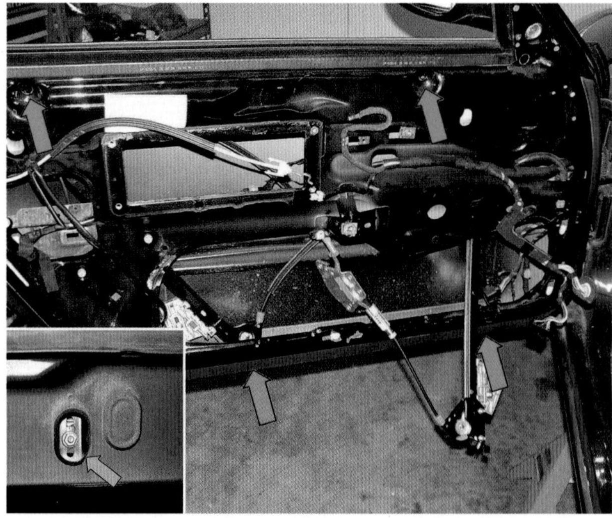

5 With the motor disconnected and detached, removal of the regulator is a snap. Disconnect the four mounting points for the regulator (green arrows) and it should slide out of the lower part of the door. On the very bottom surface of the door, you need to remove the two inner door plugs to reveal the mounting nuts (orange arrow).

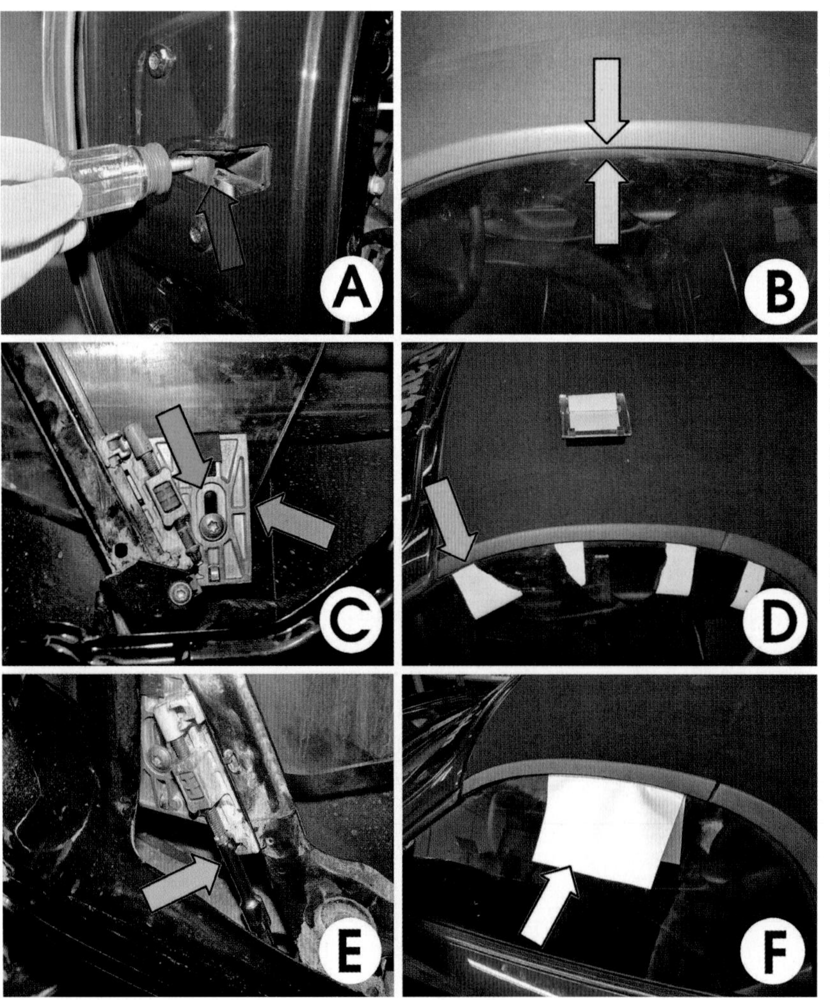

6 Window adjustment can be a bit tricky. **A:** Trick the door into thinking it's closed by putting a short screwdriver into the lock mechanism. The window should raise about 12mm. **B:** With the roof up, push the door near to being closed and measure the distance that the top of the window is located above the bottom edge of the seal. This should be about 2mm or so. **C:** Make sure that the glass is aligned properly left to right in the holding clamps. The edge/corner of the glass should be aligned with the edge of the aluminum clamp (purple arrow). To align the left-right angle of the window, use the slot indicated by the green arrow (only the rear slot is adjustable). **D:** Check the distance that the window sits into the seal by using small pieces of Post-It notes affixed to the window. Open the door and measure the distance from the top of the Post-It notes to the top of the window. This should be about 4mm. **E:** Adjust the window height by removing the outer plugs in the bottom of the door and using an E6 Torx socket to turn the stopper (counterclockwise = higher window). **F:** Check the window rake angle by placing a sheet of paper in the window and rolling it up. You should not be able to remove the paper. Adjust the rake angle by moving the position of the two lower mounting studs for the regulator, in the slots in the door (remove the inner lower door plugs to access these).

PROJECT 78
Door Locks and Handles

Time / Tab / Talent: 1–5 hours / $30–$300 / 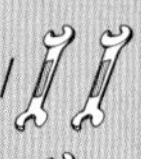

Tools: Torx set

Applicable Years: All

Parts: Door lock mechanism

More Info: www.101projects.com/Boxster/78.htm

Tip: There are lots of little plastic pieces that can easily break inside the door

Performance Gain: Able to open and close doors

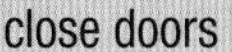

Comp Modification: Replace window regulator

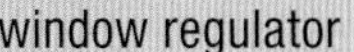

The Boxster door handles and door lock mechanism take a lot of use and abuse over the years and can experience many different failures. The first step in fixing any door lock or handle problems is to remove the door panel (see Project 76). Follow along with the photos in this project to work through the steps involved in replacing the door handle parts and also the integrated lock assembly.

One of the big failure points of modern cars are the small switches located inside the power lock assemblies. These switches get a lot of use, and when they wear out, they can cause all sorts of problems. Switches that are stuck open tell the car that the door is ajar all the time. The dashboard chime may ring continuously, the interior lamps may be on, or the gauge cluster may experience some erratic behavior. If the switch is stuck closed, then owners may have a heck of time opening and closing their doors because the window won't roll down that quarter inch or so to allow you to pull it away from the car. The integrated lock assembly also contains all of the motors for the power locks, which also tend to fail over time.

1 With the door panel removed, you can easily access the door lock mechanism. Begin by removing the inner metal door trim panel by removing the three screws (red arrows). Pull the small clip that holds the door handle cable from its hole (green arrow). Then, disconnect the door lock mechanism from the side of the door (yellow arrows).

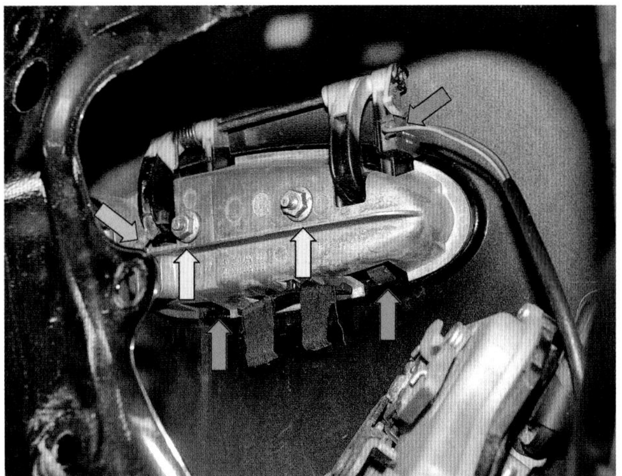

2 This photo shows the back side of the door handle assembly from inside the door. The blue arrow points to the connection where the handle itself connects to the door lock mechanism. Disconnect this in order to remove the door lock mechanism (see also inset of Photo 5). The purple arrow points to the electrical switch, which tells the car to lower the window in preparation for opening the car door when the handle is pulled. The two yellow arrows point to the nuts that fasten the door handle to the rear assembly, and the green arrows show the two clips that hold the assembly inside the door.

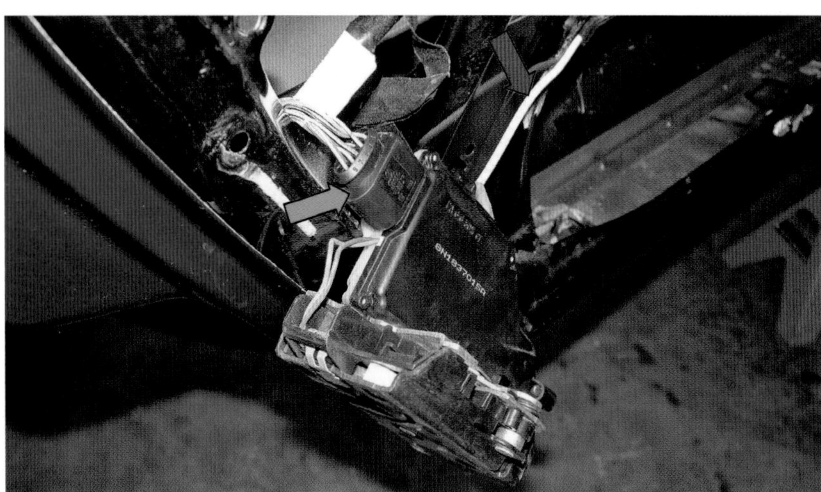

3 With the door lock mechanism disconnected, you should be able to pull it out of the door. The red arrow shows the cable that was previously connected to the door handle. Disconnect the electrical harness from the lock mechanism to remove it from the door.

4 Shown here is the removal of the door handle assembly. After removing the two nuts shown in Photo 2, press out on the clips to unsnap the door handle (see yellow and green arrows in that photo). The door handle switch is plugged into a connector located near the door lock mechanism (yellow arrow). The inner door handle housing, which contains the lock cylinder, is shown in the lower left inset photo.

5 Here's the original door lock mechanism removed from the car. The yellow arrow shows the inside door handle cable attachment point. One plastic piece that may break is the connector for the outside door handle (green arrow). If you're taking the time to refurbish the inside of your door, I recommend replacing this piece.

PROJECT 79
Replacing Hood Shocks

 **Time / Tab / Talent:** 30 minutes / $30 /

 **Tools:** Needle-nose pliers, small screwdriver

 **Applicable Years:** All

 **Parts:** Hood shocks, two for each lid

 **More Info:** www.101projects.com/Boxster/79.htm

 **Tip:** Be careful not to drop the small clips

 **Performance Gain:** No more bumping your head on the hood

 **Comp Modification:** Install the Das Schild hood and trunk protectors

Are you getting tired of having your front or rear trunk lids fall on your head? It's probably time to replace your hood shocks. These are among the most disposable of parts on the Boxster. They will fail—it's just a matter of when. Replacing them is an easy task, however one that is made easier with small hands that can manipulate tiny pieces. With a little bit of patience, you can replace your hood and trunk lid shocks in about 30 minutes.

The front hood uses two gas-pressurized shocks that hold up its weight. Start by lifting up the front hood and securing it using a long stick or a baseball bat. Make sure that this support is securely affixed, as the hood will hurt if it falls on your head. Starting with the right side, use a small screwdriver to pry out the shock retainer clip. Then use a screwdriver to pop the hood shock off of the pivot ball that is attached to the chassis. Remove the other half of the shock in the same manner.

Replace the old shock in the same place and orientation that the old one was in. Snap the new shock into place. If you can't get it around the pivot ball, then remove the retainer clip, push the shock over the ball, and then re-snap the clip into place. It is relatively easy to drop the clip down into the recesses of the trunk, so work carefully and don't rush.

The rear trunk shocks are very similar in their replacement process. The whole process should take you less than 30 minutes or so.

1 Each shock has two sockets on either end. To remove the shock, carefully pry out the retaining clip with a small screwdriver (inset photo). With the clip loosened, you can then pry off the hood shock from the car. Wrap your screwdriver in duct tape if you don't want to scratch your paint during the replacement process. The new shocks should last you several years, until they begin to wear out again.

PROJECT 80

Installing a Rear Wing

Time / Tab / Talent: 1 hour / $400 /

Tools: Drill, marker pen, tape measure

Applicable Years: All

Parts: Spoiler and mounting hardware

More Info: www.101projects.com/Boxster/80.htm

Tip: Paint match to your gas flap

Performance Gain: Sporty-looking body

Comp Modification: Replace rear lenses

One neat addition to the rear of the Boxster is a rear wing to replace the somewhat goofy stock pop-up spoiler. There are many different styles available—some incorporate a completely new deck lid that removes the third brake lamp and integrates into the wing itself. Installation is very easy—simply follow the procedure for marking and wiring the lamp in the photos. When installing the spoiler, you should have it painted to color match your car. The best way to do this is to remove your gas flap and take it along with your spoiler and have them match the paint to the flap. If your spoiler didn't ship with mounting gaskets, make sure that you place a small amount of rubber sealing compound on the spoiler so that you don't leak water into your trunk from the holes drilled in the trunk lid. You also probably want to order new rear deck lid shocks, as the added weight of the wing will stress your current ones.

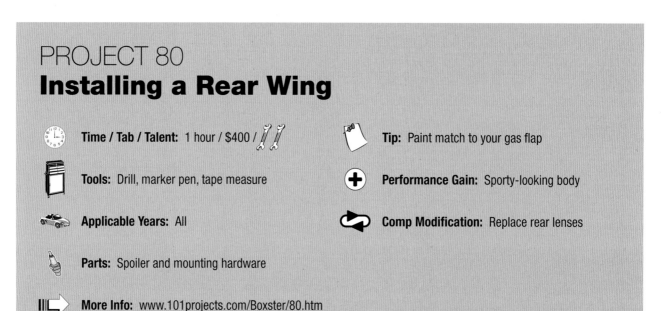

1 Here's a small collage of some spoilers on Boxsters that I photographed while at some local Porsche events. There seems to be an almost unlimited number of styles available to choose from. The two on the top are factory Aerokit I and Aerokit II spoilers that include the replacement of the rear deck lid—note that the rear brake lamp has been replaced and integrated into the wing.

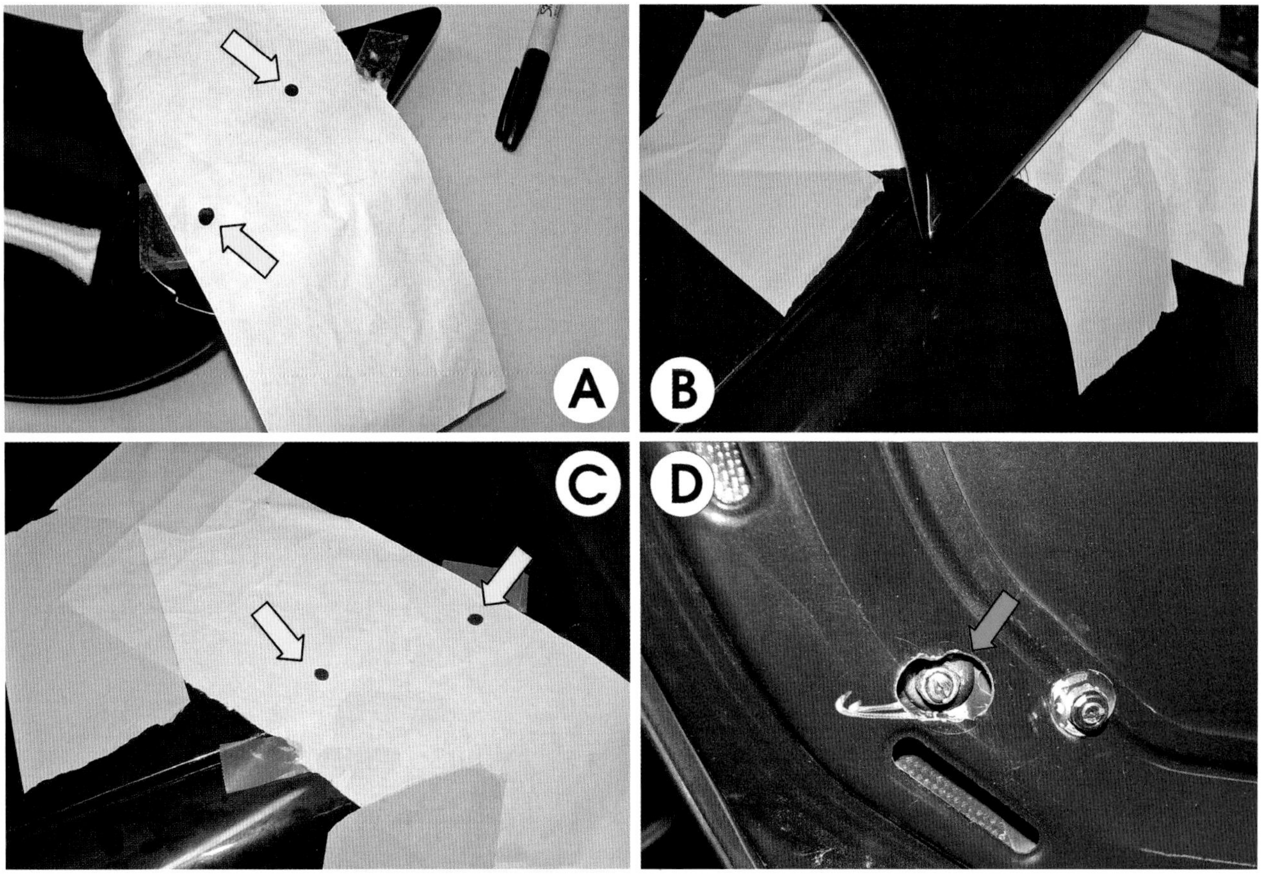

2 This photo sequence shows one of the methods that I recommend for the installation of the wing. **A:** Start by taping a piece of paper to the spoiler itself using scotch tape. Using a permanent marker that will seep through the paper, feel with your finger and mark the holes in the spoiler with the pen. **B:** Place the wing on the car in the exact place where you want it to be. When you have it positioned, then tape down the paper to the car using masking tape. **C:** Remove the wing and the paper should indicate exactly where you need to drill the holes. Take some measurements and confirm that these are in the proper spot prior to drilling. **D:** The trunk frame on the Boxster is too thick and angled too much to have a bolt run all the way through. Using a very small hole saw, cut a small access hole (green arrow) so that you can insert the bolt and a swivel-socket driver through. When done drilling, make sure that you coat the edges of all the holes with some paint to prevent the bare metal from rusting.

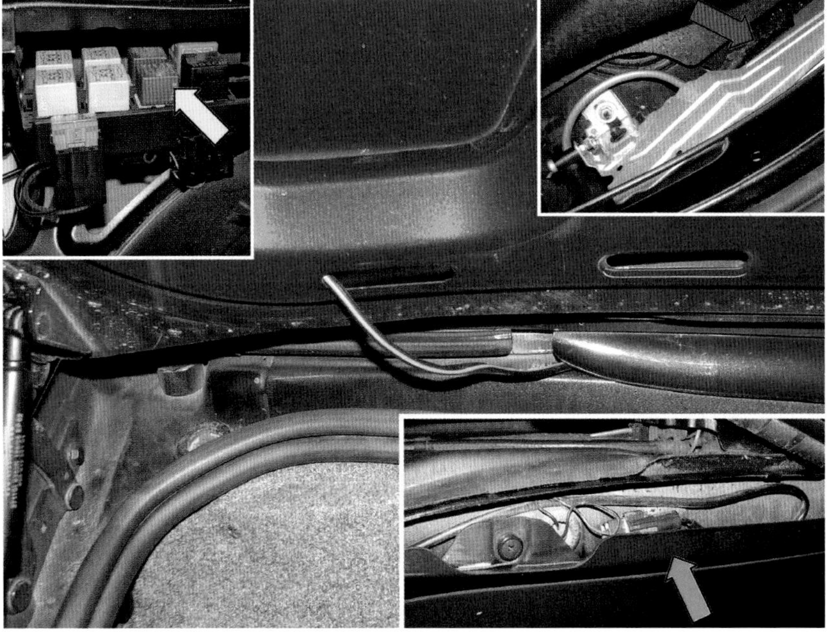

3 If your rear wing has an integrated third brake light, then snake the cable down the side of the trunk inside the deck lid. Unplug the third brake light and plug the wire in its place. Install the brake lamp block out plate (green arrow—you will probably have to have it painted body color along with the spoiler). If your wing doesn't integrate with the Boxster's built-in spoiler, then simply pull back the carpet and unplug it, or pull the two brown relays (yellow arrow) in the left rear trunk compartment instead. For pre-2001 cars, you can eliminate the spoiler warning lamp by removing the bulb in the gauge cluster (see Project 90). For 2001–2004 cars that no longer use light bulbs in the cluster, you can trick the car into thinking the spoiler is still attached. Pull the two brown relays and disconnect the connection to the spoiler (red arrow), located under the trunk carpet. Then remove pin No. 1 (blue/green wire) from the connector, and wrap it in electrical tape. Then swap pin No. 2 (gray/brown wire) and pin No. 4 (gray/green wire) and replug it in. This should stop the warning lamp from illuminating in the instrument cluster. If you have a 996 cluster installed in your Boxster (see Project 90), you can simply disable the spoiler lamp using the PST-2 tool, because some 996 cars came with a fixed wing.

SECTION 10
ELECTRIC

This section covers a wide variety of projects aimed at reducing the amount of electrical- and gauge-related problems in your car. In addition, I've also tossed in several projects that focus on upgrades and improvements to your Boxster. Whether your car has a faulty headlamp switch or has trouble turning over the starter, the projects in this section will help you troubleshoot and repair these nagging problems.

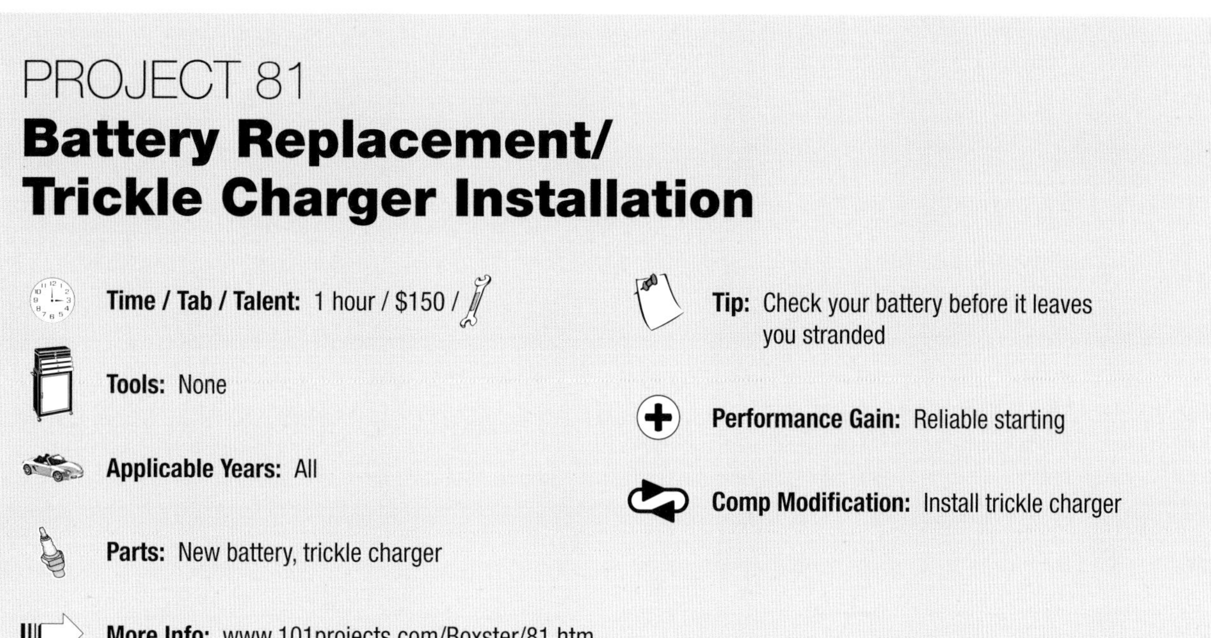

PROJECT 81
Battery Replacement/ Trickle Charger Installation

Time / Tab / Talent: 1 hour / $150 /

Tools: None

Applicable Years: All

Parts: New battery, trickle charger

More Info: www.101projects.com/Boxster/81.htm

Tip: Check your battery before it leaves you stranded

Performance Gain: Reliable starting

Comp Modification: Install trickle charger

At one time or another, everyone may have problems starting their Boxster. The first place to look for trouble in your starting system is your battery. The battery is perhaps the most important electrical component on the car, and due to its design and nature, it is perhaps one of the most troublesome. Before doing anything drastic like replacing your starter or looking at your fuel injection ECU, you should make sure that your battery is in good condition.

Begin by checking the voltage on the battery posts using a voltmeter. Place the meter's probes on the posts of the battery, not the clamps. This will give the most accurate indication of the voltage in the battery. A normal battery should read a voltage slightly above 12 volts with the car sitting still and no electrical devices on. (The small trunk light in the front trunk shouldn't make a difference in the voltage reading.) A typical reading would be in the 12.6-volt range when the battery is fully charged. If the reading is 12 volts or less, then the battery needs charging or needs to be replaced with a new one. To be certain, you can take your battery to your local auto parts store for testing.

While older batteries often exhibited deteriorating performance prior to their failure, I recently had an original OEM BMW battery fail on me in my BMW 5-Series. The car was running perfectly fine—I had just driven about 350 miles the previous day, so it should have been well charged. The next morning, I got in the car, and it started fine. I drove about 3 miles and stopped off to pick something up. I shut off the car and was inside three minutes at the most. When I got to the parking lot, the battery was completely dead. There was not even enough power left to open the power door locks. It did turn out to be a complete battery failure. I was surprised because I'd never had a battery fail like this before—it always seemed to give out slowly. Some of the informal research I've done since then seems to indicate that the newer technology used in these batteries tends to lead to this type of catastrophic failure.

When the car is running, the alternator should be outputting anywhere from about 12.5 volts to about 14.5 volts. If you don't see any significant change in the voltage after you start up the car, then your alternator could be faulty. If the voltage is high at the battery (around 17 volts or higher), then the alternator's regulator is most likely faulty and needs to be replaced. Overcharging the battery at these higher levels may cause it to overflow and leak acid all over the inside of your car. See Project 82 for instructions on how to replace the alternator.

Do not ever disconnect the battery ground strap from the battery while the car is running. The battery acts as an electrical capacitor and filter on the entire electrical system, and the car's electrical components expect it to be there, even if it doesn't hold a charge. Disconnecting the battery terminals while the engine is running can seriously damage the computers and systems of the car.

Sometimes it may be necessary to reset the computers of the car, for example, to clear error codes. Some books recommend disconnecting both terminals of the battery and touching them together to empty all of the capacitors and stored electricity in the system. While this works, it can possibly create a quick electrical shock to the system. A trick I learned from Tony Callas of Callas Rennsport is instead to place a resistor across the two terminals or simply use a diagnostic lamp that will act like a resistor. Doing this will slowly dissipate the electricity over a few seconds instead of all at once.

Once you have determined that your battery is fine, you should make sure that your engine ground strap is properly installed. The engine and transmission are mounted to the chassis using rubber mounts. While great for the suspension, the rubber mounts make lousy electrical conductors. To compensate for this, there is an engine ground strap that electrically connects the transmission and engine assembly to the chassis. It's located inside the engine compartment (see Photo 1). Check the strap to make sure it's not corroded or damaged. Make sure that you clean both ends of the strap and the areas that it mounts to on the chassis. As with all electrical connections, it's a good idea to clean the area that you are mounting to with rubbing alcohol and also to sand the area lightly with some fine-grit sandpaper or a wire brush. Doing so will remove any dirt, grime, surface rust, or other corrosion that may interfere with creating a good electrical connection. While you're at it, clean up the battery terminals as well in a similar manner.

If you have discovered that your battery is weak, then you need to replace it. Follow the steps in the photos of this project. When purchasing a new battery, I recommend the newer-style sealed, or "maintenance free," types. Sealed batteries may be more prone to damage when you deep cycle them (let them run all the way down), but require less preventative maintenance. Be sure to purchase a battery that has the same group number and CCA rating (Cold Cranking Amps). Check the freshness date on the battery that you are purchasing and avoid any batteries that are more than six months old.

You disconnect the battery by disconnecting the negative or ground lead from the battery. Always disconnect the negative or ground lead first—if you disconnect the positive/hot lead, there is a chance that your tool may touch the metal chassis. This will result in a short circuit, which would be quite dangerous. The worst case scenario would probably be where your wrench hit the chassis and becomes instantly welded there by the current. Then the battery overheats and explodes, because you couldn't break the connection. In other words, be sure to disconnect the ground first.

If your car has the original radio in it, be aware that you will need the radio code if you disconnect the battery. This code is typically included with the documentation/owners manual that came with the car. The Porsche dealer can look this code up for you if you don't have it, but that can be a huge pain, and most dealers will charge you for the service.

Leaving your lights on in your car can seriously damage the battery. Automotive batteries are not typically deep-cycle batteries, which means they do not like to be fully discharged. If you leave your lights on and drain your battery several times, then you will weaken it each time and have to replace it sooner than later. If you need to jump start your battery, then you should refer to the section in your Boxster's owner's manual. The procedure is very straightforward and very similar to other cars.

The Boxster has a few power-saving stand-by modes that it will enter after certain periods of time. If the ignition key is removed, accessories such as the trunk lamp, interior lamp, radio, etc., will be switched off automatically after approximately two hours. If the car is locked, then these will switch off after 10 minutes. If the car is not started or unlocked for more than 5 days (7 days on the 2005 and later models), then the remote control standby function is switched off, and you will need to unlock the car using the key.

After you disconnect your battery, the DME computer will lose some of its history memory used for adapting the fuel injection system. As a result, the idle may fluctuate, and the fuel injection mixture may be slightly off as the car relearns its settings.

Probably the best way to protect your battery from drain and damage is to install a trickle-charger/battery maintainer on it. This charger plugs into the wall when you are not using the car, and constantly monitors the battery, charging it as needed when the voltage runs down. Every car battery has internal electrical leakage that will cause it to become fully discharged over time if not properly maintained. A trickle charger can keep your battery fresh year-round, even if you don't drive the car for months at a time. Beware of cheap chargers though, as they can accidentally overcharge your battery, causing more harm than good. The trickle charger I like to use in all of my Porsches is the Battery Tender, available for $40–$60 at PelicanParts.com.

1 The infamous drivetrain ground strap is one of the easiest parts on the car to overlook, yet it can cause so many electrical troubles. Since the transmission and engine are insulated by rubber mounts, the ground strap is the only significant ground to the engine. If the ground strap is disconnected or missing, then the current that turns the starter must travel through the engine harness or other small points of contact. When I was working on the project Boxster for this book, I forgot to install the ground strap. When I went to start the car, it wouldn't start, and instead, the current ran through the right side stainless steel brake lines and completely cooked the line. That was a new experience for me—don't forget your ground strap!

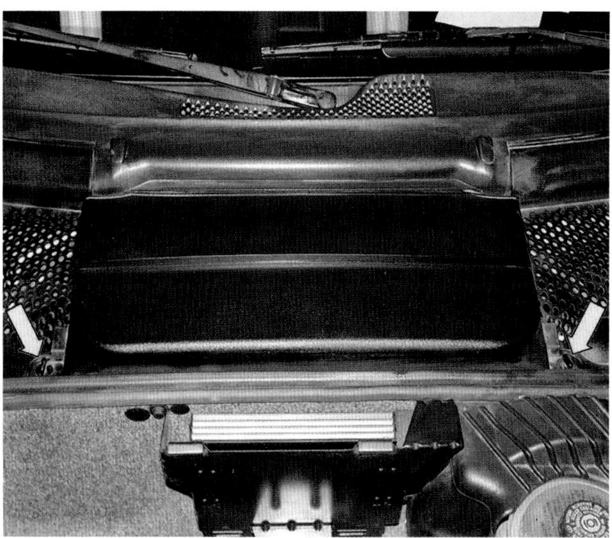
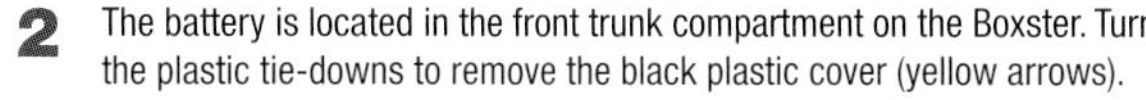

2 The battery is located in the front trunk compartment on the Boxster. Turn the plastic tie-downs to remove the black plastic cover (yellow arrows).

3 Always disconnect the black-colored negative or ground connection first from the battery post (green arrow). If you are not planning on removing the battery, then this connection is all you need to disconnect—there is no need to disconnect the positive/hot lead to the battery. When you disconnect the ground from the battery, make sure that you place or tape the ground lead aside—you don't want it accidentally falling on the terminal of the battery while you're working and effectively connecting up the battery again. If you are replacing the battery, be sure to properly hook up the vent hose once you have installed it in place (blue arrow). The yellow arrow shows the wire for the Battery Tender harness. You can route it through the fire wall (see Photo 3 of Project 85), or you can simply zip-tie it to the plastic mesh located on the right side of the car.

4 If you are removing the battery, then simply loosen and remove the hold-down clamp that attaches the battery to the chassis (yellow arrow). Stand inside the trunk and lift the battery out of the car from there (they are quite heavy). The inset in the upper left-hand corner shows the permanent attachment of the Battery Tender cable to the negative lead. A handy device I like to install on all my cars is a battery cut-off switch (lower inset). Installation of this switch on the battery ground allows you to remove the green knob and shut off all power to the car. An added tip—connect a small inline fuse from one end to the other, and a small amount of current will continue to flow, keeping your radio and DME from being cleared out when the battery is disconnected.

5 Whenever I pick up a new car, I almost always install one of these within the first few weeks. The Battery Tender is a necessary tool if you're not planning on driving your car every day. It plugs into the wall and trickle-charges the battery so that it won't run down. Although the kit comes with alligator clips for temporary installations, I prefer to hard-wire the charger into the battery, and simply leave the charging unit in the bottom of the front trunk when driving.

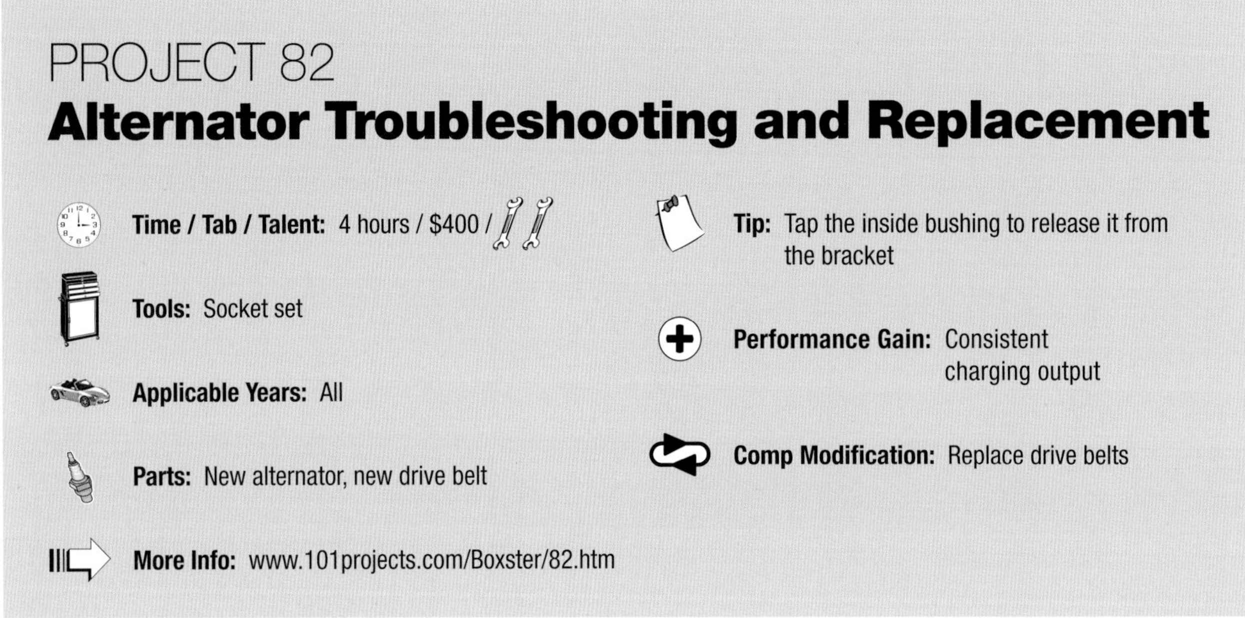

PROJECT 82
Alternator Troubleshooting and Replacement

Time / Tab / Talent: 4 hours / $400 /

Tools: Socket set

Applicable Years: All

Parts: New alternator, new drive belt

More Info: www.101projects.com/Boxster/82.htm

Tip: Tap the inside bushing to release it from the bracket

Performance Gain: Consistent charging output

Comp Modification: Replace drive belts

One of the nice things about the configuration of the Boxster engine is the relative ease with which you can replace the alternator. The alternator is nestled neatly on the right side of the engine compartment—very easily accessible. The replacement and repair process is straightforward and should take you about an afternoon to complete.

The first thing that you need to do is to make sure that your alternator is indeed the cause of the problems with your charging system. Sometimes bizarre electrical problems can be caused by a number of faults other than the alternator. It's important to troubleshoot the system prior to replacing your alternator.

If it seems to be the culprit, check the belt that drives the alternator. Is it tight and amply turning the alternator pulley? If it's worn or close to breaking, then replace it and recheck the alternator (see Project 5). Modern belts seldom break, but they do become brittle and glazed with age and can slip on their pulleys.

The next item to check is the voltage at the battery. This should read a little more than 12 volts with the engine off. When the car is running, the voltage should read at in the range of 13 to 14.5 volts with the engine at 2,000 rpm. If your battery appears to be leaking, then your alternator's voltage regulator has probably failed. The battery will usually only leak acid if it has been overcharged at a much higher voltage. If the voltage measured at the battery is more than 16 or 17 volts when the engine is running, then the regulator is probably bad. If your battery has boiled over and has acid overflowing out the top, make sure that you clean up any spilled acid immediately. Dousing the area with a water and baking soda solution should help considerably to neutralize the acid and prevent it from eating away at the metal. Be sure to wear gloves and eye protection as well.

An important item to check on your car is the engine ground strap. The engine is electrically isolated from the chassis by rubber motor mounts. If the engine ground strap is missing or disconnected, then you might have a whole bunch of problems, including electrical system malfunctions and difficultly turning over the starter. See Project 81 for the exact location of this ground strap.

Before starting any work, make sure that you disconnect the battery. The positive battery terminal is directly connected to the alternator, and it can be dangerous to work on if it's live (see Project 81).

The first step is to remove the belt that drives the alternator. Refer to Project 5 for detailed instructions on the belt removal. Removing the alternator from its bracket itself is a relatively straightforward process. Start by loosening the large B+ cable that is located inside the top of the engine compartment. See Project 3 for instructions on how to access the engine compartment.

Now, loosen but do not remove the lower alternator bolt (green arrow, Photo 3). Then, loosen the idler pulley that is located next to the alternator. Loosen the bolt and back it out about 3–4 full turns. Then, using a drift and a hammer, tap on the bolt. The purpose for doing this is to loosen up the metal bushing that is located inside the rear flange of the alternator. With the bushing loose, lift up on the idler pulley, and the alternator assembly should rotate counterclockwise. Remove the lower bolt, and the alternator should be able to be lifted up and out of the engine.

On this particular car, this bushing was a tight fit and required quite a bit of tapping and quite a bit of wiggling to remove. Specifically, I had to use a very long drift to tap directly on the rear bushing to get the assembly loose. Other mechanics seem to indicate that this is a common problem, so you might have to work at it a bit to get your alternator out.

With the alternator unbolted, disconnect the electrical connections from the rear. Reminder: Don't touch these connections while the battery is still hooked up (Project 81).

If you are replacing the alternator completely, then the installation of the new alternator is simply the reverse of the removal process. Make sure that you reconnect all of the wires to their proper terminals when you are done. If you're still not sure if your alternator is bad, you can take it to any good auto parts store, and they should be able to test it for you for a modest fee.

1 Shown here is a brand new rebuilt alternator. Unlike older-style Porsche alternators, this one is pretty much plug-and-play. The regulator is internal, and the alternator should come with the proper pulley installed on the front. The green arrow in the inset photo shows the metal bushing that may give you trouble when you try to remove the alternator. This bushing is the one that needs to be tapped on in order to loosen the assembly for removal.

2 With the top of the engine compartment open and the battery disconnected, loosen and disconnect the cable that attaches to the alternator. This will allow you to pull the unit out and away from the engine compartment.

3 You can access the alternator assembly through the engine compartment access panel behind the seats. Simply loosen both mounting bolts (arrows). Turn the idler arm bolt back about 3–4 turns.

4 Using a metal drift or punch, tap on the bolt to push out the rear metal bushing. This may require some significant tapping. If the bushing is stuck, you may end up damaging the idler pulley bolt. Don't fret though, as a new one is only $5.

5 With the alternator disconnected from its bracket. Pull the unit out of the engine bay and disconnect the two electrical connections on the rear (blue and red arrows).

ELECTRIC

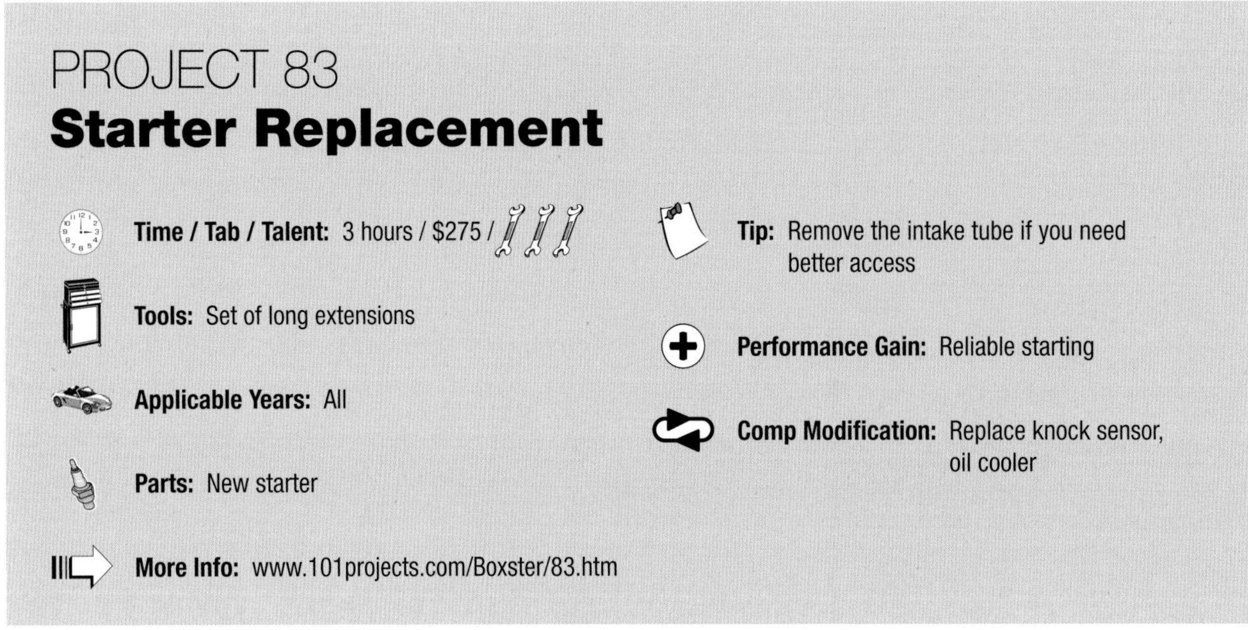

PROJECT 83
Starter Replacement

Time / Tab / Talent: 3 hours / $275 /

Tools: Set of long extensions

Applicable Years: All

Parts: New starter

More Info: www.101projects.com/Boxster/83.htm

Tip: Remove the intake tube if you need better access

Performance Gain: Reliable starting

Comp Modification: Replace knock sensor, oil cooler

Starter motors fail over time—it's just a fact of life. It may be that a starter motor is working fine one day and then all of a sudden dies the next day. Or, sometimes the motor gets weaker and weaker and turns the car over slower and slower. This is a possible sign that you should replace your starter motor. However, before replacing your starter, check the condition of your battery and make sure your ground strap is properly installed (see Project 81). Also check the clutch pedal switch (see Project 93) and also the proper operation of the electronic immobilizer system. Try a different ignition key—each key has a built-in RFID chip that may have somehow become damaged. If possible, have the system checked using the Porsche factory scan tools (PST-2 or PIWIS).

The starter is located in the engine compartment under the convertible top. The first step in the removal process is to raise the top and gain access to the engine (see Project 3). Then it's very important that you disconnect the battery. The starter has a direct connection to the positive terminal of the battery, and you can cause a lot of harm to yourself and the car if you short circuit the terminals (see Project 81). Once you have access to the top of the engine, remove the intake air snorkel that attaches to the throttle body (see Photo 4 in Project 23). Then, loosen up the clamps that hold the intake manifold tube tight (see Photo 1). Now disconnect the hoses and bolts that attach the throttle body to the engine. For 1997–1999 cars, you may have to loosen the clamp that holds the accelerator cable in place.

With everything disconnected on the throttle body, simply rotate it up and out of the way. You should now have access to the starter, the two bolts attaching it to the engine, and the three electrical connections located on the rear. If you find yourself struggling to get the starter out, then you can loosen the intake manifold tube clamps quite a bit more, slide them to the inside, and pull the entire intake tube off the top of the engine. This should give you more than enough room to remove the starter. Installation is the reverse of disassembly. Follow the rest of the photos in this project for details.

With your intake manifold partially disassembled, you can reach many components on the top of the engine. It may be a good time to replace your knock sensors, replace your throttle body, reseal or replace your oil cooler, or replace your air-oil separator.

1 On the top of the engine, loosen up the clamps that hold the intake tube that is connected to the throttle body. You will need to loosen them up enough so that you can rotate the throttle body up and out of the way.

2 With the intake air snorkel disconnected and out of the way (see Project 23), loosen up the bolts that hold the throttle body to the engine (purple arrow). The design of this mount varied slightly across the years, so you may have to improvise a bit. Disconnect the air-oil separator hose from the side of the intake tube (orange arrow).

3 This photo shows the throttle body disconnected and rotated up and out of the way. You can disconnect the air/oil separator hose from the throttle body (orange arrow) or at the separator itself, as this photo demonstrates. The starter is underneath the throttle body and now can be accessed for removal (yellow arrow). If you need additional room, then simply remove the intake tube with the throttle body attached.

4 I found it very difficult to reach one of the lower starter bolts from on top of the engine compartment. To solve this problem, I removed the cover behind the seats (see Project 5) and used some very long extensions to reach the bolt.

5 This photo shows the starter and one of the two bolts that hold it to the engine case. The intake manifold has been removed on this particular engine so that you can see how and where the bolts are connected. When you are working in your engine compartment, you will have an obstructed view. The red arrow points to the two electrical connections (terminal 30 and 50) that are attached to the starter. The green arrow points to the bolt that is generally easiest to remove. The inset photo shows how the three electrical connections are attached to the starter.

6 This photo was taken of my brand-new 996 engine during the process of prepping it for the 3.4 upgrade (Project 11). The yellow arrow is pointing to one of the two knock sensors that you can access while you have the intake manifold partially disassembled for the starter replacement. The knock sensor detects pinging on each cylinder bank. If one of the sensors is not working properly, then you may experience a drop in engine performance, or engine damaging detonation.

7 With the intake manifold out of the way, it's also a great time to replace or reseal your oil cooler. The cooler is attached to the top of the engine with four screws and is easily accessed with the front part of the intake tube removed. When you install your new oil cooler, use four new seals and carefully clean the surface prior to installation. The hose that runs out of the top of the cooler is a water coolant hose and is connected to one of the nipples that attaches to the coolant tank (see Project 33).

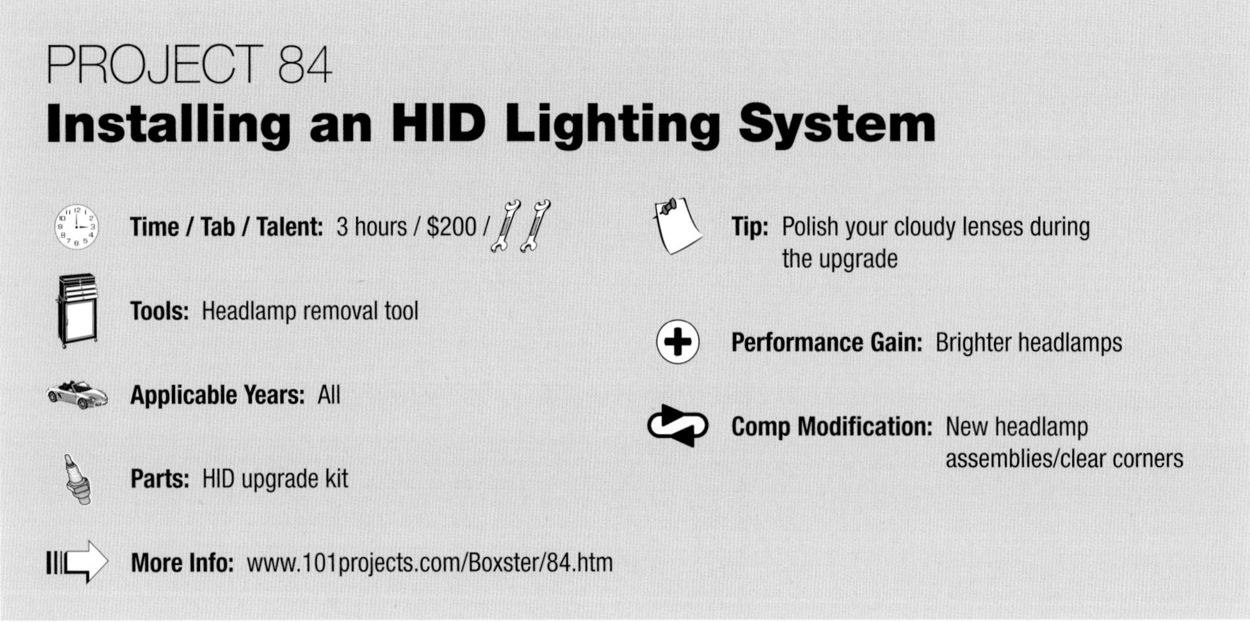

PROJECT 84
Installing an HID Lighting System

Time / Tab / Talent: 3 hours / $200 /

Tools: Headlamp removal tool

Applicable Years: All

Parts: HID upgrade kit

More Info: www.101projects.com/Boxster/84.htm

Tip: Polish your cloudy lenses during the upgrade

Performance Gain: Brighter headlamps

Comp Modification: New headlamp assemblies/clear corners

One of the more exciting upgrades you can perform on your Boxster is the installation and upgrade of your lamps to a high-intensity discharge (HID) system. This type of lighting system is sometimes also referred to as xenon lighting or under the Bosch brand name of Litronic. The lamps use electric current that runs through a xenon gas mixture to create light—not unlike the operation of an ordinary fluorescent light bulb. In order to get the lamps working, the gas mixture must be subjected to an initial voltage of about 28,000 volts. Two small ballast units create this high voltage when starting the lamps and then taper it down to about 40 volts to keep the light on.

There are two paths that you can take to perform this upgrade. The most expensive xenon upgrade is the installation of the factory Bosch Litronic kit (see Project 85). The "poor man's" solution is to use a retrofit kit that simply replaces the stock H7 bulbs used in the standard Boxster lamp housing.

I prefer to use genuine Hella units as they have a built-in safety circuit to prevent the 28,000 volts from being discharged if there is any disruption or anomalies in the circuit.

Replacement bulbs tend to be very expensive, at about $100 each. I expect this cost to decrease though in the near future as more and more cars are equipped with this technology as stock equipment. The good news is that unlike traditional halogen bulbs, the HID bulbs do not often burn out—they have no internal mechanical components and actually run very cool (like a normal fluorescent light bulb).

The lamp kits typically use 35-watt bulbs, which means that they draw about 2–3 amps of current after the initial startup. It's not uncommon for the ballast units to draw about 15 amps for less than a second as they are starting up the bulbs. The actual startup phase is typically less than a second—barely a noticeable difference from the stock configuration. With a conventional halogen lamp system, a large portion of the energy spent in the system goes toward excess heat given off by the bulb. The HID systems are much more efficient—a typical HID 35-watt bulb is about three times as bright as a 100-watt halogen bulb.

The installation is not difficult—it simply requires that you mount the ballast, integrate the bulbs into your housing, and wire up the system. The headlamps have large plastic covers on the rear that need to be slightly modified. Most of the HID kits available have a wire harness that has a large grommet on it. You need to take a small hole saw or Dremel tool and cut a hole in the rear of your plastic housing for the grommet to fit (see Part A in Photo 1). Two wires are connected to the HID bulb; the other two tap into the connections for the old halogen bulb. The harness that is included with the kit powers the HID lamps off of the power that formerly powered the original bulb inside the headlamp housing.

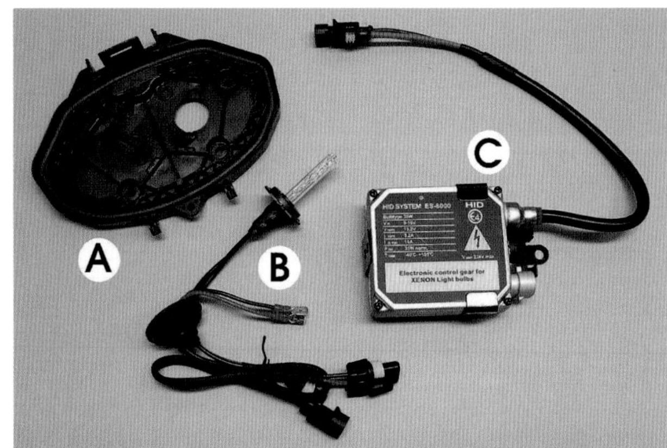

1 This photo shows the basic HID upgrade kit for the standard USA sealed-beam headlamps. **A:** Modified rear cover for the sealed headlamps. **B:** Bulb assembly and wire harness. **C:** HID ballast/controller for the HID bulbs.

Mounting of the ballast is pretty easy. Component locations changed quite a bit over the years—find a safe, secure spot near your headlamps and use the double-sided sticky tape or mounting brackets that come with the HID kits (see Photo 3). On my 1999 Boxster, I mounted it on a flat surface just to the outside of the headlamp retainer.

You can install an HID kit for your low beams, high beams, and even the fog lamps. I have seen cars with three kits installed, and their fog lamp switch modified so that all three are on at the same time. When you're finished with the installation, be sure to align your headlamps so that you're not pointing the beam into oncoming traffic. In most states, the use of non-factory HID kits are designated for "off-road use only." Keep in mind that if you don't have a street-legal headlamp system, then you may invite tickets from law enforcement.

The only downside I found from installing this type of system was that it created a lot of static on my AM radio. However, the fix for this is rather simple—just install a 12V RF car noise filter on the power lines going to the ballasts and the problem should go away.

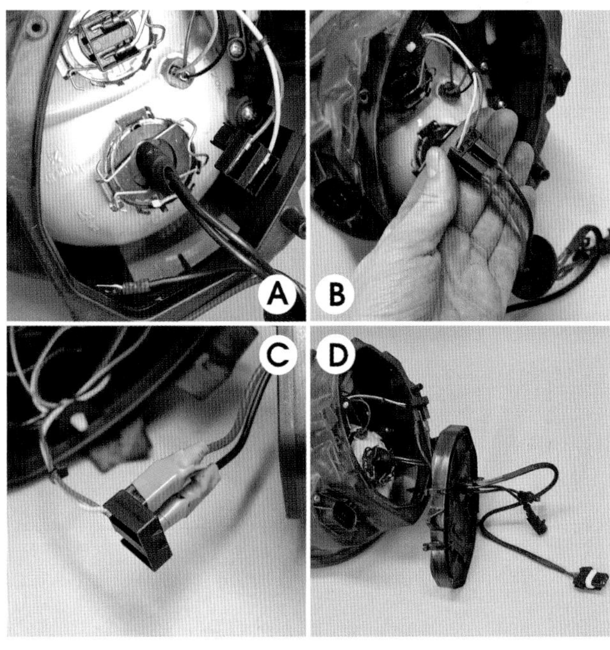

2 Here you can see the various steps of assembly into the rear of the headlamp. **A:** The lower bulb is the standard low-beam headlamp that is on most of the time. Remove the existing bulb and insert the newer HID bulb. You may have to remove the wire retaining ring completely in order to fit the new bulb. **B:** Connect the HID wires to the existing bulb connector. Brown is the ground and typically connects to the black wire on the harness. **C:** Wrap the connectors carefully with electrical tape to prevent a short from within the headlamp in case the connector bounces around. **D:** Thread the wires through the hole in the rear cover of the headlamp.

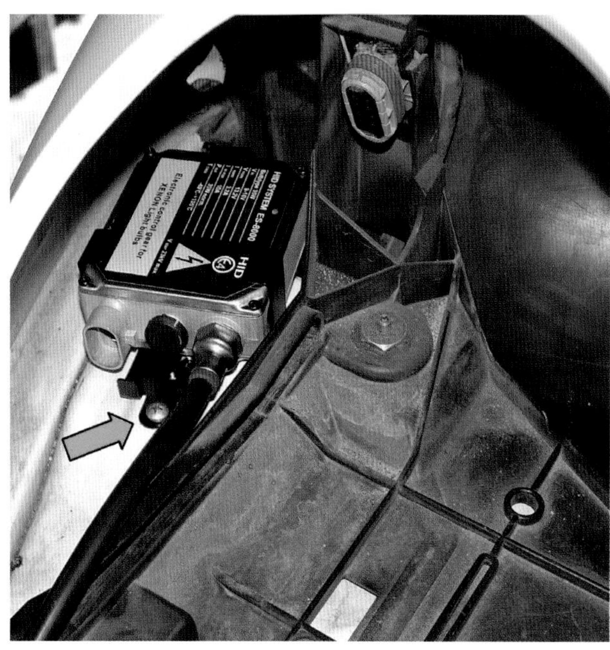

3 I found that a good mounting place for the ballast was on the side, right next to the headlamp tray. There is a flat spot there that is perfect for mounting the HID ballast unit. Clean the area carefully using isopropyl alcohol or glass cleaner and use double-sided sticky tape to secure the unit to the sheet metal. Reinforce the assembly by drilling a hole in the sheet metal and securing the bracket with a sheet metal screw (green arrow).

4 The finished product looks great and is very cost-effective when you compare the lamps to the stock Litronic ones available as a new or upgrade option on the Boxster (see Project 85).

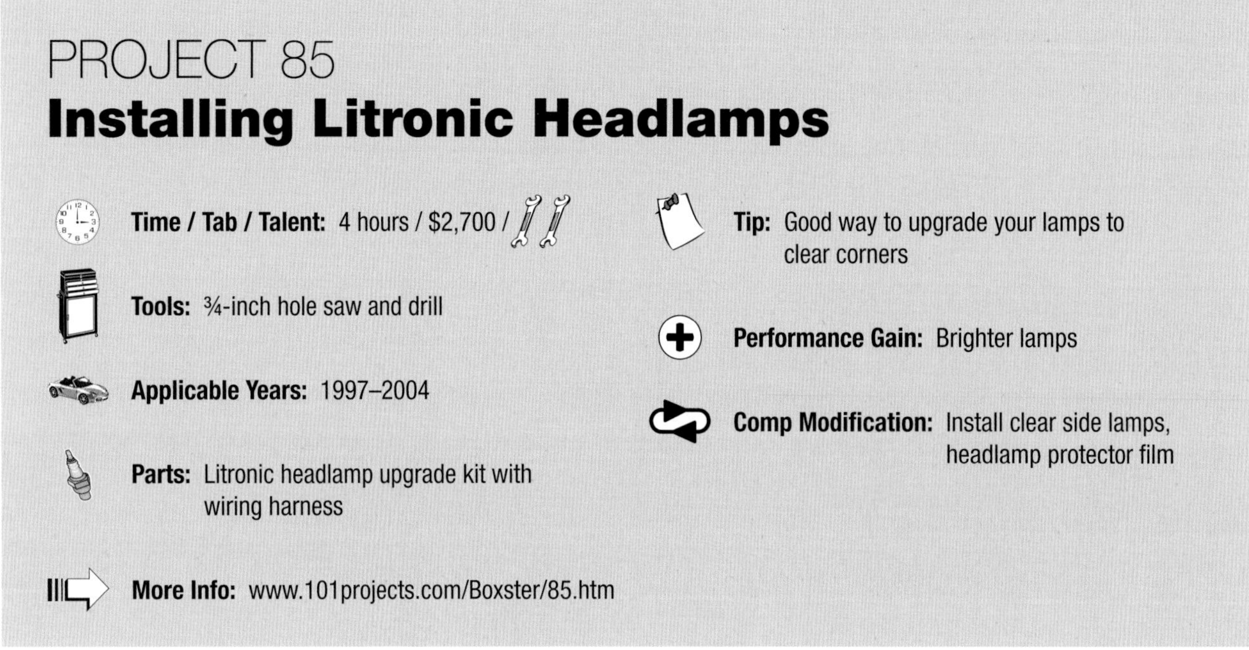

PROJECT 85
Installing Litronic Headlamps

Time / Tab / Talent: 4 hours / $2,700 /

Tools: ¾-inch hole saw and drill

Applicable Years: 1997–2004

Parts: Litronic headlamp upgrade kit with wiring harness

More Info: www.101projects.com/Boxster/85.htm

Tip: Good way to upgrade your lamps to clear corners

Performance Gain: Brighter lamps

Comp Modification: Install clear side lamps, headlamp protector film

One of the more exciting upgrades you can perform on your Boxster is the installation and upgrade of your lamps to the Bosch Litronic High Intensity Discharge (HID) system. While the "poor man's" version is detailed in Project 84, this project shows what's involved in installing the factory upgrade kit. There are quite a few compelling reasons why you would want to install the factory Litronic over a retrofit kit like the one detailed in Project 84. Firstly, the factory upgrade kit replaces your entire lamp assemblies. If your existing lamps are getting old, the lenses might begin to appear cloudy. Installing new headlamps with new lenses creates a dramatic facelift for your car. In addition, the Litronic upgrade kit uses the updated "clear corners" instead of the standard U.S.-spec orange ones.

It is important to note that the Porsche Litronic upgrade kit is different than the one installed at the factory when the cars were new. The factory-installed Litronic option is tightly integrated with the rest of the car's subsystems and as a result has additional features not found on the upgrade kit. The factory-installed kit will adjust the lamps up and down when the car is accelerating or braking to keep the light pattern aimed at the same level in the road at all times. In addition, the system is integrated with the central computer bus to pass fault codes if there is a problem. These are neat features, but they are not important enough to discourage you from installing the upgrade kit.

The procedure for installation is as simple as replacing the actual headlamp, as detailed in Project 65. However, there is an add-on controller module that you can install that will automatically rotate the orientation of the lamps up 1.5 degrees when the high beams are turned on. This change in the beam creates an improved light-filled pattern when the high beams are activated. Installation of this controller module is the primary focus of this project and is relatively easy if you're somewhat familiar with basic electrical wiring. The Porsche factory installation instructions can be found in Tech Bulletin 9415 for the Boxster.

The first step is to remove the battery cover and disconnect the battery (see Project 81). Then, remove your old headlamps (see Project 65). Unplug and remove the CD changer and/or amplifier from the front trunk if you have one. Remove the spare tire. Now, remove the front trunk liner. It's held on with plastic rivets that will almost guarantee to break. I suggest ordering new ones before you begin, part numbers 999-703-456-40 (qty 1), 999-703-432-40 (qty 8), and 999-703-455-40 (qty 2).

Next, remove the covers on the brake booster (see Photo 1 of Project 56) and the right side panel that covers the cabin filter (see Photo 6 of Project 3). Drill the wire harness holes as per Photo 3 and 4, and run the wire harness through these holes to the inside of the left and right fender. The left-side fender uses the longer portion of the wire harness. Insert the harness through the holes using the supplied grommets to seal around each hole. Next, install the pins into the connectors as detailed in Photo 5. Plug these connectors into the back of the headlamp assemblies and install them back into each fender.

Mount the control unit to the side of the front trunk compartment. Photo 3 shows an ideal spot for it where it will mount flat and be hidden under the front trunk carpet. Install the three wires that power and control the module. Attach the brown wire to ground. The white wire is tapped into the existing white wire in the connector assembly (see Photo 3)—this will signal the module that the high beams are on. The red wire is installed near the battery area where it gets constant power (see Photo 4).

After you install the Litronic kit, you should check the fuses in your fuse panel—they may need to be upgraded. Fuses A9 and A10 should be 15-amp fuses. If they are less than that, then swap them out. If you leave the stock 7.5-amp fuses in place, then they will probably blow under the increased current flow (see Photo 5 of Project 95).

Also important to note is that the small corner lenses do not come with the kit—you need to purchase them separately. The corner lenses are different depending upon whether you have a headlamp washer system or not. I recommend purchasing the clear corners instead of the standard unattractive U.S.-spec amber ones.

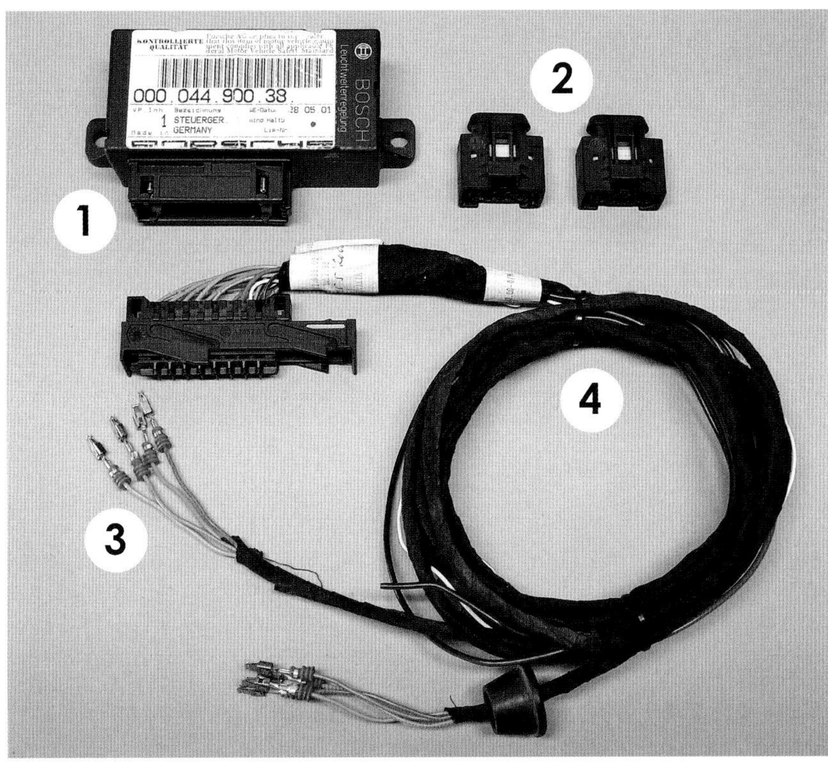

1 This photo shows the complete wiring kit that is required in order to install the factory Litronic headlamps. **1:** Electronic control unit, **2:** Harness connectors, **3:** Wire harness end-pins, **4:** Complete wiring harness.

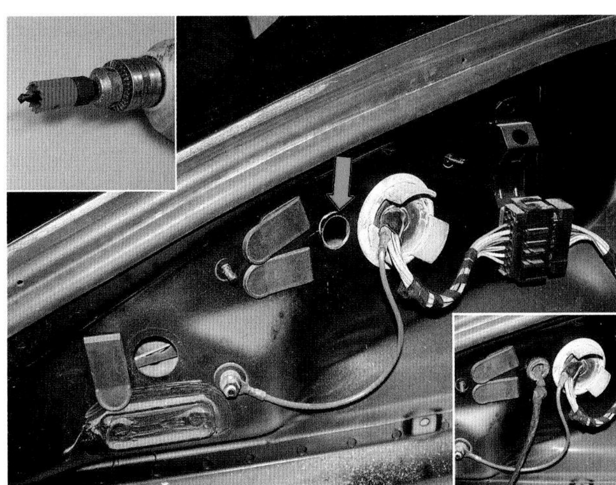

2 Begin the process by drilling a ¾-inch hole in the inside of the trunk on both the left and right side. Use a standard hole saw available at your local hardware store. The wires for the headlamp will run through this hole. Affix the grommet in place (lower right).

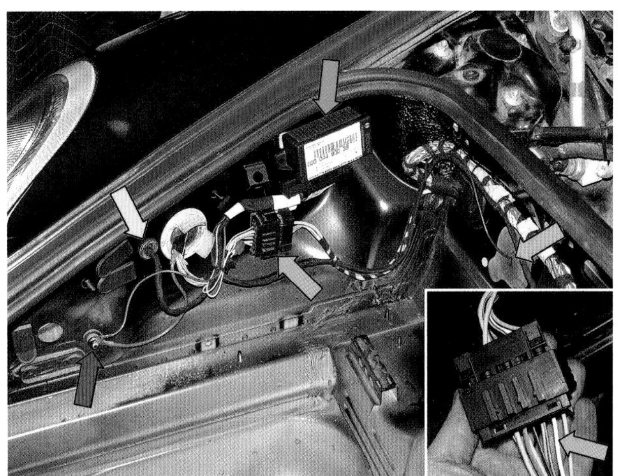

3 Install the control unit in the front trunk on the left side. Use Velcro or double-sided tape to affix the unit to the side of the trunk in the flat spot shown (green arrow). Thread the shorter of the two headlamp harnesses through the hole you drilled in the sheet metal and affix the grommet in place (yellow arrow). Attach the brown wire from the harness to the ground point (red arrow). Using a standard wire tap connector, tap the white wire from the new Litronic wire harness into the front side of the white wire exiting out of the connector (blue arrows). Finally, route the red wire up the existing wire harness and poke a small hole through the rubber plug in the firewall bulkhead (orange arrow).

4 The red arrow shows the location of where the ¾-inch hole should go on the left side of the car. The upper left shows a rubber plug located on the firewall, as shown from the side of the bulkhead right next to the battery (green arrow). The red/black wire needs to be tapped into the black/yellow wire that is connected to the plug for the right windshield washer nozzle (yellow arrow).

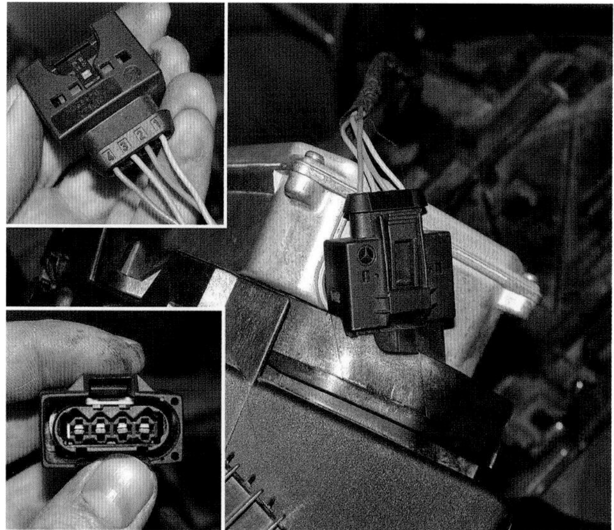

5 After threading the wire harness through the ¾-inch hole that you drilled in the sides of the front truck, place each of the pins into the wire connectors. **1:** Pink, **2:** Green, **3:** Gray, **4:** Purple (upper left). Make sure that they are well seated in the connector housing (lower left). Finally, plug them into the back of the Litronic headlamp unit.

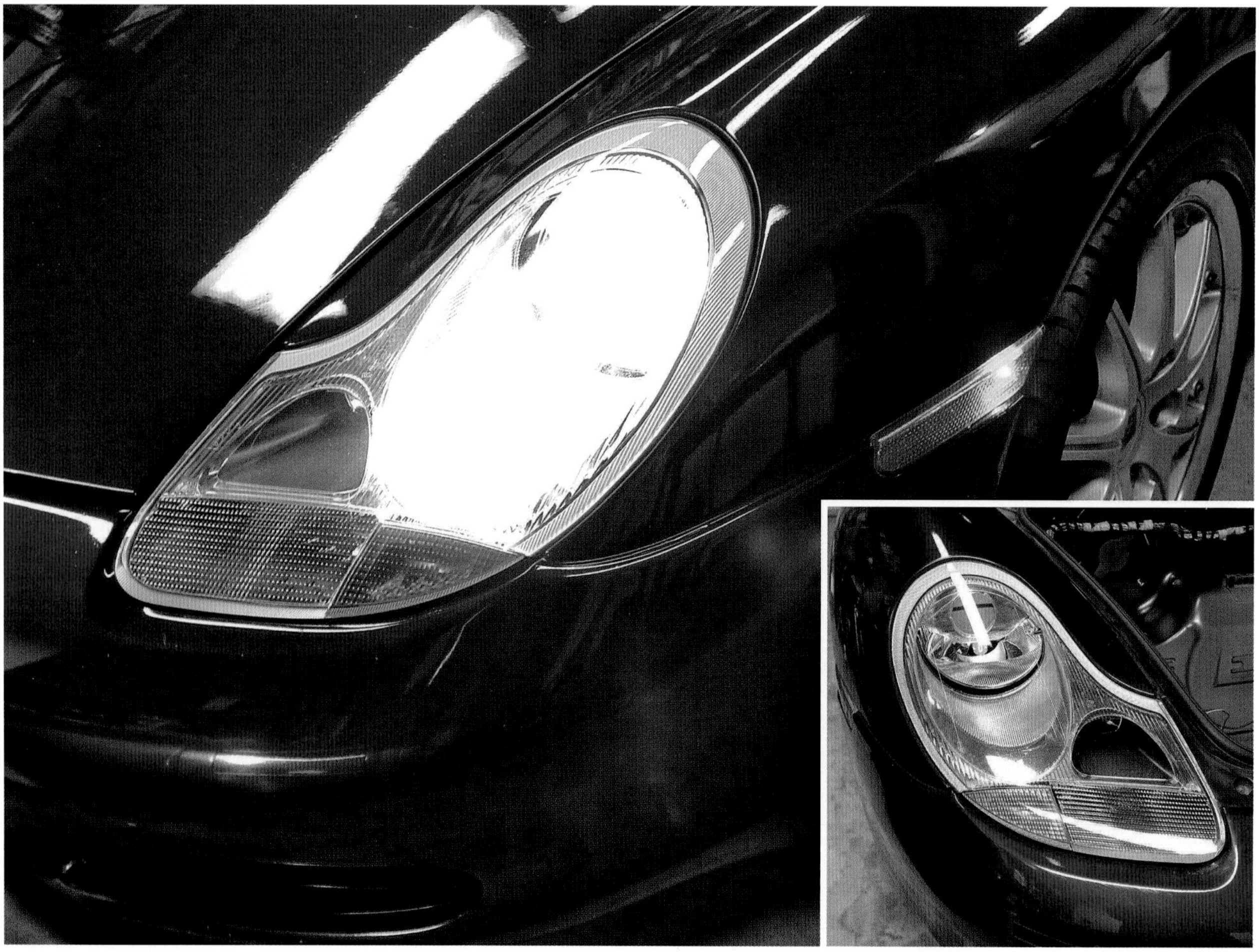

6 Not only do the Litronic xenon lamps look great at night, but you also get the "clear corner" look that vastly improves the look of your Boxster. Gone are the unsightly U.S.-spec orange turn signal lenses. The Litronic lamps use clear corners and orange-colored bulbs.

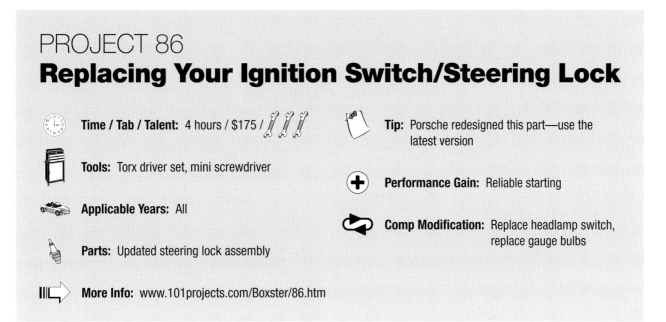

PROJECT 86
Replacing Your Ignition Switch/Steering Lock

Time / Tab / Talent: 4 hours / $175 /

Tools: Torx driver set, mini screwdriver

Applicable Years: All

Parts: Updated steering lock assembly

More Info: www.101projects.com/Boxster/86.htm

Tip: Porsche redesigned this part—use the latest version

Performance Gain: Reliable starting

Comp Modification: Replace headlamp switch, replace gauge bulbs

One of the most common electrical items to fail on some of the older Porsches is the ignition switch. This failure can show up in any number of ways. The car can refuse to start some of the time, the key may not turn too easily in the ignition, or strange electrical problems may appear. Either way, the correct solution is to replace all or part of the ignition switch.

The switch itself is comprised of two separate sections, one that holds the key and the lock mechanism and another that contains a somewhat complicated electrical switch that controls the starter and the other electrical systems of the car. The good news is that the electrical portion of the ignition switch can easily be replaced. The typical cost of this part ranges from $15–$40 depending upon which brand part you choose. If your key doesn't turn too well in the ignition, then chances are you have a worn out tumbler. You can attempt to rekey and refurbish the tumbler yourself, but the process can be quite difficult. It requires that you drill out a pin that has been pressed into the housing. If you make a mistake, you can damage the entire assembly. In other words, the ignition switch assembly wasn't really designed to be taken apart.

Early Boxsters had some problems with the ignition switch/steering lock assembly, and Porsche subsequently redesigned the part. If you're having problems with your ignition switch (as many Boxsters do), I recommend that you replace the whole mechanism. The electrical portion of the switch is different for this upgraded assembly, so be sure that you purchase the correct electrical switch to match what you have in your car. You may need to take some photos and compare what you have to the photos online in order to determine if your switch assembly has been upgraded or not. If you purchase an entirely new assembly, it should come complete with the electrical portion attached.

If you are replacing only the electrical portion of one of the early steering locks (part numbers 996-347-017-03 thru 996-347-017-06), then use part number 4B0-905-849. For the later steering lock, which was first used on 2004 cars (996-347-017-07), use part number 4A0-905-849B for the electrical portion replacement. If you're unsure of which one you have in your car, remove it first—the part number should be printed on it.

For 2005 and later models, the entire ignition switch/steering lock assembly was removed from the car and replaced with an electro-mechanical solenoid that locks the steering rack instead. You can only remove the locking mechanism after dismantling the entire steering system. In addition, removal of the locking device is only possible in the unlocked state. As of spring of 2010, I haven't heard of any reported problems with these solenoids needing replacement, but these cars are only five years old right now. In addition, the electrical switch is an entirely different and simpler design and is easy to remove. Simply pull off the rubber surround, as shown in Photo 2 and then unscrew the large nut underneath. Unplug the switch from underneath the dash and then remove it.

If you are only replacing the electrical portion of the switch (1997–2004), the project is quite easy. Simply remove the heater ductwork described in Photo 1 (it should pull out from underneath the dash with a few tugs). Disconnect the electrical plug by pulling it out of the back of the switch. Then, simply unscrew the set screws that hold the electrical portion to the back of the switch, and replace it with a new one. The switch has a locating pin cast into the housing, so there is only one way that it can be put back together.

Replacing the electrical portion could most certainly solve some ignition and starting problems. Electrical systems flickering on and off as you turn the key are a good clue that your switch is worn. Also, a bad switch sometimes causes unexplainable starting problems where the starter coil doesn't even click. I even had an experience with one car (not a Boxster) that wouldn't shut off the starter after the engine kicked over. Both the engine and the starter kept running together—even after I had removed the key!

If you are planning on replacing/upgrading your ignition lock assembly, then follow the steps laid out in Photo 2 and Photo 3. You will need to remove the headlamp switch (Project 87) and also the gauge cluster (Project 90) in order to gain access to the steering lock assembly.

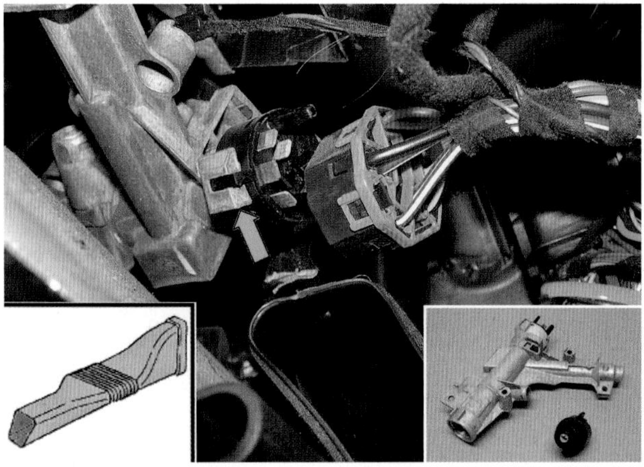

1 The electrical portion of the ignition switch can be accessed from underneath the dashboard. First, you need to remove the heater air duct (inset photo), which blocks your access to the switch. Pull out the connector and then loosen up the set screws that are located behind the red marking paint (blue arrow is pointing to one of the screws). Use a miniature flat-head screwdriver—access is tight, but the screws can be removed. Shown here (right inset) is the updated ignition cylinder/steering lock assembly. The assembly typically includes an electrical ignition switch (shown attached at the rear of the assembly and separately in the lower right).

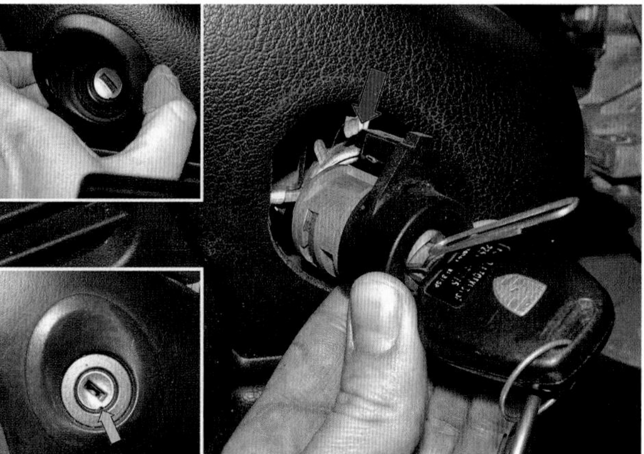

2 To remove the ignition key cylinder, first begin by pulling out the rubber ignition switch surround (upper left). Then, turn the ignition switch to position 1 (ignition ON), and insert a large paper clip into the release hole in the key cylinder (shown by the orange arrow). Push the paper clip in as far as possible, insert the key, and that should release the mechanism and allow you to pull out the assembly. Finally, disconnect the small connector that attaches to the immobilizer induction coil (red arrow).

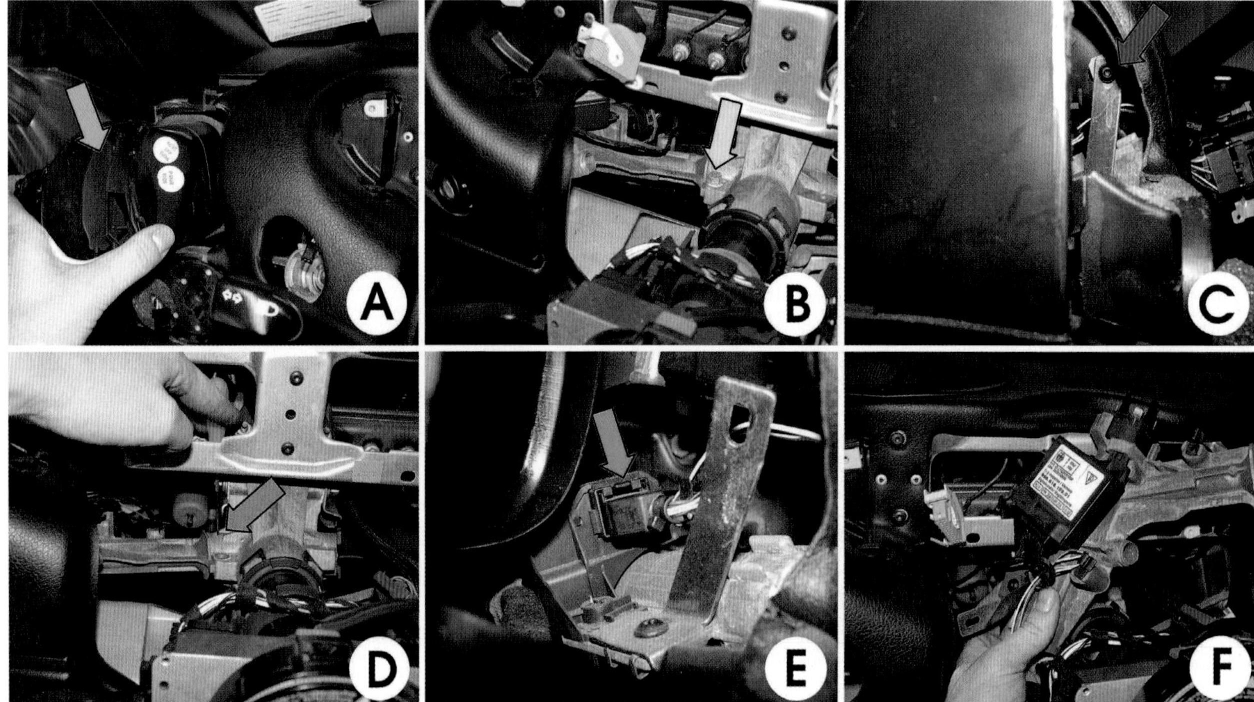

3 This photo details the steps required to remove the ignition cylinder/steering lock assembly. **A:** With the headlamp switch and side dashboard piece removed, pull out the heater duct (blue arrow). **B:** Remove the nut that fastens the lock assembly to the steering column (yellow arrow). **C:** From the left side of the dash, remove the Torx screw that holds the small bracket to the dash (red arrow). **D:** Using a small screwdriver, push down on the push lock pin to release the lock assembly from the steering column (purple arrow). **E:** Unplug the immobilizer harness (green arrow). **F:** Pull out the entire lock assembly from behind the steering column.

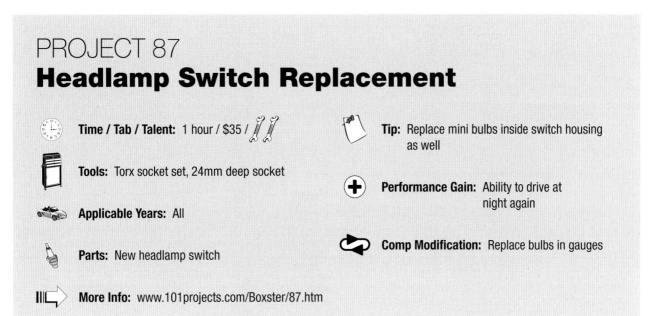

PROJECT 87
Headlamp Switch Replacement

 **Time / Tab / Talent:** 1 hour / $35 / 

Tip: Replace mini bulbs inside switch housing as well

 **Tools:** Torx socket set, 24mm deep socket

 **Performance Gain:** Ability to drive at night again

 **Applicable Years:** All

 **Comp Modification:** Replace bulbs in gauges

 **Parts:** New headlamp switch

 **More Info:** www.101projects.com/Boxster/87.htm

It's not uncommon to experience a failure of your headlamp switch. Years of repeated use and abuse have a tendency to take their toll on the switch. Some symptoms of a faulty switch include headlamps that won't turn on or perhaps inoperable fog lamps, just to name a few. In addition, there's a few small light bulbs contained within the switch housing that can burn out.

Replacement is fairly easy and only requires about an hour of your time. See the photos in this project for the breakdown of the replacement procedure. The only tricky part for some people may be the removal of the large nut that fastens the switch to the vent housing. If you have a 24mm deep socket, then you can simply place this socket on the nut and turn it by hand. If you don't have access to a deep socket this size, then you may have to resort to a pair of needle-nose pliers to remove the nut.

For the 2005 and later cars, the procedure is super simple. Press in the rotary knob on the light switch (but not to the limit) and turn the switch to the right. Then pull the entire switch assembly out.

The part number for the replacement switch is 996-613-535-00 (through 2004) or 997-613-535-01 (2005 and later), and it costs about $125 from the online catalog of PelicanParts.com.

1 Begin by removing the two screws on the leftmost side of the dash with a Torx driver. In the lower right is shown a brand new headlamp switch assembly.

2 Remove the headlamp knob by pressing on the release tab and then pulling off the knob (red arrow, upper left). With the knob removed, you can access the hidden Torx screw inside the inner bezel (yellow arrow).

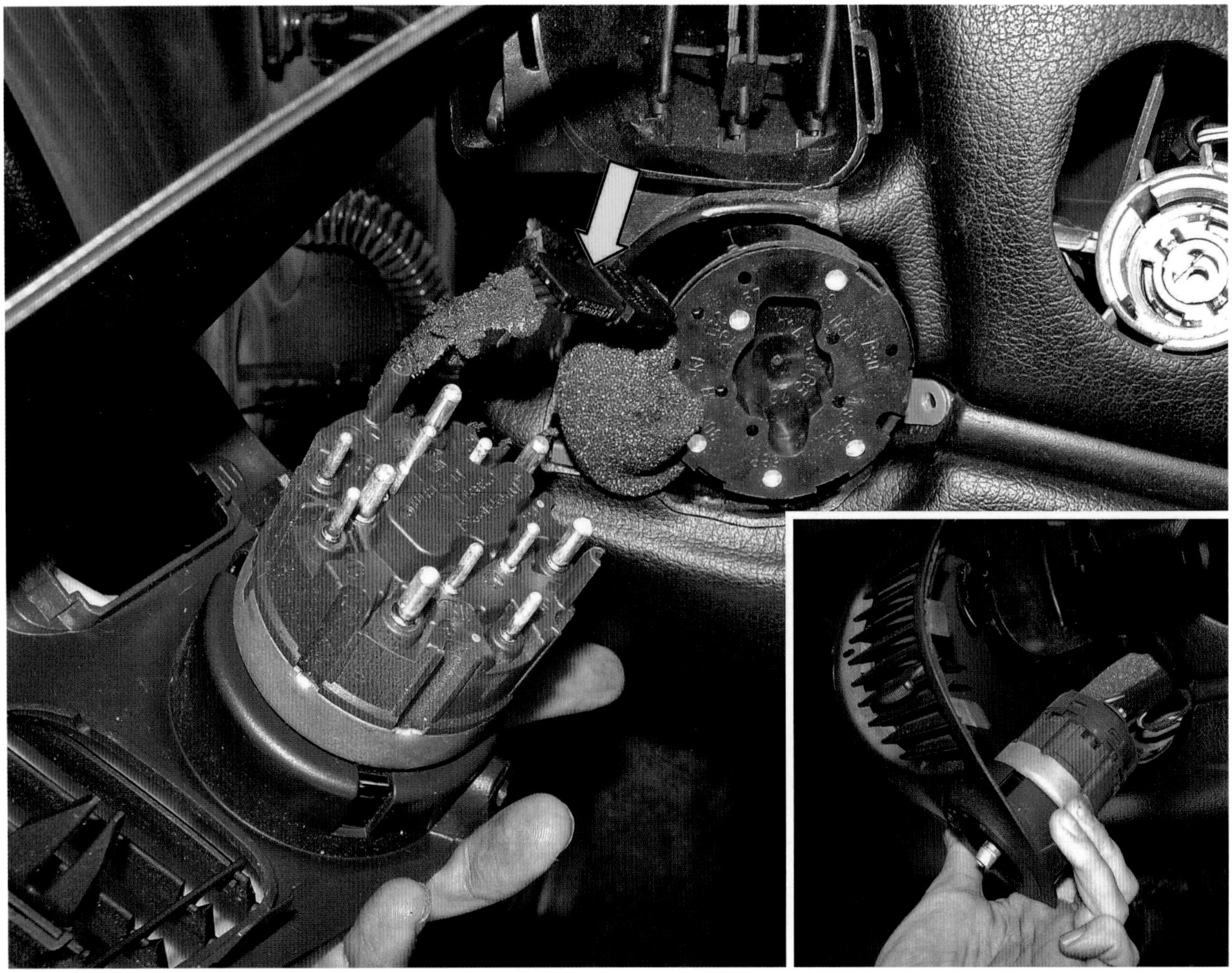

3 Pull off the side vent and headlamp switch together (lower right). Disconnect the large circular plug and then the smaller four-wire harness as well (yellow arrow). To remove the switch, simply unscrew the large nut on the face of the bezel (24mm deep socket).

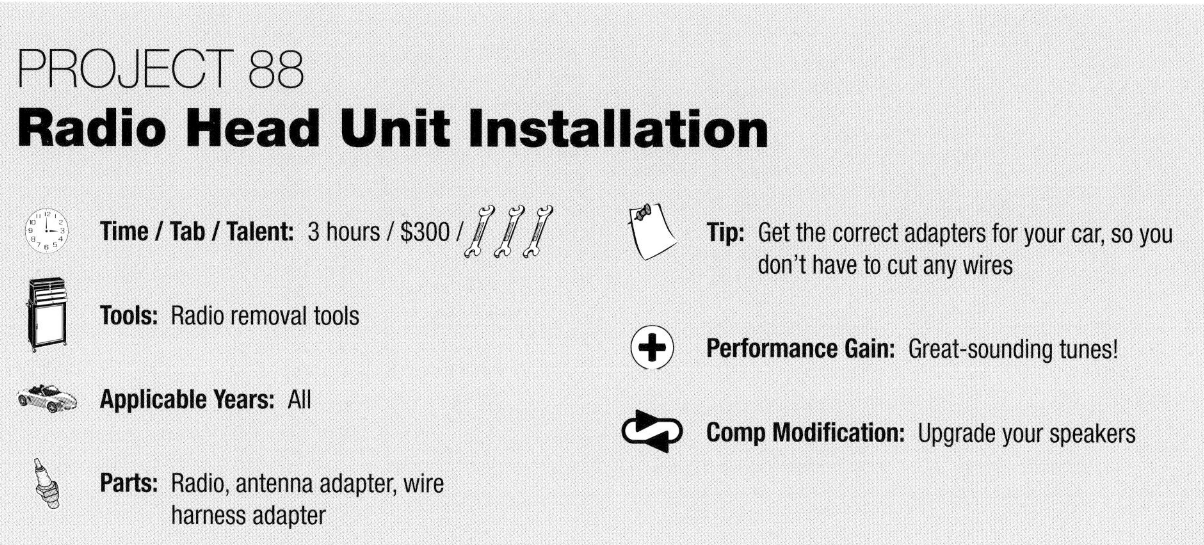

PROJECT 88
Radio Head Unit Installation

Time / Tab / Talent: 3 hours / $300 /

Tools: Radio removal tools

Applicable Years: All

Parts: Radio, antenna adapter, wire harness adapter

More Info: www.101projects.com/Boxster/88.htm

Tip: Get the correct adapters for your car, so you don't have to cut any wires

Performance Gain: Great-sounding tunes!

Comp Modification: Upgrade your speakers

One of the first projects many new Boxster owners perform on their car is to remove and replace their stereo head unit. I know that if I buy a car that has a weak stereo, it's one of the first things to go. The factory Porsche head units (manufactured by Becker) are best described as barely adequate—the technology is at least 10 years old in most cases, and the controls on the units are beyond terrible. This article specifically contains only wiring information for the 1997–2004 Boxsters, but is also applicable to the 2005 and later cars.

The good news is that the replacement process is relatively easy, providing you have the right information and the right parts. First, disconnect the battery (see Project 81). The radio harness has constant voltage supplied to it, and you don't want to accidentally blow any fuses or damage any electrical components. Using the set of factory radio removal tools (available from Becker, part number BNA-1184-989), pull out the radio as detailed in Photo 4 of Project 89. On the back of the unit, there may be a few wire connectors and a smaller antenna connector. Remove the antenna connector by simply tugging on it.

In order to install your new radio, you will need some cable adapters for the Boxster's wiring harness. The adapters plug into the factory connectors and have leads on them that you can then connect to the leads or connector on your new radio. You can cut the OEM connector off and tap directly into the factory harness, but I strongly caution against this—it's best to use the adapter cables (cost about $20). I put some spade connectors on the ends of the harness adapter and the connector that plugged into my new radio. The kits I used for my 2000 Boxster were Metra brand, PN: 70-1787 (VW/Bose AMP Integration), and the Euro antenna adapter kit from Scosche, PN: VWA-KB (Volkswagen Antenna Adapter Kit). This antenna adapter kit contains two adapters so that you can use an aftermarket stereo and/or install an inline FM modulator iPod interface (see below). These kit part numbers should be good for all of the Boxsters through 2004. For 2005 and up models, check the radio you have in your car before you order the adapters.

In general, the most difficult part of installing a new radio is figuring out how to wire it. I've done all of the legwork for you here by putting together this handy wiring chart (1997–2004). The green connector and blue connector on the back of the radio are for the operation of the CD changer, if your car has one (mounted in the front trunk, see 101Projects.com website for pinouts on those connectors).

If your car does not have an external amplifier, then the speakers for the Boxster will plug directly into the brown connector B on the back of the radio. If your Boxster has an external amplifier, then there will be a smaller yellow connector that outputs the signals from the head unit to the amplifier. If you have a factory amplifier installed, then you can simply adapt the signal from your new stereo into the leads on the yellow plug, as I have done with this stereo installation. If not, then you simply hook up the speaker leads from the new stereo to the adapter that plugs into the brown connector.

Wire your harness adapter together according to the wiring chart and the instructions included with your new radio. Plug the harness adapter into the factory connector, and then plug the harness into the back of the head unit and connect all of the spade connectors. On this particular head unit, I found that the antenna jack on the back of the unit was not compatible with the one in the factory harness, so

Color	Purpose	Connector and Pin
Gray/Pink	Speed Dependent Vol Control	Black Connector A – Pin 1
	unused	Black Connector A – Pin 2
Yellow/Black	Mute for Telecom Interface	Black Connector A – Pin 3
Red/Black (thick)	Constant Power 12 V (Fuse D8)	Black Connector A – Pin 4
White	Power Antenna Control	Black Connector A – Pin 5
Gray/Blue	Illumination (headlamps on)	Black Connector A – Pin 6
Orange	12 Volt Switched Power (Fuse E1)	Black Connector A – Pin 7
Brown (thick)	Chassis Ground	Black Connector A – Pin 8
Green	Right Rear Speaker Positive	Brown Connector B – Pin 1
Green/Black	Right Rear Speaker Negative	Brown Connector B – Pin 2
Red	Right Front Speaker Positive	Brown Connector B – Pin 3
Red/Brown	Right Front Speaker Negative	Brown Connector B – Pin 4
Yellow	Left Front Speaker Positive	Brown Connector B – Pin 5
Yellow/Brown	Left Front Speaker Negative	Brown Connector B – Pin 6
Violet	Left Rear Speaker Positive	Brown Connector B – Pin 7
Violet/Black	Left Rear Speaker Negative	Brown Connector B – Pin 8
Yellow/Red	Left Rear Line Output Positive	Yellow Connector C – Pin 1
Red/Blue	Right Rear Line Output Positive	Yellow Connector C – Pin 2
Brown/Blue	Common Audio Ground	Yellow Connector C – Pin 3
Green/Red	Left Front Line Output Positive	Yellow Connector C – Pin 4
Violet/Red	Right Front Line Output Positive	Yellow Connector C – Pin 5
Black/Red	12 Volt Switched Power	Yellow Connector C – Pin 6
Blue	CD Changer – BUS On	Green Connector C – Pin 7
Red	CD Changer – Battery	Green Connector C – Pin 8
Black	CD Changer – Ground	Green Connector C – Pin 9
Green	CD Changer – Data	Green Connector C – Pin 10
Yellow	CD Changer – Clock	Green Connector C – Pin 11
Violet	CD Changer – Reset	Green Connector C – Pin 12
Blue/Green	Telephone Audio	Blue Connector C – Pin 13
Blue/Yellow	Telephone Audio Common	Blue Connector C – Pin 14
	unused	Blue Connector C – Pin 15
	unused	Blue Connector C – Pin 16
	unused	Blue Connector C – Pin 17
Brown	CD Changer – Common Audio Ground	Blue Connector C – Pin 18
Yellow	CD Changer – Left	Blue Connector C – Pin 19
Red	CD Changer – Right	Blue Connector C – Pin 20

I needed the antenna adapter mentioned previously. Plug the adapter into the back of the unit, and then you should be able to plug the antenna cable into the unit. With the new head unit wired up, reconnect the battery and turn it on to test it. If all of the speakers, radio, and lights work, then install the radio bracket into the center dashboard. This is the bracket that comes with your new unit and typically has tabs that you bend into place once you position the bracket. When the bracket is secure, simply slide the radio into its spot on the center dashboard. Be careful though—most of these units are designed to be easy to install, but very difficult to remove, so make sure that everything works before inserting it into the dashboard.

The radio I chose to use for this project was a Pioneer head unit with a built-in CD player and iPod support. These types of head units allow you to plug your iPod into the stereo and then choose and select songs to play from the stereo itself. In addition, the stereo charges the iPod while it's playing. This arrangement is very cool, but I don't recommend it if you happen to have an iPhone. One of the coolest features of the iPhone is its ability to stream music from alternative sources like Pandora or SimplifyMedia. For iPhone users, I recommend the installation of an FM modulator interface that allows you to play music from the iPhone onto the stereo by emulating a radio station. Using this setup, you can listen to any music on the iPhone and/or any music that may be provided by a music service that streams music over the cell phone network. For example, using the DICE Electronics FM adapter installation detailed in Photo 3, I am able to listen to music streamed off of my home computer, through the cell phone network, and to the car, as I am driving. I'm sure the technology will change and get better as time passes, but this is the best that's available as of 2010.

Another way of playing through the stock radio with virtually no cost at all is by using the AUX input. The factory radio CDR-220 has the ability to take input from an external source. You can purchase a blue connector plug from Becker (PN: 1319.116-276) that will fit into the back of the radio and interface with your external source, or you can tap into the blue plug that is provided as part of the CD changer interface. Tap into and wire up your input source (iPod, etc.) using the three wires that exit out of the blue connector (pins 18, 19, 20). Then turn the radio on, and then hold down the TP button until the message BECKER 1 is displayed. Then turn the tuning knob until the message AUX OFF is displayed. Press the down arrow and change the message to AUX ON. Turn the radio off and back on, and now you have auxiliary input enabled.

The little radio knobs on the stock radios are pretty terrible and often deteriorate with age. You can purchase new ones from Porsche (PN: 996-645-901-00) or check the 101Projects.com for a tip about how to refurbish your old ones.

The Boxster alarm system has a small contact switch located to the left side of the radio compartment that detects removal of the radio. In order to prevent the alarm from repeatedly going off, you need to connect this wire (brown/blue) to ground.

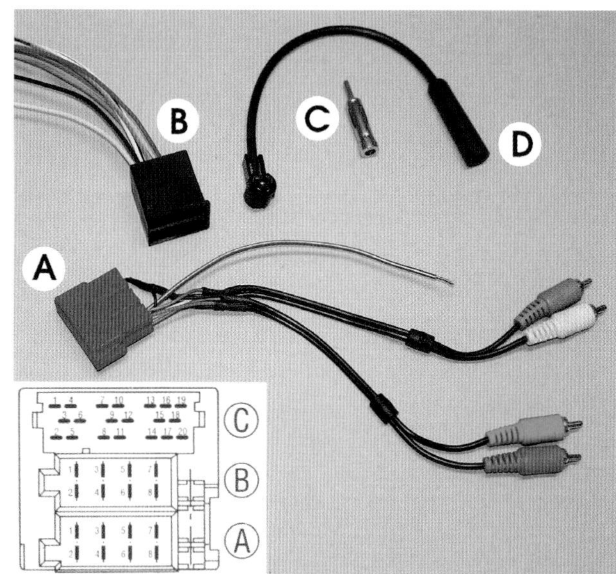

1 Shown here are the adapter harnesses I used for this installation. **A:** This harness emulates plug C on the radio and breaks the signal up into RCA jacks that you can plug into the back of your new head unit. Be sure to properly connect up the blue wire as well, which sends the signal to power up the amplifier. **B:** This plug is the main plug that supplies power to the radio. **C:** This is the antenna adapter for the back of the new radio. It converts the long tube-style plug into the smaller, European-style connector. **D:** This reverse antenna adapter is required along with the other one if you are using the iPod FM modulator interface. When connecting the harness adapters, I recommend using simple spade connectors to link the two together. In general, I do not recommend cutting wires in your car—it becomes very difficult to fix and/or restore the electrical system back to stock if anything goes wrong.

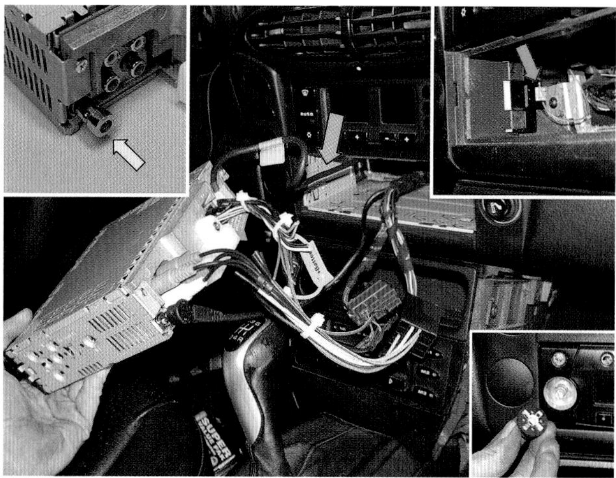

2 Shown here is the new radio ready for installation into the car. The yellow arrow shows the antenna adapter installed. The bracket is installed into the center dashboard (blue arrow), ready for the radio. The factory harness is connected to the adapter, and the connector for the radio is plugged into the back of the new head unit. It's normal to have one or two wires that are not used. In this photo, I plugged in all of the connections and then turned on the ignition to test the proper operation of the radio. I recommend testing prior to the final installation, as these radios are designed to be difficult to remove. New buttons for your stock radio are easy to install—simply pull them off and push on the new ones (inset, lower right). The green arrow shows the alarm radio detection switch, which must be grounded when installing a new unit.

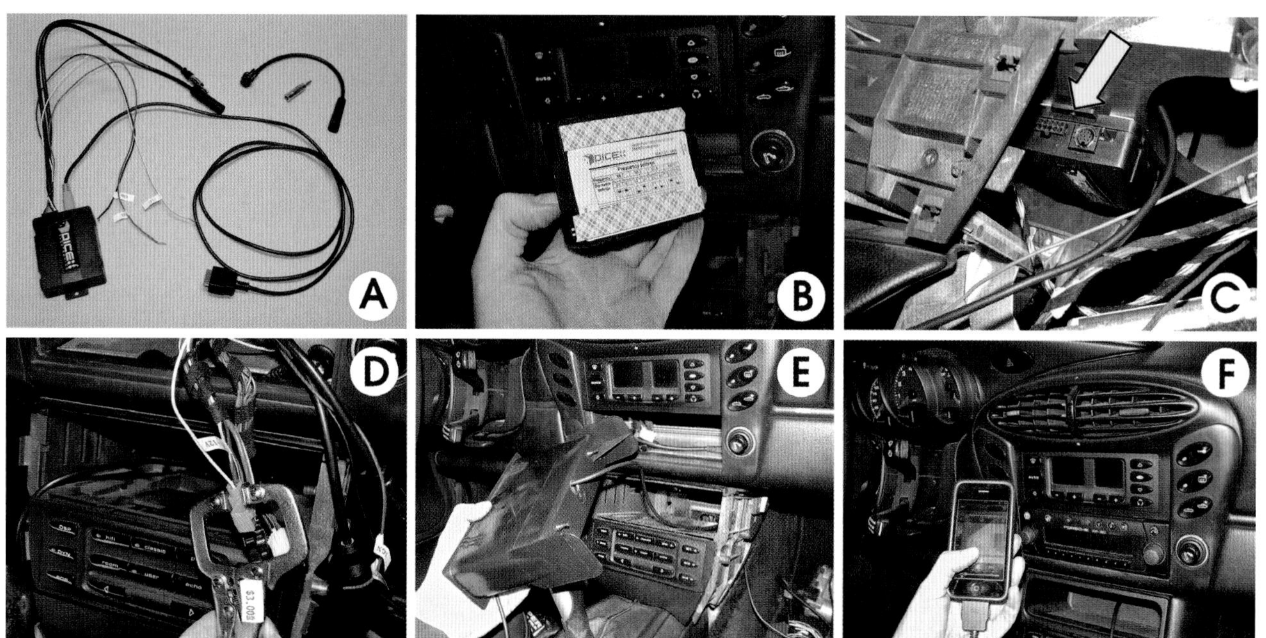

3 This photo array shows the installation of the DICE universal iPod adapter. **A:** Here is the FM modulator kit as it comes out of the box. You also need the Scosche VWAKB antenna adapter set (shown in the upper right) to work with the factory radio and its European connectors. **B:** Mount the DICE unit with double-sided sticky tape. **C:** Mount it on the underside of the center console and give yourself enough room to access the connectors (yellow arrow). **D:** Use three tap-in connectors to connect the unit to the 12V supply, the ignition 12V switched supply, and the ground. Plug in the antenna adapters and the inline antenna cable. **E:** Drill a hole in the back of the storage compartment and route the iPod cable through. **F:** Test the system and then reinstall the stereo. Although there are many different iPod adapter units available on the market, this particular one has the ability to display the iPod song and artist on the radio through the FM-RDS protocol. I tested the unit and compared the sound quality to the CD input—it was indistinguishable. The only small drawback appears to be that the volume level of the iPod interface is a bit lower than simply playing CDs.

PROJECT 89
Installing the Rear Speaker Kit

Time / Tab / Talent: 4 hours / $400 / 

Tools: Torx driver

Applicable Years: All

Parts: Rear speaker components

More Info: www.101projects.com/Boxster/89.htm

Tip: Can be used with the factory stereo or aftermarket kits

Performance Gain: Great sounding stereo

Comp Modification: Install a new stereo head unit

Almost all two-seater roadsters suffer from poor audio from the car stereo. The Boxster is no exception, as it only has a few speakers located in the doors and the dashboard to overcome the loud wind noise that often accompanies open-top driving. In order to compensate, Porsche developed a rear speaker kit that places four small speakers into the left and right compartments of the optional rear storage compartment. The result is very good—the stereo sounds great with these additional speakers—as good or better than the $3,000 premium stereo option that Porsche used to offer for these cars.

Unfortunately, the plug-in kit that was available from Porsche for many years is now no longer available. You can still create the kit from each of the individual components, which I've listed in this table:

Part Number	Description	Qty
986-551-431-00-01C-OEM	SPEAKER MOUNT, LEFT	1
986-551-432-00-01C-OEM	SPEAKER MOUNT, RIGHT	1
986-551-433-00-01C-OEM	SPEAKER COVER, LEFT	1
986-551-434-00-01C-OEM	SPEAKER COVER, RIGHT	1
986-612-085-00-OEM	SPEAKER WIRING HARNESS	1
986-645-503-00-OEM	AUTO STEREO SPEAKER	4
999-651-286-02-OEM	CABLE CLAMP CLIP	9

You can also mix and match factory and aftermarket parts to create your own speaker kit. The two speaker covers are the most important part of the project—with them in place, you can insert small 3-inch speakers of your choosing and custom mount them as needed. The 2005 and later cars came with a different speaker subwoofer package that used the rear storage compartment, but you can still install the earlier-style speaker (pre-2005) into the later cars with some modifications.

You also need the wire that connects from the back of the radio to the speakers themselves. This is dependent upon the radio that you have in your car—the factory radio uses a harness that is available direct from Becker USA for about $50 and is part number 5001.211-276. If you have an aftermarket stereo, the best option is to create your own wire harness that connects from the radio to the speaker plug where it exits out of the storage enclosure (see inset A of Photo 5).

If your Boxster doesn't have the rear storage compartment installed, then you will have to purchase the parts required for its installation. These are the following:

Part Number	Description
986 551 223 00 EMY (1997-04) 987 551 223 01 FNF (2005-)	Storage compartment with black carpet (available in different colors to match your interior)
986 551 427 00 01C	Rose
986 551 429 00 01C	Catch (2 required)
986 551 543 00 01C	Washer (2 required)

The Porsche part number for the kit was PNA 986 KIT. The kit was shipped with rudimentary instructions and a subset of information taken from the Porsche Boxster Technical Information Bulletin 0001 9142.

The first step is to remove the storage compartment from the car. See Project 3 for more information on this procedure. With the storage unit out of the car, move it over to your workbench and remove the three Torx screws from each of the two side storage bins. Use a Dremel tool to remove the glue that holds each storage bin in place. Be careful with the Dremel tool—don't cut through or damage the face of the storage compartment. Use a hobby knife to remove any excess glue, then depress the tabs on the storage bins and remove them. Work carefully during this process as the plastic material in the storage compartment unit is thin and easily damaged.

Now, snap the speaker grilles into place within the storage compartment, making sure that the top edge of the grille is properly seated in the groove in the storage compartment. Using a hot-glue gun or plastic cement, glue the edges of the speaker grilles. Doing this will ensure a rattle-free installation.

With the grilles in place, install the speakers as shown in Photo 2. Use the Torx screws that were previously holding in the left and right storage bins. Route the wires for the speakers using the wire clips. Route the wire and place the clips as shown in Photo 3. When all of the glue from the speaker grilles has dried, reinstall the rear compartment into the car.

Now, you need to route the wire from the radio to the speakers (see Photo 5). If you don't have the Becker factory harness handy, then simply run two pairs of speaker wire instead. Begin by removing the right side rear panel, which covers the seat belt and roll bar mounting point. Install the end of the radio harness clip into roll bar crossbrace—rotate it 90 degrees to snap it in place. If you don't have the factory harness, then you will need to head to your local electronics store and get a four-prong male/female connector combo.

On the side of the car, remove the umbrella compartment and remove the passenger side lower dash cover, which is fixed in place by two large plastic screws. At this time remove the radio. Route your wire from the rear speaker plug down the side of the car, up the side of the passenger side footwell, and to the rear of the radio compartment (see Project 75 for details on snapping off the side panels on the center console). Insert the pins into the connector and then insert the connector into your radio. Depending upon which radio you have, you will have to get a connector appropriate for plugging in the rear speakers. Almost all aftermarket radios have existing wires for these rear speakers. Also, if you have a car with an external amplifier, you will have to plug it into that instead of the head unit. When you're done, reconnect the battery, enter the radio code, and test your new speakers!

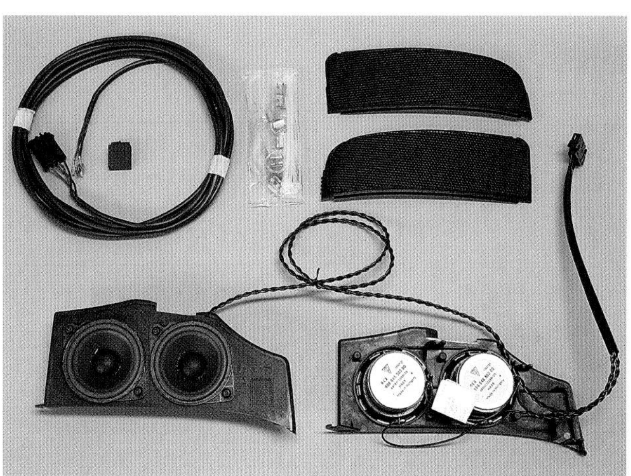

1 Shown here are the components that comprise the Genuine Porsche Boxster rear speaker kit, which was taken before they became unavailable. You can still purchase all of these parts separately, but the key component is the custom-fit speaker grilles that fit into the storage compartment.

2 The rear speakers are installed into the rear storage compartment tray. The kit was originally a factory-installed option (it came with the upgraded stereo package), so the storage compartment tray is designed to accept the speaker enclosure and the grilles as well. The upper right inset photo shows where you screw the speaker into the tray. Route the wires using the included clips as per the photo inset in the lower left. The main wire leading to the radio should be routed out the corner on the right side of the car (green arrow).

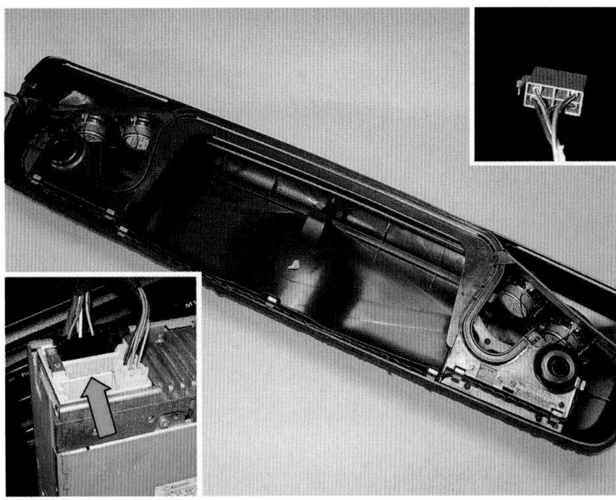

3 Shown here is the completed installation of the speakers into the storage tray compartment. The green arrow points to the spot on the back of the radio where the plug fits. The plug is a standard Audi plug and is shown in the upper right inset photo.

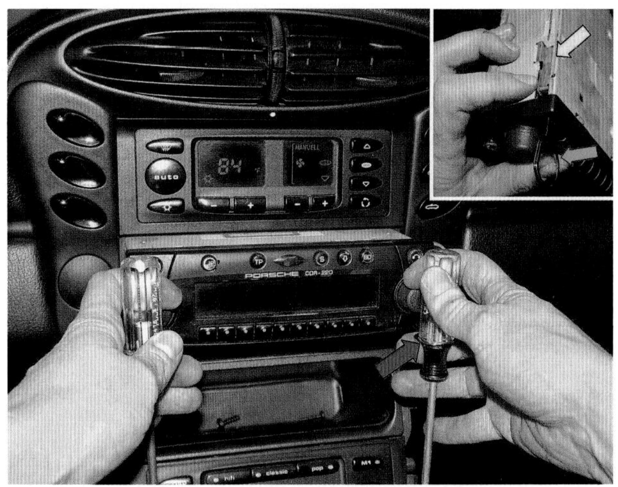

4 In order to plug in the rear speaker connection, you need to remove your radio. Use the radio removal keys (available direct from Becker and also supplied with the factory kit, green arrow) to pull out the radio by inserting them into the head unit and pulling on the two keys using two screwdrivers (red arrow). The unit should slide right out. The keys release the spring-loaded locking mechanism on the side of the radio (yellow arrow). I recommend disconnecting the battery prior to removing the radio (see Project 81). Also make sure that you have your radio security code handy when you unplug the unit.

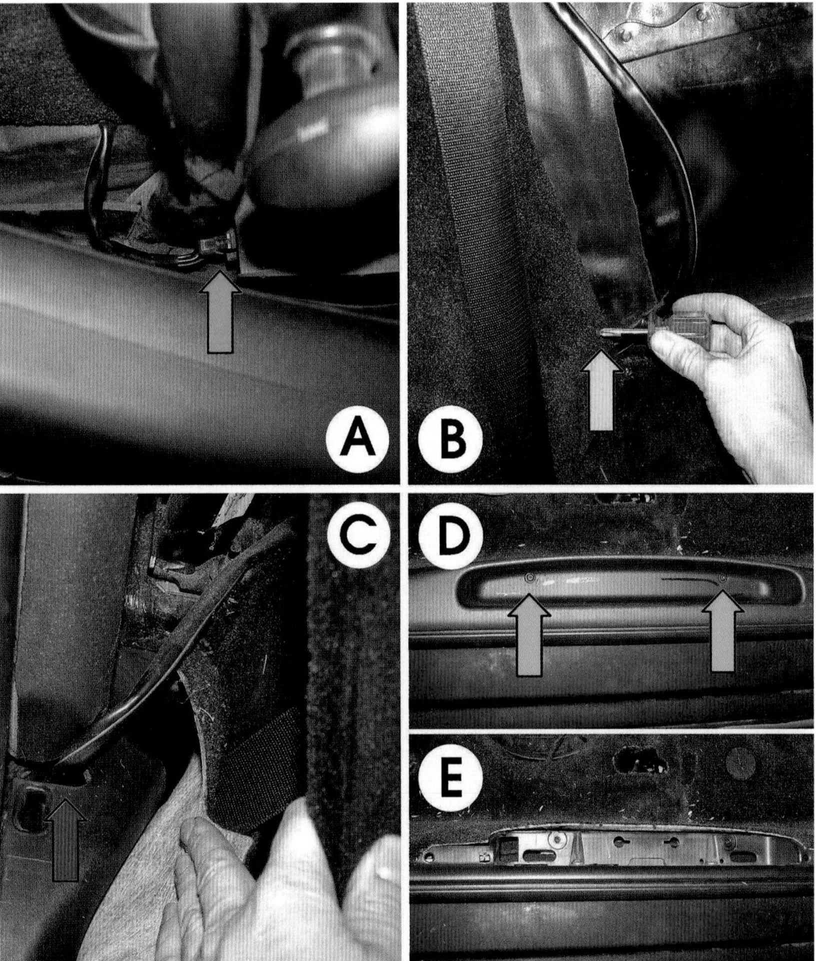

5 This photo shows the process of routing the cable from the speakers to the radio. **A:** The wire from the speakers in the storage tray plugs into the harness that runs down the side of the car. These two plugs clip into a holder on the left side of the car. **B:** Behind the passenger seat, remove the screws that hold on the carpeted panel (difficult to see with dark interiors). Remove the screw at the top too (see Photo 2E of Project 92). **C:** At the bottom of the door jamb, route the wire underneath the plastic panel that runs across the door. **D:** The "umbrella pocket" hides two screws that you need to remove in order to access the area underneath. **E:** Run the wire down the side of the car underneath this panel. Be aware of the side-impact air bag sensors located nearby.

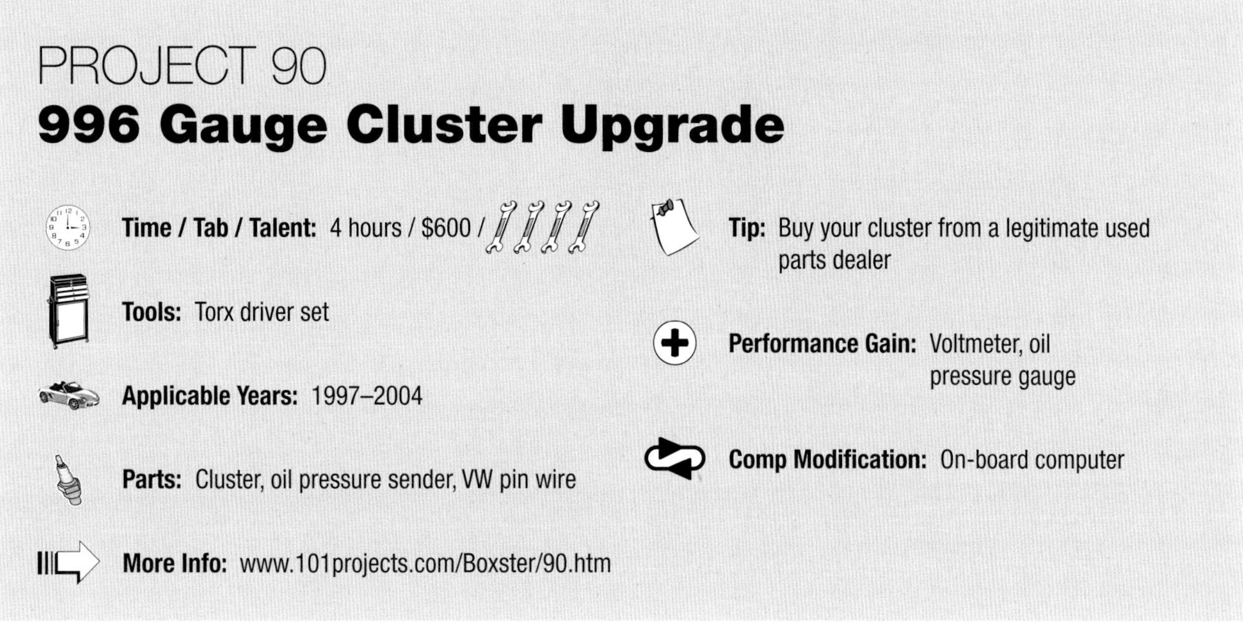

PROJECT 90
996 Gauge Cluster Upgrade
Time / Tab / Talent: 4 hours / $600 /
Tools: Torx driver set
Applicable Years: 1997–2004
Parts: Cluster, oil pressure sender, VW pin wire
More Info: www.101projects.com/Boxster/90.htm
Tip: Buy your cluster from a legitimate used parts dealer
Performance Gain: Voltmeter, oil pressure gauge
Comp Modification: On-board computer

One of the neat upgrades that you can perform on your Boxster is to install the Porsche 911 (996) gauge cluster into your dashboard. The 996 cluster has two additional gauges, a voltmeter and an oil pressure gauge, that you can hook up and make operational. In addition, the later-style 996 gauges have an improved dot-matrix-style screen that is an upgrade from the original style. The actual swap of the gauge cluster is not very difficult, but there are some elements of the entire project that can be challenging.

WHICH CLUSTER TO PURCHASE?

The first difficulty lies in figuring out which 996 gauge cluster to purchase for your Boxster. There were several different clusters manufactured for both the Boxster and the 996, and only some of them are compatible with each other. In general, there are two different types of clusters, an early-style and later improved-style with a dot-matrix display. The 1997–2000 Boxsters can only use the early style, and the 2001–2004 Boxsters can only use the late-style. You can easily tell the difference between the two by the color and shape of the connectors on the back of the gauge cluster. Early-style clusters have a blue, white, and black connector. Late-style clusters have connectors that are gray, blue, and green. The two different types of clusters are not interchangeable.

I recommend that you purchase your used cluster from a reputable used parts dealer. I'm guessing that a lot of the gauge clusters that end up on classified and auction sites might be rejects from warranty replacements. The gauge clusters can be very expensive (I paid $500 for mine from a used parts dealer), so making sure that you get one from a reputable source is very important. The cluster I used for my Boxster came out of a wrecked 996.

In addition, you must make sure that you match the transmission type and region type. If you are located in the United States, be sure that you get a cluster that is a U.S.-spec unit and has the main speedometer gauge delimited in mph. European gauges will show km/h. Also be sure that you purchase a cluster that will match the type of transmission you have. The Tiptronic clusters are different than the manual transmission ones because they have the current gear selector display on the right side of the cluster.

For the **1997–2000 Boxster,** you need to find an instrument cluster from a C2, not a C4. This is because the early C4s have a different gas tank and a different fuel sending system that is not compatible with the Boxster. If you install an early C4 cluster into an early Boxster, then your fuel gauge will not operate properly. In addition, the very early C2 cars used a different fuel level sender than the one that is used in the Boxster. As a result, installing an early C2 cluster into a Boxster may not give you the most accurate fuel gauge reading (although I did install one on my project Boxster, and it appears to be working okay). Also, the on-board computer (see Project 91) was not always included as standard equipment in the early Carreras—if you get a cluster from a car that doesn't have the computer built-in, then you will need to turn it on with the PST-2. For these reasons, I recommend using a cluster from a 2000–2001 Carrera 2. Part numbers have changed over the years, but two sample part numbers for this range are 996-641-105-02 (manual) and 996-641-106-02 (Tiptronic). The cluster may have an additional code at the end of the part number, which is the color code (70C corresponds to black, for example).

For the **2001–2004 Boxster,** you can use any non-Turbo 996 cluster from the years 2002–2004. This can be from a C2 or a C4—the clusters were modified in these later years to eliminate the problems that were inherent with the earlier C4 clusters. Ideally, you should try to find a cluster from a cabriolet car so that you won't have to recode the cluster to enable the convertible top lamp (coupe clusters can be recoded to make the convertible top lamp operational with the Porsche factory programming tool, PST-2). As with the earlier cars, be sure to match the cluster with your transmission type (manual versus Tiptronic). The on-board computer was standard equipment on all 2002–2004 Carreras, so the best cluster to use is one from a convertible within the year range of 2002–2004. I also highly recommend that you install the control switches for the on-board computer (see Project 91). A cluster from a 2001 Carrera is not correct for a 2001 Boxster—use a 2002 or later cluster. Part numbers have changed over the years, but two sample part numbers for this are 996-641-980-20 (manual) or 996-642-980-21 (Tiptronic).

WHICH GAUGE POD TO USE?

There are two methods you can use to physically install the gauge cluster into the dash of your Boxster. The standard Boxster gauge pod has a bridge that extends over the gauges, so there's a gap between the gauges and the top of the pod. The 996 gauge pod does away with this bridge. You can purchase the 996 cluster with the corresponding 996 gauge surround, but then you lose this cool-looking bridge between the gauges and the top of the pod (the 996 doesn't have this). The 996 gauge pods are also very expensive. If you do go this route, be sure to get one that matches the interior of your car and also get the hazard switch and surround included as these are different on the 996 pod.

For my car, I preferred to modify my own gauge pod. Basically, you take the existing Boxster pod and cut away some of the plastic to make the 996 cluster fit. This keeps the "bridge" look of the Boxster pod and also saves you a considerable amount of money because you don't have to purchase a 996 gauge pod. The trimming procedure is straightforward, but it requires some attention to detail and a bit of patience to complete properly. See Photo 4 for details.

INSTALLATION

Before you begin the installation, I recommend that you make sure the car has a tank of gas that is more than one-half full. There have been sporadic reports of the clusters becoming slightly confused when installed and reset with a tank of gas that is less than half empty. I recommend making sure you have about three-quarters of a tank prior to installation. To prepare your gauge cluster, make sure that it has a light bulb installed in the convertible top lamp holder (for 2001 and earlier 996 clusters). If your cluster came from a coupe car, then there probably won't be any bulb installed there.

The first step is to disconnect the battery (see Project 81). Then, remove the Boxster cluster (see Photo 2 and Photo 3). Then remove the access panel to the engine compartment behind the seats (see Project 5) and also the engine compartment lid under the convertible top (see Project 3). The Boxster engines only have an oil pressure switch, which turns on a warning lamp on the dash when the oil pressure drops below a certain level. In order for the 996 cluster's oil pressure gauge to

2 Here are the steps for removing the cluster. **A:** Pull out the microphone cover and remove the Torx screw underneath. **B:** Pull out the hazard switch button and remove the Torx screw underneath. **C:** Using some long pliers, grab the white plastic part of the hazard switch (shown in B) and pull it out of its plug (press on the two black tabs on either side of the white plastic switch and pull in the direction of the red arrow). Then, slide the black connector in the direction of the green arrow. **D:** Lift the gauge cluster up so that you can disconnect the wire harnesses on the back (see Photo 3).

1 Shown here are the Boxster gauge cluster (top) and the 996 cluster (bottom) side by side. As you can see, they are almost exactly the same, with the Boxster cluster simply missing the additional voltmeter and oil pressure gauge.

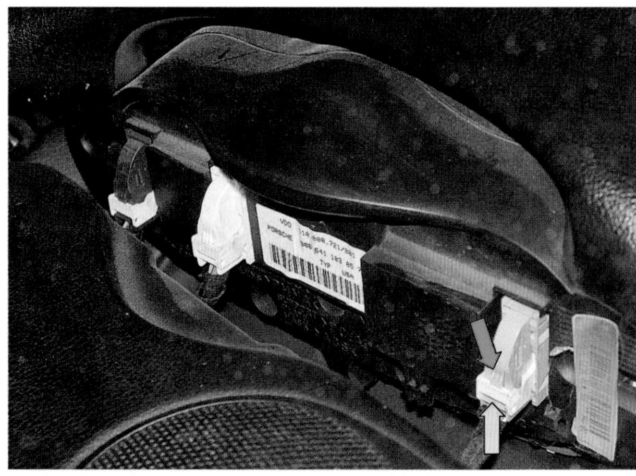

3 This photo was shot through the front windshield and shows the three connectors on the back of the gauge cluster that you need to disconnect in order to remove the cluster. Press on the small tab of each connector (green arrow), and then pull the retaining clip up (yellow arrow), and the connector will automatically pull out of the back of the cluster.

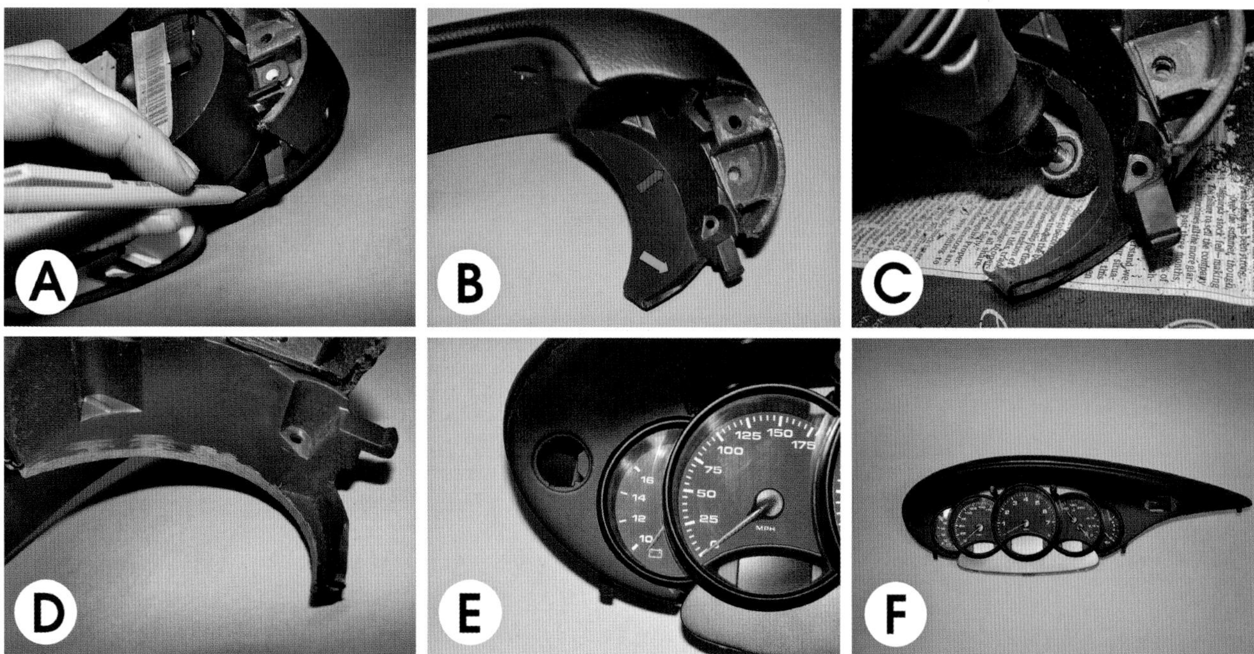

4 Here are the steps I used for adapting the Boxster gauge pod for use with the 996 cluster. **A:** Line up the new cluster with the old plastic surround and mark the area that needs to be removed with a pencil. **B:** Here you can see the pencil line (green arrow). The surround needs to be trimmed out to the wall of the plastic enclosure (red arrow). **C:** Use a Dremel tool to carefully grind the plastic until you meet the contour curves. **D:** Here's the back side of the surround with the appropriate amount of plastic removed. **E:** Here's a close-up of the final cut. Not too shabby! **F:** Here's the complete 996 cluster encased inside of the modified Boxster gauge pod.

5 This photo shows the 996 gauge cluster installed in the Boxster. The 996 gauge gives you the voltmeter on the left and the oil pressure level on the right (the oil level gauge is pegged because the sending unit is not installed yet).

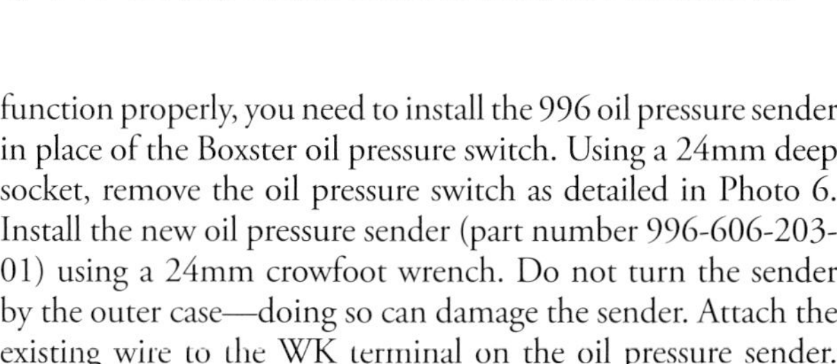

function properly, you need to install the 996 oil pressure sender in place of the Boxster oil pressure switch. Using a 24mm deep socket, remove the oil pressure switch as detailed in Photo 6. Install the new oil pressure sender (part number 996-606-203-01) using a 24mm crowfoot wrench. Do not turn the sender by the outer case—doing so can damage the sender. Attach the existing wire to the WK terminal on the oil pressure sender. This wire sends the signal for the low oil pressure switch.

Now it's time to run a signal wire from the back of the gauge cluster all the way to the new oil pressure sender in the engine compartment. Remove the shifter cover and the armrest as detailed in Project 42. Poke a hole in the rear shifter cable grommet that feeds the cables into the engine compartment.

6 This photo of the Boxster engine compartment shows the oil pressure switch (green arrow) and its connector disconnected from the sender's spade terminal (yellow arrow). The inset photo shows the 996 oil pressure canister, which contains both a low-pressure switch and a variable oil pressure sensor that powers the module in the 996 gauge. Terminal G supplies the signal for the oil pressure gauge, while terminal WK provides the low oil pressure switch signal.

Thread the signal wire through this hole. Secure it along its way with zip ties (see Photo 7). Run the wire all the way up to the front of the car and through the center console. See Project 75 for more information on removing the center console. With the wire laid out, reinstall the shifter, the center console, and the armrest. Be careful not to get it pinched under the shifter or under the armrest when you reinstall them. Crimp a spade connector on the end of the wire in the engine compartment and attach it to the G terminal of the oil pressure sender.

The oil pressure sender signal wire needs to be attached to one of the pins in the gauge cluster. Affix it to the bundle

7 It's fairly easy to run the signal wire for the oil pressure sender down the center tunnel of the car. In the engine compartment, poke a hole in the rubber boot that holds the shift cables (yellow arrow). The inset photo on the bottom shows the armrest and the shifter console cover removed—route the wire through here and use zip ties to secure it to the shift cables. The upper inset photo shows the bottom portion of the center console that you can remove to help feed the wire up through the dash board.

of wires that go into the blue connector using a zip tie or two. Project 91, on installing the on-board computer, has all the details on how to insert the wire into the plug on the rear of the gauge cluster. Use the same Volkswagen mini-wire harness (part number 000-979-010) and remember to install the proper end into the connector. For the 1997–2000 Boxster, the oil pressure sender wire needs to be tapped into pin 9 of the blue plug. For the later cars, 2001–2004, the wire should be inserted into pin 5 of the blue plug.

With the cluster plug properly wired, temporarily install the new 996 cluster into your Boxster and turn on the ignition key. It's important to note that you don't want to do this if you've removed your steering wheel and air bag, as this will cause your air bag light to come on (which will have to be reset by the dealer or with aftermarket software). With the ignition key on, you should see the voltmeter operating properly as well as the oil pressure sender (should be at zero). If the oil pressure gauge pegs to the top of the gauge, the connection is broken and you have a problem with the signal wire—time to troubleshoot it with a multimeter. If you start the car, the oil pressure gauge should go up to 4 or 5. If the gauge doesn't operate properly, you might try removing and reseating the connectors. When I installed my gauge, I was working on the 3.4 996 engine swap at the same time, and I hadn't connected the ground strap yet, which caused the oil pressure gauge to peg. Make sure your ground strap is properly fastened (see Photo 1 of Project 81).

Once you have confirmed that the new cluster works properly, you should modify your Boxster gauge pod. I don't recommend modifying it until you have at least confirmed that the 996 cluster works.

REPROGRAMMING THE CLUSTER AND RADIO

Depending upon which cluster you purchase, you may or may not need to go through a reprogramming procedure using the Porsche PST-2 or PIWIS factory programming tool (see Project 91). Most people don't have this, so you may need to buddy up with your local Porsche dealership or find a local independent shop that has one and is willing to work on this with you.

Boxster guru Todd Holyoak has developed the following programming system for updating the gauge cluster in the Boxster:

1. Connect the PST-2 or PIWIS tester and select model 996 and the DME module.
2. The only option available to you will be to reprogram the DME.
3. Reprogram the DME using the immobilizer and DME programming codes. Use the codes that you received from your dealer, and enter the same values for the old and new codes when the PST-2 requests them.
4. After programming, enter the vehicle data tab.
5. Recode the model type to 911 C2 cab; use 911310 for North America or 911311 for Rest of World (ROW).
6. Back out to the original screen and perform a complete control module search.
7. Enter the instrument cluster tab, and change any coding you would like (cruise control, on-board computer, cabriolet set, etc.).
8. Exit back to the original screen.
9. Recode back to your original 986 type using the current DME and immobilizer codes you used previously.

This procedure should allow you to change all of the settings in the 996 cluster to work with your Boxster. If for some reason you are not able to get this procedure to work, another solution is to install the gauge cluster into an existing 996 car and then reprogram it there. Of course, it's pretty difficult to find someone willing to let their 996's dashboard be taken apart for this purpose.

Unless you have purchased a new gauge cluster delivered in a sealed Porsche box, the cluster will have the mileage from the donor car programmed into it. The only way to reset the mileage on the gauge pod is to send it to a speedometer shop well versed in the secrets of how to reprogram the clusters. Palo Alto Speedometer currently charges about $200 to program the cluster and reset the mileage to a different amount. If you have a brand new gauge cluster, then you can use the PST-2 tool to set the mileage. After about 50 miles or so on the odometer, the gauge cluster will be locked and you will not be able to reprogram it any more.

For the radio, Boxster models from 1997–2002 will only need to tap in the four-digit radio code into the radio in order to make it functional again. The 2003–2004 Boxsters are installed with a new multimedia communications bus system called media oriented systems transport (MOST). The Porsche implementation of this system did away with the use of a radio code, and instead the radio looks to the gauge cluster for VIN information. If there is a match, it will turn the radio on. When you install a new cluster into a MOST-equipped car, the radio will display "PORSCHE PROTECTED." You can fix this problem by reprogramming the cluster with the new VIN information. If you are reprogramming the DME using the procedure documented above, then you can fix this problem by running the "Sports Car Handover" routine in the PST-2 tool. This is the delivery routine that is run by the Porsche dealer when the cars are received by the dealer off of the delivery truck.

PROJECT 91
On-Board Computer/Turn Signal Installation

Time / Tab / Talent: 4 hours / $300 /

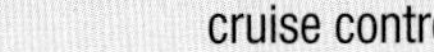

Tools: Torx driver set

Applicable Years: 1997–2004

Parts: Turn signal switch and parts

More Info: www.101projects.com/Boxster/91.htm

Tip: Buy the cruise control switch; it's cheaper

Performance Gain: Activate on-board computer, cruise control

Comp Modification: 996 gauge cluster upgrade, cruise control installation

One of the neat options that was available on the Boxster was the on-board computer (OBC). This computer adds additional functionality to your gauge cluster: range on remaining fuel, outside temperature, speed alert/gong, average fuel consumption, and average speed calculations. Many cars were not equipped with this option, but fortunately the programming and circuits are built into the gauge clusters. To activate the on-board computer, all you need to do is install the turn signal switch with the control stalk and have the OBC functionality enabled by the Porsche factory programming tool (PST-2 or PIWIS).

The table on the right shows the list of parts that are required for the on-board computer upgrade. All of these hard-to-find parts are easily available for purchase at the 101Projects.com website or PelicanParts.com.

Even if your car doesn't have cruise control and you're not planning on adding it, you might want to consider using the cruise control switch instead, as the cost is much cheaper than the one without cruise control. You can also simply purchase the new stalk and then remove the new OBC stalk portion and then transfer it to your old stalk. The two connector wires are Volkswagen parts that appear to be available only from the dealer. These are probably pretty common repair items though, as my dealer had them in stock on the shelf when I arrived there.

The four-stalk version part number is 996-613-219-10-EWC and is only currently available in the black matte/satin black finish. The early-style steering wheel switches were a glossy black. The small tabs on each of the stalks can be transferred over to the new stalk, but if they are glossy black, they will not match terribly well. The best option is to order four new tabs in the matte black/satin black finish, as per the part numbers in the table above.

The first step is to assemble your mini wire harness with the connectors and pins that you purchased. Take two of your three connector wires (000-979-009) and cut two of

Qty	Part Number	Description
1	999-650-056-40	Connector
1	999-650-057-40	Connector cover
3	000-979-009	Connector wire and pins for stalk (Volkswagen part)
2	000-979-010	Connector wire and pins for cluster (Volkswagen part)
1	996-613-219-10-EWC	Turn signal stalk with cruise control
1	996-613-215-10-EWC	Turn signal stalk without cruise control
1	996-613-509-10-A05	Turn signal cap
1	996-613-507-10-A05	Wiper cap
1	996-613-503-10-A05	On-board computer cap
1	996-613-504-10-A05	Cruise control cap

them in half. Then insert the four wires with pins attached into slots 2 through 5 on the five-pin connector 999-650-056-40. Take the remaining connector wire (000-979-009) and cut one of the pins off very close to the pin. Attach a ground eyelet on the end of this wire and then place it into slot 1 of the five-pin connector. Then snap on the connector cover. Now, cut in half your other two connector wires (000-979-010) and attach each one to the wires that exit from 2 through 5 on the connector. Label each wire with the proper pin number and then tie them together with some small zip ties. See Photo 5 for detailed steps on creating this harness. Be sure not to confuse the five connector wires—they look almost exactly the same to the naked eye, but fit into the different connectors.

Now, disconnect the battery (Project 81), pull out the steering wheel as far as possible using the lever at the bottom of the steering column, and then remove the steering wheel (Project 62). Disconnect and remove the gauge cluster as described in Project 90. Remove the steering wheel covers as detailed in Photo 1. Tape the air bag spring so that it doesn't rotate and remove it as per Photo 2. Pull the left and right rear connectors off of the turn signal stalk, mark its position on the steering shaft with a permanent marker, loosen the retaining clamp, and remove it from the steering column (Photo 3). Route your new black harness connector alongside the other wires near to the large connector on the left side of the steering column.

Now it's time to plug the wires into one of the connectors that plugs into the back of the instrument cluster (see Photo 6 for instructions). Attach the eyelet to one of the ground screws on the chassis (see inset of Photo 3). Follow the table below for your year Boxster.

If you happen to break the electrical connector plugs on the back of your cluster, then you can replace them with connector pieces from Porsche. For the 2001–2004 clusters, the kit comes with the three connectors and all three black insert plugs as well. The part number for this is PNA-721-04-300-020 and costs about $26. For the early-style clusters (1997–2000), these connectors are available in a generic repair kit available from Porsche for about $5. This "Porsche Electrical Connector Repair Kit" has a part number of CARTOOL – Nr 96-0-000 or PNA-721-043-600.

Boxster 1997–2000		
Connector Pin #2	Gauge Cluster Pin #20	Select Mode Down
Connector Pin #3	Gauge Cluster Pin #21	Speed Alert/Gong
Connector Pin #4	Gauge Cluster Pin #22	Select Mode Forwards
Connector Pin #5	Gauge Cluster Pin #25	Select Mode Backwards
Boxster 2001–2004		
Connector Pin #2	Gauge Cluster Pin #23	Select Mode Down
Connector Pin #3	Gauge Cluster Pin #22	Speed Alert/Gong
Connector Pin #4	Gauge Cluster Pin #21	Select Mode Forwards
Connector Pin #5	Gauge Cluster Pin #24	Select Mode Backwards

With the new pins installed into the gauge connectors, reinstall the gauge cluster. Reinstall the new turn signal switch, and tighten down the clamp that holds it to the steering column. When you install the switch, the top metal surface should be positioned approximately 55mm from the end of the steering shaft. Don't slide it in all the way on the shaft, as this will give you trouble with the proper operation of the turn signal cancelling function. Line up the metal clamp with the knurled section of the steering column when you tighten it. If need be, you can adjust this later on as well.

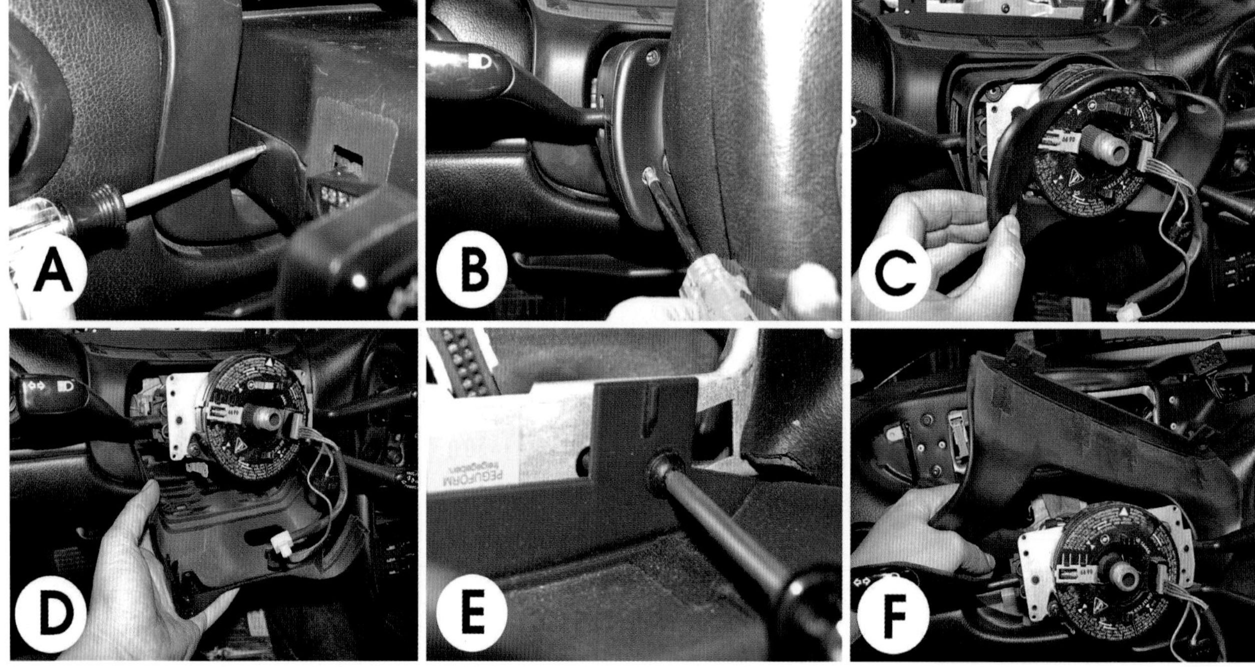

1 After you have removed the steering wheel, you can then remove the equipment that covers the stalk. **A:** The side surrounds are held on with two small screws. **B:** The front surround is held on with four screws. If the steering wheel is still attached, then rotate it until you can access the screws. **C:** Pull off the front cover. **D:** Remove both the top and bottom steering column covers. **E:** A few screws hold the upper fascia to the metal part of the dashboard. **F:** Remove the fascia to expose the steering column.

2 This photo shows the details involved in removing the air bag contact ring. Be very careful of the fragile plastic tabs on the contact ring—they are very easy to break off, and this piece is about $200 to replace. The red arrow indicates the plastic piece (shown broken here) that is very easy to snap off if you are not careful. The blue arrows show the air bag and horn connectors that need to be disconnected, and the orange arrow shows the turn signal switch connectors. Although you can simply loosen the air bag contact ring and leave it installed on the steering column, I recommend removing it completely and putting it aside, as it's way too easy to damage it while you're working in that area.

3 Here's what the steering wheel column looks like with the switch removed. When attaching the new one, you need to clamp it down by tightening the pinch bolt (red arrow). The inset photo in the lower right shows where you need to attach the grounding harness for the new stalk switch.

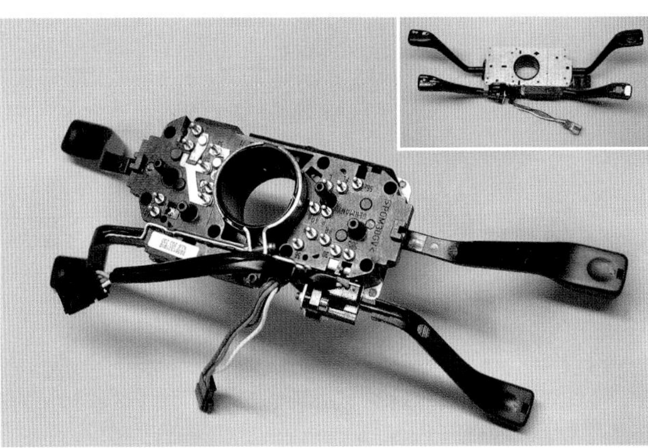

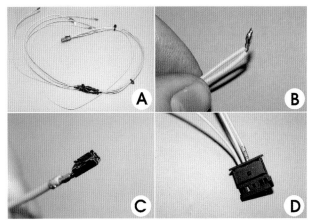

4 Shown here is the upgraded turn signal that contains all of the switches and stalks required for both the on-board computer and cruise control. If your 2000 and later Boxster didn't originally come with cruise control and you wish to add it, then you should install this turn signal switch. Shown here is the matte black version of the four-stalk switch (part number 996-613-219-10). The small tabs on each of the stalks can be transferred over to the new stalk.

5 This photo shows the process of creating the small wire harness that connects the on-board computer switch stalk to the gauge cluster. **A:** Shown here is the completed harness, with the ground lead and three pins that must be mated into the connector that plugs into the gauge cluster. Use small zip ties to join the whole harness together. It's also smart to label each wire (not shown here). **B:** I prefer to solder all my connections when possible to avoid any of them coming loose in the future. Wrap each connection with electrical tape of course. **C:** Here's a close-up of the tiny pin that needs to be inserted into the black connector. Keep in mind that there are two different types of pins, and they both look the same. **D:** The pins should easily snap into the connector. If they don't, you are probably using the wrong pin and need to grab the other one. I suggest inserting the wires and pins into the connector prior to soldering the connections, just so that you don't have to take the whole harness apart if you find you have made a mistake.

6 You can open up the connectors and remove the inner portion by squeezing the base of the plug. The inner portion, which contains all of the wires and pins, will slide out of the side of the connector. Insert your new pin into the appropriate slot. Be aware that there are two different pins used on these wires, a small one and a larger one. The small one will very easily snap into place, and the larger one will only snap into place with a lot of force. Make sure that you create your wire harness using the proper pins for this connector. As shown in the photo, I found it useful to label the wires since they were all yellow-colored.

Reinstall the air bag contact spring and the side covers for the steering column. Install the steering wheel back on the car and reconnect the battery. If your car didn't have the cruise control and on-board computer enabled, then you need to make a trip to the Porsche dealer to have them turn on this functionality with the Porsche PST-2 or PIWIS tool (see Photo 7). Once the main computer is reprogrammed, you should have a working on-board computer.

Poor Man's Version: Some people who have not wanted to go through the trouble or expense of purchasing the new turn signal stalk have instead installed extra rocker switches into the dash and wired them up to the gauge cluster to gain functionality of the computer without the installation of the expensive stalk. You can use the same wires as above, but instead use two rocker switches (PN: 996-613-980-00) that fit into the spare places in the center dash, to the left of the vents. See Photo 8 for more details.

Really Poor Man's Version: If you don't want to go through the process of installing any of the switches and have a 1997–2000 Boxster, you can simply have the dealer turn on the on-board computer function in your Boxster's computer. This will bring up the temperature display, although you cannot cycle through any of the other options. Starting in 2001, this no longer works.

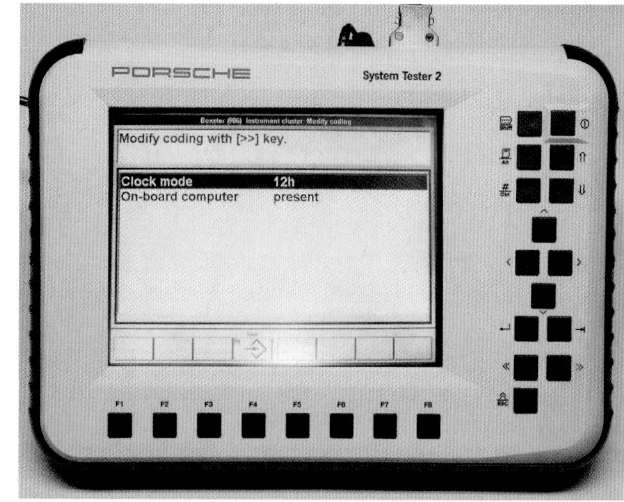

7 When the installation is complete, the computer will not work, unfortunately, until the coding is modified in the instrument cluster using the Porsche factory PST-2 or PIWIS programming tool. This tool is only found at Porsche dealers and the occasional independent shop, such as Callas Rennsport in Torrance, California. Under "Instrument Cluster," change the coding to show the on-board computer to be "present" and save the changes. After this change is made, the on-board computer should function normally. Be sure that your car is not missing the "Option Code" spec, as this will generate errors when you try to update the car with the tool.

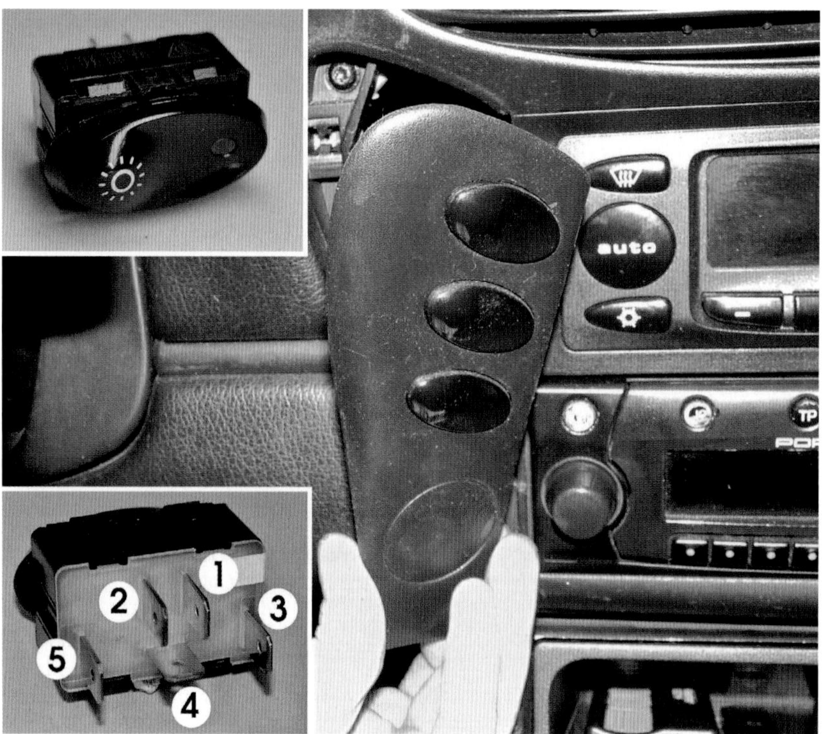

8 The "poor man's" version is a great way to get the functionality of the computer without having to install the stalk. Simply install two rocker switches into the blanks on the left side of the dash and wire them up to the pins on the back of the cluster. Wire one of the two switches to the pins that control "mode forwards" and "mode backwards," and the other switch to "select mode down" and "speed gong/alert" (see table in the text). The rocker switches that are available are pretty neat and useful. This one (for footwell lighting, PN: 996-613-980-00) contains two switches (left and right), an internal LED, and an internal light bulb for nighttime illumination. **1:** Switch left, **2:** Switch right, **3:** Nighttime illumination, **4:** Common, **5:** LED lamp. To use this switch with the OBC, wire pins 2, 3, 4, and 5 from the table above to pins 1 and 2 of two different switches, and then connect the green ground wire to pin 4 of both switches.

PROJECT 92
Cruise Control Installation

 **Time / Tab / Talent:** 6 hours / $300 / 4 wrenches

 **Tools:** Torx driver set

 **Applicable Years:** 2000–2008

 **Parts:** Cruise control switch, connectors, and wire

 **More Info:** www.101projects.com/Boxster/92.htm

 **Tip:** Easy to install with the on-board computer

 **Performance Gain:** No more sleepy feet

 **Comp Modification:** On-board computer installation

In 2000, the Boxster's engine management system was upgraded with a new system that used an electronic throttle body (E-gas). This eliminated throttle cables, and instead the gas pedal has a sensor on it that controls an electronic stepper motor located on the throttle body in the engine compartment. Because this entire arrangement is completely electronic, the car no longer needed to have a separate, complicated cruise control system. As a result, if you have a 2000 and later Boxster that didn't come with cruise control installed from the factory, then you can install the turn signal switch with the cruise control stalk, run some wires, and turn it on electronically in the computer.

This project is very similar in principle to the on-board computer installation (Project 91). Similar to that one, you need to remove the gauge cluster, the steering wheel, and the turn signal switch in order to upgrade your car. Please refer to Project 91 for specific instructions on how to replace the turn signal switch. This project will focus mostly on the additional steps that are required to wire up and activate the cruise control feature.

There are a few parts that you will need. Firstly, you will need a turn signal switch assembly that has a cruise control stalk integrated within it (see Project 91 for part numbers). You will also need a connector that plugs into the stalk (PN: 999-652-972-40), a VW wire connector (000-979-010, see Project 91) and eight female pins in order to install inside the two connectors (PN: 999-652-901-22, get some extras). You will also need enough 22-gauge wire to run four separate wires from the dashboard of the car to the Motronic computer located in the trunk. I suggest using four different-colored wires for this task.

Crimp the pins onto the five wires (four from the Motronic unit in the trunk and one from the cruise control connector to the fuse panel) and run them through the car according to the following table and also using the guidance provided in the accompanying photos. Use the pins from the VW wire 000-979-010 to plug into the back of your instrument cluster (see Project 91). Also make sure that you have a good working bulb (for non-LED lit clusters) in the cruise control indicator socket of the gauge cluster.

Cruise Control Connector Boxster 2000–2002

Cruise Control Connector Pin #1	Motronic Connector IV—pin #27 (black)
Cruise Control Connector Pin #2	Fuse B7 (black)
Cruise Control Connector Pin #3	Motronic Connector IV—pin #25 (yellow)
Cruise Control Connector Pin #4	Motronic Connector IV—pin #19 (brown/yellow)
2000-02 Boxster—Gauge Cluster Blue Connector I—Pin #16	Motronic Connector IV—pin #18
2000-02 Boxster S—Gauge Cluster Black Connector III—Pin #17	Motronic Connector IV—pin #18

For 2003–2004 cars it's much easier. The cruise control functions are integrated into the instrument cluster, and all you need to do is wire the cruise control stalk switch to the appropriate pins in the instrument cluster. This is nearly identical to how the on-board computer is wired up (see Project 91). Connect the cruise control connector to the gauge cluster using the following table:

Cruise Control Connector—Boxster 2003–2004	
Cruise Control Connector Pin #1	Plug C on the Gauge Cluster (Gray)—pin #17
Cruise Control Connector Pin #2	Fuse B7 (black)
Cruise Control Connector Pin #3	Plug C on the Gauge Cluster (Gray)—pin #4
Cruise Control Connector Pin #4	Plug C on the Gauge Cluster (Gray)—pin #1

For all 2000–2004 cars, once you have all of the wiring done, you will need to have the dealer activate the cruise control function using the PST-2 or PIWIS programming unit. The section for programming this in the tool is located in the DME module, under the Coding section. You also need to activate the instrument cluster for cruise control as well. This is found in the "Instrument Cluster" coding section within the Porsche programming tool. Make sure your car has the "order code" properly set; otherwise you may have trouble properly programming the instrument cluster. For a manual transmission Boxster 2.7, the order code is 986310. For a Boxster S 3.2 manual transmission, it's 986320. Entering either of these should be sufficient for programming your cluster.

Boxsters from 1997–1999 didn't have an electronically controlled throttle—instead they have a special servo motor that's attached to the gas pedal and controlled by a separate cruise control module. It is possible to retrofit these components to a car that did not have cruise control from the factory, but it's quite a bit more complicated. You need to purchase the cruise control pedal assembly and the control module/servo motor (see Photo 4) and then wire the assembly to the car. See diagram EWD-41 in the Bentley manual for more information on how this is wired up.

For Boxsters from 2005–2008, the installation is much easier. You need to purchase a cruise control switch (PN: 997-613-261-00), a small wiring harness (PN: 997-622-674-00), a new lower steering column cover (PN: 997-552-475-03), and a few Torx screws to secure the new switch (PN: N-909-068-01). There is a factory retro-fit kit available that includes all of these parts and instructions (PN: 997-044-903-00), but you can save money by simply buying the parts separately and looking at the 101Projects.com website for a copy of the installation instructions. Simply remove the bottom cover, install the new switch and harness, plug the harness into the connector on the switch above it, and then install the new lower cover. The cruise control function then needs to be turned on by a Porsche dealer or independent shop with a PIWIS programming tool. The whole process should take about 30 minutes—very simple.

Cruise Control Troubleshooting: If your new cruise control installation doesn't work, then check your wiring. Also double-check to make sure that the technician who programmed your Boxster's computer properly set the cruise control function in both the DME and in the Instrument Cluster section. If you are still having difficulty or if you have cruise control installed from the factory and it's not working properly, you might want to try the following troubleshooting steps:

- Check the stalk switches. Unplug the connector and use a multimeter to test the proper functioning of the switches (see the wiring diagrams in the Bentley manual for the pinouts).
- Check the brake pedal and clutch switches. Both of these deactivate the cruise control, and if the switches are faulty, they will prevent the computer from activating the system. Not only can they fail, but they can also slip out of their bracket, which causes them to not work either.
- Check to make sure the bulb in the cluster is not burned out and that it turns on for a second or so when you turn the ignition on.
- Check the B7 slot in the fusebox to make sure the fuse powering the actuator system is not blown (1997–1999 cars only).

1 The wire from pin No. 2 of the cruise control connector needs to be wired to the black wire running to fuse B7 at the rear of the fuse panel. Remove the passenger side footwell covers and you should be able to see the fuse panel. Remove the panel (be sure to disconnect the battery first) by removing the four Phillips-head screws and then squeeze the tabs on the side to remove it (yellow arrow). Attach the wire to the black fuse B7 as shown using a tap-in connector (green arrow). This will provide the cruise control circuit with the brake pedal signal to turn off the cruise control function.

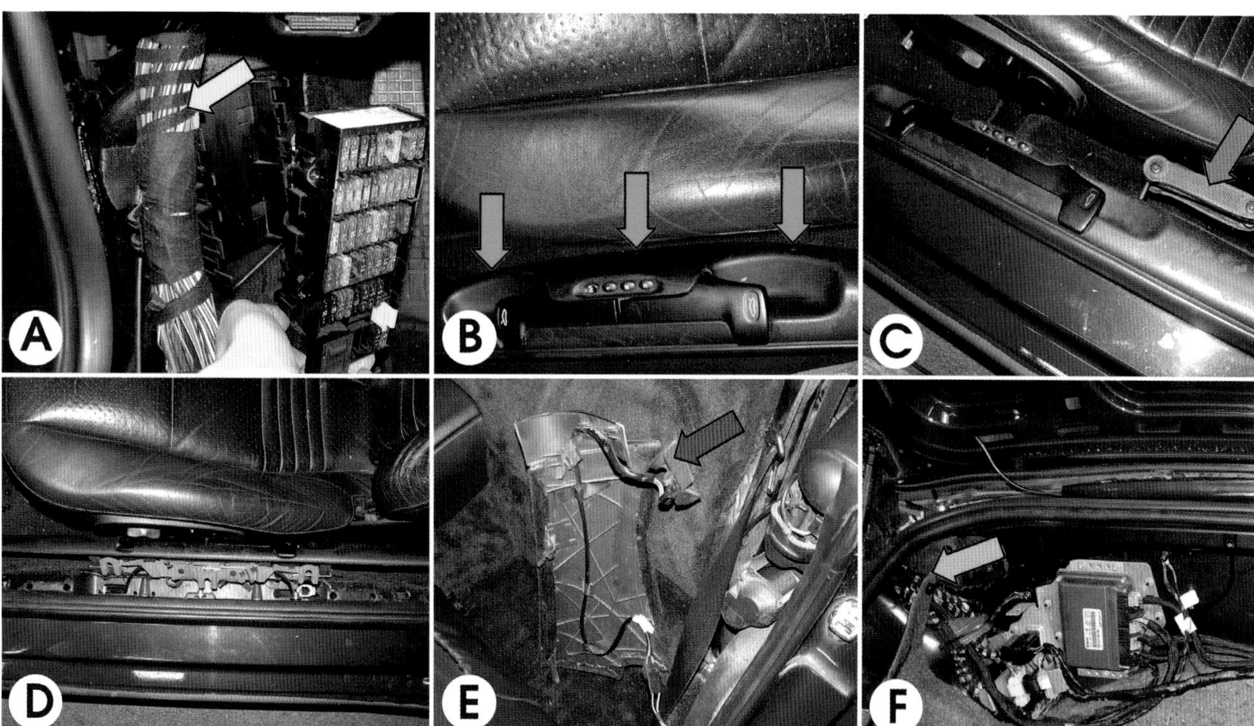

2 In order to get the control signals from the Motronic DME in the trunk to the gauge cluster and the cruise control stalk, you need to run four wires down the left side of the car and into the rear trunk. Begin by taping the four wires together to make them easier to fish through the chassis. **A:** Run the new wires attached to the cruise control connector alongside the left side harness down to the fuse panel. **B:** Pop off the three plastic rivets that hold on the covers for the hood and trunk release mechanism. **C:** Loosen the bolts that hold on the mechanism, but do not remove them. Having the right tool really works here, as this fold-up Torx set worked perfectly in this tight space (some cars may use a hex-head screw instead). **D:** Pull up on the plastic trim and the assembly unit will snap up and out of the way. Do not disconnect the cables. Run the new wires next to the existing wire harness underneath. **E:** Remove the side panel behind the seat that covers the seat belt mechanism. There is a somewhat hidden Phillips-head screw located in the bottom half of the carpet area and a 8mm hex bolt near the top that needs to be loosened (don't forget this bolt or you will snap the piece, as I accidentally did, when removing the panel). Pull on the carpet panel to remove it. **F:** Now remove the rear trunk liner—the plastic fasteners should simply snap out. Run the wires alongside the existing wire harness. If you can fit the wires through the access hole for the main harness, then run them under the foam liner in the convertible compartment area and through one of the openings to the rear trunk. Don't accidentally block the drain hole. See Project 3 for instructions on how to access the convertible roof compartment.

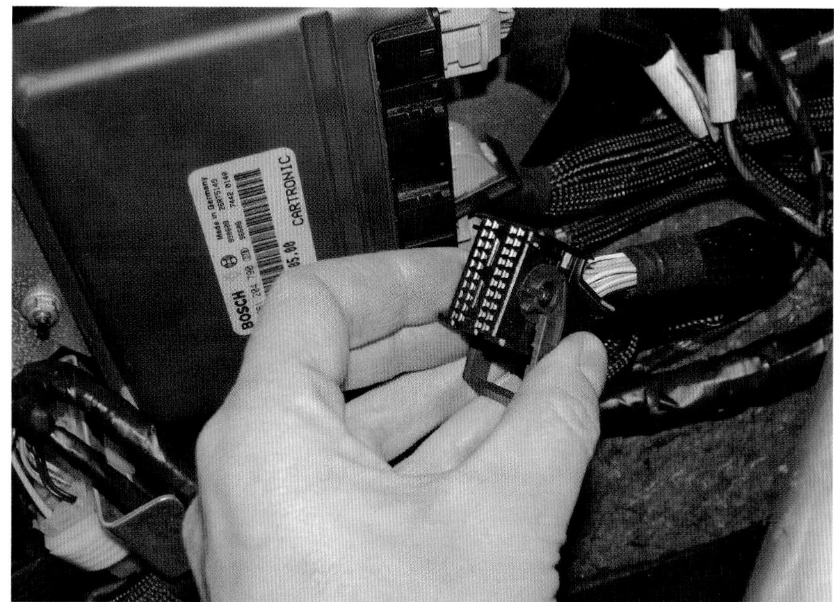

3 Shown here is the location of the Motronic DME in the rear trunk. Remove connector IV (40-pin connector) from the back of the unit (yellow arrow) and then add the pins into the empty slots according to the table in the text of this project.

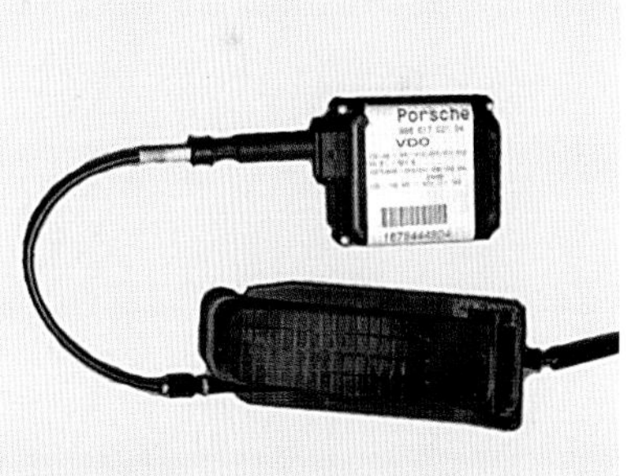

4 Shown here is the cruise control servo module and gas pedal for the 1997–1999 Boxsters with the cable driven accelerator.

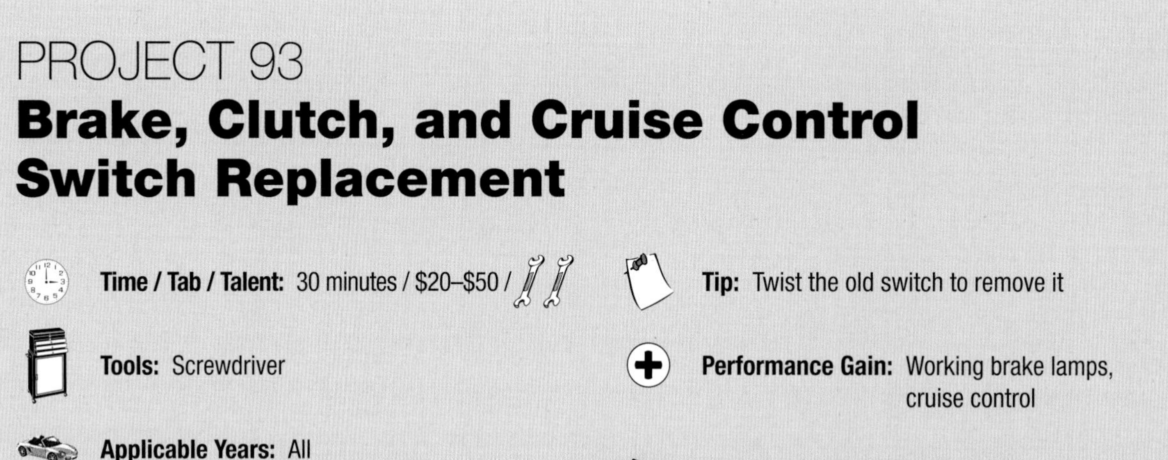

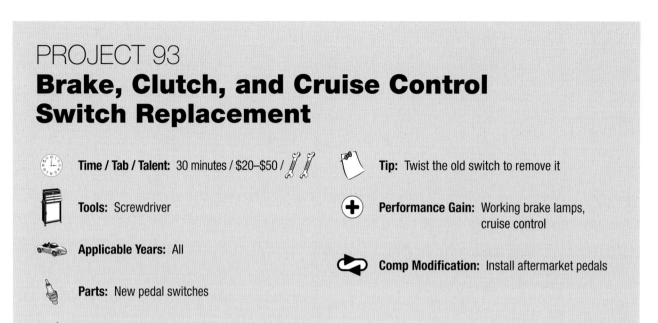

PROJECT 93
Brake, Clutch, and Cruise Control Switch Replacement

Time / Tab / Talent: 30 minutes / $20–$50 /

Tools: Screwdriver

Applicable Years: All

Parts: New pedal switches

More Info: www.101projects.com/Boxster/93.htm

Tip: Twist the old switch to remove it

Performance Gain: Working brake lamps, cruise control

Comp Modification: Install aftermarket pedals

There are three pedal switches on the Boxster, two on the clutch pedal and one on the brakes. They get a lot of use, and they all have a tendency to fail once and a while.

For the brake switch, the first step is to verify that your brake lamps are not working. If they aren't, then your switch is probably shot. It's important to note that the switch has redundancy built in, and the warning system should tell you when your switch is failing, but this doesn't always work.

The clutch pedal has two switches, although I'm not quite sure why. One switch controls the cruise control (turns it off when you push in the clutch), and the other won't let you start the car without the clutch pedal pushed in. If you're having intermittent starting problems with your car, I would look at this switch first.

Curious, but the cruise control switch is identical to the brake pedal switch except that the cruise control switch is red, and the brake pedal switch is a translucent brown. Both switches have three of the same part numbers printed on them.

The switches are relatively easy to access, as they are located right above the pedals. You will have to open the passenger door and then stick your head into the footwell to see them. Replacement is easy—simply unplug the harness from the end and then twist to remove the switch. If you need to manhandle and/or break the switch to remove it, that's perfectly okay, since you will be replacing it with a new one very soon anyways. The clutch pedal switch that prevents the car from starting is a standard microswitch mounted with screws.

To finish the job, simply install the new switch into place and reconnect the wire harness. Test the brake lights to make sure that they are working properly, and then reinstall the knee panel.

1 Here are the two clutch pedal switches. The yellow arrow points to the microswitch that prevents the car from starting if you don't have the pedal pushed in. The red switch is the one that deactivates the cruise control when you push the clutch in.

2 Here's a photo of the brake pedal switch (green arrow). Simply unplug the harness, twist the switch, and then remove it from the chassis. The lower left inset photo shows the brake and cruise control switches together. The only difference between these two is the color of the housing.

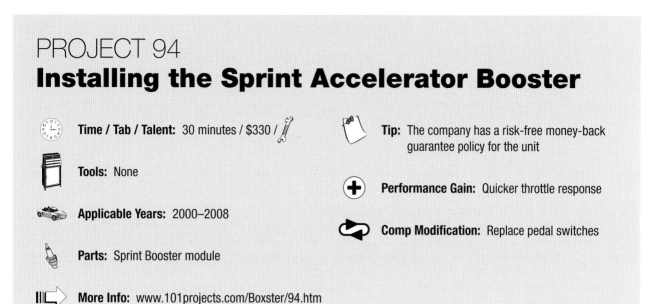

PROJECT 94
Installing the Sprint Accelerator Booster

 **Time / Tab / Talent:** 30 minutes / $330 /

 **Tools:** None

 **Applicable Years:** 2000–2008

 **Parts:** Sprint Booster module

 **More Info:** www.101projects.com/Boxster/94.htm

 **Tip:** The company has a risk-free money-back guarantee policy for the unit

 **Performance Gain:** Quicker throttle response

 **Comp Modification:** Replace pedal switches

The Sprint Booster is one of those products that are a bit difficult to explain in words. In 2000, Porsche did away with the traditional cable that connects the gas pedal to the throttle body and replaced it with what is known as drive-by-wire. Basically, an electronic sensor on the gas pedal tells the main computer (DME) how much the driver is pressing down the pedal, and then the computer opens the throttle body on the engine by the correct amount. Some people claim that the electronic throttle (also known as E-gas) is less responsive than a normal cable throttle. I have both types of Boxsters (pre-2000 and post-2000), and I haven't been able to detect a difference between the two.

The pedal has a variable sensor on it that senses the exact position of the pedal as your foot presses on it. This position is read by the computer and then used to open the throttle body. A fully depressed gas pedal makes the computer throw the throttle body fully open. Likewise, with the gas pedal at resting position, the throttle body is almost completely closed (open about 6 percent to allow the engine to idle). As you press the gas pedal toward the floor, the computer opens the throttle body somewhat proportionately to how much "gas" you're giving the car—pushing down the gas pedal halfway means that the computer opens the throttle body enough to allow air into the engine at half its maximum capacity. It's interesting to note that the relationship between the pedal and the throttle body is not linear—for example, when the pedal is pushed down 50 percent, the throttle body is only open about 27 percent. When the pedal is pushed down 85 percent, the throttle body is open 74 percent, and when the pedal is pushed 100 percent down to the floor, the throttle body is open 100 percent.

So, how does this Sprint Booster device work? Basically, I like to call it a "short shift kit for your gas pedal." It takes the signals from your gas pedal and changes them so that the computer is tricked into thinking that you've stomped down on your gas pedal when you really haven't. Basically, you reach about full throttle when the pedal is roughly halfway to the floor. The device does not increase horsepower or overall performance of the car, however the car "feels quicker." The resulting effect is real, even if the horsepower gains are not.

It's very difficult to explain the effect to someone who hasn't actually driven the car with the unit installed. It does actually feel a lot quicker. For my last book, I had an old BMW 318is project car that had about 50 or so less horsepower than my 325is. But the car was high-revving, and because of other mind tricks, it just "felt quicker" and was generally more fun to drive. I liken the effect of the Sprint Booster to that experience. It takes a little bit of getting used when you first install it, but after a few days, it will feel like second nature.

There are a few potential downsides to the Sprint Booster, however. The first one is the price—at $330 from PelicanParts.com, it's definitely not cheap. The relatively high price combined with the fact that it's very difficult to explain what exactly this unit does is probably one of the reasons why the manufacturer offers a 30-day money back guarantee on it. So, if you don't like it, the risk is about 30 minutes of your time. Another potential drawback is the fact that you may experience a decrease in gas mileage. Common sense seems to indicate that if you're an "electronic lead foot" more of the time, your gas mileage will decrease. However, an informal search on the Internet seems to indicate that most people have not experienced any decrease in gas mileage. This is one of the last projects for this book (installed winter 2010), and I have not had enough personal drive time with the device to determine what it's impact on gas consumption might be.

One more thing to note—since this is purely an electronic modification, if you are having your DME remapped (see Project 24), then you can also have the software reprogrammed to offer the same effect as the Sprint Booster. If this is something you're interested in, you might want to discuss it with the provider of your software map before you complete your purchase.

Installation is really a snap. All you do is disconnect the connector to the gas pedal and plug in the Sprint Booster so that it's now inline with the harness. The toughest part is squeezing your body underneath the dashboard so that you can reach the connections (see Photo 1). I was able to do it and take photos without disconnecting any of the duct work under the dash, but it takes some patience and dexterity.

1 Here's a shot under the dash of the Sprint Booster installation. The plug for the accelerator is up under the dashboard—simply unplug it and insert the Sprint Booster device in its place. Then, reconnect the plug that connects to the chassis. The Sprint Booster is sandwiched between these two connectors.

SECTION 11
MISCELLANEOUS

This section contains all the projects that didn't quite fit into any of the other predefined categories. Take a look at the Personal Touches project for my pick of the most interesting and unique additions that various owners have made to their Boxsters. Air conditioning recharging, track prep, wheel/tire selection, and dyno testing are also detailed in the projects within this section.

PROJECT 95
Installing the Roof Transport System

 **Time / Tab / Talent:** 2 hours / $500 /

 **Tools:** Included with kit

 **Applicable Years:** 1997–2004

 **Parts:** Roof transport system (RTS)

 **More Info:** www.101projects.com/Boxster/95.htm

 **Tip:** Third-party adapters from Yakima and Thule can be made to work with the kit

 **Performance Gain:** Able to carry lots more stuff!

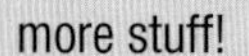

 **Comp Modification:** Buy some furniture at IKEA

The Boxster is unique among cars in that it has two trunks, one in the front and one in the back. Unfortunately, the sum of the two trunks is smaller than the one big trunk that you find in many regular cars these days. Fortunately, those clever German designers at Porsche came up with a unique and interesting way to install a roof rack system on the Boxster. As far as I know, it's the only convertible in existence to have a roof rack that you use to carry a bike, skis, or even an extra set of tires to that track day.

Installation is pretty easy, although in typical German fashion, the instructions for the kit make it seem more difficult than it really is. The roof cannot be raised or lowered with the kit installed, so decide beforehand whether you would like to travel with the roof up or down. The kit comes with two side bars, two top bars, and a black box full of fasteners and attachment tools. The first step is to install the front mounting brackets to the car. Remove the two existing screws and plastic cover piece, and install the front mounting bracket on both the left and right side of the car. Be careful not to scratch your paint. Refer to Photo 1 for details. Next, remove the B-pillar cover and install the two brackets (see Photo 2).

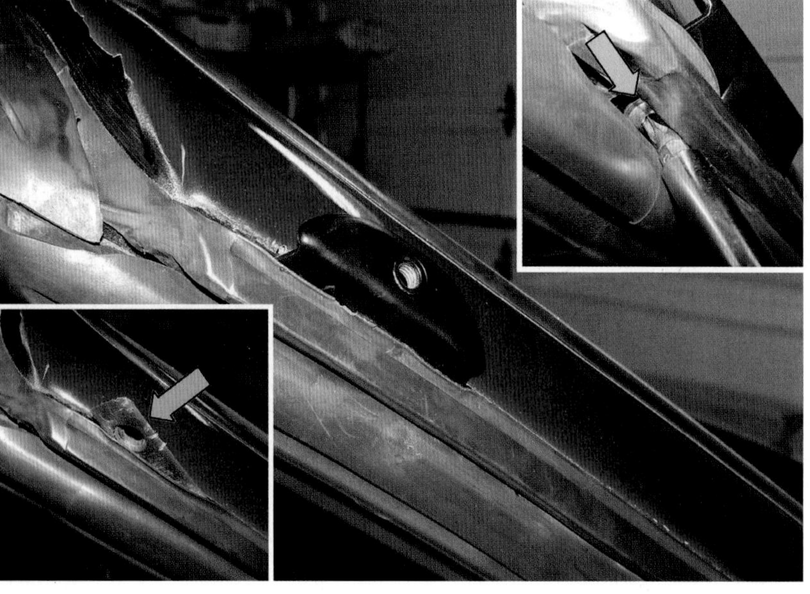

1 Shown here is the front mounting point for the roof transport system (RTS). Underneath the seal there are two hex screws that need to be removed. Remove them with the tool supplied in the kit. Then, slide out the plastic spacer through the back side of the seal (inset photo, lower left). Finally, install the front mounting bracket as shown with the Torx screws supplied in the kit (inset photo upper right). Store the plastic cover and the two hex screws in your RTS kit box (there's specific slots and compartments in the kit box to hold the hardware you remove from the car).

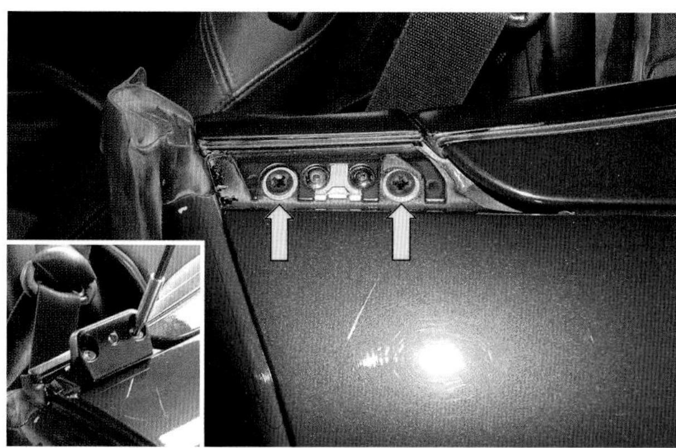

2 Using a plastic spatula or the spacer you removed in Photo 1, pry up the little cover that fits over this area and remove it. Carefully remove the two plastic screws that are shown with the two arrows. These hold on the cover piece, so carefully place them safely away in your RTS kit box when you remove them. Install the B-pillar brackets into the spots where you removed the two screws (inset photo).

3 Porsche kindly provided pieces of cardboard to use to protect your paint when installing the arches. Carefully place them around the B-pillar bracket, and then place the arch into the bracket. Using the special lock tool, install and tighten the arch in place. With the B-pillar in place, the arch will stay up in the air so that you can connect it to the front (orange arrow). Repeat for the opposite side.

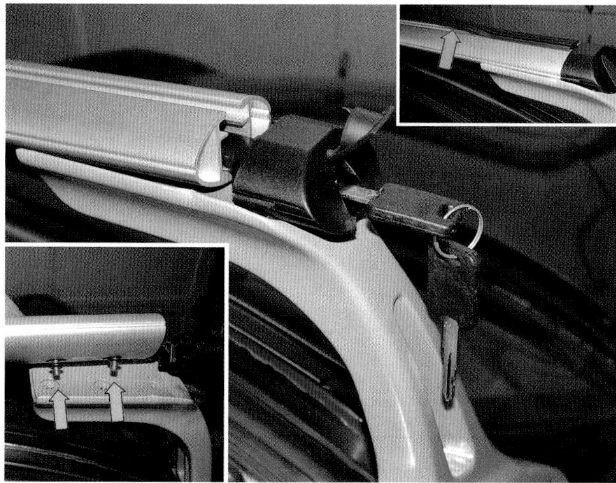

4 Install the tubes on top of the car. Remove the end caps by inserting the key, turning it, and then pulling back on the cap. This exposes the screws that mount each side of the part to each arch (blue arrow). Tighten the screws through the top slot using the tool included with the kit. Notice the black O-rings (on the screws near the blue arrow) that keep the screws captured with the tubes when they are not tightened. Install the caps on the ends of the bar, securing it with the lock and key. The kit comes with a gasket that can be fit into the groove on the top of the bar if necessary.

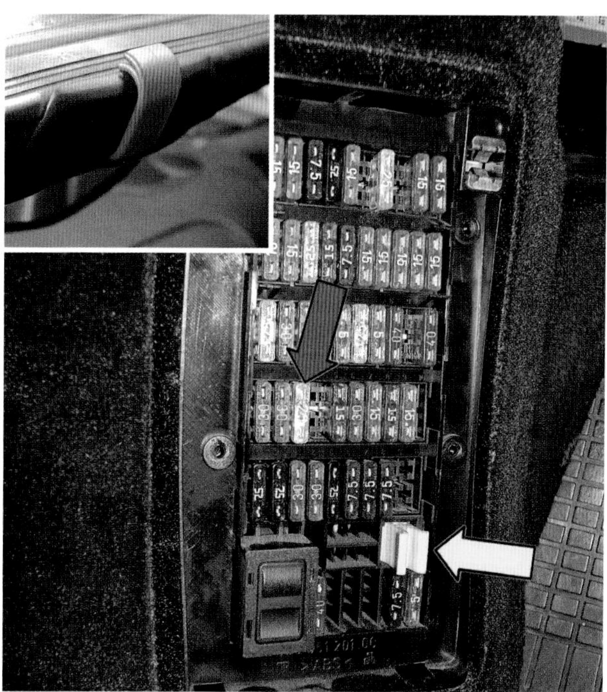

5 Once the RTS is installed, you cannot raise or lower the roof, so it's a wise idea to remove the fuse that powers the roof. Shown here is the fusebox with the plastic cover removed. The fusebox is located on the driver's side (left) of the car, near where your left foot rests. Pull the cover off and remove fuse number D3 (shown by the red arrow) using the small plastic fuse puller tool that should be clipped in the fusebox (yellow arrow). On the back of the cover there should be a little booklet showing you which fuse controls what (PN: 996-610-217-XX—the last two digits depend upon the year of your car). You can also use the factory "red clip" if you want to lock the roof in the down position (PN: 986-504-986-00). This clip snaps onto the roof and makes the car think the roof is in the up position already. This red clip is also useful because it turns on the interior motion sensor for the alarm system so that the alarm will go off if there is any movement inside of the car.

6 Here's the roof transport system installed with the factory travel box and the bike rack. It's possible to use third-party bike racks and boxes with the rack, but you will need to rig up some hardware to attach them to the rails. See the 101Projects.com website for some ideas and tips. *Photo courtesy of Mike Rentner*

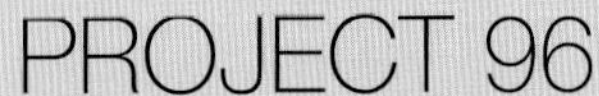

PROJECT 96
Child Seat Air Bag Deactivation

Time / Tab / Talent: 1 hour / $250 / 2 wrenches

Tools: Torx socket set

Applicable Years: All

Parts: Air bag deactivation bar

More Info: www.101projects.com/Boxster/96.htm

Tip: If you're planning on installing the on-board computer, have the dealer activate that at the same time

Performance Gain: Ability to take your driver-in-training along

Comp Modification: Add on-board computer

One of the first projects I performed on my Boxster was the installation of the Porsche factory air bag deactivation bar, so that I could take my three-year-old son along for rides. If you're not familiar with the process of preparing the car so that you can disable the air bag, it can be very confusing. In reality, it's very easy to do, as I explain here.

The "deactivation bar" is nothing more than a metal bar that holds a buckle attached to the bottom of the passenger seat (PN: 996-803-083-02). The kit from Porsche comes complete with the bar/buckle assembly and two longer bolts that replace the existing bolts that fasten the passenger seat to the chassis. This new buckle contains an electrical switch that connects to a plug under the passenger seat. All of the Porsche factory child seats have a seat belt receptacle that plugs into this buckle. When this belt is plugged in, the electrical switch is activated, and it tells the air bag computer to shut off the air bag in the car.

Installation is a snap. Simply remove the two Torx bolts that hold the seat to the chassis, slide in the bar, and then install the new bolts to reattach the bar and seat assembly. Refer to Photo 2 for the proper orientation of the buckle (it is possible to install it upside down). Plug in the connector to the empty connection under the seat. The last step is that you need to have the "Child seat occupancy" turned on by using the factory Porsche System Tester 2 (PST-2), which you can typically only find at the Porsche dealers. Some dealers will charge for performing this task, others will do it for free. It takes about five minutes total to set.

The problem with this air bag deactivation system is that it only works with Porsche factory child seats, as they are the only ones that come with the special buckle attached. For my own application, I did not use a Porsche factory seat but instead used a different seat and attached the buckle from a factory seat to the bottom of my seat. I got this buckle from an old factory seat that a friend of mine had that was too big for my three-year-old. In the same manner as the factory seat, I attach and plug in the buckle when I install the child seat into the car. I then confirm that the air bag is disabled by checking the light on the dash (see Photo 1). I have not been able to locate this buckle or receptacle separately, but the TRW part numbers are: 33000311 35 06/99680328302 for the buckle, and 56030A (part number on metal)/7670842 (part number on plastic).

Air bags are lifesaving devices, however, they can be deadly to small children. Regardless of how you install your child seat into the car, exercise extreme caution and always check that the air bag is disabled (via the blinking lamp on the dash, see Photo 1) prior to driving the car. For more information, see also Technical Service Bulletin (TSB) 15/98 6923 Porsche Child Restraint System - Installation (dated 3-7-2000).

For 2005 and later cars, Porsche used a similar, but slightly more complicated system. Dubbed the "Child Seat Fastener System," the kit includes fastening loops and lower anchorage points for mounting between the seat surface and backrest, as well as a key switch for deactivation of the passenger side air bag (PN: 997-044-800-15). Starting with 2006, the Boxster seats have a "weight sensing" system that is supposed to turn off the air bag if there isn't an adult sitting in the seat. But, these can be less than reliable when the weight of a car seat is added into the equation—I recommend installing the air bag deactivation key switch. See the 101Projects.com website for more information and installation instructions.

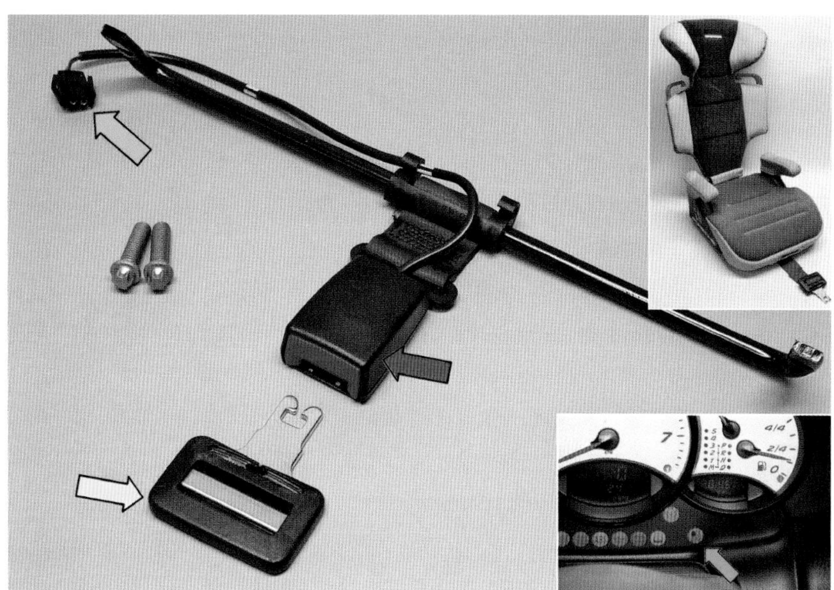

1 This photo shows the Porsche air bag deactivation bar. This part is simply a metal bar with a seat belt receptacle attached. Porsche-branded child seats come with a buckle attached to the front of the seat (upper right inset). This buckle piece (yellow arrow) mates with the receptacle attached to the bar (red arrow) and activates an electrical switch that turns off the air bag. The electrical connector (blue arrow) needs to be mated with an open connector that is located beneath the passenger seat. When the buckle is plugged in, the air bag lamp on the dashboard will blink repeatedly for 10 seconds or 60 seconds (cars manufactured after 03/31/1999) to inform you that the passenger side air bag is properly disabled (green arrow).

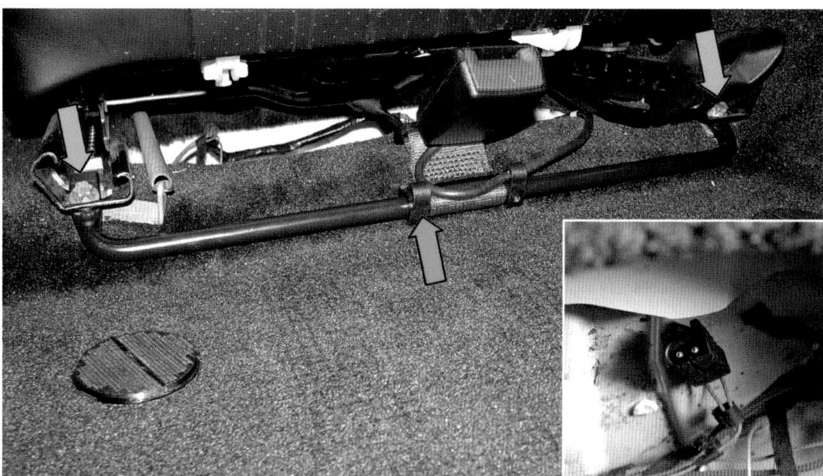

2 This photo shows the air bag deactivation bar installed in the passenger seat. Note the direction of the plastic clips on the buckle (green arrow). New, longer mounting screws for the seats come with the bar kit, as the bar is attached to the top of the seat mount (blue arrows). The electrical connection for the air bag is located under the seat (lower right photo).

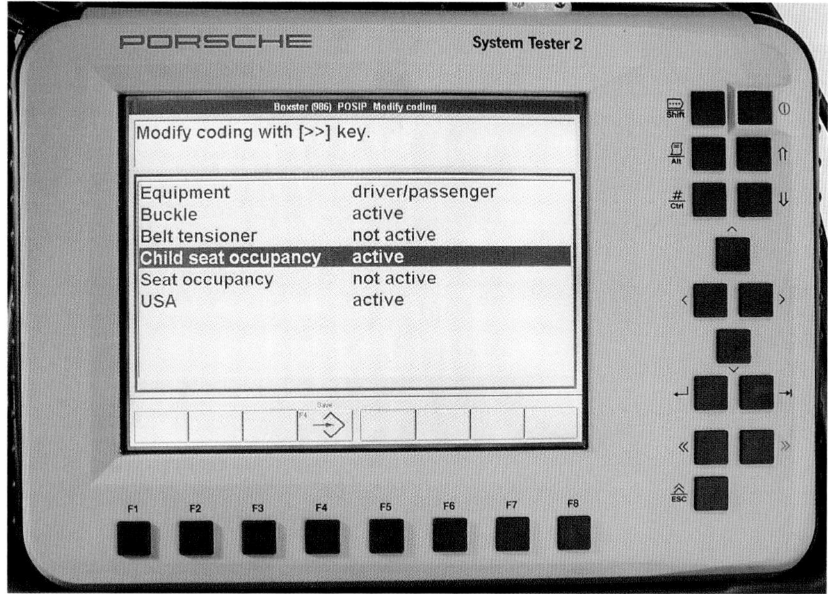

3 Shown here is the Porsche factory System Tester (PST-2). This computer needs to be plugged into your car to turn on the "Child seat occupancy" setting in the air bag computer of the Boxster. I'm not sure why this wasn't turned on by default, but most dealers will perform this five-minute task for free or for a nominal charge.

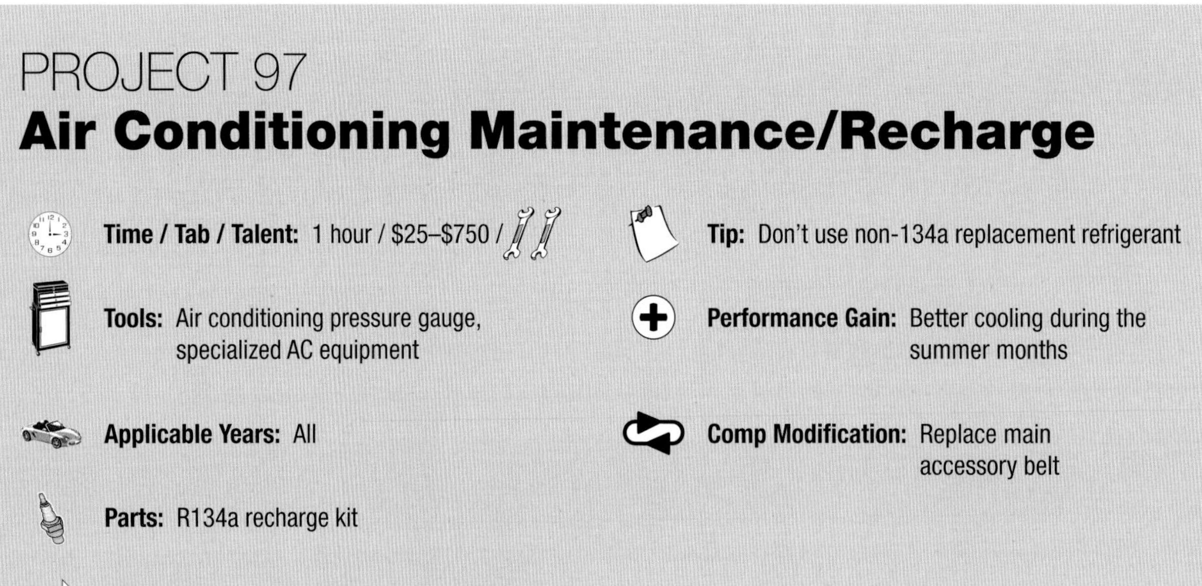

PROJECT 97
Air Conditioning Maintenance/Recharge

Time / Tab / Talent: 1 hour / $25–$750 /

Tip: Don't use non-134a replacement refrigerant

Tools: Air conditioning pressure gauge, specialized AC equipment

Performance Gain: Better cooling during the summer months

Applicable Years: All

Comp Modification: Replace main accessory belt

Parts: R134a recharge kit

More Info: www.101projects.com/Boxster/97.htm

On any car, the AC system is a complicated beast. This project is not intended to be a repair manual for your AC system but to serve more as a guide on how the system works and the maintenance involved with its upkeep.

Almost all air conditioning systems work on the theories of thermodynamics, whereby heat flows from a warmer surface to a colder one. Heat from inside the car is transferred to the cold metal fins of the evaporator. The refrigerant in the system picks up the heat from the evaporator and takes it to the compressor. The gas is then pressurized, which concentrates the heat by raising the temperature of the refrigerant gas. The gas is then sent to the condenser. The condenser cools the refrigerant and turns it back into a liquid from a gas. The liquid is then sent to the receiver-dryer, where any water vapor that may have formed in the system is removed. The receiver-dryer also acts as a storage container for unused fluid. From the receiver-dryer, the liquid flows into the expansion valve, which meters it into the evaporator located inside the car. Here the liquid absorbs heat and becomes a low-pressure gas. This evaporation, or boiling of the refrigerant, absorbs heat just like a boiling pot of water absorbs heat from the stove. As heat is absorbed, the evaporator is cooled. A fan blows air through the evaporator and into the cockpit of the car, providing the cooling effect.

The compressor pumps the refrigerant through the entire system. An electromagnetic clutch on the compressor turns the AC system on and off. In addition to cooling the car, the system also removes water vapor from the ambient air via the cooling process. It is not uncommon to find a small puddle of water underneath your car from the condensation of the air conditioning system. A thermostat control on the evaporator keeps the condensation in the evaporator from freezing and damaging the unit.

So what can be done to maintain and protect the system from deterioration? First and foremost, the air conditioning system should be operated at least once a week if the outside temperature is above 50 degrees Fahrenheit. This will circulate the refrigerant in the system and helps keep all the seals in the system from drying out. Most failures are caused by refrigerant leaking out of the system and can be prevented by making sure that the system is run frequently.

The belt that runs off of the main crankshaft operates the AC compressor. If you think that you might be having problems with your compressor, check the condition of the belt first. Turn on the system, and check to make sure that the electromagnetic clutch is engaging. If not, then you may need to replace it. Check the power connection to make sure it is live before replacing. The system also has a pressure switch located right next to the high-pressure port in the front cowl area, which will shut it off if the pressure inside the system is too high or too low. Check the pressures in the system and/or the operation of this switch if you're having A/C problems.

On the 1997–2000 Boxsters, there is also a set of diagnostic codes that the AC control unit can output to aid you in diagnosing problems. Check the 101Projects.com website for more details on this.

REFILLING A/C SYSTEMS

The biggest problem with A/C systems is a loss of refrigerant. Luckily, the replacement and top-off of refrigerant is a relatively easy task. All Boxsters use R134 refrigerant, which can be purchased inexpensively at your local auto parts stores. The Boxster air conditioning system capacity is 850 grams (30 oz) of R134. In addition, the compressor needs a synthetic lubricant for proper operation. If you're filling a completely empty system, add 195 ml (6.6 ounces) of ND 8 refrigerant oil.

The kit I used to refill the car in this project is manufactured by Interdynamics (see Photo 1). Start the car outside of your garage, turn on the A/C system and fan to full blast, and let the car run with the system on for about three minutes. Following the instructions included with the kit, connect a new can of refrigerant to the hose/gauge assembly. Connect the gauge assembly to the low-side port on your A/C system (see Photo 2). Be sure to wear eye protection and heavy leather gloves when handling the coolant and gauge assembly—if coolant leaks out at any time, it can freeze a small patch of skin on your hands quite easily and give you frostbite.

With the car running and the A/C system turned on full blast, take a reading on the pressure gauge. If your system is properly charged, it should read between 25 and 45 psi. If the pressure is low, then turn the valve on the can to release more refrigerant into the system. Be sure that you shake the can for about 30 seconds and turn it upside down when you connect it to the gauge assembly. Also be aware that the pressure gauge reading will automatically elevate as you are adding more coolant—periodically close the valve on the can to check if the pressure is rising in the system. If the pressure doesn't increase after adding one complete can, then you most likely have a major leak in your system, and you should seek the help of an A/C system professional mechanic.

With the system properly filled and measured with your gauge, you should head to the passenger compartment and check the temperature of the air exiting the vents. On a system that is operating really well, the temperature will be in the mid-30s Fahrenheit. For systems that are older and weaker, the temperature readings will mostly likely be higher. Also keep in mind that if your system is cooling air in the 30-degree-Fahrenheit range, the compressor on the car will tend to turn itself on and off, and the temperature will rise up and down slightly. This is not a defect of the system—the compressor turns itself off as the temperature in the evaporator nears the freezing temperature of water. This prevents the evaporator from becoming frozen and clogged with icy buildup.

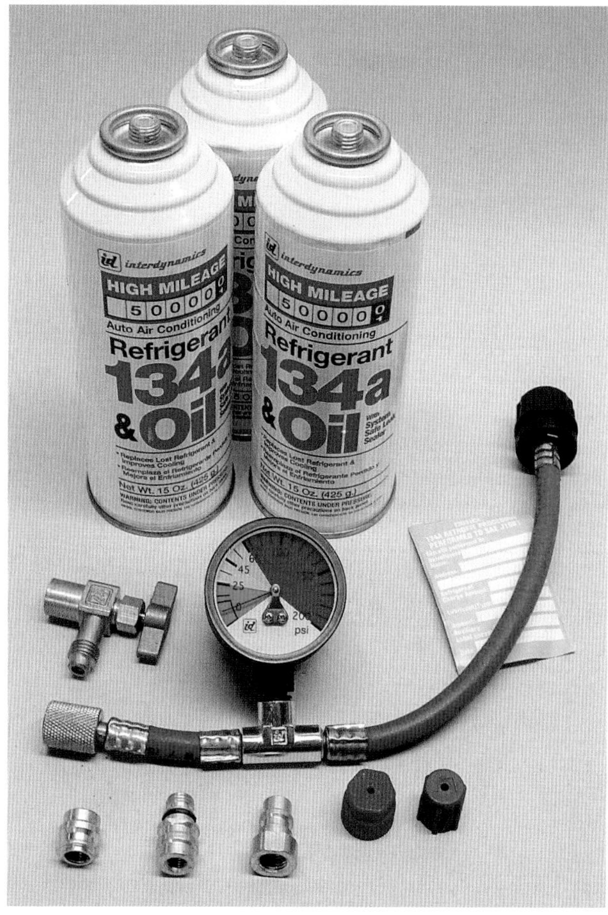

1 Shown here is a great starter AC kit from Interdynamics. This kit contains three cans of R134a refrigerant and oil and is specifically designed to replenish older cars that may have a few small leaks in the O-rings of the air conditioning system. Included with the kit are a can adapter valve, an inline pressure gauge, and several adapters that are not required for use with the Boxster. The kit is available for about $35 at most general automotive stores and contains everything that you need to recharge your R134a air conditioning system.

2 This photo shows the location and orientation of the A/C ports on the Boxster. The A/C ports are normally covered with plastic covers that simply screw off (inset). The low-side (the side that you attach the gauge and refrigerant to) has the smaller port adapter and is attached to the larger pipe (yellow arrow). The high-side (used primarily for checking the compressor during diagnostic testing) has the larger adapter (green arrow) and has a smaller-diameter pipe.

3 With the engine running and the system engaged, connect the gauge to the low-pressure port on the A/C system. The high side has a larger adapter so that you can't accidentally attach the gauge to the wrong port. With the gauge attached, you can now turn the valve to add more refrigerant to the system. In the photo inset, you can see that the pressure for this A/C system is exactly where it should be—in the middle of the white range. Remember to use heavy-duty leather gloves and eye protection when working around A/C components—it's possible that a fitting or a valve may break or leak refrigerant on your hands.

4 Your hand is a pretty poor indicator of relative temperature. In order to get an accurate reading, I recommend that you use a digital thermometer, like the one shown in this photo. Final temperature performance of your A/C system will vary based upon a number of factors: age, quantity of refrigerant in the system, and the condition of the compressor and associated components. This car is a 1999 Boxster with 80,000 miles on the odometer. The vent reading is 46 degrees Fahrenheit (8 degrees Celsius) with the A/C at full blast. Outside temperature when this reading was taken was probably around 70 degrees Fahrenheit. You should expect at least about a 20-degree drop from the outside ambient air.

PROJECT 98
Track Preparation and Weight Removal

 **Time / Tab / Talent:** Unlimited / Unlimited / Unlimited

 **Tools:** All of them

 **Applicable Years:** All

 **Parts:** Everything your money can buy

More Info: www.101projects.com/Boxster/98.htm

 **Tip:** Buy someone else's project

 **Performance Gain:** Faster lap times

 **Comp Modification:** Home equity line of credit

Any *101 Projects* book worth a grain of salt needs to have a section on preparing your car for the track. The Boxster is increasingly becoming a very popular weapon of choice as a dedicated track car. Its lightweight construction, combined with its mid-engine placement, creates an excellent starting point for building the ultimate track car. I could probably write an entire book on the subject of creating the ultimate Boxster track car, but for now I'll just give a brief overview of some of the changes I would make if I were to turn a stock Boxster into a dedicated track car:

- Install a permanent roll cage or roll bar extensions for the occasional track day (Photo 1)
- Upgrade braking system (Project 52)
- Upgrade shocks to an adjustable system (Project 60)
- Install the GT3 adjustable control arms (Photo 9 of Project 58)
- Have a full racetrack alignment and corner balance performed on the car
- Install adjustable sway bars (Project 60)
- Replace the doors and hood panels with fiberglass units (install a fiberglass hardtop too)
- Use lightweight race wheels with slicks
- Install a fully certified fuel cell
- Install a fire suppression system
- Upgrade the transmission to include a limited slip (Project 39)
- Install a real-time data logger and/or electronic dash computer
- Install racing seats and a five-point harness
- Install an Accusump and/or the deep-sump kit (Project 12)
- Install an aftermarket MOMO wheel
- Remove as much weight as possible (see next section)

WEIGHT REDUCTION

A project on track preparation would not be complete without discussing the option of placing your car on a diet. The benefits from weight reductions to rotational components in the engine are twofold—they not only reduce the rotational mass that the engine needs to spin up, but they also reduce the total weight of the car. These rotational components exist all over the car—not just in the engine. All of the rotational drivetrain components (wheels, transmission gears, axles, brake discs, etc.) have a significant effect on your car's overall performance. Using lighter-weight wheels, for example, will have a similar effect to reducing the weight of your flywheel—the drivetrain will accelerate faster, and the total mass of the car will be reduced as well. Again, the gain is twofold. It is for this reason that most racers try to remove as much mass as possible from drivetrain components when lightening their chassis.

While reducing the mass of drivetrain components can produce the most efficient gains, you can go only so far. This is because the drivetrain is responsible for delivering power to the wheels and accelerating the car. You can remove only so much weight—you don't want to weaken the drivetrain to the point where it is going to fail. The second-best thing to do is to remove weight from the chassis of the car. Theoretically, a 10 percent reduction in weight is equivalent to a 10 percent increase in equivalent horsepower. On a 200-horsepower, 3,000-pound car, it may be far more practical to remove 300 pounds than it would be to produce 20 more horsepower from your engine.

So what can you do to reduce weight? There are a couple of rules of thumb. The first place you should remove weight is from "unsprung" components. These are the parts of the car that are not supported by the suspension. Examples include suspension links, A-arms, brake discs, wheels, etc. The next-best place to remove weight is from the highest points on the car (sunroofs, windscreens, etc.). Removing weight here helps lower the car's center of gravity. Next, you want to target the mid/rear of the car. This is because the Boxster is already

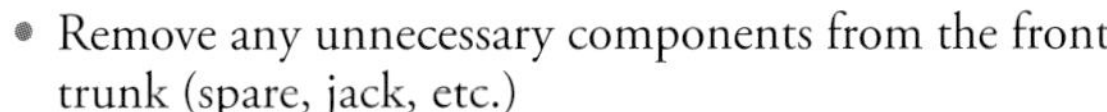

slightly tail-heavy due to the rearward mounting bias of the engine and transmission.

If your goal is pure performance, you can lighten your car significantly simply by removing or replacing the following on the car:

- Remove the entire heating and air conditioning system
- Remove window regulators/support braces in doors
- Replace glass with Lexan
- Replace deck lids and doors with fiberglass
- Remove most interior components (carpet, door panels, interior trim)
- Remove undercoating on the chassis
- Replace the driver/passenger seat with a lightweight one
- Move or replace the battery with a lighter one (Porsche has a brand new Lithium-ion battery that just came out for the GT3)
- Remove any unnecessary components from the front trunk (spare, jack, etc.)
- Remove the DOT bumpers and replace them with fiberglass
- Remove stereo system, amplifier, and speakers
- Remove the convertible top and replace it with a fiberglass hardtop
- Drill brake rotors
- Remove power mirrors

Most of this weight removal can also be done to a street car, but any weight removal must be balanced with the practicalities of daily driving. If you enjoy air conditioning and a good stereo, then you probably won't want to sacrifice these amenities for the improved performance. However, if your mission is to maximize performance, you might be surprised at how much of a difference weight removal can make.

1 Shown here is the Brey-Krause roll bar extension and padding kit installed into our project Boxster. This kit was specifically designed for use in the Porsche Club of America (PCA) driver's education events. The standard roll bar offers great protection, but only if you're not wearing a helmet. Installation of the roll bar extension is required by many events and offers very good protection against the car accidentally rolling over (yes, there have been Boxsters that have indeed rolled over at local PCA events). At about $750 from PelicanParts.com, the roll bar extension and padding kit is expensive, but it's a necessary safety requirement.

2 Any dedicated track car requires a welded-in roll cage. Be sure to have someone install it who has previously fabricated one for a Boxster. The roll cage should include the appropriate mounting points for a shoulder harness and should also accommodate the Boxster hardtop, either the steel version or a lightweight fiberglass version.

3 Shown here is a Kinesis K28 wheel, one of the best choices available in high-performance wheels. This wheel has a reputation for being one of the lightest and strongest that you can buy for your track car. The wheel centers are forged from 6061-T6 aluminum and are mated to rim sections that are spun by computer-controlled machines assuring trueness and consistency throughout the wheel. These wheels not only look cool but their performance and reliability has been proven time and again at various races like the 24 Hours of Daytona.

4 Here's a shot of two Boxster interiors that have been gutted and prepped for the track. The car on the left has had a replacement dash computer installed in front of the normal Boxster display. This programmable dashboard allows you to monitor all of the systems of the car, while also logging data such as lap times and engine performance. On the car on the right, you can see that a custom box has been fabricated to raise the gearshift lever off of the floor. This allows for less movement from the driver's hand to the lever, resulting in quicker shifts and more time with your hands on the wheel. In addition to having most of the interior gutted and removed, both cars have fire suppression systems installed, as well as lightweight seats, MOMO steering wheels, and five-point racing harnesses.

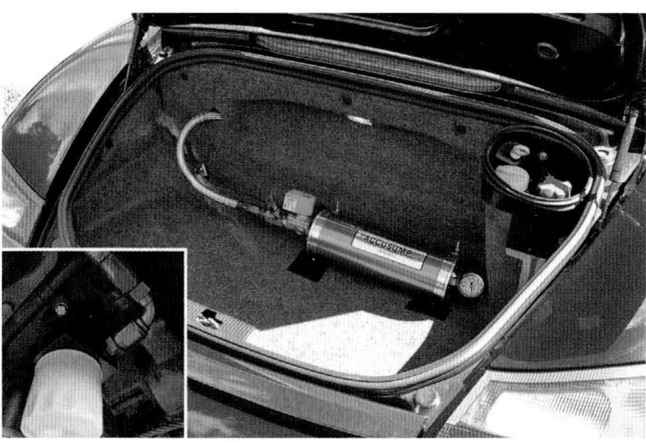

5 Here's a photo of an Accusump installed in LN Engineering's test car. The Accusump is a cylinder-shaped aluminum storage container that acts as a reservoir of pressurized oil to be released when there is a drop in the oil pressure. The Accusump is connected to the pressure side of a Boxster's oiling system (typically through an adapter on the oil filter, inset photo) and is charged by the engines own oil pump. Its simple, efficient design revolves around a hydraulic piston separating an air pre-charge side and an oil reservoir side. The oil side of the Accusump has an outlet that goes into the engine's oiling system, controlled by a valve. On the air side it's equipped with a pressure gauge and a Schrader air valve, which allows you to add a pre-charge of air pressure to the Accusump. Installing one of these on a dedicated track Boxster helps compensate for the fact that the Boxster does not have a dry-sump oiling system.

6 Nothing says fun quite like driving your Boxster on the track. The car shown here is owned by Mark Foley, driven at California Speedway. I took my wife's 1999 Tiptronic out on the track at the Streets of Willow one day mainly because every other car in my stable was temporarily out of commission. I initially thought the 2.5-liter engine and automatic transmission would be a slow dog on the track, but I was pleasantly surprised when the Boxster literally outran many of the other cars (mostly early 911s). The mid-engine placement, the balanced suspension, and the quick braking combined with the Tiptronic transmission really made the car a secret weapon. I was most surprised at the Tiptronic, which somehow figured out that I was on the track and began to shift exactly where I needed it to.

7 Big rear wings are a staple of track cars, and no matter how many events you go to, you'll always be able to find a wing that you haven't seen before. I took a whole bunch of fluid and aerodynamics classes when I was at MIT, but even armed with that knowledge, I think it would be difficult to find the optimum wing design and settings without the use of a wind tunnel. It's tough to tell whether the use of a rear wing adds enough benefit to counter the added weight and wind resistance. It's truly trial and error here. An interesting feature of this car (other than the paint scheme) is the addition of center-lock wheels, which are typically found on cars that require quick tire changes in pit lane. *Owner: Dr. Chris Murray*

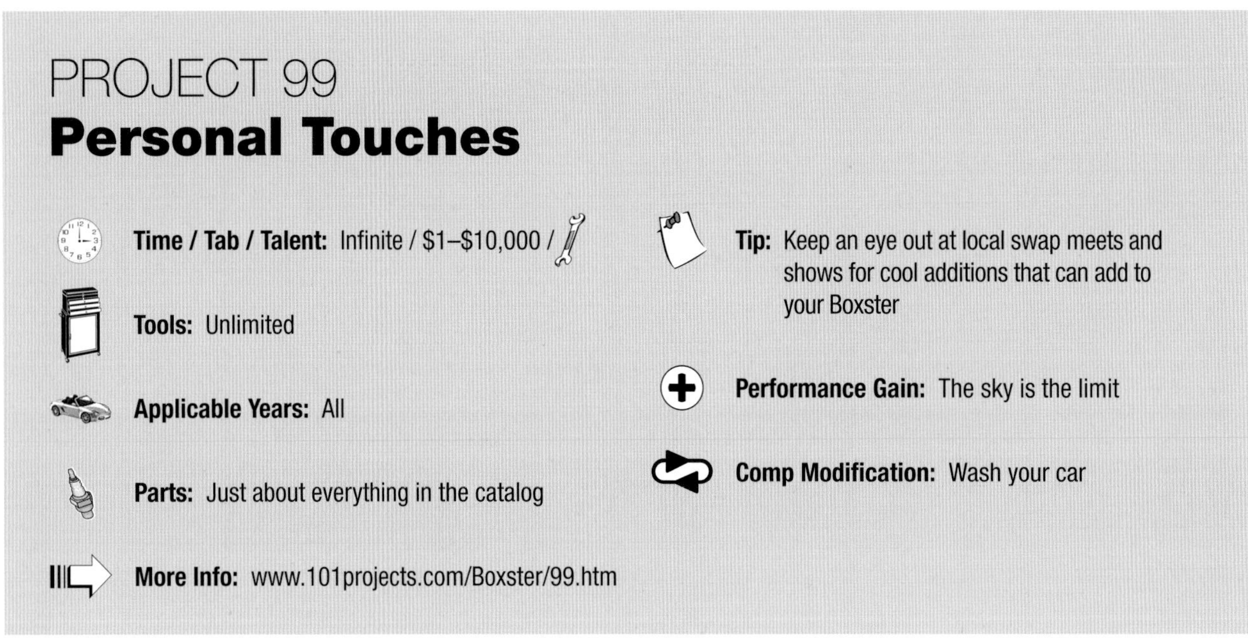

PROJECT 99
Personal Touches

Time / Tab / Talent: Infinite / $1–$10,000 /

Tools: Unlimited

Applicable Years: All

Parts: Just about everything in the catalog

More Info: www.101projects.com/Boxster/99.htm

Tip: Keep an eye out at local swap meets and shows for cool additions that can add to your Boxster

Performance Gain: The sky is the limit

Comp Modification: Wash your car

As principle photographer and owner of the Internet-based company PelicanParts.com that sells parts for Porsches, I've had the opportunity to photograph a lot of different modifications that people have done to their Boxsters over the years. While not all of them improve the looks of the car in my own opinion, it can certainly be said that Boxster owners like to modify their cars more than most people. Whether it's the addition of new wheels or a custom spoiler, if you can think of it, it's likely that some passionate Boxster owner has spent hundreds of hours and thousands of dollars to do it. This project is designed to give you some ideas for your Boxster—many of these items are currently available in the online catalog at PelicanParts.com.

1 Dressing up your interior makes sense, as it's the one thing that you look at the most. Porsche and some aftermarket companies offer almost all of the interior trim pieces in the car in genuine carbon fiber (shown in this photo). However, the real deal can cost you up to $6,000 to outfit the entire interior of your Porsche with the genuine stuff. The "poor man's" option is carbon fiber–look overlays that give the appearance of real carbon fiber for 1/100 of the cost. While not my particular cup of tea, some people may find this approach appealing.

2 Chrome trim rings are a popular interior dress-up item for the Boxster gauges. They are typically manufactured out of extruded aluminum and contain extra-sticky adhesive that you simply peel and stick to the outer edges of the gauges. The gauges are the one thing that you look at the most inside the car, so they should at least be appealing to your eye.

3 This photo shows the interior of a 996 Carrera, and while not technically a Boxster, a lot of interior parts are interchangeable and transferrable from the 996 to the Boxster. This car was ordered new from the factory with this interior. Some uncommon, yet interesting things to point out are the red seat belts ($580 option), the inlaid Porsche crest in the headrest, and the painted silver seat backs and center console (it cost $700 each panel for this option). Although I really like the look of the silver-painted center console, in reality it doesn't hold up very well to wear and tear and tends to look a bit worn, as it scratches very easily.

4 Pedal upgrades are another common accessory for Boxster owners. Beware though—you want to make sure that you get a set that isn't slippery. These pedals are great looking, but they might be a little too slippery for my tastes—particularly if I'm wearing leather-soled shoes. I recommend sets that have integrated anti-slip rubber inserts in them.

5 I've included this photo of the 2010 Boxster Spyder because it incorporates so many neat design elements that can be applied to earlier cars as well. For starters, the 19-inch wheels with red painted calipers look great on this car. Also noteworthy is the "PORSCHE" script down the side in the style originally used on the early 911s in the 1970s—very cool. Finally, the Speedster-style humps, which were an original option for the Boxster, have made a return with the Spyder.

6 Spoilers can be big on Boxsters (see Project 80). This one is unique and looks custom made (as was nearly everything else on this car). I've never been a huge fan of the stock Boxster "pop-up" spoiler from day one—I've always thought it was a bit inelegant. Adding a spoiler to the rear of the Boxster gives it a more muscular look in my opinion.

7 One of the smallest detail touches you can place on your car are Porsche crest valve stem caps for your wheels. These are really neat factory OEM valve caps, and they typically run about $20 at PelicanParts.com (PN: PNA-705-001-99 silver crest, PN: PNA-705-002-00 colored crest).

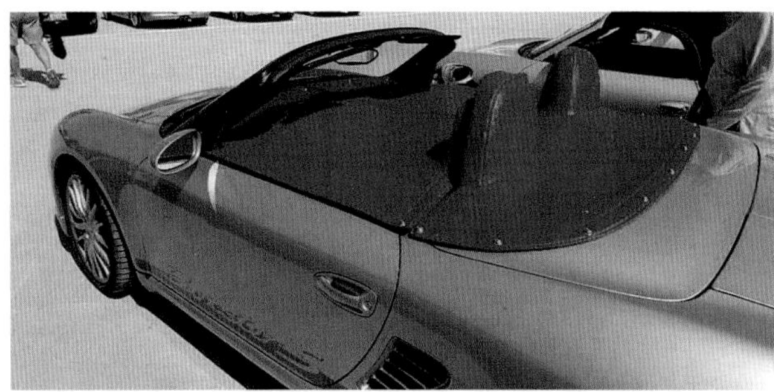

8 Shown here is what is known as a tonneau cover for the interior of your car. Originally a popular accessory on the 356 Speeders, they certainly look cool when installed. However, it takes a several minutes to unfold and install it—far longer than the 35 seconds or so it takes to roll up the top on a sunny day. Still, for car shows and displays, it's certainly an eye-catching accessory.

9 Here's the car that is featured on the cover of this book. It's a "speedster-inspired" Boxster that has had numerous upgrades, including the complete removal of the roof. In its place is a simple roof material cover for the engine compartment. Here in sunny Southern California, you can probably get away with removing the roof, but for most other climates, I wouldn't terribly recommend it.

10 If you're tired of the way your Boxster is looking, then you might want to update it with a body kit. While some body kits available on the market today are of questionable taste, I do like the "Streetster GT" featured here by Patritti Rennsport Design. It's very clear from the first glance that the design incorporates subtle elements from a variety of very successful Porsches. The front headlamps and bumper are reminiscent of the Porsche 997 Turbo, the side engine air scoops pay homage to the venerable Carrera GT, and the rear takes styling queues from the Ferrari lineup.

11 The Porsche Cayman was introduced with an entirely new-looking front bumper. With only a little bit of effort, you can install a Cayman-look bumper onto your late-model Boxster (2005 and up). You can also install and wire in the additional fog lamps so that they are fully functional. I've seen one or two Boxsters with this update, and it's very subtle, because the look is classic Cayman and is very period and factory-correct looking.

12 Here's a neat personal touch that Boxster owner Joel Lester designed. Inspired by the 2010 Boxster Spyder shown in Photo 5, it incorporates a center "Viper-like" stripe with the Boxster hardtop (see Project 69) and a tasteful PORSCHE script along the bottom of the door. Total cost: about $35 from a local vinyl sign shop.

PROJECT 100
Tire and Wheel Sizing

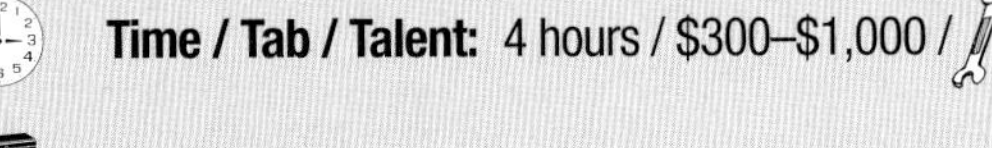

Time / Tab / Talent: 4 hours / $300–$1,000 /

Tools: Soft socket

Applicable Years: All

Parts: New tires, valve stems

Tip: Find a tire shop that will allow you to try fitting certain sizes and types of tires on your car, or find a friend who has a tire/wheel combination you like and borrow them.

Performance Gain: Good tires can increase your handling and braking significantly

Comp Modification: Upgrade to larger wheels

More Info: www.101projects.com/Boxster/100.htm

For this project, I polled a number of people on a few Internet chat boards in an attempt to figure out what the best and most popular combinations of tire and wheel sizes were for the Boxster. I confirmed what is inherently true about almost all hardcore Boxster owners—they love to modify and tweak their cars. Out of all the responses, no two were exactly alike. I've compiled and summarized the feedback here so that you can make an educated decision when equipping your ride.

Let's talk for a few moments on tires in general. Although you can write volumes on tire sizing and design, we'll try to cover the basics here. Tires are sized using a system that takes into effect the tire's aspect ratio. This aspect ratio is a function of the tire's height with respect to its width. An example of a common European tire size is 195/65R15. The number 195 refers to the width of the tire in millimeters. The second number, 65, refers to the height of the tire as a percentage of the width. Therefore 65 percent of 195 would give a tire width of about 127mm. The letter following the width and length is the tire's maximum speed safety ratings:

Q=99 MPH, 160km/h	**V=149 MPH,** 240km/h
S=112 MPH, 180km/h	**W=168 MPH,** 270km/h
T=118 MPH, 190km/h	**Y=186 MPH,** 300km/h
U=124 MPH, 200km/h	**Z=149 MPH,** 240km/h and over
H=130 MPH, 210km/h	

Needless to say, a good Z-rated tire should be more than adequate for non-suicidal driving! The last number in the tire size is the wheel diameter in inches. In this case, "15" refers to a 15-inch-diameter wheel.

Tread is another important consideration in selecting a tire. You should select your tire based upon what type of driving you are planning on doing. With the Boxster, sometimes it's a bit more complicated, because some people don't drive them in all types of weather. With a family sedan located in a snowy environment, an all-weather tire is a natural choice. However, many Boxster owners do not drive their cars in the snow or the rain.

In an ideal setting, such as on the racetrack, flat-surfaced tires called racing slicks are best because a maximum amount of tire rubber is laid down on the road surface. However, slicks have almost no traction in wet weather. The water has a tendency to get underneath the tire and help hydroplane the car by elevating the wheel onto a wedge of water as it is moving forward.

The array of choices for tire tread is way beyond the scope of this project. One rule of thumb is to make sure that you purchase a tire that is appropriate for your climate. Using a snow tire or all-weather tire on a Boxster that is rarely driven in the snow will significantly reduce the tire's contact patch area and reduce cornering performance on dry roads. However, not equipping your car for bad weather can result in disastrous effects if you are ill-equipped during an unforeseen storm. If you drive your car only during the dry summer months, then look for a conventional performance tire with a maximum contact patch area.

Another important consideration is the tread wear and traction. The tread wear refers to the average number of miles that can be put on the tires before they will need to be replaced. A tread wear indicator of 100 means that the tires should last about 30,000 miles. An indicator mark of 80 means that the tires will last 20 percent less, or 24,000 miles. Wear will be different for each car and each driver's personal driving habits, but the various ratings are good for comparisons among different brands and different types of tires. Traction is related to the type of materials used in the tire. The more hard rubber is used in the tire, the longer the tires will last. However, the hard rubber provides much less traction. A rating of "A" for traction is best. These tires will grip the road well, but will generally wear out faster than the "B" or "C" traction rated tires.

It is important to consider another factor in addition to tread wear when selecting a tire. Most tires have a shelf life based on the rubber's natural process of breaking down and becoming brittle. It doesn't pay to purchase a 30,000-mile tire if you are only going to be putting 3,000 miles a year on your car. After ten years, the rubber may be cracked and deteriorated beyond safe use, even if there is plenty of tread left on the wheel. This is also an important consideration if you are purchasing a car that has been in storage or sparsely driven for many years. Although the tires may have plenty of tread on them, they may actually be dried out and ready to fail. If the tires develop cracks in the sidewalls from aging, they can blow out when heated up from driving. A blowout is a very bad situation and can cause you to lose control of your car very quickly.

So, what tires and wheels can you fit on your Boxster? It all depends upon the wheel design and offset and which tires you prefer to run on your car. With so many different combinations out there, it's impossible to fully document them in a mere few pages. I did create a wheel collage (opposite page) that you can use for ideas on which wheels to mount on your car. This array was assembled from photos of Boxsters and 996 Carreras I took at various meets and club events over a period of three years.

Expanding the pool of options, you can also use spacers to accommodate different wheels that weren't originally designed for your car. I recommend the use of hub-centric spacers, which are located on the hub by a machined center hole. This is opposed to the lug-centric spacers that are located by the position of the lug nuts alone (see Photo 6 of Project 52).

With some older cars, the tire sizes that you can fit on the car may depend upon the condition of the car. Sometimes the chassis are perfectly balanced from left to right, and sometimes they are slightly off from being in an accident or simply from body sag. It's best to find a tire shop that will allow you to try out several tires on your car in order to find the best fit. Go in the afternoon on a slow day and talk with your tire salesman to see if he will let you size the tires on your car. If he won't, then go to a different shop—there are plenty of them out there willing to cater to you, especially if you are going to shell out some money for high-performance tires.

If you want to go with larger-diameter wheels on the Boxster, the best combination for 18-inch wheels would probably be 225/40/R18 in the front and 265/35/R18 in the rear. Moving up to 19-inch wheels, you would probably want to run 225/35/R19 on the front and 265/30/R19 on the rear. Different tires will look and perform differently with various wheels, so the best option is to consult with a good tire shop for their recommendations. You can fit 20-inch wheels to a Boxster, but at that point, the tire thickness is so small that the ride and handling suffers quite a bit. I don't recommend installing anything greater than 19-inch wheels. I currently run Genuine Porsche 18-inch Sport Design wheels manufactured for Porsche by BBS on the project Boxster for this book. It's also important to note that Porsche has released a Technical Service Bulletin warning against putting 18-inch wheels on 1997 Boxsters because the early chassis aren't as reinforced as the 1998 and later cars.

With the wider wheels, the options for the installation of tires grow exponentially. The type of offset used on the wheel and the tire size will affect whether it will fit or not. The offset of a wheel is the distance of the center of the wheel from the edge of the mounting flange on the hub. Different wheels with varying offsets will affect tire sizing considerably, so make sure that you know which types of wheels and offsets you have before you attempt to mount tires to them. It's also important to keep in mind that Porsche made very similar-looking wheels for the Boxster and the 996 Carrera, with the only major difference being the offset of the wheel. If you're buying used wheels, be sure that you purchase ones with the correct offset for the Boxster.

So after reading this project, are you still confused? You should be—and rightly so. It would appear that there is a never-ending amount of options for tire sizing. The best way to figure out what type of tires to place on your car is to inquire around. Check on the Internet at the various technical bulletin boards, like the one at PelicanParts.com. I'm also fond of the TireRack.com website—they have useful tools there for determining the right wheel/tire combinations that will fit on your car. Regardless, you will find that everyone will have an opinion to share and a wheel/tire option that they have tried on their car.

MISCELLANEOUS

1 No matter which wheels you buy, you're going to want to make sure that you protect your investment with a set of wheel locks. The factory ones available from Porsche look pretty terrible though, and I don't necessarily recommend them. Booth Designs makes an aftermarket set of locks and polished studs that are of extremely high quality and really look like they should be on your Boxster (available from PelicanParts.com).

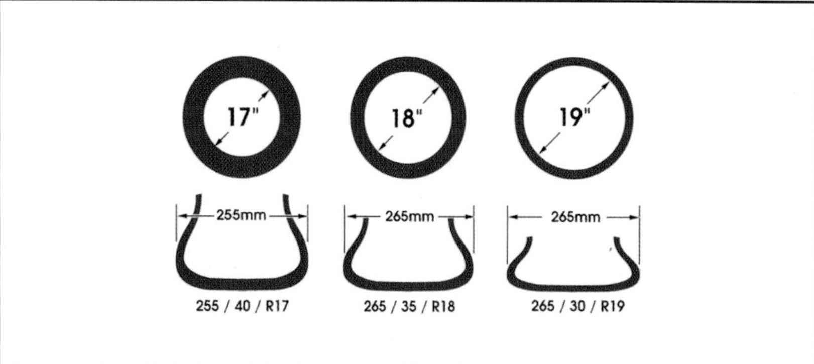

2 This photo shows how the aspect ratio of the tire changes with the change in wheel size. In general, you do not want the outer circumference of the wheel to change—this will affect handling and also change your speedometer readings. So, when you go with a larger wheel, you must go with a lower-profile tire. The lower-profile tire results in less of an air pocket under the car, and this typically reduces the ride comfort. This photo shows some examples of three rear-wheel options for the Boxster. It is generally my recommendation to run 18-inch wheels for the best combination of looks, performance, and ride.

3 The upgraded, polished lug nuts really look great on the Boxster. If you use them, be sure to use what is known as a "soft socket" (also available from PelicanParts.com). This special socket has a softer inner liner that will allow you to install your lugs without damaging them. If your center caps are looking aged, then you can try removing them and sanding them with some fine-grit sandpaper. The outer plastic covering on the crests gets old and cloudy after many years, and a few minutes of sanding can improve the overall appearance tremendously.

PROJECT 101

Dyno Testing

 **Time / Tab / Talent:** 2 hours / $100

 **Tools:** Shop dyno

 **Applicable Years:** All

 **Parts:** None

 **More Info:** www.101projects.com/Boxster/101.htm

 **Tip:** Get a group of friends together for "dyno day" and save money

 **Performance Gain:** Figuring out if your car is running at peak performance

 **Comp Modification:** Tune-up

What project book would be complete without a section on dynamometer testing? One of the neatest trips you can make is to your local dyno shop. For about $100 or so, you can make a few runs on the dyno and actually measure the horsepower that is generated by your engine. The whole process is somewhat complicated, with varying degrees of detail and accuracy, but for the sake of this section, we'll just cover the basics.

What is a dyno? Short for dynamometer, the dyno measures the horsepower output by your engine. There are two basic types of dynos: one that you bolt the engine up to and run, and one that measures horsepower at the rear wheels of your car. This is also called RWHP (rear wheel horsepower). Most modern dyno testing is performed on a rolling dyno that measures the power output at the wheels. You drive your car onto big rollers and accelerate at full throttle until you reach your rev limit. Then, you let the clutch out and let the rollers spin down freely. Large fans and environmental controls aim to keep the test environment at a steady state so that you can compare dyno runs. The dyno works by placing a load on the car, similar to how you would experience air friction as you were driving down the road at high speeds. By measuring this load, combined with the total rpm of the vehicle, a graph of the power output by the car can be derived.

Torque/Horsepower: The dyno actually measures the torque output by your rear wheels. Torque is a measurement of rotational force and is related to the overall power output by your engine. The horsepower output by your engine is equivalent to the following formula, which is derived from an early English standard:

Horsepower = Torque × rpm/5252

This translates into a power relation that horsepower is defined as 33,000 ft-lb (force) per minute. This is also referred to as the horsepower definition as defined by the Society of Automotive Engineers (SAE horsepower).

You may have also seen other definitions for horsepower and wondered what they meant. European documentation often gives horsepower numbers in kilowatts. For reference, one horsepower equals 0.746 kilowatts. Porsche's ratings are often listed in the European standard of DIN HP or kilowatts (kW). One DIN horsepower is rated as the power required to raise 450,000 kilograms one centimeter in one minute (or about 0.73 kW). The values of SAE and DIN horsepower are very similar, with 1 SAE HP being equal to 0.98629 DIN HP. For all practical purposes, you can think of them as relatively the same.

You may have also heard the term *brake horsepower* (BHP). Brake horsepower is measured at the flywheel of the engine with no load from the chassis, without any electrical or mechanical accessories attached, under ideal fuel and timing conditions. In modern terms, the brake horsepower figure would be mostly associated with what is now called gross horsepower.

Air/Fuel Measurement: In addition to measuring output torque and rpm, some dynos can also monitor your air/fuel mixture. This will allow you to adjust the mixture tables on a custom engine map to correctly match the power output (see Project 24). In other words, if you find that your engine is running lean at 4,500 rpm, you can adjust the fuel injection mixture to richen it up and produce more ideal combustion. This translates to more horsepower output from the engine.

Dyno Results: The dyno will generate a graph of horsepower versus rpm for the engine being tested. With this graph, you will be able to determine the engine's peak horsepower and peak torque. The graph will also show you the peak horsepower output from the engine. On a six-cylinder Boxster engine, this will typically be at the higher end of the rpm range, near 6,000 rpm. The engine will peak in horsepower and then fall off dramatically as the rev-limiter in the engine cuts off the ignition system.

Comparing Results: An unfortunate downside to dyno tests is that they often cannot be accurately compared to one another. Environmental conditions play a large part in these variances, as well as the fact that the large dynos cannot be easily calibrated. As a result, tests from the same dyno with the same car on different days may produce different results. Even the manufacturers of some dynamometers admit that their dyno at one location may test 5–10 percent differently than the same model at another location. When you consider that the figure may become bigger when you include dynos from different manufacturers, the ability to accurately compare results becomes significantly less useful.

An important issue to mention with respect to dyno figures is that the test is influenced heavily by environmental conditions. This includes temperature, humidity, and altitude, to name a few. Since conditions may change from day to day, dyno runs that span multiple days may produce different results.

Engine Optimization: As previously mentioned, dyno testing can be very subjective. Other than bragging rights, pure dyno numbers are not very useful. The true benefit of the dyno test comes when you are able to use it to optimize your engine. Particularly with software ECU flashes (Project 24), you really need extensive dyno testing in order to determine what your optimum operating parameters should be on the fuel ratio and ignition timing maps. The factory used the same type of procedure to optimize and program the Bosch Motronic factory maps used in the stock engine management system.

In order to gain the most horsepower out of your engine, you need to perform several dyno runs while varying many different engine parameters (timing, mixture, advance curve, etc.). Only after carefully analyzing the data can you determine what the best values are for your engine management system map. Measuring the power output of the engine will allow you to optimize your engine and get the peace of mind knowing that you are extracting the maximum horsepower that you possibly can.

Driveline Losses: Since the dyno testing is performed using rollers on your car, there are going to be forces that are going to slow down and reduce the power in between the flywheel and the rear wheels. These driveline losses include friction from the transmission, losses from brake discs dragging slightly, and friction in the wheel bearings. On the Boxster, typical driveline losses are often estimated at about 15 percent, although modifications to the chassis can raise or lower that value. Through a complicated process of calculations that are computed by the dynamometer, you can calculate your driveline losses by counting the time it takes the dyno rollers to stop when you let out the clutch. Using these calculations, you can then estimate what your horsepower output is at the flywheel.

Transmission Gearing: One of the benefits of dyno testing is the ability to design your transmission ratios to meet the exact power characteristics of your engine. Depending upon where you want optimum performance, you can install taller or shorter gears into any of the five or six speeds on your transmission. The results of the dyno test will give you specific horsepower numbers for each rpm range and allow you to tailor your transmission gearing to suit your desires.

Software Dynos: This is what I call the poor man's dyno. It is software that plugs into your Boxster's OBD-II port and estimates power and torque based upon a variety of factors. Software from AutoEnginuity that you can use to monitor OBD-II functions also has a very good dyno emulator built in. With pre-programmed profiles for the Boxster, it has proven itself to be extremely accurate in predicting engine performance. See Project 20 for details.

1 This photo shows Gary Hand's supercharged Porsche Boxster getting ready for the dyno. Engine modifications include a Turbowerx twin turbo and intercooler, ECU reflash, custom headers, EVO cold air intake, and a TechArt muffler. For this test, the car was driven slowly through its full rpm range on the dyno while carefully recording all of the applicable data. Conditions were tightly controlled using fans and air temp/humidity measurement devices to ensure that the environment remains constant between dyno runs.

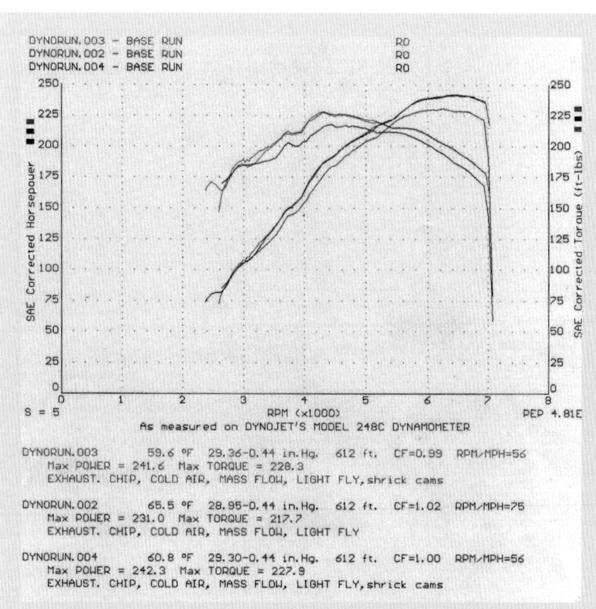

2 Shown here is a typical dyno graph for three separate runs. The graph shows rear-wheel peak horsepower of about 242. Note that as per the relationship between torque and horsepower, they are equal.

Index